WELFARE OF NATIONS

WELFARE OF NATIONS

MICHELE FIORE

PHILOSOPHICAL LIBRARY
NEW YORK

TABLE OF CONTENTS

LIST OF TABLES

LIST OF FIGURES

LIST OF FIGURES

WELFARE OF NATIONS

INTRODUCTION TO WELFARE OF NATIONS

A MESSAGE TO THE READER

Before entering the main part of this book it might be well to
present to our reader some of the objectives that this study is designed
to attain. He will shortly realize that this is not a novel, or a book that
in any way aims at entertaining or amusing him, but is an effort to
analyze in an impassioned way many of the sources of discontent, friction
and discord in the world today, either within or outside a nation.

It is quite evident that in a book of this type, conclusions cannot be
drawn until all phases of the problem have been presented and thoroughly analyzed. Because of this, the reader must muster sufficient will power
and interest to wade through passages of detail which may appear
obscure and tedious, but which are necessary for a thorough presentation
of those basic principles we like to see established. I have no doubt, as
the theme of this study unfolds and progresses that the reader and myself
shall become spiritual friends. This will spring from the realization that
we both believe in the fundamental kindness and goodness of men who
are only led astray by environments and circumstances.

The author is not pretending to have produced a work of art or a
literary jewel as he knows too well the many shortcomings of his ability
in this respect. However, he can say that he has made an honest effort
toward the amelioration and the betterment of the world and only on
this account he must ask the forbearance of the reader if ideas have not
been expressed with the artistry and fluency of a Hawthorne or Emer-
son. His fever and eagerness to vent many of the obvious causes of unrest
which keep the world in an unsettled condition was too strong to have
been left any longer concealed and repressed. As a reminiscence, we like
to confide that the idea of this book dates back to the time of the Italian
campaign in Africa when Mussolini, with his buoyant and bombastic
personality was busy trying to carve an empire against the will of more
powerful nations than Italy.

The author, while an American citizen, is of Italian birth, served in
the Italian army during the first world war, and is, therefore, familiar
with the needs, desires and aspirations of the Italian people. He knows
too well that the large support received by Mussolini during those event-

ful years was not altogether due to his leadership and personality, but rather to the fact that Mussolini adopted and became the exponent of those desires and aspirations which existed in a latent stage long before he ever entered the political picture of the world. That Mussolini and the Italian people were wrong in their purpose of conquest comes as a matter of course; that other nations should have opposed such an international act is quite understandable and yet let the pure and innocent throw the first stone. A nation and a people who from time immemorial has contributed so much and so repeatedly to human progress and achievement, a nation and a race that may be considered among the most enlightened and civilized in the world, could not be totally wrong in her attitude and in her stand unless we should assume the possibility of an entire nation suddenly losing all sense of propriety and morals. As a generality, there are always two sides in most any controversial issue and, while some tend to emphasize one side, others will do the opposite. To be sure, all may claim some degree of righteousness in their upholding and defending some particular principle. However, all are wrong when unwilling to raise themselves above petty grievances and limited horizons. Engrossed in their effort of justifying their stand, all fail to raise to that level from which the proper perspective of controversial issues could be better understood and analyzed. Italy, notoriously poor and overpopulated, tried to do in the 20th Century what other nations had repeatedly done in the past. We are not here to justify Mussolini in his quest of empire, but we refer to this instance as the one that started a train of thoughts in the author's mind that eventually caused him to examine the complete relationship among men and among nations. That the world in 1935 was in a hopeless situation does not need any particular proof or explanation; that events were then relentlessly drawing to a final showdown is now an historical fact. We all felt powerless to extricate ourselves from the whirlpool that was gradually closing on us. Now, why all this? The question was repeated thousands of times without any plausible explanation. Yet the subconscious mind was stubbornly working for that answer and with the passing of time ideas were made more clear, issues became sharper and more precise and gradually the obvious faults of periodicals and articles in the papers here and abroad came to present a challenge that could no longer remain unanswered. As previously confessed, I considered and consider myself unequal to this task and the last on earth to write a book: writing a book is not my profession or inclination, especially one that has the size and the scope of this volume. Such a notion seemed preposterous and fantastic to say the least, and yet the feeling that basic rights of man were and are deliberately distorted and made to serve definite ends and interests urged the author to scribble ideas and opinions in answer to periodicals and articles more for his own satisfaction than with the aim that this eventually would evolve into a book for the public.

While the Italian language would have seemed to the author easier to use, he soon realized that if and when such a book should ever be published, it would have to be in English. There were many considerations that brought about this decision. Some of the most important are the following ones:

(1) English has taken the place of French as the international language and by using English more people can be reached.

(2) A nation like the United States with boundless dynamic power and progressive attitude toward new ideas and new principles, was the logical nation to be chosen by the author as the one in which the new system of life could be more rapidly understood and adopted. As English is the language spoken in this country, this became a very important factor in that selection.

(3) The author had no doubts as to which contending nations were eventually to emerge victorious in World War II and naturally that was another important factor against the choice of the Italian language.

All this occurred in 1940 when the United States was still technically at peace and Pearl Harbor had yet to come. Events followed events and all contributed to make the determination of writing this book stronger than ever.

The atomic bomb has now made the first, but possibly not the last appearance on earth. The second world war has ended, but has not brought that peace for which the people expected and hoped. Dark and ominous clouds are gathering on the horizon which do not presage any fair weather ahead. The reason for all this will become obvious if we, instead of looking at the many problems confronting us from a nationalistic point of view, make the effort to isolate and study the real causes of unrest and agitation in the world today and stop placing the blame without discrimination on other people and other modes of life. "WELFARE OF NATIONS" has, with the cooperation of friends, finally been completed and as it comes to be published it will enter the turmoil of life and will no longer be our child and companion of all these years. Faced by many conflicting interests and ideals, it will have to withstand powerful forces and a scrutiny far more severe than the one given by the author. As for you, my reader, no matter the destiny of this book, if I succeed in these pages to convince you of the truth of the principles which are here advocated and established, this work will not be in vain.

One of the main purposes of this book is to establish and present some of the basic and fundamental human rights which should be made equal for all with no discrimination among nations, races or classes of people. In so far that all are born equal under the laws of God, all must be entitled to live their lives according to the qualifications and capabilities given them by nature.

A second fundamental aim of this book is that of presenting new codes, new principles and new ethics by which those rights and those liberties of men can better be established and maintained without endangering the liberties and the rights of others.

A third fundamental object of this book is that of presenting to the reader a new mode of life and a new government which, by taking those fundamental rights as the ultimate goal of mankind, makes it possible for such a goal to be reached gradually without economic strains and unrest for the good of the individual and humanity in general.

The reader unquestionably does agree with the beauty and far reaching importance of this attainment. Yet, the author freely recognizes and understands the reasonable attitude of suspicion and incredulity on the reader's part toward our presumptuousness of even suggesting such a goal in a world so far distant from those ideals. On this account he may be apt to discard this book as the work of a visionary and a charlatan.

Bear in mind that much thought has been given to what is here advocated and that this book would have never seen the light if the author did not himself feel very strongly of the soundness and constructiveness of the method which will gradually unfold in these pages.

The author is not seeking political position in this country or any country and the very fact that he is not connected with, dependent on, or in any way subservient to the dictates of any one, gives him the right and puts him in a position to say what he feels and become the interpreter of the subconscious views and aspirations of the common man throughout the world. In the effort of giving to our reader a general understanding of this book, we shall present in the following pages a brief description of the various topics that will be treated in each chapter so as to make clear to the reader what we are trying to accomplish. This was done so that he in turn may enter a subject which we hope will exert a great influence in his attitude toward ethics and problems of our modern society with better confidence and greater interest.

The first chapter gives the definition and presents the interpretation of various economic phenomena which will enable the reader to better understand the process of reasoning used by the author in his demonstration of basic causes of unrest and turmoil encountered in the world today. As a result of many wrongs and injustices and because of that fundamental instinct of man in his unceasing quest of happiness and amelioration, the second chapter presents some of the methods used by modern society in its striving toward such an attainment, strivings which eventually have developed into the different modes of life which we have come to call Communism, Fascism and Naziism. Each of these modes has been analyzed from the standpoint of what it was originally intended to accomplish, and then a study was made as to the actual results achieved. In this chapter it is proved that, in one way or another, all these philosophies of life have failed to take into account basic needs and instincts of men. In some cases their scope was limited and fundamentally unsound, and at best all they could do was to transfer wealth and prerogatives from one group to another without promoting the betterment of society taken as a whole. And even Democracy, which is what other philosophers have been trying to improve, and which in our minds, as well as in the minds of many represents the best mode of life evolved by men for the above mentioned purpose of amelioration and justice, falls far short of such a goal. Therefore, a new philosophy closer to the basic needs and instincts of men and based on more solid foundations must be evolved if real betterment is to be attained by society and humanity in general.

The third chapter assumes a hypothetical society of 400 individuals and it proves that, even for such a Lilliputian society, phenomena will appear similar to those encountered within modern larger societies which cannot be ascribed to the faults of any one within that society. By this it is implied and proved that our modern maladjustment cannot be pinned on any one particular individual or group of individuals, but that it represents the normal unescapable consequence of an economic phenomenon called scarcity. The condition called stable equilibrium point is also analyzed here. It is proved that it tends to maintain the status quo among the components of society and that it resists advancement and progress. In this chapter, the concept of money is given. Its fundamental aim, that of enhancing commerce and trade among individuals and among nations, is also stressed and analyzed. It disproves the concept that money, in itself, is wealth.

The fourth chapter deals with the evolution of a nation. It proves that, given favorable circumstances, the well-being of a population living on a land rich in material resources tends to follow a well-known pattern and cycle. The standard of living, originally low, tends to increase with the increase in population because of the greater division of labor among its components and increases also with a better knowledge of manufacturing methods. However, irrespective of technological advancements, the ratio between the wealth of the land and the size of population sets a top limit of improvement. If the population keeps on increasing, as it usually does, a time is reached when dislocations and maladjustments begin to appear that tend to disrupt that society unless that relationship between size of population and wealth of the land is substantially reduced. This explains the urge on the part of many people and many nations in the past as well as at present to acquire additional wealth which oftentimes can only be obtained through aggressions and wars. In this chapter, the relationship among nations is also considered and it is proved that, as a generality, what affects one nation sooner or later is bound to affect all the others. This stresses and makes imperative the fundamental necessity of cooperation among all people.

In these chapters, however, no effort is ever made to present to the reader those natural remedies that become evident as the various maladjustments, one by one, are taken into consideration, as all this becomes the chief topic of following chapters. Our main purpose, up to this point, is only to search and expose causes of disruption and attrition. By obtaining a wider perspective, the reader will then be assisted in pointing out the necessary reforms needed to remove those causes and permit a more rapid and enduring progress and amelioration among men. The author has adopted this method for the purpose that the reader himself, having become conscious of causes and effects, may reach such conclusions of his own free will and accord. As he reaches this stage of the book we feel confident that he will also be ready to accept and approve the suggested new system of life as presented to him and in so doing he not only will take much of what we will have to say as obvious and evident, but will add his energy and ability to the improvement of our work and come to feel and be part of the future society.

After this, let us say destructive part of our study in which so much is exposed and condemned, the second purpose of my work, or that concerning the building of the future society, is actually started and presented. The fifth chapter is mostly devoted to the presentation and moral justification of a radical reform that contemplates the gradual decentralization of wealth. As a prerequisite of progress and advancement, no one should be obstructed in his honest effort of amassing large fortunes if endowed of those rare qualities of leadership and ability. Yet, for the same reasons, this wealth should not be perpetuated in these individuals beyond their normal span of life. We mean perpetuated in their children and distant descendants, especially when the latter lack the ability and wisdom of their ancestors. Wealth in the hands of the incapable and inept is harmful to society in general and does not add to the well-being of the individual, especially when he is in possession of far more wealth than is actually needed. The new laws of inheritance will be such that, while the heirs will be left with sufficient wealth so as to maintain and enjoy the highest possible standard of living in the nation, the excess must return to society. Society's duty will then be that of returning that wealth to individuals so that the greatest benefit will accrue to society itself. By this, we do not mean to convey the idea that wealth will be taken from some to be given to others who did not work or contribute in any way to the amassing of that wealth, as this will not be done. However, by the method we shall describe, wealth will be placed in the reach of individuals of moderate means who nevertheless must work and strive for that acquisition. Independently of ownership, what is important in this world is not so much the fair distribution of wealth, but the fair distribution of the products and revenues of wealth. As a result of decentralization, the government or society in general will come to derive a given amount of revenue that will be used to improve the conditions of the population in general through a method that will become the pivotal force of the future society. It must be understood that this decentralization is advocated more from a moral and ethical standpoint than from the fact that by itself it could produce those far reaching results mentioned above. In short, the attainment of these results must rely on the contribution and cooperation of all the components of society in proportion to their ability to pay under the form of taxation as well as to new codes and regulations injected in the life of society.

The sixth chapter presents one of the fundamental pillars of the future society or the mechanism by which the basic equilibrium point can be made to advance instead of remaining stationary as at present. This can be accomplished without disrupting or changing the basic forces that create prices and profits. After a general analysis of the various economic forces that develop in society and recognizing that they cannot be changed because, emanating from basic instincts and needs of men, it is proved that any amelioration must tend to improve the economic conditions of all the components of society, rich as well as poor, in order to be enduring and everlasting. Only through such a method can real cooperation be hoped for and attained. The concept of vital commodities is extensively treated in this chapter. In brief, the term "vital commodity" represents what the average family of the lowest class of society must theoretically receive as a prerequisite of well-being and good health. Its amount, only a goal for society to attain, can be progressively raised as the original limit is approached. The reason why such a theoretical amount cannot be immediately given is because of the phenomenon of scarcity which first must be reduced and eliminated. This phenomenon is also explained in this chapter. Then a new concept is introduced by which the wage of the laborer is linked through an index with the amount of scarcity that develops in a given community. This index, by law, will represent the minimum wage.

A sub-branch of the Economic Welfare which is a part of the future government will be set up in every community of the land for the purpose of promoting that economic progress referred to above. One of its main functions will be that of buying surplus vital commodities from the various retail stores of the community as well as from wholesale stores. This will reduce the price to the indigent part of the population and will relieve the merchants and retail store owners from the anxiety of a decreased market when the supply in the country tends to increase. From the amount of vital commodities on hand, the index for the community in question will be calculated. The fact that all that reaches the market will be sold at profit in time will represent a powerful incentive in increasing supply. As the production of commodities increases so will the index and thereby the corresponding minimum wage. In this manner any increase in supply will produce the following results:

(1) A greater amount will be available to the population as a whole.

(2) The poor, because of their larger purchasing power made possible by the index, will be in a position to easily absorb any increase in supply.

(3) Any increase in supply in turn will be beneficial to the manufacturers, to the rich in general, and to the owners of stores because of the larger volume of business and the per capita increase in profit.

The ECONOMIC WELFARE (EW for short) will come to represent a stabilizing factor in the life of society. On one hand it will prevent large fluctuations in prices which tend to bring wide periods of booms and depressions and on the other, will permit a gradual and coordinated amelioration of all branches of society. It will promote the healthy economic condition of the nation on which industry and initiative in general can prosper and remain secure.

The EW, an integral part of the future government, will not be limited to the above activity, but will engage in many more that tend to exert a beneficial influence on the life of society. These will be described in the seventh chapter. First of all, a general outline of this part of the government is given. It is explained how the E.W. is divided into four separate branches. The first, more or less the nerve center of the nation, called the "CENTRAL BRANCH" will study all forces that exert an economic influence on the life of the nation. From such data, the proper directives will be formulated and given to the various sub-branches. The second branch will be mostly devoted to the economic advancement of the population. One of the sub-branches, whose activities are described in the sixth chapter, will be called "Price Stabilization." The third branch will devote its activity to the administration of wealth that comes to be owned temporarily by society as a result of the division of large estates at the death of the original owners. The fourth branch will take care of the many details that go with the division of the inheritances themselves.

The second sub-branch will have, besides the PRICE STABILIZATION, the following sub-branches: INDUSTRY CONTROL, LABOR CONTROL, HOSPITALIZATION, DELINQUENCY CONTROL and RECREATION.

The "Industry Control" will help industries on the verge of financial collapse as a result of poor management, unfair competition, and economic forces that may develop in the life of society. This is done for the purpose of promoting and maintaining the productiveness of the nation at its very best. In addition, this sub-branch will sponsor and encourage additional industries and enterprises in regions where they can be made productive and helpful to the population in general. This will also prove beneficial to the owners of the new industries.

The "Labor Control" will represent the clearing house of labor within the nation. As labor is discharged because of retrenchment or other economic reasons by any one industry, it will be used in some other industry, either in the same community or in other parts of the land eager for that labor. This will be done for the purpose of maintaining the full employment of the population. As the industry as a whole loses the capacity to absorb this extra labor, enterprises of national scope will be sponsored by this sub-branch of the government. However, as a limit is reached, the hours of work will be gradually decreased throughout the land. This will reverse the flow of labor toward industry again. By this method, while the purchasing power of the public will not be impaired, the standard of living in general will increase because of the reduced amount of effort required of the individual and the poor will no longer fear the competition of the technological advancement.

The "Hospitalization" will sponsor the erection of large and up-to-date hospitals, clinics, etc., in which the indigent, and, in general, all those who avail themselves of the services of the E.W. will find adequate help when sick or injured. Doctors and the necessary staff will be directly paid by this sub-branch of the government which will expect in turn high standards and integrity. The financial backing of this vast social enterprise, besides coming from some of the revenue derived from inheritances and taxes, will be obtained by a new system of insurance among all the population. This system, by extending the risk to such a large number of people, will permit the lowering of the necessary premium. The insurance will be divided into two parts. One will cover the actual expenditures of hospitalization and doctors and, therefore, be equal for all. The other will cover the wages and salaries lost and, therefore, will be related to the wage of the insured.

The "Delinquency Control" introduces a new concept in dealing with this social problem. Besides the fact that it will take active part in clearing the slums and find jobs for individuals and families whose environments may breed delinquency and vice, it approaches the social phenomenon of delinquency from the realization that this is only another form of sickness of the mind rather than the body. As the instruments for fighting and eradicating delinquency will have to be introduced on a pay-as-you-go basis, first attention will be given to the caring for and to the rehabilitation of children in their teens who are the potential criminals of the future, then to children of lesser age under the care of delinquent and corrupt parents, and then to the delinquents themselves. The most important activity of this branch, however, will be positive rather than negative. This means that instead of the plain physical caring for the delinquent and his prevention of escape efforts will be made toward the moral and spiritual rehabilitation.

The "Recreation" sub-branch will help small communities in the erection and establishment of recreation centers. In addition it will help the financing of good and enlightening entertainment.

This chapter also gives a preliminary description of other important parts of the future government. One of these will be the "GENERAL WELFARE" which will assume more or less activities similar to any modern government today. The other, called "PEOPLE'S WELFARE" will be made of representatives elected directly by the people and as the voice of the people, it will attain the highest authority in the land. Besides the immediate task of representing the people, it will hire the official heads of the other two branches of the government and will have the power to discharge them if and when their policy should conflict with the basic needs and interests of the people. These representatives will also have the duty of selecting the members of the "LEGISLATURE," whose functions will be that of promulgating new laws in the land and the appointment of the judges to the various courts of the nation. Mention is also made in this chapter of how the nation will come to be divided into zones and superzones depending on its size and population. All zones will have the same representation in the government so that all may have equal rights and equal power in the affairs of state.

As this comes to represent the basic structure of the future society, it becomes of interest to ascertain how this system will affect the Lilliputian society described in the third chapter. This is done in the eighth chapter. In addition, other phases of the problem are presented to the reader and analyzed. We feel that as the various influences of the new mode of life are understood and appreciated, the reader will come to realize that greater cooperation is bound to develop among all classes of the nation. This will promote a healthy and satisfied society.

The ninth chapter analyzes various phenomena confronting society which will take an entirely different aspect when viewed under the aegis of the new system of life. Unfair competition, monopoly of capital and labor, strikes, unemployment, tariffs, unbalance of trade, are some of the topics which one by one will be scrutinized under this light. In addition those positive forces that tend to raise the well-being of the individual and society in general are pointed out and compared with the destructive forces of modern time. It is also shown that any country which adopts this new philosophy of life is bound to improve its standards of living irrespective of the philosophies of other nations. Because of a more intelligent self-reliance, because of new moral codes and ethics toward other nations, international friendship and cooperation is bound to follow and expand.

The ninth chapter concludes the second part of our study or that which is devoted to the presentation of the new system of life as applied only to one nation. The two following chapters widen the horizon and include the entire population of the earth. Here also the fundamental causes of distrust and antagonism among nations are sought, not from the premise that one society or philosophy of life is better than another, but from the stand that definite policies adopted by nations spring from understandable and basic instincts of men. By interpreting those forces and needs, we shall be better prepared to point to the logical remedies.

The zone of influence of industrial centers is studied and analyzed, the profound effects on the population in general are then taken into consideration and from all this the natural responses to definite economic phenomena become plain and understandable. Historical examples are given of the perennial struggle among classes and among nations. From all this the fallacies of war and all other policies that tend to subtract from one to give to another as a panacea to betterment and progress become vivid and apparent.

We hope that our reader at this point of our study will be convinced of the necessity of a Federation of nations. The following chapter proceeds to prove how any nation, let it be poor in resources and backward in civilization, or rich and enlightened stands to gain and improve under the aegis of this new system of life. This Federation, however, will be far different in scope as well as in structure from what we call "LEAGUE OF NATIONS" or "UNITED NATIONS" which fall short of their purported goal of bringing peace, justice and amelioration among men.

The Federation will live in complete accord and friendship with other nations who follow or wish to follow other modes of life if consistent with human decency and sacred rights of men. It will not exert its influence in spreading its creeds or in obtaining economic advantages. For its name we have chosen that of "HUMANITY." In this choice we were guided by the fact that the obvious advantages that it will represent in time will convince all people on earth to live under its banner.

The twelfth and last chapter is mainly devoted to the description of the government of HUMANITY, to its setup, and also to its influence within and without the Federation. The author does not claim perfection, but he hopes that his suggested new system of life may be taken as a base by those people who, willing to establish order and justice in this world, will add their talents, enthusiasm, and cooperation to a work that visualizes a philosophy which the author believes superior to any one yet adopted and devised by men. With this understanding we end our message to the reader confidently.

CHAPTER I

SOME OF THE FUNDAMENTAL ECONOMIC CONCEPTS

THE SECOND WORLD WAR has finally come to an end, and has left in its wake an immeasurable loss of life and destruction of property.

It is not our purpose to deal with the misery and hardship experienced by millions of people as a result of the war. Much has already been said on the subject, and undoubtedly much more will be written in the future about this pivotal period of history.

What we wish to discuss is how you and I have been affected, even though spared the toil and suffering of those who fought and those who endured invasion and the constant attack of airborne armadas.

Even if not apparent, many among us have experienced a gradual transformation which has made us quite different from what we were during the easy and relatively comfortable days of pre-war times. Confronted by a cataclysm of superhuman power and intensity, all that was left to do was to go through life performing duties and tasks as if the war was not existent. Quite true, those who were engaged in war production had to work longer hours under unquestionable strain with the result of fatigue or illness and practically all had to bear many shortages, be it in labor or in food, and all kinds of discomforts which were bound to affect the mode of life of the population in general. Annoying as these experiences may have been to most of us, they were not sufficiently serious to imperil our lives, and thanks to that wonderful ability of man to adjust himself to any environment, we accepted the new mode of life as an unavoidable necessity and resigned ourselves to all its implications.

With few exceptions we have gone through life superficially unperturbed by the events taking place around us, yet our subconscious minds have been at work, imperceptibly and without pause, to bring that transformation referred to above. Nor could this have been otherwise.

Gone is the easy and light-hearted attitude toward life and the world in general. Gone is the belief that the world will find its equilibrium if let alone.

Under the impact of violent emotions the pillars on which civilization is resting seem on the verge of falling and collapsing. Honesty, temperance, religion, love, and justice are being replaced by deceit, violence, irreverence, hatred, and vengeance. The innocent are punished for the guilty, the weak oppressed by the strong, and the lowest instincts of man come to the fore, free and unhampered to add to the chaotic whirlpool of feelings and emotions.

Since the autumn of 1939 we seem to have lived in a tempestuous dream that even now frightens and torments our souls. If we overlook the many fires which are still burning in the world, the war among the great powers has finally ended, bringing to a close a bloody period of history. Yet, if the physical aspects of the conflict are over, the animosities among men are still furious and relentless and if the war has ended, this is only in name but not in spirit. Acts, which it would have seemed could not have happened in our time, are being perpetrated every second of our lives. Newspapers and radio commentators can give but a pitiful chronology of misery, death and destruction. Millions are suffering, multitudes are miserable, crime is rampant and all this proves the maladjustment of society which does not give much hope and encouragement for the future.

A great array of horrors torture our minds and make us aware of the tragedy engulfing the world, and yet we realize how utterly powerless we are to stem that trend and that tide. No one, from king to peasant is secure. No one, in the face of powerful and unscrupulous interests, at odds among themselves but allied against society, can hope to change the rush of events which, as an avalanche, overturns all in its wake, bringing chaos and disruption. Our society, standing in quicksand, seems to crumble and founder on every hand while the cries of help from the millions of afflicted go unheeded and unnoticed. This, because society has lost the moral and spiritual foundations on which it used to stand.

Many, while performing inconsequential good deeds from that force of habit and veneer of civilization, are responsible for the cruelest and most horrible crimes, denying thereby the claim to be civilized or human. The words from religion are heard, but no longer understood or practiced. We are Christians in name but not in deed, and nothing seems to change the trend and the tide, and the interminable procession of events keeps on hardening our hearts and shaking our faith in human beings. There is the mother weeping for her sons; there is the horde pushed and maltreated while on its way to the gas chamber, there is the aviator crashing to earth; there is the soldier wounded hopelessly crying for help and salvation, there is the ship plunging to the bottom of the sea and finally the city annihilated and destroyed in a fraction of a second.

Yes, all these victims in the last moments of their lives prayed that they might live and finally saw, in its true and awful reality, the utter futility of war, but no prayer now availed; their destiny was sealed forever.

This is what war has meant to millions of people all over the world: Americans, Britons, Germans, Poles, Italians, Chinese, and so on: and while these unfortunates were making their last and greatest contribution to mankind, countless mothers, wives, fathers, sweethearts, were lying awake thinking of their loved ones and hoping for their return. The unnecessary wastage of life, the sending of innocent people to such an inhuman and unjustified death does not represent, however, the greatest damage inflicted on our poor and tormented humanity. How frail is human nature. After the tempest that has devastated and laid waste such a vast portion of the world, one would think that a wave of horror would have risen everywhere against such a ghastly method of settling differences among nations; and one would think that all those who came so near being engulfed like the others by the vortices of death would at least unite to demand the abolition of war under any circumstances; one would think that they at least would realize that millions of the enemy were fighting only because compelled by their governments and by the faulty prejudices of our society, and that these individuals representing the enemy were, like themselves, killing to avoid being killed. Yet we do not see any such trend in the making. Instead hatred, one of the lowest and most depraved of human feelings, has taken possession of the masses with an intensity that far exceeds any past experience. Indeed, while we may comprehend, if not justify, the hatred and bitterness against all those reckless leaders who have been responsible for this holocaust, we fail to understand the indiscriminate hatred for millions of human beings who like us have suffered and agonized under the ravages of war merely because they happened to be born in an enemy country. Because of this hatred the great majority approves and demands regulations which will make the life of these people still more miserable and degrading than at present, and force their future generations to keep on paying for the errors of their fathers.

The flames of vindictiveness and selfishness have spread through the world, and we have been helpless witnesses to the spectacle of nations hating other nations, races despising other races, to the point of systematic obliteration of one nation or race by another, undertaken with a diabolic determination never before known. The Polish and Jewish peoples are examples. To such depths has this hostility sunk that cheers and approval greeted the woman who with her teeth tore the throat of a helpless wounded German and spat the soldier's blood in his face. What hope can we have for the future when such atrocities are called forth by the baseness of human nature?

Conscious of the vast degradation of moral standards, we still refuse to admit that all is lost. We have faith, and believe that many generous souls throughout the world are deeply concerned over the fatal trend taken by society. They do their best to promote conditions which may bring amelioration. Their efforts, however, lacking a definite plan, a definite goal, and the necessary cooperation among themselves, are too insignificant to bring even a modest result.

The end of the war finds the world divided in two camps. At one side are the vanquished nations, prostrated, helpless, and at the complete mercy of the victors. At the other side we find the conquerors, many only slightly better off than the losers. All, winners and losers alike, have lost overwhelmingly in lives and in property, and are utterly exhausted from the efforts of war.

Shall we now permit the conditions of peace to be dictated by hatred? Shall we lull ourselves into the belief that only the complete subjugation of the enemy nations will prevent a third and more devastating world war, which may spell the end of our civilization? Again, what assurance have we that the friendly nation of today may not become our foe in the future? The enslavement and degradation of entire populations are no prevention of war.

Peace was never and will never be built on hate and despotism. Let us remember that the conquered peoples are as we are: let us remember that their problems, their needs, their aspirations are similar to ours; let us remember that misery and servitude are the great breeders of war, not of peace, and that it is up to our generation to lay the foundations for a world built on justice and unselfishness if we do not want to see our children dragged toward the abyss into which we have fallen and be exterminated by a war that will not know physical or moral borders.

But if this is the lot of humanity why should we fear the atomic bomb, and all the other contrivances meant to give sure and speedy death, contrivances which we seem so able to devise and perfect? If man has fallen so low that he cannot see a better way and use better methods to adjust and solve his differences, the end of the world ought to be welcome and the swifter and the speedier the death the better.

Why have wars ravaged humanity since time immemorial? Was it because of the personal ambition of the Caesars, Napoleons and Hitlers, who were set to find power and glory no matter what the price. Or were there hidden reasons which gave them the chance and the justification for their actions? We doubt that by themselves such leaders could be personally responsible for these phenomena, and believe that something deeper was at the root of the problem.

The real causes must be found in the maladjustment of society; must be found in those conditions which promote and maintain the wide disparities among our many social levels, must be found in the eternal struggle for amelioration, must be found in the efforts of the have-nots to take from those who have plenty, must be found in the scarcity of things.

It seems to us that if we could study and analyze in a dispassionate way the basic needs of men, determine their nature and their reactions to social phenomena, that a system could be evolved by which all could be satisfied and able to find justice and contentment in whatever position they may stand on the social ladder, thus tending to relieve a great amount of friction among men and nations. At first it may seem that such a condition is utterly impossible and completely Utopian. To this we agree to a certain extent, as we know that one of the instinctive forces of human nature is that of striving for higher and higher places. But the new philosophy of life that will evolve in the course of this study does not prevent anyone, provided he has the prerequisites and the necessary qualities, from improving his lot or attaining high positions in life. But, no matter the social position, all will enjoy a full and comfortable life; the new system will maintain and encourage human self-respect and is less apt to promote strains and unreasonable feelings of greed. But irrespective of the many exceptions; it is an everyday occurrence that many with talent, ability and honesty are prevented by birth, race and nationality from attaining those positions for which they are qualified and this because of prejudices, selfishness and organized resistance. At the same time millions throughout the world are kept in servitude, ignorance and semi-starvation and thus deprive humanity of that contribution which they would undoubtedly add if opportunity were given.

Injustices among individuals as well as among nations must stop if we are ever going to see a better world. For this purpose this work has been undertaken. We freely admit and fully realize that it may have many faults and imperfections, as has everything not tested in real life. We recognize that many changes and refinements may have to be added and they will be welcome if helpful to the attainment of that goal. If this work has the fortune to inspire even a handful of men who, better qualified than ourselves, would take over with courage and determination from where we have stopped, our effort will not be in vain.

In the course of our study we must often refer to well established and fundamental economic laws. For a clearer understanding we shall present our interpretation of those laws. This will give us also the opportunity to expose some of the faults that can be found in our modern society. With that knowledge and understanding we shall then be better prepared to state the necessary reforms, this being the main purpose of our effort.

WEALTH IN ITS VARIOUS FORMS

Wealth, that great mirage for which humanity toils and strives, will be the first economic concept to come under our study. As utilized by man, it may be found in various forms.

UNRESTRICTED WEALTH: The air we breathe, the warmth and light of the sun, the water in the rivers and in the sky represent one kind of wealth which is free for everyone to enjoy. The beauty of the mountains and of the plains, the thousand blessings bestowed by nature upon us without any restriction or limitation, represent a form of wealth which cannot be destroyed or hoarded for the benefit of the few and to the exclusion of the many. This is what we call unrestricted wealth.

PERSONAL WEALTH: As the name implies, this wealth is endowed by nature upon each individual in varying degrees and forms. The possession of a healthy body and mind, which makes man fit to work, achieve, and enjoy those free forms of wealth which nature has put at his disposal, is in itself of immeasurable importance to each individual. Lack of this may indeed mean unhappiness, no matter what the material things he may possess. Intelligence, beauty, character, personality, and other qualities which may enrich an individual and make him outstanding among others are also forms of personal wealth.

Artistic talent, inventiveness, skill, ability to carry out research work, are examples of another form of personal wealth, which like the others cannot be bought or sold. Unlike the others, however, this form may and often does have great influence on the generations to come. An immortal musical composition, a beautiful poem, a glorious work of art, a great invention, or an important scientific discovery are accomplishments which enrich the world and endure long after the owner of this wealth has ceased to exist on earth. In its importance to society, this is the most valuable wealth possessed by man. Everything possible should be done to seek and recognize talent and every effort should be made to develop and promote its growth. The progress of society, it may be said, is due in the main to the efforts of people who have been endowed with this wonderful form of wealth.

These two sub-divisions of personal wealth, while of great importance to society, do not present economic problems as they cannot be bought or sold. To these, however, must be added another form which is represented by the labor and effort exerted by men, be this manual or intellectual, which can be definitely bought and sold and, therefore, has been included in our study. This third sub-division of personal wealth may be in turn subdivided into two separate forms; that which is used to provide articles and commodities needed by men which we shall call *Additive Wealth* and that which is used to give services to others which we shall call *Service Wealth.*

RESTRICTED WEALTH: In general this includes all those material things which can be damaged or destroyed, so that their usefulness to mankind may be impaired.

Uncultivated lands, forests, prairies, lakes, waterfalls and the like represent a kind of wealth which is in a virgin state. Its present value may rest only in its beauty. Its intrinsic value, however, may change if it is found to possess potentialities more useful to mankind.

Cultivated lands, mines, pastures, and the like, represent a kind of wealth whose potentialities are known. They are more valuable than the preceding type because man by adding his effort derives commodities which are useful and profitable. As we shall more fully explain, this wealth must be owned by someone to better develop its usefulness to mankind and prevent its destruction. If free, the incentive of trade and exchange would automatically stop as no one would find to his advantage the expenditure of effort in manufacturing commodities from which he could no longer derive any personal benefit. True, these individuals by adding their efforts derive a sizable profit; however, because of this effort they indirectly add to the comfort and progress of others.

Restricted wealth includes also those products, commodities, and articles which have been made useful through the effort of man. Houses, stores, and buildings in general as they satisfy many needs of society, belong to this group. Tools, machinery, all kinds of conveyances and all which is used to convert raw material into products represent another form of this kind of wealth. In appraising their worth, the potential usefulness rather than the cost of production is of importance. Indeed the ability to bring forth a given profit is the determining factor of their worth.

Millions of commodities made to satisfy the multiform needs of man represent another form of restricted wealth. These commodities may range from a plain sheet of paper to the elaborate and expensive private plane, and we may even include domestic animals as they also are useful to man.

Products of the land, such as vegetables, fruits, and the like, represent an additional form of restricted wealth. However, because of its perishable nature and consequent peculiarity of its value, which may change from a maximum to a minimum in a very short time, we shall refer to it as *Perishable Wealth*.

All these kinds of restricted wealth have in common the fact that they command a price on the market. A price which depends on supply and demand: yet we feel that, irrespective of their price, their intrinsic wealth or their aptitude to satisfy definite needs of men is the same. Any article, let this be a tree, a stone, or what have you, represents a definite amount of wealth intrinsically bound up with the article, that will not change as long as it retains the same nature and form. This wealth is represented and measured by the amount of usefulness that the article can have to mankind. We say that a land rich in gold or other material resources has greater wealth than one where only trees can be found, because men can derive greater usefulness from the first than from the second. For the same reason a cultivated land has greater intrinsic wealth than one which has been left barren and unkept. The fact that a given article is not being used or utilized does not change or affect the intrinsic wealth of that article. Quite often its real wealth is not definitely known, and naturally its price will reflect the lack of that knowledge; however, its price will be greatly affected as soon as its true worth is finally found and recognized.

The conversion of an article into another will also change, of course, its intrinsic wealth. For instance, a given amount of leather represents a definite intrinsic wealth insofar that shoes and other articles may be derived from it and as such will command a price which takes this potentiality into account. However, assuming that shoes have been made, the intrinsic wealth of the leather will be greatly increased as now the previous potentiality has become an actual ability of being useful to man and, therefore, it will be of greater value and command a greater price.

ECONOMIC WEALTH: Economic wealth is represented by money. This may be made of gold, silver, or whatever material is freely accepted in exchange of goods and services. Society gives to some of these metals a definite value which becomes the yardstick for measuring all the other forms of wealth. Being recognized and accepted by all these metals are useful because they give to anyone the power to exchange any amount for needed services or for restricted wealth which he may want to possess. The use of money promotes the smooth functioning of trade between two or more individuals or groups. Money is relatively light and easily carried, but even so may at times become too heavy, especially when large amounts must be handled. Present-day civilization has overcome this limitation by issuing paper money or bank-notes. Each is a statement that equivalent amount of gold or specie is deposited in banks or in government vaults. Giving this paper in payment of services or in exchange of goods is equivalent to giving the corresponding amount of specie printed on its face. As one may at any time go to a bank and change this paper into actual money, it has the same value.

Another form of economic wealth is represented by stocks, bonds, and the like issued by business organizations and given in return for money or any other kind of restricted wealth which is utilized by the corporation. Stocks are certificates by which the bearer is recognized as having part ownership in that operation, and therefore is entitled to the dividends and profits of the organization in that proportion. Stocks and bonds have the peculiar quality of being very sensitive to the law of supply and demand. Any small change in the market will cause wide fluctuation in their price. Quite often they produce a steady income, but because of their wide variations in price they are apt also to be bought and sold with the sole intent of profit.

CHANGEABLE VALUE OF WEALTH: Another fundamental concept in economics is that of value. Value in a sense represents the amount of sacrifice an individual is willing to make for the acquisition of an article. This sacrifice may be represented by money or by a given amount of effort or work. The more money he is willing to pay or the greater effort he is willing to exert for the possession of the article in question, the greater is the value of that article to him.

We all remember the story of the traveler who, lost in a desert, dying of thirst, gladly gave a great sum for a glass of water. At that particular time the water had more value to him than all that money. The implication of the story is that the value of things is not constant, but varies with time, circumstances, and with the individual himself.

With the proper reservations we can also state that value is likewise a measure of utility, implying by this that the greater the usefulness or utility of a given article to any particular person, the greater is the value he will place upon it. But as the utility may vary for various people, we can see that the value of an article will also be different. Indeed, the value of an automobile to a person living in the country is bound to be greater than to a person living in the city, so that assuming both individuals possess the same amount of money, the countryman will be willing to pay more for that automobile. Again, we may say that while one automobile represents a great value to the person dwelling in the country, a second will not have the same value for him even though the two may be exactly alike.

PRICE: Another fundamental concept in economics is represented by price. It is quite puzzling how commodities may vary their price when no particular reason seems to warrant that change. Consider, for instance, one of the fundamental commodities, such as eggs: On a certain day in a given season one may go to market and find that eggs cost so much for a dozen. The next day, without any particular event having taken place, one may find that the price has changed a few cents. Why the change? Who dictates or fixes such a price? To explain all this we must first focus our attention on a few fundamental qualities in man.

Consider the person who goes to market his eggs. One of his fundamental instincts is that of disposing of his eggs at the highest price compatible with the amount of demand. As such he will first inquire as to the price charged by the others to make sure that his own is equal to theirs. If he finds out that eggs are greatly needed, he may then actually step up that price a few cents at a time, and keep on increasing as long as his daily stock is easily sold.

The second fundamental interest of the seller is that of completely disposing of his stock because what is left may often turn into loss. As such the seller of eggs will first charge the highest possible price compatible on the market but will be ready to lower that price if indications are such that he may be unable to dispose completely of his stock. Of course, the variations will not occur in one day, but we may be sure, if the demand is increasing, that there will be an urge on the part of the sellers to keep on increasing their price. It may happen that a few of these sellers, greedy and over-enthusiastic, charge far more than the others. Some of them may succeed in maintaining this price and yet dispose of their stock, but more often than not their sales will gradually drop in favor of the others, so that eventually they will be forced to comply with the law of supply and demand.

The price, however, may be such as to warrant an increase in production, and in that case that producer may purchase additional chickens so as to sell more eggs. As a reverse process when some of his eggs go unsold he will first lower his price, and finally dispose of some or all of his chickens if the price reaches a level at which the producer can no longer make it worth while his remaining in the market.

Consider now the person who goes to the market to buy eggs. One of his fundamental instincts will be to buy the amount he needs at the lowest possible price. Any information as to those who sell eggs at the lowest possible price will influence him, unless prevented by distance, to buy eggs from them rather than others.

Another fundamental instinct of the buyer is represented by the fact that, having a definite amount of money at his disposal, if the price of eggs happens to be higher than usual he may be forced by necessity to reduce the amount of his purchase. On the other hand he may buy more if he finds that the price is lower than usual. This will tend to lower the price in the first case, and to raise it in the other.

These four fundamental instincts in men represent the forces which govern the price of eggs in this particular case, or of any other commodity placed on the market. Of course, in speaking of eggs we have referred to a perishable wealth that must be sold immediately, but the forces that govern the price of a commodity can still be applied to others of a more durable nature or those which if unsold could easily be stored for a more propitious market. As this is what frequently happens, we must still assume that it is to the seller's advantage to dispose of the complete stock on hand for aside from the fact that storage costs money, calls for care, and involves anxiety over fire and loss, the unsold commodity represents tied-up capital which could be profitably used elsewhere. So that even with stored commodities there will still be a tendency for the seller to lower his price even if a loss will result. Let us now consider a second aspect of price.

DISSERTATION ON PRICE: The price of an article at any particular time is set by the money an individual must pay for the possession of that article. This money represents wealth he gives in return for some other kind of wealth; namely, the article under consideration. Depending upon the amount of wealth at his disposal the article may seem cheap or costly to him. If it is cheap, he will gladly purchase the article to satisfy his need, but he will not do so if expensive. His final decision will depend on the value he may assign to the article. Indeed, if he buys it, he may have to forego some other commodity of which he may also be in need. The subconscious choice between the two commodities will be the deciding factor as to what he will finally buy.

Let us consider three men living in the country, at approximately the same distance from town, owning different amounts of wealth. To each of them the usefulness of an automobile is obvious because of its convenience in being able to go swiftly and at any time to the city for business or pleasure. The first individual is rich and able to buy the automobile regardless of what price. The cost of the automobile represents a small sacrifice to him. The second is less rich and the money he may have to spend for that purchase may represent a larger sacrifice to him. Being on the borderline he will make the ultimate decision according to his subconscious appraisal of the value of the automobile versus other commodities he may have to forego as a result of that purchase. The difference in the human behavior, the larger or smaller value attached to an article by each individual and, therefore, the amount of sacrifice he may be willing to make, external causes, as for instance prosperity or hard times, are all factors which will influence the second man in his final decision. The third person, we shall assume, is very poor and while the usefulness of the automobile is just as great to him as to the others, he is in no position to make such a purchase.

In our example we have considered the attitude of three types of individuals interested in buying an automobile. This, of course, applies to any other article. Society, however, is made up of many individuals ranging between the two extremes, who will assign to those articles different values depending on their nature, wealth, and circumstances. From the individuals willing to buy a demand is aroused for this article. If the supply is less than the demand the price will go up because of competition among the buyers for the possession of that limited amount. However, as soon as the price goes slightly higher a number of those on the borderline will drop from the market, thus establishing the equilibrium between supply and demand. If the supply is larger than the demand, the price will go down because of the competition now rising among the sellers who want to dispose of their stock even at a smaller profit. As soon as the price goes slightly lower a number of buyers · on the borderline will enter the market and again establish the equilibrium between supply and demand. The price, therefore, will oscillate about some given point which, as we shall see later, is represented by the cost of making the article. But regardless of the price, we can easily understand that there will always be individuals unable to buy those articles because they are too poor for that purchase.

DISSERTATION ON COST AND PROFIT: Two other fundamental concepts in economics are represented by cost and profit, of which we shall now give our interpretation.

We have defined the price of an article as the amount of wealth or money an individual must give for that purchase. We have also seen that this price may change and that this change is influenced by the amount of supply and demand on the market. However, as soon as the exchange has been made, at least as far as the buyer is concerned the amount he had to pay will represent the cost of the item to him.

Of all the millions of commodities which are being purchased by the components of society, not all are sought to satisfy personal needs. Many in a raw stage or semi-finished condition are bought only for the purpose of being changed into other commodities more useful to man. Thus the weaver who buys cotton from the farmer does not get it because of personal need for it but for weaving into cloth which eventually will also be sold. The cost of the cotton will, of course, be the amount of money he paid to the farmer. As the cotton changes into cloth which is equivalent to say that while it goes through the process of weaving, a given amount of work has to be done, either by the new owner or by others who must receive wages. Further expenditures may also be necessary in making the cotton into cloth. These may be required for obtaining dyes and other necessary ingredients; even for the purchase of shop and machinery, as well as their maintenance. All these expenditures as made add to the cost of the cloth. When the weaver goes to market he naturally will try to sell his cloth at as high a price as possible in order to derive the most profit, but not being the only one engaged in such production he will be confronted by a price set by supply and demand. This price may be higher, equal, or lower than the cost of the cloth to him. If it is higher he will gain a profit; if equal, he will have derived at least his wages; but if lower, he will lose money in the operation. While we occasionally find cases of factories running when the price is below cost of manufacture, this condition cannot continue for any length of time without disastrous consequences to the owners. The result is that these factories will have to close, and thereby the supply will tend to decrease, which fact incidentally tends in turn to raise the price of clothing.

Now one of the persons interested in buying cloth is the tailor. However, he does not buy this commodity to satisfy personal needs, but for the purpose of making suits, dresses, and the like. As these commodities are manufactured they also will be placed on the market. The money that the tailor paid for cloth becomes its cost to him, and represents an expenditure over which he has no further control after the purchase has been made. The individual who bought the cloth, or others in his employ, must exert a given amount of effort to make that cloth into wearing apparel, and this work must also be paid for in wages. As with the weaver, other expenditures may be required, which increase the cost of his products. When the tailor finally becomes a seller he will try to obtain as high a price as possible so as to derive the greatest profit. Not being the only tailor on the market he will likewise be confronted by a price influenced by supply and demand. Again this price may be higher, equal, or lower than the cost; and depending on that price he will be able to make a profit, break even, or sustain a loss.

Business men engage in the production of all kinds of commodities not only with the humanitarian purpose of making conveniences for their fellow-men, but with the main idea of deriving a good return for the money invested in the enterprise, a good salary or wage for their work, and a good profit if possible. They could obtain a large profit by selling their commodities at exorbitant prices far above their cost. But they can do this only when there are few sellers and their commodities happen to be in great demand. In general, however, the sellers are numerous and the competition among them is keen, so that in this instance large profits accrue only to those who are able to reduce the cost of production and, by being satisfied with a smaller profit per unit of merchandise sold, are able to increase the volume of their sales and consequently the total profit. All those whose cost of production is higher will have to be satisfied with a smaller profit, and in so far as we are confronted again by a great variety of individuals we will have some making good profits, some breaking even, and some who sustain a loss. As some of those in the last bracket will eventually drop from the market, the supply will decrease and a new equilibrium will be reached at a higher price. As the price goes up some of those who had been on the borderline or had been losing will gain at the new level, and by staying in the market will stop the decrease of supply and consequently the rising trend of prices. As any fluctuation of price around the average cost will influence the supply as well as the demand, we may conclude that the price of any one commodity tends to become equal to cost.

In analyzing the cost sustained by anyone engaged in a business enterprise we have seen how this cost may be influenced by many factors. Expenditures for raw material, labor, machinery, upkeep, depreciation, repairs, taxes, rent, heating, lighting, are a few of the items that go to increase cost. As business often is on a national and international scale, it is quite evident that this cost may be different for various persons. Indeed raw materials may have to come from distant places, and the cost of transportation may be higher for one than for another. Living conditions in various manufacturing places may also be different, thus requiring higher wages and upkeep, and so will taxes, rent, and similar charges so that other things being equal, the cost of commodity may widely vary. Of course, high efficiency, progressive methods of production, labor-saving devices, and other expedients may often offset disadvantageous conditions and permit an enterprise to prosper even against odds. At any rate, as already indicated, the difference between cost and price represents profit. As the commodity changes ownership during the process of being transformed into its ultimate state, profit is gradually distributed among all those who at some time or other became the owners of that commodity. This profit may be larger for some and lesser for others, depending on all the aforementioned factors; however, all have to break even at least or they could not keep their position in the market.

Profit then can be defined as the difference between selling price and cost. We have seen that this profit, at times exceptionally high, may become less and often turn into loss. But with the exception of glaring examples and these only for short periods of time, profits are usually small because prices tend to equalize cost. In the long run we may assume that profit represents a small fraction of the cost of an article.

BUSINESS CYCLES: There are times in which, by some psychological force within society people seem to become optimistic. As this feeling spreads among the masses, a great number of individuals are apt to spend more, buy more commodities, indulge in greater luxury. This optimism, which starts imperceptibly among few, gradually spreads to others and acquires more momentum until the entire populace seems to be pervaded. New enterprises appear, and money is exchanged at a faster pace. Under the pressure of this additional demand prices begin to climb, manufacturers are able to show profits, people are more willing to invest. With the inducement of profit, more commodities are manufactured and marketed, and as this greater activity calls for additional labor many persons find jobs or get better positions. The population in general acquires a greater purchasing power and sees a good future ahead, buys more and increases the demand for every kind of commodity. As a result we are confronted by a fortunate economic phenomenon in which prices and profits are increased by the additional consumption and demand while in turn the latter are affected by the increased prices and profits. The money that now circulates may be compared to the blood which, now full of vitality and oxygen, flows to every part of the body, bringing needed nourishment and well-being.

Because of the more liberal appraisal all the restricted wealth, in its natural form or otherwise, whose worth we know still to be the same, increases in price under the pressure of the demand. In times like these personal wealth is also more readily available to support new developments. That quality which urges men toward new discoveries, toward the improvement of things, toward greater horizons of human attainment, now finds the needed financial support and propitious ground for progress. Phenomena which were in a laboratory stage receive more impetus and are made ready for society. New processes are tried, new commodities manufactured, employment is increased, more virgin wealth utilized. New buildings, more houses, more factories come into being; mines are more intensively exploited and new ones discovered.

In all this discussion it is taken for granted that the basic wealth of society is sufficiently large and is ready to be used. No extra land can be cultivated if it does not exist; no article can be manufactured if the necessary materials for its production are not available. This, however, will be a special topic to be analyzed later on. It suffices for the present to say that society, because of this new vitality, is actually richer than before. More work is done by its components which in turn results in the production of more articles and a greater well-being. From a non-economic point of view, society is also more prosperous because the increased production makes available to people of small means a larger variety of commodities. As a result the health of the population in general is improved, and last but not least, as aforementioned, inventions and improvements seem to occur more frequently, indicating that this kind of wealth is also more active than at any other time. This activity on the part of the population is greatly spurred by what is known in the business world as *credit*. This has a vast influence in the forming of business cycles, and we will here give our interpretation of the principle on which it is based.

CREDIT AND ITS EFFECTS ON THE BUSINESS CYCLE: Let us take, for example, a bank with a given amount of money or specie in its vaults. This money has been deposited by various investors. It may represent part or al of the wealth owned by these people. The bank in turn pays them a stated dividend, so that the money they receive is given or accredited to them and is in proportion to the amount invested in the bank. The relation of a bank with the public in general can best be explained by an example.

Mr. Smith wishes to start a new enterprise which he thinks will return him a good profit. For this enterprise he figures that he needs at least a sum of $500,000 to finance the construction of the necessary buildings and machinery, to buy raw materials and pay wages. Let us assume that Mr. Smith is a rich man, but his wealth may consist of houses, buildings, lands, and the like. If the banking system was non-existent the only alternative available for the starting of that enterprise would have been that of selling a sufficient amount of his property to raise needed capital. It is easy to see how difficult it would be for him to do this advantageously in a relatively short time, aside from the fact that he might be unwilling to part with his property. Another alternative would be to raise that capital among some of his friends, which would also probably be difficult because of the large amount to be raised. It is quite likely that if these conditions existed, the starting of the enterprise would be out of the question. But the fact that there is a banking system solves the problem quite well. The bank is the repository of money put there for investment. By charging interest for money loaned the banks can pay dividends to the depositors. Mr. Smith thus goes to the bank and applies for a loan of $500,000. The bank in turn, before granting that request, satisfies itself as to the soundness of the project, investigates the character, honesty, and ability of Mr. Smith, and when all angles have been studied and analyzed to the satisfaction of the officials, the bank makes that sum available. But the $500,000 is not actually handed over to Mr. Smith, who would be embarrassed to say the least if he had to carry all that cash and provide for its safekeeping. Instead a credit to that amount is made for him by the bank, on which he may draw as he needs during the development of the new enterprise. Suppose now that Mr. Smith owes $10,000 to Mr. Green for machinery purchased from him. He will give a check for that amount to Mr. Green, who will go to the bank and receive that sum. Most likely, however, he will simply deposit the check to his account. In this exchange the actual specie has never left the bank vaults. All that is required is that $10,000 be subtracted from Mr. Smith's account and added to that of Mr. Green. For all practical purposes the check made out by Mr. Smith is equivalent to actual money. He has, of course, to pay the bank a determined rate of interest on the $500,000, let us say 6 per cent, and he must likewise pay back the loan itself in due time.

While on the subject, we must add that no matter how bright the prospects of the new enterprise, the amount of money is lent only if sufficient collateral is presented to the bank. This collateral is wealth which, while it remains the property of Mr. Smith, is given pro tempore to the bank, which acquires the privilege of disposing of it to its best advantage if Mr. Smith should become unable to pay interest or unable to reduce his debt because of the failure of his enterprise or for other reasons. This collateral, on the other hand, will be returned to Mr. Smith as soon as the loan is completely paid.

As we have seen, the transaction between Mr. Smith and Mr. Green took place without currency leaving the bank. Since the holding of the bank has not been affected, similar operations can be repeated with others. As with Mr. Smith, any new loan must be duly studied and approved by the officials whose responsibility it is to safeguard the interests of the bank. Of course, from day to day some of the money will actually leave the vaults for payment to persons who do not have checking accounts with the bank. In addition wages for labor are paid with cash, and represent an additional drain, but, nevertheless, there is always an additional influx of money, so that in general the daily fluctuation of specie does not vary a great deal. Due to the fact that lending money to Mr. Smith has not appreciably affected the amount of specie in the bank, similar lending could also be carried on with other clients without endangering the position of the bank. Through these operations large profits are made. In return the bank must pay dividends to the various investors of funds, and to all those who deposit money in the form of notes, checks, and so forth. But dividends paid out are usually at the rate of 2 or 3 per cent, far smaller than the interest from loans, and this explains the vast profits made by a well managed bank. Again the magnitude of the profit becomes apparent when we consider how much greater the credit is in comparison with the money in the vaults. It is, therefore, natural, especially in prosperous times, that there should be a tendency on the part of a bank to increase the amount of credit to the greatest permissible limit. But in contradiction of what we have previously stated, with every new lending a given amount of currency does leave the vaults. Indeed, payments in cash may have to be made to people dealing with other banks which is bound to reflect the increased volume of business, and a continuous outflow of money will be represented by payments to laborers who use cash for their daily purchases. Although some of this money finds its way back to the bank, an appreciable amount is irremediably lost, thus decreasing the actual funds at its disposal. The larger the credit, the greater the drain and if we consider the ratio between the currency in the vaults and the outstanding credit, there are cases of banks which have operated at a covering ratio as low as 5 per cent, which means that the credit is only backed by one-twentieth of its value in specie. Let us see what danger is involved in permitting that ratio to reach such a level. First, we find the general public or the small investor who deposits in the bank a small amount of money, some for the purpose of taking it back when relatively small purchases have to be made, but mostly for safekeeping and for deriving a dividend, then we find people like Mr. Green, who upon receiving the check from Mr. Smith deposits that amount to his account. For all practical purposes Mr. Green has deposited currency in the bank, because besides expecting a dividend for his deposit he has the right to withdraw either a part or all of that sum any time he may so choose. Thousands of others who likewise have deposited checks in the bank have the right to ask for such cash up to the full extent of their accounts. Should Mr. Green withdraw his money, the bank must be ready to pay at any time that amount in actual cash. The physical withdrawal of money is quite often compulsory when transactions are made with foreign countries. Of course, it is unlikely that many persons will withdraw considerable amounts of currency on the same day. In general, the amount withdrawn may be a very small fraction of the actual amount in the bank. It is on this assumption that banks go on increasing their credits to the very limit. Yet it is conceivable that occasions may arise when many people want to withdraw their holdings at the same time. If the total amount should happen to be more than the available money in the bank, it may turn to other banks for assistance, but if this aid is withheld the only way of escape from such an embarrassing situation is to call in outstanding loans. Besides the unfavorable reaction that such a procedure would arouse among the public, it is possible that these borrowers might also be unable to pay, and they would also seek help to meet their obligations. As the feeling of insecurity spreads among the depositors more are liable to go to the bank for their money until, unable to cope with such an avalanche, it has to declare bankruptcy. In order to prevent such calamities the government has established minimum safe ratios below which no bank can operate.

At any rate we have seen how by lending money to Mr. Smith a new enterprise has been made possible. If it is successful, the total amount of the loan will certainly be paid back to the bank in a relatively short time. We, therefore, observe that, because of the influence of the bank, wealth is increased. Besides being of great benefit to Mr. Smith, other investors, as a result, may have their dividends increased. Society in general is also benefitted because of the additional production of useful commodities. We can now appreciate the influence of banks. At their discretion they grant or withhold credit. While this may seem an inconsequential factor, it represents a powerful lever in speeding up or slowing down business. As credit increases, society experiences a feeling of buoyancy and well-being. This increased wealth, however, is not represented by money in circulation but appears in the larger amount of business, in the larger and more varied output of commodities now made available to society, in the better and more profitable jobs available to laborers.

Returning now to our explanation of business cycles, we have seen how the feeling of optimism beginning among a few individuals acquires momentum as time goes on. As people become aware of the new trend they enter into the spirit of things and aid the general activity, thus spreading optimism the more, until everyone seems pervaded.

As a basic truth each member of society has one important thing in mind, the welfare of himself and his family. In prosperous times when everything on the market is absorbed, no matter what the price, there is a tendency to increase production to obtain greater profits. Individuals confined to their own small enterprises usually are not aware of the trend of production on a world scale, or even on a national scale, and are apt to follow policies which will in the end work against their interests. The masses, taken in by the feeling of optimism, dazzled by the hope of luxury and wealth, more often than not resent and ignore the note of moderation and conservatism of the expert. The time must come, however, when the upper limit of demand is finally reached. To visualize better the forces which control the very life of business we may think of the waves, which starting from a ripple, gradually develop into great walls of water. As they approach the shore they gradually become top-heavy and all of a sudden crash and disintegrate into surf and foam.

As soon as the supply becomes greater than the demand some commodities will go unsold. Those business firms which have not been able to derive the expected return from the sale of their products will be unable to meet interest payments at the bank. In turn the banks may deem it necessary to sell the collateral held for such an eventuality. If the sale of this collateral happens to be made at an unpropitious time, it is quite likely that some of the firms may sustain such losses as to become unable to go on with the business and be forced into bankruptcy. But as production has been going on at such an abnormal rate all over the country, the chances are that not a few but many will find themselves in the same precarious situation.

The tottering enterprises, in the effort to save themselves from bankruptcy, will try to meet their obligations to the banks by turning to other business organizations which happen to be debtors and ask that the latter obligations be in turn fulfilled. As large amounts of money are usually involved in transactions of this kind, it is easy to see that panic will spread in the business world. As a result, corporations will fail, factories will shut down, people will lose their jobs.

As to the banks, when some of the firms become insolvent, they will protect themselves as already explained by selling the collateral they had retained as security for the loans made to them. But due to the fact that in a falling market everything decreases in value, it is possible that the banks will be unable to salvage from the sale of collateral the money they had advanced to finance the luckless enterprises, and may likewise sustain large losses.

In such critical times, individuals as well as organizations are apt to withdraw large amounts of money. Those banks which have lowered their ratio to the dangerous limit may find themselves in no position to meet such an abnormal demand. As this fact becomes known to the general public, the small investors, frantic for the safety of their savings start a stampede and a run on the banks with the result that those who are in the most precarious position will be forced to shut down. The serious repercussions of such failures are too appalling for comment.

As banks are so closely interwoven, the failure of any one may well spell disaster for others. We see then how the wonderful structure of credit, which in good times had such great influence on business expansion, now plays an important role in its retrenchment, brings on the collapse of many organizations, and spreads poverty and despair among millions.

The failure of banks and business enterprises is usually attributed to poor leadership or to risky operations, but at bottom the real cause must be found in the disparity between supply and demand. Naturally the poorly led are the first to be affected.

When banks and business firms fail, depression sets in. Banks will become more wary about lending new credits, the rate of interest will be increased to discourage new loans, a feeling of uncertainty will take possession of the masses, and we shall witness a psychological trend opposite to the one that brought about business booms. Business will retrench, work which is not vital will be postponed indefinitely, factories will close, people will be discharged, and prices will continue the downward trend. As unemployment spreads among millions of workers, the purchasing power of a large part of the population will further decrease and add to the disintegration of the business structure. In this gloomy outlook we find, however, the clever and fortunate individual with ready cash who buys up large amounts of assets at a fraction of their real worth. He knows that while he cannot utilize that wealth while the depression is on, he will eventually benefit enormously when conditions take a turn for the better.

Now, as before, the intrinsic wealth of society has not changed very radically. Houses, factories, machinery, land, are still there ready to be used. If we compare wealth at the beginning of a depression with that at the beginning of the previous upturn, we can easily see that society is now richer than before. For one it has more houses, more cultivated land, more factories, more mines. The knowledge of the utilization of wealth has been greatly advanced and could be used for better and greater achievements. But now the machinery of progress is at a standstill and this additional wealth does not add to the welfare of society. Money which circulated so rapidly has now slowed down its pace, and a good proportion of it will remain unused in government vaults, in banks, or in the strong boxes of wealthy individuals. But while society may have more available wealth, it is actually poorer because it has lost the means and capacity of utilizing that wealth. When the workman loses his job, his purchasing power usually drops far more than prices, the owner of property can no longer collect the same rent; the wealthy individual must go without commodities which are no longer manufactured.

We know that everyone, rich or poor, desires a business upturn, but each and everyone is powerless to change the downward trend of things. No one person, of course, is to blame. The reason for the peaks and depressions in the business cycle can be attributed to the uncontrolled instinct of self-preservation in all the components of society, who by trying to secure their personal advantage actually bring the misfortune of all. The cause must be traced also to the system of government which by assuming a "laissez-faire" attitude, permits these enormous oscillations to exist, causing by that immeasurable suffering.

To be sure, after an indefinite period of stagnation, favorable conditions again will appear and only a spark will be needed for a new business upturn. The causes may be multiple and intangible, as for instance a war necessitating large production of weapons, a treaty of commerce with other nations, a new invention, and so forth. There have been many business cycles in centuries past, and all have left the mark of advancement and progress, but nevertheless this has been paid for by the suffering of millions, in the intervening depressions.

RENT, INTEREST, WAGES AND PROFIT

Another fundamental concept in economics is represented by rent. When an individual gives permission to another to exploit or utilize a certain amount of wealth, he usually gets in return a prearranged amount of money. This payment, called rent, is related to the time during which the wealth is utilized as well as the amount itself.

Let us also explain the meaning of interest. Whenever an individual deposits in the bank a definite amount of money, it is understood that he gives the banker the right of its use. In return he receives from the bank a given sum of money, called interest, related not only to the amount deposited but also to the time that the deposit remains in the bank.

Whenever an individual receives a loan from the bank, he must in turn pay a specified sum related to the amount borrowed, as well as to the time he keeps the money. This sum is also called interest. The word rent is used to indicate the amount of money an individual must pay for the privilege of using restricted wealth, the word interest is used instead to indicate the sum an individual must pay another for the privilege of using money owned by the other.

In so far as restricted wealth and money are both wealth, true of different forms, it is obvious that rent and interest represent the same concept.

When we say that a certain tract of land is worth a certain amount of money, that is what a prospective buyer must pay the prospective seller. The exchange is made because in the minds of both that amount and that area have the same value; they represent the same amount of wealth. However, if this wealth is lent in the form of land, it will bring the owner a given rent; and if lent in the form of money, will earn the owner a given interest.

The word wages is used to indicate the amount of money an individual must pay in exchange of services and labor received. It is presumed that the recipient of these services derives enjoyment or profit. In this case personal wealth is exchanged for cash, and as long as the two are willing to make this exchange both forms of wealth have the same value, at least in their own estimation. In each of the three cases given above, wealth in some form is exchanged for money. By admitting this fact we can say that wages and salary are also synonyms of rent and interest. We want to make this point very clear because erroneous interpretation may lead to uncertainty and false conclusions.

There is a line of thought which holds that landlords or owners of land should not receive any rent because they do not take active part in the utilization of their wealth. We have seen that wages, interest, and rent represent the same concept; therefore, if we hold that it is right to receive wages and interest we should also agree it is right to receive rent.

There is a line of thought which maintains that the restricted wealth in so far that it is not made by men, should be free to all. This contention may sound just and fair, but the actual application of such a principle would disrupt our civilized way of life and impede the progress of humanity. In previous sections of this chapter definition was given of the various forms of wealth. We have spoken of unrestricted wealth, which includes the air we breathe, the heat and light of the sun, the water we drink, and such other things. This wealth is of great importance to us. Humanity could not exist if it were not available. But this wealth, as the name implies, is free for everybody, and fortunately no one has yet found a way to monopolize it for his selfish interest. Being free, it does not give rise to economic problems. We have also spoken of another type which we have named restricted wealth. Under this general denomination we have included land, forests, mines, and other things found in nature in unspoiled form. We have also included everything on which man has expended labor and thought to make useful to mankind. This kind of wealth is termed restricted because its beneficial effects are liable to be destroyed or altered. Thus a forest can be burned, the crops on cultivated land can be damaged, a mine can be blocked, a house or other buildings ruined, and so forth.

Assuming for the sake of argument that we should decide to take away all this wealth from the present owners and make it free to all, we should still realize that effort must be exerted to transform much of it into a form useful to mankind. On this account we may grant permission to willing individuals to cultivate and exploit any part of this wealth for the purpose of making the raw materials into useful products. To be consistent with the accepted principle of freedom of wealth we will be forced to declare that these products are also free. Under such circumstances we will never find anyone willing to labor for nothing.

To go one step further, we may allow the ownership of products which are the result of effort, but to be consistent with our assumption we shall still deny the ownership of basic wealth. For example a farmer may be considered the sole owner of the products of the land he has cultivated, but shall not be permitted to own the land itself. While this solution may seem reasonable and just, even though it may be extremely difficult to differentiate between the various percentages of wealth and effort that combine into the making of his products, we can see that it may also cause injustices. Land, generally speaking, is not equally productive, and it is natural that anyone will try to obtain some which is most fertile so that a larger return may accrue from the amount of his effort. On the basis of freedom of wealth it would be unjust to deny any applicant the permission to cultivate and exploit a definitely proven good piece of land, and it would also be unjust to deny it to those who already have been able to produce more than others. Under such circumstances no one would embark on any kind of enterprise, but work only enough to satisfy his needs and those of his family. Society would rapidly recede thousands of years when division of labor was unknown. However, the fact that society grants and recognizes ownership of wealth gives to the owner the necessary security and freedom of action to utilize his wealth for his own advantage and indirectly for the advantage of society.

From the above we conclude that for the good of society restricted wealth must be privately owned; and that the owner, since he makes that wealth useful to society either by adding his effort or by making it possible to others to do so, retains the right to receive a just compensation for that utilization which, as we have seen, is represented by rent.

Others contend that wealth should be equally divided among the people so as to promote a uniform standard of living. We can easily appreciate the enormous handicaps in the path of such an undertaking. This demands a detailed appraisal of vast magnitude before the division of this wealth in portions of equal utility is made. Consider next the fact that land poor today may suddenly become extremely valuable tomorrow. The discovery of useful raw materials could be the cause of this change. This would naturally necessitate a new appraisal and apportioning. But these are not the only handicaps which would make this mode of life impracticable and undesirable.

Assume that we have been able to divide all the land equally among the components of our society. To everyone the same amount will be given, having been previously evaluated from the standpoint of utility. Presuming that all are willing to exert effort and labor, each one will cultivate his land and be able to support himself and his family. Most likely, however, he will have a surplus produce of the land which he will seek to sell at the market. But with our arrangement of equal distribution of wealth we find that everyone, more or less, has the same amount of surplus and much the same kind of commodities to sell. Under such circumstances the exchange could not take place, and, therefore, each one would cultivate only that part of his property that sufficed for his family needs. But besides food an individual has many other requirements. He and his family need shoes, clothing, a house, many commodities and articles. Everyone, because of the equal distribution of land, must devote a good deal of his time to its cultivation, and even assuming that he could be at once a farmer, cobbler, bricklayer, carpenter, mechanic, and so forth, he could not possibly have the time to work at all these trades. Moreover in so far that many articles are obtained by combining many substances found in different parts of the land lack of necessary cooperation, initiative and division of labor would preclude their production and civilization would again recede thousands of years. The great advantage of equal distribution of land would, therefore, ebb very rapidly in the estimation of the components of our ideal society.

The division of labor, which we have found to be one of the basic prerequisites of progress would come to a stop; and everyone would have to work far more and be satisfied with much less.

Besides the various difficulties previously mentioned, which would have to be solved in the process of dividing the wealth, there is still an important factor to be taken into consideration which makes this method more absurd and impracticable. This is the fundamental inequality of men.

Taking into account aptitude, desire, and willingness to work, we may still conceive that it is possible to apportion the land among those who are apt and willing to cultivate it, and to share mines and other kinds of wealth among those qualified for that kind of work. In such cases where wealth is not suitable for dividing, we may even permit some kind of partnership among those willing and able to exploit it for their own good and that of society.

But assuming that things go smoothly for a while, what is to prevent future generations from having different desires and ambitions? It is reasonable to assume that some, if not many, will not be satisfied with their wealth. If we prohibit the exchange of property for the sake of maintaining equality, so dear to many idealists, the natural result will be a further reduction in the utilization of the wealth of the nation.

An additional cause of confusion is represented by the fact that frequently equal amounts must be divided among a varying number of heirs. Should apportioning then be made at fixed intervals of time? We are quite positive that the labor involved in keeping that wealth equally distributed among everyone would paralyze society. Equal division of wealth must, therefore, be considered as an absurdity unworthy of even passing consideration.

Once we admit that some exchange of property in society must take place, it will be just a matter of time before wealth will accumulate in the hands of fewer and fewer individuals. They will be those who work the most, who are more capable, who have more initiative and thrift, who are better able to bargain, and also those who are less scrupulous. But thereby society will exploit that wealth far more than before. Shall we then re-apportion the wealth anew, and repeat the cycle from the beginning? Society in general could not possibly improve under such a mode of life. To this we must also add that it is not ethically right to take wealth away from individuals who have proved themselves better than others, have worked harder, and shown better ability to give it back to individuals who are inept and inefficient, on the basis of equality or to punish those few who have unscrupulously amassed wealth by corruption and devious manipulations. In general, wealth finds its way into the hands of those who are more alert and active, and for the good of society it is just and fortunate that this happens to be the case.

ADVANTAGES AND DISADVANTAGES OF DIVISION OF LABOR: If we should ask which step in the progress of humanity has contributed most to its advance we would not hesitate to answer that the introduction of the division of labor among men has been largely responsible for such advancement. It would be a very poor existence if every person had to depend upon himself for the production of all the commodities which modern society takes for granted, and which he now more or less considers necessities. Take any inconsequential article, which we may pick up at random. If we care to analyze the production of this article, we will find that in its manufacture it has gone through a great variety of operations and that many persons have had to devote their knowledge and experience to its acquisition of ultimate form.

It is hard to visualize how utterly primitive life would be in a society which has not learned the great advantages produced by division of labor. Even going back to prehistoric ages we still find evidence that our ancient ancestors had some sort of division of labor, very crude and simple, but still a division of labor. We find that the males had the definite job of fishing, hunting, and defending their tribe, while the females would attend to the cooking and the care of the children. We can easily visualize that man, only slightly higher than other animals in mentality and instinct, had to rely for his subsistence on what nature would produce freely for him. He began, however, to depend upon his cunning not only to avoid fighting with animals of superior strength, but actually to kill and eat whatever animals he could overcome with his own power and strength. Slowly he learned also that what could not be accomplished by one could be done by many. Being by nature endowed with superior intelligence, he finally realized that a group could achieve things which a single man would not merely find beyond his strength and capacity but also beyond his ability. It is even reasonable to assume that the power of speech evolved from the necessity of giving and receiving information while engaged in team work. Indeed, as men began to cooperate more intelligently, signs alone would have been inadequate to convey thoughts and ideas. The capacity to understand other people's thoughts and of working together eventually made man, physically so weak, the ruler of the animal kingdom. When we consider the relatively short span of the human race, the ability of men for assigning specific tasks among themselves, which is synonymous with division of labor, is clearly seen to have raised them to a level which no other animal has attained. We observe also that civilization has advanced with the expansion and the further application of the division of labor.

When we compare man's state of development in the prehistoric era, and that of modern man, we cannot help marveling at the wonderful progress he has made in such a limited time. There have been, of course, many temporary setbacks in the evolution of mankind, but they have been of small consequence when placed in the frame of history. This progress has kept pace with the greater application of division of labor, and we can safely say that both factors are interdependent. Have we now reached the zenith of division of labor and progress? Obviously not. We still must go a long way before this maximum is reached. When we consider that the industrial era, which has applied the division of labor to a far greater extent than before, is only a century old; when we consider how many millions of people still live in a semi-barbaric condition; when we consider how much suffering and poverty is still rampant even in the richest and most civilized nations on earth, we must conclude that this zenith is still distant and that the division of labor has not yet been applied to the greatest and most advantageous degree.

In our times we may observe also that the higher the civilization of a nation, the higher the division of labor is likely to be found. Assume now that a man applies himself to the manufacture of an article. By confining himself to that activity day in and day out, it stands to reason that he will become more efficient than another with less experience and aptitude. We must also take into consideration the fact that as a man becomes familiar with his work he is usually able to find ways to increase his production. If we assume now that all the members of a particular group are engaged in the production of various articles and commodities with the purpose of exchanging them with others, it is easy to see that each component will enjoy things which would not have been possible were he left to work by himself. In a larger group not one, but many, independent of each other, will be engaged in the manufacture of a single article. Of course, even the simplest item may often require a great variety of operations. As each of these operations is assigned to various individuals, the output per capita will increase and so will the total production. This improvement is made possible because of the time saved in going from one set of tools to another and in the necessary re-organization of mental processes when a new operation has to be undertaken by the same individual. We must add that any labor-saving device discovered by any one of the group will immediately be available to all. Again standardization not only may be applied to methods of operation, but to the articles themselves which may be made into a form that will be best for the particular use for which they are intended, workmen engaged at any one given operation may be grouped in the same space of the factory under the same supervision and direction, and machinery can be introduced to increase a hundred-fold the work and productivity of man.

The life of the community which adopts this division of labor is bound to be fuller and richer in so far as it will have available a greater variety of articles at less cost.

Having enumerated some of the advantages to society caused by the division of labor, we must also point out faults which the same division of labor will involve. As the division of labor increases, each person is made to perform a smaller and smaller percentage of the work necessary to complete an article, and this tends to become tedious and monotonous. The same operation performed many times an hour every day, month, and year will tend to destroy the initiative and dull the spirit of the laborer who is so employed, and quite often he will lose sight of the total operation. This is the first unfortunate result of mass production and industrialization. The laborer who now is responsible for only a very inconsequential part of the work that goes to complete a given article can be expected to feel but a very small part of pride in its completion. The manufacture will go on with or without him. As his pride decreases, his interest will shift to the wages he is able to earn from his work, wages which become so important to him and his family's well-being. The manufacture of that article will no longer be an end in itself but only a means of subsistence.

As long as he is healthy and strong, qualities which represent wealth that he can freely exchange for wages, he will secure a living related to the condition of the market for this kind of wealth; he will become, however, a drag on society as soon as he no longer is able to work. The fact that the laborer works for someone else who may own the factory, the tools, the machinery, and the raw materials required for that production; the fact that the owner and not the worker obtains whatever profit may be made from the sale of the article, tends to deprive the man of that self-assurance and courage which make him a satisfied individual. His effort, placed at the same level as the work done by machinery, becomes a commodity whose value is subject to the ups and downs of the market. He is no longer master of himself and his destiny, and his very life and that of his family are at the mercy of circumstances he can neither change nor control.

Of course, we do not advocate a return to a lesser division of labor. The advancement of society is first in our mind, that of the individual comes next. The fact that a given change furthers the improvement of society is sufficient justification for that change. However, we believe that society in turn should see that individuals be protected from possible damaging effects and see that steps are being taken to effectively counteract any such tendency. For the present, however, we are content to point out that while society is greatly benefited by a greater division of labor, this may at times cause hardships among many of its members.

Take the case, for instance, of a family living in an industrial city where the father, employed in one of the local factories, must support his wife, several children, and perhaps his dependent parents. The high cost of living and the moderate wage of the worker will result in a low standard of living for the family. As the children grow older, their requirements will also increase, and will strain that much more the family budget. There will, therefore, be a tendency on the part of this family to take children out of the school and send them to work in order to lessen the financial burden.

In the most civilized countries of the world schools for children have been made compulsory up to a given age, and laws have been enacted which prohibit child labor. In the majority of nations, however, these improvements are yet to come, and every year millions of children, too young and too weak to do manual labor, are absorbed by industry or farming with the consent and approval of their parents. As a result the mental development of the child comes to a stop, and he may never hope to be anything else but a poor laborer unless especially endowed by nature with superior intellect and ambition. However, the vast majority of these children will simply increase the great mass of workers. Because of their youth, limited mentality and experience, they are only apt to be useful in their contribution of physical strength to whatever job may be assigned to them. The intricacies of management and operation of a modern factory are far above their comprehension. Their minds are too undeveloped to visualize and suggest improvements or refinements of operation. The fact that they are required to perform day after day some very simple task will further limit their chance of increasing their knowledge; and therefore, they will not attain the ability of bettering their qualifications and social condition. As the years go by these children in turn will become parents, and the process will be repeated over again. If they should at any time lose their health and their strength, they would automatically become a burden to society, and their subsistence dependent on charity. This may even occur while healthy and still physically strong. We have explained how periods of depression follow periods of business activity. When depression sets in, factories begin to close, industries retrench and reduce production, and millions of people find themselves out of a job. But even in the process of discharging there are factors to be considered. It stands to reason that the first person to be laid off is always the one least important to industry. At a time when drastic economies are necessary, the management of a factory retains as long as compatible those key men who may prove vital to re-expansion of business if conditions should change. Of course, the depression may be so severe that the entire factory must close. The higher-salaried workers, however, being mentally and economically in a far better position to endure the impact of depression, will be better off than the laborers, who lack education and mental keenness and are thus the least prepared for the battle of survival. No wonder, then, that quite often millions of people are actually wiped out by famine and plague in the wake of depressions.

If one should take a cynical attitude toward all this, he could state that life after all is nothing but the survival of the fittest. With the elimination of these millions of people, the world would actually improve. Indeed there would be fewer mouths to be fed and less drag on society, a great deal of ignorance and inefficiency erased; and as supply tends to increase in relation to demand the standard of living of the others would tend to go up, and this, let us remember, is one of the main factors for a new business revival.

To this kind of abominable reasoning we naturally object, as we are convinced that such a theory not only is basically false but cruel and unjustified. If people are ignorant and incapable of fighting successfully the battle of life, this is primarily the fault of society. Society, due to economic injustices, has prevented these people from developing into a full and energetic maturity. The same people, under different conditions and surroundings, with better facilities for a more normal development, would have become better in a better society. We have observed thousands of cases where men born of indigent and ignorant parents rose to the highest positions in the land. These cases definitely prove that genius and ability are not the exclusive possession of the upper classes. All of mankind is parsimoniously but evenly endowed with prodigies and talent irrespective of class and economic conditions.

Such being the case, every time that pestilence, war, and famine reap the rich harvests among the lower classes of society, future leaders, probably many, in all fields of human endeavor, are never born or become mentally warped for the rest of their lives. Needless to say, this represents an immeasurable loss which is bound to retard progress for centuries to come.

The indiscriminate application of mass production in its relentless purpose of increasing supply gives birth to an additional problem which must not be neglected. The expansion quite often is obtained by adopting automatic machines and labor-saving devices. The lower the cost, the cheaper will be the commodity produced. However, a limit is reached above which the beneficial effect of mass production is counterbalanced by the misery brought upon the many who thereby lose their jobs and the means of making a living. As this larger output must eventually be absorbed by the population in general, we must not forget that the majority is made up of people of moderate means. If we reduce the earning power of these men, they will no longer be able to absorb the increase in production. For this reason that increase not only will be unwanted, but will prove definitely detrimental to society if acquired at the expense of the purchasing power of the people. Of course, we have men of great wealth able to buy extravagantly, but they are few, and their combined spending absorbs only a small portion of the total output of the industries of a nation.

Production, in general, is mostly devoted to the manufacture of inexpensive products, commodities and foodstuffs which are bought by the poor. This, therefore, is the part of the population whose buying power must be maintained and possibly raised if we wish to keep industry healthy and productive.

Returning to the advantages of division of labor, we have seen that, in general, the introduction of factories, mass production, and labor-saving devices tends to lower the manufacturing cost of many products which in turn will reach a larger portion of the population. As the division of labor tends to improve the well-being of a particular group of people, by this meaning either a few, or the entire population of a town, city or nation, it stands to reason that a further division of labor can be accomplished when various groups can exchange their excess products with each other. Indeed there is a limit to what a group or a nation can accomplish in the production of articles and commodities for general use. Lack of raw materials, difference in climate, and other factors may prevent that group or that nation from manufacturing certain commodities. If it is allowed to exchange some of its surplus for commodities which cannot be locally produced, that group or that nation will be richer because of now being able to utilize a greater variety of things. This is equivalent to a greater division of labor and, therefore, beneficial to that group, that nation and to mankind in general.

When any person devotes his time and adds his effort to the manufacture of any given commodity, let us say shoes, not only for himself, but for society in general, he acquires the right to exchange this effort with other commodities of which he may be in need. This exchange is usually made through the medium of money. That this person belongs to a group forming a factory, or to a group forming a city, a state, or a nation, is wholly immaterial. If this individual is allowed to buy commodities made by other groups at a price that follows the law of supply and demand, we can say that he derives the greatest benefit from the introduction of division of labor.

This benefit, however, will be impaired if the same individual is forced to buy commodities from some particular groups to the exclusion of others.

Free trade eliminates inefficiency and incompetence. When each group concentrates on the manufacture of any particular commodity for which it has great skill and natural advantage over any other group, the commodity will also reach a price which is far lower than under any other condition. This decreased price is obtained without imposing starvation wages upon the workers or the individuals composing the group, and will also produce a fair profit for the owners of capital. Moreover the fact that many more people will be able to buy that commodity because of the reduced price makes this method beneficial to society.

CONTROL OF RAW MATERIALS: We have seen how important is the contribution of the division of labor to the progress and well-being of a community or a nation. Due to peculiarities of modern society, we have seen also that this progress does not keep an even pace, but there are cycles of booms and depressions, the effect of which we have analyzed. Now, while in periods of depression the utilization of raw materials is greatly reduced, in periods of boom the opposite occurs, thus bringing progress and well-being to the entire population. At any rate, independently of these factors, the progress of a nation, considered over long periods of time, is safe and assured if the nation is in control of vast and untapped material resources.

The richer the land the greater is the opportunity of a nation to improve its standard of living. Poor countries can only reach a top of well-being which must be lower than the level reached by those who are rich. This in our mind has been, and always will be, the subconscious impulse of a nation to conquer other places where raw material is found. The possession of this wealth is tantamount to acquiring that potentiality which sooner or later will place that nation in a position of self-sufficiency and dominance, it will be able to compete successfully in the world market, and as a consequence maintain a greater rate of increase in its standard of living. Without those resources this betterment will be greatly impaired.

Let us assume a country with a limited amount of wealth and

inhabited by a small population. If the people are active, enterprising, and intelligent they will utilize their resources to the utmost limit of their ability, and will manufacture as many commodities as possible as these will increase their standard of living. But as no nation on earth has all the variety of raw materials that are used in the manufacture of the millions of products utilized by modern society, it is easily understood if there was no exchange of any kind among nations, that this small group would have to manage only with those commodities made by themselves and with their own resources. Needless to say, the variety would be limited and inadequate for a modern society. The upper limit of well-being would then depend on two factors:

(a) Variety and quantity of raw materials available.

(b) Extent of division of labor among the individuals composing that nation.

The second factor will naturally depend on the size of the population itself. Up to a limit, which takes into account the amount of resources on hand, the greater the population, the greater the division of labor and the higher the standard of living. But as the size of population and, therefore, division of labor does not change appreciably in a short period of time, if that society is very active, we can see that the top limit of well-being will bear a definite relation to the wealth of the land.

Indeed, assuming again the limited variety of resources on hand and, therefore, the limited variety of manufactured products, the population soon will reach a saturation point beyond which it will be useless to go as no one will buy more of those products if already in possession of the needed amount. The total supply will represent then the top limit of well-being for the society in question. It follows that if the available amount of resources within the nation is not sufficient to produce that saturation point, referred to above, the top limit of well-being will naturally be smaller. Fortunately, however, nations do exchange raw materials as well as finished products and this naturally tends to increase the welfare of each of those nations well above the saturation point mentioned above. The larger the amount of commodities exported, the larger will be the amount of those imported and the standard of living of the population will be in direct proportion of the total amount consumed and enjoyed. A poor nation, however, does not have a great deal of surplus commodities and as such the amount imported being small, will only add moderately to the well-being of this population.

This proves our contention that a poor nation is usually unable to reach the same standard of living of a wealthier nation.

For such a nation, therefore, there is little prospect of increasing its standard of living much above that maximum permitted by the natural wealth of the land. As such it is faced by two alternatives.

(a) Self-negation of improvement over and above the top limit permitted by the land.

(b) Conquest of land where additional raw materials can be found.

The first alternative is only compatible with a small nation which does not have the physical strength for conquest, and against its will must resign itself to a lower standard of living than that of wealthier and stronger nations. The second alternative is usually adopted by all those nations which have the physical strength to conquer. Social unrest and economic pressure makes this line of action imperative. However, as soon as a nation adopts such a policy, sooner or later it will infringe upon other nations' interests and as this will generate friction and misunderstanding the ultimate result is war. When a conflict arises among nations, it is usually attributed to many factors which sometimes do not seem to have any apparent relation to the actual cause. We feel confident, however, in affirming that at least the great majority of wars in the past, as well as in the present, have had their incentive in the acquisition of that precious commodity, **RAW MATERIALS**.

CHAPTER II

DISSERTATION ON SOME MODES OF LIFE FOUND IN PRESENT SOCIETY

COMMUNISM

T HROUGHOUT HISTORY we find innumerable cases of individuals or groups of individuals who have initiated and given impetus to some new mode of life supposedly better than the one in which they lived. This urge oftentimes was a product of their religious fervor and fanaticism which made them contemptuous of those who believed in other creeds and gave them the impelling desire to sever their ties and their relations with others, and live in a world by themselves. Other times this urge sprang from the desire of alleviating and reducing some appalling injustices within the society they lived, still other times from that of ameliorating society itself.

Some of these attempts reached only a stage of pure realization as, for instance, the one visualized by Plato in his "Republic", others, lacking a solid foundation, were only temporarily applied among few individuals and failed to leave their marks in the slow but gradual advancement of civilization; others, as for instance, Christianity and other important religions in the world, left their indelible mark and became the amalgamating force among millions of people, still others lighted the torch and gave justification to uprisings and revolutions which were supposed to eradicate forever some of the injustices previously mentioned. We cannot devote much space to a study of this kind and shall refer instead to a few important attempts made within our modern society with the view of analyzing their moral worth and their method of application.

Let us consider first the view which advocates that all wealth be owned by society itself. The basic principle of this belief is that the wealth of the nation must be utilized by all under the direction of a supreme power invested in the government. The products of this cumulative effort are then distributed equally among all people. This is called Communism. A vast and extremely powerful nation, the Union of Soviet Socialist Republics, popularly known as Russia, provides an example from which much enlightenment can be drawn.

It must be stated right at the start of the discussion that complete government ownership precludes that of the individual. Rules, laws, regulations, and ways of life are determined by the few who stand in the highest ranks of the government, and are enforced by a well-trained and organized minority. These measures, presumably made for the benefit of all, must be accepted by the entire population, irrespective of class, qualification, and desire. Neglecting for the present certain considerations which will be dealt with later, the government is not in position, nor has it the necessary manpower to cooperate with all the individuals of a nation and assist them in their particular problems of the day which may spring from their efforts of complying with those laws and regulations. The government, however, has the power, through this organized minority, to severely punish all who, whether through misunderstanding or actual intent, violate or evade its laws. It likewise assumes the responsibility of distributing equally and without consideration of effort the produce of the people's collective work.

It is easy to see, however, that the individual who now has become one of the masses and is assured of a livelihood for himself and his family may slow down his pace and do only the amount of work required of him and no more. The understandable poor quality of their labor, coupled to the impossibility of the government's looking after every detail and ensuring that each contributes his best, or at least his share of the work to the general cause, is bound to be felt by society in general. The consequence will be a decreased output for the same amount of working time, with a resulting lowering of the average standard of living. We observe, thus, that in seeking to raise the standard of living of the inept and the extremely poor, all the other components of society will be reduced to living on lower levels. We must also point out that many, through submitting to orders from above for every inconsequential detail which used to be their own responsibility, forced into a life of regimentation, will gradually become more alike in no longer being able to think out things for themselves, more alike in lack of initiative and independence. This is bound to dull and destroy much of the so-called personal wealth, such as alertness, originality, perseverance, zeal, courage; all qualities which are necessary prerequisites of progress and growth.

We need not question for a moment the honesty, integrity, and good will of those who first advocated, urged, and then enforced Communism. We believe that their thoughts and actions were guided by their intense desire to erase once and for all the many injustices within the Tsarist empire. Their purpose was to establish economic equality among men, to see that all enjoyed equal rights and shares in the products of the land, and that all received just compensation for efforts on behalf of society in general. Their condemnation of democracy and capitalism still rings in our ears and their vision of the new mode of life is still vivid in our minds. There were to be neither rich nor poor, all were to contribute their best to the establishment and solidification of the new and better society, all independently of their actual contribution to the general cause were to receive an equal share of the produce of the land. Aristocracy was to be eradicated forever and capital, the prime mover of progress and industry, was to be prevented from being hoarded by individuals who thereby would be in a position to enslave millions of people.

Because of hardships and injustices arising amid the capitalistic mode of life, capital was to be placed in the sole custody of the government which, ruling over the people for their best interests, was to see that the products of capital and labor were evenly distributed among all, and see that all had equal opportunity to work and to gain the self-respect so important to happiness and contentment.

No one can question the beauty of this ideal. The time when men can look on each other with feeling and equality and self-respect, no matter what their profession, origin, capability, and achievement, will be a great one to anticipate, and we must realize how such an ideal must have inflamed the imagination of great minds, produced the necessary determination and enkindled a fervor that knew neither danger nor hardship.

At the end of the first world war the chance to seize power finally came. Russia defeated and prostrated, her army routed, the government and the aristocracy in flight, was left an easy prey to a well-organized group which was waiting for such an opportunity to step in and take over. Their great ideal, their wonderful dream could now finally be tested and if successful made to spread to other nations by aiding other idealists who were also waiting for the opportunity to rise in revolt against their established governments.

But the transition from an old to a new mode of life cannot be made with the stroke of a pen. It is true that the proletariat and the downtrodden had all to gain and little to lose from such a change, but while the new recruits came mostly from those classes of society, still the major portion of the population was too indifferent, too passive and disorganized to take any part in the shaping of the new government. At the other end the established upper class of the country, while disintegrated and disrupted by the national calamity, could still gather some resistance and opposition. All these people, some from aristocratic families, others with large fortunes, had much to lose and nothing to gain from the radical rising, and naturally used all their power to resist the new intrusion. The struggle was literally for life and death; no compromise was possible; and no room existed for both ideologies. The final victory of Communism was only possible because, with the collapse of Russia, the war still went on and the other nations, too busy fighting each other, could not effectively intervene to stop it from overthrowing the rulers and taking possession of the entire country. With these facts in mind the events which followed the downfall of the Tsarist regime and the republic under Kerensky become logical and understandable. However, as long as aristocrats and capitalists were permitted to live in the country there would have been a permanent threat and danger to the government. Under such circumstances the possibility of enforcing the new mode of life peacefully and without interruption would have been greatly endangered and the upper classes, the so-called "enemies of the people," had to be exterminated if this danger to the new dictatorship was to be averted.

Assuming that their leaders were in possession of those qualities which distinguished them from barbarians, they must have loathed the idea of ordering innumerable massacres and liquidations, yet these were deemed necessary to achieve the wonderful new world which was expected to rise from the ashes of the old. The lives of all the innocent children whose only crime was that of having been born of rich or aristocratic parents, even if too young to have any conception of the tremendous struggle that was being fought, were considered an inevitable and unavoidable sacrifice on the altar of the new ideal.

With the spread of Communism throughout the country a vast number of people met violent death, multitudes sought refuge in other countries and as a result the new regime was left free to devote more of its time to the application of the Marxist mode of life. Let us see now if all this sacrifice was justified by the results that were actually accomplished.

One of the truths which the inspirers as well as the leaders of Communism failed to take into account was the fundamental differences in human nature. We see in our daily life how things affect different persons in different ways. Individuals are fundamentally unequal, and between extremes there are a thousand and one variations. Why should not this be so? Humanity, after all, is part of Nature, and one of the essences of Nature is that no two things are absolutely alike, from leaves and snowflakes to fingerprints. Even mountains are dissimilar, so are clouds, trees, birds and insects. All kinds of animate and inanimate things seem to have an individual personality which differentiates them from all others through some peculiarity of their own. By this we wish to emphasize that men, being part of Nature, do not escape this fundamental law, and that we must expect this great variety among them.

How then can we expect to improve humanity by enforcing a system which, no matter what its ideal, robs men of those qualities which we call individuality and freedom of thought and action? This mode of life, if not changed or greatly modified, will gradually cause an ugly and unnatural uniformity contrary to human instinct as well as human nature. The personal wealth or that energy which makes men work and achieve, will slowly disappear and reduce to a herd an active and pulsating society. Under a system where geniuses are treated as equal to the backward components of society, the natural result will be fewer geniuses, and the average mentality of the population will slowly sink to lower levels.

Needless to say that, while the ideal may be beautiful, the method for its attainment is faulty. Another, therefore, must be found, one which takes into account men as they are and not as they should be. With this in mind a better world can then be planned and developed. But this will be the topic of a later part of this book, and for the present we shall abstain from considering the subject any further.

Having set forth the ideal of Communism, let us see why this mode of life, once forced upon a great nation, did not spread to other countries as its leaders had reason to expect.

The aristocrat, the capitalist, the merchant, the owner of property, the professional, and other individuals who belong to the so-called upper and middle classes of society are generally opposed to the Communist mode of life, even though we find many exceptions to this rule. Of course, they all have much to lose and little to gain by such a change. Their standard of living is of the highest, no matter in what country they dwell. They know only too well that the comfort, opulence, security, power to which they are accustomed will disappear if such a change is made. Egotistic feeling and the instinct of self-preservation will naturally bind these elements of society into a powerful conservative group which will use the utmost power at its command to oppose and hamper any effort tending to establish Communism. This feeling, perfectly natural and human, does not surprise us, and, therefore, we must expect and understand the relentless propaganda and the innumerable obstacles placed in its path.

We have observed, however, that among the vast majority of the lower classes all over the world, only a few have embraced the new creed. One reason for this failure can be attributed to the extreme ignorance of many among them, and to the vague ideas held about the system. Another reason can be attributed to the fact that many, being by nature fatalist, are resigned to life as it is, and abhor strife and turmoil. Others still, being poor and with large families to support, cannot go unaffected through periods of strikes and unemployment, and, therefore, prefer a smaller wage today to a hypothetical larger one tomorrow. Yet we do not think that these are the reasons that prevent Communism from spreading among the poor.

Deep in the heart of man burns a little light which he calls Hope. No matter how miserable and precarious the condition in which he may find himself today, he always hopes that in the future it will improve. This is felt even against great odds and common sense. Deep in his soul is the hope that some day, somehow, he will be better off. He does not know when or how, but just the same the hope of improvement is always there. It gives man courage and fortitude to endure all kinds of hardships and privations. All go through life with good and bad qualities, all struggle relentlessly to better their lot and, without exception, long for the time when the sorrow of today will just be a memory. All this, of course, applies to the thousands of men we see every day on the street, applies to the laborer as well as the clerk, to all those with moderate education and means of support. There are, of course, some who do not care for wealth or for comfort. Their aspiration is not toward worldly riches and success but toward higher and more noble ideals. These, however, represent only a small fraction of the population. Of the common man we can safely state that his life and actions are more or less guided by that inner hope of improving his lot. We do not wish, however, to go on record that all want to be rich. Wealth in this case does not necessarily mean acquisition of a great amount of money and property, but just enough to raise the present standard of living, whatever it may be. Even when actual acquisition of great wealth is desired, this may be for more noble and generous purposes than selfish well-being. In some this enrichment represents greater security; for others better opportunity to help relatives, friends, or humanity in general; and, of course, we have also those who desire wealth just for the lust of power and feeling of superiority.

At this point our reader may point out that the feeling of satisfaction that comes to the one who has been able to attain wealth and prominent position through his own efforts is only a product of modern upbringing. Men may be taught and brought up in such a way that satisfaction may be felt for nobler achievements than the pure acquisition of wealth. Examples as such are patriotic fervor and devotion to the community or the nation, emulation in greater efficiency and abnegation, thoughts and actions worthy of praise and emulation. While this applies also to other modes of life, we must not forget that these qualities can be cultivated only in great souls and minds. In the future as well as in the past, the acquisition of more than average wealth within a community will always be sought by the common man, and if prevented he will merge into the masses and his urge of industriousness will be lost to himself and to society.

Because of this basic instinct of man he will look with suspicion on any plan that promises equality and security with a stroke of the pen, a plan that promises an average standard of living, but precludes the possibility of improvement for himself and his family unless through that of the entire community, a plan that visualizes the usurpation of wealth from those who have worked and risen above others through their own efforts and initiative.

All of us, rich and poor, have something that is ours and dear to us, and all this talk of equality makes us conscious of misgivings lest we lose it if the new mode of life is enforced. This possession may be just one penny or millions of dollars, but the reaction will be essentially the same.

Searching again in our inner souls, do we really want that equality which is supposed to bring happiness and contentment and is so widely publicized to the four corners of the world? The leaders of Communism, it seems to us, failed again to take into account another quality of man which makes him different from others and differentiates society from a herd of sheep. This quality, found in rich and poor alike, is called ego. It is the innermost feeling which makes man the center of all with which he comes in contact and of which he is conscious. It could not be otherwise. Nature has endowed him with senses (sight, hearing, touch, taste and so forth), which place him in direct contact with many of Nature's phenomena. The world to him is not what it really is, but what he has learned to distinguish through his senses. As far as he is concerned, the existence of the universe is a reality only because he is conscious of its manifestations. These senses are the means which put him in contact with the world, in general, and by instinct he feels that light was made for him to see, sounds for him to hear, objects for him to touch, and so forth. Without these senses not he but the world would cease to exist. Having established this fundamental quality in men, it is reasonable to state that any individual will instinctively consider the world as it affects him and not others, because all other things considered he is apt to be mostly aware of those sensations that affect him directly. His happiness will be the greatest, his sorrow and suffering the deepest. On this account his inner ego will place him above or at least equal to others; and if sometimes he must admit to himself failure and inferiority, he will find within himself the justifying causes and explanations.

The purpose of this dissertation is to emphasize that innermost instinct in man by which, no matter what his position in society, he will refuse to admit to himself that he lacks the necessary qualities to rise above others, and it is natural that such an instinct should arouse the unconscious resistance to Communism that tends to destroy that conviction.

These two fundamental instincts, hope and ego, are great stumbling blocks to the spreading of this creed even in those classes of society where it could be expected to flourish.

The statement made at the beginning of this discussion that regimentation and imposed equality eventually kill and destroy initiative in men may sound far-fetched to our reader. We observe examples of regimentation where the initiative of men is not affected, and in many cases is actually increased. An army, where everyone is under a single leadership, gives abundant examples of heroism and initiative which should be impossible in the light of our assumption. We have all been familiar with the past regimentation existing in one of the leading nations of the world; namely, Germany. We respect and value the great contributions to progress made possible by the initiative of this country and with such glittering exceptions it would seem that our statement is erroneous and faulty.

To explain the first exception, regimentation among the individuals who make up an army, we must realize that in time of peace and in countries where service is elective, the army is made up of individuals who enjoy that kind of life. The fact that all can be promoted to a higher position if they show sufficient initiative and acquire the necessary qualifications puts the army on the same level as any other democratic organization. In those countries where conscription is enforced the period of service is usually of a limited time. While the army life may not be suitable to all, the temporary nature of the service, plus the feeling that each is contributing to the safety of the country, helps the individual to adjust himself to this mode of life. As such the enforced regimentation will not leave any permanent mark on his personality. The same can be said for periods of war. Indeed when the nation is in danger all able-bodied men are called to the colors and this necessarily includes many who in normal times would have been exempted from the service. But the sacrifice that must be endured during the national emergency is far greater than the one required of them during the period of peace and besides the loss of many liberties and comforts they must be ready at all times to yield their lives for the country. Taking into account the far greater regimentation and discomfort we must conclude that the love of the country as well as the feeling of upholding a just and worthy cause can even overshadow the instinct of self-preservation and give a great impetus to initiative and heroism.

To explain the second exception, regimentation in Germany and other countries living under absolute rule, we must remember that this spirit has been inculcated in these people for many years. It has by now permeated and become almost a second nature with them. But while this explanation may have its good points we do not believe that this is the full explanation of the phenomenon.

Right or wrong, the Germans have come to believe that the world in general is determined to prevent their improvement and expansion. They feel that a constant effort from outside keeps them from acquiring their rightful position among the nations and hampers the full development of their ability and talent. Such a feeling of inferiority complex and resentment unites the Germans in determination to break the ring about them. Their acceptance of regimentation, which is the necessary tool for achieving national aspirations, follows as a matter of course. To this add the hysterical propaganda of their leaders, which finds an easy entry into their minds and hearts. The Germans, then, live in a perpetual spirit of emergency and self-defense, and this makes them endure imposed regimentation in the hope of becoming boundlessly powerful, and with their race respected and feared throughout the world. In such a frame of mind, sacrifices and privations are easily endured, and their spirit of initiative enhanced.

But Communism under normal conditions does not spring from similar causes. It does not appeal equally to all components of society. Here the ideal is for the betterment of the average of society rather than individuals, and for this purpose takes from one to give to another, even if the loser may have honestly strived for that acquisition. This leveling system again does not allow the individual to hope for betterment unless this comes on the hypothetical assumption that the community improves and he, as integral part of a whole, shares this improvement with others. The basic discrepancy between Communism and other forms of collective activities is that its ideal is for the betterment of some through the degradation of others, and while the average person is not actually conscious of this to the extent of being able to translate it into thoughts and words; nevertheless the unconscious instincts in him, previously pointed out, make him regard the whole system with suspicion and antagonism. Communism, as conceived and applied, is not to our mind the solution for the problem of improving the lot of humanity. Shall we say that Fascism is the answer? Let us see.

FASCISM: In some respects Fascism has many qualities in common with Communism, in spite of the fact that the exponents of both ideologies are bitter enemies and intent upon each other's extermination. Some of these similarities are represented by their revolutionary nature. Both rely on a very strong centralized government, and promise support to the lower classes at the expense of the upper. We must admit, however, that in Communism the dictatorship theoretically is only a temporary necessity. If we take on faith the promises of the Communist leaders, their government will eventually transfer to the people many of the responsibilities which it has deemed necessary to assume for the setting up of the ideal society. The time when this transfer will actually take place is, of course, a matter of conjecture. It will depend on the estimation of the leaders as to when such a change is desirable. From our study of Communism we have found how individuals gradually lose their initiative and incentive to progress, and it is easy to realize that the populace will never reach the desired maturity for that responsibility. Basing their decision on such a reality, the future leaders of Communism, even if still determined to carry out the plan of relinquishing their power to the people, will realize that it would be just a matter of time before the basic principles of Communism would be greatly altered, if not completely discarded, and as such that transfer would have to be indefinitely postponed to a more propitious period which, as we know, will never come. In this they would find the moral justification for their conduct, but we must also realize that no leader will ever relinquish his power unless forced to it by a struggle and a fight.

But there is no such admission on the part of the Fascist leaders, who instead advocate the continuous growth of the centralized power. Individuals are recognized only in so far as their actions are consonant and helpful to the nation, of which they are only an infinitesimal and inconsequential part. No freedom of speech, no liberty of action, no independent appraisal of the leaders of Fascism is permitted, and this represents one of the weakest points of the Fascist structure, because it prevents a clear understanding of matters of national importance. The people must rely on the judgment of one person or of one party to form its ideas on matters which may mean the life or death of the nation. Fascism differs from Communism in its claim of upholding capitalism and personal property.

From a historic point of view Fascism was born as a reaction to Communism, which traces its origin to the teaching of Karl Marx, but really it is only a section of Socialism. Fascism was born during the turbulent years following the first world war as a countermeasure to the Communist regime which, having established its power in Russia, was forcing its influence to other nations as well.

Italy was among the first countries to adopt Fascism in her effort to suppress Communism and the wanton destruction of life and property. The leaders of this new party made the March on Rome and declared themselves the champions of capitalism, law, order, and justice. As the name implies, Fascism stands for a union of ideals as well as of interests. The ancient Roman fasces, from which its emblem was derived, was a bundle of rods tightly bound together about an axe. They represented the power of the law and its enforcement. Such an emblem was chosen to convey the idea that only in the union of all could the interests of the people be safe-guarded and protected. In contrast the Communist hammer and sickle symbolized the great attainment of the factory laborers and peasants in their reaching and maintaining the dominant position in the nation and as such meant to convey the impression that the government was finally invested in the people.

The Fascist leaders, attempting to smooth the relations among the various classes of society, realized that capitalists should not be permitted to enslave the poor, nor the poor to disrupt the life of the nation and endanger the interests of the other classes. For this 'purpose a strong central government was envisaged which could arbitrate between classes and have the necessary authority to enforce its will for the good of the nation. Branches of the government were set up for this purpose, and the influence of the central government grew so strong as to permeate all levels of society.

Theoretically the purpose of uniting all classes for the common good of blending the various interests so as to obtain a harmonious whole, of promoting peace and stability, was bound to arouse the approval of all individuals who had a sane conception of life. It is no wonder that both rich and poor entered the party. Youth, with its spontaneous response to the ideal of justice, took a leading part in the establishment of the party all over Italy. Aristocracy and capitalists as well as the middle class also gave their financial and moral support. The reasons for this enthusiastic response throughout the country is attributed to the following facts.

Fascism in its platform justified capitalism and aristocracy as necessary to the well-being of society, and as such it offered itself as their defender and guardian. Being out to defeat Communism, which was abhorrent to most of the population, Fascism promised to uphold the just interests of the poor in their dealings with the upper classes.

The rich and the nobility, aware of the fact that concessions had to be made to the poor to keep them within bounds of law and order, as the natural process of the times, felt that this alternative was vastly preferable to the outright confiscation of property and wealth advocated by Communism, and did not hesitate to use their influence in favor of Fascism.

The poor also felt equally protected by the new party because of its promises of justice and equity. The small storekeeper, the professional, the white-collar worker, the laborer, the head of the family who realized that no amelioration was possible unless the country was placed on a more solid and stable foundation, all saw reason for supporting the new party, and in a very short time only a small and insignificant minority opposed the new regime. Fascism represented the middle-of-the-road policy through which both upper and lower classes could find a common understanding, and cooperate for the betterment of all.

The beauty of such a purpose is self-evident. We realize, however, that this method even admitting the importance of the goal, had various weak points which, in time, could become dangerous instead of beneficial to society. The fact that the upper and lower classes had to rely on a single party to promote a common understanding is in itself an admission of weakness in not being able to do so on their own. It is now easy to see how such a party, chosen as arbiter and to which great power has been given, can use this power for its benefit at the cost of all other classes. This power, held by the few who have ascended to high positions in the nation, without the necessary precautions to prevent them from entrenching and establishing themselves in that position, can open the way to tyranny and to the evils involved in a dictatorial form of government.

With the abolition of the Chamber of Deputies, similar to our Congress, with the corrupt methods used at election time, when people were compelled to vote only for a definite set of candidates, the expression of free will and independent thought was bound to disappear. The national welfare came to hang only by the very thin thread represented by the honesty, capability, and foresight of the leader who represented the State. If at any time that leadership should fail, the people would have lost the power to oust him, and their fate would be irremediably bound up with that of the leader.

The evolution of Fascism can be divided into several periods. The first few turbulent years, spent by the party in establishing itself over the complete life of the nation, were followed by another period in which great social strides were made. Italy, left poor and exhausted by the long and devastating First World War, was able to acquire a leading position among her sister nations, one she had never enjoyed before. During this period Il Duce signed several commercial treaties with other countries, exerted a beneficial influence in the world at large, promoted unselfishness and understanding among his people, and improved the economic condition of the country in general. Factories and industries, which had lain idle since the end of the war, again became active; the herculean project of the utilization of the Pontine Marshes was decided upon and carried through to completion; beautiful ships showed to the world the glory of the new order; innumerable projects of a public nature were given life and support; and the country in a short time gave unmistakable signs of progress and improvement.

Fascism, in so far as it was not infringing upon the interests of others, could not and did not arouse feelings of antagonism at home and abroad, unless we except those factions in every country closely connected with Communism. Achievement of such importance disposed favorably the sane elements of all nations as they were witnessing decided benefits in a land so notoriously poor and overcrowded.

But the great enthusiasm evoked among the masses of the population finally acted as one would expect. Less power was left to the people, more transferred to the government, until it degenerated into autocracy. Only the supreme leader had the capacity to steer safely the people and the country. His word came to be taken more and more as the law of the land, and more than ever the people became willing to yield whatever freedom they had without considering for a moment that someday this authority would have to be transferred in whole or in part to another leader, or that the time might come when the dictator might prove unworthy of his role.

As mentioned, Fascism finally gave way to autocracy, and when we condemn Fascism we actually refer to the tyranny which was the natural outcome of that system. Fascism, as long as it represented the limited purpose of better harmonizing the different interests of social classes, as long as it stood for amelioration of the average standard of living without infringing upon the interest of others, definitely constituted a forward step in the right direction.

While we need not justify the impulses which made possible the surrender of political rights and liberties by such an enlightened and forward-looking nation as Italy, we must admit that these motive forces have root in human nature. It must be remembered that Fascism was born and gained momentum because of the need to establish law and order and for the purpose of combatting Communism, which at the time was fomenting paralyzing strikes and disrupting the very life of the nation. Unfortunately the leaders of the party were granted more power than was justified by the limited scope of their mission.

Regretfully we must admit that occasionally violence can only be subdued by violence, as the justice department of any well-functioning nation knows only too well. On this account we realize that at first force had to be exerted to stop the activities of the would-be Communists and revolutionists. There was not and there could not be any other alternative, especially when we consider that the law of the land at that time had shown itself utterly incapable and inadequate to cope with the problems on hand. It is to Fascism's credit that the loss of life was very small, and we must remember that the actual transition of the country from the so-called democratic to the Fascist regime (the March on Rome) was extremely orderly, considering the profound changes wrought in the nation.

Autocracy, no matter in what form, age and country, has always rested on the ability of the ruler to maintain or compel the blind and unlimited support of the masses. His words must represent the law; his actions must always be dramatic and spectacular. Failure to do so may mean the loss of that support and eventually the loss of power itself. This need of new and more grandiose accomplishments, as we shall presently see was the main cause of the downfall of Fascism.

Fascism was not born in a country rich in resources and raw materials. As explained in the first chapter, in every country there is an upper limit of progress and betterment which is closely related to the intrinsic wealth of the land. No matter what the type of government, no matter the industriousness of its people, no additional improvement is possible when that limit is reached. We are referring now to that period of history that starts from the advent of Fascism which occurred in 1922 to the financial crash in America in the autumn of 1929.

The National Socialist party in Germany had not yet gathered the enormous following that brought it to power. This period in history will be characterized as one in which all nations, under the false impression of aiding their respective economic conditions kept on raising the commercial barriers against each other. The poorer countries found increasingly difficult the acquisition of all those needed materials so important to their industries and to the national economy and they found also equally difficult the sale of their surplus commodities. All nations, in the effort to bolster economic conditions at home, took steps to curtail to the minimum all imports from abroad, and to reduce exports of all raw materials which could be used to flood their markets with articles made by cheap labor. They all, rich and poor alike, suffered severely from such short-sighted policies; but the poorest naturally suffered most. The financial crash, referred to above, and the subsequent depression aggravated conditions still more. It was the misery of the German people which eventually opened the door to Naziism. The tremendous economic strain of that country made fertile ground for the sowing of new ideas and philosophies. We shall speak of Naziism in the latter part of this chapter, but for the present it suffices to say that economic conditions usually have a vast influence in the policies adopted by a nation. Governments under economic pressure quite often collapse and give way to others under different form and leadership. It is in such times that new ideas and untried philosophies are given the chance to demonstrate their worth. Of course, both movements in Italy and Germany had many things in common, such as their origin in similar economic conditions. Only because of different circumstances, and the different nature of the two peoples, do we find dissimilarities in the two creeds. Indeed at no time did Fascism teach or further religious intolerance. Toward the end of the second world war, with Germany in complete control of the country, Italy was forced to merge her policies with those of the stronger partner. However, the Italian persecutions never approached the intensity or virulence of the Nazis.

It is also to Fascism's credit that during the best part of its cycle Italy was able to sign the Lateran Treaty with the Catholic Church, ever sensitive to human and family rights, thus ending a long standing friction between the temporal and spiritual power in that nation.

As mentioned, Italy made good progress in the first few years of Fascism but, as we know the top limit of improvement is directly related to the basic wealth of the country, and the extreme poverty of Italy is a matter of general knowledge. After the financial crash and the ensuing depression of the late 1920's, world conditions grew worse. Italy could not by herself stem the tide of depression, and in spite of Fascism's positive steps taken to counteract that trend, the condition of the people grew more pitiful and miserable. A characteristic in human nature is that of blaming the government for everything affecting a country, even when it should be perfectly clear that the government is powerless to cope with a problem of such magnitude that affects and covers the entire population of the world. Because of the need of keeping the masses hopeful and obedient, governments quite often pretend that sweeping reforms are on hand that will produce the desired results and can seldom honestly state their limitation and incapacity to improve the condition of the people. It is easy to imagine what reaction such a straightforward statement would produce among the masses so eager to solve their economic difficulties. In a democracy this resentment usually ends up by replacing those in power at the next election. As conditions improve, the government in office takes usually the credit for the amelioration, although more often than not it is no more effective than the luckless one. Under an autocracy, of course, this change which as a safety valve gives vent to dissatisfaction and unrest, cannot occur and the internal pressure of the nation is bound to attain more critical levels only controlled by suppression and force. Of course, even here, as a normal trick of the trade, the unattainable promises of far sweeping reforms are made for the purpose of decreasing that pressure, but yet sooner or later steps must be taken to bring that promised amelioration. Now the lack of the raw materials needed to raise the standard of living, the knowledge that so much is lying idle in many parts of the world, ready to be used, is a powerful incentive to any country. Under a strong economic strain it is understandable how Italy gradually began to look with covetous eyes upon resources abroad. It was not merely a matter of avenging the Abyssinian adventure of 1896 or of reviving the Venetian or Roman Empires that started this country on the path of aggression. Was Mussolini responsible for this attitude? That is hard to state. At any rate it is easy to see how a situation may become such that the leader is forced into a path which is dictated by the fundamental needs of the nation. Fascism, in other words, in order to retain its power, had to find ways and means to alleviate the economic condition of the people. This need pointed toward the forcible acquisition of raw materials beyond the borders of the Kingdom.

But as soon as any country, independently of its type of government, embarks upon this kind of policy, it is merely a question of time before it will infringe upon other nations' interests and rights, and sooner or later war will be the natural outcome. While we disapprove and are strongly opposed to any policy that justifies the taking by force of wealth that belongs to others, we must point out to our readers the logic of this policy on the part of a dynamic population which wants to work and improve its standard of living, but is prevented from reaching this goal by the poverty and limitations of its land. We also wish to point out the logic in the attitude of other countries which, being fortunate enough to possess those resources whereby their high standard of living was maintained, naturally did not want to lose them to a nation which could become a potential competitor in the world market.

We must conclude that the inevitable consequence of this state of affairs is war, which cannot be pinned upon any one nation or any one mode of life, but upon society itself, which has not been able to promote harmony of interests among its components, and has failed to apply that division of labor which extends not to the people of one country alone but to humanity itself. Propaganda, the instinct of self-preservation, prejudice, distorted explanations of facts, usually blur the real issues and keep nations in a constant fear of each other. On this account we see nations taking up arms against others for the purpose of crushing their mode of life, under the assumption that with their subjugation and the liquidation of their leaders, mankind will live happily ever after. History has not taught us any such lesson and the world has witnessed many wars fought with similar aims in mind, but the war to end wars usually turned out to be only one in an endless chain of conflicts and devastations.

Once more examining Fascism and its influence on the world in general, we have recognized but not justified the human instinct which led Italy to set out upon the path of conquest. Other peoples in history followed such a policy, and in the long run found it highly profitable. But the Italian people forgot, or at least their leaders did, that we are no longer living in times when the world was semi-barbaric and conquest was relatively easy. Today, when the land on this earth is completely apportioned, and its wealth has become the property of a few countries who were fortunate enough to have made their conquest in past eras, such a policy does not pay. Italy, having become a united nation in the latter part of the nineteenth century, entered in vain the race for colonies, although she obtained Libya from Turkey in 1911 and had held for some time the ancient coastlands of Abyssinia. But if really worth while colonies mean the opportunity of a better standard of living and less dependence on outsiders, when necessity comes, they mean also ability to endure a longer war, strength to fight a more intense war.

To be sure, Italy relied a great deal on the support of Germany. Even taking this into consideration, her ally, as regards endurance and resources, was little better off than Italy; and ultimately both nations had to succumb to superior strength. The responsibility for such an action falls, of course, on the leaders of Fascism who, in possession of all necessary information as to the relative strength of the two contending factions put their country into such a position that she entered war unwillingly and unprepared. By their action, however, they brought death and misery upon millions, and eventually disaster and ruin to their own people.

To be sure Italy, or rather the leaders of Fascism, sought to acquire territory from France and England. The concessions offered, however, were utterly inadequate to the real needs of the country, and the answer given by Mussolini from the Palazzo Venezia that Italy was not a collector of deserts still rings in our hearts. But there is where Mussolini should have stopped. He should have been aware of the extreme poverty of his country, of the fact that on a real showdown he would have had no chance of obtaining the needed raw materials by force. Still, in the face of all this, Mussolini, no longer the spiritual leader of a new mode of life but an outright autocrat whom the King did not dare to arrest and execute, embarked on an adventure which could lead only to the downfall of Fascism and to the utter impoverishment of a country already too poor to absorb additional reverses.

Before the outbreak of the second world war Italy had already started her new policy of conquest, in which the Abyssinian campaign was one episode. This proved the final parting of the ways between Fascism and the democratic world, and promoted a rapprochement with Germany which, being isolated, welcomed the new friendship. But as the clouds of war were darkening the sky, as this supreme effort made imperative a docile and obedient people, the necessity arose of weeding out all the opposing elements, as done in the Communistic regime. No dissension could any longer be tolerated, and all actual or potential enemies of the newly established autocracy had to be eliminated. This, to be sure, was done tentatively and by gradual steps. It was only in the latter part of the second world war that religious intolerance, such as the ousting of Jews from responsible positions in the government, started under the influence of Naziism, which by now controlled and dominated all Fascist policies. Returning to the Abyssinian campaign, the feeling that the outside world was willing and ready to strangle further the Italian economic life naturally gathered all citizens about their government, which never before had enjoyed such a popular support. Swayed by vicious and relentless propaganda, the people felt that to stand alone many sacrifices had to be made. The result was that the standard of living of the population began a downward trend which would not have been tolerated without hope of final victory.

Again we must stress that we do not justify the conduct of Italy during these turbulent years of her history, yet we must point out that such conduct was motivated by perfectly normal reactions in human nature. Any nation in similar circumstances and with a similar background of civilization might have reacted in a similar way. But how in the name of common sense could a nation small in population and poor in resources, wage a victorious war against almost the entire world, which by now had grown gravely suspicious of its aspirations, is beyond our understanding. Yet its leader, with the greatest lack of political acumen, driven by delusions of grandeur, was able to blind the minds of the masses under his control, who came to take his words as Gospel, to make them believe in their invincibility, and plunge them into a conflict of which there could be no outcome but utter rout and ruin.

That Italy needed and still needs a better access to raw materials is a fact valid before the advent of Fascism. That Italy will always need such access in the future follows as a matter of course, and this is a problem which future governments of Italy will have to face and solve. Mussolini and his party did not create that problem, but the pity and tragedy of the situation, which passes our comprehension, is the method he chose to solve it.

But on closer analysis was there any right way to solve that problem? The answer seemed an emphatic no. The natural instincts of men, the lack of cooperation among nations, precluded any altruistic feeling toward Italy, especially at a time when all countries, rich and poor, were going through a very severe depression, when all had a serious unemployment problem, and all efforts were toward improving their home economy. The leaders of any country, no matter what race or creed, are always the exponent of the ruling class and their actions are dictated by its interests. Indeed it could not be otherwise, or the life of that government would be very brief. With such a background how can we expect the government of a rich country to give wealth to another when such generosity is denied even to its own lower classes? England, which has jurisdiction over so much of the globe, has within itself a large population poor beyond description. If conditions were such that wealth had to be given because of unavoidable necessity, we rather think that the impoverished natives would be preferred to those of other countries who could use it against the interests of the donor. Of course, the upper class of any nation does not desire to concede anything to anybody, and under those circumstances the resort to war on the part of the "have-not" countries becomes an inevitable consequence.

Yet war will only crush the poor and the weak that much more. War means unnecessary destruction of life, war means wanton destruction of property and misery, not only for the vanquished but for the victors as well. War leaves in its wake contempt for the conquered and hatred for the winner. War separates nations further than ever. While some of its damages may be easily seen and ascertained, there are also other forms which do not easily submit to estimation and measurement. Persecution, mass slaughter of the fittest, pestilence and famine can often break the very soul of a nation and leave her crippled for centuries to come. Greece, Rome, other empires and flourishing civilizations of the past, came to their doom when either by war or by other causes they lost the best part of their population. Kill the worthiest of a country and you annihilate all the future generations which would have sprung from them. We have paid, are paying, and shall continue to pay into the endless future for the measureless damage done by the many wars of the past. Thousands of geniuses and great minds never came into existence because of those wars; and how much better off we could have been if those civilizations had been kept alive and flourishing is something no one can calculate. With the destruction of that best, darkness and barbarism was the natural result. It has taken centuries for our society to come anywhere near those ancient civilizations. Unfortunately we have not yet been able to find a way to prevent war, ever more destructive as time goes on, from claiming the best among us at such frequent intervals of time. Wars push further away that ultimate goal of humanity which will be reached only when all peoples agree to live in peace of mind and of spirit, agree to build and produce not for the destruction of others but for the betterment of the entire human race, of which they are an integral part.

From the foregoing discussion we must conclude that Fascism, like Communism, is not the answer to humanity's quest for progress and happiness. While we must grant that this philosophy has a few good points, as that of promoting better understanding and cooperation among the classes of the nation, still the tendency to degenerate into autocracy disqualifies this system as the ideal one for society. Is then Naziism the solution?

NAZIISM: In speaking of Naziism, we must first analyze how it came to power, and this takes us back to the first world war and the Versailles peace conference.

One of the most powerful and effective weapons which the Allied powers utilized against the Germans during the latter part of the war was the breaking down of their will to fight. This was accomplished by high-sounding principles of justice for all and promises of leniency and cooperation. The world was going to be made safe for democracy; there was to be freedom of the seas; and President Wilson's Fourteen Points were other commitments for alluring the Germans and their allies into submission. To a country which had borne the brunt of four long years of war, which had finally rejected and repudiated its former rulers and their ambitions, the words of Wilson came as a new hope of a better world, hope of being able to live in peace, dignity, and honor among the other nations. Truly the day when humanity was going to break the chains which had kept her enslaved to nationalist rivalry and egotism seemed finally at hand. As a life-preserver thrown to a drowning man, the new ideal gave the defeated people new life and courage, a new hope for the future, and the Teutonic empire collapsed, not only because of the pressure from outside, but also because of this new regeneration of the Germans. Expressions of relief and joy came alike from victors and vanquished. A new era of peace, of human brotherhood, was about to be molded, and everyone was expectantly happy.

In this auspicious atmosphere the Versailles conference started. What it actually accomplished is now a historical fact. One by one all the famous Fourteen Points were dropped and a cynical play for power and national ambition gradually took possession of the victors. German colonies, of course, were the first to be divided as spoils. Then German territory was granted to satisfy questionable ambitions of minority races within the land eager to join other nations, but with the definite purpose of obtaining the upper hand in the local affairs. In the Balkans, the melting pot of ambitions and races, the division of land became more pointless and absurd. Indeed, in a land in which nationalities and races are closely knitted, no fair division was possible and naturally all those who had been at the winning side of the conflict saw their aspirations fulfilled at the expense of those who had fought at the other. This, of course, could not and did not end injustices and discontent and the fairness and justice which had been promised to all people on earth were still other principles that were never applied. Germany, which by now had lost the physical and moral power to fight for her territorial integrity had become a country from which powerful and weak alike could easily extract the last ounce of national dignity. Those were hard days for the good and honest among the Germans to endure. By now they had learned to their sorrow what reliance they could put in the resounding phrases, in the ideals aired by shrewd and unscrupulous politicians who had no idea of keeping those promises. The Germans knew they were defeated and that the spoils of victory would go to the winners. It had been like that before and it was going to be like that now. If we neglect the Austrian Empire, which disintegrated into a hostile group of nations, Germany fared ill, as she had to relinquish long held territory, not only for ethnological but for economic and strategic reasons as well. She was sentenced to be surrounded by a ring of nations, the quite often referred to ring of steel, with the common purpose of preventing the Germans from expanding. The major victors would provide these nations with the necessary arms and financial support to make that ring effective, and behind these buffer states the conquerors could then relax and digest at leisure the plunder obtained.

This peace, which was supposed to bring freedom and equality of opportunity to all turned out to be very pitifully short of that goal, especially as far as the losers were concerned. However, rivalry and suspicion arose and grew also among the victors. It is a historical fact that the representative of one of the winning nations, Orlando of Italy, left the conference table because some of the promised spoils of victory were denied to his country. Amid all this show of ambition and rapacity Wilson stood great and alone. That his intentions were good no one now can doubt. He really meant the application of his ideals, he really meant freedom of the seas, justice and equity for all. We find here, however, an idealist dealing with unscrupulous politicians and realists mainly concerned with their own personal gain and aggrandizement who for this purpose indulged in long and pointless debates on inconsequential details that did not matter. This served the purpose of spreading their names, their words and their profound opinions throughout the world, while millions of people were eagerly waiting for their final decision. They were also bent on obtaining all kinds of concessions for their country regardless of their applicability and justice, but only for the purpose of not going home empty-handed. The prestige of their country as well as their own made that imperative.

Step by step Wilson had to give way to superior shrewdness and determination, until his magnificent vision of a better world stood discredited in Europe as well as in his country. Quite true, his efforts to launch a worldwide League of Nations did actually succeed, but by the irony of fate, the country he represented was the first to reject that ideal, the first to refuse that allegiance. And there stood Wilson, the dreamer, disillusioned and dejected. He unquestionably was far ahead of his time, for humanity had not yet reached that moral development necessary to appreciate that ideal, and had still to suffer on the long road to justice and happiness.

The physical war had come to an end but the animosity, the hatred, the fear of the disarmed and powerless Germany were still as strong as ever. The conditions of peace were such as to keep Germany bankrupt and hopeless for generations to come. Indemnities far above capacity to pay and all kinds of restrictions were imposed and a part of the Rhineland kept under the dominance of France for bridgeheads of occupation should these conditions not be carried out to the Allies' complete satisfaction.

The League of Nations was conceived, at least in the mind of its founder, as a body of high moral standards and great influence throughout the world, to which any country, weak or strong, could bring problems or complaints against other nations, and in turn obtain an unbiased verdict to be respected and complied with by all nations no matter their power and size.

The United States of America was at the time in the ideal position of being able to give the League the needed moral force required to make it loved and respected by all nations. She could have added also that impartial and international atmosphere vital to the settlement of quarrels in which she had no prejudice or national interests at stake. With her withdrawal, the League lost that moral authority and came to represent the interests of the remaining two powers, France and England. Indeed, with Russia paralyzed by her domestic chaos and prostrated by internal and external war, with a poor and economically dependent Italy, with the small countries of Europe and South America physically weak and dependent upon France and England for protection and trade, with a Japan too distant and too different from western civilization to take an active part in the affairs of the League, this became ever more dominated by the wishes and the interests of the two controlling countries.

The League of Nations, as visualized by its founder, was also to be an institution with sufficient elasticity to adjust itself to changed conditions and needs of the various peoples of the world, so that it could become the promoter of real brotherhood among men of different creeds and philosophies. Another goal of the League was the general disarmament, this in the firm belief that it would eventually place all nations, strong and weak alike, upon one level. Of all the leading powers, the United States stood alone, even though out of the League, in taking such a step. In doing so we must remember, however, that the United States is located on a continent in which she is supreme, and as airplanes had not at that time the great striking power developed in recent years, she felt secure from the nations of Europe and Asia. We must also remember that in making such a magnanimous gesture she was unquestionably conscious of possessing the strongest industrial organization in the world, an organization that can be immediately geared at will for war or for peace. Her phenomenal output after Pearl Harbor bears out our contention. The United States, armed or disarmed, is too powerful a nation to be trampled upon, no matter the physical strength of her enemies, as the Axis Powers found to their sorrow in the second world war. This general disarmament, however, was strictly enforced for the losers only; as to the winners they went ahead unconcerned at a still greater pace.

England built and maintained a navy beyond actual requirements. France strengthened her army and her navy and finally devised the famous Maginot Line, which was supposed to preclude forever any German invasion. Japan built an armada of her own. And all this while disarmament was forced on the losers, all this while lip-loyalty was given to a League supposed to solve all international quarrels. With the confidence born of possessing great physical power, with the acquisition of colonies taken from Germany, thus further reducing the chances of that country ever becoming a dangerous foe, these nations finally relaxed and their activities turned toward the maintenance of a very desirable status quo. They were well satisfied by the turn of events, and expected that the world should take that condition as final, without prospect of revision.

The policy of the League naturally reflected this purpose, and as earlier principles and ideals had been discarded and forgotten, gradually became an instrument of convenience alone. No wonder that its spiritual force steadily decreased with the passing of time. True, small differences among weak nations were settled by this body. However, we tend to believe that the power of the two dominating nations was the convincing factor in the settlement. Again, several international agreements were discussed and carried to a happy conclusion, as for instance, the suppression of narcotics, but the real test of keeping a big power in line against its own will was yet to come. When it did come (the invasion of Abyssinia by Italy), even though the weakest among the world powers, the League demonstrated an utter inability to deal with such a problem. It does not require much political acumen to discern the reasons for this failure. Anything which does not rest on solid foundations of justice cannot possess the moral force which will prompt people to take action, whatever it may be. Italy, embarked on a campaign of conquest, stated that she was forced to take this path to keep her population from starving. Her conduct was wrong, engineered by an autocrat who was taking the primary necessity of the country for his own personal aggrandizement, yet even in a clear case like this, the nations could not agree on a real and concerted stand. The reason for this uncertainty must be found in the fact that back home the people were also divided as to the wisdom and necessity of going to war to uphold the problematic concept of keeping a country economically stranded when, on the other hand, the League was incapable of suggesting or in any way improving the condition of that country. Again, back home, the people were also reluctant to take up arms and to submit themselves to unnecessary risk and suffering to solve a problem in which their nation had no particularly vital interest at stake. The League, in short, lacking the necessary cooperation among the members, lacking the spirit of righteousness and the willingness to face risk and danger in order to uphold established principles, lost heavily in prestige and influence. The final blow was given when the power of Germany again appeared threateningly on the horizon. As all nations took this new fact into account, the League, for all practical purposes was dead, bringing to a close a period of history of which the first world war and the League had been the outstanding exponents.

With this general background in mind, let us focus our attention on Germany.

Germany, exhausted and prostrated by the heavy economic burdens imposed upon her, had to work out her own problems the best she could to avert her eclipse as a national entity. The toll of taxation, to pay for war indemnities, was heavy. But having no voice in the arrangement, the Germans had to make the best of a bad situation and hope that this hate and distrust would eventually abate, and yield to a better understanding of the needs of the nation and of the necessity of taking her interests into account if a lasting peace was the real goal of mankind. Stresemann, one of the leaders of Germany at this period, saw the importance of dispelling among the French people the feeling of vindictiveness and vengeance toward his country, and was a pioneer in attempting a fusion of interests and a collaboration between the two nations at odds since time immemorial. Briand was the counterpart among the Frenchmen. That their efforts eventually came to nothing is a historical fact. The narrow and near-sighted perspective of the French politicians of the period, the manipulations of the politicians of England who would not tolerate any understanding that could prove detrimental to their interests, were a powerful block to the realization of this ideal. As time passed and the people of Germany continued staggering under a tremendous economic strain, their spirit of initiative, which had contributed so much to human progress, suffered a great deal. Germany was losing the moral strength to stand against odds, was rapidly becoming an insignificant factor in world affairs, and as such her vital interests were grouped with those of small and inconsequential nations about which the big powers took no thought, and left postponed to an indefinite future. Thus we assisted in the complete demoralization of Germany, and her credit beyond her boundaries sagged still further on the market. While she was supposed to continue paying tremendous war indemnities, the installments could only be in raw material, in which she was notoriously poor, and only few finished products could be exported for this purpose because of the risk of undermining the economic structure of other countries. The result of this policy was that Germany was being made poorer with no possibility of improvement. The aid which might have saved the Germans from despair and make them believe in human kindness was lacking, so that gradually a sordid bitterness and hate, a blind determination upon revenge took possession of their souls which, while subdued in their hearts, would show itself in all its vehemence if and when they should again regain power.

Although we do not know the creed or nationality of our reader, we are sure that he would have felt the same in similar circumstances. Hate of the oppressor has been and always will be one of the predominant instincts of men. To be punished for crimes committed by previous generations, for crimes committed by unscrupulous leaders who had taken possession of the country and imposed such a disastrous war, was too much to bear, especially when no prospect of amelioration existed, no hope that such a condition would ever come to an end. Their hatred for the victorious nations was bound to make the Germans more determined than ever to take revenge and destroy as much wealth as possible, seeing that they could not share in it. The Germans, in other words, were morally ready to follow any leader who could attain such a sinister goal. The democracy of the Weimar republic was only a farce that would be swept aside as soon as such a leader appeared. The author of "Mein Kampf" filled the role.

Hitler came to power, not with a positive ideal of betterment for mankind, but with the definite purpose of vengeance and destruction, with the idea of smashing and obliterating all those nations who had been intent upon the punishment of the German race, and thus started a new period of history which was to end up in the most cruel and ferocious war ever experienced by men.

We can now ask ourselves the question: Who was responsible for this state of affairs? Was Germany to blame for starting a war aimed at the destruction of those countries which were keeping her subjugated? Were Poland, England, France, and Russia, joined later by the United States, to blame for resisting with all their might the vile purpose of Hitler and eventually pushing Germany into a plight far worse than before? In our minds all were to blame in so far as all were responsible for a situation to which there did not seem to be any reasonable solution. All were to blame because all expected to gain from the destruction of the enemy power, all were to blame because no one saw the simple truth that amelioration can never be attained until all make an effort to promote real friendship among men and work together for the benefit of all.

But how could a world which had attained such a high degree of civilization ever get into such a critical state is a mystery and a tragedy. To be sure, there were millions of people in every country who saw the tragic situation into which humanity had fallen. They saw the forces of hate having full swing in shaping the world of the future, they saw the planting of seeds which eventually would bring the second world war, but they could not and did not change the trend of events because they lacked cooperation and had no definite goal to be reached. A similar condition is found now, after the second world war. All those millions scattered over the world who have at heart the good of humanity taken as a whole are sensing the dangerous trend and are as powerless now as then.

Let us review additional facts pertaining to the world as found after the first war. After four long years of fighting, after a reasonable period given to the heads of states to bring forth those ideals for which so many had fought and died the people of the victorious countries became anxious to forget the misery and tribulation of the past. The fact that these ideals had not been attained due to the interminable disputes among the nations discouraged them, and instead of persevering and expecting a just and lasting solution of world ailments, they took the easier road of oblivion. Anxious to return to their private problems, hardened and disillusioned, they gradually came to feel, because of their apparent inability to change the trend of history, that other nations should solve their own problems as best they could. They left such tasks as the rehabilitation of the world to their politicians with confidence that they had done all there was to do, and took no further thought, especially when this applied to distant countries of which they knew very little. They were through and the less they heard the better. As enthusiasm and moral backing for Wilson waned in America, as politicians everywhere took matters in their hands, leaving the people only partially informed, the gatherings of leaders became a scramble for advantages at the expense of others. What kind of world could we expect from policies of this nature? We reaped what we sowed, and shall reap what we are now sowing. That cooperation which alone could have saved the world from utter ruin was neglected and each nation was bent on its own advantage. The division of labor in the world took, in general, a definite turn for the worse.

Technological advancement made during the war, accumulation of necessary replacements in industry over a long period of time, backlogs of orders piled up in each country, were responsible for the ephemeral revival of business in postwar years. That boom, however, was based upon a very poor foundation to say the least. World trade, due to the confused and disrupted condition of each country had reached a very low level. This boom, like others was started by millions of people who recklessly started to manufacture all kinds of commodities for some future markets, and to this end bought extravagantly all kinds of materials. How those commodities were going to be sold and removed from the market no one definitely knew, but the result was that the price of stocks kept increasing and while many made money, all kinds of commodities steadily went up independently of price and more and more took part in this orgy of overproduction. The time came, however, when the castle which had been built on sand finally crashed and wiped out the ephemeral era of prosperity. The real pitiful state of the world started to show itself in its true form and intensity. Indeed, how could prosperity be maintained when millions of people were too poor to buy those commodities? Even with a large population, as that of the United States, this market was not and could not be sufficiently large to keep the enormous industry of that nation busy with all the mass production methods which had been developed and perfected since the war. This crash taught us vividly that even a rich country cannot possibly live comfortably and prosper in a world full of misery and poverty, and that even though the United States can maintain a standard of living superior to that of others, it is bound to be far lower than what the potentialities of the country permit. With the crash, conditions already had become increasingly worse. Even in the United States unemployment reached dangerous proportions, the number out of work amounting to the staggering figure of twelve million. As all the rich nations touched the bottom in economic stagnation, it was natural that efforts should be made for a comeback. The diagnosis of the responsible causes, as well as the method chosen for the revival of business as usual were wrong, and those laws which would have gone very far in establishing world prosperity and betterment were just the ones most severely curtailed. Any semblance of world trade which existed before came now to a complete stop. Emphasis was placed upon the fact that the crippled and paralyzed world trade was hurting home industry by flooding the market with articles made by cheap labor and this prevented local workers from finding employment. In consequence trade barriers were increased and reached an all-time record, and the exports of raw material, especially of the kind that could be used in competition with local products, was completely curtailed. This, of course, did not and could not produce the desired results. It was in this period that great popularity was given to slogans such as "Buy British", "Buy American", and so forth. These slogans implied that by buying home products the problem of unemployment would disappear and the depression come to an end. From what we have learned about the advantages of division of labor, such short-sighted policies were bound to produce the opposite of what was actually sought. Barriers called for counter-barriers, and instead of promoting prosperity aroused only bitterness and hatred, especially between the nations with vast amounts of resources and those who had not, the poorest naturally suffering most.

Among the "have-not" nations we naturally find Germany. Having gone from bad to worse, she was now ready for anything that could alter the trend of things, ready to accept Naziism or any other philosophy provided that it would solve the unemployment problem and assert itself in the world. The rise of Naziism to power occurred in a constitutional way, as the party obtained the required votes in the election and became the leading one in the Reichstag. Hitler, like Mussolini a few years before in Italy, taking the condition of the country as a springboard to power, called under his banner rich and poor, young and old, and with the approval of many abolished a republic which had been in some degree imposed on the people and had shown itself incapable of obtaining that national recognition sought by the people.

Naziism, in comparison with Fascism in Italy, was not a new philosophy of life, was not an attempt to reconcile the extremes of society, but an expression of the hatred which had grown and simmered in people's minds, Naziism was the apogee of hate which had been gradually growing because of the plight into which the country had been reluctantly forced by the selfishness and contempt of those nations which, by extending a helping hand, would have changed for good the course of history. In contrast to that of Mussolini, Hitler's rise to power had a definite goal in mind, the punishment and possibly the obliteration of all those who were considered responsible for the German plight. He never concealed his real purpose; "Mein Kampf" is a perfect enunciation of what he would do if and when he came to power, and when he actually emerged as a dictator of Germany, he was able to follow item by item the program outlined several years before. In his many outspoken speeches, intended to inflame a poor and dispirited population, the economic barriers raised by other nations were stressed and exaggerated, while the extermination of those countries was made imperative to the final liberation of the German race. The production of war material suddenly became the most important industry of the country, and despite the specific clauses of the Versailles Treaty, which he contemptuously repudiated, Hitler started the greatest armament program ever witnessed in history.

Feelings of this kind, especially if expressed by persons in authority, are not conducive to friendship. Whatever chance Germany may have had of receiving help from the outside was now completely gone. The only remaining hope was that of force and brutality. Animosity having been displaced by hatred, the acquisition of raw material became only second in importance to the downfall and final annihilation of those countries which were opposing Germany.

Hatred, however, does not necessarily coincide with common sense. To hate does not necessarily mean ability to overcome. Hate more often than not tends to minimize obstacles and obscures judgment. This is what Germany is finding out after the second world war. The fate of this country and its talented people will be further aggravated in the years to come, because she chose the wrong path in her efforts to attain her national aspirations.

Before the tribunal of God, it is hard to say who was wrong and who was right. As already mentioned, all nations were responsible for humanity's plight even though we must concede that each nation's policy was motivated by perfectly understandable human instincts. Nevertheless, they all turned away from the only path that led to human progress and amelioration.

Resuming the study of Naziism, we note that the eventual improvement of the poor was one of its aims. The retention of capitalism, somewhat reduced in power, was another. To prevent the country from swinging completely to Communism, this party, like Fascism in Italy, received financial and moral support from the leading capitalists. But when it finally came into power, the economic collapse of the world had already taken place and the national isolation and retrenchment on the part of the leading nations had already been in force for some time. As this precluded any betterment on the part of Germany through her own efforts only, Naziism never took a real stand toward that end by adopting sensible and accepted methods as Fascism had done a few years before in Italy.

One of the first acts of the party was to withdraw from the League of Nations, further decreasing the influence and effectiveness of that body. Moreover, the bolting of such an important nation weakened that much more the international standing of the League, which definitely came to represent the British and French interests. With the phenomenal rearmament program going full speed ahead in Germany, the smaller countries became more skeptical of the ability of the League either to improve world conditions or to defend them against aggression.

Like chickens in a storm they took shelter under the wings of the strongest and this also was in keeping with human nature. Indeed, how can we condemn nations like Hungary, Rumania, Greece, and Finland for taking sides when even a simple declaration of neutrality would have been considered by the contending parties as an unfriendly act liable to retaliation? Although they may have wanted to be left in peace and certainly never dreamed of challenging any of the big powers, nevertheless they were forced to take sides as the least dangerous step in a serious and critical situation. By following this policy if they reaped disfavor and disdain from one party, they obtained protection and favor from the other. Distance was naturally a factor in this choice. Because of this we see Rumania and Hungary ally themselves with Germany and Italy. Their geographical closeness to those countries and the greater danger if the opposite course was adopted, especially when no one knew which was the stronger of the two contending groups made that decision imperative. On the other hand we see Greece tacitly allying herself to England. Her greater distance from Germany and her extensive coastline exposed her to the powerful navy of the Britons. As to Yugoslavia, while geographically attracted toward the Axis Powers, this course was denied to her. Indeed, Yugoslavia, being a product of the Versailles Treaty, had acquired territory from other countries in the Balkans which had been faithful to Germany. It was logical, therefore, that if Germany should have emerged victorious from the impending war, that country would have been forced to lose much of her land. As a result Yugoslavia, spurned by the Axis, tried to avoid an outright allegiance with Britain as this would have meant a speedy retaliation and a very uncertain support from a weak and hesitating Chamberlain. It took a coup d'état to make up her mind for the final decision.

Although Naziism may have had some ideal of rehabilitation for humanity in general, which we very strongly doubt, it never made any effort in that direction. In its appraisal we must be guided from what it accomplished, and from the goal it set itself to attain. What it accomplished was a modest boom in industry, brought by the tremendous preparations for war. Indeed, this made jobs for millions of people who had been unemployed for years. This effort, however, being aimed at the destruction of great sections of mankind was basically wrong and condemnable. As a result rearmament booms started among other nations with a different philosophy of life. Because of its universality the consequent economic revival among all nations cannot be ascribed to the excellence of any particular mode of life and even in this country, we feel confident that the New Deal would have failed very badly if billions and billions of dollars had not been poured in the life of the nation to get ready for the impending disaster. For this ephemeral prosperity humanity has paid and will pay very dearly for centuries to come.

As mentioned before what Naziism sought to accomplish with a successful war was the conquest of all nations responsible for the previous German defeat thereby stripping them of all colonies and raw material, which had represented a large factor in their economic superiority. The Third Reich, superseding and probably surpassing in size and wealth the British Empire, would have made Germany ruler of the world.

Now anything which contemplates the betterment of the few at the expense of the many is not an ideal. Christianity, Buddhism, Confucianism, and other religions may be classified as such as they tend to improve moral standards and the spiritual amelioration of their followers, transcend physical borders and with no discrimination of race or of wealth apply to humanity in general. In this respect we would even include Communism as this also, envisages a better world on earth, but we cannot and will not call ideal any philosophy which aims at the exaltation of a group at the expense of others. Its higher standard of living is not acquired through better methods of doing things, but by the seizure of wealth and privileges. If successful this would leave the world and humanity in general in a far worse condition than before. Due to the frailty of men we understand the large following which Naziism gathered in Germany. After all it was promising that the so-called super-race was to reign over all others in a world subjugated and enslaved by them. Contemptible and foolish as this feeling and attitude may have been, can we honestly say that only Germany is apt to fall into such hallucinations of grandeur and as such punished and made to suffer the consequences? Do you not think, reader, that feelings of this kind usually spread among people in the inverse proportion of their intelligence and common sense? The pride of belonging to a super-race adds to that inner ego which lies deep in each soul. Does not such a feeling make every Briton happy to belong to a country which controls such a large section of the world, independently of the fact that he himself may be dejectedly poor? Does it not make every individual in America proud to belong to the most dynamic and progressive country in the world, although he himself is hopelessly stupid and backward. Does not a Frenchman feel proud to belong to the country which gave birth to Voltaire, Louis XIV, Napoleon, and because of the revolution gave birth to present society? Does not an Italian feel proud to belong to a country which gave birth to Dante, Petrarch, Raphael, and through Rome became the spiritual mother of the present civilization? Does not a Spaniard feel proud to belong to the land of Cervantes and Charles V who could boast that the sun never set on his empire? This subconscious passion, found among all, is more easily discernible in others than in ourselves, and while we may feel hurt and impatient in detecting such absurdities in others, still we do not realize that similar emotions and feelings are deep in our souls as well. This, however, is the subconscious feeling which demagogues in every country tend to encourage and inflame for the purpose of rousing public opinion into channels which are contrary to justice and progress. This is the feeling which serves to gather all the components of a nation about their government when issues between nations arise. This is the feeling which Hitler utilized to acquire power and become dictator. The Germans realized and understood that this wonderful world of the future was yet to be achieved, and that great sacrifices had to be endured. Guns had to be preferred to butter; enemies of the regime done away with; the Jews, resistant to assimilation, who controlled so much of the national wealth and had in their power the means of obstructing the supreme effort of the country, had to be relieved of their possessions and exterminated. Religion, in so far that it advocated peace among men, was opposed to the German philosophy of life, endangered the union of purposes of the population and in brief was a dangerous and foreign influence no longer to be tolerated. By the elimination of all creeds, by the extermination of all persons who could endanger the realization of the great destiny of the race, the country would be better prepared for the ultimate effort of war.

That the destruction of Naziism was to be sought by all who had the good of humanity at heart goes without saying. This philosophy of life which we call Naziism, being devoid of acceptable ideals, actually is only an empty word, which by association has come to represent the policies and prejudices of the now vanquished leaders of Germany.

Such policies under different forms and with different degrees of virulence are practiced by governments of other countries whose mode of life is identified by other names equally void of meaning, equally void of that true spirit and ideal which contemplates the betterment of the entire humanity, and not the betterment of a particular class in a particular country. Indeed, assuming that Germany had won the war, do you think, reader, that all classes of the new German Empire would have equally shared the spoils of conquest and victory? We very strongly doubt such an outcome. The real war was not meant for that purpose. As we see it, the leading class and the overlords of Germany aimed at the overthrow of the overlords and leading classes of other countries. The German people, the common people, beyond the doubtful glory of belonging to the most powerful nation on earth, would have continued as poor and miserable as before, just as poor as the millions within the British Empire. To be sure, with such a victory, they would have been able to gain better jobs and possibly a higher standard of living, but as to their becoming wealthy and prosperous it would have been out of the question. In short, all this sacrifice, all this destruction, all this enormous waste of life and property was made only for the benefit of the few potent overlords who were the only ones apt to gain by any acquisition of land, apt to gain from the elimination of the overlords of other countries. This has been, is, and will be the true purpose of war which, obscured by all sorts of beautiful ideals or by the great promises to the common people, has always been able to inflame and promote the necessary enthusiasm among millions to give up their very lives for hopes and ideals which are not meant to be granted. In this respect Germany is no worse than other countries. All nations, rich or poor, are made up of many classes, and the ruling one, keeping alive an unnecessary nationalism, is able to drive a docile population to fight for the betterment of the leading class and no one else.

Why were all the millions of Americans, British, and French fighting this war? Were they actually fighting to uphold the ideal of democracy and liberty in other countries? Were they actually determined to crush and wipe out from the face of the earth the philosophy of Fascism, Naziism, and absolutism? If this was the case, why is it their nations tried to get along with Communism, which we know is a tyranny in common with Fascism and Naziism? Why is it that they did not or do not declare war upon certain of the South American republics which have Fascist regimes? Do not let propaganda and a distorted sense of nationalism set you astray. The real cause of the war was that the overlords of Germany, Italy, and Japan, independently of their philosophies, set out to dispossess and crush the overlords of the democracies, which in turn aroused their countrymen, and sent them to crush and overwhelm the enemy no matter the cost or consequences.

It is a well-known fact that masses of people may, under different impulses and feelings, perform deeds of supreme beauty and abnegation or be responsible for the most horrible crimes. The multitude is like that everywhere and cases in the history of the various nations prove our contention. As we are not so much advanced in this respect, it is perfectly futile to blame and to punish the complete population of a country for having fallen prey to the viles and to the promises of bad leadership. Let us remember that this could have happened and may happen with similar results to any other country on earth. Under that influence the masses acted as could be expected of an agglomeration of fanatics no longer in their senses. They blindly followed the dictates of the autocrats who unleashed the lowest instincts in men for their own advantage and that of the class they represented.

"Vox populi, vox Dei" could only be uttered by one who did not really know human nature, or it may have been thought of by someone who had the subtle intent of lulling the people into thinking that they themselves were arbiters of their destiny, in order better to guide them along the desired path without knowing that they actually were a blind tool in the hands of an unscrupulous few.

It is more or less useless by now to express ourselves about this ideology called Naziism. Besides its lack of a real ideal of betterment for humanity in general, we feel that, had it been successful, the world would have been far worse than now. No longer would independent thought or liberty exist, but all would have been under the will of the tyrants who ruthlessly would have ruled for their benefit alone. Naziism, in other words, is not the mode of life we would advocate for mankind.

Is democracy, then, the answer to this question?

DEMOCRACY

Democracy, as the name implies, means rule by the people, in contrast to monarchy which means rule by the King, to aristocracy or rule by the nobility, and to oligarchy or rule by a few. In a democratic state those who assume positions in the government are elected by the people for a predetermined number of years, during which while they may be granted privileges not easily acquired by others, they assume also important responsibilities. Officials must relinquish their positions to any newly-elected successors at the end of their terms, and likewise be ready to abdicate their authority if and when the people no longer have confidence in them.

The functions of a government are many and varied. Among the most important we may enumerate the following:

1. It makes rules which become the laws of the land and

guides the relationship among the members of society under
its rule.

2. It upholds the sacred rights of men, it supports and defends
   the customs and the mode of life considered proper by the
   majority of the population, sets up a monetary system by
   which a better exchange may be promoted among its
   citizens, and thereby adds to that division of labor so fundamentally important to the well-being of the nation.

3. It organizes and empowers a police force to maintain the
   laws of the land, and establishes courts by which the in-
   fringer upon the rights of society may be tried and punished,
   besides settling disputes among various individuals according to those laws.

4. It assumes the burden of undertaking those projects of a
   general usefulness to the nation which are of such a nature
   that no individual could successfully accomplish them alone.

5. It represents the State in all dealings with other nations, and
   has the power to draw up treaties with them in the effort
   to enhance the progress and improvement of society.

6. It maintains military forces in order to uphold and defend
   the rights of the State in disputes which may arise with other
   countries.

Theoretically in a democratic state the government represents the
people and is elected by them for that definite purpose. This, however, presupposes that the people are cognizant of the aims that
must be attained and of the problems that must be met, and that
they have the necessary knowledge and perception for choosing the
individuals who are best qualified for the various positions.

In an enlightened community such as Athens, where the people
took an active part in national policies, democracy may be said to
have reached its zenith. Under the constant scrutiny of the citizens
the government had to follow a definite course dictated by the
people, or it could not retain their support and eventually would
have been forced out of power. Under this true democracy we see
that Athens reached the highest stage of civilization, as the architec-
tural masterpieces left behind and the great philosophic thoughts
will easily testify.

Some will say that Athens included in its population a large proportion of slaves who were deprived of human rights and liberties
and as such this fact should preclude our taking this state as a pro-
totype of democracy. To this we disagree. We must remember that

servitude and slavery, since time immemorial, has been an accepted
and normal condition of society. While slavery still exists in many
backward countries of the world, we must remember also that we
still have within us many individuals born in servitude and only
freed through a cruel and devastating civil war. As such we must
make the necessary allowance when referring to this period of
history and must take into account the fact that the slaves were not
considered part of society. With this concept clear in our mind, we
feel justified in taking Athens as the mother of democracy. But, as
we shall see, a government of this kind is always in danger of trans-
mutation and change.

The officals who are first elected to responsible positions probably
believe that the government is the people. They may have striven
ardently for the ideal, and upon election may have devoted all their
efforts, at the cost of personal sacrifices, to upholding these views.
Yet being human and making due allowance for the many exceptions, it follows that the power inherent in their position and
authority is apt to make them over-conscious of the importance of
their contributions to society. There are always a hundred and one
projects which, if approved and carried out, will greatly benefit
everyone, and because of their zeal for reform and desire to advance
society, they finally believe themselves to be the only ones who can
see those measures through. Many leaders in history followed, and
even yet follow, Machiavelli's theory that the end justifies the
means. Because of such end in mind, they frequently use their
power to influence and convince the voters at election time so that
they may continue unhampered those projects and that program
which has proved so beneficial to the people. The people in turn
feel that no harm will come of returning to power the leaders who
have done so much for society. This, however, creates a precedent
and provides the necessary justification for others who lack similar
qualifications and motives, to perpetuate themselves into office.
Enamored of their positions, the new officials will not hesitate to
use their power for this purpose. As such they also in turn will con-
fuse the people and lead them to believe that society's interests and
well-being depends on returning them into power.

Even in a small State like Athens, where people could easily
judge for themselves the worth of the laws enacted by those in
office, there were ways of misleading the masses, such as the bribery
and the awarding of government positions to unscrupulous men
able to bring over others to their views and to arouse a popular
demand for fundamentally unsound legislations. With their in-

fluence at the polls those in power can easily override the will of a more enlightened minority. This union of interests in a group eventually comes to form a party which, once in power, will not hesitate to perpetuate itself in that position. As such among good laws there may be others that are not as good for the people and only forced on them, by subterfuge and by distortion of facts. When the unfavorable consequences of such legislations are finally felt, this will logically spell the downfall of that party. There is little reason, however, to believe that its successor, the opposing party, will not follow similar tactics in its turn, political standards having been set. At this stage no longer does pure democracy exist.

Nevertheless as long as elections are the expression of the free will of the people, even though at times issues may be deliberately misrepresented and muddled, we can still say that whoever is in power rules because of that expressed free will. The people, at all times, retain the privilege of overthrowing the government if that is what they deem necessary to the well-being of the nation. We must realize, however, that the people of Athens because of their limited number and compactness were in a position to know the moral and intellectual qualities and capabilities of the candidates whom they elected, had a better opportunity to keep informed of the many issues at stake, and therefore could make a better and more intelligent choice of their leaders.

In the effort to perpetuate themselves into office we find individuals who do not hesitate to use much stronger methods than those already referred to. Such extreme and dangerous steps may vary from falsifying the ballots through bribery of election officials to the outright prevention of voting. Another method is that of using the military forces to block or to crush any attempt of insurrection by the people or any effort to overthrow the government. Of course, when such a stage has been reached, democracy is dead and absolutism has already taken its place.

In concluding the subject we must mention another factor which may endanger democracy. The government, being elected by the people for their good, assumes the duty to protect not only the rights and interests of its citizens according to definite laws, but also the duty to safeguard the nation itself against other nations. In this world of aggressiveness and expansion the interests of one nation quite often do not coincide with those of another and, even between democracies, friction may arise and lead to conflicts. When one democratic nation is defeated this may mean also the end of its pure democratic form of government. Indeed this government, even though chosen by its people, will not be tolerated if determined to carry policies that are in any way detrimental to the victor nation which now controls the very life and death of every citizen of the vanquished democracy. A government of its choosing will usually be followed by a government more acquiescent to the interests of the victor and less concerned with those of the defeated population. We have previously referred to the necessity of an enlightened, honest, and highly public-minded population to obtain what we could call a pure democracy. This unfortunately is an achievement that no country in the past or at present has ever been able to attain. First of all, even in the smallest and most civilized countries, the problem of governing the state reaches such complicated forms and magnitude that it is impossible for the average individual, who usually lacks the necessary information, given only to those in power, to judge the various issues that must be solved, no matter how intelligent and conscientious he may be. With the exception of those few who by inclination or profession make a detailed study of government in all its intricacies, the great majority of the population, even assuming they are public-minded enough to inform themselves of the merits or demerits of the various questions at stake, must form their opinion from orators and radio speakers, or from propaganda publications which more often than not tax the mentality of the average man and leave him more confused and baffled than ever. The press, which by its enormous circulation has come to represent the major influential factor for the informing of the public, may and occasionally does fall into the hands of unscrupulous men who take advantage of its power to mold public opinion.

Thus far we have considered a small state where the issues are relatively few and simple. If the nation is considerably larger, it is easy to realize how complicated the problems of government will become. Their citizens are asked to place into office and in vital positions individuals who are outside their immediate zone of acquaintances. The merits and capabilities of these citizens come to them through the usual channel of propaganda. Their opinion depends even more on the press and on the persuasiveness of individuals who, having so much at stake in the success of their party, go to great lengths in emphasizing the value of their pledges and their candidates and in minimizing whatever their opponents may offer or say on the subject. The average citizen, therefore, is usually left bewildered in making a choice among the many contradictory claims which he is in no position to prove or disprove.

In a large democracy there is again no assurance that the interests of the country may not antagonize those of another nation. Open conflict may be the consequence, and if the democracy should lose the war, this will also spell the end of its freedom, just as has been shown to be the case with smaller states.

Taking human nature as found, can we judge democracy to be the best form of government for a country? Comparing it with other forms devised by men since time immemorial, we cannot hesitate in our choice. Only in a pure democracy can the true will of the people make itself known and felt, or justice be achieved and maintained among all men. Unfortunately, however, this form of government is, to say the least, unstable and insecure. The presumption that all the citizens of a country are equally public-minded and interested in national affairs over and above their personal interest, that they are sufficiently keen-minded to decide as to what is good or bad for the nation and to have equal voice in shaping the destiny of their nation is very unrealistic. Problematic also is the assumption that such an ideal will be attained in the distant future when culture and civilization approach nearer perfection. More likely than not, only a small part of the population will ever take interest in matters of state. Of this minority only a few will be sufficiently idealistic to strive for a better society over and above their personal interest; as to the others their personal concerns and ambitions will be the prime motives of their actions. Depending on circumstances, sooner or later democracy will yield to other forms and other systems. As the new government and the new party finally shows its true aim and intent, as the people are gradually and relentlessly deprived of sacred and hard earned liberties and human rights, strife and revolution will break out and, if successful, the power of the few will be returned to the many. By this a new cycle is in the making. Pure democracy in other words is only a Utopian ideal that can be temporarily won and secured through the efforts of patriots and generous souls who, willing to suffer and sacrifice their lives, become the spiritual leaders of the people and with them promote the downfall of tyranny. But as the driving force of these individuals ceases to influence the people, ignorance and apathy will again open the door to conditions which eventually will evoke oligarchy, absolutism and servitude.

THE BRITISH EMPIRE

Considering all the countries which we are accustomed to term democracies, can they be said to have a true democratic government? Let us analyze this problem a little more deeply. Is Britain, the arch-supporter of democracy since time immemorial, herself really a truly democratic state?

We find in the British Empire a Commonwealth of nations vastly differing in civilization and standard of living. They take the dictates of and conform their economy to the main interests of the mother country; namely, England; they are forced to sell her large proportions of their resources and raw materials at prices far lower than those charged other countries. The colonies are also forced to buy necessary finished products from the mother country at a cost often considerably higher than of similar products from other nations. Due to this definite disadvantage the true interests of the natives cannot be said to have been taken into account, and hence a system of this kind cannot be called democracy.

At this point few words of explanation are in order. What we shall say about England and the British Empire may sound outdated to our reader who, within the last few years, has witnessed the liberation of two great pillars of the Empire; namely, Egypt and India, has witnessed a rise to power of a socialistic government, has witnessed many far-reaching reforms. These important steps, however, do not let us forget for an instant are the direct result of the new and powerful forces at play in the world today which not even the British can stem or alter. If those social forces that brought the second world war had not existed, it is our honest belief that those changes we have just referred to above would have never occurred, at least not at the present, and that England today would still enjoy the same predominant position to which she has been accustomed since time immemorial. What we want to emphasize by such dissertation is that these changes and reforms are not the spontaneous products of a radical change in character and way of thinking on the part of those who control the destiny of the Empire, but are the necessary and unavoidable compromises in a world that is becoming more and more conscious of those sacred rights of man. As such, the granting of freedom to those nations, the reforms tending to ameliorate the standard of living of the working classes lose the importance and the beauty that undoubtedly they would have had if they had been a result of a new regeneration in human nature and as such granted freely and spontaneously. For this the Britons are not to blame as any other nation or any other race in her position would have undoubtedly acted in a similar way. This, however, goes only to show that every step in progress and amelioration, in the past as well as at preesnt, can only be secured through strife and determination, can only be secured through the destruction of wealth and property, can only be secured through untold suffering and destruction of human lives.

With these concepts in mind, what we shall say applies to the England of prewar days, applies to the England that rested unchallenged and unchallengeable over lands and seas, applies to the England, the absolute ruler of more than five hundred millions of people scattered all over the globe.

We are conscious of the great contribution of this nation and of this race to our civilization, we are conscious of the fact that the Britons are among the most progressive and enlightened in the world and we cannot conceive any federation of nations without this race or this nation which has given us, to mention a few, a Shakespeare, a Newton, a Spencer and a Mill. We are not apt to blame the British people for acts and policies emanating from their government now as well as in the past because we know and realize how powerless is the average individual of a nation when it comes to setting the policies of the state. This may also seem an overstatement on our part as we are sure that every British citizen feels and believes that because of the power of his vote, he has a definite choice and responsibility in the shaping of those policies. After all we have said about those basic instincts of ego and nationalism, and if we admit that the Britons in this respect are not different from other people, they also, being human, respond to the same instincts and desires, and as such tend to follow blindly the ideals and the policies set by great personalities who now and then come to the fore and shape the destiny of the nation. Gladstone, Pitt, Disraeli are such leaders who, because of their great magnetic personality and talent, because of their mastery of speech and power of persuasion have been able to become the spiritual leaders of large portions of the nation and by that able to set policies that were and are taken as a base and as a guide in the future life of the nation. England is not alone in this respect. Mazarin, Bismarck, Peter the Great, Richelieu, Metternich, were also such leaders in their respective nations and they also were great factors in the shaping and reshaping of Europe according to their ideals and their interests. Partly because of the enormous power they represented, partly because of their talents and acumen in being able to take advantage of circumstances favorable to their nations and to their parties, they also did not hesitate to follow Machiavelli's dictate that the end justifies the means and as such not once, but many times, promoted and created situations by which their nation would increase its power and its well-being in relation to others. This added glory and influence to their names, this kept their party in power, this added luster and glory to their nation. But were these men actually great? In some respects we must say that they were; however, they were most of all men of their times and not men of the future, this being one of the most important prerequisites of true greatness, they were men bent at the amelioration of the people they represented regardless of the consequences in the distant future either to their nation or to humanity in general.

We are now ready to return to our topic: The British Empire. As we see, at least up to the second world war, England has enjoyed and to some extent is enjoying now a monopoly over a vast proportion of the earth's raw materials. Depending on circumstances she is in a position to strangle economically almost any other nation on earth. This power may also be exerted against any of her colonies which might seek to secede without her personal agreement. Monopoly, aggravated by trade barriers, prevents, as a generality free competition and is detrimental not only to the well-being of the people of Britain and her colonies, but also to the world in general. It is a matter of general knowledge how much misery and poverty can be found even in London, the center and capital of the Empire. Is this democracy? We can hardly think so when millions of its people spread all over the world are forced to work for the benefit of a small and powerful class which has in its power the life and death of such a large part of humanity. How long have we not observed a vast country like India futilely bid for freedom before it was grudgingly conceded? Schools, industries, and other means of amelioration were ruthlessly and cleverly forbidden, so that its people, ill-fed and ignorant beyond description, long lacked the necessary stamina and determination to rescue themselves from subjugation and servitude.

The power of the British overlords was long absolute and omnipresent. Their colonies were purposely slowed down in their advance on the path to civilization to prevent too strong a sense of nationalism and independence from taking root among their natives. Such a policy, contrary to humanity, maintains the supremacy of the leading class of England. Some of these colonies, whose standard of living is among the lowest on earth, are persuaded that the mother country is there only for their defense and protection from ravenous and would be aggressors. They do not realize that England is there mainly for her own interest and is not greatly concerned as to what happens to the indigenous population. For this reason she permits and tacitly approves the tactics and policies of key men who by force or by religious and racial prejudice keep the population in a state of darkness and degradation.

India, a vast and wealthy country with a tremendous semi-enslaved population, helpless because of its extreme ignorance, poverty, and fanaticism, was easily kept subjugated by the few Britons who did not hesitate to use immediate force to crush any attempt at insurrection. In this undertaking they were helped by local rajahs and other native potentates who amid wide-spread misery and squalor were able to amass and display great influence and wealth. Because of their acquiescence to the Britons they were long retained as nominal rulers over millions of nearly starving people. A state that permits such conditions as these surely cannot be called a democracy.

We may accept some of the arguments advanced in justification of such policies. India was not considered sufficiently civilized to govern herself. If set free she would have faced internal strife and would have been exposed to conquest or exploitation by other powerful countries which would have proved to be more cruel and selfish rulers than the British. However, under the impact of world opinion India now has been set free and some of those predictions have actually come true as the division between the two large religious groups of the country, as well as the assassination of one of the greatest men on earth will attest and prove. Her relative security from foreign assaults and domination rests in the fact that the British Empire as yet has not completely relinquished her hold on India and while she would very greatly resist any foreign invasion of this country, yet any future aggressor nation has not yet found the opportune time or the favorable circumstance for such a move. The only hope of India lies in the ability of her people to educate themselves and rise to a higher level of civilization. Progress undoubtedly was made under the Empire, but this was not due to special efforts of the British government in that direction. It would be more proper to say that progress did take place in spite of that government. How India will reach the necessary stage of civilization to keep and maintain her freedom cannot easily be foretold, but as she advances her consciousness of freedom will also increase, and not even the might of England or any would-be aggressor will be able to break their will to freedom.

As aforementioned, the British Empire is an agglomeration of states at varying stages of civilization. Some, as Canada, New Zealand, South Africa, and Australia, enjoy a great degree of freedom and initiative because of their highly civilized population. Indeed it could not be differnt or those nations would not tolerate passively such a situation. But even these nations must submit to the sway of England because they are dependent on the economy of that country. England in one way or another has always been able to prevent the industrialism of these lands. If this was promoted or permitted in any of them during the war, it was not because of any change of attitude on the part of the small and powerful ruling class, but was due to the necessity of decentralizing industry in the face of destructive and persistent German air attack. How much longer these countries will retain their allegiance to the British Empire is a matter that will depend on the way the world is left by the war. Indeed, granted the subconscious desire on the part of these nations, meaning by subconscious the opinion of few and uninfluential individuals of those nations, to bid for a complete economic and jurisdictional separation from the Empire, it is evident that in a world as insecure and uncertain as the present, it is to their advantage to retain that allegiance and by that stand to be principally protected from unscrupulous and more powerful nations. However, if conditions in the world should radically change and a just and lasting peace should follow the present turmoil, a peace in which all nations can find unobstructed their economic equilibrium, it is our guess that their bid for complete freedom will be more strongly felt than at present. These countries will then be able to buy from whomever they wish and to sell to whomever they want. In the same way that thirteen British colonies, almost two hundred years ago, seceded for economic and political freedom at a time when no real danger was felt from any part of the world, so will these countries make a bid for full sovereignty if and when similar circumstances should arise. This the British Empire, or better to say, the British overlords, will be unable to stop. The force of civilization, the true interests of these people, will be too strong for them to control any longer.

The conclusion that we must draw from this discussion is that the British Empire cannot be taken as an example of democracy.

CZECHOSLOVAKIA

Among the countries which adopted democracy as their mode of life we wish to mention Czechoslovakia, born amid the ruins of the

Austrian Empire after the First World War. This republic acquired her liberty after centuries of serfdom and subjugation and here we find a nation perfectly willing to live in peace with her neighbors and mind her own affairs. Her government, composed of men of great integrity and patriotism, was freely chosen by her 15,000,000 people, and as such represented the ideal setup of a democratic state. Under this regime Czechoslovakia prospered and advanced far above the standard of living in effect under the Hapsburg domination. Such accomplishment can really be attributed to a contented population which could devote, unhampered and unobstructed, all its energy and enthusiasm to the improvement of the national well-being. A more extensive and efficient utilization of the division of labor eventually increased the average standard of living, and made Czechoslovakia a conspicuous example of the benefits derived from a government that has at heart the welfare of its people. This, of course, was not merely the result of its democratic form, but because leaders of high ideals and integrity happened to be at the helm. However, no matter what kind of government, no matter how great the industry and capability of the people, the limit of improvement in standard of living was perforce dependent on the wealth of the land. We do not know how much potential resources Czechoslovakia has in her plains and in her mountains, and we have no knowledge of how much of these resources she had been able to utilize and exploit at the time of the German invasion. On account of the abrupt end of her national life we cannot tell if she had then reached the maximum standard of living permitted by the wealth of her land. At any rate that maximum sooner or later would have been reached, and would have set a ceiling to her standard of living. Czechoslovakia, during her prewar period of freedom, enjoyed and maintained a favorable balance of trade as so much of her munitions, pottery, and other products was sold abroad. This fact, among others, may have originated the covetous desires in her northern neighbor and greatly contributed to her downfall. Her ideal form of government could not prevent a more powerful nation from occupying and subjugating Czechoslovakia. Her physical strength was not sufficient to repel the invaders when the time of need arrived. Democracy was crushed, ultimately to rise again, but similar danger will be ever present as long as brute force is the deciding factor in dealings among men. Czechoslovakia gives us another lesson in the frailty of democracy and its power to resist change and transformation, and this is represented by her present period of uncertainty and unrest. Due to economic pressure, due to the influence of large and influential nations right on her very borders, that spirit of democracy which made that nation a jewel among the European nations, finally had to give way to other forms of government and other philosophies of life and those people who had been instrumental in her glory and in her previous achievements stand dejected and powerless witnesses to the collapse of their beautiful ideal for their country.

AUSTRIA AND THE BALKANS

As a counterpart to Czechoslovakia we may mention Austria, which was another of the republics to emerge after the Versailles Treaty. In this country of only a few hundred thousand square miles we find a population of seven million, of which almost three million are concentrated in her capital city, Vienna. The Austrian Republic definitely had not the primary requisites to become an independent and self-supporting state. The population was too large in comparison to the resources of the land. Political pressure and modest economic help from the outside was too small and too uncertain to make this country satisfied and prosperous. Economic and racial ties with the population of the north represented an ever strong incentive for a fusion of the two nations, fusion which sooner or later had to take place irrespective of help or economic assistance promised by those nations interested in maintaining the ring of steel around the defeated Germany. Feelings of liberty and other beautiful ideals, at least so far as the masses are concerned, usually do not go with an empty stomach.

This has been and probably will continue to be the main problem of all the Balkan nations. These tragic states, which together could fit into Texas, are inhabited by people of different religion, civilization, race, and outlook. They have never shown willingness to cooperate. Here, more than in any other civilized country, the lack of division of labor is appalling in its implication. Whichever race in any of these states holds the upper hand is always busy subduing the others. This naturally prevents any progress, which undoubtedly would come if the Balkan peoples joined their talents and abilities for the benefit of all. Because of this lack of conciliatory feeling among the various elements of the populations any territorial divisions which we might wish to make in the Balkans are bound to produce friction and resentment. Here, more than in any other place in Europe, poverty is rampant and general. It is evident that independently of their form of government these countries are certain to stay poor and disorganized until they decide to set aside personal and racial prejudices and ambitions, and by pooling their resources and products be able to advance toward a better way of life. Of the Balkan countries none has a democratic government and this is mostly due to the appalling privation and ignorance of the population which opens the way to the ruling class of each country to establish and enforce their local supremacy.

SWITZERLAND

There is another country in Europe enjoying a democratic government which we wish to analyze. This is Switzerland. If any nation closely approaches the pure form of democracy, it is certainly Switzerland. Because of her small size she presents the ideal condition for such a mode of life. Due to geographic conditions her existence has remained externally undisturbed and unmolested for centuries, and shows an internal tranquility not easily equalled. This country, more than any other in Europe, has had such a good fortune and has used this opportunity to educate its people to appreciate and value pure democracy. They are a blend of German, French, Italian and Romansch. Switzerland, like other nations, naturally has handicaps such as difference in religion, language, and temperament. All these animosities, however, have been lived down, and now the Swiss people present to the world a homogeneous and well-balanced unit ready to defend its land against any invader.

It seems strange that in a continent where wars of aggression have been the rule, since time immemorial, this island of democracy should have stood intact for such a length of time. There are, however, adequate reasons for this. Switzerland, for one, is located in a mountainous region and up to a few years ago, when the airplane was still unknown, any invasion of this country was bound to be costly for any aggressor. However, in centuries past Switzerland came to represent a buffer state between the surrounding powers, which found advantageous the existence of such a neutral area in their midst. This factor, perhaps more than any other, has kept this country free from attack and devastation and given her the necessary security to attain her high degree of civilization and standard of living.

Considering the subject of standard of living, we may see again how much can be accomplished by a high division of labor. The four million Swiss people, who are among the most enterprising and energetic in Europe, know only too well their physical weakness compared with the strength of her neighbors. On this account, despite their mediaeval military renown, they have never attempted to acquire additional resources which would have to be taken by force from any of those neighbors. Knowing her limitations, Switzerland has made the most of her natural wealth, and by a very high division of labor and technical skill, as in watchmaking, she has been able to reach a standard of living far superior to other countries with greater wealth and larger population. As we see it, she has reached the highest attainable level compatible with the wealth of her land and present stage of technology. Additional inventions and discoveries would obviously advance her standard of living still further, but after progress would again be dependent upon the density of population and the resources of the country.

While a great deal of credit must be given to the form of government which has been able so well to serve its people, who rank among the most cultured and progressive of the world, it is easy to foresee how different the history of Switzerland would have been if she had not been blessed by that splendid mountainous location in the center of Europe, and had not made her independence tacitly respected by the surrounding powers. Indeed not even Hitler with all his aspirations of a united German race dared to attack this country whose population is almost two-thirds Germanic in origin.

THE UNITED STATES

Among the various democracies of the world we must naturally mention our own. The fact that the United States of America is enormous in size and population prevents her, as previously explained, from being a pure democracy. Indeed here more than elsewhere the popular opinion must rely on the leading newspapers of the country and, as these can be bought or bribed, large elements of the populace may be swayed according to the interests of those who have acquired control of those papers. It is, of course, the duty of any self-respecting citizen to weigh and analyze in his mind the various contentions expounded by opposing newspapers, and in this manner to form his opinions and be guided by them at the polls. But how can we expect any individual to base an objective opinion upon any issue when charges and countercharges fill the press which he is in no position to prove and verify? More often than not he will be guided by the views of his local leading newspaper, will vote according to preconceived ideas and prejudices and will be guided also by outstanding speakers who may have much at stake in the campaign.

A more democratic course is followed in local elections, where matters of direct importance and intimate knowledge to the citizens are discussed and voted upon. In such cases the average citizen is in a position to judge for himself the soundness of reforms due to be authorized, to compare the persons standing for office regarding their integrity and efficiency, and accordingly such elections are more consonant with the actual will and interests of the majority. But even here we find conditions which prevent the free expression of the people, even here we may find bribery and distortion of facts.

We all know the power of the so-called political machines in New York, Pennsylvania, and elsewhere. The just mentioned political machines, built up by powerful groups who control millions of votes, are known all over the nation because of certain notorious episodes which occasionally come to the public attention. However, hundreds of such organizations throughout the country are prosperous and successful. Some of these groups, objectionable in their methods, are extremely difficult to expose and defeat at the polls. They base their power on graft, on bribery, on intimidation, and on the jobs so lavishly distributed to those who are in the fold. Many of these latter individuals, quite often of limited knowledge and integrity and usually referred to as small politicians, while inconsequential in the setting up of the policies of their party, will nevertheless busy themselves in convincing gullible people to vote for issues basically harmful to society because they know that their activity will be compensated by jobs to which they have no qualification or aptitude but still good and remunerative jobs. Confronted by a well organized political machine the independent and probably more enlightened citizens usually find themselves powerless to defeat such a party or expose methods of corruption detrimental to the country.

A nation which tolerates and permits such tactics cannot be regarded as ruled by a purely democratic form of government. Of course, even here the ultimate responsibility for such a state of affairs falls on the people themselves, who more often than not are apathetic and unconcerned over matters of such importance to themselves. A small, well organized, and determined group of individuals which is able to control the press, and dominate through jobs and awards a key part of the electorate which will vote for whatever issue the group may sponsor, is very hard to overcome, and in such cases the election does not represent the true will of the people, and ceases to be a valid expression of choice.

In our self-complacent belief of belonging to one of the most democratic countries of the world, we like to point out faults and shortcomings in other nations. Little do we realize that some of those faults can be found right here at home, quite as bad and just as much in need of rectification. That we have a capitalistic regime which keeps a working class helpless and insecure no one can deny. During the depression of the early 1930's we saw the number of unemployed climb to the staggering figure of 12,000,000. That the unemployed were finally absorbed by industry is no achievement of our democratic form of government or of our capitalistic system as this was mostly due to the necessity of rearming so as to meet the emergency abroad, and later because of the war which, besides taking a vast part of our youth for military service, increased production for the armed forces. With the end of the war signs of unemployment began to appear in many parts of the country, and it is possible that conditions may worsen. Although we frequently hear of technological progress and of new industries which will employ thousands of people, we neglect to take into account the unsettled economic condition in which this nation as well as all others has been left after the war, we fail to consider the staggering government debt which burdens the population and prevents the buying of the new things due to be placed on the market. It is conceivable that a boom may appear because of the accumulated demand for peace-time commodities which for so long were set aside to give precedence to government orders, but this threatens to repeat the cycle of the last war which, after the boom of the early 1920's saw the worst economic and financial crash in history at the end of the same decade. Any government which does not aim to maintain and possibly increase the buying power of the population at large and any international settlement which does not take into account the rehabilitation and the economic revival of all nations, is bound to produce still greater troubles than those we have experienced so far. This will be a certainty, no matter what our form of government in spite of our good fortune in being a large, rich and almost self-sustaining country. Accordingly, that laws and regulations need to be sponsored which give the working class a better representation in the government is a matter requiring serious thought and consideration if real democracy in our country is to be obtained.

Among other problems that need to be solved is the racial issue, which prevents millions of our people from having a real voice in matters of great importance to them. No one can deny that hate and prejudice are still rampant against Negroes in this country or that many discriminatory regulations hinder their mounting to better positions in society. That these rules or traditions act as a powerful brake against their reaching levels to which they are entitled by their qualifications is a matter of general knowledge. The postponement or evasion of laws that would bring justice, equity, and fairness among all citizens of this country is another indication that we do not possess a true form of democracy.

CONCLUSIONS

Recapitulating, we can safely say that democracy represents a decided improvement over any other mode of life, devised by man. Unfortunately, however, it has in itself the germs of decay, which sooner or later will change the governing system to such an extent that it can no longer be classified as a pure democracy. The blame for all this is due to the apathetic nature of the people who choose the easier path of indifference to that of standing up and fighting for their rights; is due to those individuals who, less scrupulous and more ambitious than others, seek their personal gain at the expense of society; is due to the fact that a pure democracy, beyond the welfare and well-being of its citizens, has no provision to stop short of encroaching upon the rights and interests of other nations, and, therefore, not being able to arouse the necessary good-will among men, is apt to involve the nation in useless competition and wars with other nations. On this account we do not believe that democracy as we know it is the best mode of life for our troubled humanity. A new form must be devised that will better promote and safeguard the rights and welfare of the citizens as well as that of all men on earth, irrespective of creed, race, ability and wealth. Reverting to our section in the first chapter in which we justify rent and profit, we must admit that to promote and maintain in man the necessary desire to make and improve things for his own benefit, and indirectly for that society in general, those incentives must be kept unaltered and unchanged. It is just that to those who contribute most to human progress a larger remuneration be given as reward of their effort. The desire of betterment is deep in every heart. Some have the necessary qualifications for the attainment of that goal and do so without appreciable or apparent effort; others, less endowed by nature, have to strive much more, and often fall short of their quest. Despite countless exceptions it is a characteristic of mankind never to be satisfied with their conditions or with what they have achieved. Frequently we see individuals, who by all appearances have reached what to many others may seem unattainable, push on relentlessly toward the attainment of still higher levels as if driven by a force that does not permit them rest or tranquility to the end of their days. Many are these individuals and varied their pursuit of life. Some devote their energies in the field of learning and science and go through life, unaffected by wealth or ease; others to amassing fortunes and riches. That the effort of the first group should be of paramount importance to society needs no emphasizing. It scans and studies the forces of nature so that these may in turn be placed at the service of mankind. The other group exerts also a great influence on our mode of life in so far as its members by their unbounded energy and initiative make jobs and forge the means of life for millions. Some of the latter fortune-builders may start even from the bottom of the social ladder. The very fact that they are prevented by poverty from enjoying the comfort and the distinction that worldly wealth will give and under the illusion that money means happiness, ensures that they will strive to obtain that wealth which they believe holds the key to the magic world of their dreams. When they finally reach this goal, they usually find to their amazement that the wonderful happiness they expected is lacking, and either their ambition is diverted toward other objectives or they will keep on piling up more money from sheer momentum and habit.

As they find out that money is not everything, and that by itself cannot produce happiness, why are men so unwilling to yield it once they come in possession? Although wealth cannot give happiness we must recognize that it gives comfort and security, qualities which are also ardently desired by human nature, and as such very few willingly will give up an advantage which either was bequeathed to them or was acquired with much labor and effort. However, the very fact that now additional wealth comes to them so easily and in such large amounts means that they will grow accustomed to it and as its value to them will also decrease, they will spend it almost as fast as it comes in. Of course, not all is squandered and spent in foolish ways. Indeed, there are persons in the upper strata of society who greatly feel the responsibility of its disposal and give serious thought to their expenditures. Depending on their inclination, background and social interest, money may be lavished on hospitals, on places of learning, on charitable organizations, on works of art, and other laudable activities. This wealth, in other words, is not dissipated but returned to society in general in so far as it represents a great and valuable assistance, quite often the only aid to the advancement of science and other farsighted enterprises, which have such an important bearing on the progress and betterment of mankind.

We are not yet ready to state if this is right or wrong. While this wealth is placed at the disposal of society, we also realize the justifications of those who contend that decency and those sacred human rights, should see that precedence be given to such enterprises aiming at the improvement of the standard of living of the poorest class in the nation. This group very often receives only scant attention from the other classes and from those in power. Their need, taken as a whole, is gravely neglected and the help that may be occasionally given to them is usually far smaller than what is actually needed. Of course, if we should dispossess all the rich individuals on earth and distribute that wealth equally among the poor, this would not appreciably increase their standard of living. Until the structure of society is radically changed, a topic which we shall extensively treat in later chapters, there does not seem to be any satisfactory solution to the problem.

As an example of how one person can influence and affect the life of others, we may cite that exerted by Henry Ford. America could never repay him for his wonderful contribution in his changing the automobile from a commodity that only the very rich could afford, to another easily accessible to millions of people. The mass production introduced in the manufacture of the automobile promoted better roads and better engineering skill which in themselves have been an important element in our progress; it has made possible a vast number of jobs; and has been a decisive factor in our attaining the present standard of living in this country. It is true that Ford died one of the wealthiest men on earth, but it is also true that his wealth, not only has not been deprived to society, but has aided our national life, and whatever anyone may feel, has proved far more efficient in the possession of Henry Ford than if divided in small parts among a multitude of incapable and undeserving individuals. The rush and the scramble for wealth is not for wealth itself, but because of the advantages that only wealth can give and because of the many things that can be bought and enjoyed. A better distribution of the products of wealth would greatly lessen that rush and that scramble. We honestly think that an equal division of wealth, so strongly advocated by many, would be more detrimental than beneficial to society, as less good would result. To this indiscriminate division of wealth we are naturally opposed as we aim at the improvement of society as a whole and not of individuals. As such we will sponsor those changes which tend to a better distribution of the products of wealth, no matter in whose possession it may be.

In this particular instance it seems proper to dispel another contention also advocated as just and necessary to the betterment of society. This applies to the contribution made by another group of persons which also claims a portion of the profit derived from the sale of commodities. We refer to the trader or the so-called middleman. In the first chapter it was stated that the owners of land, tools, machinery, and so forth, have a right to claim a certain amount of rent, interest, and possibly of profit from the utilization of their wealth. To these we must also add the middleman.

Some say that the trader, because he has in no way contributed to the making of the commodity, has no such claim on society. To our minds this is untrue and unjustified. While the trader has not taken part in the actual manufacture of the article, we should not lose sight of the fact that the article finds its way to the ultimate consumer only through his efforts.

Anything contributed by a person for the improvement of society has a just and due claim of reward. Assuming that a person is able to produce a given commodity, this does not necessarily mean that he has the time necessary for its sale or the ability of carrying it to prospective and far distant customers. The greater the sale, the greater the profit and the incentive of production. If no middlemen existed, the only consumers would be those closely associated to the manufacturing community and lacking the incentive many products would no longer be available to the obvious disadvantage of society. These middlemen invest their money in this trade. From the various manufacturers they buy products which in turn they intend to sell to retail stores and consumers often scattered far and near. Between these two operations the middleman takes the risk of being left with unsold products should the demand change very radically, naturally resulting in great financial losses to him. Other times the middleman may gain large profits if these commodities temporarily in his possession should suddenly become much sought by the public.

The fact that a middleman occasionally derives large profits from his dealings obscures the many cases when he loses his entire investment. However, aside from profit or loss, the fact remains that the middleman performs a great service to society, and this seems to us a sufficient justification for his existence. It is quite true that at times his profits are exorbitant and out of proportion to his contribution, and in these cases it may seem reasonable that law should limit such returns, which in the last analysis are collected from the poor; however, in doing this it also seems reasonable that society in turn should protect the middlemen from losing too heavily when the opposite occurs. In this light the trader or middle-man has a just claim to the distribution of profit, as he represents an important link in the chain of division of labor, which makes for a better and more prosperous society.

If we remove rents and profits from the operation of exchange we immediately destroy the ability in men to improve their conditions and seek better and more economical ways in their effort of securing personal gain which indirectly prove to be advantageous to society. As a rule no one will do anything for others unless he can likewise do something for himself. It is futile to speak of man as he should be. It is far better and much more practical to find a solution to social unrest and injustices if we take man as he is, with all his faults, desires, and instincts, with all his mixture of virtues and vices and from that point, keeping those handicaps in mind, point out to him the way to a better mode of life and a better world.

Almost every day one encounters people who, although generous and idealistic by nature, imbued with the spirit of justice and right-eousness, wish to demolish the setup of the present society to build overnight an entirely different and supposedly better one. Most of our customs and ways of doing things come to us from our fore-fathers. They also, in their time, had to contend with baffling problems similar to ours; they also had to endure oppression and injustice, which seem to be the hard reality for all too large a portion of the human race. Under the impact of economic forces slowly but surely we can discern a definite evolution toward the ultimate rehabilitation of mankind. Despite all the wrongs and the horrors of our times we must admit that strides in the right direction have been and are being constantly taken. The world as a whole is better off now than it was, say five centuries ago. Of course, in their zeal for reform, some of these would-be Utopians and idealists do not stop to discriminate between what is good and what is bad in our present setup of society, in haste they condemn the whole system and would erect a new one apparently good and just. It was because of this fervor and enthusiasm that practically every genera-tion in history has seen large and small groups of individuals separate themselves from their contemporary modes of life and launch new organizations, new types of government, new codes of conduct. In this respect our generation is no different from the others, and in our times we have seen the rise of Naziism, Communism, and Fascism which in their fanaticism have divorced themselves from democracy which, while not perfect, is still the best mode of life we have today. Democracy is our heritage of untold suffering and social struggle. Wars, revolutions, strifes and compromises which took place centuries and ages ago all had their part in making our society what it is today. Sometimes we forget that many things we now take so much for granted and as a matter of course were once denied to the great majority of the people and only enjoyed by the select few. That we are still far away from the ultimate goal we are ready to agree, that positive steps in the right direction should be taken comes as a matter of course, but let us not forget for an instant that much in our present mode of life is fundamentally good and sound, and it would be extremely dangerous to set it aside for something that is still untried, lacks the maturity of experience, and is only advocated because of temporary social strains.

Many of these new theories which have been applied and enforced in various parts of the world eventually did more harm than good, and besides being responsible for wars and widespread misery have aroused hatred and all the lowest instincts of men, blocking thereby the moral progress of humanity.

As to the Utopians who have advocated reforms in a more peaceful way, one of the revealing reasons why their wonderful system has never been put into practice or, if actually attempted, has never survived the impact with the outside world, is that they have tried to construct overnight an ideal society in which the members by some magic formula have lost all their faults, demands, impulses, all those qualities which make them live and act according to their self-interest and egotism. Utopians, pointing out to man a beautiful mode of life, a wondrous world in the distant future, have always failed to show him a practical way to reach that goal. In describing the ideal society they have omitted to teach man how to rehabilitate himself so as to gradually become worthy of that perfect world.

CHAPTER III

THE EFFECT OF SCARCITY IN THE STRUCTURE OF SOCIETY

IN PREVIOUS CHAPTERS we have shown that rent, interest paid for capital utilized, profits and high salaries received by persons who contribute more than others to the general welfare of society, are all justified if progress in this world is to be attained. With these concepts in mind we wish to analyze certain phenomena which are their direct result and fundamentally affect our mode of life. Society, in so far as it refers to the people of any specific nation, may be defined as a group of persons who, while inherently different each from the other, live within the same boundaries and under the same laws. Religion, race, customs, traditions, common economic bondage, language, love for the fatherland, all have their influence in welding this population into a compact unit different from the population of other nations. Each person, because of birth or through natural or acquired abilities, seems to find a natural equilibrium, as regards relationship with others, at a definite place in the economic structure of society.

Laws and regulations exert a restraining force of varied nature and intensity upon each individual. While favorable in a greater or lesser degree to the majority, they may hamper the free and natural tendencies of the minority. It is reasonable to expect that the re-action of an individual will be conditioned by the kind and amount of restraint brought to bear on him, and will be proportional to his opportunity to influence others in the setting up of forces which may tend to modify these laws. It can easily be seen how difficult and complicated would be any attempt to analyze all the forces acting among the components of even a very small society as a direct result of these instincts. Such forces, emanating from millions of individuals different in nature and outlook, keep our society in a continuous state of flux. To some extent we may say that through these forces and the corresponding reactions progress is promoted, since the needs, ideals, and aspirations of various groups are thereby brought to the fore. Inevitable clashes between the basic interests of different classes form social problems which must eventually be solved. In the constant action for progress, which has been going on for ages, popular needs gradually receive proper consideration, and in due time and under favorable circumstances are recognized and accepted by the other classes.

These forces and reactions, although representing intrinsic needs of men, are usually expressed and advocated by outstanding personalities rather than by the rank and file. Leaders, being human, are apt to make errors, and the confusion often times arouses misunderstandings which blur the view of basic trends and issues. In so far as we wish to focus our attention upon fundamentals unaffected by passion, personality, and prejudice, we shall analyze a hypothetical society much smaller and simpler than can actually be found in reality. Facts derived from this society may then be applied with proper perspective to larger instances.

Let us visualize a Lilliputian society of 400 people somewhere on a distant island segregated from the rest of the world, unknown and inaccessible to any other nation, yet sufficiently advanced in civilization to be compared to a cross-section of a modern society. The livelihood and well-being of each component will depend on the personal as well as the cumulative effort of all, and also on the manner in which the society is able to manage the inter-relationships among its members. We shall assume that the division of labor in this tiny nation has reached the highest degree permitted by the small number of people, so as to make it as highly progressive as possible. Its standard of living will naturally be limited because of the small population, but this must be ignored as immaterial to the problem under discussion.

Most commodities utilized by men have to go through various stages of transformation. Raw material, in general, passes from its natural state to that in which it is ready to be used by the ultimate consumer. No commodity can be produced if raw material is not available to be extracted and processed. The possession of raw material, such as ores, is a prerequisite for the survival of society, with toil on the part of men coming next in importance. As we shall explain later in this chapter, there are various requirements for a decent living, considered from a purely physical standpoint.

We know that for man to live, grow and develop, he must be able to consume and utilize a certain minimum of nourishment, and possess some protection against inclement weather. The products used for this purpose will be termed *vital commodities*. Minimum requirement of food and other vital commodities has not greatly changed from times past and, all considered, it is probably less because of the smaller physical effort required of the average modern man in comparison with those of prehistoric eras who so greatly depended on their strength for their livelihood and survival. Higher level of civilization, better knowledge and appreciation of food, general consensus and opinion of people has continued to raise this minimum from actual physical requirements so that at present what we consider vital commodities is usually far above in kind as well as in amount from the minimum requirement of times past. As this study treats of man in the present stage of civilization, the more inclusive interpretation of vital commodity must be considered. In a life as intricate and exacting as our's, the average man must consume and utilize a great amount of vital commodities (v.c.) if he is to remain strong, healthy, and able to take the responsible place in society. Let us also add that this higher level of vital commodity has added greatly to the longevity of man.

There are other commodities which, although less vital to the individual, enhance his well-being and enrich his life, again in a physical sense. Improved quality of food, great abundance of nourishment, better and warmer clothing, more protective and elaborate shelter, decorative articles, and so forth, are included in this subdivision. These things, while highly desirable, are not essential to the life of man, and shall here be termed *luxury commodities*. To these must be added what are generally called services, as they also enrich the life of man. As later noted in this chapter, they may be of various kinds and natures, requiring no raw material, but only the time and toil of those who supply them.

It will be assumed that on our island nothing is given or received either in commodities or services without proper financial compensation, and we shall analyze how the various transfers in money take place among the components of our little society.

In one day this society has produced, consumed, or utilized a certain amount of commodities and services. The larger the amount of commodities utilized and the greater the services enjoyed by the people, the higher the average standard of living becomes. We wish to emphasize again that for this production the necessary raw material must be on hand, with only effort needed to shape it. However, the raw material need not be free for everyone to use; in fact, we shall assume that it belongs to ten of the 400 inhabitants of the island. These ten represent the owners of wealth or capital, and they will permit its utilization only if society in return pays them a given amount of rent. Because of the large variety of products and the high level of division of labor, we shall assume each of the ten to be producing different commodities, although conditions may arise when more than one will make the same kind in competition with others. For simplicity we shall assume that each owner hires the same number of workers, and that the total population is engaged in this multiform production, divided according to the following pattern: 10 owners of wealth, 30 managers, 90 skilled and 270 unskilled laborers.

The managers will help the owners in directing and supervising the work on hand; the responsibility of the various enterprises will rest with them, along with the hiring and discharging of workers, and together with the owners will direct the efforts of all under them. Due to superior skill and talent 90 others will rank as skilled laborers. They will be assigned to the more advanced stages of production. The remaining 270 will count as unskilled workers. While their total contribution is very important and quite as vital to the community, that of each individual will necessarily be smaller than that of any of the components of other groups.

From the conclusions arrived at in previous chapters it is clearly right and just that the remuneration of these individuals be in proportion to the skill, amount of work performed, and importance of each person's contribution to production. Let us now indicate by "a" the average wage of the unskilled laborer. It will be paid him for work performed during a unit of time. This unit may be one hour, one week or one year and the unit of a may be in dollars, pounds, francs, or in any other kind of currency accepted among the members of our hypothetical society. Take the average pay of the skilled laborer as "2a" and that of the manager as "6a". The salary which the owner will draw for his management and direction of the enterprise will be assumed "8a" and in addition he will collect a rent for the invested money, say "a" thus receiving 9a.

No doubt this scale is crude and only partially comparable to what holds in real life, but, as earlier stated, we are interested in discerning trends rather than pointing out specific facts. We feel confident that a division such as the one chosen suffices to show phenomena similar in character to those found in actual society.

EXAMPLE ONE *a*

Say that the complete population of the island is engaged only in the manufacture of vital commodities. Assuming that each man works eight hours a day, the working time for the entire population will be 3,200 hours.

Should these be highly developed and active workers, each one proficient at his particular task, production will be relatively large. Were the workers less talented and industrious, they would produce no such amount as in the first case. The smaller the production of commodities the less there will be per capita, and the lower the standard of living. But, independently of amount produced, the people work the same number of hours in both cases, and therefore, the sum total of wages and salaries, related to the basic wage a, will remain the same. It is also immaterial what the actual amount of wages and salaries is as long as the relation among the various classes is the same. The earning power of the worker will not be different should he receive 2a or 0.5a, if the wages and salaries of all the members of other classes are stepped up or down in the same ratio.

It is evident that calculations and data should be presented in our study. Lest these become too tedious for the reader who may not wish to go too deep into the subject, they have been kept to a minimum. Since our conclusions drawn from the various cases successively analyzed are essential to a clear understanding of the reforms ultimately advocated in this book, we have included certain numerical facts vitally important to the subject under consideration, and have added in a tabular form at the end of chapter 8 the complete calculation for this and other examples to be treated in this chapter.

During the analysis we have often used the device of indicating various facts by one or two symbols such for instance as C' for cost of commodities, N for number of individuals, I for income and so forth. We feel that it would be too tedious for the reader to explain all such forms at this time. This explanation, however, is found at the end of Chapter 8, immediately before our presentation of the various examples. Each line of the tabular calculation is indicated by a number placed on the margin. This number sometimes appears also in the text as a matter of reference. This for a thorough understanding of the problem. This policy has been followed throughout our work. With these basic facts in mind we may proceed with our analysis.

Because of only one source of income, the purchasing power of each individual will be represented by his salary or wage. At first all commodities will belong to the owners of wealth, who, besides possessing raw material and the means of production, employ the workers in the requisite tasks. In calculating the cost of manufacturing they will naturally include their salary as they are also contributing to production through their talent, management, and leadership. This cost, indicated by "C'", will be given by 720a which is the income of the entire population. Each owner will place commodities on sale at as high a price as possible so as to derive the largest profit. Decreased demand, competition between sellers, or both, may force them to lower their price lest they be left with unsold stock. At times this reduced price may even go lower than cost, and in such a case sellers will sustain a loss. This condition, however, could not continue indefinitely as it is inconceivable that owners would allow the utilization of their wealth under such circumstances. The 400 inhabitants are not merely producers but also consumers, and each one must go to market and buy commodities from the owners. In the exchange between buyers and sellers there are the following factors to be considered:

(1) The buying power of each individual is represented only by his salary or wage.

(2) A definite wage can buy only a certain amount of commodities and no more; i.e. the unskilled laborer only the equivalent of his wage a, and so on.

(3) The amount each man can buy is also a function of the supply available on the market.

Indicate by "q" the ideal quantity of vital commodities which each man needs for good health and decent living. Then 400q will represent the amount which, if divided equally among the population, will ensure decent living to all. It is likely, however, that the actual production will fall short of this quantity. Say that it comes to 300q. If this was evenly distributed, no one would enjoy the standard of living which he is striving to attain. Because the commodities represented by q are vital, everyone will bid if necessary up to the full extent of his earnings, and will disregard the fact that any purchase above the average of .75q is withheld from those in poorer financial condition. As a result of this competition, the price of the unit quantity q will exceed the unit wage a. Competition among the buyers tends to increase prices while, as we have seen, competition among sellers has the opposite effect. Because of the ceaseless competition among sellers as well as buyers, it is clear that a condition of equilibrium can only be reached when the money spent on purchase of commodities equals the cost of production, or 720a. If we indicate by "Pq" the price of one unit of commodity q, then for equilibrium 300Pq must be equal to 720a. From this it follows that $a=300 \; Pq/720=.416 \; Pq$ which means that the basic wage a will only buy .416q (line 80). From the same relation the price of the unit commodity q in terms of the basic wage is given by: $Pq=720a/300=2.4a$ (line 79).

We wish to emphasize that a condition of equilibrium does not necessarily mean that everyone in our society is able to secure the desired amount as this is far from what actually happens. What it means is that the commodities on the market are sold without profit or losses, so the supply tends to remain at that particular level.

It is natural that the poorer classes, with an income smaller than Pq, in order to obtain as much vital commodities as possible will bid to the full extent of their earnings. But, as these earnings are represented by a wage smaller than Pq, that is, smaller than 2.4a, we can see that what they will actually buy will be less than q. The owners and managers could easily buy more than q, and some probably will, but as we are interested in averages rather than specific cases, we shall assume they will be satisfied with the ideal amount q, no more and no less, and will be ready to pay higher prices for that acquisition. As their financial power gives them such a privilege, it becomes obvious that what they buy over and above the average for the entire society (.75q) goes to further decrease the amount that the poorer classes can buy. It is now clear that no matter what competition the latter classes may offer the result will only be an increase in price without altering in any way the amount these classes can buy, as this is fixed by the total supply (300q) minus what is taken by the upper classes. The competition and the rise in price will stop as soon as the poor have spent all their money and are unable to bid any higher. At this price the amount that the plain laborer will secure is represented by .416q, which falls far short of the average available (.75q). However even with a scarcity as severe as this, it is possible that commodities may go unsold. Indeed given the price of q as previously calculated (2.4a), what the lower class with a total income of 270a (270 being the total number in their class) will buy will be given by:

$$U_4 = 270a/2.4a = 112.5q \text{ (line 88)}$$

The skilled labor class with a wage of 2a will receive an amount given by:

$$U_3 = 90 \times 2a/2.4a = 75q \text{ (line 87)}$$

The manager and owner class each with an average salary above 2.4a could buy a much larger quantity than q, but because q represents the needs of any one individual, no more will be sought. Assume then that both owner and manager will buy q and no more, the money not used being added to their saving. The quantity bought by these two classes will then be 40q. The total absorbed by the market indicated by U will be given by:

$$U = (112.5 + 75 + 40)q = 227.5q \text{ (line 89)}$$

which is far below the amount produced (line 75). The difference between the amount produced (300q) and that sold (227.5q) remains in possession of the owners, and accordingly is not utilized despite the evident need. This definitely indicates a condition of disequilibrium. Of course, it seems paradoxical that with such a shortage as here indicated, a condition of unsold commodities should exist, but this may and does happen in actual life. This condition is usually indicated in economic parlance by stating that the supply is greater than the market can absorb. From the foregoing we can draw the obvious conclusions:

(1) The fact that the amount produced is less than needed does not ensure that all will be sold.

(2) The fact that some of the supply is not sold must be attributed to the lack of financial ability to buy more.

The amount of money the owners will receive from sale of commodities will be given by: 227.5x2.4a = 546a (line 90). The difference between this and the cost (720a), or 174a is the loss sustained.

In consequence of this discrepancy the supply will tend to equal the demand, irrespective of the actual need of the population. Of course, a discrepancy of such magnitude is never likely to occur in actual society, for the supply would be reduced long before such a condition appears. Taking as fundamental the equilibrium between supply and demand, we must conclude that the supply in our little society will drop until this relation is reached. Such equilibrium can be attained either by decreasing the number employed in production, or by assuming that skill and technological knowledge of the society is less than the one assumed at first. The former alternative would be tantamount to supposing part of the population completely cut off from the only means of subsistence. This idea must be discarded, as it is taken for granted that the 400 islanders earn sufficient wages to live. The latter alternative, or that of a lower efficiency of society, being more plausible, will be adopted in this case.

EXAMPLE ONE

Suppose that the commodities produced is 80q instead of 300q. The cost of production, being a function of the basic wage a, can still be represented by 720a, because we assume the same relationship among salaries and wages as before. Under the new conditions the price of the basic amount of commodities q will be: $Pq=720a/80=9a$ (line 79). From this the amount bought by the basic wage a will be given by:

$$ac = 80Pq/720 = .111 Pq \text{ or } .111q \text{ (line 80)}$$

The total purchase made by each class is given in the following table:

Unskilled labor class$=270x$ a$/9a=30q$ (line 88)
Skilled   ”   ” $= 90x2a/9a=20q$ (line 87)
Manager   ”   ” $= 30x6a/9a=20q$ (line 86)
Owner   ”   ” $= 10x9a/9a=10q$ (line 85)
                Total $=80q$ (line 89)

The total amount of commodities absorbed by the market (U) becomes 80q. As this is equal to the amount produced, we can conclude that this represents the condition of equilibrium. At this level, however, the share of the unskilled laborer drops to .111q and everyone in our society, except the owner who secures the quantity q and no more, must make shift with less than desired. It is obvious that the quota of the unskilled laborer is wholly inadequate for his health and well-being. We realize, however, that such a conclusion is utterly inconsistent with what occurs in real life, since we know that many not high on the financial ladder of society are not only able to buy what they need, but to save some of their earnings and pay for services which further add to their comfort. The reason for this inconsistency must be assigned to the fact we have assumed no services are supplied in our society. This condition must be included to approximate what happens in real life, and this will be analyzed in the following example.

EXAMPLE TWO

In the first example we took for granted that the only work in our society was the production of commodities requiring raw material and that money received as salary or wages was used only to buy vital commodities. We know, howevr, that many persons, in order to increase their income, are willing to perform services for others. Such services will be paid for by those who receive them. Money will thus circulate more freely among people, even though the actual amount is unchanged. The spending power of each individual, because of the additional amount received, will be larger than before, and directly proportional to the sum and nature of the work performed, so that even the most humble will be able to improve their lot by doing more and harder work than others in their class. But as in our analysis we consider each group as a whole and regard averages rather than individual effort, when we refer for instance to the wage of the unskilled laborer it is to the average of all these, even though there may be a wide variation of income within that group. Holding this concept in mind, let us revise some of the conclusions we arrived at in the first example. As we are introducing the idea of services, we assume also that they are of various forms: they may include the work of the servant, the teaching of the professor, the assistance of the doctor, and so forth. Since such services require skill and training, we shall assume that those who thus aid others devote their entire time to this activity or profession. For simplicity we shall divide them into four main groups according to earnings. The highest-income section will be grouped with the owners of wealth, and in order of pay the other will rank with the managers, skilled labor, and plain labor classes. The new division of society into classes is shown from line 1 to 5 and 10 to 14 in the tabular form placed at the end of chapter 8. The relative wage of the individual in each class appears from line 24 to 27.

In the first example we assumed that all 400 were devoting 8 hours each day to production, giving 3,200 working hours per day. Now, the number engaged in manufacturing or "Nc α" is 280 and if no technological advancement is assumed, it stands to reason that production will sink to 70 per cent of former figures. But in consequence of the critical condition of society under our first example, we shall assume that the total working hours devoted to production of vital commodities has not changed, so the hours of work per day and per individual will be given by $3200h/280 = 11.43$ hours. Similar working conditions will be assumed for those giving services. Additional assumptions follow:

(1) The effort of those who devote their time to services, while useful, requires no raw material.

(2) Services are paid at the same rate as those engaged in the manufacture of vital commodities.

(3) Each islander will buy vital commodities as far as he can up to the required amount, and then, if he has additional money, will use it for services. This is because the latter, while important are less essential to his well being. (Here it is assumed that services and luxury commodities count as the same thing).

(4) The commodities produced are not sufficient for the needs of the islanders, or the efficiency of society (line 94) is less than 100%.

In our search for the equilibrium point we have seen that the case where cost equals price does not produce by itself a state of equilibrium but that another condition must be met. These two conditions may now be stated.

(1) The first condition of equilibrium will be reached when the poorest have used all their earnings for the purchase of as large percentage of q as possible. Indeed if we assume that scarcity is the present lot of society, competition will develop among the buyers as each goes to the limit of his purchasing power for the acquisition of q. As they will no longer be able to bid any higher, competition will cease and prices will stabilize at that level.

(2) The second condition of equilibrium is reached when revenue equals cost. Indeed any difference between them, by creating profits or losses, will tend to increase or reduce production so that ultimately that equality will be reached.

From the first condition of equilibrium we know that the total wages of the poor will be spent for the purchase of vital commodities in competition with each other and with the rich. Yet, irrespective of their effort to this end what they will actually be able to buy will be given by the difference of that which is bought by the well-to-do from the total amount produced.

Let K indicate the number of unit commodities produced. If Pq is the price of the unit commodity q, then K.Pq represents the total expenditure for their purchase. Indicate by Nu the number of people in a position to buy the full quota q. If we assume that all classes but the last are able to acquire the unit commodity q, what they will buy, irrespective of price, will be given by:

$$\text{Nu.q or } (N_1 + N_2 + N_3)q$$

and the corresponding expenditure will be: Nu.Pq.

The difference between the total price (KPq) and the expenditure made by the upper classes will represent that which must be spent by the lower classes or:

Expenditure of the lower class$=KPq-Nu.Pq$.

The total amount of money in possession of the classes not in a position to buy the full quota q is repreesnted here by: $I_L.a$ which in this case is equivalent to $I_4.a$. For equilibrium the following equation must be satisfied:

$$KPq-Nu.Pq = I_L.a$$

This equation can be presented in the following form:

$$(1) \qquad Pq (K-Nu) = I_L.a$$

Equation (1) gives the first condition of equilibrium. The second condition of equilibrium equates revenue with cost, or:

$$KPq = C'$$

From the number of persons engaged in the production of commodities, C' can be expressed in terms of the basic wage a or C' $=T.a$ so that, for equilibrium, the following equation must also be met:

$$(2) \qquad K.Pq = T.a$$

From equation (2) the price of the unit commodity q can be derived, thus:

$$Pq = T.a/K$$

Substituting this value in equation (1) we have:

$$T.a (K-Nu) = I_L.a.K \text{ or:}$$
$$T(K-Nu) = KI_L$$

From the previous equation K can be immediately derived, or:

$$K = TNu/ (T-I_L)$$

As the value of K is found, it can be used to calculate the price of the unit commodity Pq from equation (2) or:

$$Pq = Ta/K$$

This obviously must be smaller than the salary or wage of the average individual in the poorest class included in the calculation of Nu (in this case skilled labor class). If larger the calculation must be repeated with a new value of Nu and I_L until this condition is satisfied. This method has been used in the tables shown at the end of chapter 8, page 400. Referring to this table and reading the values from the column headed by 2 (which stands for example 2) we see that the unskilled laborer is now in a position to acquire the amount .555q (line 84), far larger than what he was able to buy under the condition shown in example 1. The total purchase made by the entire population (U) is 280q (line 89) which being equal to the amount produced Kq indicates that this is a condition of equilibrium.

To complete our analysis we must turn our attention to the distribution of services. In the first part of this chapter we defined the meaning of q as the ideal amount of vital commodities each person should acquire for his well-being, and assumed that no one would desire more than that quantity, after which the rest of his earnings would be spent on services.

On page 117 we gave a partial definition of services and stated that, besides being of various nature, they do not as a general rule require raw material but merely the time and toil of those who make a living by providing them to others. The man who works in our garden or the servant who cleans our house renders services that must be paid for. The taxi driver or the street-car motorman who takes us from one place to another in less time that we would do ourselves are other instances. Further examples can be recognized in actors, musicians, and others engaged in public entertainment, in lawyers, judges, policemen, firemen, and others who look after our personal security and interests, in teachers, professors, librarians, doctors, nurses, and hospital employees. Such are some of the many kinds of services available to mankind. The rich man who owns a yacht must pay for the livelihood of a large crew. The sailors supply services to him for which payment must be made in compensation. Due to the large variety of services it is difficult to choose a yardstick which will measure them in the same sense as commodities. With few exceptions, here disregarded, services add only to the comfort and pleasure of an individual, and there is no limit to the amount he can enjoy if he has that desire and the requisite resources.

Of course, even here there is a supply and demand to be considered, and the price of service will be a function of the various forces involved. For our analysis we must assume some kind of unit of service which, even though devoid of any real meaning, will help us to establish a relationship between various kinds of services and commodities. This unit we shall call "s" as the counterpart of q. The total cost of services C" will be the sum of the salaries and wages of the individuals furnishing them. Taking the wage a of the unskilled laborer as base, such cost will be given by: $C''=L.a=216a$ (line 39).

Say that the total amount of services given or received within our assumed society is represented by "Zs" where "Z" is the total number of units of service. As we are free in our choice we shall say that Z=400. If Ps is the price of the unit of service then Z.Ps will be the total price. Any amount received above that may be compared to the profit that develops when prices of commodities are too high, and will draw other people into competition, thus tending to decrease the price of services. Any lesser amount, however, will have the opposite effect and some, unable to secure a decent living, will seek more remunerative jobs. This will tend to decrease services and increase price.

Because of the chosen set-up, cost is independent of supply and the latter is a function of skill and aptitude of workers as well as amount of effort exerted (in this case 11.43 hours per person and per day). This cost or L.a is given by the sum of all wages received by those giving services which in this example is represented by 216a (line 39). For equilibrium total cost (L.a) must be equal to total price (ZPs) or:

$$(3) \qquad L.a = ZPs$$

In so far that a and Ps become respectively units of measure of L and Z can be left out. We have then:

$$Ps = L.a/Z \text{ or } L/Z \qquad \text{(line 98)}$$
$$as = ZPs/L \text{ or } Z/L \qquad \text{(line 99)}$$

where as indicates the amount of services that unit wage a can buy.

The amount of services enjoyed, however, will not be equal for all but will depend on the earning power of each individual. For any price reached by vital commodities, the amount each person will expend on services will be his wage or salary minus what he must spend for vital commodities. As the price of q is 1.8a (line 79), the unskilled labor class with wage a, insufficient to buy the unit q, will be unable to purchase any services. The skilled labor class with wage of 2a is able to do so, and (2.0-1.8)90a or 18a (line 102) represents the available funds for this expenditure. This is what we have called available income for services "A" shown in lines 100 to 103 in the tabular calculation at the end of Chapter 8. A, divided by Ps, will give the number of units of services received by each class (lines 109 to 112). In this case all classes with the exception of the unskilled laboring class are able to buy services to a greater or lesser extent.

As for the members of the unskilled working class, all their earnings go to buy vital commodities, which are a primary necessity of life. We know that the plain laborer desires services like any one else, but since his financial power is so small this desire does not sway the demand or affect the supply. As a matter of record the amount enjoyed by members of the various classes are listed:

Owners	13.28	s	Line	105
Managers	7.77	s	"	106
Skilled workers	.37	s	"	107
Unskilled workers	0.00	s	"	108

STANDARD OF LIVING

At this point we deem it neccessary to set down our interpretation of standard of living.

One person has a better standard of living than another if he can utilize within the same time a greater quantity and variety of commodities and services for which he had to exert the same effort. Money is wealth only because it is accepted in exchange for commodities and services. The miser who hoards money for the sake of its possession is much poorer, at least by a generally accepted code of life, than one who uses his lesser amount to improve his life as to comfort, enjoyment, and advancement. In our study we assume that money earned is used for this purpose, even though often it is saved for future expenditures which can be classified as advancement. That time should be included in the evaluation of standard of living is obvious since anyone able to acquire commodities and services more quickly than another is bound to have a better standard of living. Any unit of time will serve: a day, a week, year, or any period that may be desired in the analysis.

The amount of effort must also be included in this calculation for reasons which will become apparent in the course of this analysis. Standard of living can then be measured by the ratio between utilization of commodities and services to the time and effort of acquisition. Grouping commodities and services in terms of enjoyment derived from their utilization, they can be represented by "E" (for enjoyment). Then indicating time by "T" and effort by "F", the standard of living "SL" can be measured by the following expression: $SL = E/(T.F)$.

The various factors entering into the computation of standard of living must naturally be taken within given limitations. A person who acquires in unit time and with unit effort more commodities and services than he can possibly utilize and enjoy cannot be said to have a higher standard of living than another who with identical time and effort acquires only what he can enjoy in full. Again the person who can enjoy commodities and services without the expenditure of any effort (where F equals zero, the value of the ratio would become infinity) cannot be said to have attained an unlimited standard of living.

One of the factors that must be used for the determination of the ratio is what we have called enjoyment E, a synonym of comfort and well-being, as it is what each individual derives as a result of unit effort exerted in unit time. It stands to reason that the welfare of any person depends much more on the acquisition of the proper amount of vital commodities than on luxury commodities and services. To be sure, average men have diverse requirements and desires, so that enjoyment from the utilization of the same commodities and services may vary for different individuals. To simplify the problem and explain the various forces affecting our mode of life, we must assign some arbitrary measurement of enjoyment equal for all. Being free in our choice let us say that the individual who utilizes the amount of commodities q derives the unit of enjoyment e or q equals e. Let us say also that the individual who utilizes the unit of service s derives one-half of the previous enjoyment or s equals .5e. With this assumption it is plain that anyone in choosing what to buy will prefer vital commodities to services in order to derive the greatest possible enjoyment. This, however, applies only up to the quantity q since a larger amount of vital commodities would not add to that enjoyment. Summing up:

(1) If the worker can afford to buy only part of q, say .7q, his enjoyment is .7e.

(2) If he buys more than q, his enjoyment is e and no more.

(3) If besides the amount q he is able also to buy services to the extent ns where n may be any value larger than zero, from the previous assumption we can say that the total enjoyment will be represented by:
$$E = (e + .5ne) \text{ or } e (1 + .5n).$$

Time T has also a definite bearing on the evaluation of standard of living. Take two individuals as base of comparison. If one acquires the same amount of commodities and services as the other in a shorter period of time and exerts the same amount of effort, he has definitely the better standard of living of the two. Quite likely he will use this extra time either for relaxation and rest or for the acquisition of further enjoyment in the form of additional services. However, as we are not calculating the standard of living of any particular individual it seems proper to assume the element of time equal for all and say that is the yardstick by which the other two factors are measured so that effort exerted and enjoyment received will be taken in the unit time which may be one day, one week, or one year.

Effort "F" is a very elusive element that needs explanation. In defining effort we are confronted by two versions:

(1) Effort as to the amount of exhaustion experienced by anyone performing a specific task.

(2) Effort as a synonym of work and what it adds to the welfare of the individuals.

Standard of living calculated by using the first interpretation is related only to the actual individual concerned, and has no relation to that of others or of society in general. We shall call this standard of living "absolute", as it is intrinsically limited to the individual. Using this interpretation the effort of any one person could be determined if it were possible to measure the amount of exhaustion he encounters in performing a particular task. A laborer at the end of a working day may be more fatigued and exhausted than a professor who lectures to students taking the same amount of time, and yet the reverse may be true. We are inmediately confronted by the arduous task of measuring efforts required in different activities and occupations. It might be seen that such a problem would be simplified by considering workers engaged in identical tasks. Such an instance might be two bricklayers laying the same number of bricks in any one day. However, if they differ in strength, health, and efficiency, we can safely say that the best and the strongest of the two workmen is bound to be less fatigued at the end of the day. As both will probably receive the same pay for the equal number of bricks laid, it is evident that, other factors being equal, the weaker man has a lower standard of living because he must exert more effort for what he earns. It is evident that this interpretation of effort, while it gives the true factor for calculating the standard of living of any one individual, in so far that it can not be definitely known or measured, cannot be used in our analysis which is set to calculate the average standard of living of a given class or of society as a whole.

The standard of living calculated by using the second interpretation of effort will be called "relative". While it is not directly related to the individual, it is a function of his contribution to the welfare of others and of society in general. It is an established practice to pay according to amount and quality of work done rather than effort exerted. Needless to say, the professor receives more than the unskilled laborer, because his contribution to the welfare of society in general is far greater than that of the latter. In the case of the two bricklayers, such workers are generally paid according to the amount accomplished, and it is reasonable to assume that the stronger and healthier laborer will do more work, and consequently earn more money, even though the other may feel more exhausted at the end of the day.

One of the important reasons for calculating the standard of living is that of being able to compare the welfare and well-being of groups of individuals or classes within any one given society. Using the first interpretation of effort the expression of standard of living becomes:

Absolute standard of living equals $E/T.F.$

Using the second where effort is synonym of work done, in turn indicated by "W", the expression of standard of living becomes:

Relative standard of living equals $E/T.W.$

As already stated, the absolute standard of living cannot be calculated because of the impossibility of evaluating the effort for all members of society and as such we must use the relative one because based on actual work performed, which is both measurable and known. However, the relative standard of living, besides the fact that it does not bear any relation to the actual welfare of the individual, will suggest comparisons and deductions which are far from the truth as we shall prove shortly.

In the evaluation of social phenomena in which we compare the welfare of different classes of society, while the knowledge of standard of living may be of interest in its absolute form, it is not paramount to that evaluation. If we compare, for instance, the well-being of the poor with that of the rich part of the population, this comparison will not be markedly different if based on the absolute standard of living or on any other we may finally decide to adopt, provided that the standard of living of both classes has been calculated with the same method and provided also that it gives results consonant with our experience. This incidently is the reason why we will finally reject the relative standard of living.

EVALUATION OF RELATIVE STANDARD OF LIVING

From the analysis of example (2) we note that the average owner of our society derives a salary of 9a of which 1.8a must be spent for the acquisition of vital commodities, while the remainder can be used to acquire desired services. Further in the study and specifically from line 105 we find also that the amount of services which he will finally be able to buy is represented by 13.28s and, therefore, his enjoyment or amount E will be given by:

$$E = e + 6.64e = 7.64e \qquad (\text{line } 121)$$

The element of time T being assumed equal for all the individuals of our society will not affect comparison and, therefore, we shall not assign any particular unit in our calculation. As to the amount of effort this can be measured by the amount of work done W, and as this is directly related to salary and wage "W", work may be represented by 8a. The rent which he receives as compensation for the utilization of his wealth does not represent effort on his part and, therefore, must be left out of our calculation.

The owner's standard of living can then be given by the following expression: Owner's $SL = 7.64e/8a = .955e/a$.

Using the same method for the other classes we have:

Manager's $SL = 4.885e/6a = .814e/a$
Skilled laborer's $SL = 1.1185e/2a = .593e/a$
Unskilled worker's $SL = .555e/a = .555e/a$

If we take the owner as a basis for comparison (100%), this means that the standard of living of the manager is 85.2%; that of the skilled laborer 62%; and that of the unskilled worker 58.2%. Such a high rating for the plain laborer, who cannot even enjoy the necessary amount of vital commodities in reference to the owner who besides q enjoys a great variety of services is utterly absurd and contrary to common sense.

Now if we recognize the incongruity of using the concept of work in the evaluation of standard of living another must be found closer to actual conditions. To clarify our point consider the work done by a movie actor during the filming of a motion picture. Without minimizing the effort exerted by such an individual, no matter how hard and tantalizing this work may be, we cannot think it greater than that done by the farmer who tills the ground under all kinds of climatic conditions the year around, as their respective earning powers indicate. It is quite evident that such a standard of living has no relation to the actual effort of the individual. Since the work of the actor is reckoned as adding so much to the welfare of society, in the form of entertainment, he is paid in proportion to the pleasure supposedly given. To this reasoning we raise no objection. Under such an interpretation, however, "standard of living" loses its real meaning as representing the well-being of the individual. In other words, the first interpretation of effort (F) must somehow be used rather than the second (W), but since the first cannot be estimated accurately we have arbitrarily assumed that all members of society, whatever their occupation, talent, or earning power, exert the same amount of effort. Therefore standard of living becomes a synonym of enjoyment only, and can be expressed by the same symbol E.

This additional assumption, no doubt, is inaccurate and in many cases unjust, but it comes closer to the absolute standard of living than any other, and, therefore, will be used in our study. The term is quite vague in itself when measured for one individual but not so, however, for comparison between the welfare of individuals or classes. As basic level we shall use that of the owner, that is, of the class at the top of the financial ladder, and rate the other standards of living as percentages thereof. By such a method the actual condition of the various classes can best be visualized and studied.

For a detailed derivation of the standard of living of the various classes under the new concept we refer our reader to the tabular calculation at the end of Chapter 8 (lines 131 to 134). As a matter of record this relationship is set down in the following list: Owner 100%; Manager 64%; Skilled laborer 15.5%; Plain Worker 7.27%.

As to the standard of living of the various classes in example (1) we recall that there were no services available, and, therefore, they are omitted in the calculation. We find here that the owner is the only one who can afford to buy q, and his enjoyment will be represented by e, taken as 100%. The standard of living of the other groups, on this basis, will be 66.6% for the manager, 22.2% for the skilled laborer, and 11.1% for the unskilled. This, however, holds only under the circumstances prevailing in that example. To compare these various standards of living with that of the owner in the second example, we must introduce the time factor, since in the first case the working day is 8 hours and in the second it has become 11.43 (line 20). The standard of living of the owner in the first case may be represented by: $e/8$ hours, and in the second example by: $7.64e/11.43$. The ratio of the two values will give the percentage of the first standard of living in relation to that in the second; in other words by the quotient of the first fraction divided by the second one:

$$(e/8)(7.64e/11.43) = 11.43e/(8 \times 7.64e) = .187$$

which is equivalent to 18.7% (line 135).

With similar calculation the percentage of standard of living of the other classes in the first example will be: Manager 12.5%, skilled worker 4.16%, unskilled worker 2.08%. All in all we can see how much poorer society would be if no services were available. This condition, fortunately, is not found in actual life, and is given here only as a matter of superficial interest.

The unskilled laborer in the second example with his 7.37% standard of living nevertheless enjoys .555q, the important factor in his livelihood. Through his additional work in supplying services his condition, while far from satisfactory, is better than the .111q he has in the first example.

We may conclude that a supply of 280q and 400s sets up a condition of equilibrium for our society of 400 islanders in their stage of civilization. There will be no tendency to increase or decrease that supply, even though a large part of the population must live on a quantity of vital commodities far too small for their well-being. We do not wish to imply by our previous statement that the equilibrium point is fixed and difficult to move either way: as a matter of fact the reverse is true. Prices are set by a continuous competition among the buyers, and similarly among the sellers for the advantageous purchase and disposal of merchandise. The bidding that goes on incessantly, the ever-present possibility that buyers may choose other sellers or that sellers favor other buyers, keeps prices moving up and down as supply and demand change from day to day. Because of this competition, prices in the long run tend to approach costs, even though this condition is seldom attained for any length of time. As supply decreases, prices tend to raise and profits to accrue to the owners: the opposite occurs when they fall. Another factor which undoubtedly affects prices is the pressure exerted by the poorest class for the acquisition of commodities. Indeed there are occasions when its members must avail themselves of services not usually needed, such as medical requirements during widespread calamity, which have to be paid for. This naturally diverts some of their earnings along these other channels. As their pressure lessens on the market, without a corresponding decrease of commodities, prices will fall, and while this may lessen profits for some of the owners and cause a loss for others, the laborers will be able to buy as much as before with less money. This, however, applies as long as the supply is the same. If the pressure increases, prices will rise, and the laborer must pay more for the same amount, with extra profit going to the owners. This naturally holds for temporary fluctuations which are neither strong nor long enough to affect the amount of supply. If the demand should consistently vary from the supply in any one given direction, the incentive for profits or the desire of avoiding heavy losses will eventually change the supply until a new equilibrium is reached.

As a result of previous conclusions we can state that for any fixed supply the amount available to the poorest classes is independent of its earning power. Since living conditions of the laborer increased so much from the first example to the second, it would be natural to suppose that if the laboring class were willing to supply additional services, its condition would further improve on account of increased purchasing power. This is so only if the supply keeps up with the increasing demand. Assume that it cannot be rapidly increased because of factors inmaterial to the discussion. If the laboring class should seek to increase its purchasing power by additional services, it is reasonable to expect that it would seek further vital commodities, but as any additional amount they might buy would be directly subtracted from what was previously bought by other classes, it is evident that we would no longer have a condition of equilibrium. The remaining classes, seeking to secure their normal quota would pay more and prices would mount until the extra buying power of the lower class would completely vanish in its futile attempts of increasing its purchase.

Assume for instance that the plain labor class, on an average, decides to devote more work for services so that its purchasing power increases 10%. Each worker's wage will be $1.1a$ instead of a. If prices could be kept at the previous level the unskilled laborer would increase his purchase of vital commodities from $.555q$ to $.6105q$ and the total amount for his class would be $.6105q \times 270$ $= 165q$ instead of $150q$ (line 88). But as the supply on the market is still $280q$ the quantity available for the other classes will now be that much less, or $115q$ instead of $130q$. The individuals of these classes as an average would have to make with less than the quantity q. As they would naturally resist such limitation, they will offer more money for what they want. As a result prices will rise and this increase will finally stop as soon as the labor class, having spent its additional money, will be unable to bid any higher.

In passing we wish to point out another phenomenon that is a direct consequence of this competition. In our analysis, dealing with social classes, we assumed that the various economic forces affect all the individuals of one class in the same way. This, of course, is not true. We know that profits or losses are not the same for all owners, and that they depend on many factors, including the talent and efficiency used in cutting costs of production and making merchandise attractive to the public. A similar reasoning holds true for all the other classes, so when equilibrium has been reached this does not mean that all individuals of the laboring class will secure the same amount of commodities available to them, nor that they will keep on doing so as long as that equilibrium continues. For one thing, their wages will not be the same, and, therefore, those who have more will also be able to obtain more commodities. At this point we like to introduce an additional concept which will help us to better understand the various forces that develop within the modern society. We think of classes as crystallized in special patterns, giving thereby the impression that the individuals of one class are financially far different from those of another. Actually the members of a given society, with infinitesimal differences from one to the next, can be placed in a continuous line ranging from the lowest to the highest position. As a result of the economic forces rising from all these individuals an equilibrium is established. All these individuals, however, do not necessarily remain in the same position, but while some of them may climb others will fall. If the displacement of those two groups happens to be the same, it becomes obvious that their change will not affect the social equilibrium. Indeed for supply to change, it must be influenced by an appreciable change in demand. When anyone shifts his position on the financial ladder, his larger or smaller purchases are usually too small to affect the social forces and, therefore, if one member in the entire society makes larger purchases as a result of his improved financial condition he actually detracts from some other individual not necessarily connected with him. This statement, while difficult to prove, is bound to be true if the supply remains the same.

Returning to our contention that a decrease in supply tends to raise prices and produce a profit for some of the owners, we must also mention the fact that in real life that is quite often deliberately done, as when monopolies have been established. Unscrupulous manipulators of markets will purposely cut off the supply without consideration of the hardship which their action will cause. Fortunately for humanity this condition does not last because others, attracted by the profit, will enter the field and by increased supply lower the price again.

In conclusion we can say that a sudden change in demand, in supply, or in both, will set forces in motion that tend to re-establish equilibrium. But regardless of this, many of the labor class will never be able to acquire the commodities so important to their wellbeing. Their life will be poor and shabby, and the continuous lack of fundamental requirements will have a lasting effect on their health, and on the mental and physical fitness of future generations. The skilled worker, while faring much better, will usually find extreme difficulty in improving his lot, as any possibility of saving is quite problematic. The classes we have defined as manager and owner, besides being able to buy all the necessities of life represented by q, will be in a far better position to afford services, and able also to save some of their earnings to further increase their wealth.

Now, if we should deny the owner a just rent for the use of his wealth, it is easy to see that this would not materially add to the standard of living of the others. The cost of commodities would drop from 504a to 494a, and the difference would hardly be felt by the population in general. A more radical solution would be for every component of society to receive the same wages, irrespective of talent or contribution. This, as we know, is the ideal of Communism. By this method all individuals, having the same purchasing power, would be able to buy the same amount of commodities and services. Having fixed the supply at 280q, everyone would have to get along with 0.70q. We see here that what is added to one class of society is subtracted from the others. As the entire society is now undernourished and, therefore, less prepared or qualified for the quest of amelioration and advancement, the prospects of improvement would become more problematic than ever, and in the long run we could expect the degradation and disruption of society. It is now easy to see the fallacy of those who advocate an increase in wages as the solution of the problem. Admitting again the scale of earnings related to skill and usefulness, we know that raising the pay of one group, let us say the working class, is tantamount to changing that relationship of wages, and what is gained by the laborers is automatically lost by the other classes, who in turn will be resentful and will clamor for a corresponding increase. If this increase is given, equilibrium will be re-established at the previous level, the only difference being that additional money will make purchasing power correspondingly less. We find ourselves, therefore, moving in a vicious circle for which there does not seem to be any satisfactory solution. In stating these facts we are not attempting to point out the obvious remedies, which by now may have dawned upon our reader. This will be discussed in a later chapter, but we wish now to point out phenomena occurring in our society which keep humanity in a state of turmoil and perennial discontent.

In every claim made by the various classes of society, there is an element of truth not to be questioned, but each class, in the effort to emphasize its rights, usually underestimates the just claims of the others, and no one seems to go to the bottom of the problem, determine the real causes of social unrest and maladjustment, and introduce changes that will improve these conditions. Instead the solution is left in the hands of politicians who, because of the faulty setup in almost every civilized nation, are not free to make the necessary radical changes as they are unwilling to infringe upon the interests of influential people whom they directly represent. As long as there is scarcity, phenomena like those we have analyzed are bound to appear, no matter what the type of government, Communist, Fascist, or democratic. True, an enlightened government may lessen some of the most appalling injustices, and on this account we may prefer one form to another, but this is due more to the courage, initiative, wisdom and leadership of the individuals who are placed at the head of the nation than to the theoretical principles on which the government stands. Not once, but many times, in history absolutism has worked well for the people.

We have seen how in the course of time society experiences a succession of ups and downs. In these oscillations there is an element of constancy we wish to point out. Barring individual cases, the rich as a group tend to become richer, sometimes at the expense of wealthy people, sometimes at that of society as a whole. When prosperity comes, the business pulsation of society increases, and interchange among people is more active. At such times the rich have sufficient capital available for starting new enterprises which, by adding to their community as well as to the comfort of the population, represent a real gain to society as well as to themselves. It is true that valuation of wealth at such times increases, but we are not interested in the temporary value of wealth, for this fluctuates widely and cannot be taken as a base. However, in prosperous times we know that the new as well as the established enterprises yield a substantial return to the owners, who in turn will be able to acquire new properties, launch new undertakings, and generally increase the wealth in their possession. The laborer in this period usually is able to secure a good and steady job, live with more comfort and security, enjoy a higher standard of living, but is never in a position to save sufficient capital to ascend to a higher level of society. As business retrenches we know that wealth decreases in value. Houses, land, mines, and all forms of restricted wealth will be cheaper, and whoever has ready cash can easily add to his wealth by buying all sorts of products and commodities which had been expensive during the crest of prosperity.

We know that this is true, but if the amount of business has decreased why should anyone feel the necessity of selling wealth at disadvantageous prices? This phenomenon is another result of our mode of life. During good times there are always individuals who, carried away by enthusiasm and believing in lasting prosperity, invest their personal wealth to a more dangerous degree than prudence would justify, and when depression sets in find themselves driven to sell their property in order to fulfill previous obligations. In this process the shrewdest emerges on top. He is the one with substantial amount of cash who is ready to buy at great discount from persons who are obliged to sell. While wealth may have a decreased value at the time of purchase, it will always serve as the prime mover of progress, and assure power to those who hold its control.

CHAPTER IV

EVOLUTION OF A NATION AND RELATIONSHIP
WITH OTHER NATIONS

In the third chapter we dealt with various phases of the distribution of wealth among the classes of a specific society, but did not attempt to establish a relationship between average individual wealth and that of the land. We may choose either a society of a few individuals, or one made of the entire population of a nation. In the first chapter we gave an interpretation of wealth, and described the various forms it may take, such as unrestricted wealth, consisting of things which cannot be bought or sold, and personal wealth, identified with the individual. These forms, which cannot be bought, sold, or exchanged, have no economic value, and despite their importance, must be omitted from the present discussion. We considered restricted wealth, identified with land, buildings, commodities and the like; economic wealth, identified with money in general; and wealth represented by the effort of man. These three forms, as far as they have economic value, will be included in our study.

We shall now analyze the wealth of a hypothetical nation in its entirety, and its effect upon the average standard of living of its population. Assume that the population of this nation increases with the passing of time and brings conditions that need study and discussion. Due to these new objectives, it is well that we should introduce at this time additional concepts and definitions which will help us in the course of this chapter.

Wealth, as regards material objects, can be varied and multiform; some can be utilized in its natural state; the rest must undergo changes or combinations with other products to emerge as articles or commodities usable to man. It is obvious that the wealth incorporated into an article produced by the effort and labor of man must be greater than that of the same substance in its natural state, since another form of wealth possessing economic value has been added.

Disregarding in this discussion the economic forces which alter the value of things, we shall confine our study to actual wealth as capable of satisfying human needs. Wealth is a quality intrinsically linked with an article and is independent of the price it may command on the market. A ton of coal, when burned, produces certain effects desired by man and, therefore, represents a definite amount of wealth that can be measured in calories. This wealth will not change, no matter what the price or the method of utilization. Coal, usually found in the ground, must be extracted, loaded in various conveyances, transported and delivered to the consumers. These operations require work and effort that can be estimated, which, while it may not be very expensive, represents wealth gradually added as successive handlings are made to bring each load to its final consumer. This aptitude of satisfying definite needs as it has been here identified with coal will be termed *fundamental wealth*. In general, however, any substance in its fundamental state may or may not be useful to man. Coal is a commodity that can be readily used by whoever finds it free on the surface of his property and as such we may say that this owner utilizes fundamental wealth. The same also holds for anyone who eats an apple taken or fallen from a tree. Not so, however, for iron ore which, no matter where found, must go through a long and expensive process before becoming the familiar iron or steel so extensively used by man. Coal, likewise, besides the fact that it is usually deeply imbedded in the ground, may have to be transported to an ultimate consumer hundreds or thousands of miles distant from the mine. Thereby this consumer, besides utilizing the fundamental wealth intrinsic in the coal itself, utilizes also another kind represented by the toil of men. The wealth identified with the work added by men, in this case by mining, loading, and delivery, will be termed *additive wealth,* for it is needed to utilize that commodity, irrespective of the amount of fundamental wealth.

In analyzing the wealth of a nation we could visualize cases where only fundamental wealth is utilized. This would take us back to prehistoric eras when man lived on what he could find free in nature. Our study, however, covers society in the present stage of civilization in which, while some fundamental wealth is still utilized in its natural form, by far the largest proportion must be processed before it is used. On this account the case where fundamental and additive wealth are combined in the production of the commodities used by men seems to give a good representation of the wealth of a nation and accordingly will be the one used in our discussion. But independently of the amount of fundamental and additive wealth combined in the production of an article, the article itself acquires a characteristic of its own which we shall call *intrinsic wealth*. This article may have to go through additional changes if more operations are needed before reaching the ultimate consumer. In any case, no matter in which stage, it has an intrinsic wealth, that is to say, ability to satisfy given needs.

In our aim of finding the relation between the standard of living of society and the wealth of the land, it is natural that our first step should be that of establishing some kind of relationship between the various forms of wealth as newly expressed. This is the purpose of the following discussion.

First of all let us ask ourselves the question as to what constitutes fundamental wealth. It is obvious that if the appraisal of wealth was made by a society of prehistoric times with primitive knowledge of the worth and usefulness of things, they could not be expected to assign any value to commodities such as coal, oil, and hundreds of others which are so indispensable and valuable to us. But as we are making such an appraisal, it is natural that we should include these products even if referring to a prehistoric period. By the same reasoning an appraisal made by future generations and referring to our modern time would probably include the wealth of products which seem worthless to us. As to additive wealth, the following will tend to clarify its meaning.

Assume a large amount of lumber reserved for making chairs, tables, and other house furniture: The wood represents fundamental wealth to which only the effort of men is needed to change into furniture useful to people. The carpenter, being human, will only work a certain number of hours each day, and in that time will produce a definite amount of articles. The same will hold for succeeding days, and with a continued supply of material, he will maintain a rate of production easily absorbed by the population. Another craftsman, with a different degree of skill, would maintain some other rate of production. If only one man is engaged in this trade and the community to be served is large, it is plain that this man will be unable to satisfy the potential demand, however, if there are several, even if their ability and talent is different, they will come closer to satisfy the need of that population. As their number increases eventually the supply will become equal to the demand and a condition of equilibrium will be reached. The effort of the carpenter constitutes additive wealth. This theoretically should be measured by the amount of exhaustion experienced at the end of the day. However, as stated in the third chapter, exhaustion cannot be used for such an appraisal and in line with the assumptions made at that time, we shall use instead the hours of work.

Assume that two carpenters, independently of each other, use their complete working time in making chairs of the same type and quality. Of the two, however, one is able to finish a chair in eight hours, while the other, less skillful and efficient, needs, let us say, ten hours of work and, therefore, it should be said that the latter individual has added more effort to the making of that chair. It is evident that in both cases the chairs represent the same amount of intrinsic wealth; that is, the power to produce desired effects is the same, although different proportions of fundamental and additive wealth have been combined in its manufacture. This assumes that the two carpenters use only simple and rudimentary instruments in their work, yet it is also possible that they may utilize machinery and labor saving devices in which case the number of chairs finished in a working day would be considerably greater. Here again the intrinsic wealth of the finished product will still be the same, yet the effort per chair is considerably less. From this follows that the additive wealth incorporated into an article is the combination of three different factors. The first is the effort represented by the number of hours of work, the second is the efficiency of the worker, the third his mechanical ability used in his production. Assuming an inexhaustible amount of fundamental wealth, in this case lumber, the greater any of those factors the larger will be the production. From this it would seem, given vast resources of raw material in the land and sufficent number of people willing to add their effort, that an endless quantity of products should be on hand to satisfy the needs of all components of society. This is not so. Returning to our case of the carpenters engaged in the production of furniture for a given community it is plain that as their number increases, the supply will eventually become greater than demand and either prices will have to be reduced or some of the furniture will have to go unsold. In either case the carpenters will no longer derive the same compensation for their work, which is the prime mover of their efforts, and the least talented and efficient among them or those who find the hardest to sell their wares will eventually abandon this trade and reestablish by that the equilibrium between supply and demand. This example is inserted at this point to show that additive wealth cannot be indiscriminately added to fundamental wealth and that a given relationship must exist which is controlled by the amount of supply and demand.

Standard of living is another fundamental factor to be analyzed in this study. In the third chapter we saw that standard of living can be represented by the following expression: $S.L. = E/TF$, where T stands for unit time, F for effort, and E for enjoyment. From our discussion in that chapter T can be omitted if all factors are based on the same unit of time, F can be neglected if it is assumed the same for all the components of society. E stands for enjoyment derived from the utilization of commodities and services. Now it is quite plain that the wealth represented by services, while of great importance to mankind, cannot be included in a study that aims at the determination of the physical wealth of a nation as identified by commodities and natural resources. Quite true, the ability of a population to give services will materially enhance its standard of living, yet this wealth, after utilization, is usually completely destroyed and does not add to the actual wealth of the nation in the sense that it will exist in the future. We shall disregard this form of wealth in the present study even though we may refer to it only to emphasize in a general way the initiative or apathy of some given society. As a result of these assumptions, standard of living comes to be one with E where E stands for enjoyment derived from the utilization of luxury and vital commodities, that is to say enjoyment of the intrinsic wealth of the products produced by society.

With these concepts in mind let us assume a hypothetical society living on a land. This land, its size for the present being immaterial, with its trees, pastures, mines, and so forth, possesses a definite amount of fundamental wealth. To a certain extent this can be estimated with some degree of accuracy with present methods and standards of measurement. The people living on this land, i.e.; the society we are set to analyze, derive their livelihood from the fundamental wealth of their land. A small part of this wealth will be utilized in its natural form, but by far the largest proportion must be processed before it acquires utility and value. This transformation is possible only through the effort and work of man. That is to say, additive wealth must be combined with fundamental wealth to produce intrinsic wealth. The greater the number of workers and the greater their efficiency and technological knowledge, the more fundamental wealth will be utilized, and the greater the amount of finished products available. This, however, within the previously mentioned limitations of supply and demand and also on the assumption that sufficient wealth is available to our hypothetical society and nation. Such a possession is a basic necessity without which society could not possibly exist.

On a general appraisal aiming at no precise determination of standard of living, it can be said that the latter depends on the following factors:

(a) Wealth of land.
(b) Size of population.
(c) Degree of division of labor.

The first of these factors is a primary and obvious prerequisite of life and on its amount the maximum level of standard of living reached by our given society will greatly depend.

The second factor, or the number of people living on the land, gives us an idea of the amount of fundamental wealth that will be used to produce commodities.

The third factor, or degree of division of labor, will give us an idea of how efficiently fundamental wealth will be processed. This naturally will depend on the progress and civilization already attained by the society under discussion.

For a more accurate appraisal, besides the total amount of fundamental wealth, that which is actually used must be known and measured. Again the working hours of the population, its efficiency, and its stage of technological advancement must be determined. From these we shall be able to calculate the additive wealth which added to the utilized fundamental wealth will give us the intrinsic wealth available to society which is directly related to its standard of living. In all cases the total wealth of the nation will be found by adding the intrinsic wealth of the commodities produced, to that part of fundamental wealth not yet utilized.

We may be confronted by cases in which varying amounts of intrinsic wealth are produced. To this the standard of living of the population depends. This amount, however, does not have to be necessarily related to total fundamental wealth. Indeed one society may have available a large amount of fundamental wealth to which only small effort is added, yet another may possess a far smaller amount of fundamental wealth and combine with it a large amount of additive. In comparing these two extreme types of society, it is difficult to decide which is the wealthier. If we emphasize the living conditions of the population as we find them, we must conclude that the second society is the wealthier of the two. So much more fundamental wealth is combined with a greater amount of additive to produce commodities which raise the standard of living of the population. Yet such a society has no further resources to exploit if it should increase in population, as it probably will with the passage of time. Its outlook for the future is not bright, and its standard of living eventually is bound to decrease. If we emphasize instead a long period of time, the first may seem to us the wealthier. The fundamental wealth not now being used represents a potentiality both for the present and the future, and, therefore, this society has a bright prospect ahead, even if the standard of living of the population may be low at the time the analysis is made. This low standard of living of the population may be due to the fact that the society, being too small and having a limited division of labor, adds only a small additive wealth to its natural resources. It may also be due to the fact that being probably at its initial stage of civilization, it does not know how to utilize its resources to the best advantage of the population. Consider, however, a slow increase in size and civilization. As more fundamental wealth is put to use by an increasing number of people, more commodities will result, and the standard of living is bound to rise. But, as production increases, a point will be reached when the population can no longer absorb that amount. That is to say that the production of commodities made possible by the resources on hand will have reached the demand and no more will be sought. We here say that society has reached the saturation point. Additional production beyond this limit would not be useful. However, if this society is one in a family of nations, it is likely that it will export some of its surplus to other lands. In turn it will import commodities which, either because of lack of raw material or lack of technique and facilities, cannot be locally produced. As the wealth incorporated in the commodities exchanged is presumably the same, we may witness an increase of standard of living above the aforementioned saturation point. We can foresee the time when fundamental wealth decreases in relation these two forms add only in a certain proportion related to demand. Moreover, the addition of work cannot possibly increase the amount tive wealth which cannot be used, because, as previously shown, of products if the same raw material is on hand. In turn this, disto population. Society will then be confronted by a surplus of additributed among a larger population, will decrease the amount per capita and thus lower the average standard of living. This society, in other words, has started an economic decline. As fundamental wealth decreases in relation to size of population, the commodities available for export will diminish, and as this will upset the balance of trade with other nations, the commodities imported will also be less. Eventually conditions will become so serious that some must emigrate or face starvation. So far we have given only a general outline of the evolution of a nation. For a clearer presentation of the factors which bear upon the various phases of its life, a specific example must be chosen in which a definite size is assigned to each factor, their relationship established, influences analyzed, and the whole set forth in a diagrammatic form. As upon other occasions we shall only present trends, and such numerical facts as are indispensable for the clear understanding of the subject.

Let us then return to the hypothetical nation referred to at the beginning of this chapter. Fig. 7 on page 167 gives the graphical presentation of its evolution. However, before entering the main topic of this subject, some explanation is needed as to how the diagram was derived. The horizontal axis at the bottom of the page, starting from zero and stretching toward the right, represents era or period of time. The unit may be years or thousands of years, being immaterial to our discussion since we are stating trends rather than specific facts. We have then various vertical scales (a), (b), (c), etc., each of which, as later explained represents one or more factors that give the assumed standard of measurement. The first vertical scale at the right of the diagram indicates the population of the society under study at different eras, each unit in this example being equivalent to one million, but could stand for a different amount according to the scale chosen and the society represented. The curve on the graph, indicated by N, relates the size of population with time, thus, if we want to know the size of population of the nation in study at period 10, we must draw from 10, on the horizontal scale, a vertical line until curve N is intersected at point N_{10}. If we draw from point N_{10} a horizontal line, this will intersect the vertical (a) scale at point 3 which tells us that the population of the nation at period 10 is three millions. A similar procedure can be used for all the other curves shown in the graph provided that the proper vertical scale is used.

EVOLUTION OF SOCIETY AT PERIOD (O):

POPULATION (N): In retrospect let us assume that the hypothetical nation is taken at the time indicated by zero. It is here represented by one million, and the proper point on the graph can be easily found and indicated by No.

FUNDAMENTAL WEALTH (ω): The land on which our society lives has a specific fundamental wealth. Scale (b) on the left of the diagram is used for representing fundamental wealth (ω). ω_0 gives the total fundamental wealth of the land and will be indicated by a point in the vertical line passing through zero. Its magnitude, as stated above, will be determined by our mode of measuring wealth and may be expressed in terms of money, dollars, lires, francs, and so forth, or in terms of utility and potential enjoyment. At any rate, once the scale is chosen, the position of (ω_0) on the diagram will be easily found. In our case we have assumed that this wealth is represented by twenty million units, each unit being any amount we may choose.

UTILIZED WEALTH (U): If we assume that time zero occurred many centuries ago, we must also take for granted that our society at that stage was still uncivilized and backward. This being the case, what it used must have been very small in comparison with the total available. (U_0) will represent this quantity, and since it is wealth the scale used for ω will also be used for (U). We have assumed (U_0) to be 500,000 units of wealth at this time and the corresponding point has been plotted on the graph.

EFFORT (F): While society in any prehistoric age is regarded as backward, we, nevertheless, must assume that it possesses some degree of civilization. Many of the commodities used must have been in their natural form, yet many others had to go through some kind of transformation and for this additive wealth with the corresponding effort was required. As previously mentioned, it is difficult to estimate effort, but we know it is approximately a function of the hours of work. This effort, assumed equal for all, can then be found by multiplying the average hours of work per day by the number of people making up our society. This number is assumed to be five per individual and per day. It may seem strange at first that we should choose such a small average, but let us remember that the people, because of their uncivilized stage, could not possibly possess the endurance, determination, ambition displayed by present societies and let us also remember that much that was used at that time must have been in its natural form. The entire effort will be given then by: 5 x 1,000,000 = 5,000,000 work-hours per day. In this form, however, effort does not represent additive wealth that could be directly added to fundamental wealth because they are not expressed in the same units of measurement. In this particular analysis "wealth" means potentiality for producing specific effects and satisfying particular needs (enjoyment derived by those who utilize the results of that effort) and in this respect hours of work would be meaningless. However, if through these hours of work, definite results are produced which can be measured in units of wealth, then the conversion factor between effort and wealth can be established and in this form added to wealth in general. While F_H will be the effort measured in units of man-hours, $F\omega$ will be the same effort measured in units of wealth. The conversion factor between F_H and $F\omega$ is here assumed to be 8 man-hours per unit of wealth so that the expression may be written as follows:

$$F_H = 8 \, F\omega \text{ or } F\omega = F_H /8$$

In our case the effort exerted by the society in study is given by: 5,000,000 /8 = 625,000 units of wealth. The effort in this form can be plotted on the diagram through the same scale used for fundamental wealth. We wish to stress at this point that the relationship between the two forms of effort is not affected by the wage or salary received because of that effort. In other words, just as the fundamental wealth of a commodity is assumed independent of the price it may fetch on the market, and, therefore, becomes an intrinsic quality of the commodity itself, effort is independent of the compensation it may bring, so that when we consider the wealth of a product we must think of it as a mixture of fundamental wealth and of effort, irrespective of their particular price.

EFFICIENCY (e): In our definition of additive wealth we saw that an element of efficiency had to be included. Of two people working at the same task the same number of hours with similar tools and machinery, one may accomplish considerably more than another, either because he is healthier and stronger or because more interested and alert than the other. It is difficult to establish the standard of efficiency to which all others could be compared and measured, especially in a study that includes the multiform activities of a given society. Nevertheless, we know that this factor is real and all-important in the final amount of commodities produced. Being free in our choice we have assumed that the average efficiency of our society at period zero is given by ten hundreds of some hypothetical optimum value where the individual is both strong and alert. This implies that the actual effort exerted by men must be multiplied by this factor before it becomes additive wealth.

TECHNOLOGICAL KNOWLEDGE (K): We have seen that

machinery, technological knowledge, and division of labor in general may greatly multiply the effort of men. For a given supply of commodities, the larger this factor, the smaller will be the effort of men and, therefore, must be included in the calculation of additive wealth. Technological knowledge is a product of civilization, enlightenment, ingenuity of the people, inventiveness and research and there is no limit to its size and attainment. We shall assume that this factor at period zero is represented by one.

ADDITIVE WEALTH (A): Additive wealth, as previously explained, is what must be added to utilized fundamental wealth to measure the intrinsic wealth of the article and commodities produced. Its meaning has been adequately covered in a previous section of this chapter and can be directly found by the following expression: $A = F\omega \times e \times K$ and being expressed in units of wealth, the same vertical scale (b) can be used to plot its value on the diagram. In the present instance:

$$A = 500,000 \times 0{,}10 \times 1 = 50,000 \text{ units of wealth.}$$

INTRINSIC WEALTH (C): We are now in a position to calculate the intrinsic wealth of the commodities produced which is given by the algebraic sum of the utilized fundamental wealth Uo and additive wealth Ao. We realize that other units of measurement could have been chosen for measuring the various factors encountered in this study which in turn would have produced a different graph from the one we have presented. Yet the evolution of the nation would not have been materially altered and, as we are not interested in presenting actual quantities but only possibilities and trends, we feel that even the simple and crude presentation of ours will be sufficient to show causes and effects as encountered in an actual society. With this understanding intrinsic wealth, or that which is associated with the many products used by our hypothetical society, will be given by the following expression: $C = U + A$. This is expressed in units of wealth and, therefore, the same vertical scale (b) can be used to plot its value on the diagram. In the present instance:

$$Co = 500,000 + 50,000 = 550,000 \text{ units of wealth.}$$

STANDARD OF LIVING (SL): We are now ready to calculate the standard of living of the population under study. From its definition given in the previous chapter, we know that it may be expressed as follows: $SL = E/TF$ where E is the enjoyment derived from the utiliation of commodities produced, T is the assumed unit of time for production and enjoyment, while F is the effort exerted. As previously assumed, E will not take into account enjoyment derived from services, and will depend only on commodities used. T, as aforementioned, can be any length of time we may choose and as it will be equal for all the components of our society at any stage of its evolution, can be left out of the calculation. F, or effort, can be expressed by the average number of working hours H of the population, which here is 5 hours per day. The per capita enjoyment is given by $E = C/N = 550,000/1,000,000 = .55$ units of wealth. From this the standard of living SL becomes:

$$SL = 0.55/5 = 0.11$$

Under this form the standard of living has no particular meaning in portraying the well-being of the population. Of course, we can say that it is represented by the enjoyment of 0.55 units of wealth through the expenditure of 5 hours of work, and in this form will express the condition of the average individual, but in the decimal form it will be of great assistance in comparing conditions prevailing at different periods of time, and, therefore, it has been retained in our study. Indeed, if we assume 0.11 as the unit of standard of living, any other value we may calculate for another period of time can be expressed as so many units of standard of living and by that the comparison between different epochs can be easily visualized. The scale for standard of living, indicated by S in Fig. 7, page 167, is shown by the vertical scale g, on which unity is the standard of living of our society at period zero.

WEALTH OF THE NATION (W): While different definitions could be given as to what constitutes the total wealth of a nation, we shall adopt the following one. Wealth of society is given by the intrinsic wealth of the commodities produced added to that part of fundamental wealth not yet utilized by society. $W = C + (\omega\text{-}U)$. This gives both a measure of the well-being of the population at the present stage of civilization indicated by the size of C and a measure of potentiality in the future indicated by $(\omega\text{-}U)$. At this point an explanation is in order. As fundamental wealth is utilized and combined with additive wealth to emerge as intrinsic wealth (C), this does not mean that fundamental wealth is destroyed. Thus trees bear fruit year after year, vegetables grow each season upon the same land, water flows and produces electric power. This process could continue almost indefinitely, but obviously part of this wealth will be actually destroyed in utilization, as for instance, coal and oil. On this account the fundamental wealth of the land will tend

to decrease with the passing of time and the difference will be that part which is irremediably lost. Referring again to period zero, we can assume that this loss is too small to be taken into account, and, therefore, the total wealth of the nation at this epoch is given by:
$W = 550,000 + (20,000,000 - 500,000) = 20,050,000$ units of wealth.
This factor may be plotted with the same vertical scale (b) for other kinds of wealth.

PROSPECT OF THE NATION (PS): Besides the total wealth of the land we may be interested in finding out the prospect of the population living on that land. For the present we shall take the stand that intrinsic wealth C cannot be used for this purpose. Indeed C is a combination of fundamental and additive wealth and while a large portion of U will still remain useful in the future a great deal of additive wealth A will eventually disappear after utilization. To make our point clear a house made of bricks or stones may last many years but eventually, either because of changes in styles or because of new requirements, the same house will have to be demolished to make place for another. While it is quite possible that many of the bricks will be used for the new one, the work that went to build the old house will be now completely destroyed. We can say then that only part of its fundamental wealth is irremediably lost. From this we may conclude that only fundamental wealth, in so far that it is apt to be utilized by men, should be taken as base for calculating the prospect of a nation. Prospect of a nation means to represent and indicate the opportunity of the population living on that land to make a good living not only at the time the appraisal is made, but also for a foreseeable future so that if the available fundamental wealth is large, we may conclude that the prospect is good, the opposite will be said when the availability is small. The total fundamental wealth of the land does not change appreciably with the passing of time, the population, however, may change very radically and affect the relationship between population and available wealth. With the increase in population the amount per capita will tend to decrease and so will the prospect for the entire nation. From this the prospect which we shall call basic (PS) will be represented by the ratio of the actual fundamental weealth (ω) at the epoch for which the estimate is made, divided by the size of population. Thus $PS = \omega/N$. At period zero this will be given by: $PS = 20,000,000 / 1,000,000 = 20$ units of wealth. This factor, while given in units of wealth, could not be represented in the same scale used to represent other factors involving millions of units because the corresponding points would hardly show on the graph. For this reason the vertical scale (f) must be used where each unit on the scale represents one unit of wealth. Later on the interpretation of the prospects of a nation will be altered so as to include some of the intrinsic wealth produced by society.

EVOLUTION BEYOND PERIOD ZERO. Having established the relationship among the various factors affecting our society at zero period of time, we are ready to consider it at a more advanced stage of civilization. As a general rule the various factors presented above go through gradual and imperceptible changes, which, while insignificant from year to year, nevertheless exert a profound influence on the evolution of that nation in the course of centuries. We have not taken any actual society as basis of this study, but have assumed a hypothetical one stripped to fundamentals. As time goes on each of the factors may increase or decrease, and depending on these trends, different effects will become apparent. Conclusions can then be drawn and applied to actual modern societies. For convenience we shall also focus our attention upon those epochs which seem more representative to us and emphasize the message we wish to convey. This is the main purpose of Fig. 7 at the end of this section of which a partial description has already been given. In this diagram the various factors affecting society, not only give the condition of the nation at the epoch under consideration, but serve as a basis for predicting trends and future conditions. Indeed, as each factor traces its own particular history on the diagram of evolution, the shape of the line itself has its special significance that we learn to detect. Consistent with our desire to make this study as simple as possible, trends are explained without introducing complicated mathematical concepts. There will be found in note 4-1 a study on slope for a more comprehensive understanding of what is generally referred to as trend and its corresponding graph.

NOTE 4-1. Consider a curve m which may represent any function relating to different variable quantities. The scale of any of these two quantities, which we shall call X, is given by a horizontal scale originating at O and extending toward the right of the diagram. The scale of the other quantity, which we shall call Y, is given by a

vertical scale originating at O and extending upward. The curve m
relates the two quantities
X and Y in such a way
that when the quantity X
becomes X_1 the corres-
ponding value Y_1, can be
found as follows:

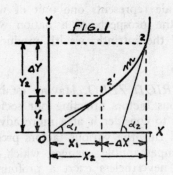

Draw from X_1 a straight
line parallel to axis OY
until it intersects the curve
m at point 1. Draw from
point 1 a straight line parallel to axis OX until it intersects the axis OY. The
distance from O to this
point of intersection gives
the quantity Y1.

If the curve m is not known, but we know the quantities X1 and
Y_1, the point 1 can be spotted on the diagram with the following
method:

Draw from X_1 a straight line parallel to axis OY. Draw from Y_1 a
straight line parallel to axis OX. The intersection of the two lines
gives the position of point 1. If several pairs of quantities as X_2Y_2,
X_3Y_3, X_4Y_4, etc., are known, points 2, 3, 4, and so forth can be
spotted by the same method. If the various quantities have been
chosen close to each other, we will have a succession of points
1,2,3, etc., which are also sufficiently close to each other. By joining
these various points by a line we will obtain a curve m which
represents the relationship between the quantities X and Y.

With this in mind let us assume two points 1 and 2 on our
curve m. The distance of point 1 from the horizontal axis is equal
to the value Y_1, and the distance of point 1 from the vertical axis is
equal to the value X_1. The same can be said for point 2. As point 2
in our diagram is placed further away than point 1 from both axes, we
can derive the following conclusions. The difference between the
two vertical coordinates or Y_2-Y_1, represents the variation in the
value of Y between these two conditions. This difference we shall
indicated with ΔY. In the same way the difference between the two
horizontal coordinates or X_2-X_1, represents the variation in the
value of X between the same two conditions. This difference we

shall indicate with ΔX. $\Delta Y/\Delta X$ represents the tangent of the angle formed by the straight line passing through the two points 1 and 2 and the horizontal axis OX. If point 2 is chosen closer and closer to 1, as for instance 2', until it coincides with 1, the line

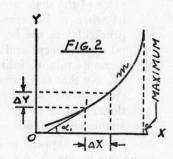

FIG. 2

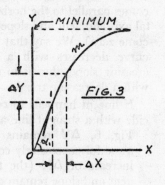

FIG. 3

passing through these points tends to approach the tangent to the curve at point 1. The value of the tangent of the angle formed by this line and the horizontal axis is called the slope of the curve at point 1. It is easily understood that if the curvature of line m happens to be upward as in Fig. 2, ΔY tends to become larger for successively equal increase of ΔX. The slope or tangent of these various points tends also to increase and the maximum is reached when m becomes perpendicular to the horizontal axis (tangent and slope become infinity). We say that this curve increases with an increasing slope, that is to say, has an increasing trend.

If line m happens to be as one in Fig. 3, ΔY tends to become smaller for successively equal increases of ΔX and when m becomes parallel to the horizontal axis, the tangent and slope become zero. We say that this curve increases with a decreas-

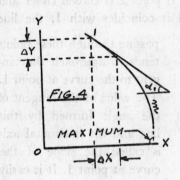

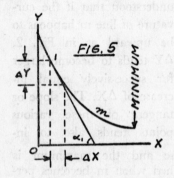

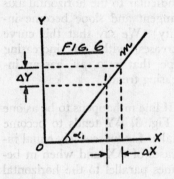

ing slope, that is to say has a decreasing trend.

If line m happens to be as the one in Fig. 4, ΔY, while negative, tends to become larger for successively equal increases of ΔX. The maximum absolute value of the slope is reached when m becomes perpendicular to the horizontal axis (tangent and slope become minus infinity). We say that this curve decreases with an increasing slope, that is to say, with an increasing trend.

If line m happens to be as the one in Fig. 5, ΔY, while negative, tends to become smaller for successively equal increases of ΔX. The minimum absolute value of the slope is reached when m becomes parallel to the horizontal axis (tangent and slope become zero). We say that this curve decreases with a decreasing slope, that is to say, with a decreasing trend.

If line m happens to coincide with a straight line as in Fig. 6, ΔY remains the same for successively equal increase of ΔX (the tangent and slope remain constant). We say that this curve has a constant slope or constant trend.

EVOLUTION OF SOCIETY AT PERIOD 5: Leaving period zero, we will consider conditions at period 5, again bearing in mind that each unit of time may represent centuries or thousands of years.

SIZE OF POPULATION (N): The size of our society will be represented by N_5. It is an established fact, barring outside interferences, which may alter the normal evolution of a nation, that society usually tends to increase in size with the passing of time. If society is particularly rich in material resources, it is also quite likely that immigration will accelerate the natural process. Accordingly N_5 is larger than N_0. As this increase is assumed constant between times 0 and 5, the straight line between N_0 and N_5 will give the population at any intervening time. Let us assume that it is now $N_5 = 2,000,000$, which value has been plotted on the diagram. Besides increasing in number, it is reasonable to suppose that our society has become more civilized and as such, having learned better methods of production the amount of commodities and consequently fundamental wealth utilized and consumed by each individual will also be greater.

UTILIZED WEALTH (U): If the utilization of fundamental wealth by each individual had remained the same during the interval of time, it is evident that the amount of utilized fundamental wealth U_5 would bear, in regard to U_0 the same relation that is borne by N_5 toward N_0, that is a ratio of 2 to 1. But through the increased appreciation of things, direct consequence of the more advanced civilization, and because of the better knowledge of manufacturing processes, it is reasonable to suppose this increase to have occurred more rapidly than that of the population, and, therefore, the curve representing utilized wealth (U) will have a greater slope than N. (See note 4-1 for the significance of slope). At period 5 the value of U_5 has been assumed. $U_5 = 6,150,000$ units of wealth.

FUNDAMENTAL WEALTH (ω): Even though small, some of the utilized fundamental wealth will be irremediably lost and this will tend to decrease the total fundamental wealth of the nation. The curve (ω), between periods 0 and 5, starting as a stright line will tend to curve as 5 is being approached, that is to say, will decrease with an increasing slope, yet, as the loss is probably very small, for all practical purposes (ω) may be drawn as a straight line. Curve (U) between these two points will have, however, an increasing slope. At period 5 the value of ω_5 has been assumed respectively $\omega_5 = 19,770,000$ units of wealth.

EFFORT (F): With the passing of time and with a better appreciation of things, we must also assume that our society gradually learns through experience that very few things in life can be acquired without some kind of effort and because of that greater ambition, result of an advanced civilization and evolution, it is reasonable to expect that the effort per individual has steadily increased from that minimum assumed at period zero. On the diagram the actual amount as well as the trend is shown by curve H which, starting from 5 hours per day, reaches a maximum of 14 hours at period 5 and then gradually decreases beyond that point. The reason for this decrease will be explained when referring to those epochs. At period 5 the total effort of the population will be expressed by:

$$(F_H)_5 = H_5 \times N_5 = 14 \times 2,000,000$$
$$= 28,000,000 \text{ work hours per day.}$$

The wealth represented by this effort, as from previous discussion, will be given by:

$$(F\omega)_5 = (F_H)_5 \div 8 = 28,000,000/8$$
$$= 3,500,000 \text{ units of wealth.}$$

The scale for curve (F_H) is shown by the vertical scale (d) in which each unit represents one million of hours of work per day.

EFFICIENCY (e): In step with a greater effort the efficiency of the average individual has also increased. As previously explained, this factor compares the result of the effort of the average individual with that of an hypothetical one, both strong and alert. For our study we have assumed a curve (e) which starting from a value of 0.10 at period zero tends to increase with time yet never reaches the theoretical perfection represented by one and, therefore, (e) is an increasing curve with a decreasing slope. The scale representing efficiency is indicated by the vertical scale (e) at the right side of the diagram. At period 5 the efficiency of our society is given by:

$$e_5 = 0.65$$

TECHNOLOGICAL KNOWLEDGE (K): This factor will also be influenced by the advancement of society, however, at variance from efficiency, will increase in relation to the amount of division of labor, increase in the inventiveness of the people, and with the advancement of science. However, inventions and discoveries do not succeed each other in an orderly manner and while we may have periods of great activity, these, either due to recognizable causes, or to imponderable factors, may be followed by periods of stagnation and as such the corresponding curve would have to be one with abrupt changes and with declines. But as we are only representing an hypothetical society, we shall assume a curve which, starting with the value of one, keeps on increasing until it reaches the value of 17 at period 15. The scale representing this factor is given by the vertical scale (g). At period 5 the value of K is given by:

$$K_5 = 2.99$$

ADDITIVE WEALTH (*A*): In possession of the factors for effort, efficiency, and technological knowledge, we are in a position to calculate the additive wealth which will be given by their product. We have then: $A_5 = (F\omega)_5$ x e_5 x $K_5 = 3,500,000$ x 0.65 x $2.99 = 6,800,000$ units of wealth.

INTRINSIC WEALTH (*C*): The intrinsic wealth of the commodities produced will be given directly by the sum of additive wealth to utilized fundamental wealth or:

$$C_5 = U_5 + A_5 = 6,150,000 + 6,800,000$$
$$= 12,950,000 \text{ units of wealth}$$

STANDARD OF LIVING (*SL*): We are now ready to calculate the average standard of living of the population at this period, which as previously shown is given by the simple expression:

(SL) $= (C/N)H$ and in this case:

$$(SL)_5 = (C_5/N_5)/H_5 = (12,950,000/2,000,000)/14$$
$$= 6.47/14 = 0.462$$

This in itself has no particular meaning, unless we express it by saying that the average individual enjoys 6.47 units of wealth through the expenditure of 14 hours of work. However, with the standard of living of the same society at period zero as basis of comparison we can state that at period 5 it is 3.16 times greater. This ratio of standard of living is represented in the diagram by curve (S) and the scale is the same as the one used for K; i.e., vertical line (g).

WEALTH OF THE NATION (*W*) *AND PROSPECT FOR THE FUTURE* (*PS*): In line with our definition of wealth of a nation $W = C + (\omega\text{-}U)$ and at period 5 this is given by: W5 $= C_5 + (\omega_5\text{-}U_5) = 12,950,000 + (19,770,000\text{-}6,150,000) = 26,570,000$ units of wealth which is considerably greater than the wealth at period zero. This, because of the addition contributed by the effort of man which has increased the utility and worth of that part of fundamental wealth utilized at that time. As to the future prospect of the nation we have seen, however, that intrinsic wealth C cannot be added to fundamental wealth and that this prospect is better represented by the ratio of fundamental wealth to size of population: $(PS) = \omega/N$. At period 5 this will be given by:

$$(PS)_5 = \omega_5/N_5 = 19,770,000/2,000,000$$
$$= 9.88 \text{ units of wealth instead of 20 for}$$

time zero. We must conclude from this that the prospect of society as a whole is not as bright now as at period zero, irrespective of the fact that wealth itself (W) is so much greater than before. The increase in population is obviously the most important factor in that reduction. Yet a factor of 9.88, as we shall see for future epochs, is considerably greater than what is actually needed both for a good prospect and a good living. To say that our nation is not as well off at period 5 as it was at period zero, would be similar if we were to state that the miser is better off or has a better prospect than the individual who, with the same money, raises himself to a better living and to a better mode of life. Undoubtedly the second individual has evolved and is closer to the final goal of humanity. We must also take into account the fact that of all the articles manufactured at any particular epoch, some and probably many of them not only are made for present needs and enjoyment, but also for the comfort and enjoyment of future generations and in this respect they become fundamental wealth. To give an example consider the pyramids of the Egyptians, the roads and the temples of the Romans the castles and churches of the Medio Evo, the dams of our present generations which we hope will continue to be useful for many years to come. Quite true that many of these structures have by now become obsolete; nevertheless, they were very important and useful for many centuries after they were built and as many of them cease to be useful, other structures take their places which tend to add to the fundamental wealth of a nation. We have now many houses in which several generations have lived, prospered and died. As these houses will gradually be replaced by better homes with better conveniences and modern facilities the loss of the old house will be replaced by the gain of the new one so that the fundamental wealth intrinsic with the house built at that particular location will not be lost but increased. Under this light our assumption of taking fundamental wealth, or that which can be found free in nature, as the base for calculating the prospect of a nation seems too pessimistic, and in order to take this fact into account we shall state that at least one-half of the intrinsic wealth (C) should be added to fundamental wealth for the determination of the prospect of a nation.

This new factor, called (PS') will be given by the following expression: (PS') = (ω + O.5C)/N. In our case:

$$PS' = (19,770,000 + 6,475,000)/2,000,000$$
$$= 13.12 \text{ units of wealth}$$

In the just finished analysis of period 5 it may have seemed that we have indiscriminately added utilized and additive wealth to derive intrinsic wealth. While it was not stated, it was, however, implicitly assumed that C was a product of a given demand born within our society at that specific stage of advancement and civilization. C is represented as a smooth curve which would tend to indicate a gradual and continuous progress from one epoch to another, but this, because each epoch represents hundreds or thousands of years and small departures from that line which would indicate periods of prosperity and depression, can hardly be shown in a study of this kind. It is only when we concentrate on any particular epoch, similar to that of using a magnifying glass to any one point of the curve that such deviations appear with all their consequences and effects. As we have seen, however, the standard of living of the population has increased enormously over that of the zero period, so that on the whole our society is now far better off than before.

EVOLUTION BEYOND PERIOD 5: The tendency shown by the various factors may continue for years or hundreds of years beyond period 5. As time goes on more fundamental wealth will be used, more commodities manufactured and enjoyed, and our society, again barring arresting factors, will steadily increase in size. However, as long as the land has additional fundamental wealth available to our society, we may be sure that almost every curve thus far analyzed will retain the same trend. This is a characteristic of a progressive, prosperous, and basically healthy society. Its efficiency will also increase, but as it advances each additional gain will become more difficult to attain. As seen, the curve of efficiency is represented by one that increases with a diminishing slope. Not so, however, with technological advancement which, due to an increasing civilization, will tend to increase at a larger rate so that even though the basic effort of man tends to decrease due to the smaller number of hours of work, the additive wealth, product of the just mentioned factors, can be represented by a curve that increases with an increasing slope. This, added to a greater amount of fundamental wealth (U), will produce commodities that tend to increase at a far greater rate than before. Needless to say that the smaller effort of man, represented by fewer hours of work added to a greater amount of commodities enjoyed will tend to increase the standard of living of the population. We can truly say then that the nation is enjoying its golden age of comfort and prosperity. Yet, as time goes on, imperceptible changes will begin to appear which will have a profound influence on the evolution of the nation and, therefore, need consideration and scrutiny. The numerical data from which the various points have been drawn are given in Fig. 7, page 167 and, therefore, we no longer feel the necessity to show the derivation of their numerical size.

EVOLUTION AT PERIOD 10: The size of population, in accordance with previous assumptions, has kept on increasing at the same rate as before and has reached the three million mark at period 10. This because of the none too rigid relation between size of population and wealth of the land.

The fundamental wealth of the land (ω), with the exception that more is irremediably lost, is still substantially the same and at period 10 has been assumed to be 19,150,000 units of wealth.

The utilized wealth (U) has kept, however, on increasing finally reaching that of the fundamental wealth (ω). This means, of course, that this factor can no longer increase in the future, but will coincide with (ω) and follow the same gradual descent which is represented by what is irremediably lost at this point:

$$U_{10} = \omega_{10} = 19,150,000 \text{ units of wealth.}$$

We know that the possibility of fundamental wealth of the nation being completely utilized in the sense implied in this study is extremely improbable if not altogether impossible because resources in general must be used for different purposes not necessarily having the same utility. If one article or commodity or what have you is used for some particular purpose, it is evident that it cannot be used at the same time for another even if this is more useful than the first which would represent the maximum utilization of the wealth intrinsic to that article. To make our point clear, if we say that the land used as foundation for building purposes is more useful to man than land where cultivation is carried, and still more useful to man than land reserved for road construction, it is plain that not all the land could be used for building purposes which would represent its greatest utilization, but that some must be saved for cultivation and some for other purposes. From this our statement that all wealth is being utilized must not be taken in an absolute physical sense but from the point that the maximum overall return is attained and that any additional amount would conflict with the basic needs of society.

The effort of man (F) represented by the hours of work, having reached the maximum value at period 5, gradually starts to decrease reaching the value of eight hours at the period in consideration, but more about effort later.

The efficiency of man (e) or ability in producing results for a given amount of effort expended will steadily increase with the increase in civilization and at period 10 will become 90 percent of the same hypothetical level.

The technological knowledge (K), result of inventions and advancement of science, has steadily increased with the passing of time reaching the value of 11.1. The factor K is and has been a major element in the decrease of the hours of work of society because it has gone to increase the additive wealth needed to manufacture commodities. The commodities, being dependent on supply and demand, cannot be increased at will and, therefore, given a needed amount of C, the larger is K the smaller is the effort required.

We can conclude that the additive wealth (A), product of the three factors mentioned above, will retain the previous trend and can be represented by a curve which increases with an increasing slope. Additive wealth at period 10 is given by 30,000,000 units of wealth.

As seen, the fundamental utilized wealth U_{10} is given by 19,150,000 units of wealth which, at this epoch, happens to be equal to total fundamental wealth ω_{10}; therefore, the intrinsic wealth of the commodities produced will be given by the sum of total additive wealth and total utilized wealth i.e.:

$$19,150 + 30,000,000 = 49,150,000 \text{ units of wealth.}$$

Up to this point the curve representing intrinsic wealth has retained the same trend. This, however, will radically change in the future.

From the knowledge of intrinsic wealth and size of population the standard of living can be easily calculated. This is given by:

$$(SL)_{10} = C_{10}/N_{10})/H_{10} = (49,150,000/3,000,000)/8$$
$$= 16.56/8 = 2,045$$

which is equivalent to say that the average individual of this nations enjoys 16.56 units of wealth through the expenditure of eight hours of work. Comparing this value with the one obtained at period zero, the standard of living can be represented by 18.6. From this we must appreciate the great progress in living conditions attained by our society. We can also say that SL_{10} is 4.43 times better than SL_5.

The wealth of the antion given by $W = C + (\omega\text{-}U)$ reaches at this epoch the value of 49,150,000 units of wealth which coincides with that of the intrinsic wealth C_{10}. This, because ω and U, being equal, cancel each other. However, irrespective of the diminishing value of $(\omega\text{-}U)$, the wealth of the nation has steadily increased at an increasing rate this because fundamental wealth, being transformed into useful products, has acquired a greater value than in its virgin form.

Of the two interpretations of the prospect of the nation, that which is based on fundamental wealth alone naturally has decreased because of both, a decrease in fundamental wealth and an increase in population and has reached now a value of 6.38. However, that which is based on fundamental wealth added to one-half the additive wealth after having reached a minimum value of 13.08 at period 6 starts to increase and reaches a value of 14.6 at the epoch in consideration. This, because the increase in population is more than balanced by the increased value of wealth. As we shall soon realize, however, period 10 represents the optimum condition reached by the nation in study.

EVOLUTION BEYOND PERIOD 10: We have seen that additive as well as the wealth of the nation have been increasing up to now at a greater rate than that of the population and this has permitted the attainment of better living conditions. This has been possible because with an increase in progress additional fundamental wealth has been utilized to satisfy an ever increasing demand of the expanding and energetic population. After period 10 this will no longer be possible because, as seen, the total fundamental wealth of the nation has been completely used and no more is available. This means also that the available wealth, rather than increasing, will gradually decrease as some is irremediably lost. The ingenuity of the people and their technological advancement will increase for a time the usefulness of the resources on hand, but this process cannot go on indefinitely and time will come when the increase in population will more than balance that of the increased usefulness of the commodities produced and as the amount per capita will become less, this will mean a decline in the life cycle of the nation.

The number of hours of work, as seen, has kept on decreasing because of the increase in efficiency and technological knowledge which, having more than balanced the decreased effort have kept the supply equal to demand. This, presumably, has kept the entire population at work. However, the decrease in number of hours of work cannot go on indefinitely because on that effort the wage of the individual and his livelihood depend. With a decreased amount of commodities (C) and a larger population (N), conditions will become precarious and as there will always be difference between individuals, those who are better equipped, both physically and mentally, will gain greater financial power either by holding higher paid jobs or by working more hours than the average. In other words, effort will no longer be dependent on the amount of commodities needed by the population, but by the amount of money needed to live and, therefore, will resist an additional reduction in working hours. This implicitly means that others will have to work less or be unemployed. For those who find full jobs, we shall assume that they keep on working eight hours per day.

At this point some explanation is in order. We have seen that supply tends to equalize demand. In a progressive society, such as described, in which ever greater amounts of fundamental wealth can be utilized, it is evident that utilization should be made only as needed. In our analysis we have shown an uninterrupted increase in commodities produced, which, being equivalent to supply, has kept pace with demand. The effects produced by the inevitable discrepancies between supply and demand as they set up alternate periods of prosperity and depression are of great importance to society, but this only in a study that focuses its attention to any one particular era of the life of the nation. By this we mean that periods of prosperity and depression are usually found in most nations no matter their stage of advancement, however, these alternate swings are too insignificant to alter in one way or another the basic nature of the lines that show the magnitude and history of these factors.

Barring these discrepancies, our society has continued to utilize larger proportions of its fundamental wealth for the simple reason that, due to advanced progress and civilization, a greater demand has made such an increase imperative and desirable. Now a greater demand implies that the population in general has sufficient purchasing power implying in turn the availability of employment and work. As mentioned before the decrease in working hours was mainly due to the advancement of science, efficiency, and division of labor. Quite likely the various classes, in line with our analysis of previous chapters, must have evolved and developed, so that while some may have received more than the calculated average, others received less. This presumably gave rise to all the phenomena analyzed in the third chapter, but on the whole our society, having sufficient fundamental wealth, was able to keep scarcity of commodities within reasonable limits. We may also add that the availability of wealth may have been the incentive for awakening initiative and devising new methods of production, thus making more and better jobs with reduced effort for many. Now, we do not mean that the standard of living changes abruptly as soon as period 10 has passed. As a matter of fact, many in the population may continue to enjoy the same standard of living for many years to come before the damaging effects of scarcity are felt in full. But it stands to reason that as the utilized fundamental wealth (U) can no longer increase, as the commodities produced cannot be very much more than those of period 10, and more likely less, and as the population still increases, it finally becomes evident that the amount per capita must decrease. The rich will remain able to buy all they want; the poor, on the other hand, being forced to accept less than before, will exert more competition for the acquisition of vital commodities. This will raise prices, and the clamor for higher wages will begin to appear; many will seek to work harder in order to earn more so that competition in the field of labor will also appear since the best qualified, not only will be able to obtain better jobs but also able to work longer hours than those who are less capable. But, intrinsic wealth of commodities cannot be obtained by merely adding any amount of effort to fundamental wealth, for a proper relation must exist to permit that addition. Thus, we cannot engage two workers to make a chair if only one is needed to do the job, especially when competition on the market becomes keen, so that as time goes on those who are less prepared for life will find it increasingly difficult to get good jobs, and must fall back on part-time work for their subsistence. This number will keep on increasing with the increase of population. Yet, even at this stage of evolution, we must still assume that all are more or less permitted to obtain some kind of remunerative work, some for more than eight hours per day (the average for period 10) others for less, with many graduations in between. Under such circumstances it would be difficult to calculate the total amount of work from such a variety of efforts. But since we are concerned with the nation as a whole rather than particular groups of individuals, it seems reasonable to divide the population into two distinct sections, one working at the rate of eight hours each day, while the other will be assumed unemployed. While this assumption is radically at variance from what we have stated above, yet it portrays the critical condition of the nation, and while it will not give the exact number of those working less than eight hours per day, it will portray the deficiency of the nation as a whole, in reference to what it requires to be prosperous and self sufficient. In our analysis the unemployed part of the population is given as a fraction of the whole and can be derived by the following method. At any particular time beyond period 10 the diagram of evolution gives us the amount of fundamental and utilized wealth of society, which at this stage are equal to each other. We have seen also that fundamental and additive wealth combine only in a certain proportion. Although not strictly correct, the relation existing at period 10 has been taken as base for all future periods of time. At period 10 the fundamental and additive wealth are respectively given by:

$\omega_{10} = 19,150,000$ and $A_{10} = 30,000,000$ units of wealth and their ratio:

$$(R) = 30,000,000/19,150,000 = 1.572$$

As such 1.572 will be assumed to be the constant relationship between A and U. Therefore, knowing the utilized fundamental wealth at any one period, the corresponding additive wealth will be given by

$$A = U \times 1.572$$

The diagram of evolution gives also the average efficiency (e) and technological advancement (K) of society at this time and the total amount of effort may be found by the following expression:

$$F\omega = A/e.K$$

By using the same ratio 8 existing between $F\omega$ and F_H the total number of hours of work will be given by:

$$F_H = F\omega \times 8$$

If we assumed now that all those who are employed work at the rate of eight hours each day their number will coincide with that representing effort $F\omega$. From this number that of the jobless will immediately follow. The ratio of this number with the one representing the entire population will give the percentage of unemployment existing at the period under consideration.

EVOLUTION OF SOCIETY AT PERIOD 15: In order better to grasp the relation between the various factors affecting the nation let us consider period 15 on our diagram and establish the various factors which can be easily calculated from the expressions previously given.

Population of the nation $N_{15} = 4,000,000$ (assumed).

Total fundamental wealth $\omega_{15} = 18,300,000$ units of wealth (assumed).

Total utilized wealth $U_{15} = \omega_{15} = 18,300,000$ units of wealth.

Factor for additive wealth (same as at period 10) $= 1.572$.

Total additive wealth $A_{15} = 28,760,000$ units of wealth.

Efficiency of society $e_{15} = 0.93$ (assumed).

Technological advancement $K_{15} = 17$ (assumed).

Effort $(F\omega)_{15} = A_{15} / (e_{15} \times K_{15}) = 1,820,000$ units of wealth.

Effort $(F_H)_{15} = (F\omega)_{15} \times 8 = 14,550,000$ hours of work.

Persons engaged at 8 hours per day $(Ne)_{15} =$
$(F_H)_{15}/8 = 1,820,000$.

Number of unemployed $(Nu)_{15} = N_{15} - (Ne)_{15} = 2,180,000$.

Percentage of unemployment $(Nu)_{15}/N_{15} = 54.5$ per cent.

Intrinsic wealth of the nation $C_{15} = \omega_{15} + A_{15} = 47,060,000$ units of wealth.

Wealth of the nation $W_{15} = C_{15} + (\omega_{15} - U_{15} = 47,060,000$ units of wealth.

Prospect of nation $(PS)_{15} = \omega_{15} / N_{15} = 4.57$ units of wealth.

Prospect of the nation $(PS')_{15} = (0.5C_{15} + \omega_{15})/N_{15} = 10.43$ units of wealth.

The standard of living of the population at this time, which could be easily derived from the previously given equation loses its significance for a society composed of two groups, of which one, lacking any commodity has theoretically zero standard of living. While this is absurd, we know that it will be small for all who have part-time jobs, and because of the impossibility of finding a factor that truly expresses the condition of the nation, we have decided to omit this factor from our graph.

For the benefit of the reader who wishes to trace the gradual change from one period to another in more detail, we have included on page 168 a tabulation of the various factors from which the diagram has been drawn.

CONCLUSIONS: We do not mean that the evolution of a nation or society must necessarily follow the trend indicated. Many factors outside our society may change conditions to a great extent, and alter considerably its mode of evolution. The annexation of additional land may vary the relationship between size of population and fundamental wealth. Our nation may itself be conquered by another, and become a unit of a greater society. Again a new discovery may suddenly change the worth of the fundamental wealth, making it considerably greater than previously calculated. On these accounts there may be abrupt variations in evolution which would be indicated in our diagram by a sudden change in some or all the curves shown, but once this change has taken place the natural trend of evolution is bound to resume its course and produce the phenomena explained and indicated in our analysis.

Between period (o) and (5) we may include all those nations with large natural resources and a population which, either because of its limited size or backwardness, produces an amount of commodities insufficient to maintain a decent standard of living. From our analysis on evolution we, nevertheless, can foresee the time when such nations, through a more advanced civilization, will be able to enjoy a better standard of living. They have a great future ahead, because the vast fundamental resources in their possession are always available for their benefit as well as for that of mankind in general. These nations may look forward to a long period of advancement and progress.

There are other nations whose stage of civilization and technology may qualify them for a period between (5) and (10) in our scheme of evolution. These nations are those which have learned to harness their wealth, at least as far as contemporary industrialization permits. Being among the most civilized in the world, they have attained a high standard of living, and may be confident of a long, active, and constructive life ahead. But as their population gradually increases, the time will come when the top limit will finally be reached. At this point forces will set in, starting the downward trend of evolution. It is true that this phenomenon could be averted by checking the increase of population, but this is not a problem easily solved. Nature, to be sure, has safety valves which in a crude way tend to retard that growth. These factors are war, plague, famine, high death-rate among children and old people. With the advent of modern civilization these counterbalances have been less devastating than in the past, and mankind has increased more rapidly than ever before.

It must be remembered, however, that we have in the world vast regions still sparsely populated, and the time when the entire earth will become overcrowded is quite distant. Of course, there is a tendency on the part of the population to concentrate in one place more than another, so that in the most congested areas the conditions referred to above may actually occur. This, nevertheless, is a local phenomenon, not to be confused with what is going on with the world at large.

Reverting to checks upon increase in population, we note that in every country the wealthiest element, comprising those individuals best equipped to support large families, are actually those who have the smallest. Various causes are responsible for this paradox. The higher the standard of living, the less profilic the population becomes. Rich people, with due consideration for the many exceptions, avoid the raising of many children. The fact that parents wish to give good education and opportunities to their offspring prevents them, from an economic standpoint, from indulging in the luxury of a large family. The softer and easier life of the well-to-do frequently makes women incapable of much child-bearing. In many cases, selfishness, the desire to avoid responsibility, the craving for opportunity to enjoy the comfort and freedom wealth brings, are other factors. We do not say this is good or bad, but merely state a fact.

Usually a nation is an agglomeration of heterogeneous peoples. While the rich have only moderately-sized families, the poor continue having many children, and this will more than counterbalance the situation, eventually bringing the nation nearer the critical condition which starts the downward trend of society. It is evident, then, that the poorest part of any population is responsible for this increase. If the standard of living could be raised among the vast undernourished masses of the nations, the problem of over-population might cease to exist.

We also find nations which appear to have passed period (10), and to be definitely on the downward grade of evolution. Of course, we must remember that throughout history we have been witness to a continuous flow of humanity from one place to another. Acquisition or loss of territory has been the experience of almost every nation on earth. It is easy to realize that a sudden change of the ratio between size of population and fundamental wealth may shift a nation to a different point on the evolution diagram. Those nations which might be identified as beyond point (10), either by war or through acquiring colonies may enlarge their possession of fundamental wealth, and their position would automatically move to one between periods (5) and (10). However, those which have made this shift were originally great and powerful. As for those which had not or have not now the physical strength to conquer and fight they must be resigned to the gradual decline of their standard of living, or to be absorbed by more progressive populations in need of manpower and additive wealth.

As previously mentioned, we shall again and again witness the ingenuity of men in making new discoveries, in thinking up new methods of utilization of the forces of nature, so that hitherto unused energies may be made available to mankind. Our concept of fundamental wealth is continually revised by better understanding and by new techniques. Coal and oil, now so abundant in nature, are extracted from the earth and lavishly consumed. As this process continues incessantly, the time will come when their supply will be completely exhausted. This will have severe repercussions all over the world. Yet, while this emergency is not pressing, great minds are feverishly working to find substitutes for these forms of natural wealth. The day is not far when forces of nature previously unharnessed may be put into practical use. Already the splitting of the uranium atom has left the laboratory stage and made its ghastly debut in the field of war. Its utilization for the good of humanity cannot be far in the future. As the splitting of the atom will not be necessarily confined to that of uranium only and other substances will probably be used more common in nature, the release and harnessing of such vast amounts of energy would completely revolutionize our concept of fundamental wealth, and place all nations in a far better economic position. Of course, all nations, and mankind in general, must learn to economize and increase their efficiency when they utilize those forms of wealth that can be irremediably lost. It is not our scope, however, to discuss at this point what mankind should or should not do. We seek for the present only to indicate tendencies which, if not corrected and stopped, may well bring about the ruin of humanity.

Returning to the nations which have surpassed the zenith of standard of living, we wish to add a few more observations to conclude our study. We have seen that the fraction of additive wealth used to calculate intrinsic wealth is related to the utilized fundamental wealth, and not to the size of population, so that if the latter increases, unemployment will gradually grow from a small to disastrous proportions. The standard of living of those who have lost their jobs will drop to a level far below the average for the nation. This, of course, is the result of over-population. From this we might think that only the poorest part of society would feel the impact of this maladjustment, but as a matter of fact the entire population, rich and poor, will be affected. Indeed if the poorest element cannot be employed, and is thereby prevented from adding its share to the well-being of society, still it must live, and either through charity, relief, or the dole from the government will be a drag upon the rest of society. Since these unfortunate people must survive, even if their requirements may sink to the minimum, what they consume will be that much less otherwise available for export and exchange. Hence, even the rich will be indirectly injured. In other words, the unemployed will devour the surplus produced by those who work, and thereby the general standard of living will be unfavorably affected.

From a theoretical viewpoint the fundamental wealth of the land is approximately the same as before. Even though a small percentage has been irremediably lost, the total is still as large as ever. In addition the potential additive wealth of the nation has increased with the gain in population, and this fact might give the impression that it is now in possession of more wealth than before. Unfortunately the relation that exists between fundamental and additive wealth prevents the latter from being utilized in full. Furthermore, the nation must face the fact that the element which in better circumstances would add its effort to the progress of society becomes actually a burden. As the strain increases, the time will come when it may seem that the only solution is that of seizing additional territory ,and thereby re-establishing a better proportion between (W) and (F). Of course, a fixed rate of propagation, as earlier stated, would solve the problem, but religious teachings, great differences in social classes, and other factors preclude such a course.

At present there does not seem to be any real solution to the problem beyond the dire calamities of war, pestilence, and famine. Yet we decline to despair of the future of humanity. As civilization advances, and dilemmas become increasingly serious, a more determined and honest effort will be made to ameliorate conditions, and a really enlightened planning will supplant the crude methods used by nature.

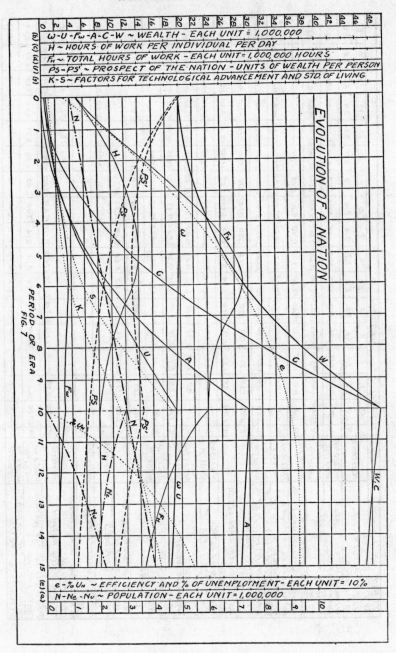

W-U-Fw-A-C-W ~ WEALTH - EACH UNIT = 1,000,000
H ~ HOURS OF WORK PER INDIVIDUAL PER DAY
Fh ~ TOTAL HOURS OF WORK - EACH UNIT = 1,000,000 HOURS
PS-PS' ~ PROSPECT OF THE NATION - UNITS OF WEALTH PER PERSON
K-S ~ FACTORS FOR TECHNOLOGICAL ADVANCEMENT AND STD. OF LIVING

EVOLUTION OF A NATION

PERIOD OR ERA
FIG. 7

e -% Uₙ ~ EFFICIENCY AND % OF UNEMPLOYMENT - EACH UNIT = 10%
N-Ne -Nᵤ ~ POPULATION - EACH UNIT = 1,000,000

TABLE NO. I — EVOLUTION OF A NATION

PERIOD OR ERA			0	1	2	3	4	5	6	7	8	9	10	11	12	13	14	15
SIZE OF POPULATION (ASSUMED)	MILLIONS	N	1.0	1.2	1.4	1.6	1.8	2.0	2.2	2.4	2.6	2.8	3.0	3.2	3.4	3.6	3.8	4.0
WEALTH IRREMEDIABLY LOST (ASSUMED)	MILLIONS WEALTH	L	0	.018	.042	.086	.152	.230	.330	.442	.568	.708	.850	1.010	1.100	1.340	1.520	1.700
FUNDAMENTAL WEALTH $Wo-L$	MILLIONS WEALTH	W	20,000	19,982	19,958	19,914	19,848	19,770	19,670	19,558	19,432	19,292	19,150	18,990	18,820	18,660	18,480	18,300
HOURS OF WORK PER INDIVIDUAL (ASSUMED)	HOURS	H	5.0	8.0	10.75	12.50	13.65	14.00	13.30	11.40	9.70	8.65	8.00					
TOTAL EFFORT IN HOURS OF WORK $=(N.H)$ OR $(F_w \times 8)^x$	MILLIONS HOURS	F_h	5.0	9.60	15.05	20.00	24.60	28.00	29.20	27.40	25.20	24.20	24.00	20.60^x	18.40	16.80^x	15.60^x	14.55^x
TOTAL EFFORT IN UNITS OF WEALTH $=(F_h/8)$ OR $(A/eK)^x$	MILLIONS WEALTH	F_w	.625	1.200	1.880	2.500	3.080	3.500	3.650	3.420	3.150	3.020	3.000	2.570^x	2.300	2.100	1.950	1.820^x
EFFICIENCY OF SOCIETY (ASSUMED)		e	.080	.230	.360	.470	.570	.650	.725	.780	.830	.870	.900	.920	.925	.930	.930	.930
TECHNOLOGICAL KNOWLEDGE (ASSUMED)		K	1.00	1.45	1.78	2.21	2.50	2.99	3.70	5.10	6.97	9.07	11.10	12.60	13.90	15.00	16.00	17.00
ADDITIVE WEALTH $=(F_w.e.K)$ OR $(1.572 U)^x$	MILLIONS WEALTH	A	.050	.400	1.200	2.600	4.400	6.800	9.800	13.60	18.20	23.80	30.00	29.80	29.50	29.25	28.95	28.76
UTILIZED WEALTH (ASSUMED)	MILLIONS WEALTH	U	.50	.80	1.50	2.55	4.15	6.15	8.45	11.05	13.75	16.60	19.15	18.99	18.82	18.66	18.48	18.30
INTRINSIC WEALTH	MILLIONS WEALTH	C	.55	1.20	2.70	5.16	8.55	12.95	18.25	24.65	31.95	40.40	48.15	48.79	48.32	47.91	47.43	47.06
WEALTH ENJOYED PER INDIVIDUAL $=C/N$	UNITS OF WEALTH	E	.55	1.00	1.93	3.22	4.75	6.47	8.29	10.27	12.29	14.42	16.54					
STANDARD OF LIVING E/H		SL	.110	.125	.180	.257	.348	.462	.623	.900	1.268	1.670	2.045					
FACTOR OF STANDARD OF LIVING $=SL/SLo$		S	1.00	1.135	1.635	2.34	3.16	4.20	5.66	8.18	11.52	15.20	18.60					
NUMBER EMPLOYED F_h/H	MILLIONS	N_e											3.00	2.57	2.30	2.10	1.95	1.82
NUMBER UNEMPLOYED $N-N_e$	MILLIONS	N_u											0	.63	1.10	1.50	1.85	2.18
PERCENTAGE OF UNEMPLOYMENT $=N_u/N$	%	U_h											0	19.6	32.4	41.6	48.6	54.5
WEALTH OF THE NATION $C+(w-U)$	MILLIONS WEALTH	W	20,050	20,392	21,158	22,514	24,248	26,570	29,470	33,158	37,632	43,092	49,150	48,790	48,320	47,910	47,430	47,060
PROSPECT OF THE NATION (BASIC) $=W/N$	UNITS OF WEALTH	PS	20.00	16.60	14.25	12.40	11.00	9.88	8.94	8.14	7.48	6.88	6.38	5.93	5.54	5.18	4.87	4.57
PROSPECT OF THE NATION (ACTUAL) $=(W-.5C)/N$	UNITS OF WEALTH	PS	20.27	17.15	15.20	14.06	13.40	13.12	13.08	13.28	13.60	14.10	14.60	13.55	12.62	11.82	11.10	10.43

INFLUENCE OF FINANCE IN RELATIONS AMONG NA-
TIONS: In our study of the relation between fundamental wealth of
the land and standard of living of the population we have failed to refer to money in circulation. The reason for our omission is that money
cannot be considered wealth when measuring the wealth of a nation.
The more the money in circulation the greater will be the amount of
commodities produced and services supplied, the more active will
be the exchange of goods, and in this respect money in circulation
is related to fundamental utilized wealth (U) and additive wealth
(A). Money, in other words, is a measure of that wealth, but in
itself has no value unless we take into account its physical aptitude
to become an article or useful commodity.

Money in the possession of a person is valuable to the extent
that people recognize it as representing wealth in his hand, and is
equivalent to a certificate given him by society. Gold, silver, copper,
nickel are the usual metals used for coinage. Their value, like that
of any other commodity, fluctuates according to the amount of
supply and demand. However, if society should cease to recognize
these commodities as money, their intrinsic wealth, while the same
as before, would cease to be sought unless for the purpose of producing some definite article or commodity. Money, in other words,
is useful to the average person because it is recognized as wealth
exchangeable for some other commodity of equal value. Using
money as a medium of exchange simplifies transactions. To own
any amount of money merely implies that someone has previously
sold, received, or earned a specific amount of wealth. Society gives
this person the privilege of exchanging with someone else that
wealth in part or in toto, now or in the future, for another kind
of the same value.

Due to this peculiar quality of money, if we visualize a case
where it passes into the ownership of one nation only, this country
will greatly impair its ability to trade with other nations because the
latter will lack the medium of exchange, as will be shown in detail
later on. The same reasoning applies to transactions between individuals, where one is very rich and the others very poor. In either

case the possession of this large amount becomes valueless, as it ceases to be a medium of exchange. Its usefulness, however, increases with a more even distribution among nations and individuals, because then it will support a greater range of exchange, which is a prerequisite for a higher standard of living.

Of course, money is not always needed in transactions. Whenever two parties have commodities they wish to exchange, and these happen to have the same value, it is evident that no cash needs to be paid or received, and that the exchange may be made without that medium. Money fulfills the usefulness only in those transactions where the commodities traded have varying values, and in such cases it covers the difference.

In the following pages we shall consider the important role played by cash or other forms of money in the smooth functioning of trade among nations. The same reasoning naturally applies to instances of deals between communities or individuals. Let Alpha and Beta be two nations. Their size, both in land and fundamental wealth, is immaterial to what we are now about to study, and, therefore, will not be considered. For simplicity we shall assume that only a few kinds of commodities are produced and required by their populations, which we shall refer to as (a), (b), and (c). The quantity of each kind will be given in terms of its corresponding value in units of money; a production of 160 (c) requiring for its purchase 160 units of money, and so on.

EXAMPLE NUMBER ONE: First assume that Alpha and Beta produce commodities (a) and (b), these being the only ones they need. Due to circumstances, varying from climatic conditions to difference in fundamental wealth of the land, the amount produced by each does not coincide with their requirement. Thus Alpha has more of commodity (a) than she can use, and less of commodity (b). The opposite occurs with Beta, and if no exchange were to take place, both countries would have a maladjusted economy and a relatively low standard of living. However, through this trade the surplus of one nation makes up the deficiency of the other, and both peoples gain in every respect.

These exchanges as a rule do not take place between the countries themselves, but between their citizens, and naturally money is used as a medium of exchange. For instance, many inhabitants of Alpha, when there is a scarcity of commodity (b), will seek to buy it from citizens of Beta, who have a surplus. The purchase by the Alphans calls for the payment of a specific sum of money, and as this shipment is resold to other Alphans it will be finally distributed among the inhabitants. Similarly the surplus in Alpha eventually will find its way into the hands of the Betans.

At this point we wish to clarify a few details, as they will aid in understanding various assumptions made in our study. We know that when scarcity of commodities occurs within any country, their' price tends to rise; and the opposite when overproduction exists. It is because of this difference in price that middlemen find it profitable to buy from a nation in which costs are low, to sell to another where prices are high. As commodities move from one nation to another, their price will tend to equalize in both countries. The reason for this change is that the transfer tends to cause scarcity in the nation that exports commodities, and abundance in the one that imports them. Since we are considering a continuous transfer extending over a long period of years, this flow from one nation to the other will stabilize at a certain level. A larger or lesser flow would reduce the profit of the middlemen. If larger, the price difference will be less; if smaller, the decreased business will more than counterbalance the increased profit per capita. The actual flow from one nation to another depends on the following factors: (1) difference in price reached by the commodity in the two nations, (2) size of the populations involved, (3) amount of supply and demand that develops in the two countries. As to the first factor, from what we have stated before, it is quite evident that the greater the difference the larger will be the flow. As to the size of population, if we assume that a given amount of commodities is being exported from a large to a small country, if this amount represents a sizeable percentage of the need of the small population, it is plain that prices in this country will drop very rapidly, tending to equalize those in the exporting country and considerably decrease the profit of the middlemen. If the same amount is being shipped to the large country, it can be easily seen that this will not greatly affect prices in that country as it represents a very small percentage of the total need of the population. Prices, however, will still be greatly affected in the small one and will rapidly climb because of the new shortage. In either direction the flow will reach a given level that will depend on the relative size of the small nation versus the large one. As to the effect brought by the amount of supply and demand, the intensity of each one developing in both nations will directly influence the prices and consequently the flow of commodities among them.

Another factor affecting the flow will be the money in circulation in the two countries, especially in the importer. It stands to reason that the smaller the amount of money in the nation, the less will be the flow of commodities, independently of scarcity. For the present, however, we shall assume that both have sufficient cash available to make the purchases required to satisfy both populations.

In our present analysis we need not consider the actual size of population in the various countries under study. We know that, due to lack of equilibrium of production between them, different price levels will be reached by the various commodities, and that the price in the selling nation is bound to be lower than that in the buying country. The final and actual price, as stated before, will depend on the relative size of the populations involved, and on the amount of supply and demand. Such phenomena, however, are considered in other parts of our study, and will not be treated at this time. For simplicity, therefore, we shall disregard the difference in price of the commodities exchanged between the various nations (which as we know is a prerequisite of such flow), and will assume that the price is the same in all of them, and that shipments move because of need rather than price. With this in mind we may resume our study.

As stated before, the exchanges between Alpha and Beta occur only among individuals, and, therefore, money should pass back and forth between the two countries as the successive operations take place. But as these transactions are made through official agencies, the respective governments will act as clearing houses, and despite the multitude of exchanges made, the amount of money that changes hands is only what is needed to balance their account. If the value of the sales to buyers in Beta happens to equal that of the products bought by natives of Alpha, no money need be transferred by either government at all.

As on previous occasions we have sought to corroborate our reasoning with examples which illustrate and emphasize our conclusions. Reverting, therefore, to example number one we shall assume that the normal commodity requirements of Alpha and Beta each are 100 units of (a) and 100 of (b). Likewise we shall assume that Alpha produces 150 units of (a), and 80 of (b), besides possessing 200 (S), where S is the unit of wealth or specie. As previously stated one unit of (a) or (b), or any other commodity we may consider, is assumed equivalent to one unit of specie. As such each unit of commodity must be thought of as made by sufficient articles of the same commodity so as to be equivalent to whatever unit of money we may choose in the study. This, of course, is a crude presentation as it neglects the effect of value and other economic phenomena that link the wealth represented by products to that represented by money and assumes a constant relationship among them, yet as these latter phenomena are not under study, for a clearer presentation of the one under consideration, we have decided to neglect their influence and effect. The unit of wealth (S) in turn may be expressed in lires, francs, dollars, or millions of dollars as the case may be. Assume also that Beta produces 50 (a) and 120 (b), and is in possession of 200 (S). Their initial position can be thus listed:

Apha: 150 a + 80 b + 200 S = 430 W
Beta: 50 a + 120 b + 200 S = 370 W

Here the amount produced and the money held appear at the left of the sign of equality, while the term at the right gives the total wealth of the country. This must not be confused with its total fundamental wealth as defined in the first part of this chapter. We are here dealing with the intrinsic wealth of commodities (C), (see page 144), and no fundamental wealth enters into the present analysis.

Comparison of production with actual needs of population swiftly shows that Alpha has an over supply of (a) and a scarcity of (b), and accordingly will seek to establish equilibrium by trading with Beta. The latter has also an unbalanced economy, and must depend on transactions with Alpha to stabilize its sufficiency. It is plain that these nations have a community of interests, and thus 50a will flow from Alpha to Beta, and 20b from Beta to Alpha, but amount in the form of money 30S will have to be sent from Beta to Alpha.

In our analysis the direction of the flow of commodities and cash to and from another country will be shown by negative (-) or positive (+) signs preceding the quantities transacted. These quantities will be written under the equation representing the position of the first country. We will express the original position before trading and then the one after the exchanges have been made. The position of Alpha is represented by the folloing expresison:

Alpha: 150a + 80b + 200S = 100a + 100b + 230S = 430W
       - 50a + 20b + 30S

From the expression above, which shall be indicated as the economic position of Alpha at the period in consideration, it can be easily surmised that Alpha being in possession of 150a sends 50 units abroad' in addition it imports 20b. Because of the difference in their size it also receives 30 units of money. At the right of the first (=) sign we find the condition of the country following the trade, with the last term giving the total wealth.

By comparing the final with the original position we can easily see that the various exchanges have not altered the total intrinsic wealth of the nation. This becomes evident when we consider that transactions mean trading of different kinds of wealth of the same value, so that what goes out of the country is replaced by an equal amount entering, although in different form, thus leaving the total unchanged.

We might think that as these commodities are being bought and utilized, a certain percentage will be irremediably lost, and, therefore, the equation is not absolutely correct; or that the wealth of the nation after the exchanges and utilization, especially when only one kind of commodity is involved, cannot be the same as before. If a person or a community as a group buys a specific amount of coal or oil, while it is true that the wealth of the individual or community is the same before and after the purchase is made, the same cannot be said after the coal or oil has been used, this so far as the consumer is concerned. As these commodities are irremediably lost, we could also say that this goes to decrease the availability of these products to others. Now the amount used by an individual, a community, or even a nation in a reasonable length of time, say one year, or even one hundred years is too insignificant to make any appreciable effect on the total amount available. For all practical purposes this availability may be considered constant meaning by this that if the individual or community or nation has the necessary wealth to be exchanged for oil or coal, the same amount can be secured time after time without impairing the available amount. Similar reasoning applies to the individual who buys apples. While it is true that his wealth is the same before and after the purchase has been made, that is not so after the apples have been consumed From the standpoint of availability in the world in geenral, we know that if all the apples have been used this year the same amount will be available in the next and the process will continue indefinitely so that, so far as availability, this also may be considered constant. From the standpoint of the consumer, the utilization of the wealth represented by the apples or by the coal goes to maintain his standard of living. The consumer when buying these commodities usually gives in return money he has received as wages or salary for effort exerted at some previous time. On this account the purchase of commodities on his part must not be considered as final, but as one in an endless succession of purchases made to maintain a given level of standard of living. As such after utilization the individual as well as the nation will again be in a position to buy the same amount of commodities if its purchasing power, result of other activities and independent of the previous utilization, is still the same.

Returning to our analysis of exchanges between two nations, the quantities shipped from one to another must not be thought of as exchanged at any specific time, but as traded in small portions over a reasonable period, such as a year. They constitute the total flow of commodities over that span of time, and go to maintain a given level of standard of living among the population. As they have been replaced by other commodities of equal value, it is evident that the total wealth of neither nation has suffered. The same holds when money must be sent from one nation to another to compensate for inequalities in exchanges, and here again it supports a specific standard of living, which after all is the primary reason for these transactions. Again we shall assume that the wealth of the nation remains unchanged after the trading. Complications will develop in time, but these will be discussed in later examples.

Using the same procedure adopted for Alpha, the transactions and positions before and after exchange can be expressed for Beta as follows:

Beta: $50a + 120b + 200S = 100a + 100b + 170S = 370W$
$50a - 20b - 30S$

Placing the expression in adjacent rows for comparison:

Alpha: $150a + 80b + 200S = 100a + 100b + 230S = 430W$
$- 50a + 20b + 30S$
Beta: $50a + 120b + 200S = 100a + 100b + 170S = 370W$

From this it appears that exports for the one are imports for the other. Disregarding for the present the fact that the amount of money in both nations has changed, they each have been able to utilize and enjoy 100 (a) and 100 (b) for their desired standard of living. We can appreciate, therefore, the influence of money in enabling such exchanges to be made for the benefit and advantage of the two peoples, as both countries enjoy better living conditions through the beneficial effects of the fusion of their economies.

EXAMPLE NUMBER TWO: As a variation upon the first example we now assume that the commodities needed by the population of

Alpha and Beta are of three kinds, designated as (a), (b), and (c). Prior to exchanges the position of both countries will be stated.

Alpha: $150a + 80b + 70c + 200S = 500W$

The only difference between this and the preceding example is that 70 c has been added. We still assume that the requirements of the two nations are represented by 100 units of each. Thus although having a surplus in (a) Alpha is deficient in (b) and (c), so if there was no other country with which to trade she would be limited to the standard of living her commodities allowed.

Beta: $80a + 100b + 100c + 200S = 480W$

At variance from the first example, Beta produces 80 instead of 50 (a), which means less need to import from Alpha. Beta also produces 100 instead of 120 (b), which in turn cuts her export, and in addition 100 (c) which satisfies her requirements. While self-sufficient in commodities (b) and (c), an isolated Beta would experience a shortage of (a), lowering her standard of living. Trade between Alpha and Beta allows successive transactions, represented by the expressions:

Alpha:

$$150a + 80b + 70c + 200S = 130a + 80b + 70c + 220S = 500W$$
$$- 20a \qquad\qquad + 20S$$

Beta:

$$80a + 100b + 100c + 200S = 100a + 100b + 100c + 180S = 480W$$

This shows that only 20 units of (a) can be exchanged, and as Beta has no surplus of any kind, money must be paid for this purchase. After the transaction Beta has acquired the needed commodity; and has less money, which, as appears from later examples, is an undesirable occurrence. Alpha still remains with a surplus of (a). This is bound to lower its price until all is absorbed by both populations, at a definite loss to the producers. On the other hand, commodities (b) and (c) will increase in price, causing much hardship for the poorer classes. As no further exchange can take place between Alpha and Beta, it is evident that another country must aid Alpha to obtain her requirements.

EXAMPLE NUMBER THREE: Three nations, Alpha, Beta, and Gamma engage in trade with each other. We could easily consider a larger number, but this would merely complicate our analysis, leaving unchanged the conclusions to be drawn from this study. As before the normal requirements of commodities for Alpha, Beta, and Gamma are each 100 units of (a), (b), and (c); their positions before trading being as follows:

Alpha: 200a + 100b +   0c + 150S = 450W
Beta: 0a + 200b + 100c + 50S = 350W
Gamma: 100a +   0b + 200c +   0S = 300W

Total: 300a + 300b + 300c + 200S =1100W

From this we can see that the economies of the three nations are complementary, since in each commodity the total production is sufficient for their combined need. The amount of gold or other money differs among them, but in this particular case is no deterrent to the exchange of commodities.

Taking into consideration any one nation, it appears that each of them, while completely lacking in one commodity, has surplus in another, and is self-sufficient in the third. If no exchange took place, all would have distorted economies. Incidentally, as all three kinds are vital, a deficiency of any one will be reflected in a low standard of living. To present a clearer exposition, we will divide the exchanges made among Alpha, Beta and Gamma into successive steps. This will let us focus our attention upon details we wish to examine, without other interferences that may take place within the same nation or elsewhere.

First Step: Beta in relation to Alpha and Gamma.
That between Beta and Alpha is:
Alpha:

200a+100b+   0c + 150S=150a+100b+   0c+200S=450W
— 50a   + 50S

Beta:

0a + 200b + 100c + 50S= 50a + 200b + 100c +   0S=350W

It is clear that Alpha can provide Beta with 100 units of (a), in which she is completely lacking, but the amount of money in her possession allows only 50 (a) to be bought, as that is all Beta can pay in exchange. Her surplus of (b) is one of which Alpha has no need, and while the latter would gladly take (c) in exchange, Beta cannot provide her with it as she has only as much as is needed by her own population.

Relation between Beta and Gamma after the above transactions:

Beta: 50a + 200b + 100c + 0S=350W
Gamma: 100a +   0b + 200c + 0S=300W

As both countries have no available money and no commodity to be bartered, it is plain that no exchange can take place between them even though Beta has 100 (b) to sell.

Second Step: Gamma in relation to Alpha and Beta at the end of the first step. Relation between Gamma and Alpha:
Alpha:

$$150a + 100b + \quad 0c + 200S = 150a + 100b + 100c + 100S = 450W$$
$$+ 100c — 100S$$

Gamma:

$$100a + \quad 0b + 200c + \quad 0S = 100a + \quad 0b + 100c + 100S = 300W$$

From an examination of the respective positions of Alpha and Gamma before any exchange we note that Alpha can and will buy 100 (c) from Gamma, and since no other commodity transactions can take place between them, Alpha must pay 100 (S) for that shipment.

Relation between Gamma and Beta after the previous exchanges:
Beta:

$$50a + 200b + 100c + \quad 0S = \quad 50a + 100b + 100c + 100S = 350W$$
$$—100b \qquad + 100S$$

Gamma:

$$100a + \quad 0b + 100c + 100S = 100a + 100b + 100c + \quad 0S = 300W$$

Gamma, with the money received from Alpha, is now in a position to acquire 100 (b) from Beta, this being the only transaction that can take place between them.

Third Step: Beta in relation to Alpha and Gamma after the second step.

Relation between Alpha and Beta:
Alpha:

$$150a + 100b + 100c + 100S = 100a + 100b + 100c + 150S = 450W$$
$$— \quad 50a \qquad + \quad 50S$$

Beta:

$$50a + 100b + 100c + 100S = 100a + 100b + 100c + \quad 50S = 350W$$

One can see that Beta is now able to buy 50 more units of (a) from Alpha by paying 50 of the 100 S she previously received from Gamma.

Relation between Beta and Gamma:

$$\text{Gamma: } 100a + 100b + 100c + \quad 0S = 300W$$
$$\text{Beta: } \quad 100a + 100b + 100c + 50S = 350W$$

The position of Beta and Gamma shows that both nations have the quota of commodities they require, and no exchange need occur between them. At the end of the third step all three nations have been able to secure what they needed through the medium of money. They also wind up with the same amount of cash as originally.

This, however, is a fortunate case in which the surplus of one nation happens to coincide with the deficiency of another, so that after the successive transactions no excess is left to reduce prices, cause losses for producers, or result in hardship among the poorer classes. The conclusion to which this example leads is that, within limits, lack of cash is no deterrent to free exchange if the nations involved are economically complementary to each other. This unfortunately is not often the case, as will now appear.

EXAMPLE FOUR: This situation, generally speaking, is identical with the preceding, having a single variation. Due to causes beyond control, commodity (a) in Alpha drops from 200 to 170 (a). Such a reduction may come about by climatic changes when (a) represents foodstuffs and similar products, or by the exhaustion of mines and of wells in the cases of coal, oil, and the like, which are also vital commodities. It will be shortly apparent the vast repercussions which this shortage will exert on the economies of the three nations under study.

It might seem that only Alpha should be affected by this shortage as after all that is where this phenomenon occurs. At any rate as this production is still far above the actual need of the population, it would seem that its effect should not be serious since it only reduces the amount exported. A closer analysis will reveal, however, that this is not the case, and that what affects one nation will in one way or another influence the others:

Let us first state the position of each country before any exchange is made:

$$\text{Alpha:} \quad 170a + 100b + \quad 0c + 150S = 420W$$
$$\text{Beta:} \quad \quad 0a + 200b + 100c + \ \ 50S = 350W$$
$$\text{Gamma:} \ 100a + \quad 0b + 200c + \quad 0S = 300W$$

$$\text{Total:} \quad 270a + 300b + 300c + 200S = 1070W$$

Here we can no longer say that the economies of the three nations are complementary to each other, for the total production of (a) is 270 instead of the requisite quota of 300 (a). We realize that a general increase in price of this commodity will result from this shortage, and this will affect all three nations, including Gamma, which produces the amount necessary for her own use. The poor classes of all three will feel the pinch of this shortage even though the effect will not be equal for all.

This can be demonstrated in detail. As explained earlier, only difference in price can promote the flow of commodities from one nation to another. The price of (a) in Beta will naturally rise to a much higher level than in either Alpha or Gamma, because of her original greater deficiency. As a result of this difference, there will be some imported from Gamma, but by far the largest proportion will come from Alpha, the chief producer. For all practical purposes we may neglect the flow from Gamma, so only Alpha and Beta need to be considered in this particular transaction. While the price of (a) among the Betans is a direct result of its original scarcity, the price which develops in Alpha will also be affected by the amount brought to market. As production drops from 200 to 170 (a) the price level in Alpha will rise, and hence many Alphans must reduce their purchases. But, since we are here ignoring the effect of price, we can still assume that the purchases made by the Alphans can be set at 100 (a). This, however, is not so for the Betans who now will be confronted by a price that is influenced, not only by the cost of transport and by the profit to middlemen, but by this new additional shortage, and thus, even neglecting the effect of possible tariffs or other barriers placed in the way of free and unhampered exchange among nations, the result will be that only a few people will be able to buy as much as before. The others will be definitely affected by the shortage.

In order to simplify our study we must make an assumption which, while it does not change the basic results derived from a more precise analysis, will help us to determine the trend of things in a more definite and understandable form. This assumption is that only the Betans will suffer from this shortage, which means that while Gamma will not export (a), Alpha will sell only up to 70 (a), her present surplus, and no more. Thereby the Alphans and Gammans will not feel the shortage, at least of (a), independently of any amount of money that may be entering or leaving as a result of this action. We wish also to stress that in this example, except for the reduced production of (a) in Alpha, everything else has remained the same as in the third example. As before we shall divide the exchanges among the nations into steps, in order better to analyze tendencies and consequences.

First step: Beta in relation to Alpha and Gamma.

Relation between Beta and Alpha:

Alpha:
$$170a + 100b + 0c + 150S = 120a + 100b + 0c + 200S = 420W$$
$$- 50a \qquad\qquad + 50S$$

Beta:
$$0a + 200b + 100c + 50S = 50a + 200b + 100c + 0S = 350W$$

From a study of these figures we can see that the only exchange possible is the sale of 50 (a) by Alpha to Beta. As this is similar to example 3, what was said then also applies here.

Relation between Beta and Gamma:

$$\text{Beta:} \quad 50a + 200b + 100c + 0S = 350W$$
$$\text{Gamma:} \quad 100a + 0b + 200c + 0S = 300W$$

As both countries have no available money and no commodity to be traded in barter fashion, it is plain that no exchange can take place between them.

Second step: Gamma in relation to Alpha and Beta at the end of the first period.

Relation between Gamma and Alpha:

Alpha:

$$120a + 100b + 0c + 200S = 120a + 100b + 100c + 100S = 420W$$
$$+ 100c - 100S$$

Beta:

$$100a + 0b + 200c + 0S = 100a + 0b + 100c + 100S = 300W$$

This exchange is similar to the one of the preceding example.

Relation between Gamma and Beta after the previous exchanges:

Beta:

$$50a + 200b + 100c + 0S = 50a + 100b + 100c + 100S = 350W$$
$$-100b + 100S$$

Gamma:

$$100a + 0b + 100c + 100S = 100a + 100b + 100c + 0S = 300W$$

These exchanges are also similar to those in the corresponding step of the previous example, and the remarks made them apply also here.

Third step: Beta in relation to Alpha and Gamma after the second step.

Relation between Alpha and Beta:

Alpha:

$$120a + 100b + 100c + 100S = 100a + 100b + 100c + 120S = 420W$$
$$- 20a + 20S$$

Beta:

$$50a + 100b + 100c + 100S = 70a + 100b + 100c + 80S = 350W$$

Relation between Beta and Gamma:

$$\text{Beta:} \quad 70a + 100b + 100c + 80S = 350W$$
$$\text{Gamma:} \quad 100a + 100b + 100c + 0S = 300W$$

At the end of this step no further exchanges are possible among the three nations during the interval of time under consideration.

The final position of the three nations is the following:

$$\text{Alpha:} \quad 100a + 100b + 100c + 120S = 420W$$

$$\text{Beta:} \quad 70a + 100b + 100c + \ 80S = 350W$$
$$\text{Gamma:} \ 100a + 100b + 100c + \ \ 0S = 300W$$

We can see that Alpha, as in the previous example, has secured the quota due her people, but has expended 30 units of cash, ending up with 120 instead of 150 (S). Beta will experience a shortage in (a), with consequent hardship among her poor, but emerges with more cash. This condition may, of course, prove to be only temporary, lacking lasting effects. In fact, the scarcity of 30 (a) in Alpha may be followed by a period of overabundance which might re-establish the previous equilibrium, or deficiency may develop in another kind of commodity elsewhere, thus tending to shift the flow of money to the opposite direction, so that for slight oscillations from normal production we may expect a corresponding financial swing from one nation to another, unattended by lasting consequences or hardships.

Gamma, on the basis of our arbitrary simplifying of trade, seems not to feel the effect of shortage in (a) and is able to secure the needed commodities even though lacking exportable specie. This proves that in this particular instance lack of cash was no deterrent to her balanced economy. Yet this, as we shall see, is merely a temporary fortunate coincidence, attributable to the fact that the Gammans secured their needs by the exchange of all their surplus. Although extremely simplified, the foregoing example illustrates the trend of things, and shows the undesirable situation which would result if the described conditions should be permitted to continue without applying the requisite remedies.

EXAMPLE NUMBER FIVE: In the foregoing example we analyzed the effects of shortage of (a) upon Alpha and Beta; and stated that if of temporary nature, no lasting damage would be incurred by the economic set-up of these nations. As an extreme case we shall assume it is permanent, and likewise that each nation instinctively will seek to acquire or retain the necessary amount of each commodity, irrespective of its financial resources or the needs of neighbors. In other words, it will buy the requisite quantity as long as its cash holds out. Alpha, which has not been able to expand her production of (a), nevertheless, continues acquiring (c) from Gamma, even though this means an irremediable loss of money. Should she persist in this policy, the time will come when her financial holdings are exhausted. Beta, on the other hand, keeps on enduring the lack of (a) at great damage to the well-being of her population, but builds up her holdings of money as a result, and eventually will

come in possession of the entire reserves of funds previously held by
Alpha. Gamma will seem unaffected by the shortage of (a) as long
as she is able to exchange her surplus in (c) to make up her original
lack of (b). We will finally see her involved in the economic unbalance that has overtaken her neighbors. Their position before any
exchanges are made is as follows:

$$\text{Alpha:} \quad 170a+100b+ \quad 0c+ \quad 0S= \quad 270W$$
$$\text{Beta:} \quad 0a+200b+100c+200S= \quad 500W$$
$$\text{Gamma:} \quad 100a+ \quad 0b+200c+ \quad 0S= \quad 300W$$

$$\text{Total:} \quad 270a+300b+300c+200S=1070W$$

Note the fact that Alpha, originally the wealthiest of the three countries, is now the poorest. This is because she has lost her entire amount
of cash, which has gone to Beta, who is now the richest of the three.

First step: Beta in relation to Alpha and Gamma:
Relation between Beta and Alpha:
Alpha:

$$170a+100b+ \quad 0c+ \quad 0S=100a+100b+ \quad 0c+ \quad 70S=270W$$
$$-\; 70a \qquad\qquad +\; 70S$$

Beta:

$$0a+200b+100c+200S= \quad 70a+200b+100c+130S=500W$$

At variance from the first example Beta is now in a position to buy
immediately the entire surplus of Alpha as she has sufficient funds
available.

Relation between Beta and Gamma:

$$\text{Beta:} \quad 70a+200b+100c+130S=500W$$
$$\text{Gamma:} \quad 100a+ \quad 0b+200c+ \quad 0S=300W$$

No exchange at present can take place between Beta and Gamma,
even though she could supply 100 (b) to Gamma, because of the
latter's lack of funds.

Second step: Gamma in relation to Beta and Alpha.
Relation between Gamma and Alpha:
Alpha:

$$100a+100b+ \quad 0c+ \quad 70S=100a+100b+ \quad 70c+ \quad 0S=270W$$
$$+\; 70c-\; 70S$$

Gamma:

$$100a+ \quad 0b+200c+ \quad 0S=100a+ \quad 0b+130c+ \quad 70S=300W$$

From the above it appears that Gamma can supply only 70 (c) to
Alpha, because 70 S is all the money she can receive from her.
This means an additional economic distortion for Alpha which,
being left without any available money to make any purchases

abroad, is now beginning to feel the scarcity in (c), enjoyed until now up to the desired 100 units.

Relation between Gamma and Beta:

Beta:

$$70a + 200b + 100c + 130S = 70a + 130b + 100c + 200S = 500W$$
$$- 70b \qquad + 70S$$

Gamma:

$$100a + 0b + 130c + 70S = 100a + 70b + 130c + 0S = 300W$$

We note that Gamma is now able to buy only 70 (b) from Beta instead of the usual 100, and this represents the first economic effect felt by this country as a result of the changed international situation. She will retain a surplus of (c), with consequent depression of prices and loss to the producers and will suffer a shortage of (b) with consequent hardship among her poor.

Beta's economy will also be disrupted, for she will likewise have a surplus in one sort and a shortage in another, with consequent disturbance in prices and lower standard of living. This condition as seen, is primarily originated from the fact that the supply of (a) has permanently decreased from the amount needed for a well-balanced economy among the three nations. However, the fact that gold or other forms of money are now concentrated in one country adds to this maladjustment. It is evident that if Alpha still possessed some money, Gamma would not be affected by that shortage, and would be able to dispose of her surplus. The final position of the three nations is the following:

Alpha: $100a + 100b + 70c + 0S = 270W$

Beta: $70a + 130b + 100c + 200S = 500W$

Gamma: $100a + 70b + 130c + 0S = 300W$

Since each nation, either through isolationism or through a government which is ruled by determined minorities, will try to do its outmost to reach self-sufficiency, we can forsee that Beta eventually will sponsor and encourage production of substitutes for commodity (a), in order to make her economy independent of others. We will assume that she succeeds in manufacturing such substitutes, which for simplicity we will include with the actual (a) produced by Alpha. The effect of this policy is discussed in the next example.

EXAMPLE NUMBER SIX: Beta, seeking to achieve economic independence, furnishes the necessary financial support to subsidize the production of 80 units of (a), that of other kinds of commodities remaining the same. Alpha and Gamma continue as before.

The new position of the three countries will be as follows:

Alpha: $170a + 100b + \quad 0c + \quad 0S = 270W$
Beta: $\quad 80a + 200b + 100c + 200S = 580W$
Gamma: $100a + \quad 0b + 200c + \quad 0S = 300W$

Total: $350a + 300b + 300c + 200S = 1150W$

We note from the above that the total production of (a) is now more than sufficient for the normal combined need of the nations under consideration. Through a superficial appraisal of the new situation prevailing, we might conclude that conditions are now improving, since the previous deficiency in (a) has been more than erased. This, however, is not the case, as presently will appear.

First step: Beta in relation to Alpha and Gamma.
Relation between Beta and Alpha:
Alpha:
$\quad 170a + 100b + \quad 0c + \quad 0S = 150a + 100b + \quad 0c + 20S = 270W$
$\quad - 20a \qquad\qquad\qquad + 20S$
Beta:
$\quad 80a + 200b + 100c + 200S = 100a + 200b + 100c + 180S = 580W$

The amount of commodities passing from Alpha to Beta is 20a instead of 70a, and as a first consequence, Alpha is stranded with a large surplus of (a), which will further aggravate her economic condition. The second result is that she will import only 20 units of cash through this exchange. As will be seen in the following step, this will represent a further disruption in her economy.

Relation between Beta and Gamma:

Beta: $100a + 200b + 100c + 180S = 580W$
Gamma: $100a + \quad 0b + 200c + \quad 0S = 300W$

From the above it becomes evident that the two nations are not in a position to trade because one of them (Gamma) lacks the necessary funds needed to buy the desired 100 units of (b) from the other.

Second Step: Gamma in relation to Alpha and Beta.
Relation between Gamma and Alpha:
Alpha:
$\quad 150a + 100b + \quad 0c + 20S = 150a + 100b + 20c + \quad 0S = 270W$
$\qquad\qquad\qquad + 20c - 20S$
Gamma:
$\quad 100a + \quad 0b + 200c + \quad 0S = 100a + \quad 0b + 180c + 20S = 300W$

The shipment made from Gamma to Alpha will now be 20c instead of 70c as in the previous example, because 20S is all the money Alpha can spend. This will leave Gamma with an additional surplus, which will further aggravate her position in reference to the fifth example.

Relation between Gamma and Beta:

Beta:

$$100a + 200b + 100c + 180S = 100a + 180b + 100c + 200S = 580W$$
$$\qquad\quad - \ 20b \qquad\qquad + \ 20S$$

Gamma:

$$100a + \ \ 0b + 180c + \ \ 20S = 100a + \ \ 20b + 180c + \ \ 0S = 300W$$

As a result of her previous transaction Gamma will be able to buy only 20b from Beta, and the effect of this additional shortage will be felt by her poorer classes. Beta will have reached self-sufficiency in commodities (a) and (c), but the great surplus in (b) will have unfavorable repercussions among her population. The final position of the three nations is the following:

$$\text{Alpha:} \quad 150a + 100b + \ \ 20c + \ \ 0S = 270W$$
$$\text{Beta:} \quad \ \ 100a + 180b + 100c + 200S = 580W$$
$$\text{Gamma:} \ 100a + \ \ 20b + 180c + \ \ 0S = 300W$$

This joint economic dislocation will naturally be blamed on Betan policies. Alpha and Gamma will rightly accuse Beta of strangling their economy and forcing them to a low standard of living, without the possibility of defending themselves or in any way improving their condition.

EXAMPLE NUMBER SEVEN: We now assume that Beta, realizing the harmfulness of her policy in competing with Alpha, a course which endangers a large proportion of her population as well, decides to curtail the manufacture of (a) from 80 to 30 units. With this new arrangement the position of the three countries before exchanges becomes as follows:

$$\text{Alpha:} \quad 170a + 100b + \ \ 0c + \ \ 0S = \ \ 270W$$
$$\text{Beta:} \qquad 30a + 200b + 100c + 200S = \ \ 530W$$
$$\text{Gamma:} \ 100a + \ \ 0b + 200c + \ \ 0S = \ \ 300W$$

$$\text{Total:} \quad 300a + 300b + 300c + 200S = 1100W$$

We can notice immediately that the total production of commodities is just sufficent for the needs of the three countries, and accordingly would expect that eventually an equal distribution should ensue, resulting thereby in a well-balanced economy. In the third example we had such a case and saw that lack of cash did not prevent Gamma from reaching the desired equilibrium. That example, however, represented one out of many possibilities and variations and only occasionally found in real life. As it is generally the case the economies of nations are not complementary and even though the total production of commodities happens to come up to the desired level, this is not sufficient guaranty that a harmonious distribution will result.

First Step: Beta in relation to Alpha and Gamma.

Relation between Beta and Alpha:

Alpha:
$$170a + 100b + 0c + 0S = 100a + 100b + 0c + 70S = 270W$$
$$- 70a \qquad\qquad + 70S$$

Beta:
$$30a + 200b + 100c + 200S = 100a + 200b + 100c + 130S = 530W$$

As before Beta will be able to buy the required (a) from Alpha for which she must pay the corresponding amount of cash. In accordance with the new policy Alpha will sell her own surplus of (a) and receive in return an equivalent sum of money, with which she can later purchase (c) from Gamma.

Relation between Beta and Gamma:

$$\text{Beta:} \qquad 100a + 200b + 100c + 130S = 530W$$
$$\text{Gamma:} \quad 100a + 0b + 200c + 0S = 300W$$

As in previous examples, no transaction will take place between Beta and Gamma because of the latter's lack of cash.

Second Step: Gamma in relation to Alpha and Beta.

Relation between Gamma and Alpha:

Alpha:
$$100a + 100b + 0c + 70S = 100a + 100b + 70c + 0S = 270W$$
$$+ 70c - 70S$$

Gamma:
$$100a + 0b + 200c + 0S = 100a + 0b + 130c + 70S = 300W$$

Here the exchange between Alpha and Gamma is greater than in the preceding example, 70 instead of 20a, because of the fact that Alpha has been able to secure more money in her deals with Beta.

Relation between Gamma and Beta:

Beta:
$$100a + 200b + 100c + 130S = 100a + 130b + 100c + 200S = 530W$$
$$- 70b \qquad\qquad + 70S$$

Gamma:
$$100a + 0b + 130c + 70S = 100a + 70b + 130c + 0S = 300W$$

The same can be said for the relation between Beta and Gamma where the exchange is now represented by 70 instead of 20b. However, this condition, while more favorable than before, is still far from being satisfactory, as each nation is left either with a shortage or surplus, or even both, although the total amount of commodities is sufficient to satisfy requirements in all three countries. This stems from the fact that the several commodities are not distributed according to need. Still it represents an improvement over the previous example since the situation cannot now be blamed upon the course taken by Beta. It is obvious that further steps are needed to promote a smoother interchange among the nations.

The final positions of the three nations are as follows:

$$\text{Alpha:} \quad 100a + 100b + 70c + 0S = 270W$$
$$\text{Beta:} \quad 100a + 130b + 100c + 200S = 530W$$
$$\text{Gamma:} \quad 100a + 70b + 130c + 0S = 300W$$

Before leaving this subject we must point out the similarity of the situation in the three nations to what is currently going on in the world at large. We must not forget that we are part of one world and one only, and if we adopt a policy to enhance our position without regard for others, its effects ultimately may affect us just as severely by leading to economic maladjustment and war. It is evident that for a better international relationship, cash no less than utilizable wealth should circulate among the nations more evenly than at present. Lack of money places a country more or less at the mercy of a richer neighbor. The tragedy of the situation lies in the fact that any nation in this condition is powerless to come to an understanding with other rich nations, especially if the latter refuse to make changes in their policies. Unless the poor country limits the use of vital commodities, so that some may be exported for needed money, there seems to be no alternative other than to clash with those who are so foolishly engaged in such strangling methods of exchange. Even so, the rich nation (in this case Beta) is justified in some respects in the policy taken, as after all she seeks to help the production of much needed commodities which she is unable to obtain abroad. Naturally it is difficult to set goals of production in a society where so much is left to private planning and initiative. The uncoordinated production of all nations may or may not be adequate to the economic condition of the world in general, and the consequences may be disastrous, as we have learned from recent history.

EXAMPLE NUMBER EIGHT: Recognizing the helplessness of a poor county (in this case Alpha) in coping with the injurious policies of a rich one (Beta) which strives to become self-sufficient in commodities the production of which comprises the very life of Alpha, ıt is possible that the latter, in the effort to equalize the shortage among her vital commodities, may decide to increase the shortage of one so as to decrease that of another. What will be the outcome of this policy? Let us see. Position before exchanges (assumed equal to example seven):

$$Alpha: \quad 170a + 100b + \quad 0c + \quad 0S = 270W$$
$$Beta: \quad 30a + 200b + 100c + 200S = 530W$$
$$Gamma: 100a + \quad 0b + 200c + \quad 0S = 300W$$

First Step: Alpha in relation to Beta and Gamma.

Relation between Alpha and Beta: From the point of view of Alpha, she is fairly sure that 70a, her surplus on that commodity, will be sold entirely to Beta. With the money derived from the exchange she will be in a position to acquire 70c from Gamma. 70c, however, is too small for her needs and in her effort to increase this quantity she may be willing to dispose of an additional amount of (a), promoting by this a scarcity in this field, in her effort to obtain additional cash with which to buy more units of (c). Beta, however, will not be interested in a larger purchase of (a) because after all 70a is what her population needs. Alpha may then decide to sell Beta some of her commodities (b), but this also will be refused because (b) represents the commodity of which Beta is essentially an exporter. Lacking the possibility of any other transaction, the position of the two countries will be represented by the following expressions:

Alpha:
$$170a + 100b + \quad 0c + \quad 0S = 100a + 180b + \quad 0c + \ 70S = 270W$$
$$- \ 70a \qquad\qquad\qquad\qquad + \ 70S$$

Beta:
$$30a + 200b + 100c + 200S = 100a + 200b + 100c + 130S = 530W$$

Relation between Alpha and Gamma: We know that, although both countries lack funds, some form of barter may take place between them. Originally their position allows no exchange to take place in commodities (b) and (c). Alpha realizes that eventually she will be able to buy 70c once her transaction with Beta is completed, but as this is far lower than the required amount, she may seek to trade some (b) for more (c). Assuming that Gamma is willing to go along with this project, their transaction will be expressed by the following relations:

Alpha:
$$100a + 100b + \quad 0c + \ 70S = 100a + \ 85b + \ 85c + \quad 0S = 270W$$
$$- \ 15b + \ 85c - \ 70S$$

Gamma:

$$100a + \quad 0b + 200c + \quad 0S = 100a + \quad 15b + 115c + \quad 70S = 300W$$

Second Step: Gamma in relation to Beta and Alpha.

Relation between Gamma and Beta:

Beta:

$$100a + 200b + 100c + 130S = 100a + 130b + 100c + 200S = 530W$$
$$- \quad 70b \qquad\qquad + \quad 70S$$

Gamma:

$$100a + \quad 15b + 115c + \quad 70S = 100a + \quad 85b + 115c + \quad 0S = 300W$$

No further exchange will take place between Alpha and Gamma beyond that shown in the first step and their final position will be the following:

$$\text{Alpha:} \quad 100a + \quad 85b + \quad 85c + \quad 0S = 270W$$
$$\text{Beta:} \quad 100a + 130b + 100c + 200S = 530W$$
$$\text{Gamma:} \quad 100a + \quad 85b + 115c + \quad 0S = 300W$$

This marks the end of transactions among the three nations, after Alpha has succeeded in more or less balancing her shortages fairly evenly, which depends on the willingness of Gamma to cooperate with her. Even admitting the attainment by Alpha and Gamma of rearranging their holdings, we must remember that Beta retains a surplus, which will mean keener competition and a general lowering of prices, with resultant loss to the producers and ultimate injury to the various populations, since the supply will gradually decrease. The sacrifice of (b) made by Alpha for the purpose of decreasing her deficiency of (c) is a poor substitute for ameliorating the condition of her people. Therefore, we can safely say that Alpha has not solved her economic problem by resorting to barter. Famine, unrest, uprising and even war will be the final outcome of such a continuous and hopeless decline, and while Alpha may be the first to suffer, the other nations will eventually follow in her wake, since the economy of each one is so closely linked to the well-being of the others.

Let us now draw some conclusions from the study of this chapter. We can state confidently that the policies adopted by our three hypothetical nations have their counterparts in real life. Indeed the various examples presented in this study could be easily used to describe the conditions found in nations of the world today. These conditions are the result of definite policies adopted by the various governments in their effort of improving the economic standing of their nation or in their effort of counteracting the unfavorable effects of policies adopted by others. The effort of Beta in acquiring self-sufficiency with utter disregard of the needs of other nations is a case in point.

At any rate these policies have had in the past, as well as at present, the definite purpose of achieving immediate results favorable to their people but have disregarded as a generality the effects on the complete family of nations. The adoption and the continuation of these policies have usually found many supporters who have gone to great lengths and used tortuous reasoning to prove their worth and desirability. To be sure, we have reduced the dealings among nations to the simplest and crudest forms and thereby we have created conditions which, while possibly exaggerated, nevertheless represent the final outcome of those policies. We admit also that during our analysis we have found it convenient to assume that nations have kept on maintaining these policies even when found beyond any doubt to be detrimental to the country itself. Such a situation appears in our assumption that Alpha continues buying vital commodities (c) from abroad even when confronted by a dangerous decline in her funds. We know that no nation in her senses would do this, but if there exists a tendency in this direction, the intensity of her economic distortion will only be in proportion to the amount she has traveled along the assumed path. If instead the nation resolves to hold onto its cash, then the shortage in commodities will lower the standard of living, and either way an economic unbalance will result. Moreover, whatever commodity is dispensed with will unfavorably affect the economic condition of others, and thereby harmonious relations among the various nations will be impaired. These policies are usually adopted and advocated as temporary solutions to problems of the day, but eventually extend indefinitely without consideration of other countries until the ultimate consequences are reached. Nevertheless, no matter how well disguised the economic panacea, definite causes are bound to promote definite effects.

We know that our country, the United States of America, holds by far the most money of any in the world, and from the example given in this chapter, we should expect an extremely unbalanced economy, with all the hardships linked to such a condition. Yet our nation is blessed by one of the highest standards of living ever enjoyed by man, evinced by the innumerable commodities available within our borders. This would seem to discredit our theory, and cause it to be disregarded as not consonant with actual facts. On the contrary we wish to point out that the immense fundamental wealth of this country, that is to say the resources and raw materials so abundant in the land, are great factors in counteracting the tendencies analyzed in this chapter. Indeed our people are blessed by a high degree of self-sufficiency, and fortunately need not depend on others for material on which their dynamic activity and industrial power is based. Add to this the fact that the extensive population, directly descended from enterprising immigrants who arrived from all over the world, and essentially of an unprejudiced nature, lends itself admirably to mass production and to exploring the unknown paths that lead to progress and advanced civilization. Yet we must recognize that in this land of plenty we have severe unemployment, nearly as bad as in other countries, and that this vast supply of commodities does not raise the standard of living of the millions who cannot find jobs and are forced to live on relief or through donations. This is a definite sign of economic unbalance. This would tend to place the United States at a point far lower than its maximum economic potentiality and, therefore, the unemployment problem and other economic dislocations could be ascribed to those temporary swings from the normal cycle of evolution described in the first part of this chapter. Yet we must realize that the zenith is being approached at a rapid rate and that the temporary maladjustments referred to above will eventually acquire far larger proportions than at present and may become the constant preoccupation of not distant future generations. Of course, our holding of so much gold in this country is not the only cause of this phenomenon, but it indicates that, even with all our resources, distribution is not properly made and that we can still improve our condition by promoting more trade with other countries, since more work will be required to furnish this greater amount of supply. Although it is true that our people enjoy, as an average, a high standard of living, this does not disprove our axiom that we could still advance to a better economic condition if a more enlightened attitude were adopted toward other nations. Add to this the fact that our future well-being must be placed on more solid foundations and in saying this we refer to all nations on earth. This requires, not only a new attitude and policy toward other nations, but also a new attitude and policy among the classes composing a nation. This will be the main topic of future analyses to be developed in the following chapters.

CHAPTER V

INHERITANCE

UPPER LIMIT OF ENJOYMENT OF WEALTH AND GENERALIZATION OF INHERITANCE

IN THE FIRST CHAPTER we gave our definition of wealth and subdivided it into unrestricted, personal, restricted, and economic wealth. We pointed out at the time that while all these are of great importance to mankind some have no economic value.

When anyone reaches the end of his life his personal wealth ceases with him and society is left that much poorer because of this loss. Despite the great progress attained in fighting disease and prolonging the usefulness of an individual, the fundamental law of nature eventually exerts its power over the will of men. While the personal wealth of the deceased is lost, his various possessions of restricted and economic wealth will remain.

UPPER LIMIT OF ENJOYMENT OF WEALTH

It is hard to define the upper limit of enjoyment of wealth. This may vary markedly for different people, and may change with age, surroundings and circumstances. A certain amount of money, more then sufficient for an individual living in a small town, may be entirely inadequate in a large city where life moves at a faster pace and opportunity for spending is so much greater. However, besides the enjoyment pure and proper that comes from comfort and luxury which only money can buy, additional wealth can only go to increase that feeling of security and in many cases adds to that feeling of power and superiority over others.

We can say that there are almost as many upper limits as there are men, the variation among them being a product of their nature, ambition, and surroundings. But there is always a period in the life of a person, who has been able to acquire great wealth, when an additional amount ceases to represent possibility of greater enjoyment. What he has is more than sufficient for his normal expenditures and further acquisition does not add to his welfare. We may conclude that this individual has reached the top limit of enjoyment in a physical sense. As a person grows older, he no longer has the same desires as when he was young. His needs are less, his pleasures are more limited, and the wealth necessary to give him what he needs is considerably smaller.

As far as society in general is concerned, we can state that if a large amount of land accumulated in the hands of one person is left unproductive, this will represent a real and tangible loss, because society at large would be deprived of its products, and the owner, while technically within his rights would fail in his duty toward society.

However, a person, instead of being the owner of a vast amount of land, may be the owner of great wealth in the form of money or capital. As is usually the case, this money is deposited in banks or converted into stocks and bonds since the hoarding of gold at the present time is quite uncommon if not altogether impossible. This capital, being invested, is performing its duty toward society in so far as it is utilized either in keeping industry going or in financing additional enterprises. Society, however, pays to the owner a large sum in the form of interest or rent which may be considered more than that person can possibly spend and enjoy. That difference goes to increase his capital without adding to his comfort and welfare, and, therefore, that wealth produces less enjoyment than it would if distributed among a larger number of people.

We do not advocate that wealth, amassed over a period of years by a person through his effort, ability, skill and good fortune should be taken away from him. Being recognized as its sole owner, he may spend it as he wishes and donate large sums to whomever he chooses. This has quite often been the case with the wealthy philanthropist who has lavished great sums to sponsor and advance worthy social enterprises. Moreover this person, while in the process of amassing that wealth, has furnished jobs, work, and livelihood for many who, without his genius and ability, would have never been able to acquire them.

The very life of society depends on possessing individuals of this kind, and, therefore, that wealth which is more or less an acknowledgment which society awards him for his leadership, rightfully belongs to him and as long as he lives he should be recognized, within proper restrictions, as the sole and only judge as to its spending even though at some stage of his life that accumulated wealth may represent a loss to society. That wealth after all exists because of his effort and ability and as such it is his in the most absolute way.

Let us consider that great genius, Henry Ford. From a modest beginning and because of his ability and wisdom, he was able to found and expand one of the great industries on earth. Thousands of people have been able to find work, livelihood, wealth and security for themselves and their families. It is true that Ford, while helping others, became one of the richest individuals on earth, so that not an entirely altruistic motive was the cause of his effort. However, we are quite sure that if his property had been taken away from him and distributed in shares of say $5,000 among as many people as possible, that wealth would not have produced as much as in the guiding hands of Henry Ford, and, therefore, would not have been as beneficial to society; and even if this was not the case, with what right could society take away from him what he acquired rightfully through his effort and his effort alone? Society has not and should not for its own sake have such a right. It is only in this way that progress can be attained.

This line of reasoning, however, does not apply to the individuals who receive inheritances. When an individual, who in his span of life has been able to amass great wealth, reaches the end of his days, his various possessions are usually distributed among his heirs who by this become extremely wealthy in their own right. We feel that such a possession, besides bringing to them a more or less exalted position among fellowmen, carries responsibilities toward society in general. As a rule these individuals have not contributed toward the earning of this wealth; it was just given to them. If they do not have the necessary ability and qualities to make it work for their own advantage as well as that of society, society stands to be greatly damaged in permitting them to retard and hamper the march of progress and universal well-being.

The acquisition of wealth, it seems to us, can be compared to the monopoly given to the inventors who receive from society the sole rights to sell and exploit new methods or inventions for a definite number of years, after which they become the property of society in general. Disregarding for the present the many phases of our problem, the wealth that comes to be owned by an individual is retained by him because of the tacit consent and willingness of society to let him enjoy and exploit the result of his labor and effort. However, we do not see why this permission at variance from that granted to the inventor, should extend beyond the life-span of the individual himself, and from a moral standpoint we must admit that at least part of that wealth should return to society.

If we assume that this line of reasoning is ethically right and just, and because of this are willing to institute laws to this effect, then the law must be equal for all, even though we know that some of the people who are deprived are also great leaders and competent individuals. Of course, we feel that the latter, because of those personal qualities inherited from their forefathers, will rapidly reach the position of leadership which is inherent to them and society will be happy to recognize that position. However, all those who do not have such ability should only be permitted to retain enough of their parents' wealth to live in comfort but no more, as society would be endangered if greater wealth was entrusted to them.

As shown in greater detail in succeeding chapters, we visualize a new society in which most of the appalling injustices that tend to retard progress are removed. In setting up the new order we have profited from the lessons taught us by the present society and, needless to say, we have retained all that is beneficial and good. In the fourth chapter we have dealt in detail with the damaging effects produced by money or wealth in general when it becomes monopolized by a few individuals or nations. It is natural on our part that we should advocate a decentralization of wealth as a prerequisite of a good society, since only by this means can the true purpose of money be fulfilled and trade encouraged among individuals and nations.

In the present discussion we shall not discriminate between wealth in general and money, which is a measure of wealth. When such discrimination was made, our object was that of measuring the actual wealth of a nation, as apt to become a tangible commodity that could be used and enjoyed independently of its distribution among the population. In the present discussion, however, we are concerned with the distribution of the products of wealth, and thus money assumes a rather different meaning. While it is true that cash is not wealth in the true sense of the word, yet it can buy wealth, and, therefore, its possession is equivalent to ownership of wealth. Those who have more money are able to acquire a greater amount of wealth, whether in a tangible form or in the shape of services. At any time wealth can be changed into money, and money into wealth, and because of this, money comes to be identified with wealth.

This being the case it becomes natural that in our study we should no longer discriminate between fundamental wealth, intrinsic wealth of commodities, and money and should consider all of them as different forms of wealth.

Returning to the original topic of decentralization of wealth, it would seem that this should start at the point when it is transferred from the original owner to others.

As later explained, we are not advocating that the wealth taken from an individual be distributed among a large number of people who have no connection with the original owner, as this would be unjust and probably very dangerous to society, but we do advocate that this wealth be made to produce the greatest beneficial effects to society in general, no matter who eventually will own this wealth. We realize that this may be obscure to our reader, but as our plan gradually unfolds and acquires a more definite shape, our statement will become clear and obvious.

One of the reasons for preventing large fortunes from accumulating in the hands of one family is that of decentralization. As later shown, the return of this wealth will raise the standard of living of the population in general, and aid in maintaining the government. This, however, is a topic to be developed in greater detail in later chapters, and will not be treated further at this time.

FUNDAMENTAL FACTS ABOUT INHERITANCE

It is traditional for a person to bequeath his fortune to his family. Among his ambitions and urges for accumulating great wealth is that of securing a comfortable livelihood for his children in future years, and this wish, since much gain has come to society because of his effort, should be respected to the point where no harm to society will result. Quite often the children of a wealthy individual have the ability and qualities of their father, and will administer his wealth just as efficiently as he himself did. Society in such a case loses very little because able hands still continue the task of providing comfort for a large number of people, but unfortunately this is not always the case. Frequently fortunes fall into the hands of persons who are neither leaders by nature nor capable of administering with skill and efficiency. Because of this society should be given the right to intervene and take from all, with the necessary restrictions, what is considered excess over that top limit previously mentioned.

In treating of the upper limit of enjoyment, it was concluded that such a limit is extremely elastic and may be affected by many factors. However, some sort of unit of measurement must be found, and it must be kept in mind that in establishing an upper limit, the heir must be able to have approximately the same comfort and welfare enjoyed while his father was alive. Again this limit must be such that if he so desires he should be able to live on the rent or interest of his wealth without the necessity of working. This point is stressed because often children of rich people, due to the easy life they have led, possess little or no ability to earn their living. Society should respect the wish of the father who has done much for humanity, and recognize that among his incentives was that of providing for his children so that they might not face at disadvantage the great uncertainty of life. This desire, we repeat, must be honored, and society must allow them to be well provided for up to but not beyond the top limit of enjoyment. Excess wealth in their hands as aforesaid, would not only injure the individual, but society itself. No claim is made here that our estimate of the top limit of enjoyment, with corresponding maximum inheritance, is correct and, therefore, be accepted as given. If the idea is approved and accepted, further study on the part of economists would be necessary to settle details.

The income that a person derives from his wealth can be usually divided into three parts. The first, and usually the smallest, is used for food and other commodities necessary to his physical well-being. The second is what he pays for enjoyment. The third portion is what is usually saved, that is, not utilized and thus adds to the wealth of the owner. In other words this unearned addition goes to increase the income of one who has reached the top limit of enjoyment of wealth.

In chapter 3 we introduced the concept of standard of living, this being a ratio of enjoyment received to effort exerted in the same unit of time. The enjoyment was represented by that which is derived from the utilization of the unit of vital commodities q, and by that which is derived from the utilization of services s.

In so far as vital commodities are a basic prerequisite of life we assumed that any one will strive first of all for its acquisition up to but not beyond the unit amount q which also represents the unit of enjoyment called e. The utilization of services only adds to that enjoyment, but, as it is not vital to the welfare of the individual, we assumed that its unit s is only equivalent to .5e so that the total enjoyment was given by the expression: $E = q + .5s$. Both q and s, as seen in chapter 3 can be given in terms of the minimum wage of the plain laborer, called a, which is also linked to a given amount of money.

In selecting the maximum inheritance we shall not try to compare standard of living between rich and poor because it is assumed that the heir or heirs are deriving enjoyment from inheritance without exertion of effort. Their standard of living in this case would become infinity, their effort for its acquisition being nihil. Instead we shall compare enjoyment and say that that of the heir should be represented by some given multiple of q to be decided by economists and by the people.

The total amount of money per year received by the average unskilled laborer, provided he works a total of 300 days at a rate of 8 hours per day, is given by: $a \times 8 \times 300 = 2400a$. Assume that a, in the locality in which the estimate is being made, is equivalent to 50 cents and also equivalent to $.55q$. $a/.55$ in terms of money is the price of the unit quantity q which in the third chapter was referred to as Pq. In this case $Pq = 91c$. The unit quantity of vital commodities per year and in terms of money will be given by: $Pq \times 2400 = \$2180$. This represents the average cost of vital commodities to a wealthy person residing in the locality and in a position to acquire the unit quantity q. Say also that the corresponding value of P'q calculated for the entire country comes to $2580. It is assumed in this study that four times this amount or $2580 \times 4 = \$10,320$ is what a well-to-do person who does not work for his living should spend for services. This will represent education for children, travel, hobbies, charities, saving for definite purposes, and all necessary expenditures in keeping with his social level. The total expenditure per year will be given by: $2180 + 10,320 = 12,500$. Any amount above this will probably be saved. Now it is true that for the extravagant spender this limit may seem small, but it is also true that for any such individual there is no limit to which he would agree and that he would spend money as fast as it comes in. These, however, are relatively few, are usually poor before their life span is over, and sink by their own squandering to the social level to which they really belong. Such money, while foolishly spent, eventually finds its way to society, so it could be said that extravagance should not cause much harm, but unfortunately much of this wealth enriches vice and corruption, and this endangers society. The proposed plan, although not wholly preventing the remains of large fortunes from being foolishly squandered, will prove a brake upon such expenditures. At any rate, despite these cases, we retain our contention that as a rule whenever anyone reaches a high standard of living, part of his income is converted into saving, and such additional income neither adds to his welfare, nor produces any real satisfaction to the owner, except that of becoming richer. This gain, however, should be reserved for those who work and achieve. Society should not set any limit to the amount such people are able to accumulate and enjoy. The limitation advocated above is for those who do not work, but live on income accumulated by others. To such people society should allow only sufficient wealth to attain the maximum standard of living, with the surplus reverting to society for use to better advantage.

At this point we state the basic principle governing our judgment in the appraisal of what is good or bad for society: *Regardless of the interest of any individual or group, whatever action on their part is good for society should be permitted and encouraged; whatever is detrimental should be prevented and condemned.*

MAXIMUM INHERITANCE

We shall now submit a plan for the determination of the maximum inheritance allowable in any community.

In the preceding study we have defined the allowable top limit of enjoyment given by the following expression:

Maximum enjoyment $= 2400.$ $(Pq + 4P'q)$ where Pq is the price of the unit vital commodity q in the locality where the appraisal is made and $P'q$ is the average price for the entire country. It will be noticed that the second expenditure $2400P'q$ has been made independent of location. Obviously for identical activities the corresponding expenditures may vary quite markedly according to location. If $2400P'q$ is sufficient for a family in a large city, it should be more than adequate for one living in the country or in a small town. To justify our assigning the same amount to people living in different surroundings, we must point out that while a person in the country might not spend that much where he lives, he must retain the privilege of moving to the city. If he desires to live more simply, his unspent revenue should be regarded as a rightful saving. While he has greater opportunity for thrift than the townsman, he may also claim that his life is more restricted, at least in pleasure and enjoyment. Assuming now that wealth produces for the owner an income of 5 per cent of its value, the amount of inheritance will be given by: $2400 (Pq + 4P'q)/.05$ or $48,000 (Pq + 4P'q)$.

If a is 50 c, Pq=91c, and P'q=1,075 the inheritance becomes:
$$48,000 \ (.91+4.30)=\$250,000$$
Each heir may inherit this amount if available. Should the total for division be less, it will be wholly left to the heirs and society will have no claim, provided that no individual inherits more than the allowable maximum. Should any surplus remain, the excess must revert to society.

This assumes that the wealth left by the deceased is concentrated only in one place. This, however, is not always the case and we may be confronted by many instances in which property and money are scattered in many locations within and outside the nation. Again, we can easily see where some of this wealth may produce for the owner entirely different percentages from the 5 per cent assumed in this study. As such the calculation of inheritance may seem more complicated than thought at first. However, this is not so. Let us bear in mind that what counts is the revenue of wealth no matter where the latter is located and that, irrespective of its actual market value, wealth can always be thought of as possessing a certain ability of producing revenue or enjoyment and from this the adjusted value, based on the standard rate of earnings, can be found.

First of all the official residence of the original owner (the individual whose property is being divided and apportioned) must be decided upon and the average index a of the community or the zone to which the community belongs will be chosen for the calculation of maximum enjoyment. The heirs may live in that community or be scattered in many other places but no matter their location no one should claim a larger amount. Again if wealth is located, let us say in an entirely different nation, nevertheless this wealth provides for the owner a given revenue and from this return the property can be evaluated, using the standard rate, and in this new form included with the total amount.

HOW THE INHERITANCE SHOULD BE DISTRIBUTED

The maximum allowable amount is what each heir may receive either by bequest or by law if no will was made. This implies that the inheritance is large enough to allow that maximum. The return of the surplus to society and the way this can be accomplished will be treated later in this chapter. The lawful heirs are defined the inmediate relatives. Each person thus may endow as many full inheritances as there are immediate relatives in his family, plus another inheritance distributable among more distant kin and friends. Naturally if no will has been made this extra inheritance will lapse. By inmediate relatives we mean father, mother, wife or husband, and all issue by the testator's lawful marriage. To brothers and sisters one-half such inheritance can be allowed. Other kin, such as uncles, aunts, in-laws, and the like have no claim on the estate of the deceased unless specifically named in a will, their share being taken from the aforementioned extra inheritance. Any one has the right to bequeath to his heirs as he wishes. He may disinherit any or all of them, but cannot leave more than the maximum amount to any one.

Cases arise in which a father is in partnership of at least five years standing with some of his direct relatives in some specific enterprise. Being a partnership it is natural to assume that its wealth, unless otherwise stated, is equally divided among the partners; therefore, at his death his share in the enterprise need be considered.

The deceased may be divorced. A divorced wife or husband is not reckoned among the inmediate family. The law may provide that a certain amount be left to them and to the children of their former union, which must be taken care of first. As this amount may be a given percentage of the total wealth, the maximum allowable inheritance will be decreased by this ratio.

EVALUATION OF RESTRICTED AND ECONOMIC WEALTH

Earlier in this chapter we defined maximum inheritance. It must be borne in mind, allowing for exceptions, that the return that wealth yields the owner is what counts most. This may be in the form of cash, ease and enjoyment, it may be tangible or merely potential, but in any case it must be translated into monetary value to estimate and determine its magnitude. As a general rule, assuming that wealth produces a return of 5 percent, its value automatically may be calculated by multiplying the yield by 20.

This will apply for the home of the owner, buildings for rent, cultivated and uncultivated land, forests, woodland and so forth. If revenue is actually derived from this property, (average over a span of five years) this should be taken as a base for calculating its worth to that family, provided it is in line with similar property in the community; if not, a market price will be chosen by responsible and competent officials.

Industries, however, require a different appraisal of worth from that hitherto used. In general, they yield varying returns at different times. As before, an average net profit may be determined over a number of years, and by multiplying this value by 20 the wealth of the industry, as far as the owner is concerned, which we shall indicate by F, can be computed. This value, however, may be quite different from what it could yield on the market, which will be based upon demand and general standing of the industry. This latter value in money will be called M. The estimation of the worth of wealth is not made with the purpose of selling out to a third party, even if this might prove the best solution for everyone concerned. If that industry is well managed, its actual worth to the family may be much more than its market price. Thus if we use M, smaller than F, for the calculation of the inheritance, society stands to lose, for the total fortune of the deceased will seem smaller than its real worth. If we use F the heirs may or may not have to pay anything to society, depending on the maximum inheritance allowable in the community, the number of heirs and the size of the estate. At any rate, if wealth has to be relinquished to society, this would be fair to the heirs as well as to society, so evaluation of actual worth F should be chosen in this particular case.

If an industry is not well managed, actual worth F may be considerably less than potential market price M. Now, if we use F for the calculation of inheritance, society stands to lose because its share would be much smaller than under more efficient management. Using the market price M, the heirs stand to lose as they would pay society far more than they derive from that wealth, so their share would be less than it may appear on paper. In this case we shall assume F, or the actual worth of the industry to the owner, as the basis for calculation of inheritance, definitely realizing that society thereby sustains a loss. We must bear in mind that society has no right to deprive the family of ownership of an industry merely because its management and policies for carrying on business are ill-chosen and out of date. Property rights have been secured by mankind after bitter and painful striving over long periods of time and should be retained within reason. This industry belongs to that family, and its owner has the sole right to decide how it should be managed. This is in accordance with principles of free enterprise and freedom of choice. Society should have only the right to claim excess wealth, over and above the maximum inheritance allowable by law, after the industry has been appraised as source of income for that family alone. Of course, in such a case, society will seek to buy that industry at market price M, which, as shown, exceeds its value to the family, and in many cases this may be preferred if beneficial to the heirs. Indeed, where there is poor management and such a state of affairs is apt to continue, the larger price paid for such industry by society will naturally increase the total inheritance, even though some may have to be relinquished.

Stocks, bonds, and investments in general have a more rapid fluctuation in price than other kinds of wealth so far considered. Generally speaking, the owner has not the power to change prices one way or another. In this field the law of supply and demand operates more effectively, and on this account the closing price on the market on the day the death of the owner occurs seems the reasonable one to be taken for the evaluation of the worth of this wealth. In passing, we can say that, at variance from previous cases, we cannot establish the worth of stocks and bonds from the amount of return it brings the owner. The reason for this is that usually stocks and bonds are bought not only with the purpose of securing a specific amount of dividends or income, but also for speculation, where price changes rather than dividends are the chief incentive for the purchase.

Money, the basic yardstick by which all other kinds of wealth are measured, needs no evaluation and its current worth should be added to that of the estate.

Another kind of wealth which may be divided among the heirs is represented by works of art, as valuable paintings, rare books, sculpture, jewelry, and so forth. Such wealth generally earns no money for its owner, unless rented to museums for revenue and as such has no real economic value in the sense of securing income. The real worth of these articles must be ascertained by impartial and specialized groups, its value in money determined, and added to the rest.

Articles of a personal nature like furniture, jewelry, books, heirlooms, and so forth, that have been in the family for a long period of time should be omitted from the total estimation of wealth, provided that their combined worth is not above a given percentage of the whole, for instance one per cent. These mementos are probably precious to those who inherit them as they may have been in the family for generations, and while society does not lose much by this relinquishment, it may mean much to the family who otherwise may have to choose the alternative of retaining wealth of a more remunerative nature.

A grand total of all these various values can then be computed. The difference between the total wealth and the amount allowed the members of the family will be the excess that must be returned to society.

TRANSFER OF WEALTH TO SOCIETY

Society, or indeed any individual, is not so much interested in wealth as in securing a return which can be more readily used. At times it may be unwise, if not outright dangerous, to divide or break up properties. It is an established fact that as a rule property is utilized more efficiently in the care of an owner who strives for the maximum income, than when held by an organization composed of a group with fixed salaries, having no vital personal interest. Whenever possible such a transfer should be avoided. Naturally each case must be considered on its own merits, and what may seem proper in one instance must be avoided in another. The fundamental guiding principle is to choose the procedure that produces the most good for society without infringing upon the rights of the individual. An example will clarify this statement.

Assume that we have to deal with the settlement of a property where a single heir is involved. A certain portion may go to him, and another, as appears from the discussion on page 201, may be distributed among friends and distant relatives of the deceased if definitely authorized in his will. The basic inheritance, as previously explained, is related to the index a of the community or zone where the original owner used to reside. This inheritance may consist in diverse proportions of all the different kinds of wealth previously enumerated. The first step taken is that of evaluating these various forms. If a will exists, the wishes of the deceased must be carried out, provided that the total assigned to anyone does not exceed the value of the maximum inheritance. Lacking any will, the heir may claim, up to the limit, any desired portion of the wealth; however, once that choice has been made and the property accordingly divided and assigned, that part which he has relinquished will immediately revert to society, and the heir ceases to have any right whatsoever therein. There may be cases where the heir wishes to utilize some portion of the wealth scheduled to go to society. In this he may and probably will be given preference over any other claimant. In turn he must pay society a rent such as 5 percent of the actual worth of the property, where by actual worth is meant what it commands on the market. Failure to pay this rent will free society from any moral obligation toward him, and rental or sale may then be made to any other claimant. In accordance with the law of supply and demand, the rent must follow the general trend of prices for similar commodities, and, therefore, must be based on the current market price.

The heir may also be given the option to buy any part of the estate at its actual worth. Payment may be made in installments, together with interest as upon a bank loan (in this case equal to rent), for any portion of the property as may still be outstanding. In noting this preference over others in renting or buying part of the deceased's property it may be made clear that such procedure is not a right on his part. Indeed, society on receiving this property becomes its lawful owner, and as such it is just that it should have the right to dispose of it to its best advantage. Of course, this prerogative of society should only be applied in cases where it is evident that the heir cannot administer that property to the best advantage to himself and society.

Assume that the total property consists of 100 acres of land, and that 30 acres represent the excess due to revert to society. This excess has a given value, and the expected return will be 5 per cent of that value. Now the heir has open the following alternatives:

(a) Give up altogether the ownership of the 30 acres; in which case society will become sole owner, with full rights to dispose of that property to its best advantage.

(b) Draw up a contract with society and rent the land in order to retain its use. He must then pay 5 per cent per annum of its value. Society retains the right to cancel the contract whenever the heir fails to abide by it.

(c) Purchase the 30 acres, and if the required sum is not given immediately, interest must be paid on that part which is still outstanding. To qualify for this precedence over any other bidder he must prove, however, that he has sufficient ability to make the wealth profitable to himself and society as well. We could conceive the case when someone, particularly interested in these 30 acres of land may be willing and anxious to pay society more than the market price. This, however, should not affect the policy of society of giving to the heir the undisputed preference referred above, because after all society, beyond the duty of safeguarding its rights and just interests, should not enter in any speculative enterprise that could tend to damage the heir.

(d) In some special cases, upon the heir's request, it should be possible for him to retain less than the maximum allowable by his inheritance, with the understanding that society in turn will pay him rent on that part of the property which he thus relinquishes. Society, in other words, will administer that property and will return to the owner all the derived revenue after the necessary expenditurs of administration have been deducted. Society, at any rate, should not assume the obligation to pay any fixed amount of rent for that wealth and while in many cases that revenue will probably be greater than the basic 5%, in others may be less and will depend on the business conditions prevailing in the community at that particular time. In those cases where those inheriting are infirm or relatively aged, this may represent the safest investment of all because they assure themselves of a good income and are relieved from the responsibility and anxiety attending administration.

What holds for cultivated land naturally applies for other kinds of wealth easily apportioned; uncultivated lands, forests, houses, and the like. As for jewels, works of art, and such things which cannot be thus divided, either the heir or society must immediately acquire the whole possession. Their value must be known so that the amount of money, to be awarded to whomever relinquishes ownership, can be determined. The reason for this rapid and complete establishment of ownership is that, due to the nature of this wealth, its value is based on the price that it commands at the market when the evaluation is made. This price may change considerably in a relatively short time and each party should be left free to dispose of that wealth as conditions may warrant. The same principle will apply for the disposal of stocks and bonds.

There are other cases again where a clear-cut division of property cannot be made. Houses for rent, theaters, restaurants, motion-picture houses, hotels, resorts, factories, are some examples of wealth that cannot be divided and final ownership established. In such cases some kind of co-partnership between society and those who receive the inheritance must be devised. After the evaluation has been made and the proportion that must go to society established, the heir or heirs may continue the utilization of that particular wealth but must pay to society a rent proportional to the outstanding part of the property. The rent may vary from a small percentage up to 5 per cent of the actual worth of the property at the time the evaluation was made. The percentage of rent may be based on the number of individuals given employment by the enterprises. For large industries that employ thousands of people, when the heirs are anxious to buy the property back from society, this rent may be reduced to as low as one half of one per cent. The rent will be raised to 5 per cent when no attempt to buy the property is contemplated and no livelihood is vitally dependent on that enterprise.

Whenever the contract is not being fulfilled, society retains the right to force the sale of the complete property and after having given the heirs their share, it may dispose of the rest as it sees fit.

In those cases where the heir does not want to retain the control of the complete property, society may buy his share and then sell or rent the whole to whoever is willing to pay the market price.

While on the subject we wish to consider those cases where extremely large fortunes are to be divided. These fortunes, quite often, are represented by large industries which somehow, while privately owned, are actually administered by many individuals in various capacities and provide livelihood for thousands of employees. Usually the owner takes for himself only a small fraction of the profit made by the industry, a fraction which, true enough, may amount to millions of dollars. Of course, the rest of the profit goes to expand the industry still further, thereby providing additional employment. We can safely say that this part of the profit is returned to society. The owner retains the control or ownership of this additional wealth, and even though he himself does not derive additional enjoyment in the sense explained early in this chapter, upon him rests the final decision and responsibility of the disposal of the entire wealth under his control, and his policies may have a far-reaching influence over millions who in one way or another are linked to his industry.

At his death his entire property will have to be transferred to others, and the new leadership may or may not be better than his own. At this stage society becomes vitally concerned with the well-being of the industry, and cannot afford to see this wealth pass to incompetent hands bringing disaster to thousands of families.

As we apply the formula of inheritance, society will become the largest beneficiary, and in so far as it will not retain but transfer this ownership to private individuals, we must conclude that the industry will pass from the hands of one person to those of many. Of course, we have many examples of large and efficient corporations owned by many individuals. Society would not be endangered by a process of this type, yet we do not think it ethically right to dispossess any family of ownership and potential leadership without giving it the chance of showing its worth. There are many instances where the sons have been able to expand and improve the work initiated by their father, and accordingly a chance must be given to them to prove to society their talent and abilities, and retain that control which was so beneficial under the guidance of their father. After all, as previously mentioned, society is only interested in the revenue of the wealth it happens to come in possession of as it will not enter into competition with private initiative so that, if the family can manage the industry efficiently and profitably, society, at least up to a given limit to which we shall refer shortly, will not be unduly concerned as to who actually manages that property. If the new management should prove inefficient and harmful it must be taken for granted that society should have the right to terminate that leadership by selling its share to others who automatically would acquire a larger voice in the affairs of the industry.

When no apportioning has been done during the owner's life time, the law of inheritance will apply in full and society will become the owner of most of that property. Yet, it will leave the heirs in complete control and, depending on the number employed by the industry, it may reduce the rent down to a fraction of the nominal amount. Society, however, will not retain that property indefinitely, even though quite often profitably, but each year will seek its sale to individuals or groups up to a given fraction of its original holding so as to be completely free after some determinate number of years. To the heirs will be given the option of buying back society's share in an unlimited amount.

As soon as the actual worth of the industry is established, bonds will be issued and society will retain its allotted number. After this division is made and irrespective of further progress made by the industry these bonds should pay society only the contracted amount. This because society had no hand in that progress. A sale to a third party, however, should be made only on the basis of their actual worth. By this method we can see that the family of the original owner, who gains a great deal by any profit made by the industry, as greatly facilitated in the repurchase of the property over and above any would be contender. Yet some and probably a great deal will be sold to outsiders, this depending on the speed with which the family buys back that property. As seen, in those cases where the family management is poor, society may speed up the sale of its bonds to outsiders and as these gain a controlling interest in the industry, they acquire also the right to ask and obtain a better and more efficient management than that of the family.

In many cases the original owner may decide to take others in partnership with him, let these persons be in the family or not. If the new partner adds the same amount of wealth to the now larger concern, at the death of any of the two partners only one half of the total worth of the industry will come under the inheritance law. There will be other cases, however, when the contribution of the new partner is much smaller than the first and it could even be in the form of skill, leadership, or plain family connection. Unless the contract that settles that partnership definitely states that it will not involve transfer of wealth from the first to the second individual, the law will request that an equal amount be assigned to society, this to be treated as in the case where no apportioning is made. In both cases society will become an interested even though inactive co-owner.

The owner at any time will be free to sell all or part of his property to a third party. In doing so, however, he must receive proper compensation for that sale or society would stand to lose when his property comes to be apportioned at his death. This is to say that no sale should be made without the permission of the proper authority. While this may seem an infringement on individual's right, it is not so if we accept the concept that wealth is only kept in trust by the owner. All this, of course, applies only where large fortunes are involved. In the vast majority of cases, where the total wealth divided among the heirs is equal or below the maximum inheritance, society has no claim whatsoever on that property and the owner is left completely free from the inheritance law if within the already established rules. This operation will only be affected by the taxation laws similar to those in force in the present society.

From this it can be seen that, while adequate protection is given to the beneficiaries of those leaders who have contributed so much to the establishment and the progress of the industry, the well-being of society is no longer endangered and a brake is placed on the growth and expansion of that parasitic part of society which, without any particular contribution on its part, not only derives dividends way above its actual need but oftentimes blocks and endangers the progress of society.

Returning to the subject of inheritance in general, society should never attempt to enter into competition with private business. The administration of wealth should be reduced to a minimum, and only where private interest cannot be found. In those cases where there is more than one heir, each may receive a specific amount in accordance with the will of the deceased, and as long as this amount is no larger than the absolute maximum prescribed by law, his ownership over his assigned property must be absolute. But whoever receives more than the maximum allowable must relinquish to society that excess and the same process previously described will apply. If there is no will, all heirs receive the same amount up to the limit of inheritance, and it is inmaterial to society how the estate is apportioned among them. But for that kind of wealth that cannot be divided, of which society happens to become a co-owner, the same reasoning earlier cited will apply, with the difference that here not one heir but several (depending upon the division of the estate) may be required to pay rent to society.

In considering the various cases of division of properties, it is plain that occasionally they can be easily divided, and both society and beneficiaries may dispose of their share as they see fit. In other cases the wealth, because of its nature, must be definitely assigned either to society or to one person only, this requiring compensation in money when the wealth is greater than the maximum inheritance. In still others, society may enter into partial ownership with the heirs, and receive from them a given return. Now obviously those beneficiaries who wish to obtain complete control may borrow from a bank to buy up society's holdings, and thereby become the sole legal owners of that property with no further obligation to society. We, however, do not consider this to be in the best interests of these beneficiaries, for reasons which we shall show in the following discussion. Our basic principle is that of producing the most good for the most people. In succeeding chapters we will analyze the various steps to be taken to help the poorer element in the population, but there are times when the rich also need aid. Conditions such as national disaster and depression may mean that wealth does not produce for its owner the income normally received. Banks, loan associations, and similar institutions are organizations which, in lending money, require collateral equal to or exceeding the value of the loan. This is done to safeguard the bank and the interest of the investors lest the borrower becomes insolvent. In such a case the bank can sell the collateral and regain the amount lent. Without analyzing the various functions of a bank, we merely note that when critical times come, loans are often refused even upon large collateral. The latter, when accepted, may even require increasing if the bank feels this justified to safeguard its investment. A bank in order to save its position, cannot hesitate to take those steps which it feels necessary to save the holdings of millions of people. If a bank is forced to sell the collateral in a reduced market, great fortunes could be destroyed. While these operations may save the bank and the investors from immediate danger, great harm is done to all those who are personally affected and indirectly harm is also done to society because the consequence of such sales on a large scale will demoralize and undermine the business world, and will increase uncertainty and confusion in the nation at large. This is the reason why loans from a bank to pay society for wealth rented or bought would be unbusiness-like, and should be avoided in the interest of the borrower, even though permitted.

The organization representing society, however, is not in the same position as a bank. Its ultimate scope is to benefit society whenever and wherever needed. If, for instance, a large number of persons cannot pay that minimum 5 per cent assumed as the rent of the wealth, the organization may reduce that rate or stop payment altogether for an indefinite period of time. In so doing, while the heir or the borrower may be the first to be benefited, ultimately all of society will feel the beneficial effect, especially if a crisis should thereby be averted. However, while this reduction of rent may be applied on a large scale, when conditions in the nation make such a course desirable and imperative, nevertheless, especially where incapacity and negligence cause failure, society must retain the right to sell the property and terminate the co-partnership.

Concluding this discussion of inheritance, it may be stated that moderate fortunes will be untouched by these laws, which will exempt the vast majority of the well-to-do in the nation. For fortunes less than a million dollars the natural division would normally reduce inheritance to an amount smaller than the maximum defined and society will have no claim upon them. Of those over a million, part will be sought. But the option of distribution among the members of the family during the life of the owner, although heavily taxed, allows the beneficiaries to receive considerably more than the maximum. Clearly they are well protected in regard to their standard of living. For those with initiative and business talent, this loss will be no unsurmountable obstacle, for others it will leave enough to live comfortably, certainly better than the vast majority of the nation.

Let us refer to a case where large fortunes are not distributed to the heirs while the original owner is alive. Some doubt may linger as to the wisdom of giving such a great proportion of wealth to society at the death of the owner. One might think that the industry will be severely taxed, while the beneficiaries use all efforts to regain its absolute possession, as much money will be spent to this end instead of being used in expanding the industry and its employment list. This might also be interpreted as unethical and dangerous, but can be shown not to be so. First of all it must be noted that individually owned industries are usually of a short duration. As the industrialist dies, leaving his property to his children, it will be divided in as many parts as there are heirs, unless only one should be chosen. Assuming equal division the heirs in time will leave their shares to their relatives, again increasing the number of owners. Considering also that many others may enter the family by marriage, it can be seen that any fortune originating through the effort of one man, within two or three generations, will ultimately be owned by many not necessarily in direct line from him. As the owners increase, their average holdings will shrink. Hence the keeping of an industry within one family, while desirable, is not altogether a necessity for survival and this phenomenon will occur as a natural process and will not endanger the well-being of the industry. We admit that the largest part will be nominally owned by society and because of that it will expect a rent that, even though as small as one-half of one per cent, may reach a yearly amount of several millions of dollars. Moreover, the beneficiaries, being anxious to acquire absolute ownership, may pay with money that normally would go to expand the industry. All this is true and, as we shall explain, it is one of our main objectives in advocating this law. As wealth is accumulated through trade and production, it remains to be seen if it will be more beneficial to society in general if plowed back into the industry or if used to sponsor new industries as would be the case if given to society. Within obvious limits, the larger an industry the more cumbersome and inefficient it becomes. The larger it is the greater will be the danger of monopoly, and the less the opportunity of others to start new enterprises which, by fair competition, lower prices and benefit humanity in general. It is clear then that keeping the size of an industry within reasonable bounds is beneficial to society. It is obvious that if money is utilized to launch other concerns and to aid those in difficulties, the benefit will be all the greater. This topic, however, is treated in greater detail in later chapters and will not be further dealt with here.

Returning to the subject of inheritance, an objection may be made also that by the proposed method the son of one who owns hundreds of millions of dollars eventually will find himself as rich as the son who has inherited from one who has less than a million. While this would still be ethically right, since both are equal in not having contributed to the building of those fortunes, we wish to stress that our method has been proposed merely as a starting point of discussion. If desired, the maximum limit of inheritance could be made proportional to the original fortune. For instance, if we indicate by M the complete worth of the property, by (n) the number of heirs and assume that inheritance should start to rise when above the 500,000 level, yet not in proportion of M, the formula of inheritance may be given by the following expression:

$$I = 48,000 \ [Pq + 4 \ (M/n \ x \ 500,000)^c \ x \ P'q]$$

where c is a factor smaller than one and to be chosen by economists and by popular vote.

For instance take the same example of page 200 and assume that n (number of heirs)=1. Then if M=2,000,000, Pq=.95, P'q=1,075 and c=.5 maximum inheritance will be given by:

$$I=48,000 \ [.91+4(2.00,000/500,000)^5 x 1.075]=471,000$$

instead of 250,000 as calculated by the original equation. What should revert to society would be given by:

$$2,000,000-471,000=1,529,000.$$

If the number of heirs happens to be four, the maximum inheritance calculated by the same expression will become:

$$I=48,000[.91+4(2,000,000/4x500,000)^5 x 1.075]=250,000$$

The amount that would revert to society in this case would become:

$$2,000,000-250,000x4=1,000,000$$

However, independently of how inheritance is determined, we maintain that the excess over the prescribed value should be returned to society, and used for the best advantage of humanity in general.

All these activities, that is, establishing the various inheritances and taking care of any property which may come to be temporarily owned by society, will represent the main concern of two branches of the government which we shall indicate as "Inheritance" and "Maintenance" group of which more will be said later in this text.

CHAPTER VI

GENERALIZATIONS ON ECONOMIC PHENOMENA AND BASIC FOUNDATION OF THE FUTURE SOCIETY

THE FIFTH CHAPTER submitted a method for transferring wealth from private ownership to society in general. Our present purpose is to analyze how this wealth can be used to produce the greatest possible benefit to mankind.

As already explained, the wealth collected from estates may be in various forms, such as money, buildings, cultivated or uncultivated land ,works of art, and so forth. It may be wholly owned, or held in co-partnership with private individuals. Money in general will be the only form that can be readily used, as it may be deposited in banks and drawn as required. Houses, factories, land, and all wealth that requires special attention and management will produce a definite return. As a general rule, such ownership by society should be avoided because it must be a firmly established policy to rent and preferably to sell these forms of wealth at the earliest opportunity to the general public at current market prices. Society must not enter into competition with private enterprises. The sooner such wealth is returned to the public the better. Large estates which cannot be easily sold or rented may be divided into smaller estates, within the means of the relatively poor, who will thereby be able to acquire and utilize rent-producing wealth. As to work of art, these can be sold to museums, national galleries, or private collectors or dealers willing to pay their price. This kind of wealth was taken from individuals and awarded to society for the definite purpose of promoting well-being among mankind in general. This result could not be achieved if handed over to museums free of charge, even though society would gain indirectly. Giving it away would merely mean that the money it represents could not be utilized for more pressing needs.

Both collection and distribution of wealth will be made by a branch of the government whose activity will be analyzed later.

We shall call this branch "THE BUREAU OF ECONOMIC WELFARE" or EW. While the collection and care of wealth from inheritances is among its activities, its main function will be that of distributing this wealth in such a manner that the maximum benefit to mankind may result. Larger or smaller units of the EW will be set up in every community. For this purpose the country will be divided into separate zones working independently of each other, yet under the direction of headquarters in the capital which will determine policies for the entire nation. The personnel will be chosen by qualification, promotion made on merit, and not based on length of service. These positions, it must be made clear, will not be political. The general policies of the EW will be similar to those of a private organization, inefficiency will not be tolerated, corruption punished and eradicated, and every one, high or low, will take orders from one or more immediate superiors, with the authority to terminate his services if necessary to the welfare of the EW and the people in general.

The activity of the EW will be known through monthly or weekly reports published in newspapers and special bulletins. These reports will list, not only the wealth on hand, but the policies being followed or due to be adopted, both in general and in great detail, so that all may easily understand what is being done in their particular community, no matter how small. Special information may be given directly to any one, and a special branch of the government will be formed to investigate complaints made by private individuals. The activities of the EW must be upheld by the law of the land, and the government as a whole, having approved its various decisions, must see that these policies are enforced and carried out in that spirit.

The following chapter analyzes in detail the general setup of the EW. For the present, in order to give a general idea, it will be enough to say that this branch of the government will be divided into four separate branches. The first will be the connecting link between the others, providing the leadership in the organization and will be called either "Central Branch" or "Policy Group", as we shall better explain in the following chapter. The second, in which we are especially interested at present, will engage in distributing wealth or its revenue to the best advantage of society. The third will devote its activity to the care of wealth in possession of society, but due to return to private ownership. The fourth will confine itself to the collecting of inheritances as they come due to society.

The activities of the second branch will affect the mode of life of the population, it will itself be divided into divisions. Some of these will be represented in every community of the land, the better to serve the people, others will have offices in the largest cities, the capital of the zone, and of the nation. A moderate amount of the activities of those divisions, not being represented in every community, will be carried on by the Manager of the organization in the community itself, as later explained. The reason is that, while the staff of the organization must be large, it needs to be no larger than necessary. The various divisions of the second group are as follows:

(1) Price stabilization
(2) Industry regulation
(3) Employment control
(4) Hospitalization
(5) Delinquency control
(6) Recreation

GENERALIZATION ON ECONOMIC PHENOMENA AS BASIS OF THE PRINCIPLE ON WHICH THE NEW SOCIAL ORDER WILL REST

Before undertaking the study of the various activities of the EW, it will be well to set down some basic phenomena which have an important bearing on our mode of life. As this is not a study of pure economics, it will only touch those topics closely related to our subject.

In the first chapter was given a description of the various forces that influence prices. These forces take root in the very nature of man, and give rise to a demand for different kinds of commodities. By demand we mean the amount the public is willing to buy at a stated price. This demand is not constant, but varies with price, so that once the amounts the public will buy at different prices are determined, a relationship can be established which can be shown graphically as in Fig. 8, page 221.

Let d represent the instantaneous demand curve of a commodity. The horizontal axis represents quantities sold, and the vertical axis the corresponding price. As a general rule the demand curve starts at a high price when the quantity sold is relatively small, and gradually decreases as the amount sold increases. Any point on this curve, say A, shows the quantity (Q_A) that would be bought at that particular time at the price (P_A). If the price is (P_B), smaller than (P_A), the corresponding quantity (Q_B) exceeds (Q_A).

Before continuing this analysis, it is well to define the meaning of *elasticity*. As any book on economics will explain, each commodity presents a different degree of elasticity. By this is meant that relationship which binds the change in quantities sold with the corresponding change in price. Assume A in Fig. 9 as the starting condition of our analysis. If we consider a small increment of commodities sold ΔQ, we know that there will be a small change in price represented by ΔP. The ratio between the increment in quantities sold and the increment in price $\Delta Q/\Delta P$ will represent the elasticity of the particular commodity at that point. The larger the increment of commodities sold for a stated increment in price, the larger the elasticity of the commodity.

For a near-perfect elastic commodity, as shown in Fig. 10, ΔQ is very large for a specific increment of ΔP, and would become infinite for a perfect elastic condition, in which case the demand curve is a line parallel to its horizontal axis. This happens when the amount of commodities sold, no matter how large, does not influence the price. The farmer going to the market to sell his wheat finds this condition. He can sell all he wants at the market price, but cannot influence that price. For a near-perfect inelastic commodity, as shown in Fig. 11, ΔQ is small for a given increment of ΔP, and becomes zero for a perfect inelastic condition, when the demand curve is a line parallel to the vertical axis. This happens when price does not influence the quantity sold. Salt, for instance, is such a commodity, since neither a decrease nor increase in price will appreciably influence the amount sold or consumed.

But as a general rule commodities will not be either perfectly elastic or perfectly inelastic, which means that the raising or lowering in prices will affect the quantity bought according to its degree of elasticity. Furthermore the degree of elasticity does not have to be constant throughout the range of prices, but may vary for different parts of the demand curve. Articles of luxury and the like are markedly elastic commodities, which people can easily go without if prices should rise, or buy more freely if prices should fall. Food and other commodities needed by the poor, especially if scarce, possess only a small degree of elasticity. The reason is that the poor, in their efforts to meet the new

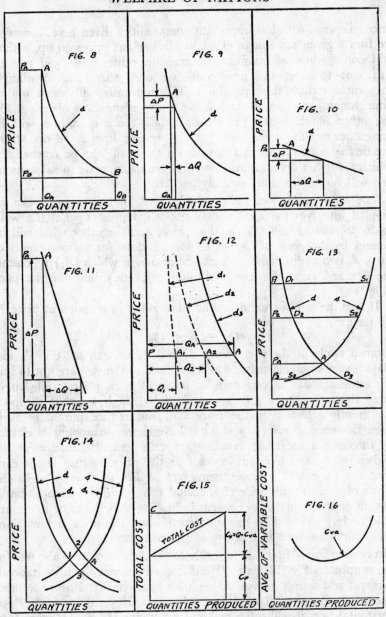

price, dispense with less important commodities. Even here, however, we find a given amount of elasticity. Indeed, as prices go up, a time will come when additional economies in other fields will not be sufficient to meet the new condition and, therefore, unwillingly they must reduce their purchase. This naturally will mean under-nourishment, squalor, ill health and a lower standard of living. On the other hand, if the price should fall, more quantities will be bought, especially by those who at the previous level could not afford the desired amount. In this direction a limit will also be reached, by which a further decrease will not produce an increase in sales, as no one will buy more than actually needed.

The amount of commodities bought at any given price can be divided into two parts, of which one will represent what the well-to-do population will take at that price, and the other what will be bought by the poor. If similar division is done for various points of curve d, two additional curves can be drawn in which (d_1) represents the demand curve for the well-to-do and (d_2) that for the poor (Fig. 12).

If A is the total demand for the commodity in question at price P, we have:

$$Q_A = Q_1 + Q_2$$

From a study of the two curves d_1 and d_2 we can see that d_1 displays a very small elasticity, which means that the rich are apt to buy the same amount of commodities irrespective of price, while curve (d_2) displays a large amount of elasticity, signifying that the poor are greatly affected by the price and will reduce purchases as it rises. However, curve (d_2) will not have the same amount of elasticity throughout its range. It will start with a small elasticity for the higher prices, and this will increase as the price lessens. This means that the poor will deprive themselves of less vital supplies in the effort of meeting the price of the vital commodities if high and will buy more if the price goes down, indicating that the poor never are able to buy the desired amount, even when the price is low, since their purchases tend to increase as the cost goes down.

In economics we find that for each demand curve there is also one for the supply. In Fig. 13, page 219, d and s represent the instantaneous demand and supply curves. Assume for instance that P_1 on the price line represents that of a given commodity. If we draw from P_1 a horizontal line, it will interset d and s at point D_1, S_1. D_1 represents, reading upon the horizontal axis Q, the quantities which the public is willing to buy at that price, while S_1, the quantities which the sellers are willing to offer at that price. As the quantities represented by D_1 and (S_1) are different from each other, it is plain that price (P_1) does not represent a condition of instantaneous equilibrium. The same holds for points (P_2) and (P_3) with the difference that, while for points (P_1) and (P_2) the supply which the sellers offer at those prices is larger than that which the public is willing to absorb, the reverse holds for price (P_3). At price (PA) the quantity offered coincides with what the public is willing to buy and, therefore, gives the instantaneous position of equilibrium for the commodity at the time in consideration.

Now either curve s or d, or both, being instantaneous conditions, at another time may be displaced to right or left of the position shown calling for a different point of equilibrium. A vivid example of the displacement of the curves is represented by the demand for eggs at Easter time compared with any other season. The demand curve for eggs during this period is shifted to the right, and assuming the same supply curve the equilibrium price will naturally go higher. Using again the instantaneous supply and demand curves of Fig. 13 (redrawn in Fig. 14) assume that s stays the same and d moves to d_1, it is clear that point 4 instead of point 3 will be the new position of equilibrium since it is the intersection between d_1 and s.

Again if d stays the same and s moves to s_1, point 1 will give the instantaneous condition of equilibrium. In general, both curves may be displaced either way, and their intersection, point 2 on our diagram, will represent the instantaneous position of equilibrium and will give both the price and the quantities sold. It can be easily seen that P_2 may be equal, larger, or smaller than P_3, depending on the amount the two curves have been displaced.

In chapter 3, while analyzing phenomena occurring in a Lilliputian society, a definition of equilibrium point was given, which is reached when the price of a commodity reaches its average cost. It was shown at that time that for the small society under consideration, this equilibrium point could not be changed, and there is no reason to believe that a similar phenomenon could not occur in a much larger society, in other words, while the price may vary from day to day, or month to month, depending on the position of the instantaneous demand and supply curves, it is clear that this change in price, unless basic variations in the pattern of society call for a different equilibrium point, cannot go on indefinitely in any single direction, or forces will enter to reverse that trend. With a consistent increase in price, profit will attract additional sellers, and by increasing the supply cause a lowering of price; with a consistent decrease of price, losses will reduce the number of sellers, and by decreasing the supply will increase price.

Although small fluctuations of prices occur within short periods of time, which tend to approach the equilibrium point, the present text is naturally concerned with phenomena extending over a long period, as they represent the actual economic position of a specific society in which society may be taken to mean either the population of a small community or that of the entire nation. On this account the equilibrium point as defined in the third chapter will still be taken as a base of analysis, and it will be assumed that both supply and demand are crystallized at a certain condition.

Now while at this level only a few can afford to buy all they want, the majority has to make shift with less than desired. Among the many commodities changing hands on the market, some, however, are so vital to the well-being of mankind that such privation must be averted and a remedy found. *Scarcity is the main reason for this phenomenon and since there is not sufficient amount of such commodities, their price reaches a level where only a few can afford to buy what they need.* If the quantity available were larger, the price would automatically fall, and the demand would correspondingly increase. While in a free country it is impossible to force individuals to produce more of any commodity, even for the sake of humanity, especially if this means lower profit, one way to obtain this result is to make this increase attractive and profitable to the producers.

Before entering this part of the analysis, the forces which combine to yield a given supply merit consideration. A study of these forces may reveal a solution of the problem. First of all, such commodities as are usually bought by the poor are very inelastic as regards this group of humanity and yet present a perfect elastic condition to each individual seller. By this is meant that in such a market each seller cannot influence the price due to the large number of competitors and the insignificant role of each seller. As stated above, such a case is represented by the farmer selling his wheat. He can sell any amount in his possession, but only at the market price. This, to be sure, follows the general rule of supply and demand, but only on a national scale, so he is powerless to change that price by selling either more or less of his stock. Under these circumstances the seller, either the farmer or a manufacturer of any commodity, will produce and sell only that amount which returns the maximum profit at that price. This maximum will be reached when his marginal cost equals price. By this is meant that whenever his cost of an additional amount of products (marginal cost) is less than the price current on the market, an increase in production will be profitable to him. But, if it is more, such an increase would be unprofitable, and he will refrain from such expansion. The maximum profit will be obtained when his marginal cost becomes equal to price. In note 6-1 appears an example of a shoe factory in which the meaning of marginal cost is more extensively explained. The attitude of the manufacturer toward any specific price on the market is also indicated and analyzed.

NOTE 6-1

Assume a shoe factory selling 55,000 pairs of shoes per year at a price of $6 per pair. The expenditure incurred for their manufacture may be divided into two main groups:

(a) Fixed cost, and (b) Variable cost.

The fixed cost (F) is represented by the interest of capital invested, salaries of officials and personnel who must be maintained whatever the output, and by other expenditures which have no direct relation to that output. The variable cost (V) is made up of the wages of the workers, the cost of material, and other expenditures having a direct relation to production and, therefore, affected by output.

At any time the manager can decide to increase production a certain percentage. This will increase the variable cost but not, within reasonable limits, the fixed cost. If this happens to be the case, the cost per pair of shoes will tend to decrease with an increased production, and, therefore, the manager will find this percentage increase desirable and profitable.

Let C represent the total cost which as aforementioned is given by: $C = F + V$. But V is a function of the amount produced (Q) and, therefore, can be expressed by: $V = Q.v$ where (v) is the average of variable cost. If (v) were constant throughout the range of production, C would bear a straight relation to the amount of production Q, given by the expression $C = F + Qv$ and, therefore, diagrammatically expressed by a line intersecting the axis of cost at a point that indicates the fixed cost (F) (see Fig. 15, page 219). However, v is not constant, but variable and can be expressed by a curve which, starting from a high value when the production is small, tends to decrease for any additional production until a limit is reached when it reverses its trend (see Fig. 16). This performance is explained by the fact that within given limits, as the production is increased, many factors tend to decrease the cost of a pair of shoes. Some of these factors are represented by the reduction of cost of raw material (leather) when bought in large quantities, by cheaper rates of transportation, by the possibility of introducing labor-saving devices and by a more efficient division of labor. However, these factors do not keep up with the increase in production and, while some will reach an absolute maximum long before the full capacity of the factory is attained, others, as for instance, the efficiency of the labor force will definitely decrease with an abnormal increase in the size of the factory, because of the decreased supervision and other causes immaterial to this study. Another factor tending to increase the average of variable cost (v) is represented by the fact that as production increases obsolete machinery is usually put into use if no expansion of existing facilities is contemplated.

At this point we must also point out that the various numerical data assumed in our study are not necessarily constant for an indefinite length of time and that various conditions of the market may alter the variable cost considerably. The same can be said for (F) where changes of salaries in the upper brackets of the factory employees, as well as changes in rates, insurance, taxes and so forth, will also tend to alter this factor. Therefore, the curves we are presenting in this study must be taken as representative of what the manager of a hypothetical factory would draw if he should assume that conditions remained constant for a reasonable amount of time. With these concepts clear in our minds we may proceed with our analysis.

Assume that the manager is well informed as to the necessary wages that must be paid for labor, the price that must be paid for leather, aware of the various discounts if bought in large quantities from different places, the rates of transportation as well as the cost to maintain a given output of shoes, and, therefore, in a position to approximate the cost of one pair of shoes for different levels of production. From his estimate he will finally be able to draw a curve (v) as the one shown in Fig. 16. Irrespective of his production, let us assume that his fixed cost (F) is represented by $60,000 per year. From this information he will be able then to calculate the total cost C for different levels of production (shown in Table 2, column 3). He, however, will be more interested in calculating the total cost per unit which will be given by the total cost C divided by the total production Q or c $=$ C $+$ Q as shown in column 6. Incidentally (c) is also given by:

$$c = (F/Q) + v$$

and if we indicate (F/Q) as (f), c will be given by:

$$c = f + v$$

c will rapidly decrease from an infinite value when Q equals zero until it assumes a value smaller than P. It is evident that for any production in which (c) is larger than price, the factory sustains a loss and, therefore, we can say that the minimum compatible production for this factory is represented by 35,500 pairs of shoes per year at which level the firm or company does not derive either gain or loss. From the shape of (c) it is evident that for any production of shoes larger than 35,500 up to 125,000 an increase in production will lower the cost per pair and, therefore, the unit profit as well as the total profit will tend to increase.

Take, for instance, the condition represented by (A) on curve (c). The corresponding point on the horizontal axis gives the quantity of shoes manufactured (55,000 pairs of shoes per year), and (OE) $=$ 5.03 represents the cost per unit under that condition. The product (OE) x (EA) $=$ \$276,650 will then be the total cost to produce (EA). This is graphically represented by the area of the rectangle bound by O-E-A-S-O. Assume now a condition G very close to A. From the diagram the quantity (KG) and (OK) will be respectively given by 70,000 and \$4.59 from which the total cost at G will be given by: (OK) x (KG) $=$ \$321,300. As before the total cost at G will be represented by the area of the rectangle bounded by O-K-H-T-O. Now the total cost of G minus the total cost at A will give the manufacturer the information as to how much his cost will climb by stepping up production from the quantity (S) to (T). T-S (15,000 pairs) represents the increase in production. Let the difference in total costs equal ΔC and (T)-(S) $=$ ΔQ. When ΔQ becomes extremely small, then ΔC/ΔQ, is what will here be called marginal cost at A, which can also be defined as the rate at which a small change in total output changes total cost. If we calculate a number of marginal costs for various quantities, and plot them on the diagram, joining these points will produce curve m, which represents the curve of marginal cost.

On our diagram assume point A $=$ (55,000 pairs of shoes), for which the marginal cost must be calculated. Take the values of c corresponding to productions equal to 5,000 units more and less than the one represented by A or 60,000 and 50,000. The values of (c) will be respectively given by $4.86 and $5.22. 1,000 pairs are the minimum variation in production assumed in this study (ΔQ), therefore, if we assume that (C) varies as a straight line between the two conditions, the variation in cost around point A for 1,000 pairs will be given by: $(4.86 - 5.22)/10 = -0.036.

At (A) the total cost is given by: $55,000 \times 5.03 = $276,650$.

At this point an increase in production of 1,000 pairs will reduce the cost $0.036 per unit, and the total cost at the new level will be: $56,000 \times (5.03 - 0.036) = 56,000 \times 4.994 = $279,664$.

The increase in production of 1,000 pairs will mean an increased cost of: $279,664 - 276,650 = $3014 = \Delta C$ which is tantamount to say that at this level of production, 1,000 pairs will cost the manufacturer $3.014 per unit, a figure smaller than $5.03. This is assumed to be the marginal cost at condition (A). If we indicate with (d) the difference in cost per 1,000 pairs of shoes at the condition assumed, the general equation for marginal cost is given by:

$$(1)\quad m = ([(Q+1000) \times (c\text{-}d)] - (Q \times c))/1000$$
$$= (c\text{-}d)(Q+1000)/1000$$

This expression has been used for the calculation of the various points of curve (m) and shown in Table 2 column 13. From an inspection of the diagram it can be seen that the marginal cost curve m after a rapid increase in the region where average of total cost (c) is larger than price and, therefore, immaterial in our discussion, tends to decrease until the condition (1) is reached (Q = 65,000) at which point it reaches the minimum value. From this point on the direction of (m) is reversed. At (2) (Q = 107,600) it becomes equal to (v), at (3) or (Q = 125,000) it becomes equal to (c), and at (4) or (Q = 155,800) it becomes equal to price P. Beyond (4) the marginal cost is larger than price.

Consider now the significance and the implication of this relation as far as the manufacturer is concerned. The profit per unit sold in every case will be shown by the difference between the curve (P) and (c). At point A this difference is represented by the distance (OD)-(OE) and the total profit will be given by: [(BA) x S]. On the diagram this total profit will be represented by the area bounded by the rectangle A.B.D.E.A. As the point A on curve (c) moves toward (1), the base of the rectangle that shows total production becomes larger, and so does the height, which gives the profit per shoe sold. An additional explanation of this increase in profit can be derived by the marginal curve itself (m). Since (m), which charts the cost of each additional pair at that level of production, is smaller than the corresponding average cost (c), this means that for any point between (j) and (1), an additional production of 1,000 units will bring the manufacturer more profit than an equal number of shoes whose cost is given by curve (c).

With the understanding that all factors used in any of the following equations are taken from the corresponding curves for the same amount of production, it is possible to state that the profit is given by PR = Q x (P-c), and the average profit per year for each unit will be: PR/Q = P-c. Using the same reasoning the total profit resulting from a production of Q + 1,000 is given by:

(2)   PR = Q x (P-c) + 1000 (P-m)
       = Q x (P-c) + 1000 (P-c) + 1000 (c-m)
       = (Q + 1000) (P-c) + 1000 (c-m)

The average profit in this case would be:

PR / (Q + 1000)   or:

(3)   [(Q + 1000) (P-c) + 1000 (c-m)] / (Q + 1000) =
       (P-c) + 1000 (c-m) / (Q + 1000)

But (p-c) is the average profit at the previous production (Q), so that the additional production of 1,000 pairs will increase that average by:

(4)   1000 (c-m) / (Q + 1000)

What has been said for the total average cost (c) applies also for the average of variable cost (v) or as long as (m) is lower than (v) any increment in production tends to decrease (v) as well as (c).

At point (1) (Q = 65,000) the marginal cost curve (m) reaches its minimum value, after which it starts to increase, but as long as (m) is lower than (v) and (c), both curves will continue decreasing with an increase in production for the reason explained above. The total profit in this case also will keep on increasing.

At point (2) (Q = 107,600), the marginal cost (m) and average of variable cost (v) reach the same value, which will be the minimum point of curve (v), as beyond this point any additional unit produced will cost more than the average of variable cost and, therefore, will tend to increase that average. (c), however, will still show a tendency to decrease as beyond this point another unit will still cost less than the average of total cost, and accordingly will tend to decrease that average.

At point (3) (Q = 125,000), (m) intersects curve (c) and, therefore, this is the minimum value of (c), beyond which, influenced by the rising marginal cost curve, the average of total cost will

also increase. It can be said in passing that at this point equation
(4) becomes zero. Indeed as the value of (m) becomes equal to
(c), (c-m) in the equation becomes zero which means that at this
level an additional production of 1,000 pairs of shoes does not
change either way the total average cost of point (3). But even at
this point we have not reached the maximum profit. It is true that
up to point (3), the rectangle representing total profit has been
increasing in area because of the lengthening of both of its sides,
respectively the quantities produced and the profit derived per
unit. Beyond point (3), however, the profit per unit produced
begins to decrease (vertical side of the rectangle). It is easy to see,
however, that if the profit per unit decreases slightly in comparison
with the increase in output, what is lost in profit on each pair of
shoes sold, is more than compensated for by what is gained in selling
a much larger number. In other words, the profit is still increasing
because the length of the rectangle is so much larger than the decrease
in height. What will be then the maximum profit? This will be
reached when the marginal cost curve (m) becomes equal to price,
or when Q becomes equal to 155,800 (point (4) on the curve).
For any value smaller than (4) any additional unit produced, costing
less than price, will return a profit. The maximum profit is accordingly given by the rectangle bounded by (4)-(L)-(N)-(D)-(4).
Beyond this point the marginal cost is larger than the price, which
means that any additional unit causes a loss, as it subtracts from
the profit attained by the previous production. Since marginal cost
(m) beyond point (3) is larger than the average total cost, (c) will
tend to increase and at point (5) (where Q = 206,000) will become
equal to price. At this point the profit per unit sold (P-c) as well
as total profit (PR) becomes zero. At this point, likewise, the
rectangle that indicates profit flattens out into a straight line coin-
cident with that of price. For quantities produced larger than 206,000
the profit turns into loss. In the diagram the total profit per year
corresponding to any amount of production is indicated by curve
(PR), which after a gradual increase up to a production of 155,800
becomes zero when the production reaches the 206,000 level.

In general the manager of a factory does not have all the facts
on which he may base the calculation of his (c) curve through the
entire range which would enable him to obtain the necessary information as to the production that will bring maximum profit. His
knowledge of his cost curve is bound to be limited, extend within
a much smaller range than that plotted on the graph. But even so

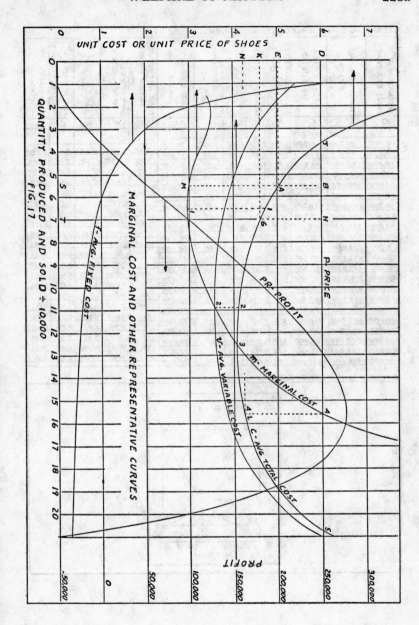

FIG. 17

TABLE NO. 2   CALCULATION OF MARGINAL COST

Q — PRODUCTION OF SHOES PER YEAR	V — TOTAL VARIABLE COST = $v \times Q$	C — TOTAL COST = $V + 60000$	f — AVERAGE OF FIXED COST = $60000 \div Q$	v" — AVERAGE OF VARIABLE COST = $V \div Q$	c — AVERAGE OF TOTAL COST = $f+v$ OR $C \div Q$	pr — UNIT PROFIT $(p-c)$ = $6.00-c$	PR — TOTAL PROFIT = $pr \times Q$
0	0	60,000					
10,000	54,200	114,200	6.000	5.420	11.42	-5.42	-50,420
20,000	92,400	157,400	3.000	4.870	7.87	-1.87	-37,400
30,000	135,000	195,000	2.000	4.500	6.50	-.50	-15,000
40,000	169,200	229,200	1.500	4.230	5.73	.27	10,800
50,000	201,000	261,000	1.200	4.020	5.22	.78	39,000
60,000	231,000	291,000	1.000	3.860	4.86	1.14	68,400
70,000	261,300	321,300	.857	3.733	4.59	1.41	98,700
80,000	291,200	351,200	.750	3.640	4.39	1.61	128,800
90,000	322,020	382,020	.667	3.578	4.245	1.755	157,950
100,000	355,000	415,000	.600	3.550	4.15	1.85	185,000
110,000	389,950	449,950	.545	3.545	4.09	1.91	210,100
120,000	437,200	487,200	.500	3.560	4.06	1.94	232,800
130,000	467,870	527,870	.461	3.599	4.06	1.94	252,200
140,000	512,680	572,680	.428	3.662	4.09	1.91	267,400
150,000	550,500	610,500	.400	3.760	4.16	1.84	276,000
160,000	623,200	683,200	.375	3.895	4.27	1.73	276,800
170,000	694,790	754,790	.353	4.087	4.44	1.56	265,200
180,000	789,460	849,460	.333	4.347	4.68	1.32	237,600
190,000	895,660	955,660	.316	4.714	5.03	.97	184,300
200,000	1,044,000	1,104,000	.300	5.220	5.52	.48	96,000
210,000	1,252,440	1,312,440	.286	5.964	6.25	-.25	-52,500
220,000	1,570,080	1,630,080	.273	7.137	7.41	-1.41	-310,200

Right-hand (marginal) columns, stepped between the above rows:

Δ — DIFF. IN COST FOR 10,000 UNITS = $p_n - p_{n+1}$	d — DIFF. IN COST FOR 10,000 UNITS = $\Delta \div 10$	K — $\frac{(Q+1000)d}{1000}$	c' — AVG. OF TOTAL COST (FROM CURVE)	m — MARGINAL COST $c' - K$
-3.55	-.355	-5.68	9.07	3.390
-1.37	-.137	-3.57	7.05	3.480
-.77	-.077	-2.77	6.09	3.320
-.51	-.051	-2.35	5.46	3.110
-.36	-.036	-2.017	5.03	3.013
-.27	-.027	-1.783	4.72	2.937
-.20	-.020	-1.520	4.49	2.970
-.145	-.0145	-1.248	4.32	3.072
-.095	-.0095	-.912	4.20	3.288
-.060	-.0060	-.636	4.12	3.489
-.030	-.0030	-.348	4.075	3.722
0	0	0	4.060	4.060
.030	.0030	.408	4.075	4.483
.070	.0070	1.022	4.12	5.142
.111	.0110	1.715	4.21	5.926
.170	.0170	2.82	4.35	7.17
.245	.0245	4.32	4.55	8.86
.35	.035	6.51	4.84	11.35
.49	.049	9.61	5.25	14.86
.73	.073	15.04	5.85	20.89
1.16	.116	25.06	6.75	31.81

(1) ASSUMED
(2) BASED ON $Q = 15,000; 25,000; 35,000$ ETC.

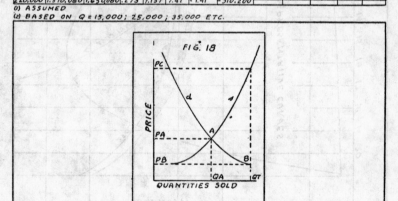

FIG. 18

he is able, from what he already knows about his particular production, to foretell whether a limited increase in production will be profitable or not, and it is evident that if his position happens to be close to the original point A that he will tend to increase his output as time goes by, until the condition represented by point (4) is attained. This will depend, among other things, on what the price of shoes will be on the market.

HOW TO INCREASE SUPPLY

To generalize the preceding explanation for any industry, it is easy to visualize that for a specific price of commodity various factories may have different cost curves, because of location, condition of labor, availability of raw material, efficiency of the organization, and so forth, so their profits will also be different. It stands to reason that the most efficient enterprises, with a much lower cost curve, stand to make also the largest profits. The conclusion follows that to increase production of commodities until there is sufficent for the poor as well as the rich, irrespective of price, a method must be devised to enlarge the supply by natural processes to the desired level. It may seem logical, from the economic forces involved, that raising the price would produce the desired result. The manufacturers would find profitable a further expansion of production up to a point where their marginal cost curves reach the new price. But close analysis of our diagram on page 228a will reeval that this is neither proper nor the most economical method. Indeed when the marginal cost curve reaches the price P, it has already acquired a tendency to increase very rapidly. This means that even a small increase in production must be obtained at a large cost. If one takes into account the large scarcity of most any vital commodity in every nation in the world and, therefore, the need of a much larger production than found at present, it can be easily seen that the price required to promote such a supply would be extremely high, much higher than the public could sustain. This fact will become evident if it is considered that while the extra production has been obtained through poor and inefficient methods (this being represented by the high marginal cost), the workers and the people in general receive the same salaries and wages and, therefore, the discrepancy between what they can buy and what is offered on the market will tend to increase. Expressed in a diagrammatic form (see Fig. 18), we can say that given a supply and a demand curve, equilibrium is indicated by their intersection, where the amount (QA) is absorbed at price (PA). If (QT) is the theoretical amount to satisfy the population in general, the price should be (PB), which can be found by the intersection of the vertical line drawn from (QT) and the demand curve (d). On the other hand such a production can be attained only if the price goes up to (PC), which can be found by the intersection of the same vertical line drawn from (QT) and the supply curve (s). Now (PC), is considerably greater than (PB) and there would be no way of maintaining that production unless a third party, such as the government, should assume the task of guaranteeing the price (PC) to the manufacturers and the price (PB) to the general public. Besides the fact that the government would have to levy all this money from the public itself, this procedure would be unjust to society, as a premium would be paid to all those manufacturers who are inefficient and posess a high curve of total cost. At such a price level artificially maintained by the government, these producers would make profits and increase their output when actually they should be facing bankruptcy for ineptness and incompetency compared to other concerns.

The method here advocated, which in our opinion offers more constructive procedure, contemplates no increase in price unless through the natural process of supply and demand, but fosters the founding of new factories, and by increasing production adds to supply. This will be accomplished by the EW through a process indicated by the following rule:

The EW will Offer to Buy Additonal Amount of
Vital Commodities offered for Sale

This is a basic principle of our new mode of life and will be analyzed in detail later in our text. All those factories whose marginal cost equals price will have no incentive to enlarge their production, as this would lessen their profit, but since our principle is tantamount to an increase in demand, other factories will come into existence, and their output added to the others will speed up the supply as long as the EW keeps its policy in operation. Obviously the method used to accelerate this output must be based on the particular elasticity of the commodity in question.

The illustration of the forces tending to affect the supply has been based on a shoe factory, but the same, with minor variations, will be valid to almost all other commodities. As to food products, a different approach may apply. We may divide these commodities into perishable and preservable kinds. If some of the latter remains unsold, the fact that it will not spoil for a reasonable amount of time allows the owner the alternative of waiting for a better market. In this respect preservable food can be dealt with in the same way as in the previous example. The incentive of the apparently inexhaustible demand will in time increase the supply and induce the sellers to dispose of the stock on hand. As to perishable products their price is usually high at the beginning of the period of sale, declines considerably as the end of that period approaches. This, because the seller, as a general rule, tries to sell as much as possible at the highest price on the market, but is ready to take considerably less if indications are such that he may be left with an unsold amount of stock. The reason for this attitude on his part is that what is not sold will be worthless at the next period of sale. A good example of the lowering of prices is represented by the Christmas trees which, originally expensive, are practically given away a few hours before the holiday. After Christmas those trees which have not been sold become worthless.

Now the fact that the farmer takes less for his product at the end of the market period is because even at such a low price the additional sale represents a profit. While less is gained per unit, the larger amount sold makes that deal profitable. A limit, however, will be reached beyond which he will not go if he knows that so much of his labor and effort will go unsold or be in effect given away. Therefore, the law of supply and demand will be once more the determining factor of that production.

Now let the EW offer to buy any amount of a certain perishable commodity at a level lower than the morning price, and to be delivered at its store at a specific time. This would allow the farmer to sell the best part of his stock to whoever is willing to pay his high price. Long before his commodity has deteriorated and to be inspected before its purchase, the rest could be sold to the EW at a moderate price, but still much higher than what he could obtain at the end of the day. The EW in turn would take the risk of being left with worthless commodities. The farmer, relieved of that risk, and with certainty of more secure profit, will find worthwhile the increase in production.

Likewise, the policies of the EW will relieve the manufacturers of the uncertainty of being left with unsold commodities and will safeguard them from the spectre of a lowering of prices. This, coupled to the assurance that any moderate surplus he may be able to produce will also be absorbed, in time will exert a powerful leverage in the country to raise the supply, without the necessity of increasing prices as previously assumed necessary. Later in this chapter it will be shown how prices can be linked with wages, so that the poor may receive a better share than under any other mode of life.

Of course, this policy is advocated only for those commodities which are vital to the welfare of the people, for all the others, articles of luxury and the like, the law of supply and demand must remain the only controlling factor in their production.

GENERALIZATION ON VITAL COMMODITIES

Food is the first commodity that comes to our mind. Doctors and dieticians can decide the kind and the quantity that a well-balanced family of four; father, mother, and two children, need to remain nourished and in healthy condition. They know the number of calories required to keep fit, and this must be the first goal to be attained for this hypothetical family. The requisite calories may be assimilated by consuming either expensive or inexpensive food products. Omitting the former kind from consideration, this discussion will concentrate on types that, while not so palatable, are still nourishing and suitable for a family in the lower bracket of society. Bread, milk, eggs, inexpensive cuts of meat, many kinds of fruit and vegetables, fall in this class.

Each has a definite value in calories and vitamins, and for a well-balanced diet a certain amount of each kind should be consumed during the course of a week. From this knowledge and from the pattern of the population as to the size of the rich, poor, and middle classes, a close approximation of the total amount needed by the people can be made. The potentiality of the land and the variation of the weather must also be taken into account. For instance, in an orange-producing land, it is natural that the orange should be included in the list of vital commodities. Where oranges must be imported and their price is far greater than other similar food products, it is reasonable that the latter should appear in that list. As to the seasonable commodities, this fact must be taken into account and omitted from the list when out of season.

The EW must collect all data pertaining to the various communities in the country. From this information, charts and lists of vital commodities can be prepared for the different places and seasons. If conditions should change in any community, allowance should be made in the list. With such information on hand it will be possible to know for any town, city or region the amount of vital commodities needed and available at any particular time. One of the first problems which the EW will try to solve will be that of increasing the production of food vital to the health of the community. In doing this there is no intention that it should enter into competition with the small business man or the owner of the corner drug store. A vast majority of its customers will consist of that part of the population which, being poor, only buys at present a limited amount of commodities and does not constitute the bulk of their business. Besides, the sale of vital commodities is a small portion of what is sold by a store, and the EW, as previously mentioned, will deal exclusively in these wares. Finally, the EW will obtain a large portion of its purchases directly from the various stores, and, therefore, tend to help rather than endanger their business. However, as it will buy more from those stores that charge less, the organization will exert a restraining influence upon the raising of prices. This will result from the free choice of the owner, who faced by a fixed price (which will be an average of the prices charged by all the stores), will decide how much he will ask for his products. At this price the owner may sell any part of his stock he thinks might go unsold, so the presence of the EW will be beneficial to him. Much of the buying, of course, will be done directly from the sources of production. Hence, by eliminating middlemen, purchases can be made at a lesser price, and this will lower the ultimate cost to the poorer classes. By varying the proportion bought at the source the EW will prevent unreasonable rise in prices and may force their lowering if already too high. Even so, the small merchant and retailer will be better off, because under the new conditions their sales will be much larger than before and this will tend to produce greater profits, even if prices in some instances have to be reduced.

The second kind of vital commodity is housing. There should be a minimum requirement for housing conditions, and people should not be allowed to live in poorer quarters. Even in the United States, where millions of dollars are spent in improving living conditions, one still finds large numbers of tenements lacking basic requirements of cleanliness and utterly unlivable. Undoutedly great strides are being made in the right direction, yet they are small compared to the great need of the population en masse. The phenomenon of scarcity mentioned above is responsible for the increase in price of apartments and houses with the minimum requirement of comfort and livability so that either rent or cost reach levels the poor cannot afford. The price of a house is bound to be high irrespective of scarcity. As earlier explained in this book, the price of commodities tends to reach equilibrium at a level equal to cost. With present technological advancements a house, no matter how economically built, is bound to be expensive, and the poor usually find themselves unable to meet that price no matter how cheap it may be.

Here again the initiative of the EW must act. Under the law of the land, it should have power to condemn all tenements, houses, and similar buildings falling short of specified minimum requirements. The owners of these properties must be notified and allowed sufficient time to undertake the improvements of their property, if feasible, or erect new buildings of suitable type. They should have the alternative of selling the unimproved property if the expenses of repairs or rebuilding are beyond their capacity to meet. Such sale could be made to individuals or organizations who by that would assume the responsibility of improving the property. Lacking such an alternative, they must sell to the EW at a price fixed by the EW officials and based on reports prepared by architects and engineers of the organization. The owners should also have the opportunity to seek financial aid from the EW if they so desire. This might take the form of a long-term loan at a low interest rate.

Besides the improvement of existing buildings, the EW will encourage the construction of new and better homes, by acting as contractor for thousands of poor people in search of a decent dwelling. By employing its own architects and engineers, by judicious purchase of construction material at a relatively low price, by competitive bidding if awarded to builders, by using standardized designs, by issuing easy terms of payment to owners, the building program could be greatly expanded.

The encouragement given the marketing of vital food products, and the construction of better dwellings must be relentlessly pursued until the chosen goal has been attained. Unfortunately, until that time, many will fall short of the standard of living which doctors and dieticians deem necessary.

The third kind of vital commodity is represented by fuel, as no family can be well unless protected from the rigors of winter. For this item consideration must be given to the climate, the season, and to the kind of heating which is the cheapest on the market.

The same reasoning will apply to the fourth item of the list, which is represented by whatever is used for lighting and cooking.

Due to the limited financial condition of the hypothetical family whose standard of living society is set to improve, it is natural that if should economize and use only the cheapest commodities on the market. However, irrespective of how small this expenditure may be, it must be borne and will represent a definite percentage of the family budget.

Clothing will represent the fifth item of vital commodity. It is difficult to establish the need of a family in this field. Here again the location, be it city or country, and the climate, dictate the kind and quantity of clothing to be bought and replaced. Again human nature must be taken into account. Of two families in the same financial bracket, one will place more emphasis on food, and economize more than necessary on clothing. Another will place instead more emphasis on clothing, at the expense of food and other vital commodities. In fixing their need we must naturally follow the middle of the road, and besides assuring to the hypothetical family the required amount of vitamins and calories, we must also provide a definite amount of clothing. It will still remain the individual prerogative as to what he prefers to buy. Society will do its best to provide the individual with what it deems necessary to his well-being by giving him the opportunity to work and earn the necessary money to buy these commodities, but in the last analysis it will be up to the individual to use his judgment and discretion and buy according to his own wishes and desires.

Lastly there are furniture, utensils, and equipment which from time to time need replacing or renewing and constitute the sixth item of the vital commodity list. These expenditures, unlike those for food, lighting, and cooking, which must be met regularly, occur only sporadically and sometimes after a period of years. Still the family has to meet these expenses as they occur, and must be prepared for such an emergency.

THEORETICAL AMOUNT OF VITAL COMMODITIES FOR THE ASSUMED HYPOTHETICAL FAMILY

Having defined what is meant by vital commodity, let us assume what modern doctors, economists and dieticians would prescribe to the hypothetical family for the latter's comfort and well-being. In a work of this kind, in which the entire population of the globe is considered, one cannot specify any amount and kind of vital commodity, which, if proper for one place, might not be so for another. However, because of the necessity of conveying ideas and establishing facts, there has been assumed a hypothetical industrial city of 100,000 population as a basis for discussion. The family referred to above will be assumed to be living in this city, its head will be a plain laborer, whose wages support a family of four: father, mother, and two children.

(1) FOOD REQUIREMENT:

The first requirement of this family is food. We present here a tabulation of calories for persons of different age:

Men engaged in hard physical work	4000	calories per day
Active women	2860	" " "
Elderly person (71 to 81 years of age)	1600	" " "
Child between 14 and 16 years of age	3000	" " "
Child between 10 and 14 years of age	2500	" " "
Child between 7 and 10 years of age	1800	" " "
Child between 4 and 7 years of age	1600	" " "
Child between 3 and 4 years of age	1200	" " "
Child between 1½ and 3 years of age	1000	" " "

Assume that this hypothetical family of four is composed of a laborer, his wife, and two children aged eight and nine. The reason why we neglect the case of a family with children older than 9 is that at that age and for that kind of family it is presumed that a child is engaged in profitable work of some kind, and obviously the extra return will help balance the budget. In cases where the children are less than 7, food requirements being less, offer the opportunity to save either for future requirements or for expenditures in other fields.

The total requirement of calories for that family per day will then be:

Father	4,000
Mother	2,860
2 children	3,600
Total per day	10,460

10,460 x 7 = 73,220 or 75,000 calories will be the requirement for the entire week. On page 268 is given a table listing some of the commodities this family may need in a week. It will be for the family itself to arrange those quantities so as to obtain a diet both varied and satisfactory. The list of commodities was chosen from the standpoint of food value and from the fact that they are the cheapest on the market. The first column shows the weight of a number of commodities on which the calories are based. The corresponding amount of proteins, fats, and carbohydrates are given respectively in the second, third and fourth column, the total amount of calories per unit weight being shown in the fifth. The sixth column shows the amount of each product the hypothetical family is supposed to use during a week, with the corresponding total calories in the seventh column. The eighth column lists the price of those products current on the market in the industrial city of 100,000 population. The cost of each commodity is given in the ninth column. Assuming that this family consumes all the products enumerated in the list, the total number of calories will be 75,295 and their cost $10.18 per week. For the present we are not interested in the money needed, but only in the amount required by the hypothetical family, so the final four columns in the list do not pertain to the present discussion, but will be needed later in this study.

(2) COST OF LIVING QUARTERS

Among the other expenditures that must be met, that for the payment of rent must naturally figure prominently. When the family owns its house, the necessary expenditures needed to keep it in livable condition may just as well be considered as rent. This house, while simple and small, must have sufficient comfort to keep the family in good health. Since the assumed industrial city is part of a well developed and progressive country it is reasonable that it should contain a large variety of houses and tenements whose price or rent will vary according to location and convenience. It is assumed that a rent of $50 per month is necessary to obtain a well-furnished home with modern facilities consonant with the requirements set forth by physicians and economists. This sum is equivalent to $11.50 per week.

(3) PUBLIC UTILITIES

As before, depending upon the locality, a certain expenditure must be borne for electric illumination and gas for cooking. If electricity or gas are not available their local equivalents will naturally be taken as base. Assume that electric power and gas are used for those purposes. As a rule light and gas are provided by public utility companies who install the necessary connections, and piping, and charge a flat rate according to amount consumed. The rich, with elaborate electric appliances and extravagant cooking, will naturally pay much more at the end of the month. But our family, living on lower standards can only afford a much smaller consumption. To be specific it will be assumed that 20 cubic feet of gas and 50 KW-hour per month are an adequate amount. Assume this to cost $1.15 per week.

(4) HEATING REQUIREMENTS

Depending on the climate and season, there will be a certain amount of fuel needed for heating the house. Being a necessity, its cost must have a definite place in the family budget. Coal, oil, wood and electricity, are usually used for this purpose. As stated, the one chosen must be the cheapest on the market. We must also say that this commodity, chiefly needed in wintertime, need not be considered for the rest of the year.

If coal is the cheapest, it will be assumed that one ton per month is sufficient for this requirement. If the price is taken as $10 per ton, and coal is required only five months each year, the money to be set aside for this purpose will be: 10 x 5/52 = 96 cents per week.

(5) CLOTHING

Climate and season again will affect requirements and expenditures. Naturally specialists on the subject will analyze and work out requirements. Lacking such information, we shall submit a list to be taken only as basis of discussion.

Requirement for the father:

One coat each five years	Say $20 or	4.00	per year
One rain coat each ten years	Say 4 or	0.40	" "
One work suit each year	Say 2 or	2.00	" "
One good suit each year	Say 20 or	20.00	" "
Two pairs of shoes each year	Say 5 or	5.00	" "
Shirts, undershirts, and misc.	Say 6 or	6.00	" "
		———	
Total	Say	37.40	" "

Requirement for the mother:

One coat each five years	Say $15 or	3.00	per year
Two dresses each year	Say 8 or	8.00	" "
Two work dresses each year	Say 3 or	3.00	" "
Two pairs of shoes each year	Say 6 or	6.00	" "
Misc.	Say 8 or	8.00	" "
		———	
Total		28.00	" "

Requirement for each child:

One coat each two years	Say $7 or 3.50	per year
Two pairs of shoes each year	Say 5 or 5.00	” ”
Two suits each year	Say 8 or 8.00	” ”
Misc.	Say 2 or 2.00	” ”
Total for one child	Say 18.50	” ”
Total for two children	Say 37.00	” ”
Total for the family per year	102.40	per year
Total for the family per week	102.40/52 = 1.97	per week

(6) FURNITURE UTENSILS AND MISCELLANEOUS

Furniture, utensils and other articles needed in the house may require at interval of years large and necessary expenditures. We may assume a saving of $10 per year to be sufficient for such an eventuality. This is equivalent to 20 cents per week. It is unlikely that the average person is willing to set aside each week such a small amount of money for hypothetical expenditures for which there is no immediate need or desire in the family. If money is saved for this purpose, it will probably be spent for purchases entirely different from those for which the saving was originally meant. Therefore, it might be practicable for any one interested in this saving to open accounts with the EW and add small sums either weekly or monthly as he may decide. This money could then be used to buy those articles referred to above at the EW stores or at any other place when such a need arises and when the accumulated money is sufficient for such expenditure. It comes as a matter of course that while this saving is in the care of the EW it will pay the owner the same dividend paid by other banks. By this simple method the strain of heavy expenditures will be avoided or lessened. Quite true, this will not prevent the owner from finally spending his money for entirely different purposes but, nevertheless, it will represent a moral obligation in this respect which many will not so easily disregard.

From the amount of vital commodities needed and corresponding price the total expenditure of the hypothetical family may now be computed. This appears in the following tabulation:

Food	$10.18
Rent	11.50

Light and gas	1.15
Heating	0.96
Clothing	1.97
Misc.	0.20
	———
Total per week	$25.96

DEFINITION OF SCARCITY FACTOR AND INDEX OF THE COMMUNITY

At this point a new economic concept must be introduced which will have a profound influence on our mode of life. It will be called *"Scarcity Factor"*.

The preceding discussion hinged upon the theoretical need of a family of four in which the father, being a plain worker and devoid of ability and skill, could only earn the minimum wage current on the labor market. As conditions make it advisable the requirements of this hypothetical family may be changed and increased. This implies that the vital commodities in the city and in the nation in general have increased to justify such a policy which must remain the constant goal for society to strive for. The case where some vital commodity is so abundant and cheap so as to be easily purchased by a family of limited financial standing, while possible, does not usually happen and naturally in such a case that commodity will not produce economic phenomena and may be left out of the list. Quite often, however, the supply of vital commodities falls far short of minimum requirements. This may be expressed by saying that the commodities in question have a scarcity factor larger than one. *By Scarcity Factor is meant the ratio between the theoretical and actual amount available to the hypothetical family.*

Were each worker given the opportunity to earn enough to buy the theoretical amount of commodities at the current price, the simple fact that the demand so much exceeds the supply would soon raise their price. This phenomenon is due to the fact that all those who are better financially situated will exert more pressure toward the acquisition of these commodities and the plain worker will soon realize that his increased wage will not improve his standard of living. A further increase in wage, if not accompanied by a corresponding increase in supply, will be fallacious as its result would only be inflation.

The only solution, as explained before, is that of increasing supply.

This, however, cannot be done in one day or in one year, and for many products this increase will depend on the understanding and cooperation with other countries, arrangements frequently difficult to achieve. A more comprehensible and reasonable approach to the problem is that of gradually working toward this increase while efforts are being made to prevent the unjustified rising of prices. This may be achieved by keeping demand equal to or only slightly above supply, so that at all times there will be a constant pressure toward increasing supply without disrupting the economic condition of the nation. This is what is here proposed.

Granted that our goal is that of increasing the supply of vital commodities to such a point that every family in the country will be able to afford and obtain what is enumerated in the list, a more realistic attitude must be adopted in the process of that quest.

We can state the following principles:

(a) *The wages of the plain worker must be such that his purchase, added to that of all the others in his class, is sufficient to absorb any supply brought to the market after what is usually purchased by the rich has been deducted.*

(b) *The economic structure of society will be based on an index (a) which will represent the hourly wage of the unskilled laborer.*

This assumes that the unskilled laborer is engaged in profitable work the current number of hours (in this country this is represented by 40 hours per week). This wage, earned and spent by those who belong to the poorest part of society, must be sufficient to buy, without causing increase in prices, all the commodities on the market after the amount usually bought by those higher on the financial ladder has been removed. Naturally money will still be the medium of exchange, but wages and salaries, instead of being referred to as so many dollars and cents per hour, will be thought of as so many times the wage of the worker, which is equivalent to saying so many times the index a. This may not at first make an appreciable improvement in the condition of the workers, but as the prices of the various commodities remain stabilized and as the supply increases under forces later to be analyzed in the course of this study, the standard of living of the working class is bound to keep pace with the expanded supply because the index will automatically be influenced by that expansion. We are ready now to calculate the economic index of the assumed industrial city.

SCARCITY FACTOR FOR VARIOUS VITAL PRODUCTS

In pages 235 to 239 an estimate was made of the amount of vital commodities needed by a family of four belonging to the laboring class. First in the list of vital commodities is food. For a clearer understanding of the subject, let us assume only one of the many commodities of this group and, as beef happens to be the first on the Table 3 of page 271,we will take this product under our scrutiny. From that list it is found that in some particular day beef has reached the equilibrium price at a level of 38 cents per pound. At this price the hypothetical family cannot afford to buy the six pounds per week needed for its diet and must make shift with a smaller amount. It is because of this self-denial on the part of such a large percentage of the population that the price of beef has reached that particular level. If all of a sudden beef should become greatly sought because of a new discovery of health conducing quality and yet its supply does not keep pace with the increased demand, it is obvious that its price would automatically go up. This is due to the fact that, while the poor are still striving to buy at least the same amount as before, the rich, determined to obtain more, are ready to pay extra for it, and as usual will succeed in their intent because they are able to afford the higher price caused by the increased demand. The instantaneous demand curve having shifted to the right calls for a higher equilibrium price. At this price, as we know, the producers stand to make greater profits. Quite true that the incentive of profit will promote new sellers but, as time is required before their influence is felt on the market, it will take some years before the stable equilibrium price or the one where price is equal to cost is again attained. However, as long as this disparity exists, the poor are bound to be unfavorably affected.

As previously explained, for each commodity there are two kinds of equilibrium prices. First, there is an instantaneous one, determined by the intersection of the instantaneous supply and demand curves. This is not influenced by the cost of producing that commodity. If the demand is greater than supply, the price will go up, if smaller it will go down. Secondly, there is also a stable equilibrium price which is equal to cost. Whenever instantaneous forces move prices away from this condition of equilibrium, forces appear which change the direction of that trend. Now, in this hypothetical case, it is evident that the sudden increase of demand, the result of the sudden increase in the worth of beef, will force the instantaneous equilibrium away from the stable condition, and so beef will be sold at a figure considerably higher than cost, resulting in profits for the sellers. As long as this condition exists the poor will be powerless to obtain the amount they bought before, because no matter what slashes in their expenditures for other commodities, this would only push the price of beef that much higher. As the new stable equilibrium point is reached the amount reserved to the poor will tend to be the same as before. This statement is based on what was found in the second example of chapter 3, where we determined the stable equilibrium point for our Lilliputian society. It was found then that this point is influenced by the cost of production as well as by the financial pressure exerted by the poor and, therefore, is related to their wages, but is independent of their need for that particular commodity. As we are not considering for the moment any change in the relationship between wages and salaries, it is plain that the pressure exerted by the poor is bound to be approximately the same as before, which will tend to reduce their share of beef to the previous level. But the new economic concept introduced in our study as well as the influence of the EW will change all this.

INFLUENCE OF THE EW IN THE NEW STRUCTURE OF SOCIETY

(1) SCARCITY FACTOR FOR FOOD.

Earlier in this chapter a general description of the EW was made and it was stated that this organization, besides the task of collecting and caring for inheritances, uses this wealth for the benefit of the population in general. This will be the special task of the second group of the EW. Let us now consider some of the activities of a special division of this group which will be called "PRICE STA-BILIZATION DIVISION" as it will aid in the analysis of scarcity factor and index of the assumed industrial city. As later explained in the text, this division will have on its list of customers the names of all those who want to avail themselves of the services of the EW. This list will include the vast majority of the poor, and will include also others who are better financially situated, this because the services of the EW are extended to all who want to join, irrespective of position and financial standing. From the number of persons on the list and from the amount of commodities available on the market, the employees of the Price Stabilization Division or PS for short will know the quantity that can be sold to its customers. As a good portion is purchased directly at the sources of production, and, therefore, at a price lower than the one charged by retail stores, and because of the many economies introduced in caring and transporting these products, we can assume that a decrease in price to the ultimate consumer will be obtained. This fact by itself will tend to increase demand, which is tantamount to consumption. The lower price of the commodities will also represent a great incentive on the part of the public in general, especially of the lower and middle classes, to make purchases through the EW and thereby receive the advantages it will be able to secure, as outlined later in the text. This fact will tend to stabilize the price, because if too high, more people will buy through the EW, and retailers' profits would be adversely affected even with the increased price.

An additional factor tending to stabilize prices on the market is the relationship between wages and prices of commodities as stated in a previous section. This relationship will be better explained later in this chapter, but it may be said now that if prices should climb, wages would also be affected, and would tend to decrease any unjust profit derived from such manipulations.

Some of the increased demand for vital commodities will be made by a minority of the well-to-do class who may decide to take advantage of the EW's reduction in price, but the vast majority will be represented by those in the lower brackets of the economic structure of society, and this is in line with the aims of the EW. As a good percentage of purchases is made from retail stores, an increased demand will also mean more business and profit for the small capitalist, who thus will regard the EW as a customer rather than competitor.

Under its policy the EW will buy beef from retail stores at a somewhat lower price than charged to the public and likewise from slaughter houses for considerably less. The elimination of un-necessary middlemen, the better facilities of transportation and care will be other factors that will lower the average cost. This will be the price of beef charged by the EW. The amount available, divided by the number of rightful customers, will give the quota each person on the list may purchase at that price. Later in this chapter we shall explain what is meant by rightful customer. However, as aforesaid this amount will probably be considerably smaller than the required theoretical one. The ratio (f) between the theoretical and actual amount of beef as previously defined will represent the scarcity factor of this commodity. In general, it will always be a number larger than one.

As the new demand for beef develops in the community, it is evident that the retail stores will have less to sell to the EW as more is being bought by the rich at the higher price. If possible, the EW will seek to make up the difference by buying more from the slaughter houses. At any rate it will never enter into competition with the rich. This means that the EW will never try to buy from the stores more than they are willing to sell. Hence, because of the lack of competition, the price will not climb much higher than the assumed level of 38 cents per pound. But as there is less beef to be distributed to its customers, the scarcity factor will automatically increase. Of course much will be done by the EW to influence the increase in supply, but as time is required for this, the poor must get along with the reduced quota for beef. As the profit from the additional demand does not materialize, a greater return can only be obtained by increasing supply, and since the scarcity factor for beef is so much higher than one, which indicates that the EW is ready and willing to buy additional amount if brought to the market, this fact will encourage the increase in production with an evident gain for the poor. This readiness on the part of the EW to buy those vital products with a scarcity factor larger than one, will represent a powerful leverage and a basic force in the new structure of society.

The theoretical requirement of beef, assumed six pounds per week, divided by the scarcity factor will give the amount that the hypothetical family of four can buy. This figure multiplied by the price charged by the EW will show what this family must spend for that commodity.

Similar reasoning can then be made for all the other commodities in the list on page 268, yielding at the end the total number of calories received by the hypothetical family and their cost.

While each commodity will have its individual scarcity factor which will reveal the degree of deficiency in the locality, a scarcity factor can also be calculated for the food products taken as a whole. This will be the ratio between the theoretical and actual calories received.

In the table on page 268, the available amount of each commodity for the hypothetical family is listed in column 10, and in column 11 the various scarcity factors appear. In columns 12 and 13 the calories and corresponding expenditures at the current price established by the EW are also shown, and thus their sum represents what the family actually receives of food value in calories, and the corresponding cost. The ratio between the theoretical requirement and the calories received gives the scarcity factor for food in the locality under consideration. This is given by: $77,295/60,980 = 1.23$. The sum of all the items of the 13th column gives the total cost of vital commodities and in this case is represented by $8.22 per week.

(2) SCARCITY FACTOR FOR RENT

The second item on the list of vital commodities is rent. It will be the duty of the "Price Stabilization Division" to study the civic housing conditions. It will hold authority to condemn all houses which do not meet minimum requirements of livability. The number of inhabitable houses as well as the number of those having the requisite facilities and comfort must be known. This study will naturally omit the homes of the well-to-do part of the population. The rent for these homes and apartments as well as the number of families and individuals living in these places must be found. Suppose the following facts have been determined:

8,000 families, representing a population of 40,000, live in tenements and homes and pay an average rent of $10 per month. Their dwellings, being of the miserable kind, have been condemned and scheduled to be replaced as quickly as possible.

4,000 families, representing a population of 20,000, live in tenements and homes and pay an average of $20 per month. Their dwellings, while somewhat better than those previously considered, have also been condemned and are to be replaced in the natural course of improvement of the city.

3,000 families, representing a population of 13,000, live in apartments and homes and pay an average of $30 per month. Their dwellings have been considered passable and their replacement may have to wait for the time when better and higher standards will measure the worth of a home.

1,000 families, representing a population of 4,000 live in homes and apartments that are considered good and pay an average rent of $50 per month.

The total number of people considered is 77,000 out of 100,000 population of the city. It is quite likely that many of these families are the owners of their homes and, therefore, the question of rent no longer holds in their case. But practically any owner is usually faced by expenditures tending to improve or maintain the well being of his home. These expenditures, of course, may be classified as rent. However, for two individuals living in the same kind of dwelling of which one is the owner of the house while the other is not, the constant amount of rent that must be paid by the latter is usually far greater than what the other will spend for improving his house. For one the rent will represent not only the necessary repairs of the house but the return of the capital invested. Be it as it may, in classifying these houses which are occupied by the owners the determining factor will be their potential rent on the market rather than the actual expenditure made for maintenance and improvement.

In analyzing the list it is found that 8,000 families with an average of five members per family pay an average of $10 a month for houses or apartments which are unfit to live in. This is also true for the 4,000 families who pay $20 a month. These hovels and tenements must eventually be replaced by suitable houses and apartments. It is taken for granted that these families are on the EW list, and this means that out of 77,000 only 4,000 persons live in quarters fulfilling the ideal requirement. The others, to a greater or lesser extent, are not housed on that standard.

The scarcity factor for any one commodity is represented by the ratio of theoretical to actual amount received by the hypothetical family. Assuming that the enjoyment is in proportion to the amount spent it can be said that the scarcity factor in this instance is given by the ratio of what must be paid for the good and comfortable home and what must be paid for the poor one or $f = 50/10 = 5$.

It must be emphasized that the rents shown in the list represent the average of what is being spent for this purpose by large sections of the population approximately of the same income group. Indeed in a large city as the one considered, not four but many variations of rent can be found. Each is influenced both by the worth of the house and by the amount of demand and as such, even though rents in many instances are unreasonably high, no one should have the authority to influence the owners as to what they should charge for their property as this would infringe upon human rights. The EW, taking conditions as found, will calculate the scarcity factor as previously shown where $50 represents the average rent paid by the moderately well-to-do on the EW list and $10 the average paid by the very poor also on the list. As such the weekly expenditures of the hypothetical family will be: $(10 \times 12)/52 = 2.31$. Under the influence of the new forces injected in the life of society, a large building program will be sponsored which will add new homes as time goes on. As a result the supply and demand will go through a continuous phase of readjustment which may call for different equilibrium prices from those assumed at the beginning of this study. But, irrespective of these equilibrium prices, the scarcity factor at any one time will be given by the ratio of the average rent paid by the well to do class on the EW list and the average rent paid by the poor, that is to say by a large section of population receiving the minimum wage.

While special interest centers about calculating the scarcity factor for rent, it must be borne in mind that many of these houses are being bought, not for speculation, but for the purpose of retention. The amount that must be paid for amortization plus interest, being equivalent to rent, must also be included in the calculation of the index. It will be assumed that the house will be completely paid up in a given number of years. By assuming the current interest rate charged by the banks, the monthly expenditure becomes related to the worth of the house. If this amount comes within the limits of the rent paid by the poor, it is natural that this house should be included with those that bear an influence in the calculation of the scarcity factor.

A person who wishes to buy a given article and has the money required, or is willing to borrow the money and thereby commit future earnings to that purchase, becomes a potential customer. Among the population there is always a certain percentage who are desirous or in need of a specific article and, therefore, become potential buyers. Mr. Smith may need a house today, and after its purchase will naturally leave the list of potential buyers, probably for many years. Tomorrow Mr. Brown takes his turn, and Mr. Green after him, from which one concludes that out of the total population there will always be a number seeking a house. Naturally, this study is not concerned with the mansions of the rich, but with the modest homes of the working people. Part of the EW program is to see that the houses of the poor measure up to a proper standard of livability, and that houses not meeting those requirements be condemned and replaced. Now the cost of a house can be divided into various expenditures. There is the cost of the material used in its building, the wages of the bricklayers, carpenters, plumbers, electricians, painters, and so forth. Besides the cost of the land on which the house will stand must be included as well the salary of the architect, designer, and contractor who draw up the plan and supervise the work, and last, if not least, we must take into account the profit of the corporation or the business man who finances the construction. As these persons make a living from building houses, they have a right to a sufficient return for their work, but yet, while the workers earn wages like any employee in a factory, the entrepreneurs are in a position of making great profits or incurring great losses. The purpose of the EW naturally is that of preventing either excessive losses or profits and to stabilize prices at a level equal to cost, taking into account the just wages and salaries of those engaged at that construction. Due to the swift strides in technology and to the many devices that cut unnecessary cost, there is a possibility of lowering costs as time goes on, but despite all kind of economies, the price of a house is always bound to be considerably more than the other commodities needed by the hypothetical family. In general, the head of a family in need of a house is seldom in a position to pay cash. He may, however, have sufficient credit with a bank to borrow the money, but, if not, he would find it difficult to finance that purchase. If he is on the EW list, has a steady job, and can give a good account of himself as to industriousness, honesty, and ability to work, he may secure the needed credit from the EW, who will be responsible to the bank for his loan. The amount of interest he will pay for that loan, as well as the necessary expenditures for keeping the house in good condition, will correspond to the rent anyone else pays for his dwelling, and, therefore, this expenditure will be included in the list for the calculation of the index. This is to say that the family will be one of the 8,000 previously considered.

It has been shown that the scarcity factor of this vital commodity is 5. This being a clear indication of the large need of the population, it may be surmised that any extensive building undertaken in the country at large will be profitable to all those who engage in this business. The EW, on its part, besides being willing to buy many of the homes sponsored by private initiative, will become the contractor of a large building program of its own, especially in those localities where private interest is lacking. These homes, naturally will be sold at cost. This in turn will stabilize prices and prevent wild speculations in this field. Since the EW holds authority to condemn building below minimum requirements of decency, and to promote the construction of better quarters, suitable homes for the poor will become more and more available as time goes on.

Returning to our city of 100,000 we find that there are 8,000 families (see page 246) in the lowest income group, who are living in places that have been condemned for unsanitation and squalor, 4,000 families who live in somewhat better houses also condemned and to be replaced, 3,000 more in better quarters for which the need for replacement is less pressing. Of course, a priority list will be made of the houses that must be torn down immediately, but this must not be undertaken unless an extensive building program is carried out to take care of the families which otherwise would be made homeless. As the building program in general becomes a reality new homes and apartments with modern facilities will continually be made available to the public. These naturally will be in great demand, and, therefore, influence their price or rent. As said, the EW will foster its own building program, and by charging the minimum price or rent compatible with the cost sustained will restrain the rising in price of all the houses in general. Be it as it may, it stands to reason that the new homes will be sought and obtained by those families who previously were on the border line, and specifically by the 3,000 families who previously paid an average rent of $30 a month. With the increase of the index these families more than any other will be able to pay the new rent. But as they move into the new homes, their former homes will become available to people of lesser means and the process will be felt throughout the line until all the 8,000 who previously were living in squalid hovels will finally occupy better lodgings. As the march of progress will be continuous, in time all the condemned houses will be replaced and the entire population will enjoy the comfort and ease of modern living. As the poorest slums vanish to make way for model quarters, and as the number of better housed families increases, it is easy to see that the scarcity factor will also tend to decrease, and the amount available to the hypothetical family will go up.

(3) SCARCITY FACTOR FOR UTILITIES

The third item on the list of vital commodities is gas and electricity, assumed the cheapest of their kind in the locality in question. The necessity of these commodities is obvious, and any family, no matter how poor, depends on their availability, otherwise its standard of living would be greatly reduced. In the study of the theoretical amount needed by the hypothetical family (page 237) it was found that this is 20 cubic feet of gas and 50 KW-hour per month, which would cost $1.15 per week. However, if this quantity was used by each family in the city, the chances are that the price would rise on account of scarcity. An understanding with the power company might overcome that limitation. If additional improvements are necessary to bring the supply to the required amount, ways and means should be found for that purpose. In the meantime, assuming that the scarcity factor is 1.11 and that the price of the 20 cubic feet of gas and 50 kilowatt-hour is $5.00, the allowance for this vital commodity will be $5.00/1.11 = \$4.50$ per month or $1.04 per week.

Let us explain this availability of light and gas as prerequisite for being considered a vital commodity. Even in this country there are many communities without light or gas. Even though they may have substitutes such as kerosene, coal, etc., it is evident that in this respect the living conditions of these people are lower than those living in a city. We are not interested in raising the standard of living of the entire population of a nation to a prearranged level. Such a goal, even if desirable, would be impracticable. Interest centers in raising it to the level permitted by the wealth and the facilities found in the community itself. In other words, to install electric light, gas, and other adjuncts of modern life in every small town and village of the land would involve an undertaking such that only future progress and technological advancement can hope to achieve. The facilities for heating, lighting and cooking, as found in the community, must be taken as a base, and their cost must be the one used in calculating the index. If inventions or other fortuitous circumstances should in time introduce into a small town or village a new convenience or commodity already enjoyed by the population of a large city, it is natural that at first it should have a very high scarcity factor. This, however, will tend to decrease with greater availability.

Assume a small village in the mountains far away from important centers, where people have only kerosene for lighting purposes. It is used by the rich as well as by the poor. Under these circumstances the price of kerosene will be taken as a base in calculating the index of the village. Now let a private enterprise install a power line between two distant cities, which passes near the village. Rich villagers may find it convenient to link up with that line at their own expense. As the price of this commodity will be very high, it will not be included in the list of vital commodities. Kerosene being the leading commodity for lighting, its price will remain the base in the determination of the index. Eventually, however, the company that installed the power line may decide to link up the village, and will incur expenses which it hopes to be covered by new customers.

Due to the high rate charged at first, only the well-to-do will avail themselves of this convenience, while the poor will continue using kerosene. But as the consumption of electric light increases and the rates abate, power will become cheaper. As a result of this the seller of kerosene will gradually increase its price in order to make it worth his while to remain in business. As the price of kerosene increases in relation to that of the electric power, a point will be reached when the kerosene becomes more expensive. It is evident that when such a condition is reached, electricity must be used in the determination of the index. At any rate, this increase in price of kerosene can only go on for a relatively short time. As the competition of the electric company will finally prove too strong for the seller of kerosene, and the increase in price of his commodity will not produce the desired profit, sooner or later he may have to withdraw from the market.

(4) SCARCITY FACTOR FOR FUEL

In our study of the theoretical amount needed by the hypothetical family (page 238) we found it to be one ton each month for five months. If the price of coal is $10 per ton, the expenditure will be 96 cents per week. The chances are that if such an amount was used by each family in the city that a shortage would develop. This automatically would increase the price of coal. We must, therefore, assign an amount that will not produce such an increase. The method will be similar to that used for food products. The EW will buy on the open market that quantity not wanted by the rich, which means in practice the amount the stores will sell at a reduced price to the EW, and, in addition, a good deal will be purchased at the mines if feasible. From the supply on hand and the number of families to be served a scarcity factor for coal will be obtained. Assuming that this factor is 1.43 and that the cost to the EW is $10 per ton, the amount the EW will allow to each family will be:

$$1.0/1.43 = 0.7 \text{ tons per month,}$$

and the cost will be:

$$10 \times 0.7 \times 5/52 = 67 \text{ cents per week.}$$

Here again it will be the EW policy to see that the supply is gradually increased so that all may have the necessary amount of coal.

(5) SCARCITY FACTOR FOR CLOTHING

The fifth item of the vital commodities list is clothing. On page 238 we have given a tentative list of the theoretical amount of clothing needed by this family. In mentioning that there would be different requirements for different localities, we intended the list to suit this particular industrial city of 100,000. The list indicates that the family should receive for its well being a sufficient amount of clothing to correspond to a weekly expenditure of $1.97. But as before, the chances are that if all workers should buy that amount, a shortage would develop which would increase the price of clothing in general. This can again be prevented by having the EW buy the clothing otherwise unsold, and after assigning a scarcity factor, sell it to its customers. Assume that the average factor for clothing comes to 1.33. Following the same reasoning previously outlined, the weekly cost of clothing to the hypothetical family will be set at 1.97/1.33 = $1.48. As for other vital commodities, the EW will seek to increase the supply, so that all will eventually be able to buy the prescribed amount.

(6) SCARCITY FACTOR FOR FURNITURE, UTENSILS AND MISCELLANEOUS

The sixth item of the list is made up of furniture, utensils, and other articles necessary in the house. There is outlined on page 239 a procedure suitable for the purchase of these kinds of commodities. It appeared that an expenditure of $10 per year, to be spent at the EW store, would be sufficient. This expense, borne by the family, must be included in calculating the index.

This item, however, being made up of many different types of articles, does not lend itself to an easy determination of the scarcity factor. A simpler method will be that of varying such allowance ($10 per year) in the inverse proportion of the average price of commodities in general. For example, choose as a basis the average price of commodities during the month of April 1954. If at a later date the average price has risen 20 per cent, this indicates that a shortage has developed to justify the increase. Since the amount assigned for this item has not been changed ($10 per year), we must conclude that our family at this later date has been forced to buy fewer articles than at the time used as a base, and that even this self-denial on the part of the poor has not been sufficient to stabilize the average price, which, as indicated has gone up 20 per cent. As the stabilization of prices in general is one of the primary goals of the EW, the demand for such articles must be purposely decreased in order to lower the level of that price, and this will be done by assigning to the hypothetical family less than $10 per year.

Of course, a study will be made of the causes that tend to increase prices, and the necessary remedies adopted. As this is accomplished the allotment will again be raised to $10 per year, and may be further increased if the situation changes in the opposite direction. For the present it will be assumed that $10 per year is sufficient to spend for this item and this is equivalent to a weekly expenditure of 10/52 = 20 cents.

With this information on hand we are now in a position to know what must be bought by the hypothetical family, and to calculate the index of the industrial city in consideration.

			Scarcity factor	Actual weekly expenditure
Item	(1)	Food products	1.235	8.22
	(2)	Rent on the house	5.00	2.31
	(3)	Light and gas	1.11	1.04
	(4)	Fuel in winter	1.43	0.67
	(5)	Clothing	1.33	1.48
	(6)	Utensils and furniture	1.00	0.20
Total for vital commodities				$13.92 per week

In this list many necessary items are not included as, for instance, traveling to and from work, amusements, medicines, taxes, and so forth. As explained in later chapters, sickness among the poor must be taken care of by society by providing hospitals and medical care, but there are minor indispositions which must be treated by simple remedies available at the nearby druggist. Besides, money must be spent for taxes, to arouse in each citizen a proper responsibility for civic and national welfare.

We realize that throughout this analysis prices of commodities and needs of the hypothetical family are only approximate, and in many cases at considerable variance from actual requirements. In a work of this kind, which is intended to include the population of all nations, rich and poor, we cannot expect to give an accurate set of figures which, if valid for one place, would be misleading for another. Our aim is only to convey ideas. Therefore, prices as well as requirements have been assumed only with the purpose of making such ideas clear to the reader.

Returning to our subject, we shall assume that all these expenditures are not larger than 15 per cent of the actual amount spent for vital commodities: i.e. 13.92 x 0.15 = 2.09 so that the total expenditure per week will be: 13.92 + 2.09 = 16.01.

If 40 hours is the accepted number of working hours per week, the minimum hourly wage as well as the index of our city of 100,000 population at the time such estimation is made will be given by:

$$16.01 / 40 = 40 \text{ cents}$$

In considering the amount that the unskilled laborer should receive as wage, it is natural that the proper choice should be $16.01 which takes into account the actual economic condition in the city rather than what the laborer needs to purchase the theoretical amount of vital commodities at the current price. If we allow more, the laborers, seeking to secure more commodities, will only push the prices up without obtaining the desired result; if we allow less, prices of commodities will fall. This, in turn, will affect the business structure of the community or nation, and will tend to decrease the supply. Thus the choice made seems the best in view of the condition of scarcity prevailing in the community. However, as the potential demand will always be there, and represented by the willingness of the EW to purchase larger amounts of commodities if brought to market, this pressure in time will increase the supply as many sellers, in the hope of securing larger profits, will do their best to achieve that result.

Only by increasing the supply will people be able to make more money. It is evident that those manufacturers who have pushed their production to the very limit (as, for instance, to point Q_4 shown in Fig. 17, page 228a, cannot hope to increase that profit as long as the price remains stationary. It may be said that, conditions being as they are, they have reached the maximum obtainable profit and as a larger production on their part would be detrimental to society because of the high marginal cost curve of their factory, they have no right to expect more. But the opportunity of larger profits will still be open to all who either start new enterprises or increase the output of their factories if their production is less than Q_4. It will also be open to all those who have an exceptionally high cost curve. By decreasing costs and by effecting economies, higher profits can be made at that price. Such aims will be encouraged and promoted by the EW.

Once the index has been calculated and published, this must become by law the minimum wage paid any person per hour for work upon which his subsistence and that of his family depends. Any other kind of work performed outside the established relation of employer and employee naturally must be a matter of agreement between the parties concerned. With the passing of time better products and conveniences may be included in the calculation of the index, and there will be no limit to the progress that may be obtained by applying the principle described and analyzed above. With the raising of the index, inheritance will also increase. This will be beneficial to the wealthiest part of the population and, as there will be general interest, rich and poor alike, in seeing that the index of their community increases, a greater degree of cooperation will arise among all classes of society in the attainment of the common goal.

As income from inheritances shrinks it may seem that this would prevent the EW from performing its humanitarian task. First of all before this effect is felt (a substantial decrease in revenue), most of the groundwork for progress will have been laid, supply increased, houses built, inefficiency in industry and in other branches of human activity lessened or eliminated, and the initial necessity of large expenditures will be greatly reduced. However, the revenue of the government is not derived only from inheritances. After all, inheritances are wealth accumulated by individuals, and are insignificant compared to the expenditure necessary to maintain the government of a nation which, as at present, must rely on taxes collected from all its people. As the index of a community rises, and more is awarded to the beneficiaries, what is lost by society will be too small to make an appreciable difference, and as new needs arise, the government will still retain the privilege of raising taxes until the necessary amount for its efficient discharge of its duties is assured. At any rate, irrespective of the share of society derived from inheritances that come to be divided, this will tend to decrease taxes, and, therefore, will be indirectly beneficial to the general public.

GENERALIZATION UPON INDEX AND WAGES

Assume now that the laborer, heading the hypothetical family, works 40 hours a week, the average period spent by the population engaged in remunerative work. His wages must be at least $16.01/40 = 40$ cents per hour if he is to be able to buy all the vital commodities available on the market. From our definition of index, given on page 240, it appears also that the index of our industrial city is given by the same amount, 40 cents, and represents the minimum wage per hour any person must receive to make a livelihood for himself and his family. As said, the worker may or may not be the head of a family, and the family may be made up of fewer or more than four. In order to choose a base that relates the work done with the wages received, we have chosen the figure of four as closest to the average family in a nation. However, once this choice is made and the relationship established, the number of persons composing the family of any laborer has no longer a social significance, and concerns only the laborer himself.

It is just and proper that wages be related only to the amount and quality of work performed, independently of the worker's family obligations. If he is unmarried, his wage will be larger than needed, if he has a large family it will be less. Since either theoretically performs the same amount and quality of work, it is natural that both should receive the same wage. It will be up to the worker with a large family to acquire sufficient skill to earn more. If his mental or physical capabilities are limited, and he is, therefore, unable to provide for his family, his case must be dealt with separately, and aid given to him in some other form than that of increased wages. As a general rule, society cannot and should not pay him more than he is actually worth. To be sure, usually large families have more than one member engaged in remunerative employment and by combining these resources, the family can add to the low wages of its head. Additional clarifications of a technical nature need be considered at this point. These will be presented in the following note 6-2.

NOTE 6-2

To better clarify the interrelation of index and distribution of commodities to the people, assume that 100 individuals of a small community have their name in the EW list. Of these 20 are bachelors, 25 represent a family of two, 25 more represent a family of four, the remaining 30 represent a family of eight. The total number of people on the EW list will be given by the following addition:

Total on the EW list = 20 x 1 + 25 x 2 + 25 x 4 + 30 x 4 = 290

out of a total population of 410.

It will be noticed that while all the individuals will be allowed to include the complete number of persons composing their family, those with a large one will only be allowed four and no more. This may seem absurd and unreasonably unjust especially for those who earn the minimum wage, yet there are important reasons for this policy. If the applicant is a common laborer, his wage is only sufficient for a family of four and, therefore, even if allowed, he could not possibly have the necessary money to buy more. As previously seen, if he has no other income but his wage, help must be given through charitable organizations and the like. If the individual has more than minimum wage, he will have money to buy additional commodities at the regular store. However, if his entire wage is not sufficient for that purpose, his case again must be referred to charitable organizations. In any case it would be unethical to allow him more than the normal amount for four as this would detract from all the others on the list. As previously explained, society should not be concerned with his private affairs and it will be up to him to earn more. It is understood that if any one of these families has more than one person engaged in remunerative work, the family may be thought of as made of several parts. Each working component may then assume the responsibility of providing for one of those parts. If the individual has a family smaller than four, it is evident that he will have more than the necessary amount to provide for his family even if he should receive the minimum wage. In so far that what is allowed by the EW does not come up to the theoretical requirement, he unquestionably would buy more from the EW if allowed. This again would be unethical as it would detract from all the others on the list. If he wants to buy more than what is allowed by the EW, he must make the additional purchases from the regular stores. With these ideas clear in mind we can proceed with our analysis.

From the foregoing the number of basic families in the assumed village will be given by: $290/4 = 72.5$. Let us now consider the distribution of beef, the first in the list of food products (table 3). The theoretical quantity of beef that should be consumed by the hypothetical family is given by 6 pounds per week or approximately 1.5 pounds per person. Approximately refers to the fact that different people have different requirements (page 236), which will be disregarded in this study. $6 \times 72.5 = 435$ # represents then the theoretical amount of beef for this village. Assume now that what is actually secured from retail stores and slaughter houses amounts to only 350 pounds and, therefore, this is what will be actually sold to those on the list. $435/350 = 1.243$ will represent the scarcity factor for beef. Again $350/290 = 1.205$ # will represent the amount per capita to be sold to those on the list. What will be secured by the families on the list will be given by the following table:

$$
\begin{array}{llll}
\text{Families of one} & = 20 \times 1 \times 1.205 & = & 24.1 \text{ pounds} \\
\text{\textquotedblright \quad \textquotedblright two} & = 25 \times 2 \times 1.205 & = & 60.4 \text{ \textquotedblright} \\
\text{\textquotedblright \quad \textquotedblright four} & = 25 \times 4 \times 1.205 & = & 120.7 \text{ \textquotedblright} \\
\text{\textquotedblright \quad \textquotedblright eight} & = 30 \times 4 \times 1.205 & = & 144.8 \text{ \textquotedblright} \\
\end{array}
$$

$$\text{Total} \quad 350.0 \text{ \textquotedblright}$$

Let us consider the problem still from another angle. The EW may be confronted at times by the case where not all its purchases find ready customers among those on the list. The fact that all sections of society may join does not necessarily mean that all will buy all that is offered to them. In previous discussions we assumed that beef could become very much sought by the public, yet the opposite might also be true. If this were the case, the sale of beef would naturally drop and as a consequence more would be offered to the EW. If this offer was still within the limits permitted by the rule adopted by the EW, this extra amount would be bought by the Community Manager. However, the unwillingness to buy beef might also develop among those on the EW list, some of which might also belong to the well-to-do class. Confronted by such a decrease in demand, what should be the policy of the EW?

Due to the decreased demand developing within the public in general, say that the offer of beef made by the various stores in town increases from 350# to 380# per week. Assuming this increase within the limits permitted by the rule, the Community Manager will buy this extra amount. As a result the scarcity factor for beef will drop from 1.243 to $435/380 = 1.145$ and the quantity allotted to each individual on the list will become $380/290 = 1.31$ # instead of 1.20#. As a result of this change two important phenomena will occur:

(1) The price of beef will not be greatly affected because the total supply of beef has been completely disposed of and sold.

(2) The index of the community will increase because of the increased supply to those on the EW list.

However, if many on that list belong to the upper class, it is understandable that, due to the new appraisal of the worth of beef, some and probably many will prefer to buy other kinds of meat at the regular stores in preference to the beef offered by the EW. As seen, the index and corresponding wages allow those on the list to buy only up to 1.31# which has been derived by dividing the total amount on hand by the total number of customers, but if many among them do not buy the allotted amount, it is evident that a good portion of beef will be left unsold in the care of the EW. We can be sure that many among the poor would gladly buy this extra amount, but they are prevented because financially unable. In so far that the scarcity factor is still above one, it is important that this extra supply be absorbed by those in need and, therefore, a correction factor must be introduced to permit this absorption. This correction factor will be called f_1, and will be changed by the Community Manager to meet the particular condition found in his community.

Say that only 260 people show any willingness to buy beef at the PS store. To promote the complete sale of the beef on hand the amount per capita must be: $380/260 = 1.46\#$. $1.31\#$ or the amount when all are included in the list divided by $1.46\#$ or 0.897 will represent the correction for beef and the official scarcity factor will become:

$1.145 \times 0.897 = 1.027$. This fact, naturally, will increase further the wages and the index within the community.

All this has been introduced to better explain the meaning of correction factor. In actual cases the number of people willing to buy more of a given commodity will not be so easily determined. Again, if the purchases during a period of sale drop to abnormally low levels, this is no proof that they will not increase in a subsequent period. If correction was made for every variation in the size of demand, the index and corresponding wages would have to be changed more often than justified and in turn tend to upset the business stability within the community. Due to the facilities of the PS stores, whenever commodities are left unsold, these will be stored for the time when the demand will again increase. It is natural, when the drop in sale becomes permanent that steps should be taken to correct this condition. This will be done by changing the correction factor a small percentage at any one time. This will gradually reestablish the equilibrium between supply and demand and the resulting index will represent more closely the actual economic condition in the community. In a future study it will be explained how commodities which tend to accumulate within one place will be exported to others as this will tend to equalize the economic condition within large bodies of population in the country.

Now besides the unskilled laborer all workers and employees will be affected by the variation of the index. Indeed their wages or salaries instead of being thought of in dollars, francs or other currencies, will be thought of as a percentage higher than that of the unskilled laborer, so that what each receives will be indicated by 1.0a, 1.1a, 1.2a, 3.0a, 10a as the case may be and will be determined by his skill and usefulness to society. As the value of (a) rises, the wage of the unskilled laborer will be directly affected, and likewise the earnings of the others. Their increase, however, will not be in the same proportion as that of the index (a). All this, however, will be discussed later in greater detail.

We may now ask the following question. What will be the influence exerted by the index on the economic structure of a community? It is easy to foresee (or anticipate) the antagonism and distrust on the part of all who do not comprehend the functioning of this concept, and on this account may seek to prevent its adoption on the theory that wages and salaries should reach their natural equilibrium established by the law of supply and demand. The difference between the two philosophies is, however, only on the surface, as both concepts take the law of supply and demand as fundamental.

By closely following the process of the determination of the index it is clear that this fundamental law has been taken into account. The larger the number of persons under the care of the EW, the smaller will be the index for a definite amount of supply on the market. Take for instance any vital commodity and assume the price which has been determined by the law of supply and demand. By this the rich element in the population has obtained the amount it desires and the poor, having bid the limit of their resources, must take what is left. Through the competition of sellers the price of this commodity will stabilize at a certain level. The EW does not change this equilibrium. Indeed the rich are still permitted to buy as much as before, and the poor, receiving a definite wage linked to the index a and, therefore, to the various scarcity factors, remain as usual stranded with what is left. If the supply for some particular reason should decrease, the rich would still be able to buy what they want and the poor, having their wages decreased, must again put up with the amount left, naturally smaller than before. Again if the number of persons under the care of the EW should increase and the amount bought remains the same, the amount per capita will be less, which also will be reflected by a larger index.

From what has been said it may seem that there is no substantial difference between the two methods, since in either case the poor can only buy what has been left by the rich, and because of the often high scarcity factor are confined to a low standard of living. This, indeed, is the case. However, in the present set-up of society the economic equilibrium point tends to remain stationary with fluctuations which represent periods of prosperity and depression. In the new system the economic forces are such that the equilibrium point is no longer stable, but increases with time more rapidly than it would be expected under natural conditions, and while there will be oscillations about that point, these will be too small to bring wild periods of prosperity or devastating depressions. Independently of these oscillations the fact remains that the continuous rise of the stable equilibrium point will mean also an increase in supply, and the lot of the poor as well as the rich is bound to improve. And this is accomplished without forcible methods or infringements of human rights and liberties.

Reference has been made to the fact that the index (a) will reflect the amount of supply on the market and will be the connecting link between the available supply to the poor and the wage needed for its absorption. It may seem at first that a rapid change in supply would affect salaries and wages to such an extent to cause confusion in the business world. But, as we shall explain now, this will not be so. In chapter nine an example is given of the method used by the EW in buying commodities from stores. It is explained therein that no purchase can be made larger than a predeterminate percentage above a previous period of time, such as a month, a year, or other desired intervals. This percentage will be chosen by the high authorities in the zone and at the capital. Thereby, should the supply increase at too rapid a rate, and thus endanger the economic structure of the country, the EW will only buy the extra percentage permitted by the authorities and no more. Since it represents the vast majority of the population, many commodities will run the risk of going unsold, which will tend to lower their prices with the resulting effect that the supply will be regulated and controlled. Wages being related to supply will also increase at a regulated pace so that, barring unforeseen causes the cost of labor will be known, not only for the present, but also for a foreseeable period of time. This will help manufacturers to estimate their cost curve with a better approximation than at present, a fact that will place business on a more solid foundation.

There may be times, however, when the supply of some vital commodity, due to disrupting factors immaterial to this study, tends to decrease. As a result the corresponding scarcity factor will rise and this will mean that a smaller quota will be assigned to the poor. As the element of competition among the classes will be averted or greatly reduced, the price of the commodity will only go moderately higher and no more. Now the fact that the plain laborer will have to pay a slightly higher price for the small amount of commodity will mean that his expenditure will be substantially the same as before and as such his wage will not be materially altered by the offsetting factor. This will serve to stabilize conditions in general. It is true that now the poor will receive less of that commodity, but, as explained previously, this condition cannot be helped as long as the supply remains at the subnormal level, and must be blamed upon that offsetting factor. In other words, wages will move only in a regulated manner, and will not be affected by small changes in prices, which as seen, will also move within narrow channels.

Now the fact that the poor must do with what is left by the well--to-do is a characteristic of present-day society. The basic difference in the two modes of life is that, while at present there is no incentive or advantage in increasing supply, this incentive will be very strongly felt in the new order because it will take momentum from the very nature of men. Being spontaneous and advantageous to all, it will have a greater prospect of success. The presence of the EW, as explained, dampens the fluctuations of prices, and can be compared to the resistance exerted by a fly-wheel to changes of rotation. To be sure even with the EW prices will vary, but their changes will be small and influenced only by actual conditions of the market. That this should be a goal of any well-wishing citizen goes without saying.

We find at present cases where, by decreasing the supply profits can be made larger, as the price will reach such a level that the difference between the new price and cost multiplied by the quantity manufactured and sold increases with the decrease in sale. The commodity, in other words, is made unduly inelastic (see Fig. 11 of page 219. This obviously is an antisocial manipulation that must be restrained, no matter what the influence of the perpetrators. The EW, with its great financial power, will see that no monopoly of this kind is tolerated, and if such a practice is adopted by unscrupulous manufacturers, it will see that the new enterprises get their share of the sale.

Once the production of vital commodities increases, wages will go up to allow the lower classes to absorb the additional supply. This in turn will increase the cost of production and should prices remain the same, the profit of the manufacturers would automatically decrease. But the law of supply and demand will establish a new equilibrium price. What will be the profit of the individual manufacturer is difficult to foretell because it will depend on the relationship between his new cost and the price of the commodity on the market. Referring to our diagram on page 228a, we can safely say that for any manufacturer whose output is much smaller than the one which produces the maximum profit (point 4 on our curve), his increased cost due to higher wages will be more than balanced from his increased sale. This is not so apparent for the manufacturer who has already reached the production represented by point 4. An additional output on his part may cost him more than what he receives because of the higher equilibrium price. Thus his final profit will hinge on what this price will finally be. It can be said, however, on his account, that he will derive the greatest profit permissible by the new order, which, as previously mentioned, may and may not be as large as before. In the eighth chapter examples have been shown in which, for definite increases in wages, the new equilibrium price is calculated and by that the relative position of various manufacturers could be easily found.

As to the industries engaged in the manufacture of non-vital commodities, it may seem on the surface that they will be more adversely affected than those producing the vital types, as their cost curve increases without corresponding rise in sales. But as already stated this difference is only superficial. As the index increases all who previously were on the border line with the raise in wage will become potential customers, and, therefore, their sale after all will increase, which will counterbalance the increase in cost. This will be explained later in greater detail in this chapter. At any rate we wish to emphasize that these contemplated changes will be so gradual that the delicate balance between capital and labor will not be upset or endangered, and readjustment to the new mode of life will be secured without any violence or strain. Technological advancements, inventions, economies in many fields of production will be important factors offsetting the increased cost of wages.

Mention must be made of the powerful influence of the EW in the relations between the various communities, zones and nations, which will tend to diminish the scarcity factors everywhere in the world by promoting trade, free exchange of goods, and utilize to greater advantage the fundamental law of division of labor. Of this more later in the text.

In so far that the index (a) is related to the amount of commodities received by the poor, which represents the largest part of the population, one should not fall into the misconception that two communities with the same index have also the same standard of living. Bear in mind that (a), besides being related to the amount of supply, is also related to the price of the vital commodities. This in turn is affected by the cost of labor, cost of material and transportation as well as by the relative position of supply and demand that may develop in any given community, all factors which may vary from one place to another. On this account equality in the index does not mean that the poor of two such communities have an equal standard of living. By definition the standard of living is expressed by $E/T.F.$ where (E) is the enjoyment derived from the utilization of vital commodities (C) and services (s) or $E = C + s$; (T) is the assumed unit of time for the evaluation of all factors entering the expression and (F) is the effort exerted. As explained in the third chapter the factors (T) and (F), being equal for all, may be neglected. If we also neglect the amount of services (s), because immaterial to the poor part of the population, the standard of living becomes one with (C). Now the index (a) is related only to commodities (C) and their price (p) and can be expressed by the simple formula of $a = C \times p$. For the same value of (a) if (p) is large (C) must necessarily be smaller and vice-versa. But since (C) in this case is synonymous with standard of living, it becomes obvious that for the same value of (a), the standard of living (C) will depend on what price the vital commodities reach in the community in study.

RELATION BETWEEN WAGES: GENERALIZATIONS

There must be a strict rule by which no one will be allowed to buy at the EW stores unless he is a registered customer. This may automatically cut off some of the rich for the simple reason that prejudice and false pride may prevent them from applying. However, all citizens will have the right to join if they so desire. When applying each must report the number of persons in his family, and according to that number he will receive ration books which will allow him to buy commodities up to a given limit, which will be fixed by the EW authorities and will depend on the supply on hand. From the knowledge of the economic forces at play, from the amount of

commodities regularly secured from the various retail and wholesale stores in the city and from the fact that the EW will have at
its disposal large warehouses where unperishable products can be
stored and preserved, it will release a constant flow of commodities
and as such it will tend to level off any moderate offsetting factor
that may develop in the market. For that kind of food products
that cannot be preserved, any abrupt excess will be sold to all
customers willing to buy more; however, for any abrupt shortage
the later customers will have to go without for that period of sale.
There may be times, however, when the change in the supply of
some particular commodity gives the indication of being of a more
stable nature. In this case its scarcity factor will be modified and
this will automatically affect the index (a).

At this point the reader may state that with this new mode of
life the laborer will be just as badly off as at present, for he still will
be unable to acquire the amount of vital commodities needed for
health and proper standard of living. While this is granted, we wish
to point out to him that our plan must avoid the errors of the
dreamers and Utopians who visualize a better world, but do not
concern themselves as to how this goal should be attained. We must
take the world as found and from this base indicate ways and
means, comprehensible to all, which will gradually lead mankind
to a better mode of life.

Naturally, as the new process is being adopted, it cannot be
expected that conditions should change overnight because of new
attitudes assumed in regard to economic phenomena. Progress is
not made in a day, nor in a single year for that matter, especially
when it is a matter of supplying steadily a large proportion of the
population. But by adopting this new mode of life the necessary
forces for progress will be kept constantly at work, and in due time
will produce the desired results. A too abrupt change would produce
dislocations more harmful than beneficial. On this account we wish
to visualize a gradual evolution which, taking the present society
as the starting point, will improve the average standard of living of
the population and produce benefits which in greater or lesser degree
will be distributed among all components of society, rich and poor
alike.

An increase in wages for those above the plain laboring class, as
explained in more detail in chapter eight, must be expected, but
will not affect unfavorably the interests of the poorest groups, as
much of the extra money received by the well-to-do will be saved

or spent for luxuries. Indeed the rich, who already have all they need or want, as far as vital commodities are concerned, are not going to buy any more with this raise in salary. The workers just above the plain labor class, whose wages also have been affected by the increased index, may and probably will buy extra vital commodities at the regular stores in addition to what they are able to secure through the EW. The higher wage gives them that privilege. This will naturally reduce the amount sold to the EW, which will mean a definite loss to the poorer classes, as their improvement is reduced by the additional purchase made by these individuals. But as long as there is betterment in their living conditions, we should not be unduly concerned. As cited elsewhere, it is a basic instinct of man to secure the greatest amount of vital commodities, limited only by his financial power, independent of the needs and interests of others. This practice neither could nor should be prevented. However, there will be others whose wage is also affected by the increased index, who will be in the fortunate position of not having to spend all the additional income in this manner. These are the ones who previously were able to secure a large percentage of the theoretical quantity of vital commodities, and as the extra income is more than sufficient for obtaining that quota, it is natural that some of it will be used for other commodities or services, or saved outright. In other words, their influence will tend to counterbalance that of the aforementioned buyers.

To clarify this statement, consider the diagram on Fig. 19, page 268. Let A,B,C, etc., represent groups receiving different wages. They are indicated in the horizontal axis at the left. The vertical scale measures wages, starting with that of the unskilled laborer, indicated by $1.0a$. Line m relates the wages of the various groups at some definite time, so that to find the wage of group C one proceeds as follows. From the horizontal axis where C is indicated draw a line parallel to the wage axis until m is intersected at point c. From this point draw a parallel to the horizontal axis. This will intersect the wage axis at a point which gives the wage of group C (in this particular case $1.4a$). Line q at the right relates the amount of vital commodities with wages at some particular price level. The horizontal scale gives the proportion of commodities q that can be bought by those wages, where q is the theoretical requirement analyzed in previous discussions. To find the amount that group C can buy: Draw the horizontal line from c until line q is intersected at point c'. The vertical line from c' will intersect the horizontal axis at a point

VITAL COMMODITY	BASIC QUANTITY FOR CALCULATING FOOD VALUE	PROTEIN	FAT	CARBO-HYDRATES	TOTAL CALORIES	IDEAL AMOUNT PER WEEK FOR FAMILY OF FOUR	TOTAL CALORIES (THEOR.)	PRICE PER UNIT QUANTITY	THEOR. COST PER WEEK	ACTUAL AMOUNT AVAILABLE PER FAMILY	SCARCITY FACTOR	ACTUAL CALORIES RECEIVED	ACTUAL EXPENDITURE
COLUMN	1	2	3	4	5	6	7	8	9	10	11	12	13
BEEF	1 POUND	282	250		532	6	3192	0.35	2.10	4.5	1.33	2400	1.57
LARD	"		3828		3828	0.5	1914	0.14	0.07	0.4	1.25	1530	0.06
OLEOMARG.	"	23	3387		3410	0.5	1705	0.20	0.10	0.3	1.66	1022	0.06
SALT PORK	"				3555	3	10,665	0.15	0.45	2.5	1.20	7400	0.38
APPLES	"	6	10	94	110	8	880	0.05	0.40	6.0	1.33	660	0.30
POTATOES	"	58	5	516	579	8	4632	0.03	0.24	6.0	1.33	3470	0.18
RICE	"				1591	4	6364	0.10	0.40	3.0	1.33	4780	0.30
SUGAR	"			1780	1780	3	5340	0.06	0.18	3.0	1.00	5340	0.18
CHEESE	"	523	1465	5	1993	3	5979	0.25	0.75	2.5	1.20	4980	0.62
EGGS	DOZEN	25	45		70	3	2520	0.35	1.05	2.5	1.20	2100	0.88
MILK	QUART	132	351	195	678	10	6780	0.15	1.50	7.0	1.43	4750	1.05
PEANUT BUTTER	POUND	507	1840	320	2667	0.5	1333	0.30	0.15	0.5	1.00	1333	0.15
BEANS	"	124	106	362	592	3	1776	0.10	0.30	3.0	1.00	1776	0.30
BREAD	"	172	74	985	1231	16	19,696	0.10	1.60	14.0	1.14	17,229	1.40
OATMEAL	"	35	32	136	203	4	812	0.05	0.20	3.0	1.33	610	0.15
CABBAGE	"	29	13	102	144	3	432	0.03	0.09	3.0	1.00	430	0.09
SPINACH	"	9	6	61	76	3	657	0.10	0.30	3.0	1.00	660	0.30
TOMATOES	"	16	17	70	103	6	618	0.05	0.30	5.0	1.20	510	0.25
TOTAL							75,295		10.18		1.23	60,980	8.22

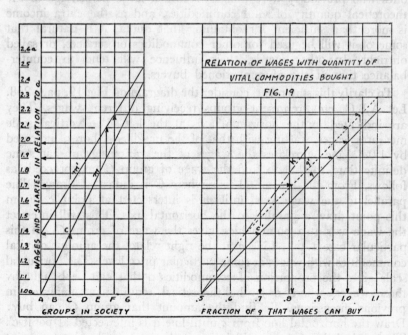

RELATION OF WAGES WITH QUANTITY OF VITAL COMMODITIES BOUGHT
FIG. 19

WAGES AND SALARIES IN RELATION TO q

GROUPS IN SOCIETY

FRACTION OF q THAT WAGES CAN BUY

which gives the proportion of q each member of the group C can buy. In our case this quantity is given by 0.7q. This assumes that the total amount of commodities secured by each family belonging to any one group is a direct function of its salary versus the basic index (a), so that for a salary equal to 2a the amount bought equals twice that which is secured by the plain laborer with a family of four. This statement would be correct if the amount of commodities over and above 0.5q was purchased at the PS store. This, however, is not so because no one will be allowed more than the allotted amount no matter his financial status. As the extra amount must be secured at the regular store where higher prices are charged, it is plain that the extra wage will not buy the amount of commodities shown in our diagram which is, therefore, faulty in this respect. However, we are interested in trends rather than actual quantities, so our presentation of the problem may be considered fundamentally sound. With this understanding we may go ahead with our presentations.

It is assumed here that all these groups buy the quantity 0.5q at the EW store. This is the amount calculated by the EW and related to the supply on hand. The difference must be bought in regular stores at the higher price, so that while a member of group (A) uses all his wages to buy 0.5q, the others, having more income, may secure a larger share depending on their respective wages or salaries. These quantities are listed below:

Group A	0.5q
B	0.6q
C	0.7q
D	0.8q
E	0.9q
F	1.0q

Any one with higher wages than 2a will only buy (q) and use the extra money for other kinds of commodities or services. Now assume that the supply of vital commodities has increased. This has influenced both the index (a) and the wages. Let line (m') represent the new relationship between the various groups and the new wages. We must notice first of all that the two lines (m) and (m') are not parallel, but tend to approach as wages increase, so that while group (A) receives 1.4a instead of 1.0a (an increase of 40%), group (G) receives 2.35a instead of 2.2a, (an increase of

6.8%). We wish to point out that these figures are only used as an illustration. Later our study will return to this subject, and make recommendations regarding relationship between increases in wages for the various groups.

Due to the new competition among buyers and sellers the cost of the commodities will reach a new equilibrium at a somewhat higher price because of the increased wages and greater pressure exerted by the poor, so that line (q') will be displaced to the left of (q), indicating that any one paid the same as before would be unable to buy as much, due to the higher price. But along with the laborers of group (A), the other groups receive an increase in wages, not in the same proportion as (A), but sufficient to buy more than before. By repeating the same line of reasoning we find that now the amount the members of each group can buy is:

Group A	0.65q
B	0.73q
C	0.81q
D	0.89q
E	0.96q

It is clear that had the prices remained stationary, members of group (A) would have been able to secure 0.7q, but because of the higher price that quantity is reduced to 0.65q which, while smaller, is still far larger than the previous 0.5q, and the increased supply constitutes an actual improvement. This drop from 0.7q to 0.65q is due to the fact that all groups with wages larger than the minimun will use the extra money to buy additional commodities from the stores, and naturally what extra is being bought by them is automatically subtracted from the quantity obtained by the EW. This is in line with the policy of bettering all classes, irrespective of position even if this may mean a slower improvement on the part of group (A). We can see then, as the supply and the corresponding index continue to increase, that the improvement of group (A) will follow a line indicated by (K). Take now a person with an original wage of 1.9a. Before the increase of supply he was able to buy 0.95q which, while far more than the 0.5q received by the laborer of group (A) was still slightly smaller than the desired amount. As the supply increases and his wage goes up from 1.9a to 2.1a, he will finally be able to buy q, and will do so regardless of what others less fortunate, are able to obtain, and so will the others whose original wage is between 1.9a and 2.0a. But as the supply and their wage increase, they will find they no longer need to spend all their income upon vital commodities, but that some may be diverted to purchase other wares. Thus the person who originally had a wage of 2.0a, and could afford to buy the quantity q, with the increase in wage is in a position to buy 1.04q, but will not do so since q is all he needs. In other words, he will no longer influence the distribution of vital supply, and his increase in wages will not be detrimental to the poorest classes. The same can be said for all whose wages are larger than 2a. As more persons reach this fortunate position, an additional supply will be distributed among a smaller and smaller number of persons, therefore, for a continuous increase in production the improvement of the poorest will become more rapid.

Under this method the wage of the unskilled laborer will gradually provide for his needs, as prescribed by doctors and dieticians. With time these basic needs can be further increased so there will always be a tendency toward amelioration.

The road to progress may be long or short, and will depend on the quantity of wealth in the country, on the alertness of the people, and on cooperation between the EW and the population in general, but no matter how long it may take economic forces will always be at work for the betterment of society and of humanity in general.

SUMMARY OF THE INFLUENCE OF THE EW

In summarizing, the influence of the EW will be to encourage the production of commodities whose scarcity factor is greater than one, keep constant the supply of those who have reached this level, and discourage the production of those products with a scarcity factor smaller than one. This by using its influence only as a buyer. With the price of commodities under its direct control, depression as well as wild booms will be avoided. As explained, booms usually take root in the fact that many producers increase their output under the assumption that demand will increase in the future. Not being in a position to know what the demand will actually be, they frequently overshoot their mark, bringing on conditions causing depression and disaster. This demand, however, will be more accurately gauged by the EW on account of its extensive information upon economic trends in the country as well as in the world in general and, therefore, in a position to take the necessary steps long before the damaging effects of those trends are actually felt by the people. At any rate all information will be made public so that any one will be in a better position to adjust his production for the maximum profit. Needless to say the business world will rest on a saner and stronger foundation. Then unless an organization is so poorly managed that, even with the constancy of prices, it is unable to derive profits its dropping out of the market will be a benefit rather than a loss to society and its place will be taken by another. Later in this study it will be shown that the EW will purchase such organizations, and thereby prevent great losses to the investors as well as the employees.

The reader may object that this slow and gradual increase in prices is comparable to a condition of stagnation. This is not true for the following reasons:

(a) Even if production must increase at a moderate pace, which will prevent a too rapid expansion of corporations, a sane and just profit will be assured to all.

(b) Whoever is able to introduce better methods of production and savings in cost will still be in a better position to derive large profits. With time his advantage will tend to decrease. But this is a natural phenomenon of our present society. To the inventor or discoverer of better means of production an interval is allowed to cash in on his skill. But it is only just after a suitable period of time, that the benefit be returned to society in general, in the form of letting competitors utilize that method or discovery. This will gradually decrease prices to a level in which they become equal to cost of production. As the greater profit derived through skill and ability, will not be impaired, the EW will not extinguish this all important form of personal wealth.

We are not interested, however, in maintaining those policies that permit the piling up of great profits on the part of the few, even though this will still remain a possibility. Our chief concern is that of improving the standard of living of the entire population. This must not be measured by the amount of dollars and cents received as wages and salaries, but by what they can buy, and by the amount of work required of them. It is obvious, then, that the new mode of life will maintain a constant and mild period of prosperity, which, without fluctuations, will steadily forge ahead toward the attainment of a better and happier society.

CHAPTER VII

A CLOSER STUDY OF THE E.W. ORGANIZATION

U P TO NOW some of the activities of the E.W. have been analyzed but only in a general way and in so far as they affect the various special forces that develop within a society. It remains to tell how the EW is composed and how it functions.

The present chapter will clarify this subject, and without stopping to discuss how the EW can be set up, expanded, and interwoven with the life of the nation, it will be assumed that it is already a vital force, promoting the advancement of society as a whole. Since the previous chapter has taken an industrial city of 100,000 population as the base of discussion, it will be in order now to describe the activities of this organization within the same hypothetical city which for that size of population will constitute what we shall call a community. Only minor changes will be needed for other cities of different size.

As stated, the EW, a main branch of the future government, is subdivided into four groups which in different ways will have a great influence in the mode of life of our community. Table no 4 page 328 will give an overall view of the organization. This will help you to understand following discussions.

The second group, or EW2, has the most immediate and tangible effect on the life of the people because it is concerned with the distribution of wealth received either through inheritance or taxes. For the purpose of presenting first those activities most conspicuous and strongly felt by the public, there will be given a detailed description of this group, followed by an account of the others later in this chapter.

In the sixth chapter (page 217) was given a list of the various branches of this group which we shall call divisions, and from it the "Price Stabilization", EW2-1 or PS for short, is selected to start with. The final title for this and other branches as well as the title of the various top officials will have to await a later discussion.

PRICE STABILIZATION DIVISION (*EW*2-1 *or PS*)

During the process of expansion of the EW throughout the country, assume that it opens a PS division in the city under consideration. The Manager of the Zone, stationed at the zone capital (another topic that must await later discussion), selects a Manager and a number of employees, and empowers them to establish the PS in that city. These employees, assisted by prominent citizens as well as by the local officials, make a survey among the groceries of the town, to choose those best fitted and equipped to serve the public. This selection will be influenced by the location and the available space for the sale of vital commodities. Meanwhile permission from the owners will be obtained and an understanding reached regarding rent paid by the EW. At times it may be necessary to build new stores if those on hand cannot offer the necessary facilities. The general policy, however, will be that of the maximum economy and efficiency, so as not to waste public money in undertakings that do not qualify as a real and positive help to society.

At the head of the organization will be the Community Manager or CM, for short, assisted in his work by special employees making this their career. His office must be centrally located, optionally attached to one of the stores selling commodities, depending on conditions in the city. As floor space is made available for the PS, this part of the store will be under the supervision of a manager under the direct orders of the CM. As a rule these employees will not be locally hired, and it will be an EW policy not to keep any store manager more than a definite number of years in any one single locality. This is desirable from the standpoint of keeping employees detached from the citizens they serve. Their mission is that of serving the people in general and not individuals in particular. This policy will also help to avoid corruption and favoritism. Clerks and other minor employees may be locally hired, and paid the current wage for this kind of employment. The CM, the store managers, and members of the staff of the organization will be paid by the EW. Promotion for these employees may be made through the recommendation of the CM.

As the various stores are organized, the necessary publicity will be gained through the local papers, the new policies explained to the public, and applications to get on the EW list will be accepted. All rich and poor, now or later, are free to apply. No statement of salary or wage is necessary but merely the information as to the number of persons dependent on the applicant. A ration card will be then issued in his name, and this will give him the right to buy from any one of the PS stores of the city a quota of vital commodities set by the CM for the period adopted, for which he must relinquish a coupon as the purchase is made.

Depending on the nature of the commodity and on the facilities offered by the city there may be several such stores. Foodstuff and the like must be sold in numerous places in order to serve the public adequately. Other commodities, such as clothing, furniture, and so forth, may be handled by a single centrally located store. As applications to become EW customers pour in, all the local stores will be notified that the PS division is on the market for the purchase of whatever vital commodity each store is willing to sell at some discount from the retail price. In chapter nine a rule will be submitted that could be used by the PS for purchases made from these stores. This rule will give both the total amount to be bought in relation to previous purchases as well as the amount to be bought from each individual store. The PS price, or the one that will be taken as base for the above mentioned computation, will be the average price charged by the wholesale stores to which a just necessary cost as well as profit may be added. The difference between the PS price and that charged by each store, while small for some may be large for others. Stores which are centrally located, besides charging more for their merchandise, will not have much to offer to the PS as they count upon disposing of their stock at high prices, but those less strategically placed will find it to their advantage to sell some of their stock to the PS, as by this both sales and profits will increase.

At the same time the wholesale stores will be sounded out as to their willingness to sell to the PS division. The amount of purchases from them will be determined by the CM, who will base his decision on conditions developing in the course of operating the organization and on the rule mentioned above. There may be times when the supply bought from retail stores drops abnormally below previous levels without apparent causes, either because of temporary scarcity or sudden increased demand, which by boosting sales of commodities reduce the amount the stores sell to the PS. In such a situation if the PS is able to buy more from the wholesale stores or, as later explained, from the PS of other communities, it will do so, in order to keep a constant flow of commodities to its customers. As the emergency subsides, offers from the retail stores will return to the previous level, and the quantity bought from the wholesale stores will again be reduced to normal. The principle to be followed is to maintain the price of a given vital commodity somewhat lower than the retail price, and to disregard as much as practicable the day by day sporadic changes of the market. The difference in price between local stores and those under the management of the PS is caused first of all by the willingness of such stores to decrease their price to the PS in their effort of better disposing their unsold stock. A second cause is represented by the fact that the PS will have at its disposal efficient methods of transportation, handling, and caring for commodities. A third cause is represented by the fact that a proportion of purchases is made directly from the wholesale stores who charge lower prices. By increasing or decreasing purchases from the wholesale stores, both a continuous flow of commodities can be obtained and the price kept at a difference from the retail price not sufficiently large to endanger the interests of the stores or in any way subtract from what is normally bought by the rich. From the total amount bought and sold, of which the staff under the CM naturally keeps records, the various scarcity factors will be calculated, and the index derived for the city, as explained in the sixth chapter. As the index is announced to the public, it automatically becomes the official wage per hour, upheld by the law of the land. By such method the PS will exert a powerful influence in stabilization of prices.

The EW is in the city first of all to improve living conditions of the local population, and secondly to blend the economy of the city with that of other parts of the zone or of the nation in general. This clearly is to the advantage of the city as well as of the zone or nation, as will be further explained. If it is proper and just for the PS to buy any excess the stores will sell, it is likewise so that it should seek out any product naturally abundant in the community in its effort to raise the scarcity factor of this commodity to a value closer to one. If this excess was unsold, (scarcity factor lower than one), its production would have to be curtailed, with a definite loss to all making their livelihood thereby. As the scarcity factor for such a commodity may be considerably higher for other communities of the zone, or for those far away from the city, it is evident that such commodities should be exported to those places.

As a general rule, commodities are not grown or made only for the local market but also to be exported. Therefore, the price of any single commodity is not only affected by the local market but by markets on a national or international scale. Whoever is willing to pay more usually gets the commodity, independently of the location of the buyer or seller. This exchange should not and will not be stopped by the EW, if within limits later explained. As the EW has branches all over the country, a flow of supplies will be maintained among them that will aid the impoverished everywhere in the nation, and this will also be beneficial to the producers, who can increase their sale to a far greater degree than if serving only their particular community.

The principle used in determining the amount reserved for the local use and what can be exported elsewhere must be based on the following facts. As a rule the scarcity factor of a commodity being exported from a locality A to a locality B, both of the same economic unit, is usually smaller in A than in B, because of the higher price reached in B as a result of transportation costs as well as additional profits to middlemen. For different economic units this rule will not necessarily hold. Were one to suppose as an hypothesis, that the EW customers in B are, on an average, wealthier than those in A, and accordingly able to pay a higher price, the flow of products from A to B will tend to be greater than if the two localities were equally rich or poor, so it may be possible, after equilibrium has been established, that the scarcity factor in B is actually lower than in A. To make this statement clear consider the instance of coffee, produced in large quantities in Brazil, exported to the United States. Because of the large purchasing power of the average modest family in the United States it is possible that it can afford to consume more coffee than the corresponding average family in Brazil, although the latter lives where coffee is produced. But, exception being made of the cases where such disparity exists, the contention as to the scarcity factors of different localities within one country, or part of a single economic unit, is bound to be approximately true, and will be influenced by the additional costs necessary to ship such commodities from one place to another. Obviously a limit must be placed on exportation and this may be set by the following rule: *The wealth of the commodities exported must be equal to that of those imported*

The reason for and the implications of such a rule must wait for a later discussion. For the present we wish to emphasize policies intended to improve the lot of the poor all over the land. If localities A and

B belong to the same economic system, meaning that the hypothetical families of both places have approximately the same purchasing power, as a result of the index and consequently of the wages received, it may be stated that the PS of B should buy from that of A only an amount of commodities consistent with the economic balance of B, and no more. At the other end, the PS of A will sell only the corresponding amount consistent with the economic balance of A. Irrespective of this rule the cost of transportation of any such commodity from one place to another, under the auspices of the EW, will be reduced to a minimum. This fact will tend to decrease prices in the community where such commodity is exported, and by increasing the local demand, will in turn increase the supply. This will be beneficial not only to the poor of B, who will buy at a lower price, but also to the manufacturers of A who will see the demand for their products increased. As a result there will be an urge to expand production, which in turn will be advantageous to all the employees of that particular industry in A.

Where there is great distance between two localities, the cost of transportation is bound to be high, despite the economies introduced by the PS, and this will be reflected by the higher price reached by that commodity in B. As a matter of fact, between A and B there will be two independent flows of commodities. One will pass through the usual channel of middlemen and eventually be sold to the well-to-do of B, the other will take place through the facilities of the PS. The latter commodities, starting from a lower price in A, will reach B with a relatively small increase in cost, due to the non-profit policy of the EW as well as to more economic means of transportation. Now we know that the PS of B will buy a large percentage of those products from the various retail stores of the community, and also an additional amount from the wholesale store which, in this case, is represented by the PS of locality A. We know also that the policy of the PS in B is to keep the price a certain percentage lower than the retail cost, a percentage fixed by the higher authorities of the EW. From this the amount of commodities that the PS of B should buy from that of A will be determined by the relation of those prices, and the PS of B should not attempt to buy more than that amount. As an example, assume that the PS of locality B, anxious to lower the scarcity factor of those commodities, decides to buy from A considerably more than what is suggested by the above mentioned policy. Even admitting that the new price to the poor further decreases in relation to the price to the rich, because of the larger percentage of commodities bought from the PS of A, still the price is bound to be higher than to the poor of A, and this difference will tend to increase with the increase in distance. Of course, this price will be incorporated in the index of locality B and, therefore, the increase in price would become immaterial. However, because of this, a greater drainage of money will be incurred by B, which may produce a condition of unbalance. This must be avoided. Thus, while this policy may be adopted by the PS of B in its effort to lower the scarcity factor, this must be consistent with the balance of trade of the same locality. But, as a general rule, the scarcity factor of a commodity in B is bound to be greater if distance from locality A is considerable. As the scarcity factor for a commodity rises above a given level, say 1.5 or 1.6, it should no longer be considered a vital commodity for locality B, and another, either locally produced or with a smaller scarcity factor, taken in its place. If this is the condition found in B, the local PS should altogether refrain from buying that commodity from A.

To make this point clear with an example, consider the State of Florida, a large producer and exporter of oranges. It is natural that oranges should be considered a vital commodity in that State because of their abundance. However, they are exported to other States of the Union and this tends to produce scarcity of oranges even in Florida. By this is meant that the price of oranges in Florida reaches such a level that the local lower class can only satisfy its needs up to a certain point, the result of so many oranges being exported elsewhere. But no matter what the price of oranges in Florida, it is bound to be lower than in Maine as this State, not being a grower of oranges, must import them from Florida, or California being that further away. This implies that not only must the oranges be bought at the price asked in Florida, but transported to Maine, an operation that requires a considerable amount of handling and a large number of middlemen engaged in business for personal profit. If the EW was operating between the two States, naturally all efforts would be made to reduce the cost of transportation and handling, so that the price of oranges in the PS stores in Maine would be nearer to that reached in Florida. Because of this the scarcity factor for oranges in Maine would be correspondingly lower. But no matter how greater the economy and efficiency of the PS division, the chances are that the scarcity factor for oranges in Maine is still too high, and that they should be considered a luxury rather than a vital commodity. Oranges, of course, would still reach Maine, but would not be sold by the PS stores, and only the well-to-do would be able to buy the desired quantity at the resulting price. In such a case emphasis would be placed instead upon some other commodity equally nourishing that could be used as substitute. This commodity might be local, or from some nearby State whence the cost of transportation is not so high. Assume now that oranges reach a scarcity factor smaller than 1.5, and, therefore, can remain on the list of vital commodities. Because of the various economies introduced by the PS, the price of oranges at their store as well as that of other vital commodities that are imported will be considerably lower than that in the regular stores. This will prove an additional incentive for many well-to-do to become EW customers. Of course, local stores could be permitted to buy such commodities through the facilities of the PS, and this would produce a general lowering of prices beneficial to all. To be sure, the middlemen would be adversely affected by such a policy. This will be the inevitable result of progress and, while one may feel sorry for them as individuals, considered as a group they have no right to endanger the welfare of the people for their own personal gain. Arrangements could be made to transfer those displaced by the PS to other trades or professions. Of this more will be said in explaining the activity of the unemployment control administration.

Returning to the policy adopted in importing and exporting commodities from a specific locality, it is evident that the final responsibility must rest with the Manager of the Zone (ZM), who has a wider perspective than the CM, and in turn must conform to the decisions of the Manager of the country.

With these basic facts in mind we may now analyze the implications of the rule that controls the flow of commodities in or out of our assumed community. Obviously, the larger the quantity exported, the greater will be the business activity in the place concerned. If the amount exported happens to be considerably more than that imported, money will enter the community to balance that difference. This will give the population a false feeling of wealth and abundance. It stands to reason, however, that if money comes in, some other community must be the loser. To reverse the process we may easily imagine the same population greatly concerned over its future economic condition. The dangers inherent in unbalance of trade have been pointed out and analyzed in previous chapters. Because of its destructive effects if left uncontrolled and unchecked, it is proper that the EW should exert its influence toward the attainment and the maintenance of the balance of trade, and disregarding short-sighted and selfish interests of minorities, favor those sound policies that produce a brighter future for the people in general.

Consider now how this influence can be exerted. A favorable balance of trade means that the community sells more than it buys and thereby derives an unproductive amount of specie. If this condition should go on indefinitely, aside from the fact that it would be detrimental to other communities with the consequent resentment and retaliatory measures on their part, the population en masse would be kept at a lower standard of living than if the trade had been kept balanced. One way to re-establish the balance of trade is to increase purchases from the outside as this will tend to increase both the actual standard of living of the people and return money to communities who otherwise would be left with an unfavorable balance of trade.

An unfavorable balance of trade means that the community buys from the outside more than it sells, and this represents a drainage on the amount of money in the community. If this condition should go on unchecked, a time will come when the community will be impoverished to a point where it may become unable to sustain trade and business activity, with a general lowering of the standard of living of the population. The condition of unbalance is recognized when money tends to go out or come into the community. The amount of unbalance, being closely related to the amount of specie in the banks and financial institutions, can be measured by the interest charged to the public. Such information is more or less a matter of public knowledge; however, an understanding with the banks and financial institutions, in order to inform the EW authorities of current trends, would not only prove a sensitive gauge of the financial condition of the city but would give the EW the required data on which to base the necessary measures long before the unfavorable consequences are felt by the population en masse. Information received by the CM would naturally be transmitted to the higher authorities of the zone so that they in turn can formulate the necessary policies to be applied throughout the area.

Among the most important causes that bring an unfavorable balance of trade we may mention the following:

(a) There may be a tendency on the part of numerous well-to-do individuals in the community to buy non-vital commodities from outside, for which money must be sent out of the community.

b) Due to unavoidable necessity the community as a whole must buy more vital commodities than it sells, and the difference will cause a drain on its financial power.

In the first case, where the rich buy too extravagantly abroad, it is true that the EW cannot stop anyone from buying what he pleases if he has the necessary money. However, a restraining influence to such expenditures could be exerted by taxing such imports. While on the subject, we wish to point out that such a policy must be adopted for an economic unit larger than the community under consideration such as a zone or the nation itself, as it would be impracticable for a community of a few hundred thousand. When such a condition exists, two types of taxes should be levied by the authorities of the zone. One tax should be placed on all the luxury commodities coming from other zones, directly levied upon all purchases; another tax imposed on all salaries and wages above a given level at the end of the year or every few months. Both taxes, directly related to the unbalance of trade, should be completely abolished as soon as the equilibrium between import and export has been established. The reason for imposing a direct tax upon luxury commodities imported is self-evident insofar as it bears on their purchasers. The reason for imposing a tax upon all salaries above a given level is to compensate for the fact that many well-to-do would go to other places to make purchases, and thus evade payment of the tax. This second tax should take only salary into account, and not property, since it is this kind of wealth that is exchanged for luxury commodities. This will tend to reduce the amount in circulation, and will also put a check upon extravagant spending. The money raised in this manner would be retained by the EW as a forced saving for the community as a whole. As the unbalance decreases, these special taxes could then be lowered, and eventually returned to the people in the form of decreased regular tax when the balance from negative becomes positive. This would have the opposite effect of putting money in circulation, and thus would promote additional buying. However, if the balance of trade should become so low as to actually jeopardize the standard of living of the poorer classes, the money that has been accumulated through these taxes could then be used to help those who have been more adversely affected. Such an extreme case, however, is not contemplated in the new mode of life.

As already stated, unbalance of trade may also be produced when the community buys more vital commodities than it sells. This may be due to the fact that the city and its surrounding zone is naturally poor in resources. In this case it will be up to the EW authorities of the zone or of the country to find a solution. Among several alternatives, they may decide on the desirability of introducing additional industries, which would tend to increase export of finished products. Of course, such a decision cannot rest on the fact that the locality needs help and assistance. Other factors must be satisfied before such a step is chosen. Availability of raw material, good roads, good transportation facilities, distance from large centers, climate and so on, are all important to the well being of an industry. It is natural that these conditions must be met by the locality in question. The setting up the industry there would do more harm than good. The industry, in other words, must not need any outside help or subsidy, as this would mean that money is spent to help a small minority at the expense of society in general, which is unethical, and contrary to the EW policy. Among other alternatives we may also mention that of finding employment for many in the population in other parts of the zone or of the nation. But more will be said later on the subject.

Recapitulating the policies that should be adopted by the CM and by the Manager of the zone in their effort to maintain the balance of trade with the outside, it may be said that these will depend on the financial and economic conditions found in the city and zone. As the policies are chosen, these must be made known to the public, so that anyone will know what to expect, and will understand the reasons for the new regulations.

In an all embracing set of policies that would tend to promote the balance of trade we may mention the following in order of importance:

For a favorable balance of trade, taxes will be reduced in cases where they had been collected above normal for a previous condition of unfavorable balance of trade. This will encourage purchases from the outside. More vital commodities will be bought by the PS from other communities.

For an unfavorable balance of trade, taxes will be imposed on non-vital commodities coming from the outside. Encouragement will be given to the production of locally made products with the aim of increasing export. As seen, this will mean the sponsoring of new industries in the community which may or may not prove practicable. The scarcity factor of imported commodities will be increased above previous levels. This will tend to cut down on the outflow of money. It is obvious, however, that efforts should be made to replace these commodities by locally produced substitutes to compensate for such enforced scarcity. When the population is too large for the resources on the land, it might be possible to move families of unemployed citizens elsewhere. This must be done intelligently so as not to deprive the community of its youth in which lies its strength. This will be averted by transferring entire families instead of individuals.

Having analyzed the fundamental rules guiding the policies of the EW, one can see how the economy of the city will gradually blend with that of neighboring places, so that the index as well as the standard of living will not markedly differ from place to place but become representative of the wealth and economic strength of the zone to which the city belongs. As the index does not vary appreciably from month to month, wages and salaries will also tend to stabilize or increase in an orderly manner. This will be helpful to business and will promote understanding and cooperation between capital and labor.

In describing the personnel of the EW, mention was made of the CM, the managers of the stores, and the staff of experts that will help the CM in operating the organization. Others are needed to keep records, to prepare information for the CM, to contact the various stores in town, to inspect the commodities being bought by the PS, to deliver them to the various PS stores, and attend to other activities advisable for smooth functioning of the unit. The larger the city the more multiform will be this activity and the greater the number employed. This staff, however, must be maintained at the minimum compatible with efficiency. At this point it may be stated that the CM, especially in small cities and towns, will be expected to represent all the EW branches, and will report regularly to the Manager of the zone or ZM. Nearby villages and towns economically bound to the city also will have a CM and a small staff of their own. They will buy and sell from the PS stores of the city in accordance with the rules. Suppose that a small village has only 200 persons under the care of the PS. Whoever does the buying for the town can only get a certain amount for them and no more. This will tend to make the scarcity factor of any particular commodity slightly higher in the town than in the city, because of the extra cost of transportation between them. The reverse will be true when commodities are bought by the city from the town. In other words, the cost of transportation must always be borne by the locality that does the buying. The CM of the small town or village will be responsible to the CM of the city.

The EW will be organized as carefully as an army, with the promotions dependent only on alertness, initiative, intelligence and integrity of character.

Parallel to this organization there will be a number of officials chosen by the citizens who will represent their interests. As mentioned in the sixth chapter, and further explained in the latter part of this one, these officials will be part of an independent branch of the government. They will have authority to discuss with the CM any policy which directly or indirectly affects the population, study any complaints against the organization, ascertain the facts, and report to their superiors. To this subject our text will return later.

INDUSTRY REGULATION DIVISION (*EW*2-2 *or IR*)

The activity of this branch of the distribution group of the EW will be that of finding ways and means of preventing tottering industries from endangering society.

The management of an industry is one of the most delicate and responsible tasks undertaken by man. Only a few persons in society have the necessary requisites to qualify for such a position. Courage, boldness, wisdom, clear thinking, and ability to make quick decisions are a few of the qualities that must be found abundantly in the person who becomes the manager of an industry. Upon him the livelihood of thousands of employees is dependent; to him is entrusted the care of frequently large fortunes which may belong to one or to many. In a world of constant change and competition, his initiative and decision are often the deciding factors that will lead an industry to the highest levels or topple it to disruption and chaos. In a corporation where the manager may be changed if he should not come up to those standards, disastrous collapses may sometimes be averted by entrusting the leadership to better hands. But there are cases where the manager of an industry is also the owner, and thus cannot be easily displaced. To be sure, changing needs of society, superseding old fashions, new inventions, discarding of old methods, or other reverses may place an industry at a great disadvantage and be the direct causes of its bankruptcy, no matter how good, honest, and efficient the management may be. To this must be added that the fact that the management was not aware of such changes, and did not have in due time the foresight to make provisions to avert disaster is, in itself, sufficient proof of incompetence. At any rate, the failure of an industry, no matter from what cause, usually means a great loss, not only to the owners but also to many helpless people who depended on that industry for their living. As explained in other parts of this book, it is cases like these that start the long cycle of depression.

A more specific discussion as to the causes that may be responsible for the failure of an industry is in order. They include:

(1) A poor and inefficient manager, who lacks the initiative and ability to make the proper decision at the proper time, is quite commonly the main and only cause of failure, no matter how good the personnel may be. Sometimes the inefficiency is made evident by his poor judgment in assigning positions of responsibility to unqualified individuals, and even when it becomes obvious, he has no courage to make the drastic changes and corrections. In the long run this will bankrupt any industry, no matter how good conditions may be.

(2) When times are good there is a general tendency on the part of an industry to increase its production to a level considerably higher than what the population can actually absorb. With few exceptions, most industries do not wait for orders to manufacture commodities. It is shown in chapter six how any industry will find it advantageous to expand production to a point where marginal cost equals the price of the commodity, and as commodities are usually produced for a future demand, this is where the wisdom and ability of a manager can be measured and appreciated. He must be able to foresee the amount of demand, the kind of products that will be in demand at some future date, and the probable price. Basing his calculation on those estimates, he will order the manufacture of a certain amount of products so that they may be ready for sale when the maximum profit can be obtained. It is easy to see that a good or bad estimate made by the manager may represent millions of dollars of profit or of loss for an industry.

It is also explained in the sixth chapter (note 6-1, page 223) how production of a commodity in a perfect competitive market depends on the marginal cost of the particular industry under consideration. Each industry has a cost curve of its own, and whenever its marginal cost is equal to price, the corresponding quantity produced will make the maximum profit for the company. But a large profit for one industry does not necessarily mean that the others are equally fortunate. It is possible that at a specific price the profit for some other industry is considerably less, or actually represents a loss (see Fig. 20, page 328. This loss may be sustained for a considerable number of years and may be due to the high cost of production (result of inefficient management). For commodities selling in an imperfect competing market, where the success or failure of an industry rests so much on the ability of the management to make its products desirable to the public, it is easy to see how a poor management may be the primary cause for the ultimate failure of that industry. Going back to the condition of perfect competition, it has been shown that each individual industry is powerless to change the price of the commodity. That price is the direct result of the general demand and supply in the country as a whole. It can be seen that the practice of manufacturing for a future demand incurs many uncertainties. For example, if the demand does not come up to that anticipated, prices will go down regardless of the cost of production. It is plain that industries which have a high cost curve will be the first to be adversely affected.

Now many industries operate on borrowed money, and as long as business flourishes it is easy for them to find additional credit. Mistakes can even be made without impairing that credit a great deal, but if they should sustain continuous losses, they eventually will see their credit withheld, and the consequence is bankruptcy.

(3) Other times the cause for failure may be traced directly to a new invention which may place on the market a better and cheaper substitute, making the company's commodity obsolete, or to some improvement in manufacturing which allows large savings to a fortunate competitor who has bought the sole rights of that process. In this case the competition may become so severe and the losses so large that no alternative is left but to close down the industry.

(4) Yet again fraud and deception may make an industry fail, but these cases enter the field of the Department of Justice, and, therefore, are beyond the limits of this text.

However, no matter what the reasons for failure, the consequences are always tragically the same: many persons lose their jobs and means of living; many lose their savings.

The method used by the IR division to stem the situation is quite simple. Money will be on hand for the purchase of any industry offered for sale because of its critical and unstable position. Assuming such a sale has been made, it will then be up to the IR to decide what policy is to be followed as to its disposal, and this will depend on conditions in the country in general.

(a) Suppose the industry being bought produces vital commodities. From the scarcity factor of each commodity it will be easy to see whether it can justify its continued existence. If the factor is larger than one, it is plain that more of that commodity is needed. In such a case a change in management may be the obvious solution of the problem. In other cases better and more up-to-date machinery and equipment, plus efficient management, may be necessary. Merging with the successful competitor may sometimes be desirable, especially if the latter is the owner of patents giving him the sole rights of a successful operation. At any rate, due to the necessity of increasing the supply of those commodities, a way must be found to keep that industry going.

(b) Suppose it produces only non-vital commodities. While in this case the IR is not much concerned with the total production of the commodity, because of its lack of vital importance to the people, it will still be its duty to keep informed of economic trends in the country and depending on those trends, a line of action will be chosen for the disposal of that industry. Of course, if it could be made to produce, without extensive and expensive changes, some vital commodity, especially if there is great need in the country, that would be the most happy and desirable solution. On this account the industry would be sold to individuals or organizations interested in such manufacture, and willing to expand their production through the acquisition of these facilities. If entirely new organizations are formed to take over this industry from the IR, a moderate amount of subsidy may be considered for a limited number of years, depending on individual cases. This would give the management of the revived industry sufficient time to establish and consolidate itself in the economic structure of the country.

On the other hand, if such alternative is not feasible because of the cost of changing the machinery, the policy might be either to have the industry absorbed by the successful competitor, or sell it to another owner or organization offering the best price.

(c) In cases where it is perfectly plain that overproduction in general is the main cause for the failure, keeping that industry in its particular field should be avoided. Here again the production of some other commodity becomes imperative, and a subsidy to other organizations willing to start in some other field may be justified.

In any case whenever possible the shutdown of the industry should be averted. If it will keep on manufacturing the same commodity, the working force should be retained on the job, pending necessary alterations to make it more efficient and self-supporting. If it will divert to some field or production, it may be impracticable to keep the same labor force. On this account whoever is willing to learn the new methods of production should be retained under the direction of expert labor brought in from the outside, work found for the others elsewhere in the country where needed, or jobs offered them by another branch of the EW whose activities will be analyzed in a subsequent part of this chapter.

Having disposed of the industry on the verge of bankruptcy to the best advantage of society, consider what should be the price offered by the IR to the original owner or owners. This refers to cases in which the help of the EW is solicited. It may happen that the owner may prefer the alternative of selling out or being absorbed by another organization in which case the problem would be out of the IR's sphere. But in cases where the specific help of the IR is requested, a price must be fixed for the wealth which is being temporarily transferred from private ownership to that of society.

First of all an inventory of buildings, machinery, tools, and land belonging to the factory must be made. Then an appraisal of their current price, with due account taken of conditions and depreciation, should be made by experts of the IR, and a total value of the industry finally calculated. This will be the basic worth, or the price of the property at the time when the appraisal is made, and will be referred to as M. All the assets and liabilities of the company must also be determined. An analysis must be prepared of all the business transactions made by the company during a stated number of years, the amount and the cost of goods bought, cost of its operation and the amount and price of goods sold. This will give the IR important information as to the ability of that industry to produce profits under that management. The gains or losses sustained by the company over the same number of years can then be compared to the theoretical return, which is a fixed percentage of the basic price of the industry.

Society, as explained in previous chapters, estimates wealth from the revenue it is able to produce. In this study it has been assumed a definite relationship between wealth and revenue in which revenue is equal to 5 percent of the wealth or to say better the worth of wealth is 20 times larger than revenue. In actual cases, however, an entirely different relationship may be found and, naturally, if we take revenue as base, we may arrive at a worth or value of wealth somewhat different from the estimate referred to above and called the basic worth of the industry. The second interpretation will be called "relative worth" and will be referred to as F. If the relative worth is chosen instead of the basic for the purchase of the industry from the original owners, it is obvious that the less the profit the smaller would be the price, down to a point where the value of the industry would become negative, yet the opposite would occur for a larger profit.

In comparing the two prices one may be confronted by the following cases:

(a) Assume that the relative price F is larger than M. This means that the industry produces for the owners a revenue larger than the 5 percent assumed as base and it may be surmised that it does not need the help of the IR. If the owners are still determined to sell their property to the IR, they will offer to pay a price given by the average of M and F or $(M + F)/2$. The final price, however, should never be under any circumstance greater than $1.1M$ which would represent a condition when F is equal or greater than $1.2M$. The owners, of course, will be at liberty to sell to any third party willing to pay more. It must be remembered that the primary purpose of the IR is only to relieve industries in danger of bankruptcy so as to save society from the consequence of their failure. A manager is not definitely committed to sell to the IR when he requests an evaluation of M and F for the purpose of sale. However, should the offer of the IR be refused, the cost of the inventory must be borne by the company. This is to prevent individuals from taking advantage of the IR for purposes of their own. This charge, however, must not be applied if the industry is actually sold to the IR because this branch will eventually recover this money from the future owners. For those industries whose relative worth is smaller than $1.2M$ it may be assumed that the owner, fearing adverse tendencies in the country in general, decides to sell while the industry is still prosperous. All that this industry needs is probably a more aggressive owner and manager who, with additional facilities and improvements, could make that industry flourish anew. Under such circumstance the IR should be willing, under the conditions mentioned above, to relieve the owner of such responsibility if requested and find another who has more faith and initiative. It goes without saying that the EW will have a clearer understanding of the economic trends in the nation at large, and the policy of diverting that industry whenever and wherever possible toward those channels that will do most good to society will be explored.

(b) Assume that the relative price F of the industry is smaller than M. This condition is found when the industry is still able to produce some profit, but less than the theoretical 5 percent of the basic price M. The causes of this poor performance, of course, must be found, and the amount paid the owner may be an average of the two estimates, or $(F + M)/2$.

As a clarification of our definition of worth, we wish to say that the actual cost of the industry at the time it was organized should not influence the value of M because conditions between the two periods may be vastly different. The appraisal, it seems to us, should be based on the potentialities of the industry and of its various facilities at the time in question, due regard being taken of similar industries in the country. If the industry derives its production through out-of-date machinery and methods, this fact will naturally decrease its basic worth. This appraisal must also be based upon the expenditures required to make the industry up-to-date and at par with its counterparts. From this it is obvious that only experts can qualify to make such an appraisal. It goes without saying that besides being just and fair to society as well as to the owners, they must have no connection whatsoever with the industry itself, and the services of the IR employees of some other zone in the country should be secured for that purpose.

F measures the worth of that industry to the owners themselves, or better to say, the amount of revenue they are able to derive, and therefore determines the value as far as they are concerned. It seems to us that the average between those two appraisals should be a fair compensation to the owners.

(c) Assume that the company has shown a consistent loss over a period of years, and the relative worth in this case becomes negative. The IR will buy the industry at a price given by $.5M$. This rule of estimating the worth as the average of the two estimates M and F being general, precise and equal for all, will eliminate the human factor and the possibility of corruption.

In cases where the price to be offered is below the basic price, it is evident that the owners of that industry must sustain a loss. Among the investors or owners some may not be appreciably affected by that loss, but for others it may represent hardship. It must be remembered, however, that whatever the critical financial condition of the industry, the price offered by the IR will not fall below half

of the basic worth. This will assure that at least that much investment is recovered. As it happens nowadays, the bankruptcy of an
industry often means also the utter loss of the investment, with
severe repercussions in business circles. That society in general
should not be called on to pay the full extent of the investment on
the part of the stockholders seems to us proper and just. Indeed,
the investors have shown, to say the least, poor judgment in placing
their capital with tottering concerns or corporations whose management was not of the highest qualifications, and, therefore, must
expect a loss even though the IR will give them the opportunity to
recover a far greater proportion of their investment than if the
industry had been left drifting alone.

In the course of the liquidation of an industry, especially in those
cases where F is smaller than M, it may be found that the industry
has previously incurred obligations with other parties in order to
carry on its operations. By law, these other parties cannot claim
more than a small fraction of their money, and this amount must
be taken into account in the calculation of F. If F is negative, the
loss to these third parties must be complete. The reason for this
policy is to prevent a further hardship to small investors. As these
corporations have been able to give assistance to the tottering industries, it follows that they are in better financial position to take
the loss. They have shown poor judgment by lending financial
support to an industry that probably would have failed long before
if it had not been for their help. It must be stated here that the
same parties or corporations have the right to buy that industry in
preference of the IR at a figure no smaller than the basic price M.
That the price should not be smaller than M is justified by the
fact that the corporation is not society in general but a group of
individuals out to derive revenue from wealth, in this case represented by M, and, therefore, it is just that they should pay in full
for what they buy. In such case the small investors will derive a
much larger share of their investment. For the IR the case is
different, because it does not buy for profit but only to relieve
hardship among people, and, therefore, should not pay the same
price as above, in view likewise of the possibility of not being able
later on to sell that wealth elsewhere. It must be made clear,
however, that if the industry is eventually sold to new owners,
these will be called to pay not only the actual worth M at the time
the industry was sold but also the expenditures supported by the IR
in connection with the estimate made at the time of sale as well

as the cost of new facilities and improvements added for the purpose of bringing that industry in an up-to-date condition. What money is gained by the IR will be returned to the original owners. It goes without saying that if conditions in the nation should change so radically so as to greatly depreciate the worth of the industry in the care of the EW, a new estimate may have to be made before selling to a third party. The loss, naturally, must be sustained by the IR.

Having set forth the basic principle on which the IR will stand, let us see how it will function. As the General Manager of an industry becomes conscious of its critical position, he will probably discuss the situation with the owner or board of directors, and together reach the decision to sell out to the IR. Such a request must be sent on a special form to the Division Manager of the IR located in the capital of the zone. According to the type of industry, the size of the organization, and so forth, one or more experts will be sent to study the situation. These experts must have access to all the books of the company, to the shops and buildings, and be granted all the facilities in order to make a detailed report to the main office of the IR. After all the facts have been ascertained and verified, the Division Manager, and the Manager of the Zone, assisted also by other high officials of the branch, will arrive at the determination of the price to be paid for the industry, which may be accepted or rejected by the company. No compromise should be tolerated, as the price, chosen by definite and rigid rules, takes into account the interests of the investors in the industry as well as of society in general. Should the price be accepted, at an agreed date the actual transfer of property will be recorded and the owners will receive a sum that will be a function of the amount of shares in their possession. The IR will then become the full owner of that property, and sole arbiter of the policies to be adopted in its management. As a rule it will not keep such property longer than necessary, and every effort will be made to transfer that wealth to private hands. However, depending on the general need of the country, and following the direct instructions of superiors in the capital, preference may be given to parties interested in the manufacture of any other kind of product more beneficial to society. As explained before, and depending on individual cases, subsidies may even be granted for the erection of buildings and machinery needed for the new production. The price of sale, nevertheless, must not be less than M unless conditions in the nation have materially changed, and the subsidy must be in the form of a loan with an interest slightly lower than the usual 5 percent.

Due to the large amount of money involved in these operations, efforts should be made to help the IR Division become as self-sustaining as possible. In other words, as a normal rule, the difference between the purchase and the sale should be such to repay the IR for the expenditures incurred in this transfer of property. Neglecting the beneficial effects to the working class, the intervention of the IR has prevented the original owners of the industry from the complete loss of their investment and has transferred it to other owners who probably will make large profits from that acquisition. As the principal concern of the IR is the good of society, and as the industry is aided in the acquisition of more modern equipment and steered toward the production of commodities most sought in the country, only good leadership on the part of the new management will be needed to make it prosper. On this account it seems to us just that the new owners should be made to pay for that difference. By this method industries that are lagging, because of the changing conditions in the country, may gradually be eliminated, and more impetus given to others that have a better chance to prosper and will benefit both their owners and the country in general.

Another activity of this unit of the EW is to sponsor new industries in new places. Because of the variety of information gathered by the IR, it will be more qualified to judge than the simple entrepreneur, who cannot have all the data on which to base his decision as to the best chance of profit, location, and kind of industry needed in the country. This selection will be made from the knowledge of several factors, such as cost of labor, distance to local centers, facilities for acquisition of raw materials, national and international demand. These facts will also be made known to the public through bulletins and the daily papers. Individuals in the process of setting up a new industry, while absolutely free to take any independent course, will do well to consult the IR officials and go over with them the various phases of the enterprise to be undertaken. If qualified as to integrity and financial standing, subsidies may be granted to them if requested in the form of loans after the industry has been organized. This is because the IR should not enter into competition with financial institutions by which loans of this kind are usually made. Such loans, however, to be granted must be justified, will require a smaller rate of interest than the one asked by the financial institutions, and will have the purpose of relieving the new industry from too heavy obligations while in the critical period of their expansion. Likewise, loans may be granted if the management of the new industry has shown unmistakable signs of following the suggestions of the IR.

The IR will constitute a small group of employees, expert in matter of finances. It will have a Manager of its own, and its ofice will be in the capital of the zone. Its policies and activities will naturally be coordinated with those of other zones in the country, all under the supervision of a general office in the national capital, to which they will report regularly and receive instructions as to the policies to be adopted. It has been remarked previously that in the long run the IR must be self-supporting. Times may come when in order to carry out their particular policies, money must be borrowed from the main office at the capital. This will be done upon the understanding that it must be repaid as soon as practicable. The rate of interest which each zone must pay to the main office must be determined from the general condition of the zone, its ability to pay, and other considerations which will be discussed in a later analysis.

LABOR CONTROL DIVISION (EW2-3 or LC)

The task of the third branch of the distribution group of the EW will be that of finding employment for those who have lost their job under the impact of economic forces, through no fault of their own. In previous parts of this chapter we have analyzed the beneficial influence of the first and second branch in stabilizing prices of commodities, and in preventing financial panics which by disrupting many industries throw millions of people out of work. Because of these constructive influences, and the more stable foundation of business, it is unlikely that great extremes of prosperity and depression can any longer occur. Society will find itself on an even keel and on the straight road to a better standard of living without the sudden jerks and setbacks experienced by our present society. But even so, the changing of fashion and the progress of technology in its relentless effort of introducing labor-saving devices will gradually displace a certain amount of labor. It is true that new inventions may make entirely new jobs, and that part of the working population will again find remunerative employment through those inventions, but one must consider the millions who by training, age, or aptitude, cannot adjust themselves so easily and rapidly to the new requirements. It is understandable that an expert who has been employed in an old-fashioned factory for many years cannot become overnight an expert in another factory with entirely new set of machinery and new methods of manufacture even though engaged at the production of the same articles. Again for these new industries young and qualified laborers will be in demand, and many others will be left out if the new enterprise is to be efficient and progressive. Mentioning this does not mean that we are opposed to technological advances. As a matter of fact, the more the better, yet while that advancement is taking place, society must provide for those who will be adversely affected. This is the problem we wish to discuss in the following pages.

Industry as a rule is privately owned, and usually engaged in constant competition. In order to survive it must always strive for the best, ever seek extra economy or improvement, not only to secure the maximum profit but often to avoid incurring large losses. When investments run into millions of dollars and a slight change may mean success or failure for that company, it is quite evident that humanitarian feelings cannot enter in the scheme of a manager who has in his power the future success of the organization. The shepherd must not stop to save a single sheep if this will jeopardize the entire flock. The task of lessening the necessary hardship wrought by this relentless progress cannot be left to private individuals but must rest with society, which is out of that field of competition.

In any country, no matter how prosperous and advanced, there are always thousands of projects out of reach of private initiative due to their vastness and magnitude, which are of great benefit to society. New roads and bridges connecting important centers, so as to lower the cost of transportation of essential commodities for the public, dams that harness new power and new facilities for large communities and zones, docks, airfield, hospitals, schools and places of entertainment in smaller communities, housing projects, libraries and hundreds of other enterprises are all projects that have in view the general welfare of society. The task of coordinating all these undertakings will rest with the LC Division. The requirements of each project must be studied and analyzed in detail, emphasis being placed on the kind and number of workers needed, and preference given to those projects that can absorb the largest percentage of unemployment as they multiply in the community.

A law must be passed by which industries are forbidden to discharge large numbers of employees on short notice. This does not apply to those few cases where a punitive reason is the cause of dismissal. Any manager of a corporation who deems it beneficial to the well-being of his industry to dismiss some of his employees must notify the officials of the LC. The number as well as the trades involved in this dismissal must be par of that information. It must be sent in sufficient time to allow the LC to relocate these workers among other industries that may be in need of them. These other industries do not necessarily have to be in the same community, but may be scattered all over the country. A similar process will be followed when any manager wants to hire extra labor. He must notify the LC officials concerning the number of individuals required and the trades in which he is interested. The LC, in other words, will act as a clearing house for labor. Since the various branches of the LC are constantly in touch with each other, relocation of labor will be greatly expedited, long periods of unemployment avoided, and each man will find a job more suited to his qualifications.

A large proportion of the expenditures involved in the transfer of these unemployed from one place to another must be borne by the company laying them off. This seems just and fair. Indeed, as a result of this layoff and eventual relocation in distant places, many families must leave behind home, relatives, and friends. If no help was given, many of these would be unable to know where they could find a similar job in some other locality, probably hundreds of miles away, and even if they knew the chances are that they could not finance the cost of transportation for themselves and their families. As a result many may have to renounce a suitable job in favor of another for which they may not have either qualification or inclination. Because of this they will be forced to earn less, overcrowd the labor market in their community, and cause conditions of hardship for themselves and others. Add to this fact that, because of the jammed labor market, many may not be able to find any job at all. Aside from all this, the company that discharges this labor makes thereby a saving benefitting the company. On this account it is proper that it should be called upon to compensate those adversely affected by this saving. This award would be set at a certain amount for each one discharged, and the money paid the LC which would utilize it to aid these displaced workers.

Those who must be discharged must be notified of their dismissal in sufficient time to plan for the future. Their names and addresses must also be sent to the LC, and some sort of grading supplied regarding their efficiency, honesty, character, and so forth. It is natural that the best available jobs should be offered to those with good qualifications, and while the LC will try to find employment for all, this may prove sometime an impossible task.

At the time of dismissal the laborers will be notified that their names have been sent to the LC for re-employment. It will be their responsibility to get in touch with the CM of the local EW to acknowledge their willingness to accept the help offered by the LC. Failure to do so within a specified time following notice of dismissal will be taken as a refusal, and if a new job becomes available, it will be offered to someone else on the list. The local CM will represent the LC in the community and, within proper limits, attend to the relocation of laborers among the local industries. The information as to the amount of displaced labor must be sent to the higher authorities of the zone. It is from such information as this, received from different parts of the country, that the higher authorities of the EW will be able to study and analyze the trends of the economic forces in the country at large. If the relocation of this displaced labor becomes impossible in the community under the jurisdiction of the CM, help must be requested from the superior branch of the zone. This, in turn, will add its service in the relocation of labor within the zone itself. If it still cannot be managed within the zone, aid will be sought from the superior branch of the country, and in turn the process repeated on a national scale.

As stated before, not all those who have been discharged can be placed in other industries. The local CM will have, however, the full list of the unemployed as well as their qualifications. Depending on that number and those qualifications the LC will decide on the magnitude and kind of project to be undertaken. This should not be, however, the only factor in that choice as the improvement of the economic condition of the community in general as a result of that project is also important. If possible, the project will be within the community and as it is selected, a job will be offered to those on the list with the proper qualifications. They must understand, however, that such a job is only of a temporary nature, the main purpose being that of keeping them employed until such time when they can be located either in the local industry or somewhere else. In this eventuality, should the new job materialize, the traveling expenses, reduced to a minimum, will be paid by the LC, which as aforesaid has received money for that purpose.

Anyone who does not avail himself of such offer, naturally, will be removed from that list, and be more or less on his own. The finding of a new job and the possible traveling expenses revert to his own responsibility if above the quota received for him by the LC, and given him on request.

The undertaking and financing of these projects needs additional explanation. Assuming that one of a public nature has been chosen, bids will be received either from local organizations or from nearby communities, and the contract awarded to the lowest bidder. It must specify that the labor is to be preponderantly chosen from the local unemployed on the EW list. The necessary key positions, naturally, will have to be given to experts in the particular kind of project undertaken, who already may be employees of the successful contractor. Several projects may be undertaken at the same time, in order to give work to all. It is important to point out, however, that just because the project is of a public nature, this does not mean that labor and money should be squandered in a wasteful way. The contractor will be strictly taken to account on the terms of his agreement, allowance, of course, being made for necessary turnover of labor which from time to time may find its way into industry again. Engineers and experts of the LC will likewise supervise the job to see that the public wealth is efficiently used, and report the progress of the project to their superiors.

Now the efficiency of these laborers, often working in trades in which they are not entirely familiar, will probably be low, and thus they cannot expect to earn the same wages as when regularly employed. The minimum wage, of course, will still be determined by the local index, and their actual wage will depend on their skill in the temporary job, but in general wages will reach a lower level in comparison with those in private organizations, this to arouse initiative on the part of the laborer himself in finding a permanent job without the help of the LC. If conditions should keep on growing worse, a limit will be reached, and the government of the land, acting on the advice of the EW officials, will pass a law by which the working hours per week of all laborers in the country are decreased. By this all industries must reabsorb a certain amount of labor sufficient to compensate for the decreased number of hours of work.

Assume that the work-hours are reduced from 40 to 34 per week. An industry which previously employed 20,000 people at 40 hours per week utilized a total of 20,000 x 40 = 800,000 man-hours.

By law it now must give employment to $800,000 \; / \; 34 = 23,500$ people, or 3,500 additional laborers must be hired. The wages per week at the beginning must not be changed, as the purchasing power of the population in general must not be reduced. However, with the new cost curves of the individual industries, which will affect the supply, and with the new demand represented by so many laborers acquiring a regular job, this affecting the demand, a new level will eventually be reached. As the index automatically takes into account all these changes, it becomes immaterial what the new price level will be, as long as the economic position of the nation is not disrupted and the laborers can still buy the allotted vital commodities set by the scarcity factor. This change will not hamper in any way those forces that are ceaselessly working for a greater supply and consequent better standard of living.

As the increase in labor force will mean an additional expenditure on the part of the industry, it may seem at first that it would not be able to retain its relative position among competing industries, but since the law will be applied throughout the country, all industries will experience the same proportional increase in cost, and thus their competitive relations will remain the same. Such a step, however, must be taken with the utmost care and consideration of present and future implications, all factors causing this unemployment problem determined and analyzed, and no change should be recommended if those causes are only of a temporary nature. In fact, a subsequent increase in working hours, if those factors should eventually disappear, would mean a lowering of the standard of living which people would resent, and for which they would rightly blame the EW.

Here it is well to point out that the necessary expenditures for such a program are far above the means of the LC. Nevertheless, this branch of the EW should and will contribute a certain percentage of the cost of any particular project. This portion will be decided by its financial standing at the time, and will be fixed by the policy group in the capital of the zone, the rest must be contributed by the community, which will so greatly gain by that project. If the project has more than local usefulness, as in the case of roads and bridges connecting centers in the zone, it is just that the population of the entire area join in covering its cost. The LC on its part will contribute a larger amount than before. In cases where the project has a national significance, the entire country and the corresponding LC branch in the capital will be called upon to aid in the financing. This money, raised by a special levy, will be collected when needed and paid over to the EW, which will become the sole arbiter of its use.

The principle upon which the contribution of the LC must rest is that no community should be called upon to finance projects in which it is not directly interested. Likewise, no zone should be saddled with projects in other zones. On this account, when a small project is being carried out in a community, such as a school house, a recreation center, or the like, the LC will first spend the money allotted to that community, which is proportional to the amount received as normal taxes and as inheritance. The same principle will apply for projects that benefit the zone as a whole. Of course, if the necessary expenditures are over and above that allotment, other communities or other zones must be called on to add. Individuals, communities, zones, since they have adopted the new mode of life, must live up to the maxim, "All for one and one for all."

As the labor force finds its way back into industry again, no further projects will be undertaken and those already started will be finished on a reduced schedule, and the special levy will gradually decrease and disappear. Due to the fact that more labor is being employed, prices will naturally rise, but as the taxes are correspondingly decreased the two factors will tend to counteract each other. It may be said that money previously used through the LC division to sponsor projects of general usefulness, such as public works and the like, is now used, through the normal channel of private initiative, for the production of commodities sought and vital to the population at large.

The LC will naturally employ the necessary number of engineers to prepare specifications, supervise the projects undertaken, and deal with contractors to the best advantage of society. Experts in dealing with labor and capital will also be required. The offices will be located in the capital of the country and of the zones, and sub-branches will be set up in the largest cities. The preparation of drawings, ordering of the necessary materials, and other like tasks will also be assigned to the employees of this important branch of the EW.

The discussion this far has been of labor absorbed by industries. The latter are organizations easily regulated and controlled, not so for farming. Here also technological advancement produces an unemployment problem which, as in the city, the LC will have to solve. The first step, of course, will be that of distributing this labor among communities in need, the second that of promoting a greater absorption on the part of industry itself. If both steps should not be sufficient, projects of a local nature must be undertaken and as before it is understood that these jobs are only of a temporary nature.

As the hours of labor decrease throughout the country, additional labor will also enter the farming industry, especially in those cases where machinery and numerous workers are employed. The farming industry, however, is not as elastic and controllable as a factory, where a definite number of persons work a definite number of hours and earn a definite amount of wages. Farming, as a rule, is carried on by the owner of the farm, his family, and some farmhands hired for a few days at a time as needed. As technological improvements are introduced on a large scale, the owner of the farm will be able to do the necessary work alone, and society has no right to force him to hire labor that he does not need. On account of this the labor force in the farming industry is bound to decrease with the passing of time.

Now either we accept progress with all the good and bad it may entail, or we do not. It is perfectly plain that 100 acres of cultivated land required a great number of slaves in the time of the Romans or Egyptians, but no one can possibly expect today that the same amount of labor should be used, when modern machinery and methods can produce far better results in less time. It must be remembered that while industry in general has the peculiar quality of supplying to the public an inexhaustible variety of commodities which gradually become a necessity of life, and thus brings into being more jobs, the farming industry has merely the task of feeding the population. Granted that here is also involved a degree of advance in producing new and better kinds of food, and assuming also an expanding population, which is not always the case, these factors are so far outweighed by technological progress that it is reasonable to expect that the labor population in the farming industry must steadily decrease. This extra labor, therefore, must gravitate toward the city, and these unemployed must be taken into account in fixing the decrease in working hours for industry in general.

As prices steadily increase as a result of the index, as profits become more closely related to the amount of production, farming in general will tend to expand and this in many cases will mean that additional land will be exploited and cultivated. This naturally will tend to increase the labor force. This phase, however, is only of a transitory nature. Food products by and large represent vital commodities. As their scarcity factors reach unity, no additional demand and consequently expansion is likely to occur, and this, coupled with technological advancement, will re-establish the trend toward a reduced labor force in the farming industry.

HOSPITALIZATION DIVISION (EW2-4 or HD)

This branch of the distribution group of the EW will help the poor during their periods of illness. In the study of the index which controls the wages in any community appeared a list of vital commodities that the hypothetical family should have to attain a normal standard of living. Among the necessary expenditures, those for accidents and sickness were omitted. Being of an unforeseen nature, such expenses cannot be included in the list, even though they may draw very heavily on a family saving. As frequently happens, especially among the lower classes, many go without medical care because financially unable and, while this makes their lot more pitiful than ever, it represents a source of danger and infection for the community and for society in general. Progress would in itself be of no avail if it did not raise the standard of living of the poor. This standard not only must include a wage sufficient to buy at least the most important necessities, but also assist the poor in times of sickness and need. It goes without saying that primary rules of health and hygiene must be taught to all in every possible way. These rules, of course, must be enforced in schools and in other places where direct control can be exerted. Safety measures where life can be endangered must be introduced and enforced. Mass injection for prevention of various diseases should be given when needed. Other measures aiming at the well-being of the population should be made available to every person in the community, not only in the interest of the individual but of society itself. But these are only preventive steps which, while of great importance in heading off accidents and illness, are of no aid when they actually occur. Obviously, it would be impossible to help all the sick people in a country, even if limited to the most severe cases. The total financial power of the EW would not be anywhere near sufficient for such an undertaking and, as has been seen, heavy expenditures will be needed in other fields of activity. While the will is there, the scheme of aid must be practical or it will not succeed. On this account a proper degree of sacrifice must be made by the people themselves, which the EW will do all in its power to make as small as possible.

Accident and illness insurance has become a common practice in most leading countries of the world. It is usually limited to a small fraction of the population, as the middle class, and in such places as factories, where it is made compulsory as a protection from law-suits against the factory. However, insurance companies are private organizations which, while beneficial to society, are formed only to derive a profit from the capital invested. From the laws of averages and probability the rates are chosen in such a way that, while the profit made upon each individual is very small, it adds up to a great deal when collected from millions of people. We have no desire to drive these companies out of business, especially those that deal in life insurance. However, as mentioned, even conceding their honesty and popularity it must be admitted that only a small part of the population avails itself of such opportunity. As is usually the case, the poorest and those most in need of such insurance have not the financial capacity to pay the monthly or weekly premium for their protection in case of accidents and illness. This is because the insurance companies while large, are insufficiently so, and accordingly the risk is distributed among a relatively small number which raises the premium far above what the poor can afford. The reference here is to sickness and accident insurance, and not to life insurance. Since life insurance is important to the individual himself rather than to society in general, it is just that he should make the necessary saving toward that attainment. Accident and sickness insurance, however, is extremely important to society, and should be made compulsory among all who avail themselves of the services given by the EW.

With the information obtained from existing insurance companies the number of accidents and cases of sickness apt to occur among a specific population, say a nation, can be approximately estimated and the probable cost calculated. Consider now what the insurance should cover as far as the average laborer is concerned:

(1) Money paid to the hospital
(2) Money paid for necessary medicine, treatments and so forth
(3) Fees to the physicians
(4) Loss of wages during the period of illness

The first three items are related to the sickness or accident of the insured, and being unknown must be apportioned among all who take part in the plan. From the probable cost of these items, and the total number of prospective applicants, a premium may be chosen by which the insurance companies can still derive sizable profits. These profits, however, will not be in proportion to the increased number of insured. That is to say that the profit per capita will be considerably less than present standards. Again the premium, for the same amount of insurance, may be made somewhat higher for those belonging to higher income classes. This will permit a smaller quota for those in the lower class. Yet the difference between maximum and minimum rate should not be anywhere near in proportion with salaries. This is because the risk should be fairly evenly distributed among all components of society. The last item, while related to the kind and severity of the sickness or accident of the insured, since as a result he is forced to stay out of work for an indefinite time, should bear a more strict relation to the applicant's wage, and accordingly vary from one person to another. Thus the quota paid by each individual to the insurance company will be composed of two parts. The first will insure the applicant and his family against sickness and accidents, meaning thereby that if he or anyone in his family should be hospitalized, a certain percentages of the total expenditure for medicines, hospital, and doctors will be paid from insurance. As already stated, this quota being practically equal for all and being distributed among a large number of people will be relatively small. The second will cover the wage of the insured, presumably the head of the family. It will be left to the applicant himself to decide as to the minimum contribution that he is willing to make toward this kind of protection. This minimum will be represented by the quota that must be paid in order to receive a compensation related to the basic wage. By this arrangement, if the applicant should be hospitalized, the insurance company not only will contribute toward the payment of the total bill but will refund or pay his family, while he is sick, a certain percentage of lost wages, related to the quota he had previously chosen to contribute. While on the subject, we wish to add that a statement of wage must be submitted when the application is made, because no one should be allowed to ask for higher quota than the one related to his actual wage. We have seen that he will be permitted to choose a smaller one even though this will tend to increase his risk. It has been mentioned that the insurance will cover only a percentage of his total expenditure, and that the difference will represent the amount of sacrifice made by the individual himself. For those receiving the minimum wage this sacrifice could be made 5% of the total cost of his illness. This is done also for the purpose of discouraging the few who would dishonestly take advantage of the plan and stay away from work longer than necessary. The doctors, of course, will have the final say-so as to when the individual is ready to return to his normal occupation. In note 7-1 a case is presented which will clarify our thoughts.

NOTE 7-1. Say that 5 % of the total expenditure represents the amount any worker receiving the minimum wage is supposed to pay as his share of this cost. This percentage may be increased with the income of the insured. What this change in percentage will be is left to the time when the plan is put into practice. Take the head of a family, receiving the minimum wage, who must be operated upon. As a result he will be out of work for a total of ten weeks. The expense incurred in his operation may be as follows: Cost of hospital, doctors, and medicines $300. If the local index is 50 cents $200 will represent the unreceived wages. 200 + 300 = $500 will represent then the total cost of his illness and 5% of this ($25) will be his share of that cost. The difference (500 — 25 = $475) will be paid by the insurance. From this the insured will easily appreciate the great benefit of the plan, since under normal conditions he would have had to pay $500 instead of $25, with the probability that the necessary operation would have never been done.

. . . .

If non-supporting members of his family happen to need medical care, this will also be covered by insurance and again 5% of the expenditure will represent his personal share.

As already mentioned this insurance distributed over such a large percentage of the population could be easily undertaken by already existing insurance companies, if willing to abide by protective rules of the HD and permit some degree of supervision and inspection. If existing insurance companies should fail to cooperate, the HD should assume this assignment at least for that part of the population not covered by insurance. In those cases in which the insured cannot even contribute the 5% of the total expenditure, this payment, in part or as a whole, given or lent, could be made by the HD. All this is for a normal expectancy of sickness among the population. In emergency cases, as for instance floods, earthquakes, and other major disasters, it is plain that the HD will be unable to cope alone with the situation. Such cases are usually

taken care of by the Red Cross and other similar organizations in
the country. It is natural, however, that the HD should cooperate
with them and add its facilities as well as financial power.

Additional explanation is required at this point. Those insurance
and accident plans which are in force at present in different factories must be retained and possibly extended to all factories and
industries in general. This is important because such plans have
been greatly responsible in the past for the introduction of all kind
of safety devices in industry, safety devices which have considerably
expedited the cutting down of accidents, and unnecessary loss of
life while individuals are performing their duties. Such steps would
never had been taken had the management not felt responsible
for the safety of its employees. Of course, such insurance only
covers the worker while on the premises of the factory and does not
apply if he should injure himself outside. Depending on the kind
of insurance that is in force in the factory, adjustments could be
made so that the insured and his family may be protected at all
times. This means that if the company pays a certain amount of
money for the insurance of its employees, the difference must be
paid by the applicant. In cases where workers become chronically
ill and their chances to recover normal health are very small, they
must, naturally, be weeded out of the plan and taken care of by
society by placing them in rest homes, sanitariums, and other places
to be erected in each zone for this purpose. The cost of such activities
must be contributed directly by the HD in cooperation with
charitable organizations and philanthropists.

It would seem that under this plan anyone on the EW list who
needs medical attention will have the right to enter any hospital,
sanatorium, or nursing home in the community and receive the aid
needed as the bill would be paid, within the limits referred above,
by the insurance company. But it must be realized that once this
method is applied, hospitals and the like will be filled with new
patients, for whom their accommodations will not be anywhere
sufficient. Since the insurance company will analyze each bill as
to its reasonableness and fairness, and pay no more than a just
amount, the law of supply and demand will again be felt, and as
usual the rich will secure advantages over the poor because of their
greater financial resources. Because of this the plan cannot be put
immediately into effect, as it would not be right to collect money
from the poor when accommodations in hospitals for which it
would pay are not available to them. Thus at the beginning the

insurance should apply only to the loss of wages, and if practicable, also to the fees due to doctors. Only when the necessary number of hospitals and nursing homes have been established, will the time be ripe to extend the insurance to all the expenditures referred to above.

This is the mode in which this division of the EW will function. The HD will receive from its headquarters an appropriation each year in order to perform its humanitarian duties. Some of this money will pay the insurance companies, some for those financially incapacitated, but the main part will be spent to build large hospitals devoid of unnecessary frills but with all modern facilities. These will maintain a permanent staff of doctors and nurses, and since the question of remuneration between doctors and patients will be eliminated, all will receive the same attention, according to the highest standard, made possible by the good salary paid each member of the staff. Only persons on the list of the EW will have the right to enter such hospitals and as these are erected all over the country, the full plan can be put into operation. Needless to say, the insured will have the right to be treated in all hospitals of the country reserved for this purpose.

Leading physicians could then be made honorary members of the HD and receive a nominal salary. In return they should promise to devote a certain amount of their time, without compensation, to care for patients in these hospitals who need their particular type of skill but unable to pay the fee normally charged their patients.

Additional sanatoriums, clinics, and so forth should be founded as needed and naturally their erection must await the financial availability of the HD. In this respect, the HD will join forces with the Labor Control Division which is also interested in providing work for the unemployed in periods of business recession. The same can be said for the erection of homes for the aged which, though neither elegant nor pretentious, must be sufficiently livable to make them attractive to those who, due to unfortunate circumstances, are alone in the world and financially unable to take care of themselves.

The main office of the branch, as stated, will be located in the capital of the zone. The CM will administer this branch for the people. The money received for insurance, collected directly or from the respective employers of the applicants will be sent to the main office which in turn will pay the insurance companies if the latter have accepted this plan. If this does not happen to be the case, the money will be invested and drawn as needed.

DELINQUENCY CONTROL DIVISION (*EW2-5 or DC*)

Delinquency is a social evil that must be eradicated, or at least reduced to a point where it will no longer endanger society. No one can deny that delinquency is a direct product of our civilization. Children born of poor families, hungry and dejected, often huddled in houses and huts not worthy of the name of home, who are not taught even the most elementary principles of honesty and personal dignity, who live in a world of their own, unwanted and unaided by the rest of society, make the potential criminals of tomorrow. If we consider the type of parents from whom many children learn to know the world, the innumerable cases of children who are abandoned by their parents to wander alone, it is a wonder that there are not more criminals. This background, plus the social disgrace in which a released prisoner finds himself, tends also to leave a criminal unchanged.

The efforts made toward decreasing unemployment and improving housing conditions as well as the enforcement of universal education will all be beneficial factors in reducing delinquency. It is now a general practice to send to the reformatory schools all the children who have committed minor crimes. More often than not they emerge from these places further advanced in delinquency. Forcing on a child the companionship of others who are closer to becoming criminals, is in itself a sinister influence upon his plastic mind. Lack of understanding on the part of the teachers in a reformatory of the mind, background, ability, unconscious desires, and idiosyncrasies of any individual child prevent the realization of the results intended when sending him there. A better solution for this problem must be found if real progress in the right direction is to be made.

It seems to us that the possession of a criminal mind should be grouped with other forms of diseases, moral instead of physical, that need to be treated as such. Only in cases where it is found that this disease is incurable should steps be taken to prevent the criminal from endangering society any longer. However, irrespective of crime, capital punishment should be abolished as a remnant of the uncivilized past. Indeed what right has society to end the life of any one and thereby echo the same crime for which the individual is punished? No matter how strong the evidence brought against an accused person, there are too many cases on record in which an innocent victim is sent to the gallows for a crime he never committed. Circumstantial evidence placed him in a position of not being able to disprove his guilt. This, however, is not the point. Criminal attitude, as stated, should be considered a form of illness, and treated as such. While we all agree that it is ethically right to exert all efforts in saving the life of an individual who is afflicted by a dangerous malady, it seems to us equally just that all efforts should be exerted in saving the individual whose mind is so unhinged that he has become a danger to society.

It remains to be considered how the EW can approach the solution of this problem. As said, by improving the standard of living of the poor, by raising their wages to a point where they will be able to obtain the necessities of life, and thus get the proper nourishment for the normal development of themselves and their family, by gradually demolishing the slums while replacing them by intelligent housing projects, the poor will live in healthful surroundings, more conducive to the acquisition of that mental and normal stability that makes a person a better citizen, more observant of the law, and more contented with himself, with life, and with society in general. The attainment of such a goal, however, once the new mode of life is adopted, is bound to require considerable time, and meanwhile the evils which breed criminals will still be doing their destructive work. The above-mentioned improvements, however, consider the problem from a physical approach and in themselves could not and will not cure delinquency unless a different attitude is taken and efforts made toward the moral rehabilitation of the delinquent.

Assume first the case of a child caught in a criminal act, and thus brought to the attention of the law. With few exceptions, the present approach is not to search any too deeply into the causes that made that child a lawbreaker. These causes may be few or many, but even if found and recognized, no attempt is ever made to correct them and see that the child is reared under better surroundings. Instead, he is usually sent to a reformatory where the effect on him is far from good, and should he be the proper age he is sentenced to jail with the misguided assumption that physical punishment and fear of the law will plant honesty in his mind. In many cases the child comes from a large family whose parents are poor, separated, or living in vice, so that quite often he is subjected to a punishment that should be reserved for his elders. Of course, every case presents its own peculiarities which should be studied with common-sense and an enlightened approach. For instance, with a poor family vainly striving to improve its condition, effort should be made to find a job for the father or mother, help should be given to locate them in better surroundings, and so forth. In cases where the family has been broken up and debased by corruption and vice, the parents should be considered responsible for the children's criminal acts and their case treated accordingly. The fact that a child has gone so far in the ways of corruption is in itself a proof that the parents have not given him proper education, and society has a right to regard them directly responsible. In cases where it is obvious that the parents are too far gone in moral corruption to expect an early reform, their children should be taken away independently of the fact that only one was caught in a criminal act, and all placed in better environments.

As these children come under the direct supervision of society, a study should be made of their physical and mental development and aptitude, and from this examination a place chosen that will best improve their minds, develop good qualities, and eventually make them responsible citizens. If the intelligence test of a child shows that he is unusually bright, he should be sent to a school that will give him the opportunity to learn; if of average mentality or less, he should be sent to a farm or school where trade may be learned, but in any case he must be completely separated from his parents and early environment, and given a chance to start life anew with better probability of success.

Every important city in the country should have in its zone a farm or a school with facilities for taking care of a large number of children (ten years of age or more). As a child, whether guilty or not of a criminal act, is sent to the school, steps should be taken to discover and analyze his subconscious personality by competent physiologists, and his nature, attitude and general qualifications established. While living in his proper section of the school, the child will receive the food, vitamins, and general teaching needed to improve his health and his mind. After a suitable period of normal life the proper rehabilitational school will be chosen on the basis of the qualifications of the child. This is necessary because each school will specialize in the taking care of children with definite inclinations and aptitudes. For instance, one may emphasize the teaching of trades, others farming, still others higher education and so on. The mental and moral development of the child will be under

the scrutiny of specialized teachers, and from time to time they will
have to go through additional examinations and tests. The surroundings of the school must be the best, and while the gates of the
outside world will be closed to them, they will have opportunities
they did not receive from their parents. Good food, plenty of exercise
and recreation, libraries, good lectures, and so forth should be
available to them. The time of confinement will be independent of
the crime committed, but must be conditioned on the causes that
tangled the child in the toils of the law. The mode of life of his
parents must be considerably improved before the child is returned
to them, and they must be in a position to take better care of him.
The child in turn must show sufficient mental and moral progress
to justify his release. In those cases where it would be criminal to
return a child to parents who are still corrupt and in no position
to guide him toward an honest life, this reunion should be prevented. In those cases where the children have shown definite mental
and moral improvement and have become worthy of freedom but
yet remain isolated for the reasons specified above, efforts should
be made to place them in private homes, or they may take a more
responsible position in the school itself as substitute instructors. In
such capacity they would receive a salary and the school gates would
no longer be closed to them. As soon as they reach a suitable age,
the school will find them honest and remunerative jobs consonant
with their aptitude and training.

The rehabilitational schools may be built to take care also of
children under the ten years of age who should be located in a
separate wing or in another building. These children may also have
committed a crime or may have been taken away from irresponsible
parents. Their moral, and physical well-being will likewise be fostered
by well-trained and qualified teachers, and only the improvement
of their homes will be required for their release. As the child grows
older he may either go home or be included with those who are
in their teens.

Consider now what should be done with the criminal whose
physical development has reached maturity. The first question that
society must ask in dealing with him is what were the factors, the
circumstances, the training that made him a criminal. There exists
a great variety of crimes, ranging from minor robberies to brutal
premeditated murders. Even when a murder has been committed,
different impulses may have been the causes of that action. In some
cases the original intention may have been robbery, and the murder

only an effort of escape. In considering his case we must keep in mind that the intended crime was robbery. As he was bound to be under terrific nervous strain, his being detected, added to the apprehension of arrest, made him lose his self-control and, impelled by the instinct of self-preservation, he became a murderer in his attempt of freedom. Other crimes are committed under similarly strong emotional feeling, as hunger, jealousy, despair; some are due to intoxication or drug-taking, in which case, more often than not, the person shows signs of an unbalanced personality and should be treated accordingly. We have also the cases of cold premeditated murder, committed with the calm faculties of the individual in arranging the necessary details as for instance the case of kidnapping a child for ransom, the poisoning of individuals to gain inheritances, insurance, and so forth. And even here the background of the person may have been such that his mind was distorted to the extent of becoming a potential murderer or kidnapper. Murders sometimes are committed to acquire prohibited drugs frantically desired. By curing an individual of that craving, he may still be restored to society.

All these causes that may have contributed to the forming of a criminal must be considered and ranked in proper importance. Society, while often injured by the loss of a useful, honest, and prominent citizen, should, nevertheless, give these criminals the chance to amend, and with the proper approach to their inner souls make them worthy of recovering their standing as valued components. A separate branch of the rehabilitation farm or school should be devoted to these individuals. A treatment, based upon the diagnosis of their shortcoming, would be given, and their confinement would depend on their moral rehabilitation. In variance with the present policy where a lawbreaker goes to jail and is often forced into an inactive and useless life that breeds in him greater hate against the institutions that sent him there as well as society in general, the setting should be another orderly society, similar to that of the outside world where everyone assumes responsibilities toward others and is required to perform duties consonant with his capabilities. Society should not pay out more money for their subsistence than necessary. All these rehabilitational schools, farms and the like, should have sufficient ground on which cultivation could be maintained. All kind of trades should be fostered, not only for the welfare of the school but also for manufacturing articles to be sold outside, quite likely through the facilities of the EW. Wages on the same level as those in the outside society should be paid these men, and with their approval whatever surplus is saved beyond living expenses, could be sent either to their families or accumulated for the time they have earned their freedom.

A system of promotion should also be in vogue. This would be based, of course, on the ability and efficiency of the individual. A primary prerequisite of such promotion, however, will be his moral and spiritual progress, recognized by the officials of the school. As many of the responsible positions will involve leadership among other inmates, some could be awarded through elections among the latter, a procedure that will also tend to teach good citizenship and sportsmanship. Any individual entering the institution must start with the minimum wage, whatever his skill or qualifications. As his moral rehabilitation begins, he will be promoted to a better position and receive better wages. This is bound to enhance his self-respect, and eventually prepare him to re-enter society with a different outlook and a greater feeling of responsibility toward himself and his fellow-citizens. Freedom will be restored to him as soon as the officials of the institution have sufficient proof of his moral advancement and not after some specified time set by the judge who based that sentence on the seriousness of the crime rather than that needed to rehabilitate the criminal and become worthy of being restored to society. As he advances, better quarters may be provided for him, and he will also receive the privilege of inviting his family for a few days each month. Besides an active and useful life (in fact, the institution will depend a great deal on their work), their minds will be developed and improved in all possible ways. People here should be able to study, learn different trades, attend special lectures, cultivate useful hobbies, and as much as practicable be able to have some kind of relaxation and privacy during part of their day. This will teach them the habit of thinking and of being with themselves and their conscience. All should be treated with kindness and sympathy by the institution employees, and have easy access to the officials of the institution from whom they should be occasionally invited to better determine their progress. This will help to build up a better understanding between inmates and officials, and will greatly help the latter to gauge the moral rehabilitation of each man, as his freedom greatly depends on this. On this account, the school should be large enough to accommodate a sizable number of inmates, so as to decrease the total cost of this humanitarian project, yet should be sufficiently small to permit a close supervision on the part of the officials. Again in a small school the criminal will not feel isolated in a crowd and by becoming a conscious unit of a small society, he will have greater chance of rehabilitation and progress. We realize that instinctive aversion of an official toward anyone in the school could prevent him from receiving his freedom. However, his release should not depend on the judgment of any one official, but on the majority of the secret votes among several officials who independently of each other have had the opportunity of studying each individual whose name, at stated intervals of time, will come up for consideration. It will be well to divide all inmates into various groups depending on their ability and on the activity required of them. Therefore, those who will be mostly engaged in making shoes will have a room or shop by themselves, so will the tailors, carpenters and so forth. Those who will work on the farm will also be divided into groups and assigned to different locations depending on where they will be mostly needed. Each of these groups, besides a leader chosen among themselves, position which should only last a specified amount of time, will be also under the supervision of an official who will be moved to different groups at the end of each month. Besides the task of supervision and direction, the official will have also the duty to study the moral progress of all under him during that month and before leaving he must write a report about every one of them, describing small and large incidents which may help to gauge the moral development of his men. This report will be duly filed and at the time when any one particular individual comes up for discussion, as to his gaining his freedom or not, will give valuable information and assistance before the secret vote is cast by all the officials who at some time or other have had the opportunity to know this man and study his qualities. Good health and medical approval will also be required before anyone can be returned to society. It comes as a matter of course that to all those in need of medical attention, it be given freely, and any deformity or remediable defect, which often is the subconscious cause of their warping of character and personality, be removed and cured.

The walls of these institutions must be well guarded and attempts to escape prevented. We have spoken of the inhumanity of capital punishment. There is one case, however, when the taking of life is justified. This is represented by the action of the officer of the law who forcibly resists violence on the part of a criminal seeking to escape. At the split-second in which the criminal is shot and probably killed by the soldier or guard on duty we see society defending itself from the criminal who, by trespassing, endangers society. From the standpoint of the criminal he may only be dashing for liberty, but for society it is a matter of self-defense and a justifiable attempt to shield itself from future criminal acts by that outlaw. In this light society is right. For the criminal the way to freedom is always open, as he is encouraged to rehabilitate himself and earn his liberty. Any other way should and must be blocked even if the taking of life is necessary.

As implied before, courts should not fix a definite term of confinement, which must be left to the officials of the school to decide, as they will be better qualified to judge the moral progress made by the criminal. Two individuals sent to the institution for the same criminal act may stay widely different periods of time. The justification for this is that they must remain confined until their moral rehabilitation is such that their release will no longer endanger society. When an individual, having served time in one of these institutions is set free and then is again apprehended by the law, his case will be handled much more severely than before. Here again, of course, the circumstances of his new crime must be analyzed and weighed, and depending on this he may be returned to the institution or sent to a more rigid place where his confinement may not be less than ten years and may last for the rest of his life. Indeed, in cases where it is found that his mental distortion and degradation is incurable, society is justified in segregating such a lawbreaker in places where he will no longer be able to endanger anyone. Similar action will be taken upon anyone attempting to esacpe from the school, or who if successful is later apprehended. In either case he should be sent to places of detention where he will be held a minimum of ten years. But even in these places the inmates must be kept active and mentally alert and their life must be similar to that of society outside, within those limitations that must be taken to prevent their escape. As mentioned above, the confinement of some may be for the rest of their life, but even this will depend on the degree of rehabilitation, under the scrutiny of a more strict and exacting set of officials. In other words, the hope of freedom will never be completely lost.

In this vast program of rehabilitation, foremost will be the contribution of the Delinquency Control Division (DC). First of all, the leaders of this crusade against delinquency, corruption, and crime must be DC officials especially qualified through talent and understanding of human nature. Schools for training those who wish to make a career of this branch of the EW should be attached to several universities. These men, placed in key positions in the various institutions of the nation, should be directly responsible to the head of the branch at the capital of the country or of the zone. The granting of the necessary ground, the construction of the buildings, the acquisition of the necessary facilities, the training of the personnel, including teachers of various qualifications, doctors, specialists in neurology, detectives, and so forth, will require a considerable amount of money that must be spread over a number of years and undertaken on a pay-as-you-go basis. Most of the work necessary for the erection of schools and installation of facilities will be provided, as much as practicable, by the members of the institution, who will receive suitable wages. The design of the buildings will be left to specialists who have made a detailed study of the requirements previously analyzed, and, of course, an undetermined amount of outside labor must be provided to promote the maximum efficiency and economy. The program may be carried out in successive steps, and efforts made whenever possible to coordinate it with the activities of the LC.

The number of schools or institutions may be increased from time to time as necessity requires and as money becomes available. Precedence should be given to the quartering of children over ten years of age, then to that of those under that age, and finally to that of criminals above 21. Separate quarters for boys and girls, men and women must be provided and the sites carefully chosen from the standpoint of health and hygiene.

As said, schools will be attached to various universities for training candidates who are choosing a life career in these institutions. Emphasis must be placed on the fact that their duties, rather than the negative ones of physical caring for the institutions inmates and preventing their escape, will be the positive ones of aiding and supervising the moral and spiritual rehabilitation of their charges. They must have the natural ability to reach their inner soul, to win their friendship, trust and confidence, to find the causes of their maladjusted life and personality, to help them to raise themselves from the moral degradation into which they have fallen, and eventually inspire them with the necessary determination to face life with courage and enthusiasm. Lastly, they must be able to teach them that happiness and spiritual peace can only be attained by self-sacrifice and abnegation, and by learning to respect and love their fellow-men. These persons, whose duties will not probably change with the passing of time unless exceptional qualities should raise them to more responsible positions in the organization and in the country, will receive a salary based on the length of service. This salary should be sufficiently large to attract a class of persons of the highest talent, qualifications, and integrity.

RECREATION DIVISION (EW2-6 or RD)

From the analysis made of the activities of the EW it can be concluded that the hypothetical family will eventually obtain sufficient food and other vital commodities, possess a better home, and will be helped in time of illness. Its standard of living is bound to be far above what may be found even in the most advanced countries of the world today. With the progress of technology and subsequent decrease of working hours, the head of the family will have more leisure time, and will enjoy better things in life. Some of this time may be used for well-deserved rest, relaxation and companionship with the family, some spent in libraries open to the public and in the attainment of higher education and improvement of the mind by attending schools and lectures made available to the public in general and some given to the pursuit of happiness and satisfaction by devoting more time to their creative talent and industry, such as painting, gardening and so forth which does not have to be necessarily expensive. In the problem of furnishing more entertainment for the public, by far the largest part must come directly from the people themselves through their initiative by joining forces in promoting folkdances, picnics, parties, cruises and so forth. But up to a certain extent additional channels of recreation and enjoyment could be facilitated by the EW through the Recreation Division or RD.

In times when the labor population is being gradually shifted from industry to the care of the EW, part of the projects undertaken to give work to the many unemployed could be of a social nature, as for instance halls in various small towns to be later leased or donated to the Y.M.C.A. or other organizations serving the public in general. These halls would be provided with the necessary equipment for gymnastics, basketball, moving pictures, etc. Most of the entertainment in these public buildings must be of the inexpensive kind such as dances, amateur plays, etc., but occasionally, as financial conditions permit, the RD will subsidize more expensive and elaborate entertainment like learned lectures, dramas by famous playwrights, ballet performances, concerts and so forth. As a matter of patriotism and devotion to humanity, these noted organizations and artists should not charge for these tours as much as if the audience were made up of well-to-do people. The difference between the actual cost of the entertainment and the quota provided by the RD must naturally be raised among the inhabitants of the town, either through contribution by wealthy people of the community, sale of tickets, or both. When such an entertainment is provided, two prices may be charged, a lower one for those on the EW list and their families, who take precedence above all others, especially when a large attendance is expected, and another for the general public. Donations from generous citizens of the community will form the nucleus from which funds will be drawn to pay the artists or companies, as this money must be paid ahead of time and will be independent of the attendance. What is collected at the door will go to replenish that basic fund. It is likely enough that more money is made than spent, and this surplus may be used in future to pay for similar or more splendid shows, once the community learns to appreciate and anticipate this sort of mental recreation. The choice of artists, the planning of their tour, the amount they are to receive, and other details will be discussed and determined by this special branch of the EW whose central office will be in the capital of the country. This branch may also keep smaller offices in the capital of each zone.

Whenever a small community has succeeded in accumulating some minimum amount for the purpose of securing one of these entertainments, the CM may be notified and correspondence opened with the RD at the capital of the zone, which will give valuable information and suggestions on the subject. Interested citizens will then be appointed by the people. They will carry on the necessary correspondence, make the selection of the kind and quality of entertainment, take care of the details pertaining to the coming attraction and necessary to the success of the show, and take care of the financial matters. Since the RD will act as a go-between among artists and public, small communities will have now and then the opportunity to meet and enjoy artists which otherwise would have been out of their reach.

EW1 OR POLICY GROUP OF THE EW

Having analyzed the activities of the second group of the EW in all its details, there will now be given a preliminary description of the all-important branch of the organization that will be referred to as the POLICY GROUP. This branch, in our estimation, will represent the core and nerve center of the entire organization and its main activities will be the following:

(1) It will collect the information necessary to guide society along beneficial channels.

(2) It will keep a constant watch on the general conditions of the country, and will measure changes in its welfare, in response to various policies adopted by the organization.

Wages, indexes, prices of commodities and corresponding scarcity factors, condition of labor, standard of living, condition of industries, financial pattern of society, work being done and money being spent, amounts exported and imported, are some of the data that regularly every month or every week each CM in the country must send in duplicate form to the Policy group of the respective zone. An account of all the steps taken in the solution of problems brought to their attention must also be included. In the office of the EWI of the zone all this data must then be classified and forwarded to the respective offices specializing in each particular activity. Here they will be studied and analyzed. Charts, graphs, tables, and other means used in assembling data in a clear and concise form will then be prepared and eventually submitted to the EW Manager of the zone who we shall indicate as the ZM. Regarding what comes under his direct supervision and responsibility he will issue the proper orders and directives. All else, together with a detailed analysis of the various steps taken in his zone, will go to the EWl in the capital. There a similar process will be repeated before all data reach the Manager of the EW, who will thus have a comprehensive and overall view of the organization activity throughout the country. He will then be in a position to formulate the proper national policies.

All this information must be published at specified intervals in special bulletins, available to the public on request at any post office or other public building. The first section will include all the information and data pertaining to every locality in the zone. Anyone sufficiently interested will be able to ascertain thereby the financial condition of his town, what is being done for the locality itself, and what are the immediate or distant prospects for the future. In a separate part of the same section similar data will be given for the zone as a whole. It is easy to see that such bulletins may be of great value to any business man, who may gain valuable information on which to base his future activities.

In the second section of the bulletin a succinct analysis of the economic position of the various zones in the country will be given, as well as an analysis of the economic welfare of the country in general. The bulletin should also include a description of the various goals to be achieved, as well as the measures being contemplated or taken to that end. The purpose of these publications will be first of all to maintain a check and restraint on the EW activities, which should be above reproach and open to discussion from every quarter. As will be seen later on in this chapter, a parallel branch of the government will be set up for the purpose of making sure that the best interests of society are actually cared for and protected. But independently of this, the publication will help to enlighten the public in general, or at least all public-minded individuals, upon issues of vital importance to all. It will encourage discussion, criticism, and suggestions which, if sent through the proper channels, can eventually be tested and accepted.

HOW THE EW SHOULD BE STARTED AND EXPANDED

In describing the functions performed by the second group of the EW, it was assumed that the latter had reached in the country its full growth and development. We shall now analyze the various steps that could be chosen for setting up this branch of the government. It is easy to see that to build an organization of this character and magnitude may require long and careful planning on the part of many persons of ability. Experts in different fields must give thought and consideration to innumerable details before the organization takes form.

For obvious reasons the new policy must not be applied in full forthwith throughout the country, but should expand gradually from some central locality, say the capital. As knowledge and experience accumulate, expansion throughout the zone adjoining the capital, and then to other zones, may be considered and undertaken. This cautious process is advocated for the following reasons:

1) Expert personnel cannot be found and made available in a short time. As individuals are hired to serve in the organization, only a few will have the necessary qualifications to discharge their duties properly and efficiently. The others will have to go through some kind of training and thereby acquire not only a general knowledge of the vast activity of the EW but be able to specialize in some particular field to which they may feel attracted. As new recruits

are taken in, some in turn will become instructors for additional personnel, so that the process of expansion from a slow start will acquire momentum with time.

(2) As the personnel is originally limited, it can only take care of a small part of the country, therefore, the choice of one zone or locality seems appropriate, as it will also give the first test of the organization. Changes made necessary as experience is acquired will be passed on to the new personnel which will eventually serve a larger population.

(3) As the mode of life in the new system will be somewhat different from the present, time must be given to people to become accustomed to it so as to prevent dislocation and strain.

Now assume that a nation, under the pressure of public opinion, decides to adopt the new mode of life. This desire will be manifested by articles in leading newspapers of the country and by the many appeals to representatives in the government. The actual decision of transition must await the results of a general referendum throughout the country.

Congress, or whatever else in the government represents the people, must then elect a committee. This will appoint a number of prominent citizens, outstanding for their achievement as well as for their humanitarian qualities and integrity. These appointees must be chosen from every part of the country, efforts being made to have one representative for each three millions in the nation. These individuals will form the "PEOPLE'S WELFARE BRANCH" of the government or "PW". Their main task will be that of representing and upholding the interests of society and their position will be for a term of twelve years. Later the same number will be added after four years, and the same process repeated after eight years until complete representation exists for each million people in the country. Disregarding for the present the important activities of this branch when the new government is completely organized, it will be part of its duty to select the MANAGER of the EW which we shall indicate by M. This official, as earlier explained in this chapter, must be a proved leader of organizations, and his normal term of office will be four years. His contract may be renewed if he discharges his duties to the satisfaction of the PW branch and of the country in general. It can be cancelled at any time if 90 percent of the members of the PW vote to terminate his term. The EW M with the aid of the PW will then select four "GROUP MANAGERS" or 1-2-3-4GM who will be in charge of the four main groups of the organization. Additional officials will be then selected by them and by the PW to hold other responsible positions. The four Group Managers will have the title of first, second, third and fourth Group Manager of the EW. The 1GM will be the titular head and coordinator of the EW1 of the nation, the 2GM will hold the same rank in that part of the organization that distributes wealth to the people, 3GM in that part that takes charge of wealth temporarily entrusted to the EW, and the 4GM in that which administers the settlement of inheritances. Mention has been made of these Group Managers in order of importance, and in that order they will substitute for the EW Manager if absent on business or ill, and during the period in which a new EW Manager is being chosen in place of the one who is discharged.

Personnel will be hired by the four Group Managers to help them in the subdivided duties that will fall in their particular field of activity. This choice will be made with the cooperation and approval of the EW Manager, according to a fixed and previously arranged plan. This personnel, which at this level in the organization will still have executive position, will possess the highest qualifications, and must be selected among lawyers, engineers, bankers, business managers, and the like, depending on the duties they will be called to assume. All must be well-known and respected leaders in the nation at large. As the various assignments are distributed among these individuals, more enlargement will be made so as to further divide the work among a greater number. They will all, while assuming diversified activities, be part of what will be called the Central Branch or CB and will form the nucleus from which the necessary personnel must be chosen to assume responsible positions in the various zones that eventually will have to be set up throughout the country.

While the organization is in the process of taking a more definite shape, the still constituted government must pass and approve the new CONSTITUTION on which the foundation of society will rest.

It is well at this point to remind our reader that this work is not meant to apply to the United States or to any other nation in particular but to all nations in general which at present may or may not have a Constitution of their own. It follows that the Constitution to which we refer will be somewhat different from any we may find at present even though it will include and adopt many of the ideals and principles of the others. As such we shall refer to it as the "CONSTITUTION OF HUMANITY" or just "CON-

STITUTION" even though at first it may be applied to one or only few nations. This Constitution, headed by a proclamation of basic and fundamental rights of men will have to be formulated and written by men of great vision who will become the spiritual leaders and spear-heads of the new philosophy of life. The clauses of the Constitution must be gradually enforced as the organization becomes ready for its successive assignments.

Returning to our analysis as to how the EW will grow and expand, it is plain that the activities of the fourth group, being the simplest of them all, may be temporarily and immediately assumed by the CB of the nation, pending, of course, the formation of the branch itself. Such activities as the collection of inheritances will give rise to many problems and in solving them, valuable experience will be acquired. Each case that may occur anywhere in the country will also give a practical test of the organization, and as they will not occur very often, the latter will have ample time to detect and correct any flaws.

We wish to emphasize at this point that such a pyramidal organization must grow from the apex toward its base, and thus the CB at the capital will be the first to be formed. This eventually will become the CB of the nation, the core and nerve-center of the entire organization. The CB itself, which will mostly be a policy making body, will be divided into four groups, each under a Group Manager. These groups will continually feed the necessary personnel into the respective divisions of the zones as they take form, and naturally into the various divisions of the zone capital which, while residing in the capital of the nation, must not be confused with the CB of the nation.

It is plain that the EW at this stage of development will not be in a position to perform those duties analyzed in the first part of this chapter, which pertain to the second group of the Zone EW. The CB of the nation will be busy, however, collecting the necessary data in the capital zone and elsewhere in the country so as to plan the future policies for the country at large. Needless to say, as the various branches of the capital zone acquire the necessary and specialized personnel, they will assume their normal duties within the capital itself later to be expanded to its zone and as such will take over many duties from the CB of the nation.

The CB of the nation will first limit its activity in and around the capital zone and will expand its influence as experience and knowledge is obtained and personnel trained. Its activities will be many and far-reaching, and besides the immediate task of taking care of the activities that will eventually be taken over by the zones' governments as they come to be formed, some of the most important tasks are given in the following list:

1) The CB will establish a minimum requirement for a healthy person as to food, clothing and kind of dwelling.

(2) It will determine those commodities that are very important to the well-being of the hypothetical family and these will be recognized as vital commodities.

(3) It will assess the availability of such commodities in the locality under study (capital of the nation at this stage) with the purpose of establishing their scarcity factors.

(4) It will make a study of the market price of various commodities, special emphasis being placed upon vital commodities needed by the hypothetical family.

(5) It will make a survey of housing conditions to establish rules and regulations on which the grading of all dwellings must be based. It will consider comprehensive housing projects, and the ways for their attainment.

(6) It will study the condition of labor as to wages received in the local industries.

(7) It will ascertain the pattern of the population as to wages and financial conditions in the locality.

(8) It will make a survey of the local industries as to financial position, quality and quantity of products manufactured, kind of management and respective cost curves in relation to current prices, zone of influence, and other information that may aid in establishing a standard by which all other industries may be measured.

(9) It will make a survey of the various projects that could be sponsored in the community in case of necessity, emphasis being placed on general usefulness as well as on the amount and kind of labor needed.

(10) It will determine the percentage of population that takes hospitalization insurance with the purpose of coming to agreement with existing insurance companies so as to include practically the entire population.

(11) It will make a comparison of the policies followed by various industries as to compensation in case of accidents and sickness, in order to establish rules and regulations to be eventually enforced in all industries.

(12) It will make a comparison of the fees charged by doctors

and hospitals with a view of establishing insurance rates and the amount that must be added by the EW.

(13) It will make a survey of the kind and amount of delinquency in the community and zone, and determine the type and amount of facilities available.

(14) It will make a study of the recreation places that could be sponsored when the organization will become sufficiently wealthy to give attention to this kind of activity.

(15) The CB will establish inheritance rules and will take care of any wealth that comes under the jurisdiction of the EW.

Now some of this information will be relatively easy to obtain because it is more or less a matter of public knowledge; other items may be more difficult. At any rate, common sense and an enlightened attitude will be valuable assets in such an undertaking. We wish to say, in addition, that such data gathered at this or any other time by the EW may always be revised and made more in accord with actual fact, so that any rule or regulation issued as a result of such information can be changed if needed, and, therefore, keep pace with the normal evolution of society.

As this information is gathered and analyzed, plans as to the line of action to be taken will become more clear and definite. Of course, each activity will need its own personnel under a specialized leader who can coordinate their actions. As their knowledge in their particular field increases, their assistance will be invaluable in setting up the four groups within the various zones of the country, where they will occupy positions of leadership and responsibility.

In conjunction with the personnel that covers the field, others will be needed to receive their reports, translate such information in a condensed form, prepare charts, diagrams, and the like, and provide the EW Manager and the immediate assistants with the fundamental facts on which to base their policies and instructions.

As inheritance wealth accumulates from distant communities, care must be taken to set it aside for the time when the activity of the EW will extend to those places. In the meantime, experts will be sent throughout the nation with the task of dividing the country into zones.

At this point consideration of the formation of the EW in the capital zone is in order. A MANAGER OF THE ZONE or ZM must be chosen from among the best-qualified candidates of the nation CB. Four Group Managers or Z(1-2-3-4)GM will head the four main branches of the EW and take orders only from the ZM. The necessary personnel will also be selected and will concentrate on problems pertaining to the zone rather than the nation. In the development of this branch of the government within the zone emphasis will be put on the development of the second group or the one that comes into contact with the public. The other groups will gradually increase to their ultimate size but since they will be mostly located in the capital of the zone (in this case it coincides with the capital of the nation), they will not represent any particular problem. As to the first division of the second group or PS, this should be developed immediately in the capital. A COMMUNITY MANAGER or CM of the city must be chosen, stores in which the EW will sell its wares must be selected, and in general priority given to the setting of the "Price Stabilization." It is natural that before such a step is taken that funds be on hand, and the CM as well as the ZM will have valuable help from the National CB also located in the capital. In the meantime, industry and labor control divisions, as well as hospitalization, delinquency control, and the like within the zone will gain impetus. As conditions permit, the activity of the Price Stabilization will spread to other communities of the zone.

CLOSER ANALYSIS OF THE CENTRAL BRANCH OF THE NATION OR CB

At the beginning of this chapter we gave the general set-up of the EW and said that it will be divided into four main groups. This set-up will be maintained throughout the organization either if applied to a zone or to the nation as a whole. The EW of the nation, mostly a policy-making body, will be referred to as the Central Branch or CB. For a more comprehensive visualization of this branch we shall submit two tables of which the first will give the name of the groups and corresponding divisions, while the second will give the title of the officials that will be at the head of these groups and divisions (see Table 5, page 328).

The EW Manager and the four Group Managers will form the "Executive Board" of the CB.

The "Policy Group" (EW1) will be divided into three divisions.

The main task of the "Upper Division" (EW1-1 will be that of studying the economic condition of the nation as a result of policies previously taken or to be taken in the future. It will also study the economic relationship of the nation versus other nations. Many of the leading economists of the country will be part of this division

TABLE NO. 4

BRANCH OF GOVERNMENT		
ECONOMIC WELFARE ~ EW	POLICY	EW1
	DISTRIBUTION	EW2
	MAINTENANCE	EW3
	INHERITANCE	EW4

FIG. 20

PRICE LEVEL — COST CURVE — A B C
UNIT COST / QUANTITIES PRODUCED

TABLE NO. 5   EW ORGANIZATION

		BRANCHES AND DIVISIONS			TITLE OF OFFICIALS·					
	GROUP	DIVISION ~ D			G.M.	DIVISION MANAGER ~ DM				
ECONOMIC WELFARE BRANCH ~ EW	POLICY / EW1	UPPER	EW1-1		GENERAL MANAGER ~ M / 1ST GROUP MANAG. 1GM	1ST DIV. MAN.	1ST GROUP			1DM1G
		INNER	EW1-2			2ND " " " "				2DM1G
		LOWER	EW1-3			3RD " " " "				3DM1G
	DISTRIBUTION / EW2	PRICE STABILIZATION	EW2-1		SECOND GROUP MANAGER 2GM	1ST " " " 2ND "				1DM2G
		INDUSTRY REGULATION	EW2-2			2ND " " " "				2DM2G
		LABOR CONTROL	EW2-3			3RD " " " "				3DM2G
		HOSPITALIZATION	EW2-4			4TH " " " "				4DM2G
		DELINQUENCY CONTROL	EW2-5			5TH " " " "				5DM2G
		RECREATION	EW2-6			6TH " " " "				6DM2G
	MAINTENANCE / EW3	HOUSE	EW3-1		THIRD GROUP MANAGER 3GM	1ST " " " 3RD "				1DM3G
		LAND	EW3-2			2ND " " " "				2DM3G
		INDUSTRY	EW3-3			3RD " " " "				3DM3G
		SALE	EW3-4			4TH " " " "				4DM3G
		FINANCIAL	EW3-5			5TH " " " "				5DM3G
	INHERITANCE / EW4	HOUSE	EW4-1		FOURTH GROUP MANAGER 4GM	1ST " " " 4TH "				1DM4G
		LAND	EW4-2			2ND " " " "				2DM4G
		INDUSTRY	EW4-3			3RD " " " "				3DM4G
		ART	EW4-4			4TH " " " "				4DM4G
		LAW	EW4-5			5TH " " " "				5DM4G

TABLE NO. 6   EW ORGANIZATION IN ZONE

		BRANCHES AND DIVISIONS			TITLE OF OFFICIALS					
	GROUP	DIVISION ~ D			GM	DIVISION MANAGER ~ DM				
EW BRANCH OF ZONE GOVERNMENT ~ ZEW	POLICY / ZEW1	UPPER	ZEW1-1		ZONE MANAGER ~ ZM / 1ST GROUP MANAG. Z1GM	1ST DIV. MAN.	1ST GROUP			Z1DM1G
		INNER	ZEW1-2			2ND " " " "				Z2DM1G
		LOWER	ZEW1-3			3RD " " " "				Z3DM1G
	DISTRIBUTION / ZEW2	PRICE STABILIZATION	ZEW2-1		SECOND GROUP MANAGER Z2GM	1ST " " " 2ND "				Z1DM2G
		INDUSTRY REGULATION	ZEW2-2			2ND " " " "				Z2DM2G
		LABOR CONTROL	ZEW2-3			3RD " " " "				Z3DM2G
		HOSPITALIZATION	ZEW2-4			4TH " " " "				Z4DM2G
		DELINQUENCY CONTROL	ZEW2-5			5TH " " " "				Z5DM2G
		RECREATION	ZEW2-6			6TH " " " "				Z6DM2G
	MAINTENANCE / ZEW3	HOUSE	ZEW3-1		THIRD GROUP MANAGER Z3GM	1ST " " " 3RD "				Z1DM3G
		LAND	ZEW3-2			2ND " " " "				Z2DM3G
		INDUSTRY	ZEW3-3			3RD " " " "				Z3DM3G
		SALE	ZEW3-4			4TH " " " "				Z4DM3G
		FINANCIAL	ZEW3-5			5TH " " " "				Z5DM3G
	INHERITANCE / ZEW4	HOUSE	ZEW4-1		FOURTH GROUP MANAGER Z46M	1ST " " " 4TH "				Z1DM4G
		LAND	ZEW4-2			2ND " " " "				Z2DM4G
		INDUSTRY	ZEW4-3			3RD " " " "				Z3DM4G
		ART	ZEW4-4			4TH " " " "				Z4DM4G
		LAW	ZEW4-5			5TH " " " "				Z5DM4G

which will be closest to the EW Manager. Data received from other divisions will be analyzed by this division and the policies for the entire nation formulated and approved.

The main task of the "Innner Division" (EW1-2) will be that of collecting all data from every part of the country. This data, after the necessary time required for filing and sifting, will be transmitted to the proper division of the CB.

The main task of the "Lower Division" (EW1-3) will be that of translating the directives given by the EW Manager into proper orders to be later transmitted to the various zones.

The normal procedure will be the following: As data are received by the EW1-2 division, a routine amount of work will be required in sifting and selecting all such information which will be sent to the proper division for study and recommendation. As the proper study has been made by the various divisions of the CB and recommendations made, these will be sent to the Upper Division (EW1-1) where final decisions will be taken in collaboration with the EW Manager. It is possible and likely that some of these recommendations will be sent back to the original division for further study and changes. As the policies are finally chosen and adopted, these will be sent to the Lower Division which will issue the orders to the Managers of the zones, after the signature of the EW Manager has been affixed.

Among the most prominent duties of the EW1 GROUP are the following:

(a) Study, analyze, and coordinate the policies issued so that they may agree with the pattern set by the Constitution.

(b) Prepare the final data to be submitted to the EW Manager for approval and receive from him the broad directives for the organization.

(c) Give shape and substance to the policies to be applied, and provide the necessary leadership to the Managers of the zones.

(d) This group, in collaboration with the other groups of the CB, will issue the bulletins to be made available to the entire nation.

THE "DISTRIBUTING GROUP" OR EW2 will be divided into six divisions, each under a Division Manager. The activities and aims of these divisions have already been analyzed in detail in the first part of this chapter. However, as an overall summary of their activities we may mention the following:

(a) It will study the economic forces within the country as well as in the world, and will co-ordinate the activities of similar branches of the zones.

(b) From information received all over the nation through the EW1-2 it will study the effects of the policies issued in the past, with the purpose of making corrections and improvements.

(c) It will study and analyze all wealth in possession of the EW and make plans for its utilization to the best advantage of society.

(d) It will study the industrial situation of the country and provide coordinated leadership to the "Industries Regulation Divisions" of the zones.

(e) It will set up standards of measurement of wealth for the nation.

(f) It will determine the conditions of labor in the country with the aim of aiding those zones in need of assistance. It will serve as a clearing house of labor throughout the nation.

(g) It will give attention to projects of a national nature when conditions of unemployment in the country make their undertaking desirable.

(h) It will co-operate with the proper divisions of the zones to solve problems of hospitalization, delinquency, and recreation with the purpose of providing leadership as well as unified effort.

THE "MAINTENANCE GROUP" OR EW3 will be divided into five divisions, each under a Division Manager. The activities and aims of this group have been analyzed in detail in the fifth chapter. As an overall summary of its activities we may mention the following:

(a) It will handle all problems related to the caring and upkeep of wealth that comes into the direct possession of the EW.

(b) It will direct and co-ordinate similar activities in the zone. Its policies, presented to the EW Manager for approval, will be eventually enforced throughout the nation.

(c) Up to a certain extent, it will assume direct responsibility in cases in which more than one zone is involved in solving a situation.

(d) It will collect a percentage of wealth from the zones, this to be eventually distributed in accordance with established policies.

THE "INERITANCE GROUP" OR EW4 will be divided into five divisions, each under a Division Manager. The activities and aims of this group have also been analyzed in the fifth chapter. As an overall summary of its activities we may mention the following:

(a) It will set those policies that unify and co-ordinate the activities of the branches in the zones dealing with the settlement of inheritances.

(b) From the data received it will determine the maximum inheritances within each zone.

(c) Its policies, like those of the third and second group, will be transmitted through the EW1-1 division to the EW Manager and after their approval will be sent, again through the EW1-3, to all the zone managers to be applied throughout the country.

As to the "Executive Board" this will meet as often as necessary. The zone managers may be called upon to take part in these meetings when dealing with problems of the zone they direct and thereby achieve more comprehensive formulation of policies issued in the capital. The Board will discuss with the representatives of the PW any complaint coming from the people. It will be seen later how, on certain occasions, the Executive Board must comply with the dictates of the PW. All the policies issued for the country in general must first be discussed with that body and receive its approval to become effective. These leading officials must be of the highest caliber, and possess in great abundance those qualities found in leaders of industries and of large organizations. Besides business skill, they must also have the understanding of the far-seeing type and able to feel and share the great needs of humanity. Besides imagination and vision, so as to discern and recognize the proper path ahead, they must have the character, fortitude, courage, and determination to forge ahead toward humanity's goal. Similar qualities must also be found in the Zone Managers, as they also may be advanced to the supreme position in the nation. Upon these leaders the nation's rate of economic advancement will rest and, as mentioned before, their position will not be a political one. For the entire hierarchy, merit will be the only key to success and promotion. But, irrespective of the qualities of these leaders, fundamental policies in the land will be set in the Constitution of Humanity so as to eliminate the human factor as much as practicable. Only the interpretation of those policies will be left open to the officials of the EW and, as said, this must coincide with that of the PW branch. In a later chapter will be submitted a more detailed study on the subject, but for the present we wish to mention that the Supreme Court of the land will settle any dispute that may rise between the two branches regarding interpretation of fundamental policies.

The amount and kind of help given the zones must be independent of politics or minority pressure, and must conform to rigid rules that take into account the wealth held by the EW as well as conditions in the zone itself.

EW WITHIN THE ZONE

The EW Manager of the zone, or ZM, will be the titular head of the EW within the zone. He will only take orders from the EW Manager of the nation. Suggestions, however, may be received from the various Division Managers in problems pertaining to their particular field of activity. Any discrepancy that may develop between any of these managers and the ZM will be referred to the EW Manager, who will have the final word in any such dispute. The management of a zone will be made as independent as possible of unnecessary interference from above, but in the last analysis it must conform with the general policies issued by the management of the country.

For a comprehensive visualization of the EW branch of the government in the zone, we shall submit two tables of which the first will give the name of the groups and divisions forming that branch, while the second will give the titles of the EW officials in the zone (see Table 6, page 328).

The ZM and the four Group Managers will form the "Zone Executive Board" (ZEWB). With the exception of the "Price Stabilization Division" or ZPS, all the groups and corresponding divisions will be made up of highly specialized employees who will go whenever and wherever needed within the zone. As a result, the EW will not require an exceptionally large staff. This will be located in a government building of the zone capital.

The activities of the FIRST GROUP will duplicate those of the CB of the nation with the exception that it will concentrate on matters pertaining to the zone. Its set-up as well as its policies will also be the same. Among the most prominent duties and activities of this group we may mention the following:

(a) It will be the connecting link between the zone and the capital.

(b) It will be notified of the policies to be applied and after study it will translate them into orders to the various communities of the zone.

(c) It will receive from all CM of the zone the data pertaining to their respective communities. These, translated into tables, charts, and so on, will go to the ZM who, basing his directives on policies issued from the above, will give the proper orders and directives.

(d) It will transmit to the CB of the nation all data received from all parts of the zone for further study and coordination.

(e) It will assist all the CM with problems of management and replacement of personnel.

The *"Distributing Group"* or ZEW2 will be divided into six divisions, each under a Division Manager.

The activities of these divisions have been already described, and at present need no further elucidation. We shall say in passing that with the exception of the Price Stabilization the other divisions will have the largest representation in the zone capital with some skeleton staff in the largest cities as needed. The Price Stabilization, however, will have most of its staff scattered among all the communities of the zone. These will follow directives given by the ZEW and will also provide it with the necessary data pertaining to its multiform activity.

The *"Maintenance Group"* or ZEW3 will be divided into five divisions, each under a Division Manager. The activities of this group have been analyzed before. As an overall summary of its activities we may mention the following:

(a) The first division or ZEW3-1 will specialize in the collection of rent from dwellings, houses, apartments, hotels, and so forth, where owned in co-partnership with individuals. It will attend to maintenance and repairs of similar property when under the complete control of the EW.

(b) The second division or ZEW3-2 will specialize in caring for lands, farms, and so forth, held under temporary control by the EW.

(c) The third division or ZEW3-3 will specialize in caring for industries under the supervision of the EW.

d) The fourth division or ZEW3-4 will specialize in the advertisement and sale of the above mentioned property.

(e) The fifth division or ZEW3-5 will specialize in the financcial aspect of the activities of the other divisions. It will prepare contracts, collect and deposit money as directed by the ZM.

The "Inheritance Group" or ZEW4 will be divided into five divisions, each under a Division Manager. The activities of this group have been analyzed before. As an overall summary of its activities we may mention the following:

(a) The first division or ZEW4-1 will specialize in estimating the value of houses, dwellings, and so forth.

TABLE NO. 7   EW ORGANIZATION IN COMMUNITY

EW BRANCH OF COMMUNITY GOVERNMENT ~ CEW	POLICY GROUP CEW1	MADE OF CAREER MEN IN THE EW ORGANIZATION AND UNDER THE DIRECT CONTROL OF THE COMMUNITY MANAGER (CM)
	DISTRIBUTION GROUP CEW2	MADE BY THE PRICE STABILIZATION DIVISION (CEW2-1)

TABLE NO. 8   PW ORGANIZATION

PEOPLE'S WELFARE BRANCH OF THE GOVERNMENT ~ PW	COMMUNITY CPW	MADE OF REPRESENTATIVES FROM THE COMMUNITY TOTAL 3 FOR EACH COMMUNITY	CPW
		ALL SUCH REPRESENTATIVES WITHIN 5 COMMUNITIES	CPW-C
		" " " IN THE ZONE	CPW-Z
		". " " " " SUPERZONE	CPW-S
		" " " " " FEDERATION	CPW-F
	ZONE ZPW	MADE OF 3 REPRESENTATIVES FROM EACH GROUP OF 5 COMMUNITIES IN THE ZONE TOTAL 18 FOR EACH ZONE	ZPW
		ALL SUCH REPRESENTATIVES IN THE SUPERZONE	ZPW-S
		" " " " " FEDERATION	ZPW-F
	SUPERZONE SPW	MADE OF 3 REPRESENTATIVES FROM EACH ZONE TOTAL 27 FOR EACH SUPERZONE	SPW
		ALL SUCH REPRESENTATIVES IN THE FEDERATION	SPW-F
	FEDERATION FPW	MADE OF 3 REPRESENTATIVES FROM EACH ZONE	FPW

(b) The second division or ZEW4-2 will specialize in estimating the value of land, forests, farms, cattle, and so forth.

(c) The third division or ZEW4-3 will specialize in estimating the value of industries, factories, corporations, and other financial enterprises.

(d) The fourth division or ZEW4-4 will specialize in estimating the value of works of art and luxury commodities.

(e) The fifth division or ZEW4-5 will represent the legal branch. It will prepare deeds and represent the EW in taking possession of properties and in collecting inheritances. It will eventually transfer this wealth to the fifth division of the third group (ZEW3-5).

The amount of personnel of these divisions will, naturally, vary from one zone to another, and will depend on the needs of each. In such cases as involve the maintenance of the EW property, sufficient personnel must be available, and a large part of this may be temporarily secured from the local population. The personnel outside the capital must be under the direct supervision of the Community Manager.

ZONES AND VARIOUS PROBLEMS CONFRONTING THEIR POPULATION

Up to now frequent reference has been made to zones and government of a zone, and it was implied that this is an important factor in the mode of life of the future society but no explanation or description has been given of the zone itself. This will now be supplied.

By zone is indicated a group of communities which, from an economic standpoint, are closely related to each other. Zone can also be defined as a land with natural resources and climate more or less equal, producing the same kind of commodities and forming a compact economic unit. Indeed, in a zone the transportation facilities are such that commodities will be exchanged with a minimum of cost, and the economic interests of the several communities are such that they naturally gravitate toward each other. Thus, the agricultural part of the zone will be the natural area where many finished products of the city are sold, and on the other hand the city will be the most important market for local farming products. Of course, a zone may have more than one large city within its border, depending on the number of zones into which a country is divided. As shown later on, it will be a good plan to have the zones of approximately the same population, say two or three millions, so that each will have equal representation in the government and exert equal influence in the shaping of national policies. In cases where this division is not possible, as where a city alone has more than two or three millions population, its zone must include sufficient surrounding territory to make itself approximately self-sustaining from an economic standpoint, and being so much larger than other zones will have a greater representation in the government of the country. That, however, will be the exception rather than the rule. On the other hand, in regions sparsely populated it may not be convenient or advisable to have a zone of great size because of the great distances involved between one place and another which in turn may not be necessarily bound by economic interests. In the latter case these zones will be laid out more according to their geographic area than population, but in order to have their interests protected and properly cared for, they will have the same number of representatives in the government of the country.

Let us consider now the principle to be followed in assigning a border to any zone. Assume as an example that three large cities are not far distant from each other and their respective regions of influence are to be grouped together in a zone.

Some of the nearby towns and villages that obviously gravitate toward any one of these cities will be considered part of the zone without further study. Doubt may arise regarding communities located between one of the cities and a fourth that belongs to another zone. Experts of the central branch of the nation will be sent to these doubtful communities, and they will make studies of the vital commodities imported and exported, special emphasis being placed as to where they are sent and whence imported. Generally, the main part will come from or to some nearby city, either because of its nearness or better transportation facilities. At any rate, it will be decided that the town or community gravitates toward the center with which the greatest exchange of vital commodities is being maintained, and, therefore, from an economic standpoint, it is more closely related to that center. From a similar study in other doubtful communities, which could be completed in a relatively short time, especially if several experts are assigned to the task, the areas of influence of the three cities and thereby the border of the zone will be determined. It is of passing interest to note that with such a system no city can ever be at the border of a zone unless located by the sea or other natural barrier. This is explained by the fact that the zone of influence of any center, barring geographical or man-made obstacles, such as tariffs and the like, will naturally spread outwards and, therefore, the border is bound to be some distance away from that center. It is evident that our proposed division of the nation into equal zones is more consonant with the interests of the people than many present-day borders where we find hundreds of cases in which the economy of a community is made to gravitate toward distant centers rather than a nearer one, because the latter happens to belong to some other country or state. This is an arbitrary division imposed by men, and quite often detrimental to the interests of many towns and communities. By such division they are compelled to buy or to sell at a disadvantage commodities that are important to the well-being of the population involved. With this in mind we feel that our present divisions of land should be superseded by one which takes into account the interests of the population itself. This border, of course, must not be made permanent, and as improvements of transportation are introduced, the result of which makes a community gravitate toward some other center, it should be transferred to the zone in which the latter belongs.

As each zone receives its geographical border, as the necessary data is collected, as the financial position of the EW becomes stronger the same procedure followed for the capital zone will be applied for the one under study, and this will be repeated until the influence of the EW comes to cover the entire nation.

It is natural that the most capable men should be chosen ZM while others take key positions in the new zone, to insure a smooth and efficient organization. It has been stressed before that time must be allowed the personnel to become familiar with the intricate and innumerable problems it will have to solve in the discharge of its normal duties. Besides the fact that the project must be on a pay-as-you-go basis, the new mode of life must be introduced at a slow and orderly pace to permit unavoidable readjustments. While some commodities must be increased, others may have to be curtailed, which means a disadvantageous retrenching for the producers of the latter. Again the well-being of the zone may have been hinged in the past on economic barriers and tariffs and as such any abrupt change in policies would produce chaos and disruption. This naturally must be avoided and, while those barriers and tariffs must eventually be completely removed, this change will occur at such a rate that it will give ample time to all industries affected to redirect their activity into more profitable channels. In short, the general policy of the EW will be that of helping the population in general when-ever and wherever assistance is needed. While it is right that the poor should be helped and their standard of living increased, this must not be secured by disrupting the industry of the zone and causing confusion among the components of the higher classes of society, as such a policy would tend to defeat rather than attain the desired results. Instead, even if the increase of standard of living must take a slower pace, care should be taken that the manufac-turers be protected from bankruptcy and ruin. With this end in view, the chance must be given them to adopt a course which is consonant with the policies of the EW, who, after all, has their welfare in mind as well as that of the poor. If the EW deems it necessary to curtail the production of a certain commodity, this decision is reached from a study of the economic forces at work between zones and countries. It is to the interest of the entire pop-ulation of the country that each zone devote its main effort to the production of commodities that can be made cheaper and better than elsewhere, and cease producing those that are at disadvantage in the open market. Such a policy will benefit the producers and consumers of each zone and arouse a more sympathetic understanding between the populations of the zones. These facts, with trends, prices, statistics, etc., will be made known to the public through bulletins which, as we have seen, will be issued by the CB of the nation. Such facts, with the proper interpretation and significance will better explain the various policies of the EW so that all may understand and comply with those policies.

But, as in any human activity, not all producers will respond quickly to changing conditions. Some to be sure, immediately grasping the new trends, will take advantage of the EW's advice and redirect their business into more profitable fields reaping thereby great profits, others, more timid, will follow at a slower pace, yet an obstinate minority may persist in manufacturing commodities com-peting with better and cheaper products imported from elsewhere. While some of the latter may still be able to make some profit and a living, others may dangerously come closer to bankruptcy. But even here the EW, through one of its divisions, will come to their rescue by offering to buy their industry at a fair and just price to them-selves and society. In any event no tariff must be kept indefinitely, nor uneconomic support given an industry, as this would benefit the inefficient few to the detriment of society in general. As the supply of such commodities decreases tariffs may be gradually lowered. This will open the door to a larger volume of better and less expensive commodities coming from places where the cost of production is so small that they can easily compete with the local products even with the disadvantage of distance and tariffs.

Another subject to be analyzed is that of the disposal of inheritance wealth. In describing the formation of the CB of the nation it was mentioned that inheritance wealth collected from places that are still outside the immediate influence of the EW should be set aside for the time when this influence can be extended to those places. This is in line with the policy that the main portion of such wealth should be used for the amelioration of the particular zone from which it came. Indeed, it would not be right otherwise. Of course, as the entire nation comes under the new mode of life, the fact that all the zones are part of the same nation and are united by the same economic bonds obligates them as a duty to contribute some of their wealth toward the welfare of the nation as a whole. Just as at present, where a large part of the taxes collected are locally spent while the rest goes to the national government, some of the wealth of each zone must be sent to the CB of the capital where it will be apportioned from the standpoint of general rather than local utility. On this account, depending on circumstances, more aid and assistance may be given to one zone than another but this will be done less in the specific interest of that zone than because spending that money in that way will produce the best results so far as the entire nation is concerned. Indeed, projects of a national scope will be sponsored and contribution made by the nation itself. But as a general rule the average standard of living of each zone, while considerably higher than had it remained alone and out of the community of zones, must be necessarily lower than the average standard of living attained by a richer zone, that is to say in natural resources, possessing a better climate, and so forth. It is obvious that for a poor zone raw material may have to be imported and other factors being equal, the cost of the finished products will be correspondingly higher, unless the cost of production is reduced by a lower level of salaries and wages which, as long since noted, is equivalent to a lower standard of living. Now the influence of the EW will not be exerted toward the increase of production of commodities that would be at such disadvantage on the open market but toward that of those that can be made cheaper and better than elsewhere, either because the raw material is on hand or because that zone is particularly fitted for that production. This will tend to increase export, and correspondingly to increase import of valuable commodities, with a consequent increase in the average standard of living of the population. The EW influence will also be exerted toward the improvement of such facilities in the zone as tend to increase this production. It can be said that if the industry of the zone is encouraged toward those fields which are more promising from the standpoint of raw material and of other factors which necessarily must enter into the determination of the cost curve, the zone in general and the manufacturers in particular stand to gain and prosper by this policy. In giving this assistance it is reasonable that money originating from this zone should be used first, and if not sufficient further aid be given by the CB of the nation since the increase in standard of living of the population of this zone in one way or another means a gain for the others.

A strict balance of trade must be kept among the various zones, to limit to the very minimum the flow of gold. For this reason the EW will keep a constant watch on any such tendency. This will be determined by observing the fluctuations of specie in banks and institutions of credit. Depending on the direction of that flow, the necessary steps will be taken to restore equilibrium. See page 281 for a detailed analysis of this subject.

In a zone poor in natural resources and hence incapable of raising the local standard of living above a certain level there will be a tendency of many in the population to emigrate to other lands. Lack of large manufacturing facilities, stagnant condition of business, difficulty of finding remunerative work, will cause a severe unemployment problem. It goes as a matter of course that the EW in the zone as well as the national organization will consider all possibilities of introducing in the zone whatever industries have good probability of success. If this is done, even on a modest scale, many jobs will be available. An additional step will be that of sponsoring projects that besides giving employment have the more distant aim of improving the economic structure of the zone. A third step, probably taken simultaneously with the others, will be that of finding employment for many in other zones where they can be easily absorbed. As these emigrants and their families depart, the population will decrease and a better equilibrium between its size and the wealth of the land will be established. As a consequence the standard of living will tend to go up. However, if this flow of population was left uncontrolled, the tendency would be to emigrate to places that are highly industrialized and probably already overpopulated.

Thus this flow would tend to decrease the standard of living of that particular zone, which, naturally, would resent this unsought immigration. Friction and misunderstanding would follow. But if this emigration is controlled in an intelligent way, no damaging consequence will appear. If some of the rich zones need additional manpower, this should come from those zones that are able to supply it, but by far the largest part of the flow will be channeled toward those places that are underpopulated and have large resources to be exploited. This policy not only will help the emigrants and their families, and decrease the pressure in the overpopulated poor zone, but will aid also the population of the zone where such flow is directed. Some of these immigrants will find work on the land while others will increase the business activity and in general will tend to increase the production of vital commodities which is beneficial to this zone in particular and to the others in general.

Needless to say, one must also realize the impossibility of obtaining the same standard of living for the entire nation. People in the country are limited to a standard of living far below that attained by the population of a city. Among the reasons for this discrepancy are that in the city improvements and conveniences abound on a larger scale than in a town or small community and may be obtained more cheaply, and so reach a poorer strata of population, but it must be remembered that while in the city more comfort may be had from conveniences provided by men, the city lacks many other things just as precious and valuable to human happiness, which are enjoyed only by those living in the country. When it comes to measure standard of living it is difficult to define which is the best, as this depends on different points of view, and is a direct result of the fundamental difference of human nature.

From the large amount of information and data gathered by the EW as well as by other branches of the government, each zone will be assigned a definite economic index, that is to say its relative position in reference to the other zones of the country. According to this index the amount and kind of aid will be determined, which will be such that no zone will receive more or less than its due. We believe that such a policy is right and fair to the entire population of the nation. This position or zone index will be the product of three factors:

(1) The first, indicated by (x), will represent the balance of trade of the zone. When x becomes unity this will mean that the zone has reached economic balance. It also means that the value of

the commodities exported is equal to that of those imported, and that the amount of money in the zone is constant. However, as the wealth exported becomes larger than that imported, or vice versa, it is evident that this balance is broken, and in either case the condition must be corrected. But it is easy to see that a moderate favorable trade is much better than a moderate unfavorable one, and that assuming the same amount of swing from the condition of equilibrium, the population with an unfavorable trade, other things being equal, must receive assistance before the population with a favorable one. In other parts of this study it has been seen that there are cases when a moderate favorable trade may be desirable to raise the economic position of a zone poor in money, and naturally the nature and amount of unbalance to be maintained must be left to the M of the EW to decide and control. In short, the factor (x) is the ratio of two quantities, in which one is related to the value of the commodities exported and the other to that of the commodities imported. Indicating by (e) and (i) respectively the values of exported and imported commodities, then (e-i) or (i-e) represent the amount of favorable or unfavorable unbalance. This unbalance will be indicated by Δ. In either case the factor x will be given by the following expression:

$$x = 1 - \Delta/e$$

The fact that (e) rather than (i) is assumed as denominator in the expression of x will tend to give this factor a smaller value for a condition of unfavorable unbalance than for an equal swing in the opposite direction, which is in line with the policy outlined above.

(2) The second factor will be the ratio of two quantities. One quantity will be related to the actual average standard of living within the zone, the other to a hypothetical one. This hypothetical standard of living will be found by a study of the wealth of the land and the size of its population. The ratio between these two quantities represents the factor (y), and gives a measure of potentiality of this population as to the amount of wealth in its possession and ability to exploit it. The average degree of culture of the population of a zone must also be taken into account when calculating the factor (y). Indeed, for a zone in which the population is extremely ignorant and illiterate, it cannot be expected that it should be able to use the necessary initiative and resourcefulness so as to be able to exploit to the best advantage the natural resources of its land. This factor (y), which we have indicated as the ratio of size of population versus natural wealth would give a misleading interpretation for two pop-

ulations with different levels of civilization. The introduction of industries and the like into a zone in which such a large illiteracy exists would be of no avail in raising the standard of living of that population. In such a case, while efforts should be made toward raising the productiveness of the zone, the enlightenment of the population should receive by far the largest consideration. The degree of civilization of a given population may be measured by the proportion of people who have gone through grammar schools, high schools and colleges. By taking a given proportion as base, that degree can be easily found. The factor (y), therefore, should be the product of two quantities. The first will represent the ratio of population versus the wealth of the land, the second will represent the cultural factor.

(3) The third factor, referred to as (z), will be the percentage of the actual average standard of living of the zone compared with the actual average standard of living of the country in general. This will give a measure of the amount of support that the zone may need from the outside in order to raise its standard of living. If it is assumed that both factors (x) and (y) have reached the equilibrium point while (z) is still less than unity, this reveals the following facts:

(a) The zone has reached the optimum condition in its interchange with other zones, as any change in that condition would tend to decrease rather than increase the average standard of living of the population.

(b) The zone has utilized to the utmost the economic resources of the land, and future improvements in this direction may have to await technological advancement or better knowledge of the wealth in its possession.

(c) The wealth of the land is too small to sustain the population of the zone. This is equivalent to saying that the population is too large for that land, and accordingly emigration must be considered.

Now assume a zone designated by A. Assume also that the three economic factors for this zone are as follows: $x = 0.9$, $y = 0.8$, $z = 0.7$. The index or position of the zone which we shall indicate by P will be given by:

$$P = 0.9 \times 0.8 \times 0.7 = 0.504.$$

Now if some other zone, B, has a smaller value of P than A, it stands to reason that B should have priority in receiving assistance from the EW branch of the government. This rule, of course, must be rigid and, since the index P of the several zones will be a matter of public knowledge, everyone will realize the justice and fairness in the policies that the EW may follow in regard to different zones, and each zone, knowing its rights, will recognize and respect those of others. But even in giving assistance to any one zone, priority must be given first of all to those policies that tend to increase x, or the ratio that represents the balance of trade, then to those that tend to increase y, which is tantamount to say, that tend to bring a more efficient and intense utilization of the natural resources of the zone; and last attention must be paid those policies that tend to increase the standard of living of the population in relation to the average standard of living of the country in general. As already mentioned, the third kind of policy deals with the transfer of population from one zone to another, and while this emigration will be channeled toward those zones that are in need of personal wealth, theoretically this will represent the improvement of a zone at the expense of another, and, therefore, should be used as a last resort, and only after the other policies have been tried and exploited.

By this discussion we do not want to convey the idea that the zones will be helped one at a time, according to the economic index P referred to above. As a matter of fact all, in greater or less degree, will receive some kind of assistance from the CB of the nation if that need exists, but more emphasis will be placed on helping those zones that have a lower index because that indicates that they are in greater need. Of course, each zone will represent different problems, and the raising of the standard of living of one zone may require an entirely different kind of assistance from another, so that the policies used to help both may be vastly different, and may be applied at the same time and independently of each other, but in all cases in which two zones need the same kind of assistance from the CB it is obvious that the larger amount must be given to the one that has the lower factor. In other words, each of the three factors that make up the economic index of the zone requires different kind of approach, and if the zone A has a factor x lower than B it is natural that for policies intended to raise x in both zones, A should receive precedence over B, even though the economic index of B may be lower than A.

EW IN THE COMMUNITY

A general description of the EW's activity within a community has already been given during the study of "Price Stabilization" which, as noted, has the largest representation in the communities.

However, for a clearer presentation of this branch of the community government we shall submit Table 7 on page 334.

The only official will be the Community Manager or CM. The CM, the managers of various stores and key men in the CEW1 will form the "Community Executive Board" on CEWB. All the CM in the zone will be under the jurisdiction of the ZM. Naturally, they will have some freedom of action in the discharge of their duties, but even so they must conform to directives imposed from above meant to co-ordinate the activities of all the communities within the zone. Similarly to the Managers of the zone those of a community must have the highest qualifications as to character, honesty and ability as they, more than anyone else, will be in direct contact with the public and hence exposed to criticism and slander. Again their personality will be paramount in achieving collaboration and cooperation among the people, and thus they will be responsible for the smooth functioning of the EW in the communities. They will have the following assignments:

(1) They will supervise all the CM of nearby towns and villages.

(2) They will supervise all the Managers of the various stores in the community.

(3) They will have under their charge the necessary personnel for the efficient discharge of the many duties toward the public.

(4) They will have under them a small but efficient group of career men who will represent the CB of the community with the special task of helping the CM in all problems outside the Price Stabilization activities.

(5) They will represent the other groups and divisions of the EW.

PEOPLE'S WELFARE BRANCH (PW)

Consider now more closely the branch of the future government which, while completely independent of the EW, assumes the duties of supervising its activities, and in general, will represent the people and safeguard its interests. This is the People's welfare branch, or PW. As said, Congress or whatever branch of the government represents the people, will form a committee to select a group of men who will form the nucleus of the PW branch of the future government. This will be done once the nation decides to adopt the new mode of life, through a general referendum within the country. There must be one individual for each three million population. As said, when this group is formed and organized, one of its first and most important assignments will be that of selecting the EW Manager and, with his approval and cooperation, also the four Group Managers of the CB. As these five officials form the CB EXECUTIVE BOARD, the people's representative or PW members will discuss with them the future policies of the EW, and take a vital part in the policies adopted by that body with the particular duty of safeguarding the interests of the people as far as they are consonant with the new Constitution of the nation. It has been mentioned that after twelve years they must relinquish their position to an equal number of representatives whose election will now be described.

The final and total number composing this branch will be three times that chosen by Congress. One third of the total number will be elected after four years from the time the new government becomes active, and the other third after an additional interval of four years. It is obvious that the election of these representatives must take place after the new government has passed a proper period of consolidation, as it may not be convenient to elect additional representatives until the nation is ready for such an undertaking. Much time may be required for a satisfactory development of the EW and, as shown in a later study, time must be given for other branches of the government to take shape and form. As such it is desirable from the standpoint of balance and equilibrium that the PW be in step with the other government branches until all will be ready to assume in full their duties toward the nation. Another reason for the increase of the PW by steps of four years will soon become evident in the course of this study. At any rate, the progress of the new government will be known and gauged, and at the proper time a general election must be called throughout the country. The procedure and the many details required for such an election must be left to the already constituted government of the nation. The period between the referendum which will express the willingness of the people to adopt the new mode of life and the aforementioned election, may be termed the interregnum or period of transition. During this interval the official positions in the outgoing government will be crystallized. In other words, if the country is a republic, the individual who happens to be President at the beginning of this period will retain that position until the new government is ready to take over, no matter how long this term of office might be. If the country is governed by a King, he will hold his rank and power throughout the interregnum, at the end of which he must abdicate. The same will apply, of course, to the other important positions in the outgoing government.

During this period of transition the outgoing government, besides the normal discharge of its duties, acquires also the duty of facilitating in all possible ways the gradual formation of the new one. At the proper time as mentioned, the people will go to the polls and elect a PW representative for each 100,000 population. This position will last for a period of twelve years. These individuals, in any normal problem concerning the nation, will directly represent the people. They will discharge their duties to the best of their ability, with only conscience as a guide, and will not be dependent upon or influenced by minorities among the population. By the time the election takes place, the EW will be sufficiently organized and many economic problems will have been solved for the benefit of the population as a whole. As a result the people, instead of selecting individuals for the expressed purpose of influencing some particular economic advantage for the community or region, will be apt to choose them instead for their character, honesty, and popularity. Each representative, being one of them, will unconsciously partake of their problems and just aspirations, which will make him a real representative of the people. It is our guess that such individuals will be mostly persons of culture, and that it will not be very difficult for them to familiarize themselves with their new duties. All similarly elected in the nation will form the "Community PW of the Nation." After a specific time (two months), the representatives of nearby communities whose total population comes to approximately 500,000 will assemble and elect one representative to the zone branch of the PW. Representatives of the communities as well as respected and prominent local citizens may be eligible and chosen for this position. This candidate, as the others similarly elected by other communities, will form the PW branch of the zone to which those communities belong. All similarly elected in the nation will form the "Zone PW of the nation." They will be selected for their character and honesty, and will be left free to use their judgment in matters that may come up in the zone with the assumption that their integrity and the knowledge that great trust is placed in them will be sufficient guarantee that they will stand for what is just and fair for the people they represent as well as for the zone in general. There will be one elected for each 500,000 population and their position will also last for twelve years. At the next election which will also take place four years later, another group will be elected to this branch and the same process will be repeated in four years until the entire representation is of three for each 100,000 in the Community branch of the PW and three for each 500,000 in the Zone branch of the PW. At the next election, four years later, all the representatives who already have served twelve years will step aside and an equal number will become part of the "Community PW of the Nation." Similar process will be followed for the "Zone PW representatives of the Nation."

One of the main duties of these representatives will be that of safeguarding the interests of the people, their liberties and their rights, which means upholding the fundamental liberties and rights of any individual if impaired and endangered. These representatives will also have other duties treated in more detail in a later study.

After a specified time (say two months) the representatives of the zone will get together and elect a representative to the highest branch of the government. It will be shown in later study how a number of zones may be grouped to form a superzone, but for the present it will be assumed that only a nation of average size is in the process of changing its mode of life, and, therefore, the government of the nation will be directly above the government of the zones. These representatives, also elected for a period of twelve years, will join the original representatives elected at the beginning of the interregnum or period of transition, and, therefore, besides adding their number to that body will bring with them new ideas and new needs of the people. After four years the same process will be repeated until all zones have reached a total representation of three each. These may be elected either among the representatives of the zone or among prominent and esteemed individuals of the zone itself and, like the other representatives, will be free to discharge their duties according to their conscience and ability, unhampered by minority pressure and interests. Each individual of this highest branch of the PW will have the duty to uphold just grievances of individuals or groups in the zone they represent against the highest officials of the EW of the nation. Of course, there will be times when such differences will not be settled by the individual representative alone, and must be referred to their branch taken as a whole. This body in turn will appoint a committee from its members with the purpose of studying grievances that may originate from any part of the country. The committee will finally present a report to the general assembly of the national PW branch. After due discussion a vote may be taken and if the majority considers the grievance justified a group may be chosen to represent the PW at a special meeting with the CB EXECUTIVE BOARD. If this representation is still of no avail, the matter must be referred to the SUPREME COURT of the country, which is the highest authority on the interpretation of the CONSTITUTION.

The PW branch of the nation in certain circumstances has the authority to terminate the services of the EW Manager, if such an important decision is expedient for the good of the country. The PW will not have such authority, however, unless a large majority of the votes (at least 90%) is obtained among all the representatives in a special election in which the impeachment of the EW Manager is discussed and considered. A vote of such magnitude must be taken as the true will of the people, and the EW Manager, by law, must relinquish his position. Such procedure will seldom be taken, unless the EW Manager is held definitely accountable for incompetence and corruption. As a general rule, if he should prove to lack the high qualities expected from one in his position, and unless he should become definitely obstructive to the interests of the nation, at the proper time his contract will not be extended and his duties will come to an end after his normal four years of service. This is a matter of policy only but the right of the PW branch of the nation to discharge the EW Manager, even if seldom used, must be actual and absolute. If a strong sentiment should develop among many representatives of the PW as well as in the country in general to terminate the duties of the EW Manager the aforesaid 90% majority among the representatives of the highest branch of the PW will adequately represent the will of the people. However, if this vote does not reach the 90% level but is still larger than 85%, this body disqualifies itself to pass on this matter and the retention or dismissal of the EW Manager must be referred to the "Zone PW of the Nation" where a similar procedure will be followed that may take the case even to the Community PW of the nation and to the people themselves.

In those cases in which the position of the EW Manager is not an issue, but still there is a definite difference of opinion between him and the PW branch, it has been said that this matter will be referred to the Supreme Court. If this body upholds the view of the EW Manager, it is plain that the PW can no longer impose its will in the matter. However, in cases where the Constitution is definitely faulty and no longer consonant with the times and with the new needs of the people, the PW will have the authority to ask for a new referendum, and thereby change one or several clauses of the Constitution. Needless to say that in all disputes that may arise among these two branches of the government such matters must be covered by the bulletins and by all the newspapers in the country, first to keep the public informed of such issues, secondly to gauge its reaction.

There may be cases in which the EW Manager does not feel equal to assume alone the responsibility of some major change in the policies to be adopted throughout the nation, even though, let us say, he may happen to be in favor of or against such an adoption, and thus he may refer the matter to the PW branch to decide. The National PW branch will first study this policy and eventually come to a vote. If the vote happens to be greater than 80% for or against this will represent the will of the people; if it is less than 75%, it will be assumed that the people have no clear idea of the implication of such a change and the EW Manager will be free to use his judgment in the matter. For a vote larger than 75% but smaller than 80% the National PW branch disqualifies itself, and the matter must be referred to the ZPW of the nation. By a similar process it is possible that decisions may go up to the people themselves if the ZPW and CPW in the country fail to give a clear vote on the matter. All this will probably be clearer if submitted in a tabulated form:

	Percent	Percent	Percent
National PW Branch	100-80	80-75	75-50
ZPW of the Nation	100-75	75-70	70-50
CPW of the Nation	100-70	70-65	65-50
People through Referendum	100-65	65-60	60-50

Any vote taken by the PW representatives that falls between the limits shown in the first column will represent the will of the people and the Manager of the EW will by that receive a definite answer to his question as to the policy and path to be chosen. Any vote that falls between the limits shown in the third column will indicate that the people have no clear idea of the contemplated change and give to the EW Manager the freedom to follow the path which in his own estimation is the best pending the time when a clearer understanding can be obtained. Any vote that falls between the limits shown in the second column disqualifies that body and the matter must be referred to a lower branch of the PW and quite possibly to the population itself.

The reason for this gradual decrease in the required majority among the members of the various PW branches is that the one below any one considered is closer to the people, and therefore more apt to give a true interpretation of their interests which must be considered supreme in this new mode of life.

From the previous discussion we may conclude that even a numerical majority among the people and the representatives of the PW branches is not sufficient to dictate important EW policies and this is right and just because the EW Manager, having at his disposal far greater information on which to base his decision is more qualified to grasp the implication of such changes. Of course, in this particular instance the EW Manager has shown no definite preference for or against the policy and this implies some degree of hesitancy on his part, yet if final decision has to be taken, it is natural that he, rather than anyone else, should take the initiative on the matter pending the time when causes and effects will better define the issue. Where the EW Manager takes a definite stand on some issue which does not happen to coincide with that of the PW national branch, the natural procedure will be that of referring the matter to the Supreme Court of the Nation. The Constitution should include a regulation by which any vote or decision of the PW of the Nation can be cancelled and annulled if a given percentage of the ZPW of the Nation are not satisfied. This will be known by a special petition made among the ZPW members which must be sent to the upper branch. As a result the matter must be settled by the ZPW of the Nation. The same procedure should be followed in those cases in which a certain percentage of the representatives of all the communities are dissatisfied with any specific vote either of the zone or national branch. Such a case will rarely occur, but the Constitution must provide for such an occurrence. At any rate, the fact that in certain cases major policies may come before the ZPW and CPW of the Nation, whose representatives are closest to the people, will guarantee a truly democratic government.

In cases in which some representative, either in response to his conscience or through strong public opinion, does not feel equal to give his unbiased judgment on some particular policy he may refer the matter to the people through a referendum within that particular community, even though in other places other representatives, more confident of the will of their constituents, will see no such a necessity. When the public opinion has been found, the representative becomes duty bound to vote according to it.

We may say here in passing that the vote of each representative does not have to be 100% in favor or opposed to a definite policy, but that he himself may decide how much he leans toward the adoption of a policy, and thus he may vote accordingly by stating that he is only 80% in favor or opposed. All these percentages added together will represent the true will of the PW branch and of the people they represent.

Going back to the election of the community representatives, a given amount of electioneering is bound to take place, for the simple reason that those who are willing to accept such a position must make their willingness and desire known to the public in general, who make the final selection. Of course, there may be cases of prominent personalities in the community who may be asked to run for such a position without any electioneering, but this is immaterial to this discussion. At the polls there will be a list of candidates, and the one who receives the largest number of votes wins that position. If any of these representatives later on should be elected to a higher branch, the vacant place must be taken by the candidate immediately following in number of votes. If any tie should develop among the candidates, the eldest should be chosen. Similar procedure must be followed in case a representative for some reason becomes incapacitated to discharge his duties toward the people. The community representatives will not receive a large salary because their duty will not require a great deal of their time and will not be asked to relinquish their profession or trade, yet their salary must be sufficiently large to attract people of good qualifications. This will also discourage any tendency of graft and bribery even though any such desire on their part will be extremely difficult to translate into practice. As to the representatives of higher branches, these must have an office of their own, sufficient personnel to help them with the necessary correspondence and other activities, and their salary must be consonant with their position. Since they must give individual attention to their new duties, they must relinquish their profession or trade for the twelve-year period. The PW branch will have other duties which will be described in a future study when the relationship between the several branches of the government will be stated and stressed.

To better visualize the set-up of the PW organization in the nation we will submit an overall view of this branch of the government in Table 8, page 334, this to be further expanded and detailed in a further study.

OTHER BRANCHES OF THE GOVERNMENT
(GENERALITIES)

For the present we wish to mention that besides the EW and the PW branch of the government there will be another one called the "General Welfare Branch" (GW) whose duties, similar to those of any modern government, will be to attend to all tasks of a general nature necessary to the well-being of the nation. Its activities will, naturally, be complementary to those of the EW branch, and as will be seen it will be independent of politics and under the supreme jurisdiction of the PW branch of the government, which becomes the supreme guardian and protector of the people's liberties and interests.

In line with a predetermined and arranged policy, set in the Constitution, as soon as the PW branch becomes more active and organized within the country, the officials of the GW will be selected and, starting from the top, a method similar to the one described for the EW will be followed. A large number of the officials who are part of the outgoing government, career men and so forth, familiar with their intricate duties, will naturally be retained so that only the highest officials need to be replaced at the end of the transition period. Simplification will be introduced gradually in the life of the nation, and it can be safely said that the transfer from the old to the new mode of life will occur in an orderly and uneventful manner.

Other branches of the government will be given by the "Legislative" and "Judiciary" branch, but of these more will be said in a future study.

GENERALITIES AND CONCLUSIONS

As can be noticed, it has been our effort to set up a system in which no individual or group of individuals may become supreme in the life of the nation. No one, no matter what his position or station, can arbitrarily dictate the laws of the country and all, either considered as groups or as individuals, will have some other group or individual with the authority to overrule them and actually terminate their term of office if necessary for the good of the nation. In order to prevent individuals from perpetuating themselves in the PW branch, any representative at the end of his service, by law must not become a candidate again for any similar position until after a lapse of four or even eight years.

We also wish to note in passing that no dole is ever contemplated by this new system of ours unless the recipient is physically unfit to work. As a general rule the EW will provide any one in need the means for working and improving his station in life through his own efforts, and will seek to conserve and stimulate that self-respect and confidence so important to human happiness.

CHAPTER VIII

GENERALITIES AND COMPARISONS BETWEEN THE PRESENT AND THE FUTURE MODE OF LIFE

IN THE FIRST CHAPTER of this work the advantages resulting from a large division of labor were analyzed. The comment was made that the division of activities among men, dating from time immemorial, has been an important factor in making them what they are today, and many things now enjoyed and taken for granted are its direct consequence. In addition, this analysis pointed out the fact that division of labor tends to produce disparity of earnings, and classes markedly differing each from the other are the direct result. These disparities rarely make for a peaceful and happy society. Quite often the wages paid the working classes are utterly inadequate for a decent living. This generates dissatisfaction which now and then comes to the fore, arouses strife, and frequently takes a violent form that bodes ill for our civilization, since it further divides the two extreme classes of society.

It will be well to analyze in greater detail the forces causing the wide rifts in society, so that with these facts clear in mind, we shall be better prepared to discern the obvious solution. That division of labor is beneficial to society is by now beyond question. The greater that division, the more commodities will be manufactured, and the more abundant will be the supply available to the public in general. When we think of division of labor it is natural to visualize it as represented by numerous groups engaged in the production of a specific commodity. As these workers are apt to concentrate upon a certain detail of production, in a position to exchange information on improvements and the like, to join together in the same building and utilize the same machinery, it is obvious' that their output should be far greater than if each was engaged in production by himself. However, conceding the great improvement made possible by the division of labor where all the workers become proficient in the manufacture of the same commodity, we feel that this method is far surpassed by another that contemplates diversified activities only partially linked with that manufacture. An example will explain this statement. Take 100 cobblers engaged in manufacturing shoes separately, and more or less in competition with each other. Let us join them together under one roof, using the same machinery, and each concentrating upon one operation alone. The production of this group, even though it represents a great improvement over that of the 100 cobblers working separately, is still short of the possible output that can be obtained by still another group which, besides cobblers, includes persons proficient in other trades and professions. It is easy to conceive that the 100 expert cobblers who have resolved to join forces and form a partnership, may be quite incompetent at other tasks equally as vital to the well-being of their association. Many blunders are bound to be made, and as they lack the necessary leadership and the qualities that will put them at a good advantage in a world of competition in which intelligence, knowledge and business acumen are paramount, this group cannot last but will soon fail and dissolve.

When we refer to division of labor, we have, of course, in mind this second interpretation, in which many individuals of different ability and talent join forces for the production of a certain commodity. This being the case, we must state that in any such group or association, not everyone will exert the same effort or will be equally vital to that production. Turning back to the factory analyzed in chapter six, there is found a great mass of employees whose combined effort maintains a certain output of shoes per unit time. There is the plain laborer who does nothing but the simplest kind of manual work. His ability is limited, and all the intricacies of the factory are a mystery to him. He will be assigned the simplest of tasks, and his activity will be directed and guided by his immediate superior. Quite often the laborer himself is unable to comprehend the relationship of his particular work within the frame of the whole enterprise. There is also another kind of laborer who, through skill, talent, or training, is able to perform more important assignments. He naturally will be engaged in more delicate and taxing operations, and besides his manual effort, he is required to use some initiative and intuitiveness in order that the final product may be of the finest quality and successfully meet the requirements of experts. Over these workers is generally placed a foreman, who has usually reached that position by demonstrating greater knowledge to the satisfaction of officials, and has proved to possess leadership traits so important to a successful organization. He generally has been employed in the factory for a number of years, has its interests at heart, and has gained the trust and respect of his superiors. As the factory may be composed of a number of shops, these may be operated under the supervision of a superintendent. The factory will also employ experts some of whom will devote their activity to the inspection of finished products, some to the care of machinery in need of repairs or improvements, and others to the study of time-saving devices and better methods of production. It must have several departments, manned by clerks, draftsmen, engineers, and so forth. Each of these groups will have a surpervisor who will assign and coordinate the work of the employees under him. Then there will be a business branch, made up of the salesmen whose assignment is that of calling upon or attending prospective customers. On them will rest the responsibility of expanding the sphere of influence of the company. Correspondence, record-filing, bookkeeping, and other details will be carried by employees who are specialists in the subjects.

Because of the possibility that workers may injure themselves at their tasks, infirmaries are usually set up adjacent to the factory. The nurses and the doctors who receive their salary from the company are not actually engaged in the production of shoes but still represent an important factor in the organization's well-being. Through them many hours of labor are saved, minor injuries cured, and the company is relieved from heavy compensation expenses and lawsuits. There are also lawyers whose time is devoted to the interpretation of the laws governing the relationship between capital and labor. They steer the company clear of patent infringements and the like.

Directing all this are the top officials, headed by the general manager. Upon the latter rests the responsibility of the whole organization. He is the supreme authority in the factory, and much of the organization's success is owed to the quality of his leadership. He must have the complete confidence of the workers as well as that of the investors. There is seen here a perfect application of the division of labor. It is difficult to say which group in the factory is more vital to the good of the organization. Undoubtedly all elements are important, since only their combined effort keeps the factory going and just as the delicate watch needs the perfect condition of each part, large or small, the same can be said for any group of people intent upon a common purpose.

To analyze the problem one step further, while it is true that all groups are vital to the well-being of the factory, the same cannot be said of each individual employee. Consider the manual laborers at the bottom of the factory organization. They usually represent the largest group of employees. While collectively, the work performed by them is paramount, the individual contribution of each one is a very small percentage of the total amount done in the factory. If necessary, the individual's contribution can be easily replaced by a well designed machine that will perform not only his particular work but that of many others like him with a decided economy to the organization. As a matter of fact, as new inventions are made, as tools, instruments, and machinery devised or perfected, a large amount of this labor is actually displaced. To this phenomenon there must be added also the severe competition among workers in search of a job. The laborer's work not requiring much skill or intelligence, naturally attracts a large number of persons from the lower levels of society, who are willing to accept any wage, no matter how small. If only 100 workers are needed and 110 apply for the position, it is plain that, because of competition, only those willing to accept the minimum wage stand a chance of securing the job. This low wage spells a decided economy to the organization which thereby attains a more advantageous position toward its competitors.

Analyzing now the group next above the plain worker, we find here a more skillful person whose individual contribution to the production of shoes is greater, and whose bargaining power is higher. These specialized workers, who have gone through some kind of training and have given proof of skill and talent naturally comprise a much smaller group. As the need for their talent is greater than that for the plain laborer, the wage of the former must be higher than that of the latter. Also, because of the limited number of such specialized individuals, the relative position between employer and employee is completely reversed. Instead of the skilled worker looking for a job in competition with others, the different industries compete against each other for such men. If a skilled worker is dissatisfied with his wage he can easily secure a better job from some other concern willing and frequently eager, to pay that much to increase the necessary skill so important to the organization. On this account, any manager who wishes to keep his specialized labor force must be prepared to pay high wages. What has been said about skilled workers naturally holds for all the other groups above them. The higher wages or salaries paid are determined not only by their higher skill and usefulness to the organization, but also by their greater bargaining power, which is a direct result of their limited number. This condition repeats itself until the highest position is reached, that of the general manager himself.

Now, that wages should be in proportion to skill is almost self-evident. No one could employ intelligent and educated persons and expect to pay them the same wages given to the plain laborer. Of course one may think of coercive methods from above which would enforce the same standard of living upon all persons, irrespective of talent and contribution, but would the output of that factory be the same? Decidedly not. It must be concluded that the wage scale is necessary and beneficial to society, and even though it may represent hardship to millions of people, it assures progress, encourages the perseverant, and compensates those who work the hardest, produce the most, and make themselves more vital to the advancement of society.

In our present set-up of society the work of the laborer, as any other commodity on the market, finds its equilibrium point through the fundamental law of supply and demand. The larger the supply, the lower the price, and vice-versa. As all know, manual labor is abundant in every nation, and this is the main reason for the extremely low wages that many are forced to accept. Under this condition, as we have seen, they find themselves incapable of making a decent living.

As noted in other parts of this book, there are commodities which, being of a luxury nature and quite expensive, are completely out of their reach. The commodities more essential to their subsistence are available to them only in limited quantity. One reason for this limitation is that the amount of vital commodities produced for the entire population is, as a generality, far less than what it should be. Disregarding hoarding on the part of the well-to-do, it is reasonable to assume that the latter should buy more than the average of the entire population. Having more money at their disposal they will buy at least the amount necessary to their well-being, irrespective of scarcity, and this further subtracts from what is left to the poor, who make up the vast portion of the population. As noted in the third and sixth chapters, the supply is unaffected by the theoretical demand, but stops at the level which results in maximum profit. This level is reached when price equals marginal cost. Reverting to the case of the shoe manufacturer analyzed in note 6-1 page 224, it was noted that if he should decide to go above that production he would actually decrease his profit, and that even though the number of shoes in the country at large may be definitely less than actual needs, the manufacturer will not increase his production just for the sake of humanity.

It may be concluded that the low standard of living of the poor is the result of three powerful forces which operate against his advancement. The first is represented by the unskilled nature of his work, the second by his large number, the third, by the phenomenon of scarcity that raises the price of commodities far above his purchasing power.

In contrast, we wish to state that in the new system of life wages will be related to the amount of vital commodities produced or on hand, irrespective of price. The purchasing power of the poor will become a most important factor in the economy of society. At any time, assuming that he is willing to work, any person will have sufficient money to buy at least up to the amount permitted by the scarcity factor, irrespective of prices. If hardship must be borne, this will be due to the fact that the quantity produced is not yet sufficient to allow the desired amount, and it is inevitable that the lower class should bear the brunt of the unfortunate situation. It must be remembered, however, that the new economic forces tend to increase production at all times, so that critical scarcity will only be a temporary condition. In the new order, the purchasing power of the lower class will become the foundation of the economic structure of society and as long as this vast element in the population remains undernourished, this fact alone will impel the increasing of production to the limit where even the poorest will be able to make a better living. How will this influence be exerted? It has been explained that the EW will purchase vital commodities for the millions of moderate means. Now if each one may represent individually a very unconsequential factor in the economy of the nation, the same cannot be said for the EW which stands for them all. With such representation, the poorest class will automatically increase its power to a degree undreamed of in the present set-up of society. Assume that lack of sufficient raw material, inadequate knowledge of mass-production and time-saving devices, inefficient and backward enterprises, all combine to cause a shortage of vital commodities. Their scarcity factor will naturally be high and consequently the amount available to those under the care of the EW will be correspondingly small. The wage scale, however, will be such that any laborer, no matter how poor, will be able to buy the amount assigned by the EW, whatever the price, and in this respect he will be protected, whereas now, with the dislocation of wages and unemployment, he runs the risk of not being able to buy even that much. But as long as wages are kept related to the amount of commodities produced, an increase in production will be encouraged and fostered because of two dominant forces:

(a) As long as the scarcity factor of any commodity is larger than one (indicating that consumption has not reached the saturation point) there will be no fear on the part of the sellers to be left stranded with unsold commodities. Therefore, there will be a more buoyant attitude toward an increase in production, especially on the part of those manufacturers who have not reached the maximum limit of profit.

(b) As prices will be kept under control, the manufacturers will no longer find to their advantage the charging of indiscriminate prices by setting up monopolies and the like, as the corresponding increased cost of labor as well as the positive steps taken by the EW would cut their profits. As a result, increased profit will be possible only by introducing better and cheaper methods of production, and of course by increasing production itself.

Returning to our analysis of the shoe manufacturer, it was found that given a price level for shoes he can gain more profit by increasing his production up to a point where marginal cost equals price. Beyond this point profit will decrease, so it must be taken for granted that there will not be any incentive on his part to increase production above that level, unless able to reduce his cost by introducing additional economies. It may be assumed, therefore, that he will maintain this production as long as the price of shoes does not change. But since we have assumed a shortage of shoes, there will be a potential profit in this field which will encourage other manufacturers to enter the market. Keen and cut-throat competition between established firms and new comers will not result, as the profit of the older organizations will not be impaired by the presence of the others. As the price is kept from wide fluctuations by decreasing competition among the consumers, there will be no advantage to the established manufacturer in setting up a monopoly and in increasing prices through scarcity. As long as these methods are prevented, the profit will depend essentially on his ability to cut costs and increase production and will not be affected by the output of others. The new manufacturer, however, will seek to increase his production to the point of maximum profit, and his output of shoes, added to that of the others, is bound to increase the total supply. The poor, as production increases, will be able to buy more of these commodities because of the automatic adjustment in wages provided by the index, and their standard of living is bound to advance with the general improvement in the country.

But why doesn't this happen in our present society? The answer is simple. Business and capital, as a rule, are usually over-cautious because of the ever present uncertainty of the future. The price of shoes as we know, is not affected by the production of any single manufacturer unless in possession of a patent that gives him the sole rights of production and sale of some particular kind of shoes, but is governed by the combined output of all the shoe manufacturers in the country. Accordingly production is set to derive the maximum profit at that price. If production in the country at large should materially increase above that level, it will tend to produce a general lowering of prices. The established firms, being conscious of this, are not apt to make any increase unless they should come in possession of a new and patented method that puts them in an advantageous position among their competitors. Because their marginal cost, and thus cost itself, is so greatly reduced, they will not hesitate to step up their production to the new equilibrium point, irrespective of others. However, without that advantage, their output will not tend to change. Now, if the country, in spite of this policy, should experience an increase in supply with a consequent decrease in price, it must be taken for granted that this is the result of new enterprises coming into being. As the price of shoes goes down, the established firms will find that the old profit can no longer be obtained. At the lower price the maximum profit can only be attained by a reduced production as this tends to equalize the new price with marginal cost. At this new level, however, not only the profit per shoe will be less but the total profit will tend to reduce. On this account they will find the entry of new enterprises into the market detrimental and annoying. As the new firms continue to expand in their quest of maximum profit, gained when their marginal cost equals the current price, this additional output will further injure the established organizations. It is plain that the latter, left with lesser profit because of the intruders, are apt to retaliate by cut-throat competition in order to block the setting up or expansion of these new comers. The latter, faced by such strong and determined opposition, will find it difficult to expand their business, and only those with gifted and courageous leadership may hope to survive the assault. Such a struggle may also develop between two strong organizations especially when one is in possession of patents and tries to undermine its competitor. One, therefore, must conclude that with the present set-up of society, an increase in production is often out of the question even for those commodities that are extremely scarce. This means that progress is made at a slower pace than justified by the immeasurable want and privation in every nation of the world.

Returning to our search for a system that will bring progress and betterment to the peoples in general and the poor in particular, we shall assume again the Lilliputian society analyzed in the third chapter, because it quickly responds to different systems of life. Conclusions, with proper perspective, may then be applied to any actual society. In the analysis made, it was found that even for such a small group, phenomena will appear that keep many at a low level of standard of living. In this chapter additional facts will be cited which we consider important.

As before, it is assumed that this small society is composed of 10 owners who control all the restricted and economic wealth, 30 managers, 90 skilled workers, with the rest of the population belonging to the unskilled laboring class. The efficiency of this society, or its ability to manufacture vital commodities, is taken as 70%, as in the second example of that chapter. At that time, taking the wage, a, of the unskilled laborer as base, the cost of the entire production of vital commodities was calculated and found to be 504a. This cost was made up of the wages of the skilled and unskilled workers, the salary of the manager and the owners, and the cost of the raw material, assumed equal to a. It was also explained at that time that if the effort of society was utilized for the production of vital commodities alone, (example 1) the owners would have been the only citizens able to acquire the basic amount. The others, with more limited financial resources, would have to make shift with less, in proportion to salary or wages received. As this is inconsistent with actual experience, it was concluded that our assumption was basically wrong and that services had to be included to reproduce phenomena occurring in an actual society. This was done in the second example where part of the population was diverted toward the production of services and of non-vital commodities. However, due to the already limited amount of vital commodities, and being free in our choice, we deliberately increased the number of working hours so as to maintain the same rate of production of the first example. As a consequence of these new assumptions, the equilibrium point for vital commodities rose from 8oq to 28oq, and the share of products available to the poor from a mere .111q increased to .555q. This was because the larger purchasing power of the poor, as a result of the greater number of working hours, permitted this new equilibrium.

Our reader is reminded that equilibrium point means the level at which the cost becomes equal to price. At this point the manufacturers or owners, as an average, do not make any profit, and suffer no loss, but are able to secure the rent for their wealth represented by a as well as the just compensation for their work set at 8a, and taken by them as salary. With this supply on the market the people in general are in a financial position to meet this equilibrium price and each citizen is able to buy a portion related to his wage or salary. As stated, the share of the unskilled laborer is .555q.

.555q, however, is still utterly inadequate, and there is no way for him to improve his lot so long as production of vital commodities cannot be increased. A greater amount of work on his part, in the effort to secure more money, will only tend to increase prices, and ultimately merely increase the profit of the owners (see chapter 3, page 129). However, the fact that the purchasing power of the unskilled laborer has gone from .111q, when no services were supplied, to .555q when the hours of work were changed from 8 to 11.43 per day, may start a train of thought as perhaps here we shall find the solution to the problem. Indeed, it is natural to expect that if the time allotted for services could be further increased, the economic forces would tend to expand the amount of money in circulation and this, by promoting an additional demand, would further increase the supply of vital commodities.

First of all we must emphasize that the example where services were omitted represents a hypothetical case not consonant with reality, as one can hardly conceive a serviceless society. The increase from .111q to .555q is, therefore, meaningless. No doubt if Lilliput should succeed in increasing the number of hours of work, even if merely at giving services, it would add extra purchasing power to all and especially to the laboring class. This would affect the demand for vital commodities, as well as the supply, which in due time would also tend to increase, but only up to a definite limit. Bear in mind that these people are already compelled to work approximately 12 hours per day and longer hours cannot be expected of them. This limitation linked with the assumption of a certain amount of skill and technological knowledge, which may be applied to any particular epoch of the nation under study, will establish the amount of vital commodities that our society can produce.

The next thought to come to our mind may be that if we are not willing to increase the number of hours of work, a greater output can be obtained by increasing the number of workers engaged in producing vital commodities. This is presented in the following example 3 which is a continuation of the analysis started in the third chapter. We shall adopt the same conventional method used at that time, shall restrict our calculation to the minimum and refer to the end of this chapter (under example 3) for the additional data needed in our presentation.

CASE WHERE THE NUMBER OF PERSONS DEVOTING THEIR TIME TO THE PRODUCTION OF VITAL COMMODITIES IS INCREASED

EXAMPLE 3

It has previously been indicated how undesirable it would be to expand production of vital commodities through an increase in working hours, as the men thus engaged are already toiling approximately 12 hours per day, five days per week, and any lengthening of working time would subtract from, rather than add to, their standard of living. Expansion of production, therefore, must be obtained through an increase of the number of workers. This increase will naturally involve a decrease in services, as a certain number of persons must be transferred from one activity to another. But this fact, for the present, must be considered immaterial to this discussion.

The number of persons employed in the production of vital commodities is assumed to have increased to 320 from the original 280 of example 2. Assuming the same technological know-how ($Rc = 1.0$ line 77) and sufficient raw material on hand, the amount produced will increase in proportion of number of workers and will become 320q (line 75). These people will be paid a total of 576a (line 33).

Those in the upper division of society, already able to buy the amount q essential to their well-being, are not going to buy more just because the production has increased, and therefore it must be taken for granted that they will buy the same quota q as before.

The full benefit of the greater production therefore will go, in greater or lesser degree, to those who previously could not obtain that optimum quantity q.

Now 130Pq represents the amount spent by the upper classes, the difference, or 190Pq, will be spent by the unskilled labor class. As this represents a condition of scarcity and as there will still be competition among the buyers, prices will go up to a level where the labor class will be forced to use up to the complete amount of its earnings. This requirement is expressed by the following equation:

$$190 \ Pq = 270a \quad \text{from which}$$
$$Pq = 1.42a \quad \text{and}$$
$$a = .704q$$

From this we could conclude that the laborer is now able to buy a far greater share than before, because the price has decreased from the previous level on account of the lesser competition among the buyers. But is this a position of equilibrium? To have equilibrium all conditions must be satisfied. One of these is that cost must be equal to price. The price of q as calculated, is represented by 1.42a and, therefore, the total amount the owners will derive from the sale of vital commodities will be:

$$1.42 \ a \ x \ 320 = 455a \ \text{instead of } 504a.$$

But the cost as we know, is 576a, so that the owners would lose:

$$(576\text{-}455) \ a = 121a$$

if they should persist in maintaining such a volume of production. This, we know, they will not do, and sooner or later some must drop from the market, the unemployed will revert to supplying services, and gradually the old production of 280q will be re-established. Hence this method will not solve our problem, as the gain of one class will have to be made through the loss of another.

INCREASED PRODUCTION THROUGH SKILL AND TECHNOLOGICAL ADVANCEMENT

EXAMPLE 4a

Assume now that the expanded production results from the increase of the average skill of our society rather than in the number of workers. Those in the upper branches of society, as in example 3, will be satisfied to buy the amount q and no more, therefore extra commodities produced will be spread in larger or smaller degree among all in the lower classes. But as this increase will only be a small percentage of the total production at any one time, the phenomenon of scarcity will again be present, and this means that the poor will still have to use all of their earnings for this purchase. It is known, however, that due to the increased supply, the prices of vital commodities will drop. This lowering of prices, without changing cost, will mean a loss for the owners and some of them, by withdrawing from the market, will again limit the production to the original level.

But then how can anyone say that an improvement in skill or technological knowledge represents an advancement in progress and standard of living? Our reader must forgive our slowness in coming to the point, but we must explain all the phases of the problem so as not to leave any doubt or uncertainty about what we are trying to prove. An improvement in skill or technological knowledge does mean an advancement as will be explained in the following discussion.

Whenever skill is increased (bringing about better and more economical methods of production), or whenever we are faced by an advancement in technology (such as new inventions and discoveries), the amount of time devoted to the production of vital commodities is correspondingly decreased. This phenomenon can be easily proved by reminding the reader that the hours of work from 16 and more per day have been steadily reduced in the last century to a standard of 8 hours at the present time. This reduction has kept pace with the new discoveries and advancements. It is also reasonable to assume that this trend will project into the future as new inventions and discoveries are made. This reduction in time of work has had the tendency to keep the supply equal to the actual demand, so as not to produce the inequality between cost and price of commodities mentioned above. As this reduction occurs, available energy is set free for producing other kinds of commodities as well as for supplying a larger volume of services for the same amount of working hours per day. As the cost of vital commodities has decreased in relation to the total purchasing power of the laborer, this will produce an additional demand which, after the inevitable ups and downs around the new equilibrium point, will aid the increase of vital commodities and consequently the average standard of living.

Say that as a result of a new invention the ability of producing commodities increases for our society from 1.0 to 1.14 (line 77). The number of hours of work per day and per individual will still be taken to be 11.43. If the number of individuals engaged in production of commodities is still 280 (same as in example 2) the new production will become: 280 x 1.14 $=$ 320q (line 75 of example 4a). The cost of production, however, will still be represented by 504a as we have not changed either wages or number of individuals. Since 320q still represents a condition of scarcity, the price will rise to a level where the poorest will be forced to use all of their earnings. Yet, irrespective of price, the upper classes will secure the amount q so that:

$$320q - 130q \text{ or } 190q$$

will be the amount the poor can buy at that level of production for which they must spend their entire wages. This can be expressed by the following relation:

$$190Pq = 270a$$

where Pq is the price of the unit commodity. From this relation the price Pq becomes:

$$Pq = 270 \ a/190 = 1.42 \ a \quad \text{(line 79) and}$$
$$a = 190Pq/270 = .704Pq \quad \text{(line 80)}$$

From this we could conclude that the laborer is in a position to buy a far larger share of q than before, because the price has decreased from the previous level on account of the larger supply and consequent smaller competition among the buyers. However, for this to be true, both conditions of equilibrium must be satisfied. The other condition, as we know, is that cost must be equal to price. As the price of q in relation to wage a is given by Pq $=$ 1.42a, the total price, or the amount which the owners will derive from the sale of commodities will be:

$$1.42a \times 320 = 455a \text{ instead of } 576a,$$

so that the owners will lose:

$$576a - 455a = 121a$$

This loss will be distributed unevenly among the owners, and those losing most will be forced to withdraw from the market, tending to decrease production toward the old level. But as many shift their activities from the production of commodities to that of giving services, fewer persons will be left in the field, and therefore, production will tend to decrease from 320q to the original 280q. This takes us to example 4b.

Example 4b. We must note immediately that this level of production is attained by a smaller number of people. However, this released energy is now utilized to supply more services to society in general and it can be said that on this account alone society is bound to be that much richer, even if the production of commodities is the same.

Assume for instance that 245 persons, made up of 6 owners, 18 managers, 55 skilled laborers, and 166 unskilled laborers, utilize their entire energy in producing commodities. The rest of the population, or 4 owners, 12 managers, 35 skilled workers and 104 unskilled laborers, use their time in supplying services. The total hours per day for the production of commodities will be:

$$245 \times 11.43 = 2800 \text{ hours}$$

instead of the 3200 of example 2, or about 12.5% less than before. As to the purchasing power of the laborer, this has not changed since the total number of hours of work as well as wages remain the same. As usual he will spend all he makes to buy as much vital commodities as possible, as essential to his subsistence, consequently the price of commodities will depend on the pressure exerted by this class.

The total amount, influenced now not only by the total hours of work but by the increased skill of society which is 14% more than before will be:

$$320q \times 245/280 = 280q.$$

The cost to the owners, as a result of fewer workers being engaged in this activity will become 438a instead of 504a (line 33). On account of this reduction in cost it is plain that 438a rather than 504a will determine the new equilibrium price. The amount of commodities available to the lower classes becomes:

$$280q - 130q = 150q \quad \text{(line 88)}$$

for which they must use their entire wage. Reasoning as before:

$$150Pq = 270a \text{ from which:}$$
$$Pq = 1.8a \text{ and}$$
$$a = .555q$$

From the above it could be said that the laborer has not improved his condition through the increased efficiency of society, as he must still make shift with the same amount of commodities (.555q of example 2) which is not sufficient for a decent living. But is this a condition of equilibrium? To have equilibrium, cost must be equal to price. The price or the amount received by the owners from the sale of these commodities is given by:

$$1.8a \times 280 = 504a,$$

and as this is greater than the calculated cost (438a) it is plain that the owners will now realize a profit of

$$505a - 438a = 66a.$$

This profit will promote two effects:

(a) It will increase the production on the part of the owners already engaged in this activity.

(b) It will encourage the entrance into the field of additional manufacturers who want to share those profits.

Both of these factors, as already noted, will tend to increase production and decrease prices, so that after an indeterminate number of fluctuations a new equilibrium price will be established between 438a and 504a.

Example 4c. Taking the just finished example 4b as a base for the following analysis, we know that 2800 working hours per day will produce 280q which will cost the owners 438a, and will be sold at a price of 504a. The new condition of equilibrium will be reached when cost becomes equal to price and the profit is reduced to zero.

The new time devoted to the production of commodities shall be assumed at 2800X, where X is for the present an unknown factor larger than one which will produce a condition of equilibrium. The amount produced will be given by 280qX as this quantity, because of the same amount of skill, will be directly proportional to the effort done. The cost of the total amount of commodities will also increase in the same ratio, and will be 438X (more people enter the field of production). By adopting the same method described in example 2, that is, by equating the amount of commodities received by the lower class with their wage and then solving for the factor X, this turns out to be:

$$X = 1.08.$$

Substituting now this value in the various expressions of example 4c, the numerical values have been derived and shown in example 4. From this the following facts can be established:

Price of unit commodity q or Pq = 1.57a	line 79
Commodities bought by unit wage a or a = .638q	line 80
Commodities produced Kq = 280q x 1.08 = 302q	line 75
Commodities bought U = 302q	line 89
Cost of commodities Cq = 438 x 1.08 = 474a	line 33
Price of commodities Pq.U = 474a	line 90

Price and cost as well as commodities produced and absorbed are equal to each other. This indicates that a condition of equilibrium has been reached. It can be noted that the amount which the wage a can buy is now .638q much larger than .555q of example 2. As this is now a new condition of equilibrium it can be stated that barring additional improvements in skill or technological knowledge, this rather than the previous level will be the point at which the economic forces tend to stabilize the price. This level, as has been seen, is a direct result of that improvement. It follows that an increase in efficiency or technological advancement does produce a better standard of living for the laborer, and this fact must be recognized by any person who compares living conditions of the modern laborer and the living conditions of the average laborer of 100 years ago.

CONCLUSIONS REACHED FROM EXAMPLE 4

We have seen that technological advancement and better methods of production tend to improve the standard of living of the people, but such improvements are not commodities that can be manufactured overnight and at will. Inventions spring from the minds of geniuses and gifted individuals who devote years of their life, and endure great hardship and discomfort for that attainment. And even then, as soon as the knowledge has been acquired, made available to society, and contributed to the raising of the economic equilibrium point economic forces will take over and maintain it until additional discoveries and inventions push it to a higher level.

We must conclude that this wonderful world we live in, this abundant variety of things enjoyed in our every-day life, is due in a large portion, to the achievement of the men of talent who have scanned the forces of Nature and gradually opened up new horizons and laid the foundations of our present society. That this process is going on right now is evident, that the pace of discoveries is accelerating rather than otherwise is also a well-known fact, especially when one considers the improvements in education and the facilities made available to a large number of scientists constantly at work in laboratories at a great variety of problems. But what we like to emphasize in this study is that this improvement which we now enjoy is the direct and sole result of this phase of human activity, and not of any particular mode of life, as some would like us to believe, whether Communism, Fascism, or Democracy. True, one system may be better than another, as set forth in detail in previous chapters. This, however, is not due to any particular positive contribution of their own to human welfare, but to the degree of restriction they impose on human life, which has a powerful influence upon the free development of man's marvelous mind and ability. A pure democracy, which to our mind is easily the best among the others, if set up in a nation devoid of these imponderable qualities herein termed personal wealth, would not have in itself the motive power to foster progress and betterment. Even in a pure democracy the tendency to raise prices and consequently profits through scarcity would keep the population in general on a low standard of living, even though it could boast of possessing freedom of speech, freedom of worship, and freedom from fear. In later years freedom from want has been added to the others, but notwithstanding the sincerity and goodwill of the would-be sponsors, modern society does not have the necessary power to make good such a boast, as so many factors will change or divert that aim. It seems to us that such an ideal and offer is only aimed at the weakening of the enemy's will to fight, and no real effort is ever made for its true application because too many obstacles are placed in its path. The inability of our civilization to achieve such a goal is clearly an evidence of its maladjustment and weakness. If we take into account the millions of honest thinking individuals of all classes and nations who would gladly welcome the realization of such an ideal and as such represent a powerful force in its favor, it must be concluded that its application is beyond the power of one man, one class or one country and that only a complete change in our ethics and mode of life can hope to attain such a goal. Freedom from want should not rely on improvements introduced by science and the inventiveness of the people which, as already seen, are slow and unregulated, but should rely on changes in the way of life itself, so that the raising of standard of living could be achieved, no matter how great or how little the ability and inventive quality of the people happens to be.

From the examples given in chapters 2 and 3, and those in this chapter, it must be concluded that with the exception of the benefit brought by inventions and technological advancement, there is no mode of life in modern society that by itself could produce such improvements. Confronted by the economic chaos of the modern era, with all its moral and physical damaging effects we must conclude that the introduction of the advocated mode of life becomes an imperative necessity. This is not only from the point of view that this system will aid human advancement, but from the point that it will stop the trend toward a more disrupted and chaotic humanity without endangering in any way those human rights secured in the past with so much hardship and toil.

FACTORS THAT TEND TO CHANGE THE EQUILIBRIUM POINT

In the course of the present discussion it was found that price of vital commodities tends to oscillate around what is here termed the equilibrium price. To be sure, prices do not stay at any fixed level for any length of time, but when they move too far from the equilibrium point, economic forces set in and tend to reverse that trend. It has also been shown how technological advancement and improvement in skill will eventually change this point. Now we may ask ourselves the following questions:

(a) Are there any other factors besides technological advancement that will change this level?

(b) Why is it that our particular society under study has a level at 280q rather than at say, 290 or 270q?

(c) What are the forces or conditions in society that make possible this particular level instead of any other?

(1) In answer to the first question it may be stated that there are several other factors that change the equilibrium point.

(2) In answer to the second: 280q has been reached because of the assumption made at the beginning of this discussion, or better to say the equilibrium point has been a result of the pattern we have arbitrarily chosen for our society in study.

(3) In answer to the third: There are at least three factors that will change the equilibrium point (if we assume an unlimited amount of raw material available to society). These factors are the following:

(a) The number of persons engaged in manufacturing vital commodities.

(b) The number of persons composing any one class.

(c) The relation between wages and salaries.

Other factors are represented by the amount of saving done within the society and by the magnitude of unemployment. These factors, however, will be dealt with in a latter part of this chapter and shall here be neglected. Another obvious factor is that of the number of hours of work linked with the efficiency of society.

At the beginning of this study (chapter 3, page 111) an assumption was made as to the number of owners, managers, and so forth, composing our society, and a stated relation between the number of individuals turning out commodities and the number of those furnishing services, likewise a fixed relation between wages and salaries. From those assumptions the equilibrium point turned out to be 28oq. Any other assumption would have given us a different equilibrium point.

It will now be explained why a change in any of these relations will affect that level. In order to simplify this study we shall assume again our Lilliputian society, and taking case 2 as the basic condition, we shall change one factor at a time so as to follow the effect produced by each change.

The numerical analysis of these three examples (5 to 7 included) is shown in the tabular calculation placed at the end of this chapter. It will be noticed that we have changed only one factor at a time leaving the rest equal to example 2 which has been taken as a base of comparison.

CHANGE IN NUMBER OF PERSONS ENGAGED IN MANUFACTURING VITAL COMMODITIES

EXAMPLE 5

First we shall study the effect of changing the number of persons manufacturing vital commodities and say that the owners of wealth, for reasons immaterial to this study, all of a sudden are reduced to five. It can be said that with fewer receiving a salary the cost of commodities will drop to 486 from 504a (line 33). This at first will produce profits for the owners because revenue becomes greater than cost, yet, this fact will stimulate additional production of commodities which will eventually become 292q (line 75, considerably more than the 280q of example 2. By following the various steps indicated in the tabular calculation it is proved that this is a condition of equilibrium or cost equals revenue and production equals amount absorbed by the market. With such a pattern if production should be less, prices will go up because of the greater competition among the buyers, if production should gain the consequent decrease in price will represent loss to some of the owners who in turn will decrease their output.

It may be observed in passing that the quantity the poorer class will buy is somewhat larger than in the basic example or .6o instead of .555q. There is, therefore, an advantage in decreasing the number devoting their time to the production of vital commodities and this fact is obvious when it is considered that the cost of production is lowered because of that reduction.

A similar reasoning may be followed if one assumes an increase in the number of owners engaged in the production of commodities. Of course, in this case the condition is reversed and naturally Kq, or the commodities produced by society becomes less.

CHANGE IN THE NUMBER OF PERSONS COMPOSING ANY CLASS

EXAMPLE 6

Another factor that will tend to change the equilibrium point is a variation in the number of persons composing any class, and again for simplicity this will be done only for one class with the others left unchanged. Assume that owner class to be seven instead of ten, and in order to keep constant the number of 400 individuals, the labor class, and specifically that which devotes its time to giving services, is now 84 instead of 81.

The equilibrium condition in this case will be broken by the fact that the number of individuals able to buy the amount q becomes 127 instead of 130 of example 2 (line 50). By following the various steps indicated in the tabular calculation, it is found that the production which will reestablish equilibrium is 277 instead of 280q.

It may be observed in passing that the quantity bought by the individual in the lower class is somewhat smaller than in the basic example or .55 instead of .555q and this fact becomes obvious when it is considered that a smaller production (Kq) has meant no reduction in cost (C^1) and therefore the price of the unit commodity Pq, which is the ratio of the two, has correspondingly increased. Quite true that the amount to the poor is the same, yet, this must be distributed among a labor class of 273 instead of 270.

A similar reasoning may be followed if one assumes an increase in the number of owners engaged in the production of services with a corresponding decrease of those belonging to the labor class. In this case the condition is reversed and Pq will become smaller.

CHANGE IN THE RELATION BETWEEN SALARIES AND WAGES

EXAMPLE 7

Consider the effect of a change in the relation between salaries and wages as the third factor affecting the equilibrium point. As in the previous instance everything remains as in example 2, with the exception of a single factor. This change is that the income of the owners is reduced from 9a to 8a. All the others will retain the same wage as before.

The equilibrium in this case is broken by the fact that the cost of vital commodities will drop from 504 to 497a (line 33). By following the various steps indicated by the tabular calculation it is found that the production which will reestablish equilibrium is 284.6 instead of 280q (line 75). This because a decreased price will stimulate additional demand which in time will establish the equilibrium at a higher level. Because of the larger production the laborer now will be able to obtain .572q instead of .555q and the price of the unit commodity becomes 1.746 instead of 1.8a. The reverse will occur if the salary of the owners is increased.

CONCLUSIONS REACHED FROM EXAMPLES 5, 6, AND 7

This dissertation is presented to prove that the position of equilibrium is related to the pattern of society. It is evident that in any society the number belonging to any class is governed by imponderable factors out of our economic field of discussion and may range from personal ability, ambition, and chance, to old established human rights handed down by previous generations. This pattern, while fixed at any particular time, nevertheless, goes through gradual and imperceptible changes over a period of years. As a result of various economic phenomena, and of the personal ability of individuals, it is always found that some advance to a better class while others lapse to a lower. Thus the number of members making up any class will vary with time and circumstances. To be sure, the change will be small and undetectable, sometimes in one direction and other times in another. However its effect over a long interval of time will bring about variations of the equilibrium point according to the relation we have established. As we see it, all consciously or unconsciously tend to improve their conditions and in this relentless struggle for advancement some will go or stay on top while others will drop or remain at the bottom. As this phenomenon is rooted in the very nature of men, it should not be altered or influenced in any way if we want to retain the inviolability of individual rights within the law of the land. Since most of our problems consider society at any stage of its evolution, this variation among classes cannot and should not be controlled. Our avowed policy of non-interference places this problem out of our field and thus, whatever the pattern of society, this must be considered fixed and unchangeable.

As to the relation between salaries and wages, these are governed by the usefulness and contribution to society in general as well as by the law of supply and demand. It was noted in previous parts of this study how a moving picture artist can secure a payment for his work far greater than the laborer who toils year in and year out without ever being able to attain economic independence. As earlier explained, the effort of these people is paid in relation to usefulness to society, and, therefore, cannot be altered if we do not want to restrict or tamper with the fundamental law of supply and demand. This being the case, how can the pattern of society be changed so that the equilibrium point will increase and hence raise the lot of the poor, who make up the vast majority of a nation?

Discarding any attempt to change either the number of people belonging to any class of society or to force any profession or trade upon any one, a certain amount of change in wages and salaries must be considered in order to correct the injustices of present society. Now if this is done in such a way that no one will be adversely affected, but all will actually gain, there is hope that this method will be well accepted by the rich as well as by the poor. It remains to be seen how this can be accomplished.

RELATION BETWEEN SALARIES AND WAGES AS VISUALIZED FOR THE FUTURE SOCIETY

As the EW becomes organized, the salaries and wages of those who receive compensation fixed by a regular contract or agreement between employer and employees will be related to the index a. This will be true no matter whether the compensation is in terms of dollars, francs, lires and so forth. But as a represents also the minimum wage in the community under consideration each individual will receive an income indicated by 1.1a, 1.2a, 10a as the case may be.

At the beginning, these wages and salaries will be assumed the true measure of each individual's worth to society, and we shall assume that they have been reached by the natural law of supply and demand, which, as explained before, will not be changed or altered. Under the beneficial influence of the EW the production of vital commodities will increase. As graphically shown in Fig. 19 this extra amount of commodities will be mostly absorbed by those lower

on the financial ladder of society, and their individual quota will
depend on the percentage of q their wage or salary can secure. All
those already able to obtain the quantity q will not be interested,
as a generality, in buying a larger amount. We know also that if
the wages were not increased so as to absorb this additional supply
that loss would result from this change in production and consequently the supply would decrease to the original level. This
obviously must be prevented. As the supply increases, the quantity
available to the EW, and therefore to the poor in general, will
increase also. Since as a general rule the EW will seek to hold the
fluctuations of prices between narrow margins, we are justified for
the sake of simplicity to assume them stabilized at a certain level.
However with the increase in supply the scarcity factors for the
various commodities will drop. This, in turn, will increase the basic
wage a and the poor automatically will be able to make greater
purchases as explained in the latter part of the sixth chapter. That
exposition however, was more concerned with presenting the idea
than in giving specific facts, and thus the increase in salaries and
wages was indicated but not specified. This will be the topic of the
ensuing analysis.

First of all, the idea of increasing all wages in the same proportion
must be discarded as the purchasing power of each class in relation
to the others would not be affected but would only mean a change
in the value of money. We shall assume instead that ALL SALARIES
AND WAGES ARE INCREASED BY THE SAME AMOUNT so
that if Y is the difference in wage of the unskilled laborer before
and after the increase, the same amount will be awarded to all
engaged in remunerative work. If a stands for the original average
wage of the laborer and a_1, for his wage after the raise, Y will be
given by: (a_1-a) and a salary for instance of 10a will now become
$(10a + Y)$. In other words, Y stands for the necessary adjustment
in salaries and wages so that the supply may be completely absorbed
by the general public. Since this raise is made for this definite
purpose it is just that it should not be related to skill and ability
and since it is equal for all, rich and poor alike, it should not be a
cause of resentment among the various classes. The poor will use
this extra money to buy additional vital commodities, now available
to them, the rich for additional services and luxury commodities.
Of course as wages and salaries are raised, the cost to produce
commodities will also increase, and this will tend to raise their price,
which in turn will affect the index in the opposite direction. But as

the variations are small, one can foresee a gradual increase in prices as well as salaries and wages, with fluctuations about an equilibrium point that is now definitely on the upgrade. All this is explained in greater detail in example 8 with the complete analysis at the end of this chapter.

NEW RELATION BETWEEN SALARIES AND WAGES

EXAMPLE 8

Assume that under the influence of the EW organization of our small society of 400 that the amount of vital commodities produced has increased from 280 to 320q or an increase of 14% above the level reached in example 2, again assumed as a base of comparison. It shall be taken that this increase has been induced by the fact that the producers, confident now of disposing of their complete stock, are more willing to expand their production. It must be realized that such an increase is out of proportion to what will actually happen in real society, where the influence of the EW will be exerted long before such a gain is attained. Indeed, without such influence on the part of the EW prices would drop and bring losses to the owners of wealth but, being anxious to show unmistakable trends, we will consider such condition as possible. The number composing each class as well as of those devoting time and energy in manufacture of vital commodities will be the same as in example 2, the only difference being in the increased amount of production (320 instead of 280q). The problem on hand, therefore, is that of calculating the increase in the salaries and wages of all components of society under the new concept.

As explained previously this increase will be equal for all and will be indicated by Y pending its evaluation through the usual method of equating the two conditions of equilibrium. By following the tabular calculation in example 8a we find that the cost of commodities is now given by: 504a + 280Ya where a is the basic wage before increase, 504a is the original cost and 280Ya is the addition in cost necessitated by the increase in wages and salaries. Note that 280 coincides with the number of people engaged in production of vital commodities and this is consistent with the assumption that all components will receive the same increase. Substituting all known factors in the equation of line 58, Y works out to be .282a. With this information the new condition of equilibrium can be presented in the adjoining column 8. Note that a is still the basic wage before increase in production.

It can be seen that the poor now receive .705 instead of .555q (line 84) and that the price of unit commodity Pq is 1.82 instead of 1.8a (line 79). All have received an equal increase in pay, yet the percentage increase is not in the same proportion to their original basic pay and is largest for the unskilled laborer while smallest for the owner. This, of course, means that a different relationship is established between salaries and wages. Indeed, if the new wage of the laborer is taken as base of comparison, as it will be done if the system is accepted, the new scale of wages and salaries will be the following:

Unskilled laborer	$W4$ = 1.00a	or	(1.282/1.282)
Skilled laborer	$W3$ = 1.78a	"	(2.282/1.282)
Manager	$W2$ = 4.90a	"	(6.282/1.282)
Owner	$W1$ = 7.23a	"	(9.282/1.282)

It may appear that the reduction in wages and salaries of all classes in comparison to the labor class has had to suffer greatly but this is only on the surface. To make the point clear consider the large number of people in this country who receive an annual income of $200,000 and more. Assume also that the income of the laborer is only $2000. The ratio between the two or 200,000/2000 = 100. Say now that under the suggested mode of life the new wage increase is $200 per year so that the new wage scale will be represented by 200,200 for the owner and 2200 for the laborer. The ratio between the two wages now becomes: 200,200/2200 = 91 which is considerably smaller than 100 yet it can not be said that the owner is much poorer than before and that he stands to be greatly affected by this arrangement. The opposite, however, is true if one considers that this new increase will have a powerful influence in preventing depression and large scale losses to the rich. At any rate, the fact that all have gained and that the extra amount of money is used by the poor mostly for the purchase of vital commodities not in competition with the rich will make this changed relationship agreeable to all. It remains to be said that this general increase in pay will not prevent any one from receiving an additional raise or promotion as individual. This will be the personal concern and privilege of his superior who will pay him according to his worth and usefulness and, therefore, beyond our scope of discussion.

EFFECT OF Y ON THE DISTRIBUTION OF SERVICES

It will now be considered how the distribution of services will be affected by this new imposed rise in salaries and wages. Having contemplated an increase in commodities, it is reasonable to assume that a similar process has taken place in the amount of services given as one cannot easily conceive progress in one direction with none made in another. The new forces make society more vital and efficient. On this account, again taking example 2 of chapter 3 as the basis, it will be assumed that the amount of services is now 456 instead of 400s (line 97). This increase of 14% is equal to that assumed for commodities. It will be assumed again that this increase has been induced by the fact that more money is in circulation which, by increasing the price of services, tends to increase service itself. The number of people giving services has not changed and is still 120 of example 2, yet the salaries and wages have been increased by the amount .282a so that the cost of services La (line 39) now becomes 250 instead of 216a.

The first condition of equilibrium is that V equals Z where V is the amount of service bought (line 113) and Z is the amount of services rendered (line 97). The second condition of equilibrium is that VPs (line 114) equals La (line 39) where VPs is the total amount spent for services by the people in general and La is the total cost of services based on the assumed wage scale. It can be seen that the amount of services by the individual of each class (lines 105 to 108) with the exception of the unskilled laborer who is completely out of the field of competition, has increased in relation to example 2 which is consistent with the fact that the total amount of services has also increased. The addition, however, is largest for the skilled laborer (.844s-.37s=.474s) and smaller for the owner (13.6s-13.28s=.32s). This results from the fact that the larger number of individuals in the skilled labor class exerts now a larger pressure on the market which tends to reduce the amount available to the rich. Indeed, in example 2 the pressure exerted by the owner and skilled labor class was:

Owner's class   72a/216a=33.3 %
Skilled labor class   18a/216a= 8.35%

For example 8 the respective pressure becomes:

Owner's class   74.62a/250a=29.8 %
Skilled labor class 41.58a/250a=16.6 %

Yet the owner enjoys by far the largest proportion of services and this discrepancy should and probably will not give rise to feelings of jealousy and injustice as all, rich and poor alike find themselves in a far better condition than before.

SUBSTITUTION OF MONEY TO BASIC INDEX a

EXAMPLE 9

In all our previous examples we have taken as base of comparison the wage index a. Yet salaries and wages must be paid in cash and it is understandable that this may raise a feeling of doubt in the mind of the reader as to the applicability of the system when real money is involved in the various transactions among the members of our society. In order to dispell such a doubt, example 9 has been calculated as counterpart of example 2 and "a" becomes a definite value in money. For the sake of presenting also the change from the laissez-faire policy of example 2 to that where the EW exerts a beneficial influence in the economy of society, example 10 has been given as counterpart of example 8.

Let us first translate the second basic example of chapter 3 in terms of money and say that $40.00 is the weekly wage of the unskilled laborer now taken as a base. If Lilliput works six days per week at the rate of 11.43 hours per day the index will be approximately 58 cents. The wage or salary for the other classes will be increased by the same ratio and will be as follows: Skilled laborer $80, manager $240, owner $360. The total amount of wages and salaries per week is given by $28,800 which will represent the total circulation of money. It must be understood that while this is quite small in our society of 400 individuals it would be represented by a far greater amount for an actual society. Let us now make the additional assumption that the actual amount of gold in the banks or in the government vaults is $8000 which means that the ratio between specie and money in circulation is: $8000/28,800 = .278$, well above the critical ratio established by the government, say 5%. With this money in circulation our society has reached the economic equilibrium at a level of 280q and 400s.

The cost of vital commodities, as shown in the calculation at the end of this chapter, is given by $20,160 and the number of units of commodities, as already stated, is 280q. From this the price of unit q becomes: $Pq = 20,160/280 = 72 which can still be represented by the expression $Pq = 1.8a$.

It can be seen that the distribution of vital commodities among the various components of society is still the same as in example 2 and it is also proved that this is a condition of equilibrium.

The total amount of services given is still represented by 400s and its cost will be $8640 (line 39). From this the price of unit services becomes:

$$Ps = 8640/400 = \$21.60 \text{ (line 98)}$$

which can still be represented by .54a. Just as for commodities the distribution of services among the various components of society is still equal to that of example 2 and it is also shown that this is a condition of equilibrium.

EXAMPLE 10

This example, like example 8, assumes the same pattern of society considered in example 2 with the provision that the adjustment in salaries and wages must be made so that the commodities produced above previous levels will be completely absorbed by the population. As we know, this adjustment is indicated by Y and, as the pattern of society has not changed, the equations of example 8a apply also to this case. This adjustment is represented by: .282a or .282 x 40 = $11.28 which will be given to all members of society engaged in productive work. The new wage scale per week becomes the following one: Owner $371.28, manager $251.28, skilled laborer $91.28, unskilled lavorer $51.28. The amount of money in circulation in this case will be $33.312 of which more will be said later. The amount of commodities produced, like example 8, will step up to 320 from 280q and its cost, due to the increased wages and salaries becomes approximately $23,318. From this the cost of unit q becomes: Pq = $33,318/320 = $73.00. The distribution of commodities is equal to example 8 and while all those who are placed up in the financial ladder maintain their consumption of one q, the unskilled laborer increases his share from .555 to .705q.

The amount of services likewise is increased from 400 to 456s and its cost, in line with the increased wages and salaries, becomes approximately $9993 per week. From this the price of unit service becomes Ps = $9993/456 = $21.92 which is slightly above that in example 9. The distribution of services remains the same as in axample 8 and it is also proved that this is a condition of equilibrium.

From examples 9 and 10 we can conclude that the substitution of money in place of the index a does not change the results arrived at in the example 2 and 8. These cases were included, however, for the purpose of showing that the circulation of money in the new system of life will tend to increase 33,312 for example 10 against $28,800 for example 9). The amount of gold in the banks and government vaults, however, is still the same or $8000 therefore the ratio between specie and amount in circulation will have to drop from the original ratio of .278 to a new one given by:

$$8000/33,312 = .240$$

But as long as this ratio is above the critical level, this to be established by economists, no harm is done by following the assumed policy. It becomes as a matter of course that as the ratio tends to decrease toward dangerous levels, that efforts should be exerted toward the replenishing of the supply of gold or specie. By this decrease in the ratio the business activity of our society will materially increase and, while the owners are still the absolute possessors of wealth, as nothing has been detracted from or added to their holdings, the products of this wealth are apportioned in a more intelligent way and tend to increase the standard of living of all.

Quite true that as prices increase, the value of money in relation to actual wealth will drop. This will mean, for instance, that a type of house originally costing $10,000, with the passing of time will cost more and anyone who has saved such a sum for that purpose and then for some reason postpones his purchase will find later on that the same sum is no longer sufficient. On this account, he may feel that he has sustained a loss. This, of course, is a chance that all who save money must take. Money, as we have seen, is only a medium of exchange and as long as it remains unspent, the exchange having not taken place, it is natural that while that sum may represent a certain amount of wealth at some given time it will represent an entirely different one at another. In our visualized new system of life where the economic index continues to increase, the value of money in reference to wealth will tend to decrease. Therefore, it will be wise for the hypothetical saver to invest his money in actual wealth as this will also increase in price with the passing of time. This could be represented by the purchase of stocks, bonds, and other commodities that can be easily sold when the saver is ready for his final purchase. As we know in our present system of life prices may go up but can also go down so that the original $10,000 house will cost considerably less in periods of depression. This will be prevented in the new system of life and, therefore, the intelligent investment of money will be paramount in the future. This will tend to maintain an ever increasing rate of circulation which will prove beneficial to society.

EFFECT OF UNEMPLOYMENT

While on the subject, we feel that additional topics need consideration. In all our examples we have emphasized that the entire population is at work. We know that this is not so in the actual society and that in all classes there is always a given percentage of unemployment. Quite true in the upper classes this may be due to the fact that many individuals, already in possession of what they want and need, do not feel compelled to work. However, in the lower class unemployment usually is the result of economic forces within society which may call for a certain amount of labor force and no more. As a result some will only be able to find part-time jobs while others will be entirely unemployed. What is the effect of this social phenomenon? It is plain that for different proportions of unemployment among the various classes of society different equilibrium points will be obtained. This is shown in detail in examples 11 to 18 where various conditions are considered.

EXAMPLES 11 TO 16

Take again the basic Lilliputian society of 400 and for the sake of retaining the assumptions made in previous examples it is established as a base of comparison that 280 individuals are usually employed in the production of vital commodities, and 120 in giving services so that for other conditions the respective numbers will be given by 280α and 120β where α and β are usually smaller but in given cases can be larger than one. In previous example the values of α and β have always been taken as one, or the change in the number of individuals employed in the two main basic activities was actually shown so that the effect of α and β has not been felt; not so, however, when they differ from unity. The 280 and 120 individuals referred above come from all classes of society so that by applying the factors α and β we imply that the unemployment has the same percentage for all classes. This, of course, is not true. However, it simplifies our problem and, as it does not change the nature of the phenomenon, conclusions from this and following examples can be applied to the actual society.

Say that α and β (line 11) are respectively .9 so that the total number of people working at production of commodities and services will be given by 252 and 108. It will be noticed that in this and following examples the number of people employed may not be given by whole numbers. This because of the assumed small number of individuals in our society and the necessity of maintaining the proportion equal for all classes. As a result of unemployment the cost of vital commodities will drop from 504 to 453.6a (line 33) while the total circulation of money drops to 648 from the original 720a of example 2 (line 44). The amount of commodities that will produce a condition of equilibrium is found by substituting the known factors in the expression shown in line 58. This works out to be 280q. We shall refrain from showing our surprise in finding that production has not decreased from the basic example 2 because of unemployment. A complete explanation of this fact will be given when all examples have been shown.

As to services it seems reasonable to assume, barring technological advancement, that this should be in proportion to the skill and number of people giving services. The ability of producing services in example 2 was chosen to be 3.33s per person. This factor Ms (line 96) will be retained for the condition under study, therefore, the total services rendered within our society will be given by:

$$Z = Ns \ \beta \ Ms$$

where Ns is the basic number of people giving services, Ms is the ability of producing services and β is the unemployment factor. In our case Z becomes:

$$Z = 120 \times 3.33 \times .9 = 360s \quad (\text{line } 97)$$

The cost of unit services s becomes:

$$Ps = 194.4a/360 = .54a$$

From the detailed calculation at the end of this chapter it can be seen that the amount of services received by the average individual of each class is less than what is received by the corresponding one in example 2. This because it is assumed that those in the class who are not working will have to be sustained by the working population of their class this tending to decrease the amount which the latter would normally obtain had the complete group been employed.

At the beginning of this discussion a statement was made that α and β are usually smaller but occasionally become larger than one. This will occur when individuals, usually employed at producing commodities, shift their activity to that of giving services or vice versa. This shift will increase one group at the expense of the other and naturally α and β will measure that change. Therefore, if we assume a condition of full employment, a definite relationship will exist between α and β which can be expressed by the following equation:

$$280\alpha + 120\beta = 400$$

As a value of α is being chosen that of β can be equal or smaller but not larger than:

$$\beta = (400\text{-}280\alpha) / 120$$

For the same reason the maximum value of α when β has been chosen is the following:

$$\alpha = (400\text{-}120\beta) / 280$$

No attempt will be made to give a detailed analysis of each individual case related to this study and shown in detail by the proper column of the tabular calculation at the end of this chapter (examples 11 to 18 included). Each example was chosen from the standpoint of bringing forth different trends and economic phenomena which have a counterpart in real life.

The first important conclusion that can be drawn from a study of these examples is that the quantity of vital commodities produced by the Lilliputian society, which we have called Kq (line 75), tends to be the same ($280q$) for values of α equal of smaller than one. This can be surmised from examples 2, 11, and 12 where α becomes progressively lower. This means that, even when the number of individuals employed in the production of commodities decreases, the tendency for our society is to keep on producing the same amount .Therefore, while the efficiency of society (Rc) remains the same (line 77) that of the individuals (Mc) increases (line 78). This may seem a startling result because, not being conscious of technological advancements, we would tend to believe that the smaller the number of individuals employed, the less the production. First of all, let us bear in mind that we are only giving a condition of equilibrium and that time may be required for its attainment. However, we can see that supply usually tends to respond to a given demand. The fact that a number of people do not produce is not a deterrent to that production and means are usually found to counteract that effect or the technological advancement after all will increase as α decreases. Of course, we are stating a tendency and if α should change abruptly from one value to another it is understandable that time will be required before that condition of equilibrium is established. As it is usually the case it is not the change of α tha tends to promote the technological advancement but improvements in techology tend to lower α and when viewed from this point that is what happens in the actual society. Of course, this analysis only assumes the first unfavorable effect of technological advancement and as shown in examples 4b, 4c, and 4 an increase in vital commodities will be the final result. This, however, does not change our conclusion that when α decreases, irrespective of what cause, the forces in society are such that they tend to maintain the same level of production. Not so, however, when α becomes larger than one. Indeed, if α is larger than one, this means that more than 280 individuals of the Lilliputian society are engaged in the production of commodities. This automatically detracts from the number of those who give services and as such society tends to approach the condition of example one of the third chapter in which the complete population is engaged in the production of commodities. We saw in that example that the production tends to decrease (in our case 80 instead of 300q as originally assumed) until only the individuals of the owner class are able to secure the basic amount q. The numerical data of this case are shown in example 13 of the same table where the production of commodities decreases to 225 from the original 280q of example 2.

As to services these will be directly affected by β. Indeed, as no change in the art of giving services has been considered, the output is still taken to be 3.33s per person (line 96) and, therefore, unemployment in this section directly affects the total amount of services being given.

For β and α equal to one (example 2) the skilled labor class, besides the basic amount of vital commodities q (line 83) is also able to secure some services (line 107). As β decreases while α remains unity the production of vital commodities is unfavorably affected and drops to 270 from the original 280q. This is shown in example 14 where the unemployment is only 10% of those giving services. At this point the skilled labor class is still able to secure some services above the normal amount q of vital commodities and specifically will receive .14 instead of .37s. However, all classes are unfavorably affected and the upper classes at this level will also receive a smaller amount of services. If unemployment should keep on increasing, a point will be reached ($\beta = .83$ of example 15) when the entire wage of the skilled labor class will be only sufficient to buy the amount q but no services. Any value of β below this, the skilled labor class as well as the unskilled one will receive less than one q.

The fact that α is unity does not prove that the efficiency of society in producing commodities (Mc in line 78) has remained the same (actually has dropped). In both cases the smaller purchasing power of the unskilled labor class tends to decrease the demand for vital commodities and supply, naturally, responds to the new economic condition. This means that lack of incentive in the market tends to lower output of commodities and the per capita production, (Mc of line 78) tends also to drop from the original level of 1.00 of example 2. In both cases also, the purchasing power of the unskilled labor class is such that the pressure it exerts on the market raises the price of q to such a level that the revenue becomes equal to total cost and this is all it matters in conomic parlance. Examples 14 and 15, however, where β decreases without a corresponding decrease in α, are not apt to occur in actual life where unemployment in a greater or lesser degree is equally spread throughout society. These cases have been presented only to explain the influence of β.

A decrease in α, as shown in case 11 and 12, tends to increase the production of vital commodities. This is more clearly shown by case 16 where the value of β, being one, has no particular influence on the corresponding equilibrium point and the change is directly accountable to α. This equilibrium point under such a condition has definitely increased (291 instead of 280q). This means that the efficiency of society increased and on this account society as a whole has definitely improved even though some within the society, being out of work, are forced to a low standard of living. For the sake of showing the effect of α when β remains unity it has been assumed that skill in giving services (Ms of line 96) has not changed from the basic example 2 and, therefore, the upper classes will receive less services than in that case (line 105 to 107 of example 16) because of the greater pressure exerted by the skilled labor class on the same amount of services rendered. This case, however, like examples 14 and 15 is not apt to occur in real life because progress in skill, in greater or lesser degree, is made in all branches of society, but was given only to better explain the influence of α.

Example 17 shows the case where the entire population is at work and therefore for a value of α equal to .9, β becomes 1.232. This condition shows also an increase in production of vital commodities when α is less than one (321 instead of 280q) indicating that the technological advancement in this group has further increased from the previous level example 16 or Mc=1.274 instead of 1.155 (line 78) even though in both cases the number employed is the same or 252 individuals. Services have increased, if not because of an increase in skill which was still kept at 3.33s per person but because of the shift of workers and salary persons from the group which produces commodities to that which gives services. But this, like previous examples is also an unlikely condition because progress in one branch of society does not keep pace with progress made in other branches. The optimum condition, of course, is given in example 18 where not only the entire population is at work but skill is assumed equal in the two branches of society.

The fact that α is smaller than one means that some who were first engaged in the production of commodities are now employed in giving services and, therefore, the factor β becomes larger than one. As a result, while the cost of commodities in reference to a is less, (453.6a) instead of 504a), the production of commodities is more (321 instead of 280q). This indicates a technological advancement of 1.274. If we assume the same progress made by society in the art of giving services, that is, if we assume the factor Rc (line 95) as being equal to 1.274 (line 78) then the total amount of services becomes 627 (line 97), far above any other condition assumed. As a result of the great activity of society, the plain laborer will secure .71q for his work and all classes besides q will enjoy a far larger amount of services so that the standard of living of all components of society has materially increased above any other previous condition.

This, of course, is the aim of the new system of life, i.e., that of keeping the entire population at work while taking advantage of all technological advancements promoted by individuals within the society.

From this analysis we do not want to convey the idea that the smaller α is the better will be our society. The decrease in α must be compensated for by an increase of β up to the point where the complete population is at work (with the exception of those not willing to do so). If this is not the case, many in the labor class, being unemployed, will not be able to share in the larger production of vital commodities even though the average for the class is larger than before. This is the condition found in many countries of the world including our own in which, irrespective of the large production of all kind of commodities, many cannot find work and the financial means to improve their living. Needless to say, this represents a maladjusted situation that needs correction and remedy.

EFFECT OF SAVING (EXAMPLE 19)

In all our examples it has been implied that no saving is ever done by the individuals of our society. We know that this is not so, and that many do save some of their income either for the sake of accumulating capital in their hands or for some large anticipated expenditure. Society is made up of many individuals and while many are in the process of saving others are in the process of spending what they had previously saved so that the influence of such economic occurrences compensate each other and are seldom greatly felt at any particular time. On this account this subject has no definite place in the overall frame of our study. However, for the sake of exploring all possible causes that may affect the well being of society, we have prepared example 19 to which we refer our reader if interested in this particular subject.

Assume again the basic example 2 of chapter 3 as base of comparison and say that within our Lilliputian society all of a sudden saving is being done in sufficient amount to influence the economic equilibrium. The problem on hand is to determine the new one and then observe the changes brought upon the economic life of the people. It is immaterial which class or individual does the saving, the effect is always the same, i.e., that of withdrawing money from circulation. For obvious reasons we must discard the assumption that saving is being done by the unskilled labor class because we shall still retain the basic desire of each individual to secure as much vital commodities as possible. We know, of course, that saving can also take place among them. This, however, is bound to be small and inconsequential in its effect on society as a whole. The same can be said for the skilled labor class. Saving then will be done by the owner and manager class.

The pressure exerted by the unskilled labor class in securing vital commodities and that exerted by the skilled labor class in securing services raises their price to such a level that as both commodities and services come to be entirely sold the total revenue (U and V) become respectively equal to total cost (Ta and La) and, therefore, the two basic conditions of equilibrium are attained. However, if money is saved, this cannot go to equalize those costs and, therefore, the condition of equilibrium is broken. This means that some of the owners will have to sustain a loss.

Now while saving may be done in large scale when times are prosperous, it is obvious that it will shrink as the economic equilibrium tends to decrease so that stable condition will be reached only when no further saving is being done. Even though it could be easily calculated, there is no point in determining the equilibrium during the period of saving, therefore, it will be assumed that the total

amount finally taken out from circulation sums up to 120a. Obviously
this sum will only be saved at the expense of services because the
rich will still require one q of vital commodities. This fact, naturally,
brings a state of unemployment in that section of society that gives
services and as the skill and technological advancement has not
changed from that of example 2, services as well as number of
workers will shrink in proportion to the amount that is being spent.
This amount from 216 drops to (216-120)a=96a or to 44.4% of the
original level so that the number employed and services rendered
become respectiely 55.3 individuals and 177s. As in previous analyses
we can represent this condition of unemployment by saying that β =
.444. As a result the total income of the unskilled labor class will diminish (216+81x.444=252 instead of 270a of line 43) and this factor
in turn will affect the requirement of vital commodities. As usual production of commodities responds to the need of society. It is reasonable
that the skill of the workers in the commodity field like that of those
giving services has not changed from that of example 2, therefore,
reduced production means that unemployment will also appear in
this section of society. This indicates that the assumption of α equal
one is faulty. The determination of the value of α which will produce
equilibrium is shown in example 19a where α rather than k is the
primary purpose of the calculation. By making use of the equations
shown in lines 49 to 53, α and β turn out to be respectively .9107
and .653. These equations, however, are for those cases where the
skilled labor class is in a position to secure services over and above
the amount q. In so far that this fact cannot be predicted from the
information on hand, the price Pq and the average wage W_3 of the
skilled laborer are calculated from the equation shown in lines 61 and
62. As the price of the unit commodity q turns out to be larger than
the wage of the skilled laborer, this definitely proves that his class as
well as the unskilled labor class are not able to secure services of any
kind and that the values of α and β must be recalculated. This is done
in example 19b where the unemployment factors turn out to be
respectiely α=.887 and β=.709. With this information example 19
has been calculated. In this example it is found that the commodities
produced become 248q (line 75) and the unit price Pq becomes
1.89 (line 79). The tabular calculation shows this is a condition
of equilibrium.

In so far that vital commodities as well as services have decreased
from the original level of example 2, it can be said that all elements
of society have been unfavorably affected. The opposite will occur

in periods of dissaving, that is when additional money is placed in circulation. If it is assumed that no other factor is injected in the life of society, it can be said that definite amounts of saving or dissaving will move the equilibrium point some definite distance after which it will remain constant at that level.

At the beginning of this discussion it was stated that while some in society may be in the process of saving others are usually in the process of dissaving so that the resultant effect will be far smaller than the one shown in example 19. Not so, howeer, when the decrease in circulating money is the result of losses sustained in the sale of commodities for which large sums had to be paid previously for their production. In such a case the economic dislocation comes from the inability of many of the owners, who have sustained heavy losses, to maintain their business as well as from the fact that the same individuals can no longer buy the same amount of services (forced saving). As it is unlikely that dissaving should be done at this time in sufficient amount to counteract or even lessen the effect on the national economy, the equilibrium point will sink in proportion to the original disturbance. This is what is usually referred to as depression.

Going back to the effect of saving, it is reasonable to assume that all those who have lost a job will try to find a new one even if their pay should be less. Up to now it has been assumed that all those who have lost a job make no attempt of finding a new one. This, of course, is against human nature and if not all many will be willing to accept a smaller wage for the sake of being employed and by that improve their lot. This desire will be mostly felt by those in the lower class who more than any other will feel the effect of a decreased production of vital commodities. In a case of this nature it is difficult to predict how wages will change due to the competition that now is developing among the laborers. It will be assumed that all wages and salaries, in smaller or larger degree, are affected by this new condition and being free in our choice a new wage scale is here indicated.

Unskilled labor class		$1.00a^1$
Skilled	" "	$2.05a^1$
Manager	"	$6.30a^1$
Owner	"	$9.70a^1$

The calculation corresponding to this case shown in example 20.

The a^1 of example 20 is obviously smaller than the a of example 19 because of the decreased amount of money in circulation, yet it may seem strange that the new wage ratios should be larger than in previous examples. This can be explained by pointing out that the urge of securing a job is mostly felt by those in the lower class now willing to accept a much larger cut than the others. This automatically increases the ratio of all classes in reference to the new wage a^1.

As to the magnitude of a^1 in reference to a it can be said that the total income of society is given by the difference of the income of example 2 (720a) minus the amount saved (120a) or 600a. The total income of society under the new condition is given by:

$$740.5a^1 \text{ (line 44)}$$

$$a^1 = 600a/740.5 = .81a$$

With this information it is possible to calculate the new salaries and wages in terms of a. These are presented in the following table:

Unskilled Labor class	.81a	instead of	1a	or	19.0%	reduction	
Skilled	"	"	1.66a	"	"	2a	"	17.0%	"
Manager	"	"	5.10a	"	"	6a	"	15.0%	"
Owner's	"	"	7.85a	"	"	9a	"	12.8%	"

It may be of interest to note that the owner, even with a smaller salary, is able to secure more services than the owner in example 2 This comes as a result of the greater reduction in pay sustained by the skilled labor class.

From the fact that the equilibrium point of example 20 is higher than the one of 19 it can be stated that a reduction in pay with the object of increasing employment tends to lessen the effect of saving. Yet, this is not always possible as for instance in those cases where some of the owners, having sustained heavy losses, can no longer go on with their business. The shut down of many industries precludes the possibility of full employment in the nation no matter the reduction in wages. In general the larger these losses the lower will be the final equilibrium point and the ability to provide jobs for many individuals.

COMPARISON OF STANDARD OF LIVING

To complete the analysis a comparison should be given of the standard of living of each class of our Lilliputian society first in relation to that of the owner's class of the particular example under consideration and then to that of the owner in the basic example 2 of chapter 3. The same assumptions as to relative enjoyment received for services and vital commodities as well as the assumption that all work the same number of hours and exert the same amount of effort made in chapter 3 will apply for all the examples of this chapter. These calculations are covered by lines 119 to 130 included where total enjoyment received by the average individual of each class is the sum of enjoyments represented by services and vital commodities received. This enjoyment, in so far that time and effort are the same for all individuals, becomes equivalent to absolute standard of living. Lines 131 to 134 give the standard of living of the average individual of each class in relation to that of the owner which is taken to be 100%. It can be seen that in case 4, which measures the effect of technological advancement, the absolute standard of living has improved for all classes. It can be noted also that the poor has made a larger percent improvement than the rich because his relative standard of living stands now at 7.35% instead of 7.27%.

The same can be said for case 8 which measures the effect of the new mode of life, that is, the effect made possible by the presence of the branch of the government identified as Economic Welfare Branch.

Example 18 represents the case where all branches of society, through the beneficial influence of the EW advance in skill and technology while the population is maintained fully employed. The large increase in standard of living enjoyed by the well-to-do of this example is due to the large increase in services made possible by the more active society represented by this case. It may seem strange that the relative standard of living of the unskilled laborer of this example should be lower than in examples 2, 4, and 8. In case 17, that is, the example immediately preceding the one in consideration, this ratio is actually higher and this is what it should be. It will be noticed, however, that example 17 was derived by assuming that no technological advancement had taken place in the art of giving services (Rs = 1.00 of line 95). As such the total amount of services for society in general increased only because of the larger number of workers in this field some of which had previously been released from the activity of producing commodities. Under this condition the absolute standard of living of the unskilled laborer rose to 7.10e (line 130), considerably higher than any of the examples 2, 4, and 8. However, as soon as we consider an advancement in the art of giving services, which is what will occur in real life, the total amount of services from 494s rose to 627s (line 97). These extra services, distributed to all the well-to-do classes, reduced the relative standard of living of the poor even though their absolute standard of living remained the same. In chapters 6 and 7 it was explained that the unskilled labor class theoretically will never reach the position of obtaining services. This, however, is only on the surface because, as economic conditions permit such as in example 18, some of the commodities and services now called non-vital and as such included with services, can be made vital. Because of this change the standard of living of the poor will increase in greater proportion than that of the rich for the simple reason that the wage increment Y, given to all in society, represents a larger percentage increase for the poor than for the rich. This will tend to equalize the large discrepancy among all classes.

Example 19 shows the effects of saving in those cases where society is unable to find employment for all those who have lost a job. The standard of living of all members drops to a lower level than the corresponding individuals of example 2 and this fact is shown also by lines 135 to 138 which measure the standard of living of each class in relation to the owner class of the basic example 2. This example, besides the effect of saving, shows also that of depression caused by some given disturbance (in this particular case saving).

Example 20 considers the same amount of saving of example 19 with the difference that now society succeeds in finding employment for all those who have lost a job. While the economic condition of society is far from ideal, still it is far better than the one represented by example 19. As often explained, one of the primary objectives of the EW is that of decreasing unemployment throughout the nation by one or several of the methods enumerated in the text. Such being the case, any disturbance that may strike the nation beyond the power of the EW to alter or control, will not have the devastating effects that would certainly follow if the EW was not there to cushion and reduce.

EXPLANATION OF SYMBOLS AND
EQUATIONS IN TABLE 9

1 N_1 Total number of individuals in the owner's class. This may also include individuals prominent in their field with income comparable with those who own the means of production.

2 N_2 Total number of individuals in the manager's class. This may also include high officials, doctors, lawyers, etc., with income comparable with the general manager and high officials of industry.

3 N_3 Total number of individuals of the skilled labor class. This may also include the moderately paid professionals, white collar workers, clerks, etc.

4 N_4 Total number of individuals in the unskilled labor class.

5 N   Total population assumed.

6 α Ratio of number of individuals engaged in the production of vital commodities to similar number used in example 2 (taken as base of comparison) as a result of unemployment. Aditional explanation will be given in line 55.

7 β Ratio of number of individuals engaged in giving services to similar number used in example 2 (taken as base of comparison) as a result of unenployment. Additional explanation will be given in lines 48 and 56.

8 X   Factor representing the increase in number of individuals engaged in producing vital commodities as a result of the additional demand made possible by the new system of life. Additional explanation will be given in line 59.

9 Y   Increase in wage given to all components of society so as to produce equilibrium between production and consumption of vital commodities. Aditional explanation will be given in line 60.

10 $n_1\alpha$ Number of individuals in the owner's class devoting their time to production of vital commodities.

11 $n_2\alpha$ Number of individuals in the manager's class devoting their time to production of vital commodities.

12 $n_3\alpha$ Number of individuals in the skilled labor class devoting their time to production of vital commodities.

13 $n_4\alpha$ Number of individuals in the unskilled labor class devoting their time to production of vital commodities.

14    $Nc\alpha$ Total number of individuals of all classes devoting their time to production of vital commodities.

15    $n_5\beta$ Number of individuals in the owner's class devoting their time to giving services.

16    $n_6\beta$ Number of individuals in the manager's class devoting their time to giving services.

17    $n_7\beta$ Number of individuals in the skilled labor class devoting their time to giving services.

18    $n_8\beta$ Number of individuals in the unskilled labor class devoting their time to giving services.

19    $Ns\beta$ Total number of individuals of all classes devoting their time to giving services.

20   h   Hours of work per day and per individual.

21   Hc   Total hours of work per day devoted by society to the production of vital commodities. $Hc = Nc\ \alpha.\ h$

22   Hs   Total hours of work per day devoted by society to giving services. $Hs = Ns\ \beta.\ h$

23   H   Total hours of work per day for the entire population. $H = Hc + Hs$

24   W_1 Ratio of what is received by the owner and that which is received by the unskilled laborer.

25   W_2 Ratio of salary received by the manager and wage received by the unskilled laborer.

26   W_3 Ratio of wage received by the skilled laborer and wage received by the unskilld laborer.

27   W_4 Ratio of wage received by the unskilled laborer in reference to unit wage a. Unless comparison is made to some other condition, this factor is usually one and, therefore, W_4 is a synonim of a.

28   T_1 Salary and rent received or paid to all the owners engaged in production of vital commodities. $T_1 = n_1\alpha\ W_1$

29   T_2 Salary received or paid to all managers engaged in production of vital commodities. $T_2 = n_2\ \alpha\ W_2$

30   T_3 Wages received or paid to all the skilled laborers engaged in production of vital commodities. $T_3 = n_3\ \alpha\ W$

31   T_4 Wages received or paid to all the unskilled laborers engaged in production of vital commodities. $T_4 = n_4\ \alpha\ W_4$

32   T   Sum of the wages and salaries received or paid to all components of society engaged in production of vital commodities. $T = \Sigma_1^4\ Tn = T_1 + T_2 + T_3 + .T_4$

33   C'   Cost of production of vital commodities. This is given by the product of T (which is a ratio of wages and salaries to unit wage) and the unit wage or: $C'=T.a$

34   L_1 Salary received or paid to all the owners engaged in giving services. $L_1=n_5 \beta W_1$

35   L_2 Salary received or paid to all the managers engaged in giving services. $L_2=n_6 \beta W_2$

36   L_3 Wages received or paid to all the skilled laborers engaged in giving services. $L_3=n_7 \beta W_3$

37   L_4 Wages received or paid to all the unskilled laborers engaged in giving services. $L_4=n_8 \beta W_4$

38   L   Sum of all the wages and salaries received or paid to all components of society engaged in giving services. $L=\Sigma_1^4 Ln=L_1+L_2+L_3+L_4$

39   C"   Cost of services. This is given by the product of L (which is a ratio of wages and salaries to unit wage) and the unit wage a.

40   I_1 Income o fthe owner's class. $I_1=T_1+L_1$

41   I_2 Income of the manager's class. $I_2=T_2+L_2$

42   I_3 Income of the skilled labor class. $I_3=T_3+L_3$

43   I_4 Income of the unskilled labor class. $I_4=T_4+L_4$

44   I   Income of society. $I=\Sigma_1^4 In=I_1+I_2+I_3+I_4$

45   Im   Income of society in terms of money. $Im=Ia$ where a (unit wage) is given in terms of money.

46   S   Saving done by society. In so far that saving disrupts the economic equilibrium of society, this in turn produces forces which tend to reduce the rate of saving. Saving (S) represents the total amount of saving done during this period of disequilibrium. With the exception of examples 19 and 20, saving is not taken into account because it is assumed that the effect of saving is counterbalanced by the effect of dissaving.

47   I   Income of society at the end of a period of saving. $I=I_B-S$ where I_B is the income taken as base before saving. I and I_B are given in units of basic wage a. In so far that I and I_B represent conditions of equilibrium the following expression holds:

$$I_B.a—S=I.a'$$

The basic wage a' (after saving) is different from the basic wage a (before saving) and is given by the following expression:

$$a' = (I_B.a - S)/I$$

48   β   β, or employment ratio in the field of services, is usually related with its counterpart α in the field of vital commodities.

The fact that α (or β) happens to be smaller than one should not be interpreted that unemployment exists in the nation in general if the factor β (or α) rises to a level where the entire population is enployed. This only means that some who previously were engaged in producing vital commodities are now engaged in giving services. For a condition of full employment such as the one indicated above, the relationship between α and β can be derived from the following equation:

$$Nc\alpha + Ns\,\beta = N \qquad \text{from which :}$$
$$\beta = (N - Nc\alpha)/Ns$$

This condition can be found in examples 2, 13, 17, 18, and 20. While the same condition is met by other examples such as 4, 5, 6, and 7 the value of α and β were not given because in such cases the size of the various classes was assumed and not compared with that of example 2 which is taken as base for all the other examples.

Quite often, however, this is not the case and the previously given relationship does no longer hold. In all these cases there is a definite amount of unemployment to be considered.

When unbalance begins to appear between supply and demand, whatever the cause, the economic equilibrium of society is broken. If supply becomes larger than demand some of the supply must go unsold or lowered in price below the original cost. If supply becomes smaller than demand its price will go up and profit will be derived by the owner even though it is also possible that some of this supply may actually go unsold if the people in general cannot meet such a price. This case is described in example 1a and 1 where the assumed supply of 300q units of vital commodities must be reduced to 80q for equilibrium.

In either case the income of the population in general is affected and in so far that income is related to cost of commodities and services or: I=T+L (line 44) any change in I is bound to affect T or L or both. With less money in circulation there will be less jobs available to the public and a new equilibrium will be reached at a level consonant with the new income. The decrease in circulation of money does not necessarily indicate that the amount of specie is less (which as we know is much smaller than the total volume of credit). This only means that the credit has been reduced because of the stagnant condition of business (fewer enterprises are started and less money is borrowed at the banks). Such a case is considered in examples 19 and 20 which describe the effect of saving.

Saving is usually done at the expense of services and luxurious commodities as less essential to the welfare of the individual. As such, the field of services will first feel the impact of saving and some will lose their job. This, however, tends to decrease the total income of those who give services and the poor in this field will have less money available to buy vital commodities. As a result the demand for vital commodities will drop and tend to produce unemployment in this field, that is, α becomes smaller than one. When a new condition of equilibrium is finally reached, both α and β will be less than one and will stabilize at some new level. The relationship between α and β in this case can be found in the following manner. Let the subscript (B) stand for the basic condition before saving. We have then:

Income before saving $I_B = T_B + L_B$

But T and L are functions of a given wage scale with the wage of the unskilled labor class as base (a). While this relationship has been kept constant (the salary of the manager is still 6a as before) the actual worth of a before and after saving will be different and will tend to decrease with a decrease of total income. Yet this decrease will not cover in full the original disturbance (amount of saving in this case) and as in everything in life some will still be able to earn more than the average. The difference can be made up by a decreased income for others which is tantamount to say by unemployment. While we are conscious of this and because of the need of referring to only one issue at a time, it has been assumed that the difference in earnings is made up only by the loss of income of those who lose a job.

If S indicates the total amount of saving, the income of society after saving becomes:
$$I = I_B - S = T_B\alpha + L_B\beta$$
From this equation the value of β in relation to α becomes:
$$\beta = (I_B - S - T_B\alpha)/L_B$$

49   K   Gives the number of units of vital commodities produced by society in the unit time. When shown in this line it may and may not represent a condition of equilibrium. It is given by the following expression:
$$K = N_c\alpha R_c$$
where $N_c\alpha$ (line 14) is the total number of persons employed in this field, R_c (see also line 77) is the technological advancement of society in the condition in which it is being analyzed versus that of example 2 taken as base of comparison. It stands to reason that the product of these three factors will give the amount of commodities produced by society irrespective of demand.

50   Give the necessary equation that must be solved for the
to   calculation of the condition of equilibrium when it is
62   assumed that all classes, with the exception of the unskilled labor class, are in a position to acquire the unit q of vital commodities.

50   Nu   Stands for the number of individuals in the upper class in a position to acquire the amount q of vital commodities irrespective of price. This number can be used also to represent the units q taken by the rich from the complete production K. Because of the assumption made, Nu becomes equal to: $N_1 + N_2 + N_3$

51   I_L Represents the income of the lower class which in this case is the one that cannot afford to buy as an average the full quota q of vital commodities. Is given by I_4 (line 43) which is the income of the unskilled labor class. From the first condition of equilibrium given in chapter 3, page 119, here repeated:
$$Pq(K - Nu) = I_L$$
we can state that line 51 must be equal to line 54 from which, knowing three out of four terms, the fourth can be easily found.

52   By implication (K-Nu) represents the number of com-

modities available to the poor (in this case the unskilled labor class).

53 Pq   Represents the price of the unit commodity q. From the second condition of equilibrium (chapter 3, page 119) here repeated:

$$K.Pq=T.a \quad \text{we have:}$$
$$Pq \ =T.a/K$$

In so far that a represents the unit of measure, it can be left out, and Pq can be expressed by the following relation:

$$Pq=T/K$$

From the first condition of equilibrium

$$Pq(K-Nu)=I_L \quad \text{and from this:}$$
$$Pq=I_L(K-Nu)$$

When Pq is derived from this latter equation it is shown surrounded by brakets, thus ( ). The reason for the dual expressions is that at times different ways of approach seemed expedient.

54   From the amount of commodities bought by the unskilled labor class (K-Nu) and shown in line 52, it follows that the corresponding expenditure will be given by:

$$(K-Nu).Pq$$

55 α   As indicated in line 6, α is the ratio of the number of individuals engaged in production of vital commodities in the example in study and similar number in example 2 where the population is assumed fully employed. In some cases (such as in examples 19a and 19b, α is not known and can be found from the condition of equilibrium given by equating lines 51 and 54. In all such cases K is given as a function of α (line 49) and α rather than K is the unknown quantity that must be found from the condition of equilibrium. As the values α and β are found from lines 55 and 56, these can be introduced in the various equations and the unknown value of K finally determined in example 19.

56 β   As indicated in line 7, β is the ratio of the number of individuals engaged in giving services in the example in study and similar number in example 2 where the population is ssumed fully employed. In those cases where α and β are not known (such as in examples 19a and 19b) β can be calculated from the equation shown in line 48

where β is given as a function of α which is calculated in line 55.

57
58

It was stated in chapter 3, page 118, that the economic equilibrium of society is reached when both equations (1) and (2) are satisfied. From these conditions the amount of vital commodities K that will produce equilibrium is given by the following expression:

$$K = (TNu)/(T-I_L)$$

where T is shown in line 32; Nu in line 50; I_L in line 51 and $(I-I_L)$ in line 57. All this, however, on the assumption that only the unskilled labor class is unable to purchase the full quota q. Lines 61 and 62, to be described later, will prove if this assumption is correct.

59   X

As indicated in line 8, X represents the increase in number of individuals engaged in producing vital commodities as a result of the additional demand made possible by the new system of life. It was proved in examples 4a and 4b that as society in general becomes more efficient the production of vital commodities tends to increase above what the general public can absorb. As this brings a condition of disequilibrium many, who previously were engaged in production of vital commodities, must shift to the field of those who are engaged in giving services. Yet with the passing of time the purchasing power of the labor class will increase and as this will increase the demand for vital commodities additional labor will be sought in this field in order to keep up with the changing condition. When a new equilibrium is finally reached the number of those engaged in the production of vital commodities, while not as large as that shown in example 4a, will be larger than that shown in example 4b. This latter increase, as previously stated, is represented by the factor X. In so far that example 4c represents a condition of equilibrium the two basic equations of chapter 3, page 119, must be satisfied. With a fixed technological know-how, indicated by the factor Rc of line 77, which indicates also the average output of the individual in reference to the average individual's output of example 2, the factor X will express also the increase in production of vital commodities (more people being engaged in this activity) and, therefore, the amount produced will be given by KX.

The ratio Rc, assumed equal for both conditions, can be left out of the expression. In this example it is also assumed complete employment and, therefore, α and β are not considered. Again the cost of production, being proportional to the number employed, will be indicated by TX. Introducing these new values in the equation shown in line 58 we have:

$$KX = (TX.Nu)/(TX-I_L) \quad \text{or} \quad K_B = T_B.Nu/T_BX-I_{LB})$$

from this: $\qquad X = (T_BNu + K_BI_{LB})/K_B.T_B$

where T_B, I_B and K_B are taken from the basic example (in this case 4b). As X is calculated its value is used in example 4 and the unknown production K can be derived from the expression shown in line 49.

60   Y   As indicated in line 9, Y represents the increase in salaries and wages given to all components of society so as to produce equilibrium between production and consumption of vital commodities. If Y is not large enough, people in general will not be able to buy the large amount of commodities made possible by a more buoyant society. As a result some of the owners will sustain heavy losses and as they will drop from the market production will tend to decrease. If Y is too large the larger pressure exerted by the poor toward the acquisition of vital commodities will tend to raise prices above cost. This will tend to increase the profit of the owners without any particular benefit to society in general. In short, Y must be such that a condition of equilibrium will be maintained as society moves toward higher levels of standard of living.

The text gives the justification for choosing Y equal for all, rich and poor alike, and, therefore, such a choice trascends the scope of this discussion.

In all cases, like example 8a, the production of vital commodities, referred to as K, is usually known (in the text it is assumed). The problem on hand, therefore, is that of finding the value of Y that will produce a condition of equilibrium, that is, it satisfies the two basic equations of chapter 3, page 119. In so far that Y is equal for all, the most of commodities becomes:

$$T + NcY$$

while the income of the unskilled labor class (assuming

that all other classes are in a position to buy the full quota q) can be expressed by:
$$I_4 + N_4.Y$$
where N_4 is the number composing the unskilled labor class. By substituting these values in the equation shown in line 58, Y can be easily found. Again, by substituting this value of Y in the various equations in the tables all the unknown factors can be calculated and here shown in example 8.

61
to
62

When K is calculated in line 58 the price Pq will immediately follow by using the second condition of equilibrium:
$$Pq.K = T.a \qquad \text{From this:}$$
$$Pq = T.a/K \text{ or } Pq = T/K \text{ for short.}$$

The previous calculation hinges on the assumption that only the unskilled labor class is unable to acquire the full quota q of vital commodities. This now may be proved by comparing the price of q with the wage of the skilled labor class. If the assumption is correct the wage of the skilled laborer (W_3) must be equal or larger than Pq or he would not be in a position to buy the amount q. If smaller (as in examples 1, 13, and 19a) the assumption must be revised. Indeed, for all those cases where unemployment eixsts, W_3 would no longer represent the average wage of the unskilled labor class because some would be out of work. It is assumed in this study that all those in each class who happen to be out of work will be helped by the others of the same class and this tends to decrease their average wage. In all cases such as 11, 12, and following the average wage is obtained by multiplying the theoretical wage and the ratio of income with and without unemployment or:
$$W_3(I_3/I_{3B}) \; ; \; W_2(I_2/I_{2B}) \; ; \text{ etc.}$$
When this is done the number indicating the average wage is included into brackets.

63
to
74

Lines 63 to 68 give the necessary equations needed to calculate the value of K when the assumption is made that the skilled labor class as well as the unskilled labor class are not in a position to acquire the full quota q of vital commodities.

Lines 59 to 74 give the necessary equations needed to calculate the value of K when the assumption is made that only the owner's class is in a position to buy the full quota q of vital commodities.

The process of reasoning for all three cases is the same. To simplify our presentation we shall group those lines for which the same explanation apply.

50, 63, 69. Number of those who can afford to buy the full quota q. This number is indicated by Nu.

57, 65, 71. Information needed to calculate the condition of equilibrium. (T-I$_L$)

58, 66, 72. Value of K that will produce a condition of equilibrium.

61, 67, 73. Price of the unit commodity. (Pq)

62, 68, 74. Average wage or salary of the class which is the poorest among the assumed upper classes.

75   K   The value of K appearing in this line is either assumed or chosen from the four shown in lines 49, 58, 66 and 72. Depending on the nature of the example in study the K finally selected is the one that will produce a condition of equilibrium.

76   fc   Is the ratio of actual to potential output of the individual engaged in the production of vital commodities or:

$$fc = Mc/Rc$$

In so far that actual output must satisfy the basic conditions of equilibrium, Mc may be larger or smaller than Rc and consequently fc larger or smaller than one depending on the needs of society.

77   Rc   Represents the technological advancement of society in relation to that of example 2 taken as base of comparison. It indicates also the potential output of the individual in producing vital commodities. Rc is usually taken as one which means that in any of the examples in the tables society is assumed in the same stage of advancement as that represented by example 2. Exception is made for examples 4 and 8 where the effect of technological advancement and social progress are actually considered.

78   Mc   Represents the amount of vital commodities actually produced by the average individual and is given by the following expression:

$$Mc = K/Nc\alpha$$

Mc may be equal or different from Rc (potential output). It may seem strange that Mc should ever be different from Rc as we would tend to believe that potential output Rc multiplied by the number of individuals actually engaged would give the total production for the entire society. To explain this discrepancy we like to point out that irrespective of know-how and number of individuals engaged, the actual production must satisfy the economic need of society. Even excluding a change in the efficiency of those engaged in production, although this may actually occur, depending on social needs better methods of production may be introduced to increase the output of the individual such as in examples 11 and 12 while in other cases such as in examples 13, 14, and 15 no effort will be made toward this and machinery may be left unimproved for lack of incentives.

79   Pq   The price of the unit vital commodity shown in this line is derived from the value of K given in line 75 which may be either assumed or chosen from those shown in lines 53, 61, 67, and 73 depending upon which of the four represents a condition of equilibrium.

80   ac   a, the unit wage of the unskilled laborer, will be usually expressed in terms of money. a, however, can also be expressed in terms of amount of vital commodities that it can buy and is indicated by ac. Under this form a becomes equivalent to some given fraction of Pq or q whichever is convenient in the process of study. It can be derived from the second condition of equilibrium of chapter 3, page 119.

$T.a = K.Pq$ from which $ac = (K/T).Pq$

In so far that Pq becomes now the unit of measure it can be left out and ac becomes:

$$ac = K/T$$

81   The equations shown in these lines give the maximum
to   amount of commodities that can be bought and utilized
84   by the average individual of each class and is expressed by the following equation:

$$Un = (In/Nn).ac$$

If Nn is the number composing any of the four assumed economic classes and In its corresponding income, then the ratio In/Nn gives the number of unit wage a received by the average individual of that class (In is a function of quantity of vital commodities (line 79) the product or $(In/Nn).a$ will give the potential purchase of the average individual of that class. However, because of the assumption that no one will seek a larger amount than one q, whenever the equation gives a larger number than one, the unit quantity will be shown in the tabulation and this number will be shown surrounded by brackets, thus: ( ), indicating that it is not derived from the equation given above but just assumed.

85 to 88   Give the total amount of commodities utilized by each class. This obviously is given by the product of u (lines 80 to 83) and the number of individuals in the assumed class (Nn). We have then:

$$Un=u.Nn$$

89   U   Represents the total amount of commodities used. This is given by:

$$U=\Sigma_1^4\, Un=U_1+U_2+U_3+U_4$$

90   Gives what people must pay for the acquisition of the amount U of vital commodities. This is given by the product of quantity bought (U) and price of unit commodity (Pq) or U.Pq.

91 to 93   These lines tell if the two basic conditions of equilibrium have been met in the example in study.

When the amount bought by the people, indicated by U in line 89, is equal to K or the amount produced (line 75), this means that the first condition of equilibrium has been met and that demand equals supply. This is stated in line 91.

When the price paid for the purchase of vital commodities indicated by UPq in line 90 equals the cost of production T in line 32, this indicates that the second condition of equilibrium has been met and that the price has the tendency to stabilize at that level. This is stated in line 91.

When both conditions of equilibrium have been satisfied, the example itself represents a condition of equilibrium, as far as vital commodities, and this is stated in line 93.

94   Ec   Represents the economic progress made by society in producing and utilizing vital commodities. This is obviously given by the ratio of K, that is, the entire production of

vital commodities given in line 75, and total population N given in line 5 or: $Ec=K/N$.

95   Rs   Technological advancement of society. At this point the condition of equilibrium for services needs some clarification. At variance with the basic conditions of equilibrium for vital commodities where the pressure of the lower class establishes a given price for the unit commodity q, this cannot be said for services which lack the impelling need for their acquisition. Unquestionably the need and the desire for their acquisition is there, yet this is not so strongly felt and people can easily go without if the price is above what they can afford. Therefore, we are still faced by a supply and demand curve and even though what is available for services is fixed by what must be spent for the purchase of vital commodities, generally people will try to secure services where cheapest and sell services where they can receive the most. Because of the incessant competition between buyers and sellers it becomes obvious that all those who are engaged in giving services will strive to acquire the greatest skill compatible with their education and ability either for the purpose of holding or securing a better job or for that of securing or maintaining as large an income as possible among many competitors. On this account it is possible to state that the amount of services is linked with technological advancement and is independent of cost. It seems logical that the technological advancement of society in giving services should keep in step with that of producing commodities or:

$$Rs=Rc/Rc_2$$

where Rc is the potential output for the example in study (line 77) and Rc_2 is the potential output for example 2 taken as base of comparison. In so far that Rc_2 happens to be one, Rs becomes equal to Rc. This assumption, however, needs some clarification. In many cases the actual output of the individual (Mc) is larger than Rc indicating that at such times, whatever the cause, the productivity of society is greater than in example 2. In all these cases such as examples 5, 7, 11, 12, and 17 it would seem reasonable that such advancement should spread also to the field of giving services and that Rs should be equal to Mc rather than Rc. This has been done only for case 18 because of the desire of bringing into focus only one phenomenon at a time. In other cases, however, such as examples 6, 13, 14, 15, and 20, because of economic pressure, Mc becomes smaller than Rc. Due to the competition referred to above, those engaged in giving services will still give the most compatible with their skill and ability and this will tend to maintain Rs equal to Rc, even though Mc drops below Rc.

96   Ms   Indicates the amount of services given by the average individual. This is given by:
$$Ms=Ms_2.Rs$$
where Ms_2 is the productivity of society in example 2 and Rs the technological advancement (line 95). Ms_2 has been assumed 3.33 units of services per individual.

97   Z   Total number of unit services (s) given or received by society. It is given by the following expression:
$$Z=Ns\beta \ Ms$$

98   Ps   Is the price of unit service s. It is given by the total cost L (in line 38) divided by total services Z of line 97 or:
$$Ps=L/Z$$

99   a*s*   Rrepesents the unit wage of the unskilled laborer expressed in terms of services, that is, amount of services that unit wage can buy. From the condition of equilibrium given by the following expression: $(La=Ps.Z)$, a*s* becomes equal to: $(Z/L).Ps$. In so far that Ps is now the unit of measure it can be left out and a*s* becomes:
$$as=Z/L$$

100   An   These lines represent the income of each class available
to   for the purchase of services. This is given by total income
103   In (n stands for any number between one and four) minus the amount of income needed for vital commodities (Nn.Pq) or:
$$An=In-Nn.Pq$$

104   A   Is the total income of society available for the purchase of services. This is given by:
$$A=\Sigma_1^4 \ An=A_1+A_2+A_3+A_4$$
For equilibrium available income for services must be equal to total cost of services L (line 38) or: $A=L$.

105   vn   The equation shown in these lines give the amount of
to   services bought and utilized by the average individual of

108   each class. This amount is expressed by the following general equation:

$$(An/Nn).as$$

If Nn is the number composing any of the four assumed classes and An the corresponding income available for the purchase of services then the ratio An/Nn gives the number of unit wage a which the average individual of that class can devote for this purpose. In so far that as corresponds to a given amount of services (line 99) the product or (An/Nn).as will give the number of unit service bought by the average individual of the class in consideration.

109   Vn   Give the total unit of service bought and utilized by each
to   class. This is obviously given by the product of v (lines
112   105 to 108) and the number of individuals in the assumed class (Nn). We have then:

$$Vn=vn.Nn$$

113   V   Represents the total amount of services bought and utilized by society. This is given by:

$$V=\Sigma_1{}^4Vn=V_1+V_2+V_3+V_4$$

114   This line gives what the people must pay for the purchase of the amount of services represented by V. It is given by the product of quantity bought V and price of unit service Ps or: V.Ps.

115   These lines tell if the two basic conditions of equilibrium
to   have been met in the example in study.
117   When the amount bought by the people, indicated by V in line 113, is equal to the amount produced Z (line 97) this means that demand equals supply and that one condition of equilibrium has been satisfied. This is stated in line 115.

When the price paid for services, indicated by V.Ps (line 114) equals the cost indicated by L (line 38), this indicates that the second condition of equilibrium has been met (price equals cost) and that prices will stabilize at that level. This is stated in line 116.

When both conditions of equilibrium have been satisfied, the example itself represents a condition of equilibrium as far as services and this is stated in line 117.

118   Es   Represents the economic progress made by society in

giving and utilizing services. This is obviously given by
the ratio of total services Z (line 97) and total population N given in line 5 or:

$$Es = Z/N$$

119
to
130

En In these lines the enjoyment of the average individual in
the owner's class is calculated. In chapter 3 the basic unit
of enjoyment, indicated by e was assumed to be that
which the average individual derives from the utilization
of one unit of vital commodity q or: $e = q$. In so far that
the average individual of this class usually buys only one
q, (line 85) the corresponding enjoyment will be given
by: $U_1.e$ which is equivalent to $1.oe$ and this value is
shown in line 119.

In chapter 3 it was assumed also that the unit enjoyment e is equivalent to that which is derived from the
utilization of two units of service or: $e = 2s$. The enjoyment derived from services will be given by $.5v_1e$ where
v_1 represents the services bought by the average individual
of the owner's class. This is given in line 120.

The total enjoyment E (equivalent to standard of living) of the same individual is given then by the sum of
enjoyments received from the untilization of vital commodities and services and shown in line 121.

The enjoyment of the average individual of other classes
is calculated in the same manner and given in lines 122
to 130.

131
to
134

Enjoyment En is synonim of standard of living (SLn).
Lines 131 to 134 relate the standard of living of the average individual of each class to that of the average individual of the owner's class taken as base of comparison.
This relation is given by the ratio of En (where n stands
for any number between one and four) and E_1 or:
En/E_1. On a percentage basis this ratio must be multiplied by 100 and in this form has been shown in the tables.

135
to
138

It is often of interest to know the relationship existing between the standard of living of each class in the example
in study and some other standard of living taken as base
of comparison, say that of the owner's class in example 2.
This is given by the following general expression:

$$Sn = (En/E_{1B}) (h_B/h)$$

where En and E_{1B} give respectively the enjoyment of the average individual of the class in the example in consideration and that of the owner's class in example 2 while h_B and h represent respectively the hours of work or average effort made by the individual in example 2 and average individual in the example in study.

Table No. 9a — Example No. 16&1 — Ref (Chapt-Fg) 3-112

TABLE NO. 9b

TABLE NO. 9c

EXAMPLE NO.		1	2	3	4	5	6	7	8	9	10	11	12	13	14	15	16	17	18	19	20
95	R_1R_2		1.0	1.0	1.143	1.0	1.0	1.0	1.143	1.0	1.143	1.0	1.0		1.0		1.0	1.0	(1.274)	1.00	1.0
96	M_1M_2		3.33	3.33	3.80	3.33	3.33	3.33	3.80	3.33	3.80	3.33			3.33				4.24	3.33	3.33
97	N_1N_2		400	400	512	406.7	400		512	456	400	456	360	320	360	332	400	494	427	283	400
98	L/Z		54	54	48	.576	.48	.533	.549	.85	.85	.85								.54	.556
99	Z/L		1.85	1.85	2.08	1.738	2.083	1.078	1.82												1.80
100	$J_1-N_1P_1$		72	72	74.3	73.5	503	62.5	74.62	2800	2482.8	64.0	57.6	65.7	68.78	66.4	68.2	75.8	77.8	57	77.1
101	$J_1-N_1P_2$		126	124	133.0	130.2	1255	127.6	138.86	5040	5348.4	113.4	100.8	107.1	108.86	113.6	120.7	137.5	137.5	96	131.7
102	$J_3-N_1P_1$		18	18	38.7	30.5	162	12.9	41.58	720	1645.2	16.2	14.4		6.76	0	27.1	53.1	53.1	0	12.6
103	$J_3-N_1P_2$		0	0	0	0	0	0	0	0	0	0	0	0	0	0	0	0	0	0	0
104	$\Sigma_i J_m = L$		216	216	246	234	192	213	250	8640	9276.4	194.4	172.8	172.8	194.4	178.6	216.0	266.4	264.4	153	222.2
105	$(A_1/M_1) a_3$		13.28	13.28	15.40	12.770	14.93	11.7	13.600	(13.28)	(13.600)	12.000	12.640	12.13	12.71	12.30	12.63	14.07	17.8	10.54	14.02
106	$(A_1/N_1) a_3$		7.77	7.77	9.22	7.543	8.733	8.0	8.140	(7.77)	(8.140)	7.000	6.212	6.62	7.33	6.76	7.45	8.50	10.8	5.92	7.90
107	$(A_3/N_3) a_3$		.37	.37	.895	.585	.372	.418	.844	(.37)	(.844)	.332	.296	.14	.14	0	.56	1.09	1.39	0	.252
108	$(A_3/N_1) a_3$		0	0	0	0	0	0	0	0	0	0	0	0	0	0	0	0	0	0	0
109	$V_1 N_1$		132.8	132.8	154.0	127.7	104.5	117.0	136.0	132.8	136.0	120.0	106.6	121	127.2	123	126.3	140.7	178.0	105.4	140.2
110	$V_2 N_2$		233.6	233.6	277.0	226.3	262.0	240.0	244.1	233.6	241.1	210.0	186.8	199	220.2	209	233.4	254.8	324.0	177.6	237.1
111	$V_3 N_3$		33.6	33.6	61.0	52.7	335	43.0	75.9	33.6	75.9	30.0	26.6	0	12.6	0	50.3	125.0	125.0	0	22.7
112	$V_4 N_4$		0	0	0	0	0	0	0	0	0	0	0	0	0	0	0	0	0	0	0
113	$\Sigma_i V_m$		400	400	512	406.7	400	400	456	400	456	360	320	320	360	332	400	494	627	283	400
114	V_3		216	216	246	234	234	213	244.84	8640	9995.5	194.4	172.8	172.8	194.4	1786	216	266.4	2664	153	222.2
115	$(113)-(97)$?		YES																		
116	$(114)-(38)$?		YES																		
117	EQUIL. ?		YES																		
118	$Z \cdot N$		1.0	1.0	1.28	1.017	1.0	1.0	1.14	1.0	1.14	.90	.80	.10	.10	.83	1.0	1.23	1.56	.71	1.0
119	$u \cdot e$		1.000e	1.000e	1.000e	1.000e	1.000e	1.000e	1.000e	1.000e	1.000e	1.000e	1.000e	1.000e	1.000e	1.000e	1.000e	1.000e	1.000e	1.000e	1.000e
120	$5u \cdot e$		6.640e	0	6.305e	6.365e	7.465e	5.850e	8.000e	6.640e	4.800e	4.070e	3.500e	5.330e	6.045e	3.665e	6.150e	6.315e	7.035e	9.100e	5.270e	7.010e
121	$(u_1+5u)e$		7.640e	0	8.700e	7.385e	8.465e	6.850e	7.800e	7.640e	5.070e	5.070e	4.500e	6.330e	7.045e	4.665e	7.150e	7.315e	8.035e	9.100e	6.270e	8.010e
122	$u_4 e$		.666e	0	1.000e	1.000e	1.000e	1.000e	1.000e	1.000e	1.000e	1.000e	1.000e	1.000e	1.000e	1.000e	1.000e	1.000e	1.000e	1.000e	2.410e	3.950e
123	$5u_4 e$		0	3.885e	4.410e	3.771e	4.364e	4.000e	4.070e	3.885e	4.070e	4.070e	3.500e	3.105e	3.300e	3.665e	3.480e	3.725e	4.250e	5.250e	3.900e	4.130e
124	$(u_4+5V_4)e$		.666e	4.886e	5.410e	4.771e	5.366e	5.000e	5.070e	4.885e	5.070e	5.070e	4.500e	4.105e	4.310e	4.645e	4.480e	4.725e	5.250e	6.400e	3.910e	4.130e	1.000e
125	$u_5 e$		222e	1.000e	1.000e	1.000e	1.000e	1.000e	1.000e	1.000e	1.000e	1.000e	1.000e	.824e	1.000e	1.000e	1.000e	.920e	.920e	1.000e	.926e	1.000e
126	$5V_5 e$		0	.185e	.447e	.372e	.464e	.239e	.185e	.185e	.422e	.422e	.146e	.148e	.070e	.070e	0	.290e	.545e	.695e	.926e	.126e
127	$(u_5+5V_5)e$		222e	1.185e	1.447e	1.372e	1.464e	1.239e	1.185e	1.185e	1.422e	1.422e	1.146e	1.148e	.824e	.810e	1.000e	1.280e	1.545e	1.695e	.926e	1.126e
128	$u_6 e$		.555e	.555e	.638e	.600e	.550e	.572e	.705e	.705e	.555e	.705e	.355e	.555e	.412e	.520e	.500e	.596e	.710e	.710e	.463e	.523e
129	$5V_6 e$		0	0	0	0	0	0	0	0	0	0	0	0	0	0	0	0	0	0	0	0
130	$(u_6+5V_6)e$		.111e	.555e	.638e	.600e	.550e	.572e	.705e	.705e	.555e	.705e	.355e	.555e	.412e	.520e	.500e	.596e	.710e	.710e	.463e	.523e
131	$(E_1/E_1)100$		100	100	100	100	100	100	100	100	100	100	100	100	100	100	100	100	100	100	100	100
132	$(E_2/E_1)100$		66.6	64	64.5	64.7	43.3	73	65	64	64.36	64.36	44.3	64.8	61	63.5	42.7	44.6	45.4	44.7	42.3	61.8
133	$(E_3/E_1)100$		22.2	12.5	15.5	17.5	14.0	18.1	18.2	18.2	15.5	18.1	16.65	18.1	11.64	14.55	14.0	17.5	18.25	17.1	14.78	14.04
134	$(E_4/E_1)100$		11.1	7.27	7.35	8.12	6.5	10.64	9.05	9.05	7.27	7.05	1.11	8.77	5.82	7.07	7.0	8.15	8.95	8.85	7.36	6.53
135	$S_1=(E_1/E_m/L)n/100$		10.7	100	114.0	96.7	110.9	89.7	102.00	102.00	100	102.01	91.62	82.85	92.47	94.27	93.54	95.75	105.17	129.50	62.0	104.80
136	$S_2=(E_2/E_m/N_1)n/100$		12.5	64	73.5	62.5	70.5	64.5	64.36	64.36	64	64.36	58.10	33.73	56.41	61.06	58.64	61.84	68.71	83.00	51.10	44.80
137	$S_3=(E_3/E_m/N_1)n/100$		4.16	15.5	17.0	16.82	16.54	14.21	18.61	18.61	15.5	18.61	15.24	18.1	14.00	14.00	15.03	7.80	20.21	22.00	12.0	14.74
138	$S_4=(E_4/E_m/N_1)n/100$		2.08	7.27	8.35	7.85	7.10	7.50	9.23	9.23	7.27	9.23	7.26	7.26	5.39	6.81	6.54	7.80	9.32	9.20	6.05	6.84

SOME ADDITIONAL THOUGHTS AND CONCLUSIONS

It has appeared that an increase in supply will increase prices as well as salaries and wages throughout our society. The reverse phenomenon will occur if for any unforeseen reason the production of vital commodities should drop. This fact, as already stated, would be reflected by the index which then would decrease. By law the salaries and wages would automatically abate, and as the poor will be less able to endure any financial loss, they will be most affected. But as this is a fundamental law of nature, its effect must be accepted as an unavoidable necessity. However, even in this case the beneficial influence of the new mode of life will be felt, as it will tend to cushion the impact of any damaging force that may oppress society. The loss, distributed equally among all members of society, will fall more heavily on the poor, yet their lot will be far better than if this new mode of life had not been adopted. Since all lose by decreased production, rich and poor alike will be vitally interested in reversing the trend of things and this fact will bind rather than part the classes in a common purpose of betterment.

The EW, with its knowledge and resourcefulness, will be in a strategic position, and since it can analyze the causes of this trend will quite often be able to take the necessary steps to counteract those forces. But even if these causes should be beyond its power to cope with, as in case of a national disaster or the shutting off of some material important to the well-being of our society by a more powerful nation, its influence will tend to mitigate those disastrous effects, and make life more bearable than if the present mode should remain the lot of the nation.

At this point we wish to emphasize the fact that all our examples have dealt with a limited number of classes, and with a small and insignificant society, so that on the surface it may appear that only one set (the unskilled workers) are deprived not only of any form of services but also of the acquisition of the ideal amount of commodities q. In an actual society, however, one is concerned with millions of people and thousands of gradations of wages and salaries, and it is easy to see that all, in greater or lesser degree, will be affected by the economic phenomena described. The sixth chapter has also dealt with this subject, and from the conclusions reached at that time, as well as at this point we have no doubt as to the powerful and beneficial influence that the new mode of life is bound to bring to any group or nation willing to adopt this system.

It has been assumed that as the index changes from one value to another, by law all the wages and salaries will be affected according to that change. While this may be enforced upon all who receive a fixed amount each week, month, or year, it is easy to see that in an actual society many will be able to slip through the lattices of the law. A great doctor, a great lawyer, a great musician demands his own price according to his worth rather than to economic conditions in the country. Even if he is in a position to do so, however, the fact that a greater or lesser amount of money is in circulation will eventually force him to adjust his demand according to what he can obtain, so indirectly his income will be altered. The same can be said for the owner who possessing great wealth lives mostly on rent and on the dividends received from invested money. Indeed his rent is fixed by the law of supply and demand and as such is indirectly affected by any variation of the index. The same holds for dividends received from corporations which pay certain sums according to the profits made on the market. If we disregard the efficiency and well-being of the corporation these dividends are related to the economic condition of the nation and, therefore, are also indirectly affected by the index.

Before closing this chapter, we wish to cover two additional subjects in one way related to the analysis just completed. One of these deals with the pension awarded individuals, either by the government, or by private organizations after they have reached retirement age. At present the old age pension is usually based on the salary received at the time of retirement, as well as on the number of years of employment. We are not discussing here the proper amount, even though we feel that a pension should never be less than the minimum amount of wage a, in order to prevent making paupers of people who have given their best during their lifetime and are only prevented from achieving independence through causes outside their power. In short, we feel that any pension, no matter of what amount, should be related to the index of the community, so that purchasing power will not be affected by subsequent changes in the index. By this is meant that if a pension is fixed at 0.8a at the time of retirement, a being the minimum wage established by law for any person performing useful work, this value of 0.8a should be kept constant in the years to come, no matter what the relationship between a and actual money. In this way, and only in this way, can we alleviate the lot of millions who, unable either through sickness or by advanced age to withstand the shocks of life, see their purchasing power reduced if prices of commodities should go abnormally high through no fault of their own.

The second subject deals with life insurance, and to be more specific, with that kind through which the policy-holder, after making the specified payment of premium, starts to draw an income from the accumulated savings for the rest of his life. While no objection can be raised against this kind of investment we feel that there should be an additional kind of policy, especially if the new mode of life is adopted, by which the insured at the end of a predetermined number of years should receive an income proportional to the current index. In this way anyone will be in a position to provide for a definite purchasing power, rather than for a sum of money which may or may not assure the desired security.

In conclusion it may be stressed that the fusion of interests among all members of society, the positive help and assistance given by the EW, and the elimination of many causes of unrest and uncertainty are bound to have telling effects toward the well-being of society.

CHAPTER IX

BASIC CODES AND ETHICS OF THE NEW SOCIETY

IN THE FIFTH AND SIXTH chapters of this work are presented definite sets of rules by which specific steps are taken to advance the standard of living of the population in general. These rules, however, merely stated as a clarification of certain themes, often apply to a hypothetical society with requirements and needs that may be widely different from actual instances, and thus should not be taken literally. This was mentioned at the time, and allows us to consider our reader sufficiently forewarned of these limitations. In the seventh chapter appears also an account of the branch of the government (EW) which devotes its activity to the formulation of these rules and to their practical application among the population. These rules, dictated by economists dealing with actual and not hypothetical facts, will naturally be based on the condition of the population for which they are made. However, a rule would not be valid unless it springs from definite ideals, principles, and ethics which represent its spirit and significance. Rules may differ in order to serve different needs and populations, but must have a common denominator on which they are based. They can be changed if faulty, or if dealing with changing conditions, but not their spirit. These ideals and ethics must be incorporated into a constitution to form the foundation of our future society. This unwritten topic underlies the present chapter dealing with problems that may confront society in general. As the various analyses are presented, the spirit in which these problems should be dealt with and solved will be submitted. In some degree, topics already presented will be taken up again and reconsidered. The subjects that of necessity were merely indicated, and introduced as a corollary to the main theme under consideration at the time, will be now examined in detail and clarified. We shall likewise consider how this new mode of life affects the individual himself, discuss the restrictions it imposes on his personal activities, as well as the positive advantages resulting from the new structure of society. In conclusion, additional aspects not previously mentioned or cited only as obvious, will be set forth in their proper order and importance.

SECTION 1.

FORCES INTRODUCED BY THE NEW MODE OF LIFE THAT TEND TO INCREASE THE ECONOMIC EQUILIBRIUM POINT OF SOCIETY

First to be considered is the setting up of certain principles guiding the effort to raise the standard of living in general. The previous chapter has analyzed in some detail the equilibrium point and proved that it is related to the specific pattern found in society. Since this equilibrium point also represents a definite amount of supply, it is linked to the standard of living of the society itself. Hence, any increase in the equilibrium point constitutes an improvement in the standard of living of all classes of society, as well as a change in the aforesaid pattern. The latter is represented by a decrease in the large variations between classes, a fact both desirable and necessary to their well-being. By pattern of society is meant the cumulative influences exerted by the relative size of the several classes, the number of people engaged in producing vital commodities, the relation between salaries and wages, and the size of society itself in relation to the wealth of the land. The last factor was not considered in our analysis on the subject, nor presented in the eighth chapter, but it is easily seen that this relation is paramount in establishing the upper limit of standard of living. This last factor again, while essential to the very life of society, exerts an influence that is discernible only over long periods of time, as shown in our analysis of the fourth chapter. Thus for problems of the moment, this factor may be considered constant. The other three, however, may and sometimes do, change very rapidly and, as they spring from basic instincts in men, can produce results both detectable and measurable. Insofar as these factors tend to assign to each member of society a definite position on the social ladder, they influence the equilibrium point as well as the standard of living of every citizen. We have said that these factors change more rapidly, but this is a misstatement because the word rapidly is only used in contrast to the slow change produced by the relation of society versus the wealth of the land. In normal times this change is only slightly detectable, and many at the bottom of the social ladder barely see any difference during their normal span of life. However, in periods of great activity and strain, as during a war or revolution, these factors change both rapidly and abruptly, and naturally their influence on the equilibrium point is more readily recognized. Such changes do not always represent an improvement. A disastrous defeat or a great national calamity will see a lowering of the equilibrium point, while a victorious war or great strides in science will result in the opposite effects.

Barring these violent strains the equilibrium point, as already mentioned, tends to remain stationary, or to rise at such a slow rate that no definite betterment can be felt by a single individual in any appreciable length of time.

The establishment of the new mode of life, however, introduces forces that tend to speed up this process and yet the improvement is gradual and systematic, and avoids social strife and turmoil.

One of the most important factors bringing this change is the increase in wages and salaries paid all for the purpose of building up the necessary demand which in turn will promote the absorption of the additional supply. As prices will automatically go up in line with the increased cost, the manufacturers not only will be protected from financial losses but will actually benefit by the larger amount of commodities sold. With such a prospect they will increase production to the limit permitted by the wealth of the land.

The increased wages, at the other end, will give the poor the financial ability to absorb the increased supply. Since the poor will no longer come into direct competition with the well-to-do element of the population, the subsequent increase in supply of vital commodities will also represent an increase in standard of living, irrespective of prices.

Increase of production, it is true, must be gradual and coordinated with the other activities of society so as to avoid breakdowns and recessions. We have seen that financial collapses and depressions occur when many individuals independently of each other embark upon a policy of business expansion far above the actual need of the people. For a time such policies may produce moderate prosperity but once commodities begin to accumulate unsold, depression is bound to set in, bringing in its wake damage and loss. Our reader may point out that if abnormal increase occurs for commodities with a high scarcity factor, it would benefit society that much sooner, and accordingly no strain or depression should appear, especially if the index increases with expanded production. To this we agree, but only to a given extent, because while this contention is justly taken it is very unlikely that production will increase only for scarce vital commodities. As is usually the case, when an abnormal increase occurs in any one field it will occur in many others as well, these however, probably beyond the control of the EW, and as this in turn may bring about a depression, the situation may wholly elude regulation. Again in saying that this increase must be gradual, we are not placing any particular restriction upon the time required. While for certain commodities it may prove quite desirable that increases should occur as fast as practicable, the opposite may also be true. At any rate this increase, no matter how rapid, will always be under the direct supervision of the highest authorities of the EW who alone are in a position to gauge and appreciate its influence within the framework of society as a whole. As stated in chapter five, one of the basic ideals of future society is that irrespective of the interests of individuals or groups, the policy chosen must be one that proves to be the most beneficial to society as a whole. In other words, if from data gathered throughout the country it is found that any one commodity is accumulating at a rate that may endanger the economic structure of the nation, it is obvious that steps must be taken to curb that production. This emergency quite likely will very seldom occur, and our dissertation may prove to be only superfluous, but the ideal and regulation must be there to justify the conduct of the EW if confronted by such an occurrence. If private interests are endangered by such a policy, the affected individuals will register their complaint with the PW branch of the government which will consider their case with the proper authorities of the EW. There will be times, of course, when the EW will give ground and as a result will modify its policy, but likewise other times, when, feeling its responsibility toward the nation, it will disagree, and the case must be appealed to higher authorities in both branches of the government, and eventually reach the Supreme Court, which is the final interpreter of the Constitution. This procedure will be dealt with later.

The influence exerted by the EW is due to the fact that it will be able to control prices as well as amount of commodities produced. The almost unlimited purchase promised for all commodities vital to the population as a whole will apply only to those with large scarcity factor, and even for these the EW reserves its right to limit that purchase if the resulting increase in output becomes excessive and endangers society. This in turn will set a definite rate of improvement geared to the capacity of consumers to absorb the extra supply, so that, apart from minor fluctuations about the equilibrium line (formed by the successive equilibrium points), both production and wages will gradually move toward higher levels and improved standards of living.

Mention has been made of the fact that the EW will buy a certain amount of vital commodities from the retail as well as wholesale stores, this to be eventually resold without profit to all who take advantage of its services. As the EW represents the interests of such a vast portion of the population, and yields a large purchasing power, it can select the sellers from which commodities must be bought as well as their amount. This, of course, will not be done, as the EW is not a coercive organization used by society to limit the free enterprise and self interests of the people. As long as anyone finds sufficient customers willing to pay high prices he imposes for his commodities, this is strictly a matter between owner and customers to be solved for the best of their interest. If, as a result of the high price, the owner asks the EW to buy his unsold stock, we feel that he should receive this assistance, but naturally the EW acquires the right to decide as to the amount it will purchase from him at his price. As a rule the majority of EW purchases must be made from those charging low prices. This will tend to keep prices from rising unreasonably high, and irrespective of other benefits, will constitute a definite gain for the people in general.

These purchases, as far as is humanly possible, must not endanger anyone's rightful interest. All stores of any community must have the right and privilege of submitting to the local EW at some specified time a list of vital commodities they are willing to offer the EW at a desired price. Pending the final counteroffer of the EW officials, what is offered must be earmarked for the contemplated transaction because the EW may at any time decide to buy part or all at that price or an adjusted one, as later explained, and naturally it must be available for a reasonable period subsequent to that offer. Failure to comply with such an ethical rule would gravely impair the standing of these stores versus the EW.

From the reports received from all stores and the amount the local EW is allowed to purchase, what will be actually bought from each store will be calculated from a rigid rule that excludes personalities and preferences. Once the formula is determined and published, anyone who feels discriminated against or financially injured will have the right to lodge a complaint with the local PW branch which exists, among other reasons, to disclose and eradicate possible injustices within the EW organization.

The final formula will have to be worked out by economists, and must be changed if its application happens to produce unforeseen and undesirable results. For the present we shall submit one of our own to make our point clear. However, it will be well to explain first what the rule must eventually accomplish, and this involves the analysis of basic instincts of men which by giving rise to certain economic phenomena set a pattern in the structure of society.

Take the owner of a shoe store and say that his rate of sale is represented by Q. By rate is meant the amount actually bought and sold during the unit of time, which may be any desired length. Q, in other words, gives a measure of continuity, as the store, though selling a different number each day, tends to approximate the same number each month, or each year, or other unit of time chosen in the analysis. Then if the sale of shoes in this store tends to be 2000 per month, Q will have that value for that unit of time.

If the demand tends to increase the owner will very likely be tempted to raise the price of shoes, and if able to acquire additional stock from wholesale stores or manufacturers, will do so as this tends to increase his profit. Under such circumstances he will have no incentive to reserve any part of his stock for the EW, and consequently the latter will have no control over him.

This analysis does not give excessive importance to emotional feelings such as greed, ambition, neighborly love, and so forth, to explain impulses and actions of individuals in an economic parlance. While certain feelings affect the masses, such as optimism, which often is the mainspring of prosperity, and those of fear and pessimism frequently the basis of depression, still they have no place in a study of this nature, and we must assume that each individual under all circumstances tends to do what, in his judgment, is the best for his interest. Of course, this does not always turn to his advantage, but again this is beside the point and does not disprove our contention.

Let c and p represent respectively the cost of one pair of shoes to the owner of the store, and the price he charges his customers. Then $(p-c)$ gives the profit per shoe sold, and his profit in unit time will be: $Pr. = (p-c)Q$.

We have referred above to periods in which the demand tends to increase. This is not always the case and the owner is often confronted by periods in which it tends to decrease. What he paid for

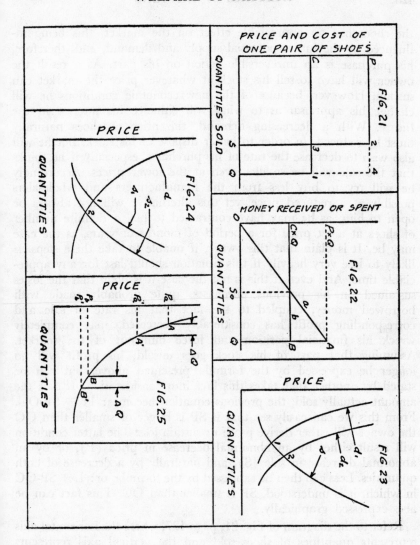

the shoes has no appreciable effect on the market, this being influenced by the future potential supply and demand, and, therefore, his purchase is an unreversible action on his part. As a result the owner will have to sell his stock at whatever price the market can sustain. However, because of the new economic conditions he will change his appraisal as to what will enhance his interest in the future. With a decreasing demand, the price of shoes naturally must be reduced, in order to better dispose of his stock, but he will also wish to decrease the rate of his purchases, especially if he thinks that the sale will be smaller even at the lower prices. Accordingly he will try to buy less from the manufacturers and wholesalers possibly at a reduced price, yet this alternative will not always be open to him, as he may have contracted to buy a definite number of shoes at a set price for a period of months or years, as the case may be. It is plain that this owner, if unable to take these steps, is likely to lose very heavily if this situation should last for any appreciable time. And even if this is not the case it is plain that the losses sustained on his previous purchases, quite probably made with borrowed money, coupled to the fact that his rate of sale and corresponding profit has considerably decreased, may completely wreck his financial position and force him out of the market. Assuming that part of his stock goes unsold, his profit will no longer be expressed by the formula presented above, but can be stated by another that takes this fact into consideration. If S is the amount actually sold, the previous equation becomes: $Pr = SP\text{-}QC$. From this we can easily see that if SP is larger or smaller than QC the owner will either derive profit or sustain loss. The latter condition will result either by an abnormal decrease in price (P), or by an abnormal decrease in sale (S), and naturally by a decrease of both quantities. Loss can then be expressed by the formula, or: $L = SP\text{-}QC$ in which, it is understood, SP is smaller than QC. This fact can be also expressed graphically.

Refer to the diagram of Fig. 21, page 427, where the horizontal axis represents quantities of shoes sold and the vertical axis represents prices. C on the vertical axis represents cost of shoes to this particular owner, and P represents the price charged to the public in general. $P\text{-}C$ then represents the profit upon each pair sold. On the horizontal axis Q represents his rate of sale, or the number of shoes he has contracted to buy from the various manufacturers at price C while S represents the actual number of shoes sold. If we draw a horizontal line from C and a vertical from Q, the two lines intersect at point 1. We have then a rectangle in which one side represents cost per pair of shoes and the other represents number of shoes bought. It is plain then that the area of this rectangle represents the cost of the entire stock to the owner. If we draw a horizontal line from P and a vertical line from S, they intersect at point $_2$. Another rectangle will then be formed, in which one side gives the amount of money derived from the sale of a single pair of shoes, while the other shows the number sold. It follows that the area of the rectangle O-P-2-S-O represents the amount of money he takes in, and the area of the rectangle O-C-1-Q-O the money that goes out. The difference between the areas of the two rectangles then represents his total profit or his total loss, depending on the relative size of the two rectangles. It can easily be proved that the rectangle C-P-2-3-C shows the profit derived from the sale of S pairs of shoes, and the rectangle S-3-1-Q-S the loss sustained for the fact that (Q-S) pair of shoes have not been sold. When S becomes smaller the profit decreases, and the loss increases. For S equal to zero the profit is nil, while the loss reaches its maximum value, indicated by the area of O-C-1-Q-O. For S equal to Q the profit reaches its maximum value, represented by C-P-4-1-C. This is equivalent to say that it is the area of the rectangle O-P-4-Q-O minus the area of the rectangle O-C-1-Q-O. We wish to emphasize that no matter the amount of sale represented by S, the expenditure of the owner is constant and is given by (QxC).

These factors can be represented still in another form probably somewhat clearer than the one just given, because it shows losses and gains as ordinates rather than areas.

Let the horizontal axis of the diagram in Fig. 22 represent quantities of shoes. Q still stands for the rate of sale, and S for the actual amount of shoes sold. If P is the price charged the public, any amount S multiplied by P will give the money received. When S equals zero, zero is then received; when S equals Q it is QP. Let the vertical axis repreesnt money received or spent. For the condition of $S = O$, the corresponding point on the diagram will be the intersection of the horizontal and vertical axes. For $S=Q$ it will be the intersection of the horizontal from point PQ with the vertical from Q. They intersect at point A. The line between O and A, indicated by a, will give the money received for any particular quantity of shoes sold.

If it is assumed that, irrespective of sales, the quantity bought is always Q, and if C remains the cost of one pair of shoes to the storeowner, then CQ will represent total cost. This can be found on the vertical axis, and if a horizontal line is drawn from this point, it will intersect the vertical from Q at point B. BQ will then show total cost, and AQ the money received when the sale of shoes is Q. But the total cost is the same under any condition, which can be represented by the horizontal line b passing through B.

Line a intersects line b when the sale is So. There the amount received is equal to the amount spent, and, therefore, the profit is zero. For a sale less than So the owner sustains a loss given by the difference of line b and a, where b is larger than a. For a sale larger than So a profit is made, shown by the difference of lines a and b, where a is larger than b.

With these basic facts in mind we can proceed with our analysis. It has already been mentioned that whenever the owner of a store encounters an increase in demand he will be tempted not only to increase his price but to increase his rate of sale, and at no time will he wish to sell any of his stock to the EW. However, when sales begin to drop his position will be radically changed and, as will be explained, the EW will hold control over him. With decreased demand and with sales (S) tending to lessen if he is still bound by contract to buy the amount Q at price C, it becomes evident that his profit will rapidly decrease as S comes closer to So and will turn into loss once that point is reached and surpassed. Facing stronger competition from other sellers, he may be forced first of all to charge a lower price in order better to dispose of his stock and still maintain the same rate of sale, but it is possible that even then sales may shrink below Q. If he succeeds in selling the amount Q it is evident that his total profit will be less because of the smaller price charged to the public. Almost every store has to cope with a heterogeneous group of buyers in which some can afford to buy what they want at almost any price while others, less financially able, are greatly affected by the variation in prices and usually abstain from purchasing the same amount of commodities if the prices are too high. It is because of the necessity of keeping this purchasing power in the market that prices are lowered, because the others, as mentioned before, will buy the same amount at any price. Should the sale drop below So (Fig. 22) the profit would turn into loss, but if the owner could dispose of the unsold stock to the EW at a moderate profit, he not only would avert disaster but his position would be made secure. The fact that the EW can absorb the amount Q-S will obviate the necessity of decreasing his rate, and consequently the pressure on the various manufacturers will also lighten. In brief, the entire business structure would gain stability.

Now, whatever this owner may choose to charge, it is evident that the EW must consider his offer when requested to buy commodities from him. Naturally the EW must be fair to all parties concerned, and while it will buy some from him, it will buy more from those who charge a lower price. We have seen that cost varies for different individuals and organizations, and depends on their efficiency and ability to introduce savings. If the EW should accept their estimates of cost and buy all they offer at their price this would not only encourage graft and corruption but would tend to place a premium upon those less capable than others. Thus the official cost of the commodity must be considered equal for all and might be either the average of prices charged by wholesale stores or what must be paid to the EW of other communities for merchandise imported from there. By adding a reasonable allowance for middlemen and for transfer as well as a given percentage as just profit, this will represent the cost which the P.S. will take as base.

This cost is fair to the public as well as the owners. From the previous discussion it may appear that the influence of the EW in decreasing prices is non-existent because all stores will feel secure in setting whatever price they may choose, since any surplus unsold can be easily unloaded upon the EW, quite true, at a lower profit, but a profit just the same. This, however, will not be the case, as it will be explained now.

The purchase of vital commodities made by the EW and referred to in previous chapters as unlimited needs at this time additional clarification. If unlimited purchase was actually made this would only result in a disorderly and abnormal increase in supply that would seriously impair the well-being of society. As previously stressed this increase must be gradual and orderly and, therefore, the EW Manager of any community cannot buy indiscriminately all that is offered to him even at just and fair prices. The purchase from one period to the next can only increase a certain percentage and this to be determined by the higher authorities of the zone and of the nation, who are in a position to gauge the various economic forces acting within the society. Of course it will be left to the EW manager of the Community as to the amount that must be bought from day to day, but he must ultimately conform to the rate set by the previously referred authorities.

We should not be unduly concerned of the seemingly large control exerted from above on private initiative. It must be understood that for all those commodities with a large scarcity factor through-cut the nation, only a small control will be necessary if all that is produced is easily disposed among the entire population of the nation or elsewhere because any surplus within any zone will readily find its way to other zones and, therefore, the larger the production the better will be the condition of the nation. The strict control and limitations referred to above, naturally, applies to those commodities with a small scarcity factor and it is plain that if an abnormal production should develop because of the unlimited purchase promised by the EW, this would not so easily find its way among the population and, therefore, such a control tends to help rather than endanger the producers and sellers. It must also be mentioned in passing that the higher authorities of the zone and of the nation will usually concern themselves only with large fluctuations of commodities that may affect the entire zone or nation and sporadic ups and downs in production that may develop within a community will be left to the General Manager of the community itself and to the General Managers of adjoining communities to solve among themselves to the best advantage of the populations they represent. Because of this large freedom and authority of the Community Managers great flexibility in the system will be possible and the EW organization will not be as top-heavy as a superficial estimate would indicate. As mentioned at the beginning of this chapter our purpose is that of establishing laws and principles to be used as base of necessary actions to be taken when confronted by definite needs. While such actions may not be necessary and possibly prove harmful in many cases still must be taken in others and, therefore, their application must rest on the judgment of those who have the ultimate responsibility of the well being of the nation. If misjudgment should develop among the higher officials of the EW we know that the new system of life has effective methods either to enlighten those leaders of their errors and misjudgments or to substitute them with others more qualified and adept. With this understanding we can state that if supply under the impetus of the new economic forces should expand to a point that may endanger society, it is natural that the EW should act and correct that condition.

As a general policy, whenever the supply drops to a lower level, the latter and not the former must be taken as a base for a subsequent interval of time because the rate of increase must be kept rigid from one period to the next. If the supply is equal to or lower than the pre-established amount, it is evident that the Community Manager will buy all that is offered at the price described above.

This willingness to buy will prove a great incentive toward production, and thus the EW influence will be favorably felt both by the population and producers. However, if the supply is larger, some commodities must go unsold, and the policy of the EW under such conditions must be further examined and analyzed.

In the previous case, when supply is small in relation to demand, the EW has no direct control over prices charged by the retail stores. Scarcity awards that privilege. The fact that some of that supply must still be sold to the EW will keep prices from soaring too high because otherwise many well-to-do would buy from the EW instead of the retail stores, to the definite disadvantage of all charging exorbitant prices. Beyond this no direct control is exerted by the organization, but when the supply is greater that it can absorb, its influence will be direct and tangible. Other factors being equal, the EW will buy more in proportion from stores that charge less.

Consider first the moral justification of this rule. Assume two stores selling a certain vital commodity; one is more centrally located or closer to the best residential part of the city and charges a far higher price than the other. If both happen to have an unsold part of their stock they will turn it over to the EW. Let Po be the EW base price, and Pa and Pb respectively the prices charged by the two stores. Before starting this study let us introduce a few thoughts that will help to clarify our subject.

The first part of the sixth chapter explained the relationship between the curves of supply and demand as well as their influence on the final price at which exchange can take place. It was shown that for a stated supply, the larger the demand the higher the equilibrium price, and vice-versa (see Fig. 23). Likewise for a given demand the larger the supply the smaller the equilibrium price, and vice-versa (see Fig. 24, page 427). Now the demand, especially for vital commodities, does not vary appreciably from one period to another. We must conclude then that marked variations in prices are mostly due to wide fluctuations in supply. It was also found during that analysis that the stable equilibrium point is the cost of the commodity itself. By a closer analysis of this economic phenomenon we find that while this statement is correct for the nation in general, or for any place where averages are taken into consideration rather than individual cases, yet one can easily see that the particular supply and demand that may develop in localized places, such as a city, a town, or district thereof, may call for an equilibrium price quite different from the average calculated for the nation, the city, or the town. In fact it could not be otherwise. Since most individuals, regardless of ethics, do what seems to them best for their interest, it is natural that those able to charge more will do so as long as sufficient customers are available to make it profitable. It is also true that even at top prices some will make larger profits than others because of their particular cost curve. This dissertation is introduced to prove that even when a store charges a seemingly exorbitant price, it is still the result of a supply and demand. In this case, however, the demand is made by people who can afford to pay the higher price. In other words, the owner of such a store is confronted by a very inelastic demand curve, by which a large variation in price produces only a small variation in quantities sold.

Returning to our analysis, it must be stated that, even for this individual, if his price was lower the amount sold would increase, and the fact that he is left with a surplus proves that his price is above what it should actually be. Up to a given extent, the same can be said for an owner charging lower prices because he also is unable to sell his entire stock.

In cases where the EW buys only part of what is offered it is natural that those who charge less should be favored over the others. While this preference has an obvious moral justification, one cannot expect the Community Manager to exercise such discrimination lest he become open to graft and bribery. Instead a rule will be devised by which this discrimination is automatically taken into account and yet is independent of personalities and special interests. Let line d of Fig. 25 be the demand curve of a specific commodity. A and B on this curve give the relative position of the two independent stores. The price they charge can be found by drawing horizontal lines from A and B until the vertical axis is interested at points Pa and Pb. ΔQ represents the amount unsold, which is here assumed equal for both stores. These two quantities, needless to say, are offered to the EW. From the same diagram it can be easily seen that if both stores should wish to sell their entire stock to the public in general they would have to decrease the price of their commodities, respectively to points Pa^1 and Pb^1. While the reduction by store B is small, that of store A is considerably larger. This, of course, is due to the fact that both stand in different positions on the demand curve, and while A faces a demand with a small degree of elasticity, B is faced by one that is very elastic. Thus to produce the same increase in commodities sold ΔQ, A must reduce his price far more than B. The EW, however, should not take this into account, but should consider instead the fact that both pay approximately the same for their commodities, and that all stores in the same position of A, as an average, not only make much higher profits than those in the same position of B but actually derive a profit above what is fair and just. It might seem that a system could be devised by which the owner of store A would find it more profitable to lower his price to (Pa^1), rather than maintain his original (Pa), and then sell his surplus to the EW. This would entail either a marked reduction in the price offered by the EW, or a marked reduction in the amount purchased from him. However, such a policy would be unwise. First of all, price (Pa) is an equilibrium point between supply and demand. At this price the profit of store A will be the difference between Pa and its average cost, and depending on the owner's efficiency and ability his profit may be large, normal, or small. Since the EW will not be in a position to know his actual profit, it seems unjust to adopt coercive methods against dealers who, even at high prices, may make less than others who charge less. Yet the opposite is probably true and it is more likely that the profit made on that part of his stock sold at price Pa is much greater than what he would derive if he should decide to sell his entire stock at price Pa^1. Thus if the EW should refuse to consider his offer of ΔQ, the lack of this additional profit would still be preferable to that of lowering his price to Pa^1 and he will do so even if that surplus should go to waste. Thereby the chief aim of the EW to increase the supply of vital commodities would be defeated by its eagerness to lower prices and curb profiteering. Moreover, we do not feel that the EW has the right to adopt coercive methods against anyone, even on the problematic assumption that they may benefit society in general. We must realize that the commodities sold at price Pa are transacted through a free and unhampered agreement between owner and customers, and the EW has no right to interfere. However, when the EW becomes a customer it acquires the right and the duty to safeguard its interests and the interests of those it represents. As previously explained, some kind of discrimination against all those who charge exorbitant prices is just and fair, and in following this policy the EW does not endanger the interests of anyone, especially when it is bound to buy only a certain percentage of the commodities offered.

In brief, our rule is as follows:

If we indicate by P the price charged by a store, not necessarily equal to Pa, and by Po the basic price determined by the EW, the ratio

Po/P will give the factor K_1. If the amount offered by the store is indicated by M, the amount that the EW will offer to buy at price P will be given by MK_1. The sum of all such quantities bought from stores in town and calculated by the same formula will be indicated by W. Let now Wo be the actual amount of commodities that the EW is supposed to buy, which as previously explained, is derived by adding a fixed percentage to what was bought in the previous period of time. Indicating by K_2 the ratio Wo/W, the final amounts bought from the various stores will be: MK_1K_2. As previously mentioned this is only a tentative rule not to be accepted without further consideration and study. If desired, the penalty for charging high prices may be made more or less severe by introducing an exponent to the factor K_1. If this is done the quantity to be bought from a store would become: $M(K_1)^n K_2$ where n is the exponent to be finally selected by economists of the future society.

Consider again the position of owner A. He will, naturally, maintain the price Pa as long as profitable. However, in the course of time the supply will increase at a far greater rate than at present. Due to a greater competition among sellers, and to the natural readjustment in prices, more and more well-to-do may cease to be his customers in preference of stores that charge less, while taking advantage of the services of the EW. If this condition should materialize the amount sold at price Pa may become so small that he may find it profitable to lower the price of his entire stock rather than sell the surplus to the EW. He will do so since it is to his advantage. It is clear from this discussion that the EW, even though indirectly, will exert a powerful influence in reducing prices in general, and this will be accomplished by securing an increase in supply, which in turn will step up competition among the sellers. Obviously this is to the advantage of society in general.

Because of the close interrelation among the communities forming a zone, prices will not differ appreciably throughout each zone, and therefore the same scale of salaries and wages will be maintained: a fact that in turn will assure a stable economy.

Since helpful counsel will be given all whose cost curve is very high and who are, therefore, limited to lower profits, variation in prices among stores will tend to decrease, and all eventually will be able to sell to the public a good portion of their stock. What remains unsold can then be offered to the EW at a reasonable profit. This will be a good incentive in increasing supply, especially for commodities with a large scarcity factor.

As new forces enter the economic structure of the nation it is natural that their effects be taken into account in the shaping of policies. A new treaty with a foreign country, a decision to lower an economic barrier, action to improve the economic condition of a zone, will naturally affect policies, but as long as the general principle is maintained that no one need lower his standard of living to increase that of others, no one should fear the presence of the EW. Indeed even those stores which may be forced to decrease their prices will eventually be able to maintain a far larger rate of sale than before, and thereby increase rather than decrease their profits.

By such a method the pattern of society will be transformed from a stationary condition to one where the equilibrium point not only is higher but tends continually to climb, bringing better standard of living to all. The poor will be able to get a larger amount of vital commodities (these, as earlier explained, in time can be expanded to include others previously listed as of the luxury kind), those with larger wages and salaries not only will be able to acquire more than before but also to enjoy more services, and the same, naturally, holds for those already rich. But for the latter more than actual increase in salary the intangible benefit will be found in the healthier economic condition of the country. Because of the greater purchasing power of the population, more commodities will be manufactured and made available to mankind, and of these the rich will, naturally, secure for themselves the larger portion, and thus improve their lives to a limit undreamed of before.

SECTION 2

COMPETITION AND THE INFLUENCE OF THE EW

Competition, by definition, is the effort of two or more parties acting independently to secure the custom of another party by the offer of the most favorable terms. This gives no idea of the multiform gradations, quality, and intensity which competition may assume; no idea of the feelings that result in millions, such as hope, worry, happiness, sorrow, uncertainty, and so forth; it gives no idea of the fundamental changes it will foster in society. Competition may also mean emulation, or the desire to excel, having no reference to the feeling of those who also have worked hard for that attainment but must step aside; competition again may mean rivalry in which the contest is directed toward selfish ends, and leads to envy, jealousy, and so forth. Competition in any event is a battle which in many cases comes to be one with the fundamental law of survival and with the battle of the fittest. Competition it must be admitted, may come to resemble a war which, even though not fought with the sword, has consequences which may mean economic strangulation, life and death for millions of people, and for entire nations.

In the first part of our study, and specifically during the analysis of price, we referred to four fundamental instincts of men which give rise to forces that affect the price of commodities. These forces spring from the combined actions of millions of individuals and no one seems to be able to alter them, no matter how harmful they may turn out to be to some individual's interests. We know also that prices tend to equalize cost, so that for any decrease in price many sellers see their small profit turn into loss. For all unable to lower their cost of production it is evident that the only way to obtain profit is to decrease the supply, and in the fundamental egotistic nature of men this can be done by forcing other sellers to withdraw from the market. Competition among such sellers is the natural result.

In our study we wish to consider two forms of competition. One kind is wasteful and dangerous to society, the other is more constructive and beneficial even though some of its phases may be harmful to individuals. To better convey our meaning let us take the example of two individuals competing against each other for the privilege of selling lumber to a factory which in turn serves the needs of a small community. If the two will fail to come to agreement by which both can sell a specific amount of lumber and still realize a moderate and just profit, the consequent result will be that each will try his best to force the other out of the market. To achieve this purpose each will offer lumber at a decreased price in the hope that the other, faced by heavy losses, will be forced out of business. The decreased price, however, will stimulate a larger demand, so that both individuals will have to work harder for their meager return. As each is set in his purpose, he will go on cutting more and more wood than needed by the community, so that the part of their stock remaining unsold will have to be put to uses where a lower grade of material would be more profitable so far as society in general is concerned. It is a matter of common sense that the cutting of trees in a forest must be done intelligently and that the rate of cutting must be at such a rate to give time for new trees to take the place of those that have been felled, and thus keep a constant rate of production. The policy of the two men is wasteful, to say the least. If they keep on cutting their trees indiscriminately for the sake of keeping up with the increased demand, and also each with the purpose of pushing the other out of the market, it is likely that some day one or the other, or probably both, will find their forest exhausted, and besides being unable to continue with their business, they will be powerless to compete with a third who may enter the market. This is one phase of competition which happens to be harmful to those who compete. Let us assume now that the third man, having disposed of the others in short order, remains undisputed in the field. He probably will have bought their property at considerably reduced price, and from that point on he will be able to control the supply of lumber so as to derive the greatest profit. But his best interests are not necessarily the best for the community, as a whole, consequently we see that lack of competition may become detrimental to society. Of course, through competition, the strong and often times the unscrupulous are able to drive the weaker out of the market, and this opens the way to the setting-up of monopolies. In our modern society competition sometimes deprives many of the only way of earning their livelihood and is responsible for the continuous transfer of individuals from the middle to the lower classes. From the example above we may conclude that competition, while necessary to society, sometimes may be wasteful, and on this account needs a stricter control which, while it will prevent wastefulness, will help those who are unfavorably affected as it will prevent the setting-up of monopolies detrimental to society itself.

In actual life we are also confronted by another form of competition which is constructive and beneficial to society. This is represented by the emulation that develops among individuals of great talent and knowledge for the attainment of better things in life not necessarily of great benefit to those who compete but of unquestionable benefit to humanity in general. Often times competition may develop for the attainment of a better station and position in life and quite often only a small difference will be needed for one person to be displaced by another. Of course competition, no matter in what form, can always be thought of as one individual displacing another, and in this respect the loser stands to suffer. However, through competition humanity has reached heights undreamed of only a few years past, the ablest and the worthiest reach positions of leadership and open the way to others, the unfit are pushed aside for the good of humanity. In this form competition is a necessary form of progress. By limiting competition we limit initiative and progress, and society would acquire a sameness and apathy which in its effects would be far more detrimental than the problematical advantage gained by allowing the unfit and inefficient to block the way to those who have talent and ability.

There is a fundamental law in nature by which the weak is overwhelmed and crushed by the strong, the timorous supplanted by the courageous, the unfit replaced by the qualified. The survival of the species and the process of evolution does not admit any other alternative, and we find this law rigidly applied not only among the most primitive forms of life but also up through the animal kingdom to the human race. But while we must admit and comply with this fundamental law of nature, still we cannot place ourselves at the same level as beasts. Man is much superior to that. While in principle we agree that leadership belongs to the fittest we must also remember that progress relies not only on the effort of the few but on the cooperation and well-being of the many, and while it is just and proper that qualification should be the key to advancement we must remember that the well-being of the masses is the prerequisite of a good and healthy society. On this account, while we favor a free and constructive competition, steps should be taken to lessen its most appalling and harmful consequences.

In our study we are not concerned with that kind of competition that takes the form of emulation for the attainment of higher things in life, such as in science and so forth, but shall deal with that kind of competition for personal economic advantages that affects such a large portion of the population of any community, competition that develops among various stores of a small community, among analogous industries and the like. Such competition, as long as it is done with fair and honest methods, is very beneficial to society, since it tends to give the public a fair return for its money. Those who are more efficient stand to gain the most, many will be able to obtain a reasonable profit in return for their investment, or a just wage for their work, while a few will have to withdraw because of inefficiency and ineptitude.

In chapter seven, in the section where we describe the activity of the industry control branch, we have analyzed the influence exerted by the EW in alleviating the plight of those who find themselves on the verge of bankruptcy as a result of competition, and need now to go no deeper in the subject, however, referring to that part of our study we may point to several beneficial effects brought by the activity of the EW.

(a) It will weed out from positions of leadership persons who are inept for such a responsibility. This will be done without applying unjust regulations or using methods that would infringe on human rights. Indeed, their misfortune will only be a result of their ineptitude and incompetence. Yet, by being rescued from the IR, a good portion of their property or investment will be saved. This would not have been the case if they had been left alone to extricate themselves from their untenable position. Needless to say the same wealth could then be reinvested in profitable enterprises under the leadership of more capable men and they would still add to the common good by assuming less prominent roles as salaried men and experts in their particular field.

(b) It will avoid crippling losses to the various small investors of the failing industries, which will prevent hardship among many individuals of small means.

(c) It will place industry and business in general in the hands of those more efficient and able to benefit themselves as well as society in general.

It is true that often the one who goes ahead is not necessarily the best qualified for the advancement, and often the unscrupulous reach places of prominence by dubious and objectionable methods. Destestable as this fact may be, we must admit that these are the exceptions rather than the rule, and again we must refer to the essential egotistic nature of society. Indeed, as long as an individual placed at the head of an organization is able to guide it efficiently and to the satisfaction of the employees and investors he will be retained in that position. As long as one merchant is able to sell at a lower price than another, society as a rule will buy from the former rather than the latter independently of the moral qualities of the sellers. However, the world is always in a state of change, and the stronger today may become the weaker tomorrow, and in turn must submit and obey the law of the fittest.

Now we may ask ourselves the question. Is it ethically right to spend the wealth of society to buy enterprises on the verge of bankruptcy, possibly of no use unless large expenditures are made to transform these industries into others more useful to society? We must first realize that the EW exists only because it can be of benefit to poor as well as rich, to old and young, to the strong as well as to the weak. Since the principal aim of the EW is that of helping society, taken as a whole, to counteract tendencies which may become harmful, any step taken in that direction is ethically right. If, as a consequence of that step, individuals are benefited, that must be considered to the good. Buying those enterprises, besides helping those individuals personally involved, will be beneficial to society, and this is sufficient justification for this step. As the unfit are gradually and continuously weeded out from positions of leadership and responsibility, the best qualified for those positions will take their place. Again as those who are so replaced cannot blame anyone but themselves, and even then the fact that their loss will not be as great as if they had been left alone to extricate themselves from their untenable position, in time they will realize and appreciate the fundamental justice behind this continuous reshuffling of individuals to places of leadership and power.

SECTION 3.

INFLUENCE OF FOREIGN COUNTRIES ON
THE WELL-BEING OF A NATION

Another important subject to be dealt with in this study is the pressure exerted by a foreign country on the economy of a nation. This influence is measured by the magnitude of the demand or supply originating from that country.

Before entering on this subject let us first analyze the influence of a sudden change in demand within the country itself. In previous parts of our study we have analyzed the four basic forces that affect the price of a given commodity. Neglecting those forces that tend to equate price to cost of production, as a rule, the day by day price is determined by the instantaneous position of the supply-and-demand curves. If the demand should decrease greatly in relation to the supply the price will drop and many manufacturers will sustain a loss. We know that if such condition should persist that many manufacturers and sellers would be forced to leave the market. The unfavorable effects produced by their withdrawal on the population as a whole are quite obvious. If the nation is one of those that has adopted the new mode of life, such variations of price will be greatly reduced, and the supply and demand within the country are not apt to experience large and abrupt changes that tend to dislocate the economic condition of the nation. The demand for a given commodity can be divided into four different components.

We have the demand represented by the population of the community, then the demand exerted by the population of the zone. Following we have the demand exerted by the population of the nation, and that exerted by the population of other countries. The presence of the EW as we have seen, will exert a stabilizing factor on the economy of the nation and even the supply and demand of luxury commodities, confronted by a stable economic condition, will also move in a coordinated and orderly manner. Of course, offsetting factors may and will appear from time to time to upset that equilibrium. A new bridge, a new highway, a new railroad, may change the balance of trade either in favor or against a community, and thereby many manufacturers may find that the relation between their cost curve and the new equilibrium price has altered. If, as a result, the price of the commodity has decreased, this, irrespective of other considerations, indicates that the population as a whole has benefited, and therefore the innovation is justified. Those manufacturers adversely affected by that change will in turn receive from the EW valuable advice and cooperation in their effort of decreasing their cost curve and thereby regain the original profit. In extreme cases, as previously explained, the EW will be ready to rescue those industries that are on the verge of bankruptcy. Since the labor population will always be employed either by the industry of the nation or by the EW, the unfavorable effects resulting from the foundering of any sporadic industry which is forced to close because of the new improvement will not be excessively felt by the public in general. Now it is plain that such improvements as a new railroad, a bridge, or the like result from competition among manufacturers, and represent a great factor in the advancement of society.

The subject of competition from abroad will now be considered, and we shall also analyze the course that should be taken to enhance to the maximum the economic condition of the country under study. In an expanding and dynamic nation, if at any time the supply exceeds the demand, the price will fall, with detrimental effect on the population. However, should it be able to export its surplus, the price will remain at a profitable level, making more work available. In return other commodities will be imported, which will go to increase the general standard of living. The exchange might be in gold or in other monetary forms internationally recognized and accepted. Indeed, as explained elsewhere, a proper amount of money in circulation is essential to healthy business activity, and there may be cases when the importation of gold rather than other forms of wealth should be emphasized for the overall well-being of the country.

As a generality many commodities are exported because of the fact that middlemen, citizens either of that or other countries, find it to their advantage to buy products in one place and in turn sell them at a profit to middlemen elsewhere. Their purchases, representing a certain fraction of the total demand, are a factor in establishing the equilibrium price of commodities. If these middlemen buy more, prices will rise, if less, they will fall. If a foreign government should abruptly introduce excessive tariffs or other restrictions upon the free flow of trade, some middlemen will find profits greatly reduced or even vanished, and naturally cease further operations. As a result the supply, which hitherto has kept step with demand, will become unbalanced, prices will decline, and many will be unfavorably affected. Of course the influence exerted by foreign demand depends on its size in relation to the total. If it is small, few will suffer in consequence, and the policies of the EW may prove more than sufficient to avoid economic strain, but if it is large the repercussions in the community and the nation are bound to be more serious. Due to the heavy drop in demand, the supply will be finally disposed of at a far lower price than before, and because of the severe losses suffered by many, a depression may set in affecting the entire population. The new equilibrium, which in the course of time is bound to be established, will be at a level far lower than before. The consequence will be decreased employment and lesser purchasing power. As it is assumed that the nation under consideration has adopted the new mode of life, the proper authority will seek to reach an agreement with the country imposing these tariffs, or with other nations in order to correct the off-setting factors. In addition, vast public works will absorb surplus labor, and in extreme cases a nationwide reduction in working hours may be imposed. Be that as it may, trade restrictions by a foreign country are bound to produce vast changes in the nation under consideration, which can be partly offset by policies of the EW. Of course abrupt methods as described above are not apt to occur very often, but are gradually brought about by the changing conditions in the world market. As a generality, in a free market the demand exerted by a foreign country, say Beta, is influenced by the same factors as the local market. The producer who supplies the best commodities at the lowest prices is sure to sell most, irrespective of local or foreign demand, and this is just and proper. These basic facts, having been stated, the main subject of this analysis may now be introduced.

Using as a base of discussion the welfare of a country, identified as Alpha, with due regard to its financial and economic position, the policies that benefit her most in foreign relations will be analyzed. The resulting welfare of other countries is incidental, and figures only in so far as it affects the well-being of Alpha. Alpha is a progressive and dynamic nation which up to now has traded only with one other, Beta. As their exchanges have proved beneficial to both, there has been no need of change in their relations. But now a third country, Gamma, comes to the fore and begins to compete with exports originating in Alpha. This competition does not end trade between Alpha and Beta, yet it is sufficiently severe to disrupt the internal economic condition of Alpha. Now the fact that Gamma gradually edges herself into world markets may be because her population, rapidly advancing in civilization, progressively adopts better methods of production and labor saving devices, and following a natural instinct toward the acquisition of a better standard of living, exerts pressure increasing with time. With the emergence of Gamma, it is plain that Alpha would be adversely affected if she should embark upon policies intended to block the progress of her neighbor. But if she adopts an open-minded attitude it can be shown that Gamma will definitely aid the well-being of Alpha. Alpha having adopted the new mode of life, is willing to follow the basic rules intended to promote cooperation among nations. At any rate, in dealing with this third country, the following alternatives arise:

(a) Gamma is able to undersell Alpha because of being closer to raw materials.

(b) Gamma is able to undersell Alpha because of her lower standard of living.

(c) Gamma is able to undersell Alpha because she has adopted more efficient methods of production.

(d) Gamma is able to undersell Alpha because of a change in the tariff of Beta advantageous to Gamma rather than Alpha.

(a) *Gamma is able to undersell Alpha because she is closer to raw materials.* Her manufacturers, other factors being the same, can acquire basic material at a lower price than their rivals in Alpha, and in consequence their products will be cheaper on the open market. One cannot see any justifiable method which Alpha should adopt to counteract this situation, since the advantage of Gamma is a natural one. If we are to advocate a free exchange of goods among men, it is plain that those nations distant from any raw material must reconcile themselves to the fact that their products for which that material is needed, must be more expensive than when made by others who can acquire it at less cost of transportation. Other factors remaining the same, those nations have a great advantage in world markets. As raw materials of different kinds are found throughout the world, it follows that it will be to anyone's advantage to emphasize and concentrate on products for which the raw material is close at hand. This instance will be further treated in dealing with subsequent cases.

(b) *If Gamma undersells Alpha because of her lower standard of living,* the fact that she now trades more with Beta will in time increase her standard of living, and simultaneously manufacturing costs of commodities will rise. Thus her present advantage will gradually diminish and disappear, this giving opportunity for Alpha to recapture a large percentage of her lost market. Gamma, having improved her standard of living, will consume more commodities, and some of these will have to be bought from Alpha. This will tend to balance the losses sustained in reference to Beta. It is true that people are impatient and this waiting period may seem entirely too long. Yet what right has Alpha, or anybody else, to prevent Gamma from improving her standard of living if in possession of the necessary prerequisites for that advancement? These advantages may well be represented by a better climate, better strategic location, possession of vast quantities of raw material and many other factors immaterial to this study. Alpha in the position of Gamma would certainly follow the same policy, with the difference that she now would be influenced by entirely different needs and situations than those assumed. If Gamma is able to undersell Alpha in some products, effort should be made by the latter to substitute others for which she has a natural advantage, and business then could be built up with Gamma as well as Beta. As a result Alpha would achieve a better economic standing than when she dealt only with Beta. Of course in any forced readjustment, individuals would suffer, and those affected by the competition of Gamma would strive to impose legislation endangering the economy of that country. Such policy is shortsighted, and ultimately detrimental to all countries concerned. This is what actually happens in the world of today. However by adopting the new mode of life the EW, by sensing new changes, will be able to counteract the detrimental effects on the individual, who in turn will abate his hostility to the concessions that must be made to another country in the process of expansion, and the time will come when the entrance of Gamma in the world market will be regarded as a blessing rather than a scourge.

(c) *If Gamma is able to undersell Alpha through more efficient methods of production,* this fact should be accepted as a worthy and necessary lesson. There is no reason why the industrialists or business men of Alpha could not also improve their facilities and methods, and thereby not only benefit their countrymen but regain some of the lost trade relinquished abroad. As in the previous case, room must be made for Gamma to expand and improve her standard of living, and if possible the economic structure of all three countries should be linked to the advantage of all. Each will thus reach the highest standard of living compatible with the resources on hand.

(d) *If Gamma is able to undersell Alpha because of changes in tariffs by Beta,* before condemning the Betan officials for such unethical procedure, it would be well to examine the causes that led them to take such a step. It is possible that while Beta can absorb all the surplus products of Alpha, in return Alpha cannot do likewise. In such a case, gold would flow from Beta to Alpha in payment of purchases, and as it has been previously shown how dangerous it is to a country to lower abnormally her holding of specie, it is possible that her better relations with Gamma spring from this basic need of that nation, this to a definite disadvantage of Alpha. As the latter is the country being studied it is well to analyze this economic fact in detail.

If Alpha is a poor country in that respect, the influx of gold would be highly beneficial to her business activity. Still the gain of gold, while potentially important to business, does not add to the standard of living of the population if the commodities utilized are unchanged and working hours stay as before. In chapter 3 was given our definition of standard of living, (SL), which now requires additional explanation.

Anything that adds to the comfort and enjoyment of anyone will increase his standard of living. If a person is in possession of a large quantity of apples, greater than he wishes to use, and is able to exchange some for oranges, the fact that he has gained the latter means a better standard of living than had he only apples alone or only oranges. Again one who works fewer hours than another for his livelihood, even though commodities consumed by both are the same, enjoys a better standard of living than the other on the basis of time and leisure. Reverting to the barter of apples for oranges, money may be received instead, in lieu of direct exchange. Now if the apple-trader spends that money to buy oranges, his standard of living will reach the same level as before, but as long as he does not utilize that cash his standard of living will remain at the original level when he had only apples to eat, and, therefore, that sale has not produced any change in his welfare. Unless he is one who finds pleasure in the plain possession of gold, an accurate yardstick for measuring his standard of living will be the amount and variety of products he is able to utilize and enjoy.

Now it stands to reason that any action taken by Beta in regard to Alpha must spring from definite economic needs, for no nation will take a step it does not think advantageous. It is true that the policies of a nation are often directed by individuals who provide for only the immediate problems of the day, and are not overly concerned with effects that may develop in a more distant future. Suppose that the raising of tariffs by Beta was dictated by the necessity of preserving her holdings of gold. In this case one can safely say that Alpha must bear much of the blame. Indeed, as a dynamic and expanding country, Alpha has been receiving gold from Beta which has gone to enrich only few of her citizens and has accumulated in the vaults of the government or of the banks. To the extent that this gold has not been used to buy commodities abroad, this hoarding not only has decreased the amount available in the world but has not even increased the well-being of the Alphans. This indicates that Alpha has been producing at a greater rate than was justified, and that her population has been maintaining an unreasonable output in the futile effort of importing not really needed gold. Once she has adopted the new mode of life this error will no longer occur. If it should become evident that Alpha must retrench because of the expansion of Gamma, the hours of work for her entire population will be decreased. As Alpha abates her production many commodities will have to be imported both from Beta and from Gamma, which means that they will no longer sustain the siphoning off of their gold while the Alphans still maintain the same level of available supply. However the fact that the population works less than before for the same amount of commodities is a clear indication that its standard of living has improved. It is true that now the rich will no longer realize the same profits but the good of the few should not and must not block the good of the many. The diverting of industry into different channels, the adoption of better methods of production, and the assistance given by the

EW will counteract the disturbing effects previously mentioned, and all affected by the new competition of Gamma will soon see, under the guidance of the EW prosperity ahead not only for themselves but for mankind in general.

We must also realize that discordant conditions among nations are not always the direct result of definite policies adopted by their governments, but are caused by individuals in each country who indiscriminately engage in the production of all kinds of commodities which later on cannot find ready markets. As they are concerned with their own particular field, they cannot possibly regulate their activity so as to comply with fundamental laws of international exchange. Lacking coordination and guidance they precipitate, by their actions, distorted and chaotic international situations only partly relieved by the day-to-day government policies which apply only to that particular problem and leave unsolved the fundamental problem on hand. For this reason a higher and better informed organization above minority pressure is necessary if a comprehensive effort is to be made to improve society as a whole.

If Beta has not already adopted the new mode of life this policy on the part of Alpha is bound to be acceptable to Beta since it aids rather than endangers her internal economic structure. If extreme wealth and poverty are to be found in Beta, this cannot possibly be attributed to Alpha. It may be expected however, due to Alpha's happier and more harmonious internal condition, that Beta will eventually be willing to change to the new mode of life. This will facilitate an understanding among the two nations along the lines described above and made possible by the accepted new ethics and this will further enhance the economic unity of both countries for a better standard of living.

Assume now Alpha is poor in raw materials and totally dependent on other countries. Her striving for survival will become much more severe, and she must check any leakage of whatever gold may be in her possession.

As a first case say that none of her neighbors have yet adopted the new mode of life. Their quest for a higher standard of living will not be in a spirit of cooperation and regard for other peoples' rights and needs, but with motives of greed and mistrust which will arouse not only bad feeling among the countries concerned but will breed misery and poverty among their people. When individuals allow greed to sway their code of life, it injures members of the same family as well as outsiders. Needless to say, the consequences

of such a philosophy can only be disorder, chaos, war and all the
disastrous results that have plagued the world from time immemorial.

An impoverished Alpha can do little toward the improvement of
world conditions. Her poverty in raw materials will place her at
an extreme disadvantage in dealings with other countries, either in
imposing her will in a friendly way or in waging war to safeguard
her liberty and interests. Alpha, accordingly must find her equilibrium
compatible with whatever resources she happens to have on hand,
and abide by the dictates of the strongest, no matter how absurd
they may be. If she has adopted the new mode of life, among the
first things she must tackle will be that of using her resources to the
utmost limit permitted by her technological knowledge. Nevertheless she must make shift with a relatively low standard of living
and must guard against loss of specie, realizing the fact that the
greater the outflow of gold the closer she will be to foreign economic domination. If gold must be exported, it must be done only
to acquire durable wealth, as machinery, tools and the like, which
will give the opportunity of regaining that gold through a larger
exportation of products. No expenditure should be made abroad to
buy perishable wealth, as foodstuffs and the like, and, of course,
luxury commodities should be prohibited unless under the form of
barter. With such a strict policy Alpha may reach a safe degree of
self-sufficiency never-the-less must always remain on the lookout for
all exchange that tends to increase the specie on hand. In other
words, her position does not permit her to adopt a bold policy in
international affairs, and by following the conservative dictates of
the EW she will attain the best standard of living compatible with
the wealth on her land. A further increase could ensue only if and
when humanity should awake to the fact that progress lies in cooperation among peoples instead of rivalry and antagonism. Alpha's
economic and physical insufficiency does not let her take a leading
position in the world, possible only for a rich and powerful country
which, fearless of other philosophies or physical might, can lead its
people and those of other countries toward a better and brighter
condition for all. But if leadership in this respect is denied Alpha,
she will still have ample opportunity to enlighten and inspire others
by her indomitable faith and example.

At any rate, no matter what the basic wealth of the country,
the change to the new mode of life will have advantageous effects,
as it will tend to raise the standard of living of the population to
the maximum attainable with her resources. A higher standard for

Alpha can only be made possible if one or more of the surrounding nations should adopt the new mode of life and extend to her the necessary aid which will eventually enrich the benefactors as well.

Consider now what will become of Alpha if Beta, considerably stronger and wealthier, should be one of those to adopt the new mode of life. The simple fact that Alpha can only attain a low standard of living in comparison with more fortunate countries indicates that she possesses a large amount of unutilized labor wealth. Without taking into consideration the possibility of emigration from one country to another, a move basically opposed to human instinct if better methods are available, agreement could be reached between Alpha and Beta by which the latter would sponsor the setting up of industries in Alpha. Raw materials then could be sold to Alpha with the positive assurance that finished products would be bought by Beta in free competition with her industries. While the raw material will probably be more expensive to Alpha because of the greater distances involved, the lower standard of living of Alpha, which is tantamount to admit her lower wage scale will place her industry on an equal footing with that of Beta, and therefore Alpha will be able to raise her standard over and above the previous level. Obviously Alpha stands to gain, but would Beta lose by such an arrangement? Definitely not. Indeed, the simple fact that the Alphans better their lot means also that their country will have more money to spend. Some of this money will go for commodities and articles abroad, and because of the friendly economic relationship existing between the two countries it is reasonable to expect that a large proportion of the importation of Alpha will come from Beta. This, incidentally, will represent for Beta an additional demand and a greater volume of business. The industries of Beta adversely affected by those opened in Alpha can be easily guided into different channels, and thereby both populations stand to gain. However no Betan industry actually need be affected by the competition of Alpha if the EW Manager, who supervises the federation of both countries, decides to sponsor the setting up in Alpha of industries engaged in the manufacture of commodities with a large scarcity factor. By such methods direct competition among the industries of both countries may be averted or lessened, and both will gain by the fusion of the two economic systems, without endangering the freedom of Alpha or the interests of Beta.

In conclusion we wish to say that integrity, honesty, and fair play should be the ideals governing all dealings with foreign countries.

If these ideals are accepted and actually applied the sacrifices we may make today will be generously repaid by the benefits we shall reap tomorrow.

SECTION 4.

ELIMINATION OF MONOPOLIES

It has been shown that monopoly is a device by which an individual, or group in partnership, controls the exclusive supply of any commodity or service in a market, and is thereby enabled to raise the price above that fixed by free competition. As a broader interpretation we can also say that the few who have some monopoly profit at the expense of the many. Disregarding the many exceptions, such as that granted to inventors for a definite number of years, as a general rule monopolies are antisocial, selfish devices of the few to obtain possession of wealth, which they do not really honestly earn, and hence should be resisted and eliminated.

In our study we shall consider two kinds of monopolies. One deals with the control of the production and distribution of commodities and raw material; the other with the control of the labor market.

Through financial manipulations, unfair competition, oftentimes sheer weight of wealth, and the like, cases are found when few people buy the interests or come to control less financially able enterprises. Using these methods they continue to expand their holding to a point where no one dares or is able to stand their competition and is forced to leave the market. As this stage is reached these individuals are at liberty to increase the price of their products to a level far above the actual cost of production, at a definite loss to the general public.

For the establishment of a monopoly many methods, of course, can be used but the following is the most typical one. The individual who succeeds in setting up a monopoly usually starts like anyone else by selling the commodities produced by his factory. Fortuitous circumstances put him in a position to take advantage of other people's weaknesses and set him on the road to monopoly which he will pursue unless endowed with exceptional integrity, honesty and self-abnegation toward others' rights. Of course for establishing a monopoly he must already be in possession of a large amount of wealth or at least more than that in possession of those who gradually become his competitors. Fair competition, as previously explained, is beneficial to the public and to business in general and his setting up of the new enterprise should not and must not be considered harmful to society. However with the passing of time the competition may become unfair. This is done when the individual, because of his greater wealth, decides to sell his products at a price that is considerably lower than cost, deliberately subjecting himself to a loss. As the public in general makes its purchase where the price of commodities is lowest, it will buy from him rather than his competitor, who is charging cost plus a moderate profit. This will, naturally, endanger the competitor's business, as he will be forced either to sell his products at a price lower than cost or see his sale drastically reduced if unwilling to lower that price. As the latter business man is not as financially strong as the first, no matter what his choice, sooner or later he will be forced to sell his enterprise or declare bankruptcy if he wants to salvage a small fraction of his capital invested. As it is usually the case, the first individual, who deliberately lowered his price, is also sufficiently wealthy to buy the tottering enterprise at a fraction of its actual value, regaining thereby the money previously lost. The same method can be used to undermine the position of other established enterprises in the community or zone until he becomes the sole producer and seller of that particular kind of commodity. As this stage is attained, he will be at liberty to increase his price to a level far above his actual cost and also above the equilibrium price that would result if many competitors were in the market. Usually, however, monopolies cover vast regions of land and this control is very often acquired with the following method:

If an individual wants to extend his monopoly to region B he will use there the same tactics that were so successful in region A. Now, however, he does not even have to sustain the initial loss necessary to force the competitors of region B out of the market. By increasing prices in region A he will balance this extra profit with the losses he must sustain in region B. He can easily keep up this pressure until all the competitors give up the struggle and sell their enterprises to him who, because of his large wealth, can easily outbid any would-be competitor who may wish to enter the market. As his position in region B becomes secure his prices will be increased and this again at a decided loss to the general public.

That methods such as these are harmful to society needs no further explanation, that methods such as these should be easy to detect by the EW officials goes without saying. Consider now what counter-measures can be taken by the EW against such practices.

Reviewing the purchasing rules used by the EW it will be noted that where production increases at a slow rate or remains stationary the EW will buy practically all that is offered on the market within the limitations stated in the first section of this chapter. Considering any one store if M is the amount of commodities placed at the disposal of the EW and P the desired price, what the EW will actually buy will be determined by the following relation:

$$Mo = M. K_1 K_2 \text{ or } Mo = M. Po.Wo/P.W$$

where Po represents the price offered by the EW and Wo the total amount it expects to buy from all stores while W is the cumulative amount offered by all the stores in town. Wo, a fixed percentage greater than previous purchases, is usually equal or larger than W and unless P is exorbitant in relation to Po it can be easily seen that M will be equal or very close to Mo. This will automatically prevent mono-poly because any one who is undersold by another will have that much more to offer the EW who is anxious to increase its purchases. Quite true that the sale to the EW will be at a reduced profit but yet it will be sufficient for that store to remain in the market and effectively minimize the influence of the would be monopolist.

Where the production increases at an over rapid rate, the policy of the EW, like before, will still be that of buying a fixed percentage above the previous purchase and no more. This will bring an un-balance between supply and demand and theoretically some of that supply should remain unsold. Actually the price will tend to decrease until all is absorbed by the public. This price however in many cases may be lower than cost. As a result some of those who have sustained severe losses will drop from the market and by their withdrawal prices again will approach the average cost. This condition is directly attributable to the EW policy to maintain the increase in produc-tion under control and affects all producers and sellers.

Another fundamental policy of the EW will be that of being only partially influenced by the market price of a given commodity. In other words the price the EW will offer to the various stores will be based on the average actual cost plus a reasonable profit and will not be appreciably affected by the market fluctuations. As a result of this policy there will be times when the EW will actually offer more than the market price and this will tend to decrease the losses of all those who have been more severely hit by the exceptional increase in production. This, however, is a general policy and does

not describe the influence of the EW in curbing would be mono-
polists. In a decreasing market, as the one contemplated above in
which the price drops below the average cost, the would be monopolist must lower his price far more than when the market is on the
upgrade and this fact, by itself, may represent a loss he may not be
willing to sustain. However, assuming his determination of establishing a monopoly his policy will tend to decrease the number of
customers to his competitor who, as a result, will have that much
more available for the EW. Of course not all he offers will be
bought by the EW and his surplus must be disposed at a lower
price to the general public. At this point a note of clarification is
in order. While the market price may at times and in sporadic cases
be lower than what is offered by the EW, we do not foresee such an
occurrence to remain for an indefinite amount of time because
many of the EW customers would find it to their advantage to buy
more from those stores and the increased demand would soon raise
the price of that particular commodity. At any rate the fact that
any store will be always in a position to dispose a good deal of his
stock at a moderate profit to the EW and unless the individual has
a poor and unefficient organization meaning by this that his cost
is much greater than the price offered by the EW, he will be able
to sustain the policies of the would be monopolist almost indefinitely.
The latter, needless to say, will soon desist in his scheme and fall in
line with the others. It may be said, then that with vital commodities
the possibility of using unfair methods of sale with the intent of
setting up monopolies is quite remote. As regards manufacturers
or owners of stores dealing in non-vital commodities, the situation
is radically different because the EW does not exert a direct control
over their sale. In other words, it has no power to prevent unfair
competition or the setting up of monopolies, unless one considers the
aid extended by its Industry Control division to all in need of
assistance either in decreasing costs of production or acquiring industries approaching bankruptcy. We feel, however, that the consequences of monopolies in such a field would affect only the relatively small rich part of the population, and hence would not
have widespread economic repercussions.

Let us now consider the second kind of monopoly, which is one
of labor. To treat this subject in detail would require more space
than we wish to allot. Monopoly of labor is only one of the many
phases of the all-important relationship between capital and labor,
and we cannot adequately discuss this phase unless something is

said about the relationship between capital and labor which constitutes the setting of many economic phenomena.

Misunderstanding and friction between capital and labor is something real and vital that has long been afflicting our existence as well as our mode of life, and the solution of this problem is of tremendous importance to the entire civilized world. Expedients have been applied in the past and continue into the present to that end. That we are not solving it yet is evident from the increase in the number and the seriousness of the strikes continually paralyzing industry and society itself.

Since the emergence of the industrial era society has slowly evolved into two main blocs or classes of people. Neglecting the thousand variations of groups between the two blocs it may be said that on one side are those who own wealth and, generally speaking, the means of production, and on the other those who possess none and depend for their livelihood on the others. The author has already placed himself on record as to the necessity of the private ownership of wealth, and therefore does not deem it necessary to revert to a topic already discussed. Reference has also been made to the many advantages of division of labor, industrialization being only one of its phases. At any rate, many of the modern evils of society can be directly traced to the uneven distribution of wealth and to the division of labor, which while highly beneficial to mankind, have in themselves potentialities of coercion and economic strangulation from which society, or rather the working class, tries to extricate itself by futile and unreasonable efforts, producing convulsions often detrimental to itself, which fall short of the desired results, and make the lot of the poor more unbearable than ever.

Let us first consider and analyze in a dispassionate way some of the efforts intended to wrest economic advantages from the owners. First on the list is the strike. Either carried on in an orderly and peaceful manner, or accompanied by violent and unlawful acts, it has the intent of halting the production in an industry or factory, thereby inflicting upon the owners heavy financial losses through that stoppage, and thus punishing them for policies which seem to conflict with the interests of the workers. Often strikes are called as a sympathetic gesture toward the laborers of another industry. Their immediate result is the crippling of production. Independently of the kind of commodity produced, one of the most important consequences will be that of raising its price. This comes as a direct result of its greater scarcity throughout the land. If the commodity is vital the immediate effect will be felt by all laborers in the land whether or not they have any personal quarrel with the owner of the industry in question. If the commodity is not vital, the repercussions of this stoppage, while less easily recognizable, nevertheless do exist, and are of great importance.

Let us assume that the automobile is considered a luxury commodity, and that a strike develops in that industry. This implies that all engaged in the manufacture of automobiles cease, during the period of shutdown, to receive the wages and salaries which buy bread, butter, and the other necessities of life. Many, with sufficient savings on hand, will continue buying the same amount of commodities as before throughout the strike; others, less fortunate, must reduce their purchases. Again, any industry, and the automobile industry is no exception, buys raw material and a considerable line of finished products from other industries. Now that the automobile industry has come to a halt as the result of the strike, other subsidiary industries will also be affected, and some will have to shut down or reduce production. Thus the effects may be felt by millions of people who have nothing to do with the original strike. One of the consequences of the decreased purchasing power of the laborers affected in one way or another is the fluctuation of prices of consumer goods. As many persons will naturally buy less, prices will drop and bring financial losses to many small enterprises and investors some of which, being on the border line, will have to drop from the market. As the supply of vital commodities decreases to meet the reduced demand, prices again will climb, eventually reaching and probably surpassing the original level. This will inflict additional discomfort and hardship upon the poor and will be a direct consequence of a strike in an industry devoted to the production of luxury commodities.

This is the first effect of the strike while in action. Unquestionably great financial damage is done to the owners of the industry suffering its direct assault. As a result, the ownership may or may not continue with the same individual. But the fate of the owner, taken as an individual, has no importance in a study that considers society in general. In other words, that the industry should still belong to Mr. Green or pass to Mr. Brown does not have any appreciable effect on the phenomena that will appear after the strike. Since any industry must resort to all kinds of devices to keep abreast with the competing interests and still show some kind of profit upon the capital invested, which is the main reason for its financial existence, the same emphasis on economy and efficiency has to be stressed and attained, no matter under what ownership. Settling of the strike may be obtained by granting all or many of the financial demands made by the unions. As a result of this the cost curve of the industry is bound to go up, and therefore may cause not only a decreased profit but often an actual loss. To offset such a damaging factor the industrialist is confronted by two technical alternatives. One is an increase in efficiency of his labor force that will justify the increased wages; the other is the introduction of additional machinery tending to replace as much labor force as possible.

Now we all know how uncertain is the increase in efficiency of a labor force, which very often only looks to its immediate advantage without regard to the interests of the industry. For this reason more workers are continually replaced by well-designed automatic or semi-automatic machines that perform all kinds of intricate operations at less cost, and add to the stability of the industry itself. But no one with common sense can consider such substitution as an ideal economic improvement. As these machines effectively compete with and finally replace human labor, more and more workers enter the ranks of the unemployed; more and more people, driven by privation and destitution, turn to crime and try to acquire by force what society prevents them from earning with honest work. The population as a whole loses its buying power, and this in itself defeats the purpose of the introduction of machines. To push our argument to absurdity, we can conceive the day when all commodities may be manufactured by machines of wonderful intricacy and efficiency that need only the pushing of buttons installed at the desk of the president of the corporation, who no longer requires any labor or help of any kind. In all this sea of plenty no one will be left, however, to buy the commodities produced, as all will be unemployed and with no means whatsoever to pay for what they need. As stated, this is only mentioned as fantasy, and none foresee the day when this could happen, yet the problem is one of gradation. The trend now is in that direction, and the resulting effects will only be in proportion to the amount of displacement caused by these innovations.

As the increase in wages is granted, the immediate effect will be that this extra money is used for all kinds of commodities, mostly vital, of which there is a definite scarcity, resulting not only from the strike just ended but by hundreds of similar shutdowns forced by other unions in industries elsewhere in the country. As the rivalry for scarce commodities between the poor and the rich becomes keener, the usual consequence will be that prices will rise, and those who can afford them will always be able to outbid the others lacking their funds. Even when ceiling prices are enforced by responsible authorities, black markets and other devices based upon the fundamental law of supply and demand will appear, and leave the poor as miserable as before, if not more so. Besides those who have been able to obtain an increase in wages we find, however, millions of workers who have not struck and, therefore, are still paid as before. Considering the problem from the point of view of these laborers they are justified in demanding an increase, and many eventually will strike if this is not granted. If all these strikes prove successful, at least so far as the laborers are concerned, and all receive an increase in wages, their purchasing power will not have gained in relation to what it was before, but it will decline considerably because of the decreased supply. Indeed, due to the fact that so much manpower has been wasted, scarcity will be more severe and equilibrium point will be considerably lower and will make life less endurable for the poor. Indeed, at this level these will consume less, irrespective of their increase in wages. In other words inflation has begun, which reduces the value of money in reference to commodities, and the higher wage actually buys less than before. To top all this, business failures, uncertainty for the future, and retrenchment of invested capital, will further aggravate the situation.

All because the problem has not been approached with a clear understanding of the origins of these phenomena. Instead of following policies that look ahead and have wide perspective, the authorities have usually pursued a "laissez-faire" attitude in the hope that conditions will eventually right themselves. This, of course, could not and does not happen, and because of the continuous tug-of-war between the rival classes of society, things have become worse instead of better. Besides the fact that all components of society stand to lose from such a condition, it is natural that the poor will be more severely affected because of their limited financial power. Driven to desperation, the workers try to solve the problem with the only weapon at their command; the strike, which more often than not turns to their own disadvantage. In all this disheartening picture, selfishness and egotism usually come to the fore more virulent than ever. Indeed in a world as uncertain as ours, where unfair competition, trickery, unscrupulousness, dishonest ambition, are the order of the day, the average man learns to be selfish and to adopt similar methods lest he be engulfed by the raging whirlpool that relentlessly destroys the weak and all who fail to fight for their very life.

This is the background of modern society. Out of this struggle a new factor has come forth to aggravate the matter: the monopoly of labor, nominally termed the closed shop.

Frequently bad feeling between labor and management starts and gains momentum with the passing of time; usually strikes are settled by some kind of compromise between labor and management, in which the workers feel that they have not received enough, the management that it has granted too much. As the economic repercussions of successive strikes are finally felt, both parties become convinced of their point of view and naturally veer toward a more determined stand, either against yielding further concessions by the management or for the full acquisition of advantages they consider their due, on the part of the workers. In quarrels of this kind, personalities are bound to become involved, and as the leaders of labor run the risk of being singled out and discharged on the most trivial pretexts, leaving the labor group without guidance, a close and compact unity of interests among the laborers becomes paramount to the success of their mission. For this reason unions are organized. They include not only workers in a specific factory in a certain city, but gradually also those in similar industries throughout the land. The power of these unions, as their size increases, plays a major role in the life of the nation, and because of the strict regimentation among their members, one word from the leader may paralyze the entire country. With such vast power in their hands, concessions have been extracted from management which would have seemed out of the question only a few years ago. This, however, has not brought the laborers the expected economic improvement, and as conditions have continued to grow worse for reasons now familiar to our reader, additional strikes have started and the end is not yet in sight. As already mentioned, manufacturers have come to rely more and more on machines to the exclusion of manpower, and this shift is going on at as rapid a pace as technology permits. In this country, shortly before the second world war, the number of unemployed reached the staggering figure of 12,000,000. The unemployment problem was solved only because of the war which, besides calling millions to the colors, put many more to work in factories engaged in the production of war materials. Now that the war is over, the unemployment problem is beginning again to assume alarming proportions, and what the outcome of all this will be is at present hard to foretell. However as more and more manpower is displaced, as many unemployed begin to compete for jobs of any kind, the selfishness aforementioned becomes evident in its brutality and ugliness. All fortunate enough to have a job not only clamor for a higher wage but for the closed shop, which binds the management to cease hiring more workers, or at least those who do not belong to the union. Besides the immediate necessity of making jobs secure, there are other reasons for the closed shop. Large as the various unions are in any country, these do not usually include its total labor force as many either because they see the ultimate danger to the nation because of this regimentation of labor, or for various other reasons, do not join the unions, yet indirectly profit by any advantage gained by the members. This, naturally, starts a feud among the workers themselves. Those in the union feel that any advantage which has been secured through their effort should be shared only by the union members, and as it is impossible in any factory to increase the wages of one group without raising those of all the others, the natural solution is the closed shop, by which only members of the union can get jobs in the factory. The closed shop has been obtained in many places through strikes and intimidations, which have further aggravated the position of industry in general. Closed shops, besides the economic necessity referred to above, have been sponsored by the union leaders with the object of enlarging their membership. The increased size of their union magnifies also their bargaining power with the management. A major union likewise receives a large revenue from the dues paid by the members, and this is of great importance as heavy expenditures are necessary during the period of a strike to support all who in one way or another take active part. Again, their greater wealth means a higher salary for the leaders, some of whom, as in other organizations, profit by fraudulent appropriation of union funds.

Advantages for the few at the expense of the many are dangerous to society, and such injustice naturally must be opposed. There is also another effect produced by the closed shop which we wish to point out while on the subject. When it is established, those who are included gain a false feeling of security. Many will toil harder and more efficiently, confident of not losing their jobs, but others relax and loaf, feeling that as long as their jobs are secure there is no need to work hard, or at least to produce as much as if their jobs were at stake. On this account it is an everyday occurrence to witness the spectacle of a simple operation being undertaken by a large number of workers drawing sizable wages, when a few could do the job quicker and better. That industry can not go on with such methods is obvious, and that a general collapse is ahead if such trends should persist follows as a matter of course. Unfortunately the illusive idea is spreading among people in general that one can get something for nothing, and one expects others to do the work he himself usually does not care to do.

No such thing could happen under the new mode of life. Like the monopoly of capital, the monopoly of labor must end. All must be given freedom to improve their standard of living in proportion to their ability and industriousness. It does not seem right to us that any minority, no matter on what ground should deliberately prevent others from acquiring positions for which they may be better qualified. Quite true that these unions were originally intended to prevent the industrialist from discharging undesirable and unnecessary employees in favor of better machines, or from replacing workers drawing high wages by others willing to accept lower pay. But two wrongs do not make a right. While we do not approve the conduct of the industrialist who uses such methods, the unions as well as the closed shop do not solve the problem, and neither operates to the good of society nor produces the benefits sought and therefore lacks justi- fication.

It has been seen that in the advocated new mode of life emphasis is placed not on the amount of wages measured in dollars and cents, but on the quantity of commodities and services those wages can buy. Thus a scale is chosen with a minimum wage sufficient to buy a quota of commodities compatible with the economic progress of the nation. When this method is accepted, indiscriminate increases in wages for many persons without corresponding increase in supply lose their importance, because the physical well-being of the worker now depends on the amount of supply, which in the last analysis represents the real wealth, rather than on money, whose elusive purchasing power can rise or fall without close relation to the actual standard of living of the individual.

A worker employed at a certain trade in one city receives a given wage. Another, employed in a similar trade, in another city, may be paid a smaller amount. However living conditions in the two cities may be such that the worker with the lower wage may be able to buy more than the other. It is evident that he enjoys a higher standard of living, despite his smaller pay. As the increase of the index is represented by an increase in supply, and is equally beneficial to poor and rich, cooperation between capital and labor will be the natural result, and all will work for this end, eliminating useless waste of energy in combatting each other for illusive advantages. As the friction between labor and capital tends to lessen and finally disappear, as the EW aids industry in ways already explained, as it weeds out all enterprises showing no possibility of improvement, the industry of the country in general will be able to rely on more stable conditions, resulting in great economic strides. It has been explained and proved that the new forces in the economic life of the nation will tend toward increases in supply, and irrespective of price levels all will enjoy greater abundance.

As said, tension between capital and labor will disappear. Of course, all with any degree of common sense realize that better qualified workers earn their right to receive higher wages. It is true that nepotism, likes and dislikes between manager and employees, may prove exceptions to the rule, but these cases will be infrequent, and the EW will always be ready to aid in finding another job for whoever is unhappy and dissatisfied. At the other end, the capitalist or industrialist also has sufficient common sense to recognize that a satisfied and well-paid labor force, besides adding to the stability of his industry and improving the efficiency of the factory, helps to build a bigger demand for his products, as directly or indirectly they must be bought by them as an integral part of the general public. Moreover, it has been shown how any technological improvement in this new setup of society will be the supporter rather than the competitor of the poor. New inventions, new machines, instead of supplanting the manual laborer and causing unemployment, will serve to alleviate his task, and make life easier for him, through a decreased number of working hours. The advancement in technology, without undermining the financial position of the workers, will eventually yield hundreds of new and improved products, of which a good share will benefit them, as their purchasing power will increase instead of decrease as so often occurs in our present mode of life.

In conclusion we can say that the basic principle to be adopted in solving problems caused by conditions covered in this subsection should be one that prevents the selfishness of the few from holding sway over the many. Since the new mode of life is planned to eradicate injustices and enslavement, any independent action taken by the few loses its justification, and should no longer be tolerated.

Regarding monopoly of capital, it has been shown that this will be effectively counteracted by the EW, at least for enterprises dealing in vital commodities. In the new society, in which basic principles of justice and decency are made the foundation of every business transaction, monopolies of industries outside the immediate responsibility of the EW will become extremely unpopular, contrary to the Constitution, and punishable by the law of the land. As to monopoly of labor, it is equally clear that practices originally intended for the amelioration of the worker, but which ultimately injure the workers themselves, will no longer be needed, and should be also eliminated by the laws of the land.

SECTION 5.

UNEMPLOYMENT PROBLEM

Another scourge of society is the spectre of unemployment which as a consequence of depression, occurs when the poor are least likely to receive adequate aid from friends, relatives or charitable institutions. Famine, plague, actual obliteration of vast areas of once populated lands, are among the most tragic results of past economic dislocation. It is true that such phenomena have usually appeared when civilization could be considered in its infancy, but let us not lull ourselves into believing that these disasters could not occur right now, when our civilization has at its command so many means to counteract such tendencies. This is a false belief, because famine does exist in several sections of the world today. India and China are examples confirming this statement. Although one may say that the second world war is responsible for this situation, and to this we agree, such ghastly methods for settling disputes among nations have not yet been discarded, and there is no assurance that still another war may not break out to play havoc with humanity, nor can one tell who will be the next to suffer. Even the highly civilized countries of Europe can be prey to famine and other calamities, and even this vast and prosperous country of ours, under certain circumstances, might endure similar experiences.

Our civilized society is like a delicate and sensitive instrument, in which the smooth functioning of all parts is a prerequisite of the functioning of the whole. The forces that set up and maintain the relationship among men must be balanced, or confusion and distortions will appear. As to the assumption that such evils could not possibly occur to us because our people are so highly civilized, bear in mind that this high level of civilization has made us more and more dependent on its achievements, so that, if it should fail, it would leave us that much more unprepared and helpless. It is enough to recall how we feel when the electric power fails in our home.

Unquestionably the problem of unemployment can be directly related to that fine balance of society referred to above. Many theories are presented as explanation, even justification, of this phenomenon. Some of these causes have already been analyzed in detail. However, among the theories there is one which contends that mankind is too numerous, and therefore unemployment with consequent famine, plague, and finally obliteration of people is the course taken by nature to reestablish the equilibrium between supply and demand, especially in countries with poor, over-crowded, and primitive population. We emphatically do not agree with this theory, and believe that unemployment is mainly due to faulty relations among men. Indeed the simple fact that such calamities occur in periods of depression, when economic forces are most strained and distorted than at any other time, is a proof of the correctness of our point. It is not reasonable that a land in which all could find work and plenty in periods of prosperity should change so radically when depression sets in, and especially when we consider that the same land will again support better living conditions as a new period of prosperity approaches. The contention that the land becomes too small for the people has been advanced time and again in years gone by, when world population was far smaller than today. This gives us assurance that such a limit, that is to say the amount of population the land can sustain, is still distant in the future, and that there are yet vast resources in the land sufficient to provide for a population far larger than ours. That some countries are richer than others, and therefore able to maintain a better standard of living, goes without saying; that a more judicious and intelligent distribution of wealth among men is needed if we are to reap the full benefits of a greater division of labor, comes as a matter of course; but let us not forget that a land which may be considered poor by present standards may become vastly richer if some of its raw material, probably abundant but worthless, should in time increase in importance and value. We are now at the threshold of the atomic age. The disintegration of the atom with its vast release of energy may free humanity forever from want and scarcity, as the relation between fundamental wealth and size of population will be so radically changed. On this account there is no need to be unduly pessimistic regarding the possibility of the land not being able to sustain our population. If unemployment exists, if famine, pestilence, and obliteration of populations occur, these are mostly due to a poor and faulty system of production and distribution of wealth, as well as to the selfishness of men.

It has been explained that even in a land of plenty the pattern of the population will set a theoretical and stable equilibrium point between supply and demand. This equilibrium will also set a limit to the amount of commodities produced. As previously stated, the actual equilibrium point tends to oscillate about the theoretical one. When the shift is in one direction there results prosperity and abundance for all; when it is in the other direction there comes depression with starvation for many. As these equilibrium points are the result of the cumulative and subconscious attitude of each component of society, no one by himself can alter or counteract such tendencies, and while some will be left untouched and even enhanced by such phenomena, others will be badly affected and liable to lose jobs and livelihood. As in a storm, depending on the severity of the waves, many will be swept to their destruction.

In the new mode of life such conditions will vanish. Since the equilibrium between supply and demand will be maintained within narrow margins the oscillation referred to above will be prevented. This in itself will be a great factor in reducing unemployment. However, as new inventions and technological advances are made, a certain amount of labor is bound to be temporarily displaced. This, however, will not reach such devastating proportions as at the present time, for new industries, the direct result of these inventions, will supply new jobs and more employment. Thus those who hold responsible positions in the country will not face the same staggering problems as today. It has also been stressed that as technological improvements are being made no manufacturer will be allowed to discharge labor without previously notifying the EW officials, who will have ample time to find them new jobs. As re-employment in other industries becomes increasingly difficult, vast projects of general usefulness will be undertaken by the responsible authorities of the land and effectively counteract unemployment. The EW, as the sponsor of such projects, will act as a shock-absorber, and due to its capacity to expand or retrench will be complementary to the industry of the nation, keeping the population constantly at work. As the ratio between the workers engaged in private industry and those employed by the EW reaches some predeterminate level, the official working hours in the nation will be reduced some definite amount. This will tend to divert the flow of labor toward private industry. Through using such regulated methods every section of society will come to consider technological advancement as a blessing. Since these advances will not affect the purchasing power of the nation, all will be able to enjoy greater comfort and a higher standard of living.

SECTION 6.

TARIFFS

Since time immemorial, groups of people, communities, or nations have taken the shortsighted policy of raising economic barriers between themselves and other groups, communities, or nations. The purpose of these tariffs, ostensibly, has been that of safeguarding the interests of minorities of these groups. Such barriers usually have been in the form of levies imposed by the local authorities on commodities coming from the outside, so as to raise their price to a level equal or higher than that of those manufactured by the minorities in question. This has tended to protect the interests of industries and enterprises which otherwise would not have been able to compete with their foreign counterparts. Tariffs therefore have averted financial losses by the owners, and as a consequence have kept at work many who found livelihood therein. Undoubtedly this was among the purposes of early tariffs, but we are inclined to believe that other factors were also responsible.

If one goes back a few centuries in the history of the civilized world, he will find that most of the countries that now form the various nations were divided into hundreds of small communities and principalities, under the rule of counts, dukes, and other nobility, and practically all were maintaining at the expense of the people an extravagant ruling class, which extorted high taxes in money and in products. Under such burdens the people did not progress beyond a very low standard of living, and it was under such conditions that plague and famine frequently decimated the population, retarding humanity to an extent that can never be estimated. Those people, being only human, were bound to be resentful toward their government, and whenever possible made a determined stand against the continuously increasing taxes squandered in high living or petty wars by their rulers. As further levying of taxes often was impractical due to the impoverished condition of the population, and the heavy expenditures required to collect them, tariffs were introduced into general use in lieu of levies. The rulers pretended to their people that tariffs meant a saving on their part, since any additional tax was imposed upon the outside world rather than on the people themselves, and thus constituted a magnanimous gesture toward their dependents. As tariffs also helped local industry, this gave the people, ignorant of policies that did not have an apparent or immediate effect on themselves, the impression that these were desirable devices. Under this delusion tariffs came to be considered an integral part of society.

Ultimately those who had fattened at the expense of society came to an ignominious end. The miserable condition of the population as well as the enlightenment given by great philosophers and humanists, finally struck the spark of revolution, which though in many ways destructive, changed the world from the medieval to the present age. That people are better off now than they were then needs no proof, although many customs and habits, surviving from those days, still linger and paralyze progress. One of these is the tariff. In the fourth chapter of the present text we analyzed the effects of tariffs in greater detail than need be reviewed ,and came to the conclusion that tariffs, besides endangering the economic structure of other nations, are also detrimental to those who impose them. Commodities available at lower prices from the outside become expensive because of tariffs, which is tantamount to say that the supply is made abnormally smaller, at a definite loss to the consumers. At any rate, if the tariff exists for the purpose of protecting the local industry, this means that it is not as efficient and well-managed as its counterparts in other countries, and thus their competition is beneficial in forcing the former to improve its methods of production. If the advantages of the foreign industries are not due to better methods of production or greater efficiency but to conditions independent of the industry itself, such as a better climate or a lower standard of living, the exclusion of their exports not only prevents those countries from improving living conditions, but endangers the local population itself by preventing the purchase of cheaper commodities. This follows because of the problematic advantage given the local industries which thus protected, will no longer exert the necessary effort to increase their efficiency. It seems to us that industries so disadvantageously situated that they will never successfully meet foreign competition have no reason to exist.

If tariffs are imposed by the government or local authorities to raise additional revenues, this is a tacit admission of ineptitude or extravagant expenditure. Indeed, this means only that the government has not the courage to reveal its financial situation to its people, and in order to avoid open discussion, which might be embarrassing to many in high places, turns to tariffs to cover extra costs. But whatever the cause or the purpose the consequence is always the same, many suffer for the benefit or shortcomings of the few. Thus this policy is antisocial, and should be eliminated as soon as conditions permit. This is one of the aims that the new mode of life will pursue. Trade among people of the same or different nations should be free to reach its equilibrium as this is the method most beneficial to humanity in general as well as to the nations in particular. We could say that as a result of this policy, those local industries disadvantageously situated in reference to others may be forced to shut down. This would be the natural consequence if this policy should be adopted at the present time, but since the EW will be ready to give all industries assistance and advice either to improve their efficiency and strengthen their competitive position, or to change their production toward more profitable lines, this will preclude these disastrous effects.

Of course we visualize a world in which all countries, setting aside their animosities and jealousies, join in a vast family of nations united by strong economic bonds. As they work together for the good of humanity they in turn will also prosper and improve. In such a world wars and threats of war will no longer exist, yet we realize that for the present they remain a hard and unfortunate reality that each nation must take into account when settling important policies of state. We realize also that in a world as unstable as ours the policies advocated above could easily endanger and impair the very life of the nation. Indeed, the losing of skill in manufacturing special commodities could easily become the deciding factor in the outcome of a war against would-be aggressors. Because of this reality, as long as the world remains as it is, industries possessing paramount importance for the life of the nation must be maintained and protected. For instance, Europe in general and England in particular can build ships at a cost far lower than ours due to difference in wages and standard of living. Under the policy advocated above, instead of being built by our own yards, ships would have been bought from England, or other countries of Europe. This procedure would have injured our yards to such an extent that they would no longer have been able to find adequate activity and sooner or later would have been forced to convert to other types of production. This would have meant loss of valuable experience and technical staffs qualified to maintain or to increase the necessary construction of ships should the European market for any reason be shut off from us. Instead the fact that this industry was kept alive and healthy before the war, gave us the power to expand production when the need of the nation became imperative. We all know the wonderful contribution of this industry to the winning of the second world war, especially when England, under the relentless bombing of her yards, lost much of her ability to build or even repair the thousands of ships needed to carry war cargo. By maintaining our yards in a going condition we were able to meet the enemy challenge when the crisis arose, even though our ships in the world market may not compete with those of other countries.

What has been said of ships naturally applies to other commodities needed to defend our rights and liberty. On this account we realize that the removal of tariffs, while basically sound and requisite for the well-being of society, must await a better world, as it cannot possibly be expected that the new mode of life will be immediately accepted by all nations. This dual policy of ours must be maintained as long as aggressions and wars darken the sky. But with the exception of tariffs that apply to industries and commodities vital to the security of the nation or federation of nations, and therefore subject to control by the military command, all must be gradually reduced as drastically as possible, because this objective will benefit people in general. But among the nations that have formed the federation the necessity for tariffs of any kind will no longer exist, and accordingly they all must be completely ended. For instance, no one in the United States would consider the building of shipyards in the cold and utterly unsuitable expanses of northern Alaska just for the sake of helping the local economic conditions of that land. Ships built there would be extremely expensive, with no chance of competing successfully with those from yards with better climate, better facilities, and nearness to the thousands of products used in their construction. But as Alaska is an integral part of the economic system of the United States, there is no need for her population to feel endangered because of the inability of building ships, or to feel insecure because of her lack of shipyards, since as once her territory was threatened the entire economic system would rally to her defense. A similar bond of unity will hold when several nations anywhere in the world join in a strong and compact federation. While the necessary key commodities must be on hand to be used against would-be aggressors, these products will freely reach their equilibrium point within the economic unit of the federation, without reference to the fact that they may have to be manufactured in one nation rather than another within that economic system. This topic is one to be discussed at greater length when treating of the relations among nations. The idea intended to be stressed at present is that tariffs are definitely detrimental to the nation imposing them, even though they sometimes may be of benefit to minorities and entrenched groups, and consequently disregarding the influence on other nations whether friendly or unfriendly, they should be decreased and finally eliminated. As a result of the abolition of tariffs the price of many commodities will drop, which means that the supply will correspondingly increase, thus achieving one of the primary aims of the new mode of life.

SECTION 7.

DIVISION OF LABOR

The present text has had occasion to consider and analyze the advantages and disadvantages of division of labor. Not only have the nations not reached the same level in this respect, but in many backward and primitive countries division of labor can only be considered still in its infancy. Even in a country like the United States in which this subdivision has reached perhaps the highest degree in the world, there is still a great deal to be achieved, both for its own benefit and that of the world in general. Division of labor involves mass production, which assures an increase in the output of each individual allowing him in theory to enjoy greater abundance and a higher standard of living.

Here again the pattern of any single society with its fixed equilibrium point tends to set an upper limit to the desirable amount of division of labor. Let us explain the meaning of this statement.

In the example of our Lilliputian society it was shown that as a result of assumptions made regarding its pattern, meaning by this a specific wage scale as well as a fixed number of the components of the various classes, that the amount of commodities that could be absorbed by our society was represented by 280, and no more, even though the potential demand was considerably larger. The economic forces within that society were such that 280 represented the actual equilibrium point. As a result conditions were such that any increase in supply of any commodity would tend to lower its price and thus cause an immediate loss to the owners. It is natural that this part of society which was apt to lose by any increase in production would seek to keep the supply at a level where they could at least make a reasonable salary. For this reason an increase in the division of labor not only was considered unnecessary but actually harmful to their interests and, therefore, applied in a moderate scale.

This is the condition found in many countries, where the upper classes are instinctively opposed to any advance in division of labor. This attitude is taken because of the immediate loss they would suffer if it was permitted, even though they could expect greater profits in a subsequent period of time as a result of the expanded purchasing power of the population. Since technological advancement and inventions tend to increase production and supply, even in a backward and moderately civilized country, if they were permitted the condition described above would appear. How otherwise can we explain the unwillingness and hesitation on the part of those nations to introduce such improvements?

If the reader reviews the case where we analyzed the improvement produced by technological advancement (example case 4, page 366, he will find that one of the first effects is a reduction in price of the commodities affected, involving an initial loss to the owners in general. In a backward country one can expect and understand a conservative upper class unwilling to make any change or take any risk likely to upset a well-established equilibrium or status quo in which they enjoy a fair standard of living, certainly far above that of any other group in their nation. Lacking the necessary vision, courage and initiative, and often wholly devoid of interest in the betterment of their fellow-citizens who belong to a lower class, they are apt to take not only an apathetic attitude but often a definite opposing stand toward any kind of improvement involving industrialization. Lacking the interest and initiative of the only class with wealth, culture, and ability for leadership in such radical changes, the people in general, being too poor, ignorant, and helpless to achieve their amelioration, retain the same standard of living century after century, despite the progress made elsewhere.

It is evident that a higher standard of living in these countries not only would be beneficial to themselves but of great advantage to other nations as well. With their increase in civilization the commodities needed and utilized would be far larger than any amount they use at the present. Their expanded imports of manufactured products would accelerate activity in other lands. In turn they would be able to export those products and commodities for which they have better natural advantages, and by contributing to the total supply of the world would raise the standard of living of all. Unfortunately under present conditions, the advance toward the improvement for these lands is bound to be slow and imperceptible.

Now consider the influence of the new mode of life. First of all it is plain that such a system must start, take root, and eventually expand elsewhere, from a civilized and enlightened country. Only in such a nation can the leaders and their fellow-workers in this crusade find the proper soil for sowing the seeds that will raise humanity to higher levels of civilization and attainment; only in such a nation can one find the culture, courage, and vision among many of the masses who, because of their facilities of transportation and means of exchanging and disseminating information and ideas, would transmit the enthusiasm and inspiration to still many others and so impart a powerful impulse to an ideal that would eventually spread all over the world.

Assuming that this has already taken place, let us see how this mode of life could enter and eventually win over a country relatively passive and backward. First of all, the free and unobstructed will of the people must be respected and upheld, as one of the main pillars of society on which human relations must rest. This author means by this that he does not approve, advocate, or endorse in any way coercive or revolutionary activities aiming at the substitution of the new for the old mode of life, neither in our country nor in any other. Any such act would mean the imposition of the few upon the wills and desires of the many, and thus would become anti-social notwithstanding its elevated aims, tending to upset the social equilibrium and the established institutions of the country. We base our hopes and our faith for an ultimate realization of this goal not on such methods but on the honest conviction that in time, with full understanding of the aims and ideals to be attained, the cause will win over the rich as well as the poor, the old as well as the young, and gradually, with the brilliant example set by the nations that have already made that change, all others with their freedom of choice will approve and actually join their sisters in a system that will make a single nation or federation out of the many peoples of the world.

We want to emphasize that this new system of life must be consciously accepted and endorsed by all classes of society within one nation. Indeed, while it will represent a premium, it will also indicate that the nation is morally prepared and equipped to join the sisterhood of nations. This can only be done when all classes of society know and appreciate the step that is being made. We do not mean to infer by this that the vast majority of people in the nation must reach a high level of culture and enlightenment before such a step can be taken as this would preclude its adoption for many centuries to come but we refer to that moral rehabilitation that takes root in the hearts of men and makes us all conscious that we are all brothers and all equal in the presence of God. Moral rehabilitation does not mean knowledge, skill, academic or scientific accomplishment which often times are used for the downfall rather than improvement of humanity but it means goodness of heart, unselfishness, abnegation and respect for the sacred rights of men. Those with these qualities represent the actual spearhead of humanity and they can be found among the poor, the ignorant as well as the great and if they represent a small and inconsequential minority today, let them enlighten the others so they may become a majority. Then, and only then the nation will be ready to adopt the new mode of life.

Assuming that a backward nation has joined the federation, while this implies that the majority of the people desires and accepts such a change, we must still assume that many in the population will be opposed. In a country such as this in which suspicion, ignorance, and fear of losing prerogatives which have been handed down from ancestors, the EW could not be financed by revenues collected from inheritances. Such a radical change from ancient customs and methods would alienate a large proportion of the upper class and quite possibly prove an insurmountable obstacle. At first the law of inheritance must allow the heirs considerably more than visualized in this study. Only after a long period of time and when civilization and the standard of living have made great strides in the country, a larger part of the cost of the government may be made to fall more heavily on inheritances. Instead the EW, and other branches of the government, may have to rely at first on a moderate increase in taxes among the population in general, as well as on financial support from wealthier and more enlightened countries of the world. Once this minimum has been established, both the rich as well as the poor will gain from any increase in the equilibrium point, and thenceforth, due to the new fusion of interests, the path of progress will be clear of impediments and obstacles.

This subject will be taken up again later on when discussing relations among nations. For the present we wish to emphasize that an increase in division of labor, no matter in which form or in what part of the world, is bound to be highly beneficial to humanity in general.

As the production of all kinds of commodities increases and is absorbed by the population, as a greater subdivision of labor is attained, we know that sooner or later the faults of division of labor will likewise appear and be resented. Industry, originally on a domestic scale, will evolve into larger and more complicated forms in which the workers in greater numbers will have to be grouped in factories and the like where the means of production can be found. As a result of this change many individuals would lose their freedom of action, and independent initiative would be hampered and hindered. Again the well-being of workers would come to depend upon that of the industry, they would be obliged to live in the city in more restricted and crowded surroundings, and their feeling of importance would correspondingly decrease in keeping with their smaller individual contribution. But in a country in which the new system is well established, active, and organized, such offsetting factors will be hardly felt or noticed. All the advantages and improvements made possible by the new mode of life will be available to them, and as the number of work hours will be gradually reduced in relation to new inventions as well as to the basic wealth of the land, their higher degree of general culture will make them appreciate their blessing, and they will advantageously and usefully fill the extra leisure in happiness and enjoyment.

SECTION 8.

UNBALANCE OF TRADE

Another important factor introduced by the new mode of life is the rigid balance of trade maintained not only between distant countries but also between adjoining zones and communities. It has been noted in previous studies how important it is to the well-being of a nation to possess a certain amount of gold. While gold is not wealth in the sense herein assigned to this term, yet it has tremendous importance in initiating and maintaining a high degree of trade, not only within the nation but with others as well. It has been shown that as gold accumulates in the hands of a few men or nations, the consequences are detrimental not only to those who now own only a deficient amount, but also to those who wind up with much more than is needed. Under this unequal distribution of specie its real function (that of maintaining a high degree of trade) is dangerously impaired, and as the exchange of all kinds of necessary and useful commodities slackens, the standard of living of all nations is bound to suffer. In one respect our purpose of raising the purchasing power of the population in general and preventing too high a concentration of wealth among a few rich individuals (this accomplished by the law regarding inheritance) must be considered as a part of the all-embracing problem of keeping a balance of trade among men, communities, and countries. Modern thought tends to give the impression that a favorable balance of trade is highly beneficial to a country. While this may be true in special cases, it is not valid if applied indiscriminately to all nations. Undoubtedly a favorable balance of trade is beneficial to a country lacking sufficient specie, because this tends to establish equilibrium among nations, but for this very reason it is detrimental to one already possessing such reserves, because the tendency is to disrupt that equilibrium.

Gold, for one reason or other, has been accumulating in the vaults of the United States government and banks, and while this hoarding cripples trade among nations, it does not save us from the economic unrest general in our time. Assuming that all recognize the wisdom of a better distribution of gold among the nations, how can one determine the ideal amount that each country should seek to obtain honestly, without disrupting the equilibrium of the others? Turning to the fourth chapter of the present text, in which was analyzed the trade among three nations, and the effect produced either by lack or abundance of gold in any single country we must come to the conclusion that the amount that each should have cannot be definitely given, as it is related to imponderable factors dealt with in the following discussion.

Specie in some respects is related to and measures the total intrinsic wealth of a country, so that one which utilizes vast amounts of fundamental wealth, implying that it has great aptitude in manufacturing useful commodities for itself and for other nations, must obviously possess more specie than another either too poor in material resources or unable to develop them, and consequently maintains no such level of business and production. As any country's activity increases, specie is needed to keep it going. If the available gold in the world is too limited to perform this essential function for many countries, some other commodity internationally accepted as a medium of exchange, such as silver, copper, and the like, must be used in addition. By such a method the scarcity of gold will be remedied, and the disturbing effects of its scarcity entirely removed or relieved.

It may also be stated as a general rule that the amount of money that each country should possess must be such that it sustains a healthy international economic activity, and able to enhance to the maximum the local market. In other words, if several countries are operating under an economy by which many commodities cannot be imported for lack of money, this is a clear indication that the international economic balance is distorted, and that, while some hold a surplus of gold, others lack a sufficiency. The problem of establishing a more harmonious balance can be solved in steps. The first important move to be made is that of setting up among all nations that join the new mode of life a complementary economic balance by which their total supply of all commodities shall prove sufficient for the entire population of the federated system. This means that the excess possessed in some commodities by any nations must satisfy the deficiency of others without resort to abnormal prices. A second move will be that of equating in each country prices to costs. Then each must import an equivalent amount of commodities to balance the value of those exported. By following this policy the amount of gold imported or exported will be reduced to the minimum.

As shown in example three, page 176, the three countries, Alpha, Beta, and Gamma, by reason of their complementary economy were able to exchange their surplus products without any loss or gain in their amount of gold, and as an extreme case even Gamma, assumed devoid of exportable specie, was able to sell and to acquire her needed quota of commodities.

Now if a nation within that system should begin to import more than it can export, with a consequent outflow of money (Alpha in example four, page 179, this condition must be prevented from reaching the more serious situation in example five, where Alpha loses all her gold. So far as Alpha is concerned this can be attained by deliberately curtailing the importation of commodity c by such an extent that her balance of trade is again established. As this policy in some measure will affect other countries, a general agreement must be reached, by which Alpha should again be able to export more of her products in exchange for commodities imported. This is the attitude that the officials of Beta should have assumed in example six, rather than sponsor an increase in the local production of commodity a in an effort to reach self-sufficiency, which as was seen disrupted the economic balance of the three nations. In line with this attitude Beta would have sponsored instead an increase of commodity *a* within Alpha. As assumed in the fourth chapter, Alpha became unable to maintain the output of *a,* and from an original production of 200*a* dropped to 170*a*. Since substitutes had to be found by Beta to re-establish total production to the original 300*a,* these substitutes should have been developed in Alpha so that this nation could have maintained her balance of trade.

No doubt that our examples are quite crude and fail to represent in full the many intricacies of the trade relations among nations. Production of many commodities is usually undertaken by individuals intent upon their own profit, who are not apt to know or care about the implications that such and such an action may exert on the general economic equilibrium among nations. It is natural that as commodity *a* becomes scarce within Beta that its price should go much higher than cost, a fact not taken into account in our examples, yielding high profits for those engaged in that production. It stands to reason that because of these profits, many others intervened and introduced substitutes. We know what is the result of this policy when referred to the general background of the international exchange.

But in a well-managed federation of nations such results would have been avoided or greatly lessened and, as stated above, the increase would have been encouraged and sponsored in Alpha rather than in Beta when the normal production of the latter country started to fall. As the situation grows worse we may even justify some production of *a* in Beta, especially if the inability of Alpha's greatly increasing that production has been determined. As above stated, when a commodity tends to decrease, competition increases and its price rises to a level far above cost, enriching all engaged in its sale, and attracting others to seek success with substitutes. This, of course, cannot and should not be prevented if one wishes to uphold freedom of choice. Yet the fact that money now enters the country at an abnormal rate and that other commodities are becoming exceedingly difficult to export is a clear indication that international trade is becoming unbalanced, and regardless of the interests of minorities who may welcome such a situation, steps must be taken to prevent a further aggravation of conditions which would eventually be detrimental to the population of Beta, even if we disregard the repercussion upon other countries.

In the example only three varieties of commodities (*a, b, c*) are considered, whereas in actual society thousands are manufactured and exchanged internationally, so that in the above situation the officials of Beta could have easily sponsored in Alpha not merely *a* but many other commodities which, while not in direct competition with the manufacturers of Beta, would have still added to the world supply and kept the purchasing power of Alpha in as good condition as ever. Such a policy would have been the most sensible and beneficial to all concerned. In short, the rule that must be adopted in the new mode of life is that of maximum business activity within one country and maximum exchange among them all. Then if the imports and exports of each nation, whatever their size, are kept equal to each other, no abnormal amount of money need be exchanged, and each country will be left free to increase its production as it will not endanger the business activity and well-being of others.

Now what is meant by sponsoring the manufacture of commodities in Alpha? Since she lacks adequate money, and is, therefore, without the means of starting or sustaining new business activities, some capital from outside must be invested. As this puts money in circulation in Alpha, a greater volume of business can be maintained. The amount that needs to be invested does not have to be large. Business activity is usually related to credit and, as shown in previous parts of this text, credit may increase and expand to many times the actual value of money. If the EW encourages this business expansion toward those profitable fields indicated by the international economic situation, it is plain that this policy will be highly beneficial to Alpha. It will also aid others, because due to a greater international division of labor more useful commodities will be added to the world supply.

As capital is invested in the country, and business begins to improve, it is reasonable to expect that conditions cannot swing from bad to good in a short period of time. Reverting to Alpha, it is evident that in her effort to re-establish the equilibrium between import and export, she will seek to curtail the entrance of many luxury products. This will be done by imposing moderate tariffs. On the other hand she will try to export as much as possible. By agreement among her neighbors Alpha should be permitted to maintain during this period a favorable balance of trade, which means the value of exports should exceed that of imports. This trend will be measured by the increase of gold in the vaults of the government and banks.

We can then ask the question as to how long this trend should exist. As the money flows in while business improves, the average standard of living of Alpha will gain through the introduction of the two beneficial factors, namely the reduction of expenditures upon luxury commodities which had been a drain on the country, and the expansion of exports. As soon as the ratio of the money to credit reaches a predeterminate level set among the neighboring nations, the tariffs which had to be imposed will be gradually abolished. As a matter of fact, these tariffs should always be mild, only intended to prevent abnormal strain on the supply of gold, yet not apt to endanger the economies of other countries. As the level is reached Alpha's trade will be kept balanced from that point onward. This is not to imply that the standard of living will no longer improve, but that the progress and amelioration of Alpha will become integral with that of her neighbors. It must be borne in mind that her favorable balance of trade has been unfavorable for the others, and now it is just that she should join them in striving to improve their joint standard of living. In short, the nations should be compared to a group of men intent upon the attainment of a goal in which the effort of each is important. When any have fallen behind, the others must await their arrival so that all may join in exerting the supreme effort essential to the common goal.

As standard of living rises in a country, it signifies also that a greater exchange of commodities has taken place with other nations, and that more have been produced for its own population. However as credit can expand only to a specific ratio of the gold in the country, it is clear that sooner or later a limit will be reached above which it would be both improper and dangerous to go. If the country is rich in raw material or in other kinds of wealth, and money alone is needed for their utilization, additional funds could be invested or borrowed from abroad. At any rate, efforts should be made to keep the economy of the country complementary to that of the others. This, however, should be a matter to be left to the EW officials to decide, as they are in touch with their counterparts in other countries and jointly determine the kinds and amounts of commodities to be produced in each place.

We have considered so far the balance of trade among nations in a general way, and have also referred to the fact that on special occasions some favorable balance of trade may be permitted with the object of accelerating the recovery of nations which for any reason have fallen behind their sisters.

In some respects this rule must also apply to zones and small communities, because similar undesirable effects will be the result of causes that foster unbalance of trade. Referring to small communities, we all know that a large variety of products are continuously being traded with each other, some adding to their well-being while others, for instance the luxury type, proving detrimental. We wish now to concentrate upon this subject, and direct our reader's attention to a small community whose average standard of living is lagging because of its unfavorable balance of trade. We have noted that a large outflow of commodities tends to enrich the community in general, as this represents, among other benefits, a steady employment for many and a larger importation of money. Heavy import of goods, for similar reasons, tends to have the opposite effect. While it may temporarily add to the average standard of living, it means exhaustion of the available gold of the community as a whole. Generally speaking, and with all due exceptions, articles imported are usually more of a luxury kind than those locally produced. Therefore, it is reasonable to assume that these commodities are bought in a far greater proportion by the well-to-do element, who are able to spend more lavishly than the workers. As a general rule imports should be divided in two groups; in one we should include those bought to enhance the productivity of the land, as for instance, machinery, tools, and other kinds of equipment; in the other, those not essential to the welfare of the community, as expensive food products, jewels, works of art, furs, ornate furniture, and the like. These latter commodities, while of great importance to those who are willing to pay large sums for their acquisition, are superfluous on the whole to the welfare of the community, and may even be detrimental, if they should greatly impinge on the reserve of gold within the community. It has been explained that business in general, and therefore business within a community, is related to the amount of gold held. From this postulate one must conclude that whenever money leaves the community its business activity will be proportionately reduced. Take a village where a wealthy citizen has deposited in the local bank a sizable sum. Other people may have also banked their money, but say that the balance of the capitalist is by far the largest of them all. Because of these funds,

business in the community has developed to the advantage and betterment of the inhabitants. Assume now that the rich depositor withdraws a large portion of his money to buy some luxurious commodity.
Unquestionably he has the right to use money whenever he chooses,
but because of that withdrawal the rural bank will probably be left
in an embarrassing position. Because of that withdrawal the ratio
between money and credit may abruptly approach, even pass, the
critical level. It is obvious that efforts will be made by the officials
of the bank to extricate themselves from such a situation. This will
be done by retrenching and by reducing credit, and many individuals,
who had previously borrowed from the bank, will now be asked to
cover part or all of their loans. Even if disaster is averted, it is reasonable to expect that in future less credit will be available to float and
finance new local enterprises. This community, in short, has dropped
to another financial level on which fewer jobs will be available, and
the average standard of living will be correspondingly reduced. All
this ensues because of the original heavy withdrawal. Of course in
a free country we must not prevent the investor from using his
money at his own discretion, but a way must be found to avert or
at least decrease the effects of a situation of this nature, and the
EW will prove equal to the problem. Whenever the community
finds itself facing unbalance of trade, by law a tax should automatically be imposed on purchases of a certain kind of commodities,
related to the amount of unbalance. The larger the unbalance, the
higher the tax, and vice versa. The revenues thus raised will be used
by the EW to cushion the effects of such purchases on the local
people, and naturally will be expended at the discretion of its
Manager. They may be deposited in local banks to protect them
from bankruptcy; or otherwise loaned to sponsor enterprises intended
to improve the economic position of the village. At any rate, the
tax should prove a brake to all purchases that tend to unbalance
the economic position of the community. How much the tax should
be, and how it should be levied, are details immaterial to a study
of this kind. If the new mode of life is finally adopted, additional
study will have to be made by those at the helm, and a formula
found that takes into consideration the kind of commodity, its price,
and the amount of unbalance in the community. As the condition
improves, this tax should be gradually reduced, and finally cancelled
once the balance of trade is re-established. We realize, however, how
easy it would be for anyone who wishes to avoid payment of such
a tax to withdraw money from the bank and make his purchase in

some other part of the country. One way to prevent this evasion would be that of taxing any withdrawal larger than some stated amount within a specified period of time. If the individual can then prove that he has spent that money on non-taxable commodities, his tax will be refunded. For small items of luxury a tariff can be applied also, as they enter the community, so that eventually it will be paid by the ultimate consumer. In any event, the money so collected must not be used to pay the expenditures of the city government but used to counteract the local unbalanced condition. With such a plan the community will protect itself against wanton and irresponsible squandering.

SECTION 9.

MORE REASONABLE REGROUPING
OF THE POPULATION

The division of land into zones will help to set up efficient economic units, better serve the people, and facilitate rather than hamper their progress and that of a nation.

In the present set-up of society, mankind is composed of small, medium-sized and extremely large nations. The small nations often do not have the prerequisites for a self-sufficient economic system. Because of the variety of interests controlling a nation, millions of people are made to gravitate toward centers other than those to which they feel attracted. Needless to say that such divisions prove a heavy burden to them, and a great obstacle to the advancement of society. In the new mode of life these factors will no longer exist, because no matter to which zone any community may belong the primary interests of its people will always be paramount, and all communities will remain free to gravitate toward any center, independently of the main interests of their zone. The division of the land into zones, instead of being dictated by ethnological or religious considerations, will be made with the purpose of arranging uniform economic units, and this course will best serve the people of the zone. When a community is found to gravitate toward one center rather than another, it is reasonable that it should be assigned to the zone in which its economic center belongs. However, even in this case the free will of the people will be taken into account, if the opinion of the majority differs from that of the experts to whom has been assigned the task of dividing the country into zones. Likewise if that relationship should change in the process of time, every community will be permitted to transfer to another zone if that is the will of its people and of the zone to which it wants to belong. One of the purposes of dividing a land into zones is to simplify the problem of production and distribution, which now will deal with a relatively small and compact population, bound by similar economic bonds and interests. All the PW representatives of such a population, no matter which part of the zone they may happen to represent, will have similar interests in the handling of the economic problems affecting the zone as a whole. This will facilitate the choosing of a harmonious and unified body of men who will represent the people versus the higher branches of the PW.

Besides the unification of interests among small and compact groups of people, this subdivision of the land into zones has an additional valuable advantage. Throughout history there has been the tendency to join people under the same flag and the same government. Often enough no opportunity was given the people to express their wishes on the matter. While certain nations have valid justification for their existence, such as economic background, religion, customs, language, and traditions, others are merely an amalgamation of races of various origins, frequently with entirely different civilization, interests and aims. Yet the central government, made up of men who consciously or unconsciously represent the strongest class of the nation, usually lays a course beneficial chiefly to this class, dragging their enslaved minorities in their wake. Serious dangers evolve in the existence of these great nations. Frequently quarrels, disputes, and feuds flare up between communities of different nations close to each other, which eventually are taken up by their respective governments. Nationalism will soon distort and magnify those misunderstandings, and from insignificant incidents they rapidly become serious threats to the peace of the world. Not once but many times they have produced the spark that ignited war, and brought destruction to millions.

There is also another factor that must be taken into account. In any dispute between two communities of different nations, there is always a certain amount of right and wrong on each side. Quite true, one community may be more in the right than another. However if it belongs to a country poor and insignificant in comparison with the other, there will be little chance of seeing its rights respected and upheld. "Might makes right" has always been and remains at present a decisive policy in the life of a nation. This is wrong and unsound. Because of this kind of injustice that is apt to develop among nations of different size and power, we see an additional advantage in the advocated division of land, as this serves to place people on an equal level as to rights and responsibilities. The nations that unfortunately have fallen prey to dictatorship would no longer have their youth and resources placed at the disposal of unscrupulous minorities who do not hesitate to spread terror throughout the world for their selfish aims and interests.

Let us assume for example that Mexico, the United States, and Canada have joined into a nucleus of nations living under the new mode of life. In line with our plan, these countries have been divided into zones, by taking into account the economic interests of the communities concerned. Some of those which were integral parts of one country may find it to their advantage to be incorporated with zones originally belonging to another. Religion, language and customs, will be respected and maintained, no matter in what zone they now belong. In such a system as this, nationalist feeling will gradually abate, and eventually blend into brotherhood and love for all people. This, of course, is an ideal, and its realization must come through the gradual evolution of man. Meanwhile one can expect that discrepancies and disputes may arise among communities of different zones. If no agreement is reached among the authorities of the two contending communities they may be appealed to the officials of their respective zones and again lacking agreement to those of the federation. Quarrels such as these are bound to be viewed by the federation with impartiality and justice, and nationalism will be less apt to intervene. Since each zone represents a small fraction of the combined population of Mexico, the United States, and Canada, the overwhelming opinion of the federation, unswayed by sectionalism, race feeling or fanaticism, is certain to give an unbiased verdict. Its judgment and counsel will prove on the other hand, a powerful factor in maintaining peace and cooperation among zones.

Even so, it is well to remind our reader that such quarrels are not likely to occur. With few exceptions, disputes among zones are bound to be rooted in clashes of economic interests. Since each zone will be assigned a specific index related to the standard of living of the population and to the total wealth of the zone, each community will receive the advice and assistance its index entails. To the extent that the index is intrinsically bound up with the particular economic condition of the zone and is not influenced by favoritism and re-gionalism, each community will know its rights as well as its duties. As this policy will be rigidly applied by the EW officials of every community it is evident that friction and feud will rarely occur.

All zones will have the same voice in the PW branch of the federation and none will be afraid to protest if and when their rights are infringed, as they have the assurance that they will receive a just and sympathetic consideration of their problems. Within this great agglomeration of zones, people not only will be free but will be conscious of their freedom. We say that the people in the Balkans are free, in that they have governments of their own, and somehow are able to steer their national affairs without apparent domination by others. But is this true? Each of those countries, poor in material resources and gold, lacks the prerequisite of a self-sufficient and independent economic whole. The life of any nation depends on its ability to acquire vital raw materials and commodities, either from countries like themselves or, more likely, from the larger and more powerful nations of Europe. Because of this dependency their actions and allegiance must be consonant with the interests of those coun-tries, and thus their freedom is only hypothetical. Add to this the fact that the rivalry and animosity that has always existed with each other and between the races bound together to form each of the Balkan nations, prevents the attainment of even that minimum economic level that might be expected from the wealth of the land. Again their limited physical power, as well as their dependence on outside assistance, makes them highly vulnerable to foreign dictates and threats. How different their lot if they were part of a federation of nations that had adopted the new mode of life!

We have explained in the course of our study that the standard of living cannot be the same throughout the federation. While each community and zone under the auspices of the new mode of life, will reach a level far higher than that under present standards, it will still reflect the wealth of the land. We are confident that such differences will not promote feelings of resentment and greed. We base this assumption on the honest belief that, influenced by the new codes and ethics, no one will covet wealth which he has no right to possess. It is to be expected that the opportunities enjoyed by the people of New York and London (at the center of important highways of the world) should be far more than those enjoyed by the citizens of other communities not so generously endowed. The same holds for zones or for nations. Now it is unthinkable that conflicts should arise between two adjoining zones because of this discrepancy in standard of living. The fact that the rich zone contributes like the other and probably more than the other to raise the well-being of the poorer zone, will kindle friendship rather than antagonism between the two populations. Moreover, as previously shown, this difference will be mostly represented by the amount of effort required by the respective inhabitants. At any rate, no matter what their wealth and importance, all zones being represented by the same number of people will have the same power and weight in matters of national policy. If hostile feeling should ever arise between two of them, the fact that they represent a very small percentage of the total population of the federation means that the wealth and importance which either may possess in relation to the other will be greatly minimized and disregarded by the other zones, who will consider only the moral merits of their claims. Thus their verdict will exert a powerful moral pressure because of being based on righteousness and equity. As their judgment is rendered it will be up to the contending zones to abide by the will of the others, with the assurance that justice has been done.

SECTION 10.

INFLUENCE OF THE EW ON THE INDIVIDUAL

Let us see now how the new mode of life will change the life of each citizen. It is plain that those in the poorest class of society will be favorably affected. If they are willing to work and contribute their share to the betterment of society through their intelligence or plain physical strength, their wages will be such that they will be able to enjoy and utilize a proper amount of commodities and services, no matter what price these may reach on the market. With the passing of time these commodities and services will gradually increase, and this will be to the advantage of such workers and their families. The time devoted to monotonous and uninteresting work will be gradually reduced without affecting their purchasing power. The reduced hours of work will mean more leisure for enjoyable activities and pleasures. If properly used, this will enrich and fill each worker's life and make him a better man and citizen. The road to progress and betterment, the road to a higher and better level in society, will always be open to him if in possession of the necessary qualifications and ability.

It is also plain that anyone on a higher level of society will enjoy additional commodities and services consonant with his larger wage or salary, as the direct result of his increased contribution to the well-being of society. In those cases where prices of various commodities have to be raised to build additional demand, his wage or salary will also be increased. If he is among those fortunate who can afford all the necessities of life, the extra pay will mean a larger supply of services. As with the worker, the reduction of hours will further increase his standard of living.

The professional and the artisan whose livelihood depends on services supplied to the public will have all to gain and nothing to lose from this new mode of life. The wealthier and the more stable society is bound to be to their benefit and advantage.

The business man or manufacturer, as a general rule, will find in the EW a just and sympathetic organization willing to furnish advice, assistance and cooperation so that he may increase his contribution to society and to himself in particular. Naturally he must conform to and abide by well-established codes and ethics that prevent abuses and injury to society in general. This aid may save him from bankruptcy in times of crises, and even when this cannot be avoided, the EW will save. him from exorbitant losses by giving him the opportunity to sell at just and moderate prices. No limit will be placed upon the amassing of wealth if honestly pursued.

The heir of large fortunes will be allowed to receive a sufficient percentage of inheritance to live in comfort and ease. With that wealth left to him, if old and sick he will not have to fear for the future, if young and healthy he will own a powerful lever that may raise him to his father's position of importance and leadership. We wish to repeat, while on the subject, that the law of inheritance, as submitted by us, is only an attempt to place wealth where it will be most beneficial to society. If and when the new mode of life is accepted and given a trial, better and more enlightened minds than ours will bring to the subject the necessary consideration as to the practicability of such a far-reaching reform. As seen in a previous part of this study, the maximum inheritance is made up of two quantities. One is represented by a fixed amount of wealth equal for all in the nation; the other takes into account the index a of the community where the wealth is located. Thus if this index should greatly increase in a subsequent period of time, one can easily see that the heir will feel he has not received the full extent of his due, and that his standard of living is not as high as it should be. To this interpretation of the inheritance law we wish to present the following objections:

(a) Not one but several inheritances may be received by the various components of a family, and this will greatly add to his standard of living.

(b) The inheritance as given by us has been calculated with the view of providing a standard of living far above the level where subsequent increases or decreases of that index could produce any appreciable difference. If one person enjoys an income of $10,000 per year in comparison with another who receives $9,000 it cannot be said that they have a different standard of living, especially when all they need for an easy life may be furnished by an income of only $2,000.

(c) Unless the heir is physically and mentally unfit to work and produce, the return from his wealth will only be part of his income.

(d) The taxes that each individual will be called upon to pay will take into consideration for a limited number of years the fact that the index was varied. This clause in the law of the land, therefore tends to correct that obvious injustice, such as it may be, and defeats the previous contention.

Due consideration given all exceptions, great wealth as well as great business enterprises tend to become cumbersome and uneconomical as they expand. We would like to believe that the instinctive desire of those men who are in possession of fortunes and wealth is not only that of providing for the well-being of their children but also that of their grandchildren. However many in ages gone by, no less than contemporaries, have not hesitated to dispossess other children in favor of one, for the sake of perpetuating their fortunes. Thus we are forced to believe that this particular distribution of wealth is not made for the sake of their heirs but, bluntly stated, only to perpetuate themselves in that wealth. Now this new mode of life, while it upholds to a large extent the will of the original owner of wealth, prevents such injustice from being perpetrated by placing a limit to the amount anyone can inherit. As the passing of great fortunes from one individual to another will no longer be possible, all who under normal circumstances would have been left out of the inheritance will find in the new mode of life a protector of their rights and interests.

SECTION 11.

SHIFT OF POPULATION WITHIN THE LAND

At this point of our study we wish to add a few ideas and suggestions which, if adopted, will aid our new society to acquire a stable relationship within itself as well as with other societies that have not chosen the new mode of life. First in mind is the question of the shifting of population from one land to another in the quest for better opportunities and advantages. It has been emphasized in previous discussions how the standard of living of a people settled on a specific area will improve because of the beneficial influence of the new mode of life. However this improvement cannot go on indefinitely, but taking into consideration the technological advancement and the knowledge of how to utilize to the best advantage the basic wealth of the land, that improvement will finally reach an upper limit, related to the wealth of the land itself and to the size of population settled thereon. The richer the land, the higher the standard of living the population can reach, so that in a country poor in resources only a moderate standard of living can be attained, compared with a richer one. For the purpose of discussion assume that the population is living on a poor land. Let us see then what can be done to increase its standard of living. The region in question is one of many others forming a country that has adopted the new mode of life.

It is a well-known postulate that in any nation wealth is not equally distributed over its entire territory. Of course when one refers to the amount of wealth on a land we imply that it is measured with the yardstick of present knowledge of recognizing wealth as, after all, that is what counts. This wealth of the land may be known either in the form of actual value, as that of mineral resources or high agricultural potentiality; or in desirable location, as situated on the main highways of commerce between prosperous places. Whatever the kind enhancing this land, there is a tendency for people to gather in great numbers in key places, where they form heavily congested cities, while other areas retain few inhabitants. A case in point is the state of New York, and in greater or lesser degree the other states located at the extreme East or West of the country. Meanwhile vast expanses in the Midwest and the South have in comparison only a small population. The reason given above is responsible for this condition. Even admitting that much of this sparsely settled land is unsuited for comfortable living, as in the middle belt where heat, drought, and wind erosion make it unfavorable for cultivation, or in the mountainous region with its extremely cold climate, there is still in this country a tremendous area that could easily sustain a far larger population. Usually in these latter-cited territories life is hard and monotonous, opportunities to make a decent living are few, and the general tendency of a part of its population is to emigrate where prospects are brighter. It is not pretended that the entire central part of the United States or the South is in anything like the situation described, as this would be an utterly absurd statement. Everyone knows that there are many important and flourishing cities in this part of the country, which derive their wealth from the fertile surroundings and are a great factor in making the United States the fabulous country of the modern age, but one must admit that the population per square mile in many of these states is extremely scanty compared to that of Connecticut or Massachusetts. Even in a sparsely settled state, such as Nevada, there is a tendency to drift to the biggest towns of the state, because there will be better opportunities than in the country. Since no law prevents this sort of shift from one place to another, there ensues a vast emigration toward the metropolis. Cities like New York, Philadelphia, Chicago, grow by leaps and bounds, due to this influx. In times past much of this increase was due to immigration from other countries, but this is no longer so at present. Although the city offers more opportunities, there is a limit above which the condition of many living there becomes far worse than if they had remained in the country. People dwelling in the poor quarters or slums of a city, without being conscious of the fact, are far worse off than those of the same class and background in the country.

In this world of quick and cheap communications between distant places this condition should not prove a serious problem. In the course of our study we have seen that part of the EW program is that of sponsoring new industries, especially those devoted to the manufacture of vital commodities with a scarcity factor larger than one. Many such industries, especially where location is not paramount to their success and well-being, could be opened in small towns far from the large centers, with the aim of decentralizing population as much as practicable. With the combined effort of several of its branches as for instance those of the "Industry Regulation" and "Labor Control", such a program could be carried out successfully throughout the land, both in the rich regions and the areas that are not so fortunate. This would raise the standard of living of the population as a whole, because now all sections of the country would cooperate to that end. As the standard of living of the population rises to reach a uniform level, the urge to emigrate elsewhere will be greatly reduced. Of course an absolute leveling-off of the standard of living of the entire population is unattainable, because of the upper limit set by the basic wealth of the land itself; but such a policy will go far in decreasing these differences without subtracting from that maintained in the most prosperous parts of the country.

Even if people residing in the city are able to enjoy a larger variety of commodities and services, and, therefore, from an economic standpoint reach a higher standard of living than those in a small town or in the country, one should not forget that there are many other imponderable factors that enrich the life of an individual, such as for instance the far healthier and invigorating air of the country compared to the congested and vitiated atmosphere of the city, which decreases considerably the aforementioned discrepancy. Since the world is made up of many individuals of varying outlook and desires it can be easily foreseen that, while there may be a transfer of population from the country to the city, there will be also an approximately equal one in the opposite direction, especially if the standard of living in both places is not so disparate as at present.

The problem presented by the population leaving the country altogether for another one is a topic to be treated later on in this text when relation between nations comes under study. For the present it may be noted that in the vast majority of cases emigration takes place from a poor or over-populated country toward a rich or sparsely settled one, as people are eager to move where more opportunity for a decent living can be found. From the standpoint of the poor or over-populated nation, whose standard of living is low, sending some of its surplus population abroad solves serious dilemmas. As these emigrants depart, the effects of over-population decrease, and permit better conditions for the rest of the nation, as the ratio between wealth and the number of people dwelling thereon tends to increase. To this it must also be added that as many individuals leave the country in quest of better opportunity a good portion goes without family and is likely to send back commodities and money, the circulation of which improves the national financial structure. This exchange of manpower may also prove a blessing for the rich country, especially if it is in an expanding period of its life-cycle. This influx or immigration of individuals, especially those who are young, healthy, and strong, constitutes labor wealth needed to utilize the fundamental wealth of the land, to the great benefit of its population. But as we are concerned with the welfare of humanity in general, rather than that of any one country in particular, the transfer of population, if carried above a reasonable limit, may be detrimental to all. To be sure, when the United States was at the beginning of its development, and had only a few millions living on its land, immigration from Europe was highly desirable and equally helpful to the new country as well as to the old. At present the United States has a population of 150 millions, and its peak of development is still far ahead, however we do not dare to visualize what would be the outcome if its gates were left wide open to immigration. It is easy to guess that if this policy was adopted, the population would rapidly increase because of the stampedes from other lands, and in a relatively short time congested conditions would develop, with consequent lowering of our standard of living. On the other hand, Europe would be left exhausted, as so many of her youngest, healthiest, and strongest people would have left for America. This would mean that much of the imponderable wealth represented by the human factor, the emigrating element, would leave Europe much poorer, even though actual wealth in the form of funds, food, and furnishings had been sent back to give their kinfolk a false and illusory feeling of enrichment. As a result the remaining people of those European countries would no longer be a vital factor in the advancement of humanity. Without detracting from the great and positive advantages added by moderate immigration which tend to establish a better balance between wealth of the land and population, one should not lose sight of the fact that a far better method for improving world conditions consists of our ability to aid the economic structure of Europe to such an extent that the urge of emigration will not be so strongly felt. But this again awaits later discussion, when the present text will submit ways and means for the solution of this all-important problem.

SECTION 12.

BANKING SYSTEM

Among the factors that exert great influence on the well-being of a nation a solid and healthy banking system must be considered among the most important. It was pointed out in the first chapter of this study how powerful is the effect of the banks and lending houses on the economy of a community or nation. We have also observed that, due to the private character of most banks in any country, they are apt to look first after their own interests, and secondly after those of the nation. During periods in which an excessive amount of gold flows out of the country, the position of the banks becomes increasingly precarious as the margin between specie on hand and outstanding bank notes tends to reach the critical point. Any bank so affected, in order to safeguard its own standing, becomes reluctant to finance new enterprises which would draw further upon the reserves. This attitude affects the general public through the higher interest charged upon any new loan. The result of this policy is a slump in business activity, and together with other factors is responsible for the resulting retrenchments and depressions. Likewise in those periods in which an excessive amount of specie enters the country, a large percentage of this gold finds its way into the banks. This fact, it is true, will stimulate and maintain a business revival, as the banks now become very anxious to lend more money, and accordingly reduce the rate of interest required for new loans. But the possession of large amount of gold, while an important factor in business activity, is not the only one, and if times are not ripe for an economic revival the banks will find themselves paying an increasing amount of dividends while still collecting the same rate of interest on loans made. Again to safeguard the bank, the dividends paid the depositors will be decreased. Among these many will be found who depend on dividends for their livelihood, as the money deposited in the bank may be all they possess, the result of lifelong saving. It is evident that abrupt variation in the amount of gold in the country is likely to injure many people. Needless to say, the stabilizing of these fluctuations will go a long way toward maintaining a stable economy throughout the nation.

Consider now how the influence of the EW can be exerted to the best advantage of the nation. In the course of time the EW will accumulate vast funds used for purchasing commodities and transactions of various kinds based upon its multiform activities. This money will be kept in vaults under its own supervision, and in case of necessity deposited in banks. Any bank that finds itself short of specie because of the necessity of financing local enterprises, and forced to reject others as a result, could apply directly to the EW organization for a sum of money to be deposited in its vaults. This will increase the ratio of the specie on hand to the notes outstanding, and therefore will aid the stability of the bank. The EW before making this deposit, will satisfy itself of the sound and reliable status of the bank, and review with its officials the loans contemplated to new enterprises; and not until all phases have been analyzed to its own satisfaction should the specie be transferred. This deposit naturally will draw the normal rate of dividend. This is just and proper, as the bank derives a profit from the financing of enterprises only possible through the EW's aid.

In the same way, if a bank should find itself flooded with too much specie it could avail itself of the fact that the EW organization can be asked to take some of this surplus. This means that the EW assumes the duty of paying dividends to the depositors of that extra specie in the bank. Hence the rate of dividends will not be decreased by the bank, and the investors will be correspondingly protected. In turn the EW may be asked to deposit part of this specie with some other bank anxious to obtain it. The EW then would act as a clearing-house for the banks of the country, and become an important factor in maintaining the banking system on a solid and healthy foundation. Now as long as specie can be shifted from one bank to another to the best advantage of all through the medium of the EW, the financial position of the latter will not be affected because what it receives from a set of investors will pay to another, and this will retain the same rate throughout the country. However if a large amount of gold enters the country, the chances are that the EW may become the depositor of far more than it will be able to dispose of among the various banks and as a result the rates of dividends will have to be proportionately reduced. This will influence the rates throughout the country, which, while it may encourage a larger volume of business will also decrease dividends for many investors. Such influence, however, will be felt by all the banks of the nation, and since this decrease is spread to the entire population, the offsetting effects produced by a large amount of specie will be minimized. At such times as these the EW will change its policy from a rigid balance of trade to one in which some specie may be exported in return for luxury commodities and the like, which tend to increase the average standard of living. This may be accomplished by the removal of any kind of regulation adopted for the purpose of maintaining the balance of trade, and as many of the rich will make more purchases abroad, the equilibrium will tend to be re-established. Likewise the EW will consider the financing of new enterprises in countries that have adopted the new mode of life, with the purpose of increasing supply of such commodities as cannot be efficiently produced at home. This financing will be done directly by the EW if the banking institutions are not willing to assume that large responsibility and risk. Thereby it will increase world production of commodities that can only be manufactured in certain localities, will improve the economic position of poorer nations and zones, and by stimulating business activity there maintain a wider exchange of products at a decided advantage to all.

To a certain extent such financing could also be extended to nations that have not adopted the new mode of life. Such steps however must be out of the EW's jurisdiction, and must be taken directly by private organizations and financial institutions abiding by the advice of another branch of the government which considers the political implications of such a policy, and takes the final responsibility. By using the methods described above heavy fluctuations of specie in the nation will be prevented, and since the EW will act as a superbank, the interests of the population as a whole will be protected.

NOTES ON GOVERNMENT AND ELECTION

In closing the second part of this study it is well to make some statement on the future form of the government, reserving until later a more detailed analysis of the subject. It is quite apparent that many duties that now are performed by our government must be transferred to the EW which as noted, will be one of the branches of the future government. As earlier explained, the EW is made up of experts qualified for their particular task. They have reached their position of responsibility through promotion after many years of experience. No one in this organization achieves preeminence, because whatever his position, he will always have one official or group above him, with power to terminate his services if this is deemed necessary to the well-being of the people or the organization itself. With a system such as this we can feel confident that corruption will be eliminated or greatly reduced, and the interests of society protected and upheld. There are, however, many more tasks belonging in the proper powers of the government that are not taken care of by the EW. These may include those of a protective nature, as for instance the national defence, which requires an army, navy, and air force; the domestic security, which requires a police force, courts, etc., the maintenance of moral standards and the protection against fire, flood, and storms on land and sea. Other tasks are typified by those intended to develop spiritual and material qualities, as for instance education, and religion; caring for rivers and harbors; conservation of the nation's resources; and maintaining a monetary and postal system. These are a few of the government activities that could not very well be undertaken by the EW or by private enterprise.

The kind of government is immaterial to the well-being of society, as long as the fundamental liberties of the individual are respected and maintained. A monarchy, a republic, a democratic or absolutist administration, can be equally good or equally bad for society, and their influence will depend on the type, integrity and honesty of those who happen to be at the head of the government. In the second chapter of this study, in which were analyzed the philosophies underlying the governments of several of the most important nations in the world, the conclusion was reached that, with the exception of Naziism, in which no philosophy at all was identified, all aimed at some kind of ideal supposed to raise mankind to a higher level. However all, in more or less degree, fail to take into account the nature of man, and behind the high-sounding phrases of brotherhood and universal progress, all governments exist first of all to protect the interests of minorities to the exclusion of the majority within a nation; and next the interests of one nation to the exclusion of those of other nations. And even democracy, which in our estimation springs from a nobler philosophy than the other forms of government, since it represents the people and from them derives its power, has an unstable nature as to capacity for remaining a pure democracy, and not only can harbor corruption and injustice but lacks the prerequisites necessary to improve the people's standard of living. Obviously the adoption and establishment of the EW in any nation along the lines indicated in the present text would be in itself such a formidable advance in the right direction that the actual type of government would become of secondary importance. However as successive countries choose the new mode of life and form a federation rigidly bound by economic interests, it seems best that they should adopt the same form of government, for the sake of avoiding confusion and possible friction with each other. We naturally visualize the future government as one that represents the people, and from them holds its power. As each nation decides upon the new mode of life and enters the federation its population must be willing to have its country divided into economic zones. Nine such zones or states, formed on the basis of economic considerations rather than race or religion, will constitute a superzone.

Each zone will maintain its own EW organization as well as its own government, with the duties described in previous chapters. The EW of each zone will take orders from and work in cooperation with the Central Branch located at the capital of the superzone. The government of the zone will perform the duties enumerated at the opening of this discussion, with the exception of defense against external foes. Since all zones will have approximately the same population, and are bound to cooperate with each other for the betterment of all, it is unthinkable that animosities should ever arise among them. The fixed and rigid rules of the EW will maintain justice toward all, and no minority, whether a group of individuals or of zones, will ever be in a position to dictate or impose upon others as they will lack the means of aggression. Just as it is unthinkable to us that any of the forty-eight States in our Federal Union would physically clash with another, or one province in Italy declare war upon another, this will be more or less the prevailing condition among the zones of the coming federation of nations. No effort will be made to change the customs, language, or religion of the various populations, and any change that may develop will be only through the natural process of evolution. In cases where one or more zones fall into disagreement with the government of other countries which have not adopted the new mode of life, the solution of such problems will be left to the individual governments of those zones with no interference on the part of the federation. Thereby it is certain that many international clashes will be eliminated, since this great agglomeration of nations, due to its governing laws, will not make its weight felt against other countries, within reasonable limits, and therefore the economic strangulation often referred to in this study will no longer exist. However any aggression on the part of a foreign country against any zone of this agglomeration of nations will automatically become a declaration of war upon the entire federation.

It was mentioned that the government of each zone will be left free to follow local economic policies of special benefit to its population, and to some extent zones will even be permitted to sign economic treaties with foreign countries. However, for the sake of coordinating the interests and aspirations of the entire population of the federation, we must visualize a supergovernment over the zones, to which will be assigned the important task of representing the entire federation and safeguarding its interests throughout the world. This government will also organize the military defense of the federation.

As stated, the actual form of government is immaterial to the progress of the country, as this depends wholly on the uprightness and probity of its officials, however from the nature of the new system of life, it would seem that a monarchy or empire are not particularly suited for that task. With no animosity or preconceived antagonism against any King or Emperor, much less against this form of government, one must suspect that the life-cycle of the kingdoms and empires is fast approaching its natural end. Monarchies had their important place in history, and in past periods came to represent the natural form of government for numerous peoples who had different needs and outlooks from ours. As the vast majority of the people belonging to any remaining empire or kingdom will eventually realize the tremendous advantages inherent in the new mode of life, and will begin to desire its adoption, as it could be indicated by a referendum, one cannot doubt that the King or Emperor, if truly concerned with the betterment of his subjects, should freely and willingly abdicate for the good of his people, and for this magnanimity be remembered with gratitude and affection in the years to come.

In passing we wish to say that the system of taxation will have to be similar to those enforced by the most civilized countries of our time. Future economists will naturally devote their knowledge and talents to this important subject, and work out improvements and simplifications. At any rate, the revenues from inheritances, used mostly for the betterment of society, will be too small to cope with the multiform expenditures of the government, and therefore all people must be called upon to contribute according to each individual's capacity. In a modern country the government's revenue is derived from four chief sources: Industrial earnings, taxes, fees and loans. In a study of such nature much space cannot be devoted to this topic, which is exhaustively treated by any textbook on economics. However, what we wish to emphasize in these pages is that every effort should be made to reduce to a minimum the amount of indirect taxes. This statement is made in the firm conviction that every citizen should know, and feel the amount he is actually paying for the support of his government, so that he may take greater and keener interest in public affairs, and be better prepared to fight graft and incompetency. The views of the people will be made known at election time, and the more enlightened the public the better chance the country will have to elect honest and capable citizens to important positions.

At this point it seems proper to advocate a new method of election which, although imperfect, represents a forward step in the effort to obtain a clearer picture of the public will. First of all, it is pleasing to note that in various countries women, who make up half the population, are now allowed to vote, and thereby enabled to express their will and to exert their influence in public matters. This is definitely a step in the right direction, and it is to be hoped that the day is not far distant when all nations will follow the example set by these pioneer countries. But does numerical majority represent the true will of the people? To us it seems irrational that, at least at the polls, the vote of the most ignorant individual of the country should have the same weight as that of a justice of the Supreme Court. True, this is one of the fundamental axioms of pure democracy, but is democratic only on the surface, as we shall seek to prove in the following analysis. As repeatedly expressed in this text, one of our main concerns is that of bringing about changes that will be for the good of society in general, irrespective of the fact that their application may be harmful to individual interests. Dedicated to these principles, and emboldened to raise the call to action whenever and wherever we feel that injustice is being done, we refuse to call just and democratic a system that gives the same importance to the opinion of the most backward and the most enlightened member of society. And again numerical majority, especially when one considers that so many votes of the lower classes can be easily swayed by unscrupulous politicians, does not necessarily mean that issues adopted by such methods are the best for the community or for the country in general. Bribery and political machines are devices that influence multitudes into voting for or against particular candidates or issues. As a generality such tactics, cleverly disguised under the form of enlightening the public opinion, are actually used to foster the schemes of the few at the expense of the many, and often to the exclusion of those who have so voted under the impression that it was to their advantage. Such tactics would not and could not take root and flourish if the vote of the public was revised to represent its intellectual and moral power rather than its number. Of course we cannot entirely prevent bribery and intimidation from being used, as any method of coercion would be antisocial, no matter how justifiable its purpose but the new method will decrease considerably the influence of these practices, without any application of force or compulsion. That all eligible citizens should vote comes as a matter of course, since all are components of society, all directly affected by current issues, and their opinion should be made to exert its just and proper weight in the final expression of the popular will. However for any election to be a true democratic expression it must give every individual his proper importance, not because he is one of the many but because he is a responsible and reasoning citizen who backs up his vote with his judgment, knowledge and experience. It is natural that those who are best qualified should be given greater authority at elections. In short, our method is as follows:

As at present, 21 remains the age when boy or girl becomes eligible to vote. In itself each vote will be counted as one. If the young voter has completed the elementary school and can display the proper certificate to the electoral board, this vote will automatically be counted as two. The ballot issued in this case will have a different color from the one first mentioned. In the same way the value four will be awarded the vote of a citizen who has graduated from high school, the value eight to that of one who has graduated from the university. All these separate values will be on ballots of different colors, so that in computing the election returns the proper value will be recorded for each ballot, according to its color. Age also should be considered in the evaluation of the judgment an individual can bring to bear on problems that come to the public attention. The value of the vote of anyone would be increased by one when he reaches the age of 30, again at 40, 50 and 60, in turn. Under this method a professor who has reached the age of 60 will have a vote of 12, of which 8 will represent his education and 4 is based on his age. His vote, in other words, will be equivalent to that of twelve essentially uneducated boys of 21. We realize that it is difficult to evaluate, much less to compare, the judgment and wisdom of citizens who may be far apart in background and outlook, but since it is impossible to reach any perfect method, we can feel that an election held on these lines will better represent the sane and responsible part of the poulation, and be less apt to be influenced by corrupt minority groups.

We wish to emphasize the fact that we have not included in our evaluation of the voters' influence on the election either his salary or his wealth. The fact that he is rich does not give him the right to a higher level in the electoral vote. After all he may have come into possession of great wealth through bequest or inheritance, and this is not proof of his judgment or wisdom in public matters. If any person is elected to a responsible position in the government, such as PW representative, it is just that he be awarded a greater influence at the polls. The simple fact that he was chosen by the people is sufficient reason to qualify him as an outstanding citizen. His vote will be comparable to one who has graduated from the university. It is understood that at the end of his public service his vote will revert to the original level. This is done not because his judgment and wisdom are less than before but to prevent other people of similar background and education from feeling unjustly treated.

Our reader may object that advanced education does not necessarily mean greater wisdom in solving problems of public interest, where often only a higher degree of common sense is needed, and this quality is more or less ingrained in the individual rather than acquired through school and study. Again our reader may point out that by such a system a far greater representation is given to the upper levels of society than at present. Such power in the hands of those who have more knowledge, more culture, and in general belong to the upper and middle class of society is no assurance that they in turn will not use it to enhance the interests of their class to the exclusion of the lower. The educated individual can be just as selfish as any one else, indeed more successfully so, and the basest instincts of men unfortunately are not erased by culture or knowledge. After all the poor have acquired such privileges through many centuries of hardship and suffering, and certainly should not lose the only tool they possess that gives them the power to make their will known in matters in which they may lose so much and so decisively.

Answering the first contention, we agree that common sense is not a privilege of those who have more culture, and that there are many cases in which individuals of limited education can and do display far greater acumen and wisdom than others who have gone through long periods of schooling. These, however, represent the exception rather than the rule, and while such may be the case in numerous instances, by and large those who know more are also more alert and interested in public matters than the average of the great mass of uneducated people, who are not in the habit of thinking out things by themselves, have only a scant knowledge of issues that affect them only indirectly, and rely on the judgment of others when it comes to decide the pro and con of questions that come to the fore. Their vote often does not represent their interests or their views on the subject, but only the interests of those who either through coercion and bribery or more subtle methods of persuasion lead them to vote one way or another. Viewed from this angle, the universal ballot is not a true democratic expression and another form, closer to the will of the people must be found.

As to the second contention, we wish to warn our reader that such methods of election must be used only when no economic matter of great importance, or change in the set-up of society, is to be decided by the population. In any such case the referendum and not the election must be chosen to gauge the true will of the people. Indeed in all cases where people are liable to be so greatly affected and where the issues will be so simple, fundamental, and clearly defined, we believe that the vast majority will vote according to their true interest, less apt to be swayed and therefore all, no matter what their education or position, must have the same standing at the polls.

Now who is going to decide which method is to be used when various issues come to the fore in the life of a nation? The PW whose duty among others is to supervise the activities of the EW, is in our estimation the best qualified body for such decision. The components of this body, as already noted, do not receive a high remuneration for their services, retain their particular profession or trade for their livelihood, and have been chosen by the people because of their character, integrity, and honesty, so they act as protectors of public rights and interests. Their knowledge of economic issues that come to them through the normal discharge of their duties as members of the PW gives them the necessary basis upon which to judge which method should be chosen. At a reasonable time before election the various questions that have to be voted upon must be submitted to that body, and through an election of its own, it will decide which issues will be settled by regular election and which by referendum.

In this manner the fundamental and basic rights of the people will be preserved and protected. In cases in which no great or fundamental economic change is at stake it seems to us that an election conducted in the newly-evaluated style is by far the most desirable solution. This will put an end or at least a brake to all

kinds of political manipulations and methods that decide issues by
sheer numerical weight.

As a generality we can say that a large proportion of the issues
that arise in the life of the nation will be settled by election rather
than referendum. The reason for this statement is that with the
acceptance of the mode of life most fundamental economic issues
important to the welfare of the people will be incorporated into
the Constitution, form part of the laws of the land, and accordingly
will be automatically enforced by the EW in the normal discharge
of its duties. As soon as the necessary motion is imparted to the
new mode of life in the nation, no one, either inside or outside the
EW, will be able to change or alter these policies. The many balances
and counterbalances introduced in the activity of the government
will be sufficient guarantee against that possibility, and the life of
the nation will run smoothly and without deviation from the path
that was chosen for the good of the people and of humanity in
general. It comes as a matter of course that any change in the
policies of the EW must be approved by referendum among the
people, not only of the zone or superzone which may desire that
change, but of all the nations forming the federation.

CHAPTER X

CAUSES OF STRIFE AND DISUNITY AMONG NATIONS

IN PREVIOUS chapters we have considered relationships among classes within one nation. Various causes of strife and attrition were analyzed and we finally submitted a plan that should promote unity and cooperation among them. We feel confident that as a result the population in general will improve independently of outside forces. The maximum attainable standard of living of an isolated nation is related to the wealth of its land. This maximum, however, may be easily surpassed if better relations and greater volume of trade can be established and maintained with other people and nations. In this part of the text we shall widen our horizon and include in our discussion all the nations on earth, large or small, at whatever degree of civilization and life-cycle. Their needs, aspirations, fears and instincts will be studied, in order to single out the negative forces that guide their conduct and their policies. These forces, mainspring of friction, suspicion, and misunderstanding, bring in their wake war, chaos, and misery. If we could add to these forces that tend to alienate nations from each other, others that besides effectively counteracting the just mentioned negative ones, bring order out of chaos, cooperation out of distrust and selfishness and prove also beneficial to all, we may expect humanity to rise to un-dreamed heights of understanding, achievements, and happiness.

For a clear study of these negative forces, and a better under-standing of the resulting economic dislocation of the world, there must be presented first what might be called a brief resume of the economic evolution of mankind.

At the beginning of civilization, when modes of transport were in their infancy, trade was by necessity limited and crude, while the division of labor, chiefly responsible for our present progress, was still insignificant. The manufacturing centers of those times depended on whatever raw materials could be found in the immediate vicinity.

Many products, which we now enjoy because of our ability to acquire raw materials from distant lands were wholly unknown and the standard of living was bound to be far lower than we now can comprehend. In passing it must be noted that progress in the last 100 years far surpasses that achieved since the beginning of civilization. This makes one wonder why it was so slow in earlier times. It can be safely said that before the last century humanity has advanced at a very slow pace, and whatever now seems simple and obvious to us actually took thousands of years to evolve and reach the actual application. One of the main reasons was the abysmal ignorance of most of the population in those days when whatever education and knowledge existed were limited to a small fraction of the population (the priesthood and nobility) who more often than not let the rest of humanity wander in ignorance, first because of the enormous undertaking required to spread knowledge and enlightenment with the limited means available, and second because of the great power inherent in knowledge and culture which it did not serve their basic interests to share with the lower classes. By this it is not intended to convey the idea that education was prohibited to those who did not belong to the nobility, as this would be misleading, but little or no effort was ever made to popularize education among the masses. With their knowledge and culture, the upper class had the tools with which to guide the country to its own best advantage and interest. Since the egotistic nature of men is the underlying motive of their actions, the upper class was never willing, as a body, to relinquish its power and conscious of this, never made an honest effort to raise the cultural level of the people. An ignorant and dormant set of serfs was easier to dominate and enslave. Because of this all the advances of mankind in the past were attained through tribulations and suffering of multitudes of martyrs who even gave their lives for the establishment of sacred rights of men. These souls, coming from every walk of life, were animated by a higher ideal than their own betterment or that of their own class, and fascinated by their beautiful dream became insensitive to persecution and hardship.

Man, the ruler of the earth, man who slowly unfolds the laws and the secrets of nature, man who is gradually learning how to control the forces of nature, can also be and has often shown himself the cruelest being upon earth, cruel not only to beasts but to his fellowmen as well. Since time immemorial how much craft and cunning he has shown, how much ingenuity he has developed merely for the purpose of devising more terrible weapons more thoroughly to destroy and even annihilate his fellowmen? Are we in this century of ours any better in this respect than our progenitors of antiquity? Definitely not. The issues seem to have changed, but on the surface and in name only; the incessant struggle between the powerful few and the weak many has been going on from the beginning of time, and is raging right at present. This fact is of such importance that we feel justified in reviewing some of the many instances of strife and upheaval that have occurred in the past.

ROMAN EMPIRE

Take for instance the rise of Christianity under the Roman Empire. This new religion taught by Christ and spread by His apostles was bound to inflame the imagination of the millions who belonged to the lowest class of Roman society, and of the millions of slaves who in their utter misery and abjection must have clung to the feeling of being human, as much as anyone else. The wonderful and idealistic principles proclaimed by Christ, the promises of a better world beyond, the implicit statement that all men are equal in the presence of God, did naturally arouse in these people feelings of self-respect, and the necessary courage and determination to stand by their convictions, despite the dictates of the dominant classes. This religion, as can be easily understood, naturally made its greatest strides among the poorest elements of society. These people, by embracing the new faith, learned also to hope for a better life in the future, and this gave them the moral force to endure the toil and misery of their lot that lacked any prospect of betterment or amelioration. The dignity and self-respect that was acquired by those who had accepted the new religion, this moral force of being able to stand up against the powerful of the time, despite the suffering and martyrdom involved, could not help but disturb and alarm the oppressors over the significance and implications of these theories as opposed to their well-established supremacy. Instinctively, to protect themselves against this new challenging force, they resorted to the usual methods of disseminating slander and calumny among the ignorant who composed the majority as yet unacquainted with the ideals of Christianity. Using falsehood and prejudice to win the mob's allegiance and support, the ruling class sought to erase the new religion from the face of the earth, and in the name of the ancient laws and of the established religion slaughtered and massacred the Christians by the thousands, and used human beings for the entertainment and pleasure of barbaric masses. As a result many Christians went to their deaths as human torches, many Christians were fed to the beasts. But in the face of so noble death, of so much courage, calmness and joy displayed by the innocent and helpless many who went to their martyrdom with faith and hope and love, the people as a whole became increasingly conscious of the nature of the new creed and this led to further martyrdom among the newly converted masses. But as Christianity kept on making further inroads in the hearts of men, the upper class finally became powerless to cope with the unmistakable fact that Christianity had started a new civilization with new codes and new ethics, had supplanted the old myths of the Roman religion and in short that Christianity was here to stay.

Now was this upper class actually defending its pagan creed, as some of the writers of the time wished people to believe? We doubt it and reject this purpose and intent. This naturally was the official version, but the real issue, as always, was the unwillingness of the strong to grant the weak any concessions which might diminish and endanger (no matter how faintly) the prestige and power of the upper class. Thus this one-sided fight lasted for centuries until more and more aristocrats, realizing by instinct that the struggle was hopeless, decided to join the victor's camp and acknowledge the new creed (whether in spirit, or in name only, is immaterial). This eventually shifted the scales in favor of the new religion, and the martyrdom of the Christians finally came to an end. Emperor Constantine, however sincere he may have been, was nevertheless an opportunist. By becoming a Christian he prevented the threatening disintegration of the Roman Empire, and not only kept himself in power, but likewise the class he represented, which by now was rapidly losing the leadership that had made Rome the capital of the civilized world. However, the fall of the Roman Empire did not take very long to come. The high ideals of the new religion, along with other factors, did not furnish the fighting spirit necessary to repel and subjugate the hordes of barbarians that constantly were battering at the gates of the empire. The spirit of sacrifice and resignation to events in this world could not very well stem the tide of the invaders, who saw in the ebbing empire an easy prey for their ambition and hunger.

Between the time when the new religion took over and that when the empire succumbed to the onslaught of the invaders, did humanity gain because Christianity had won? It seems to us that the physical and moral gains acquired in those centuries were too small to compensate for the enormous suffering earlier endured; too slight compared to the great number of people who had given their lives for the new ideal. In retrospect, and without entering the field of religion, its aims and its dictates, was that sacrifice justified in relation to the benefit that humanity was actually able to derive? From a moral and ethical standpoint it was justified. The new religion, in establishing itself through that sacrifice, taught mankind a new and better mode of life consonant with the principles of justice, fraternity and love among men, and set a goal for humanity to aspire to in the endless centuries to come. As to actual moral rehabilitation of man, that sacrifice was not justified, because notwithstanding the physical progress which we have witnessed up to the present era and which has given us a veneer of moral standards, the actual teaching of Christ has never been fully applied and adopted. The realization of those ideals for which so many have given their lives has yet to come. Therefore, when in saying that sacrifice was not successful, there is no intention to imply that no effort should have been made to bring those ideals to earth, and that things should have been left as they were. This is not what we have in mind to convey. As a matter of fact, even if that sacrifice had been ten times as great it would still have been justified if it had only succeeded in keeping alive somewhere in the world the longing for justice in the hearts of men, and the determination to raise humanity to the level that represents its ultimate goal and the very essence of its existence. Our statement that this sacrifice was not successful must be interpreted only in the sense that, compared one against the other, the suffering of humanity during this period far surpassed the moral rehabilitation it was able to achieve. As to the physical amelioration of the people in general, history is not clear as to the actual condition of the people at the time when the new religion was adopted, but with the incessant invasions and the disintegration taking place throughout the empire during that period, the standard of living of the poor was bound to be very low, and to this extent the sacrifice was not justified.

The reason for this absence of amelioration among the poor, and the lack of defensive military power on the part of the Romans in general, can also be ascribed to another fundamental factor. The entire elite of the empire, having lost its previous position and prestige, eventually disintegrated and dropped to approximately the same level of the masses. Lacking leadership, the empire became easy prey to the outside.

As it is generally the case when the people are not morally and intellectually prepared to take advantage of fortuitous situations, the dispossessing of prerogatives hitherto belonging to the upper classes does not necessarily mean that the rank and file of the poplation will be benefited. The only result is that the upper class sinks to the same stratum as the lower, and leaves the nation open to foreign rule. The decadence of the Roman aristocracy, that had been the bulwark of the national power and greatness, eventually allowed the barbarians to surge in, and while the conquerors were less civilized than the vanquished, they were sufficiently strong and ruthless to subjugate their victims as they saw fit, and once they had stripped the people of the few prerogatives they had gained through centuries of struggle, the civilization that had produced Cicero, Virgil and Caesar sank into submission and servility for centuries to come. Humanity, to free itself from serfdom and oppression, had to start the fight all over again.

FRENCH REVOLUTION

Another classic example of clash between classes of society is the French Revolution. Here one has an uprising of the lower class against the tyrannical barons, counts, and the king who, by claiming the divine right of possession over lands and peasants, ruled the country for their shortsightedly selfish interests. As a generality, no thought or consideration was given to improve the condition of the people who starved, toiled and suffered under the crushing load of poverty and of taxes, the latter imposed to sustain the glittering life of the nobles. Again, little effort was made to eradicate ignorance and superstition among the people, who thus took their misery for granted and as part of their lot that could not be improved because imposed by the will of God.

But slowly, with the passing of time, and because of glaring and scandalous injustices which now and then were perpetrated by many in the upper classes, a feeling of resentment took hold among many in the masses. These, however, were too divided and disorganized to exert a restraining pressure against the brutal and organized minority. Those among them who dared to challenge those supposedly divine rights paid with their lives for their audacity while the others unwillingly had to bow to the will and dictates of the tyrants. But, as is evident in nature, there is a cycle for every-thing. Civilizations come and go, nations reach greatness and then decline, nothing is absolute and stable in this world. The life-cycle of nobility was fast reaching its end. The aristocracy, which had in the course of history its proper place and justification, had long ago reached its zenith and the forces that had brought about its advent and development in the life of society were ebbing before other forces. Great minds such as those of Voltaire, Rousseau, and others, too powerful to be silenced by methods used against the poor and ignorant few, came to challenge these privileges and divine rights in their publications. The pitiful and unjust condition of the poor was emphasized and made vivid in their immortal prose and in their ironic poetry. The dawn of the new mode of life was be-ginning to appear on the horizon. Many of the young generation who were sufficiently wealthy to acquire education and thus able to enter that special group of the middle class that gradually was becoming more powerful, were the obvious leaders of any popular insurrection that aimed at the breaking of the chains that were keeping the people enslaved to a decadent and corrupt nobility. As usual in such circumstances a minor incident (in this case the storming of the Bastille) started a train of events which eventually evolved into the great revolution that was to be felt all over the world. While in many countries the incipient uprising was suppressed at the very beginning, the upper class of France was unable to stem that tide, and the nobles found themselves confronted by the necessity of fleeing the country, or perishing. If captured by the mob or the Committee of Public Safety that by now had reached a stage of savage lust and uncontrolled desire for blood which did not discriminate between innocent and guilty, they would surely lose their heads under the blade of the ever-busy guillotine.

Much life was sacrificed on the altar of the new ideals, Liberty, Fraternity, Equality. But did this show of force on the part of the people against the powerful few give humanity that liberty, fratern-ity, and equality so prominently proclaimed? NO. Mankind, as a whole, was still too ignorant and ill-prepared to realize and enforce those principles, too apathetic to raise itself from the miserable condition in which it had existed since time immemorial, and after that turbulent and futile show of force was again ready to serve a new master and a new tyrant. By this we do not wish to infer that the French Revolution did not bring some betterment to the people.

Indirectly humanity did actually improve because of that titanic eruption. As a result of the Revolution the nobility was definitely on the wane in all nations, and the great power held by kings was markedly reduced. But to our mind the greatest contribution of all was the greater opportunity given the masses to acquire knowledge and education. The new ideas, because of this new factor, swept the oceans and the continents, and planted in the heart of man the seeds of future progress and advancement. But even these great strides in educating many among the people were too small to change the nature of men bred down the centuries to suffer and slave away for heartless masters. Those who, through their talent and knowledge, could benefit because of the new changes made possible by the Revolution, became the middle class and, as will be presently seen, some of them eventually supplanted the upper class and became the new masters of society. But despite this negative result, the education now spreading at a far greater pace than before eventually produced telling effects in the world in general. Tremendous progress was made in all branches of science. This in turn gave rise to the industrial era to which we now belong. Humanity, however, freed from the serfdom of the nobles, once again fell prey to a new master and tyrant: Capitalism.

While everyone now is nominally a free man, free in his choice of work, free in his quest of happiness, contentment, and economic sufficiency, yet a dense tangle of imponderable obstacles and circumstances prevent him, unless endowed with more than average talent and ability, from reaching that goal, and instead make him an unconscious slave of a new master: the capitalist. The products of his work, his skill, and his very life have become a commodity bought or sold according to the law of supply and demand. The set-up of society is such that he has no other choice but to become an instrument in the hands of those who control the capital and who at times, are hardly less ruthless and unconcerned over his well-being as in times gone by. In other words, the enslaving of humanity has changed its form but not its nature. How long this condition will last no one can really tell, but the struggle and strife between the weak many and the powerful few has been going on for a good many years already, and it will still go on until that freedom of choice, that equality of opportunity, and fraternity in the sense of cooperation and understanding will exist in reality rather than in an abstract form as now.

RUSSIAN REVOLUTION

To be sure, the French Revolution took place more than a hundred years ago, and is fast becoming past history no longer consonant with our times, but the clash among classes has a glittering example in modern times as well. This refers to the Russian revolution, which is a direct result of our modern civilization and mode of life.

It is a matter of general knowledge that Russia before the revolution was one of the most backward countries among the civilized nations of Europe. Under the Tsarist regime, the great mass of the people, ignorant and extremely poor, toiled under the dictates of a small and powerful upper class. The lack of even the most rudimentary system of communications, an industry resembling the pre-industrial era, the insufficient number of schools and institutes of high learning, contributed to keeping the population apathetic and ignorant. That the people suffered under such a regime, there cannot be any doubt in our mind, but it was too ignorant, too weak and disorganized to revolt against the powerful and efficient minority. However, the unavoidable contacts with other civilizations such as those of Germany, France, and England could not prevent ideas filtering across the borders, could not prevent many of its people from observing and comparing the miserable standard of living of the Russians in general with that of other countries, and thus give rise to a determination in their hearts to find a remedy for that appalling injustice. The great thinkers and the leaders among them, baffled and distressed by the lot of the proletariat in the world in general as well as the poor people of Russia in particular, likewise became resolved to eradicate injustice wherever found. However, conscious of humanity's innumerable failures in the past to break the chains of slavery they came to realize that equality among men, which had become the supreme goal of their life, represented a too remote possibility if sought through peaceful methods, and that stronger and more violent steps had to be taken if that goal was to be attained. In their eagerness to establish the new order they formed the Communist party, and dissociated themselves from the Socialists, who were aiming at similar results through peaceful and constitutional methods. Among their important aims we may mention the following: to promote a union among the proletariats of the world, to place them under a single international red banner, to assist one another to overthrow their respective governments, to displace the existing established and controlling minorities or upper classes, and to place the various states in the hands of the proletariat, that is to say, of the many rather than of the few. Uprisings and abortive revolts within Russia were attempted even before the first world war, and as a consequence many Communists were deported to Siberia, while others fled to various countries. This was the fate of many leaders, among them Lenin, Stalin, and Trotsky. This persecution, however, intensified their determination, and by clandestine methods they kept in touch with other leaders scattered all over the world and despite many setbacks, they worked incessantly upon the expansion and consolidation of their party, and made plans for taking over the reins of the government. Their chance finally came with the defeat of Russia in the first world war. Because of the disorganized condition of the country it was easy for them to start the revolution and eventually place themselves in power.

The first part of this study has already analyzed the ideals and the goals which the Communist party seeks to establish. At that time we also gave our views as to the faults and merits of their system, and shall not add more on the subject. What we wish, however, to emphasize at present are the following facts: The Russian revolution in effect was not made by the people of Russia, but by a small minority composing the Communist party, which even now, after many years, constitutes a very small fraction of the Russian population. Humanity in general was not ready, as in the past, to take advantage of situations that had worked in their favor and, as usual, the power shifted from one minority to another. The Russian population, because of its extreme ignorance, had no clear idea of what the revolution was supposed to accomplish, and while many of them, idealists as well as opportunists, joined the rank and file of the party on their own volition, the new order had to be imposed by force upon the rest of the population. This, of course, meant that, while the previous upper class was being dispersed and destroyed, a new one was taking its place, and this new dominant class was now the Communist party. The Russian people, as a generality, had no more to say in the affairs of the state than when the Tsarist regime was in power, had merely changed their masters, but had not acquired that liberty and that justice which is the goal of all generous and free thinking people.

At this point we wish to inject our pessimistic appraisal of the situation, and state that the time when humanity will be ready for such responsibility will never come. Some of the reasons on which we base our statement are the following:

(1) Government policies, which usually embrace many branches and activities of the state, are usually too complicated and complex matters for the average individual of any population to comprehend and judge for the good of the country.

(2) The average person, as a rule, is mainly interested in his own private undertakings, and only pays scant attention to matters that do not seem to affect him directly.

(3) The average person is apt to take sides, add his weight as vote-getting power, or use other means for exerting pressure, to promote or defeat issues that seem to affect him personally one way or another. His attitude, as a generality, will be that of preserving and possibly improving his own interest, irrespective of the effect that such issues may have on the population in general.

(4) Due to the usual apathetic attitude of a large portion of the population, unscrupulous politicians often work out tortuous methods to establish themselves in power, and thereby derive advantages for themselves as well as for the class they represent.

(5) When conditions become unbearable and revolution is necessary to displace entrenched minorities, because of the nature of things, that revolution can only succeed if guided and organized by superior individuals. These, in turn, having overthrown the previous dominating minority, are apt to take their place in the affairs of the state, because after all the government can only be administered by a relatively few persons. The rest of the population has no other choice but that of placing their trust in them for their own good and that of the country. As these leaders are human, and, therefore, with the same basic instincts of men, either they themselves or those who in the course of time will replace them in office, will take advantage of the power in their possession to perpetuate themselves for their benefit at the expense of the others and thus start a new cycle in which the minority oppresses the majority.

In stating all this we have no nation or type of government in mind. Such cycles have occurred in the past, and we see clear evidences of their recurrence at present, and since instincts of men are not apt to change materially in the future, we can foresee that conditions are not apt to improve, at least not so long as our mode of life remains what it is at present.

Now the obvious solution of the problem is that no person or minority should ever be allowed to assume and retain power, no matter what the contribution to the public welfare and the importance of the position, and that there should always be either another official or group of officials with the necessary power to check and regulate the activities of the others. This principle has been adopted in the EW organization. If the EW ever flourishes and takes over many of the present government activities, we can easily see that not even the FM, a position that could be compared to that of a king or president of a country, is the actual head of the state, as he no less than anyone else will depend on a higher body or authority to retain his position. All have to contribute their best for the good of the country and humanity in general, and yet no one will ever be placed in a position where he could retain his power against the will of the majority should his policies not be consonant with the interests of the country. On this account, we feel that the basic liberties of men will be protected. As to the economic interests of the population in general we know that the standard of living of each class as well as of each zone will be known, measured and compared with the basic wealth of the land and with the standard of living of other classes and other zones. As the policies planned to improve the economic welfare of each group will automatically take that situation into account and will be incorporated in the Constitution, they will be out of the political field and un-affected by minority pressure. The necessary steps will be enforced by the law of the land, and this is bound to be advantageous to the people's interests. Only in this way can the human factor in the affairs of the state be properly checked and counterbalanced, and the true interests of the population protected and enhanced.

Returning to the analysis of the Russian revolution, we pointed out in the first part of our study the fallacy of the Communist ideals.

Personally, the author does not believe that people are born equal. Equality cannot be attained, no matter what efforts are made to that end. It is not in the nature of things. To expect then that all people should share equally from the efforts that are made collectively would be just as much an injustice as when a favored few, of which a good percentage were without qualification, took the lion's share of the produce of the land. This would mean a swing from one extreme to another. It is true that in recent years a system of dis-crimination has been introduced, by which those who do not work are publicly condemned and punished, while those who do more than their share are praised and granted a higher standard of living. The great incentive of accumulation of capital is, however, removed, either by inducing the individual to donate to the state whatever capital he may have been able to save, or by its outright confiscation before or after the death of the owner. For all practical purposes the building of fortunes becomes ineffective as an incentive to greater achievement, and barring a few glittering exceptions, the vast majority will do only so much and no more. This is bound to have a detrimental effect on the quality and quantity of commodities produced. It must be admitted that great strides have been made in both quantity and quality, that the average standard of living has increased considerably during the various five-year plans, and we must pay homage to the tremendous efforts and sacrifices of the Russians during the second world war. On the other hand it is not right to state that these achievements were possible only because of the new ideas and mode of life. In a country as poorly managed as that of the Tsarist empire, yet rich in natural resources, and with vast expanses of fertile land, any improvement in the management of the affairs of the state was bound to increase production and raise the standard of living. This, however, does not mean that this progress will continue indefinitely. Time alone will tell. As to the aggressiveness and heroism displayed by the Russians in the war, this also cannot be ascribed to the new mode of life, as the instinct of self-preservation, the instinct of defending family, home, and country, is one of the basic reactions of men, and any country will defend itself to the best of her ability. In possession of the necessary weapons and manpower, it will not only stop the enemy legions, but is also apt to repel and destroy the enemy to prevent future aggression. Greece did all she could to halt the Germans, but, despite the innumerable heroic deeds of her people, she was too weak to stand for very long against the panzer divisions and confronted by such a superior power eventually had to give up open resistance. What we wish to emphasize is that the fall of Greece cannot be ascribed to any inferior mode of life possessed by this people in comparison to Russia, and thus less morally prepared to resist the impact of invasion. This phenomenon proves only that no matter how great the courage, the heroism, and the spirit of sacrifice, the size and wealth of the country are also extremely important factors to be taken into consideration. Russia did well but so did Greece, France, England, Germany, and in short, every country that was involved in the war.

It must be emphasized that the new ruling minority of Russia, in the effort to find solution to the many problems with which they were confronted, and yet consonant with the principles of Communism, tried several large scale experiments of which many caused untold hardship and misery to millions of people and were also responsible for actual obliteration of populations. Among the many trials and errors, the Communist party deserves some praise and commendation for the intensive educational program carried out in the lower classes. Yet this educational program is not carried out in that spirit of openmindedness and fairness by which all are free to judge by themselves the pros and cons of many controversial issues that separate Russia from the rest of the world. Many young Russians, born after the revolution and quite skillful in many fields of human activity, have a very scant idea of the prerevolutionary history of their country or that of other nations. In this we see a definite purpose on the part of the new ruling class to keep the people as ignorant as possible of what is going on in the world today. This purpose is made evident by the Iron Curtain enveloping Russia and minor satellites. In short, in this educational program we do not detect any altruistic desire of spreading the knowledge among the masses for the sake of raising their intellectual level and ability of reasoning, but for the definite purpose of imbuing as many of the youth as possible in the principles of Communism. This one-sided education serves and has served also the purpose of creating a vast number of fanatics completely blind and deaf to what is being done or said in other countries and by this the Communist party hopes to perpetuate itself into office because of the blind subservience and fanaticism of the many who have come to take Communism as their very life and religion. This blind and powerful tool in the hands of the new rulers can be then unleashed at any time and depending on needs, not only against other people, but mostly against the people of Russia if they should ever revolt against the new tyrants. But in this, as in other instances previously discussed, the Communist leaders have failed to take human nature into account. Granted that the one-sided educational program will make many blind and fanatic and ready to any action no matter how brutal, many others will resent this brutality as, after all, we believe in the basic goodness of men. Many of those who will naturally acquire the capacity of intelligent thinking will revolt against these dogmas which are utterly inconsistent with human nature and tend to endanger rather than improve humanity. Of these, many will be ruthlessly suppressed and murdered but, like the advent of Christianity, their blood will go to germinate millions of others and at the end the Russian people, like all others, will finally become free and willing to adopt the new system of life and join the new family of nations. We must conclude that the intensive effort to educate the people, even though serving a different purpose, will finally prove beneficial, not because it will help to keep Russia in the communistic side in the years to come, but because with that knowledge Russia, finally freed from the shackles of Communism, will become a very important factor in the advancement and evolution of humanity.

At present it is still too early to gauge the results of the Russian revolution. As we see it, it is still in a state of flux. Its ultimate influence on humanity has yet to appear, and one can only guess at what will be and what trend it will finally take. Right at present a great spirit of nationalism seems to have pervaded the Soviet Union, and the Communist leaders appear officially to have temporarily abandoned any design of world revolution in favor of more practical objectives. Russia, as a result of the war, has annexed entire nations, as Lithuania, Latvia, Estonia, part of Poland, and much of Rumania, besides additional areas fringing her large empire. Needless to say, these populations were not anxious for annexation. Because of her new power and prestige, Russia is also forcing herself into the affairs of other countries with the specific purpose of installing governments serving Russia rather than their people. That this will eventually stir unrest is a matter of course. We see also that Russia is working for the establishment of a vast sphere of influence far beyond her immediate borders. How this power will be used if acquired is also a matter of conjecture. Taking history and human instincts as a guide, we fail to discern any altruistic motive in the action of the Russian government in extending her power outside her borders. Whenever one nation conquers another with the purpose of subjugating its people and making them economically subservient to its own interests and dictates, it will never attain its objective, because resentment and hatred will be the natural result which in turn will breed uprising, revolts, conflicts and massacres. The Russian leaders, who so valiantly opposed the oppression by the Tsarist regime, are in turn becoming the oppressors.

Will the few advantages won by the Russians be permanently retained? Will the present leaders, or those who in due course replace them, perpetuate themselves into power to the exclusion of others, and form a new upper class and a new tyranny? Again time alone will tell. As a conclusion we must restate our previous assumption that at least for the present the advancement of mankind can only occur by jerks and hard fought battles and that its progress cannot be continuous because for every step forward there is always a recession that cancels a good deal of the gains.

CONCLUSIONS AND ADDITIONAL THOUGHTS

Keeping the previous examples in mind, it is easy now to see why humanity made such slow improvement in the past. The reason becomes apparent when we consider the abysmal ignorance of the people in general, too weak and helpless to stand up for their rights. This explains the presence of so many backward countries in the world today, explains the existence of colonies, as no country with an enlightened and progressive population can ever tolerate foreign domination. But, because of the enormous strides continually being made in educating the lower classes of the world, one may feel confident about the future of humanity. As this enlightenment increases, more people will acquire the necessary willpower, ability and determination to erase injustice, discern for themselves what is best for their interests, and no longer tolerate impositions from above, whether within or outside the country. That this education is still very thinly spread among the people of the world is self-evident. One need only focus his attention upon the vast populations of China and India where only in recent years has a feeble consciousness just begun to appear. At present turmoil and unrest are apparent in many parts of the globe indicating that this consciousness is just beginning to exert itself more and more in the affairs of the world. We can safely say that those countries with a more enlightened population have gone very far in the acquisition of liberties in relation to backward ones. This because the masses, conscious of their rights, have been able to exert a more determined stand toward the recognition of those rights which would have seemed out of the question only a few centuries past. This process we anticipate will continue at a far greater pace than at present, but as no class will ever relinquish any advantage without a struggle, we foresee also in the near future great disorders in every nation unless a way can be found by which the gains of one class will not endanger or injure in any way the interests of another. The same principle likewise will apply to nations. We are confronted at present by nations possessing great wealth, while others are utterly impoverished and unable to maintain a decent standard of living. Usually the poorest nations are also economically dominated by the rich ones. Those whose populations have still a low degree of education take their lot as a matter of course. To nations that have reached a high stage of civilization, this economic subjugation is unendurable, and it is only human that they should react against that condition. As raw materials represent the basic sine qua non for progress, it is natural also that there should be a frenzied competition for their possession. Now if a way can be found by which all could obtain a just quota of these essentials without endangering the standard of living of other nations, a great step would be taken in alleviating the apprehensions of humanity regarding war and famine throughout the world. To this topic we shall return later on in our study.

The foregoing has been included in our analysis to stress the gigantic struggle carried on by humanity since time immemorial. This is still going on under our eyes, and will continue until rich and poor, aristocrats and peasants, races and nations, awake to the simple truth that progress is open to everyone only through cooperation, friendship, and understanding of each other's rights and needs. A unanimous effort toward a better life for all without regard for nation, race, minority is imperative. That day when this basic principle is really understood and actually put into practice, when men cease to destroy their brothers and extend instead a helping hand to those in need, will represent the dawn of a better era, and the present period will seem as the Middle Ages to future generations.

From the discussion just ended we are able to identify at least three of the chief negative forces that stop or slow down the advance of progress and civilization.

(a) *The ingrained reluctance of men, classes, and nations to grant opportunities and prerogatives with even a semblance of endangering their interests.* As a result selfishness, hatred, and intolerance find ready soil in which to grow and thrive. Conflicts are in due time bound to ensue. Due to the magnitude and intensity of these feelings the chance to reach a just solution of the inequality among men is bound to be small. Such instincts and feelings, which have had so long to develop through years of suffering, subjugation, and squalor, give rise to forces which like a tornado are bound to destroy all in their path, and conditions from one extreme rush to another.

(b) *The extremely low level of education among the vast majority of the population of the world.* This puts them at a great disadvantage in the struggle for survival. The statement may be made that strife is more apt to occur among people with a higher degree of civilization and, therefore, our contention may seem faulty. However, what we wish to point out to our reader is that the fundamental clashes that occur within the most forward societies of the world today only indicate that they are in a period of change, and that these disorders will come temporarily to an end when a new condition of equilibrium has been reached. What this condition will be we are not prepared to say at present, but from what has been inferred above, this new future equilibrium may be compared to that instantaneous position of the pendulum at the end of its travel, ready to start a new swing in the opposite direction. This because excesses will be made in one direction, which, after a short period of time, call for adjustments; i.e. a swing in the opposite direction. As for those nations in which education is so low that the people are not even conscious of their degradation and misery, it can be said that they are in a dormant and lethargic condition, and sooner or later, either this century or the next, they too will wake up and give rise to phenomena similar to those now encountered among the most civilized nations of the world. There is no doubt in our mind that this awakening is bound to come, but the when and how will depend on many factors that take into account the interrelation among nations and people. We can easily see that in our modern era events of great importance to society take place at far shorter intervals than before, and it is easy to foresee that in a relatively short time the entire population of the earth will be in a state of flux. It is on this account that we must state that, while education is a prerequisite for the advancement of society, gains will be secured after a period of great strain and distress, and that new ethics and a new mode of life must be injected into the life of society to stop these gigantic convulsions that are liable to annihilate the entire human race.

(c) *The faulty set-up of society that grants to individuals power that they should never possess.* This power, as a general rule, is used to enhance the interests of the few to the detriment and subjugation of the many. We no longer see the need to elaborate further on this subject as this becomes obvious from what we have already explained in other pages, especially if one cares to analyze the conditions encountered in every country in the world today, where irrespective of their form of government, nations lie prostrated under heartless tyrannies, while others are made equally miserable through the bickering and continuous tug-of-war among selfish and irresponsible minorities for the supremacy and for the furthering of their interests to the exclusion of the basic interest of the people.

Of course, what is really needed in this world, far more than physical or economic progress, is the moral evolution of man. In a hypothetical society that has attained this ideal, injustice and other negative instincts would no longer exist. This represents the ultimate goal of humanity, and this goal, we are confident, will be eventually reached in a far-distant future. However, this evolution cannot be imposed from above, but must gradually grow from within through the normal process of maturity. All we can do at present is to facilitate this process by introducing a new mode of life which, while it will restrain the negative and detrimental forces, it will add positive ones that will better direct humanity toward its ultimate goal. Freedom from want is one of the prerequisites for this evolution. It does not, however, necessarily mean that all will have an easy life of abundance and leisure, and that the law of survival of the fittest will no longer exist. The battle for survival represents one of the powerful tools of nature in promoting evolution. The day when man will cease to look ahead and become complacent will also mark the end of his progress and the beginning of his downfall. Those better prepared and qualified for progress and advancement are bound to take over the leadership, and thereby bound to displace the unqualified and inept in the future as well as in the past. Yet the leaders of today are not necessarily the leaders of tomorrow. If society permits the obliteration of populations, even if composed of ignorant and backward people, the number of leaders who tomorrow would have added their talent for the attainment of greater progress and betterment will automatically decrease. Therefore, freedom from want, as previously mentioned, does not mean that man must no longer work and strive but means that he will be permitted to reach a level of well-being such that will awaken in him those inner qualities that, even though latent, would never develop in a dejected and starving condition. We have no illusion that these potentialities are only inherent in members of one race or of one nation. We, ourselves, are the product of many civilizations, and of many people that in older days had their periods of glory and greatness. For similar reasons we have no right to believe that only our civilization and our race will produce the ideal civilization of the future. Let us not forget that future generations may come to consider our civilization as one with that of Greece and Rome, and that our direct contribution will be considered as one among the many that will combine in the evolution of the future society. Given favorable conditions and proper development, other races will probably come to play a prominent role in the shaping of the future civilization. And even those peoples and branches of mankind who now to us seem backward and many centuries delayed in development and in progress, have probably inherent in them qualities and aptitudes that may prove very important in the shaping of the future society. After all, hundreds of years represent an insignificant interval of time compared to the many thousands that were needed to form our present civilization, and to our descendants the discrepancy in this respect, will seem trivial and non-existent in the general background of evolution.

SPHERE OF INFLUENCE OF DIFFERENT MANUFACTURING CENTERS

Up to now only the general background has been given of the inter-relationship among men and among nations, and negative forces have been mentioned as if inherent in human nature and not a product of circumstances and environment. The subject will now be more closely scanned, to see how some of these forces or instincts take root in the hearts of men. Since such instincts spring from basic needs of men as well as of nations, they are bound to exert profound influences in their relations. With the knowledge of the causes that bring about these conditions, we will be better prepared to discern those remedies which are able to change the unattainable ideal of society into actual reality. Because of the complexity of the problems which will come under scrutiny, we are compelled again, for clarity's sake, to simplify the various subjects under consideration to such an extent that may seem at times absurd compared to actual life. However, this simplification, without altering the basic nature of the problem, will be true to life and has the advantage of setting aside factors not pertinent to the subject, and bringing into focus in its true form and expression the particular one which is being analyzed.

Let us consider a locality Alpha which, for the reasons expounded above, is assumed the only place where a certain raw material can be found. In the vast majority of cases the effort of man is needed to extract that raw material from the earth and as is often the case, not in a form that can be readily used by the final consumer, but must undergo a series of operations until it finally becomes a finished product. Of course, this raw material may be only one of many required in the finished article, but this would merely complicate the analysis without affecting the conclusions to be drawn. Therefore, dealing only with hypothetical cases, it is assumed that this raw material[1], found in Alpha alone, is also the only one needed in the manufacture of the particular article chosen as an example.

The fact that Alphium is mined in Alpha does not necessarily mean that it can be processed in the same locality. Quite often this is the case, but not as a generality. Alpha may be atop a high mountain, or other places not suitable for manufacture. Therefore, Alphium, after being extracted, must be sent elsewhere for the final conversion. These places may have definite advantages over Alpha which may include proximity to large industrial centers, railroads, rivers, and so forth, and, therefore, strategically located from the manufacturing and distributing standpoint. In analyzing the various steps that will be needed to change that raw material into finished product and make it ready to be used by the ultimate consumer, the first step, of course, will be that of extracting the raw material from the earth. The owners of the land, or whoever represents their interests, will engage the workers required for that extraction. This labor, naturally, must be paid. Again, machinery, warehouses, all kind of conveyances, and suitable buildings must be on hand for efficient operation, all of which represents capital invested by the owners, who naturally will take this into account when figuring the cost of the raw material. As in everything else, the law of supply and demand will establish the price of Alphium, from which some of the owners will make high profits, while others may sustain losses. This is immaterial to our discussion, but through this exchange, possession of Alphium will pass from the owners of land to those engaged in the manufacture of the useful article. Of course, it stands to reason that the price of raw material must be such that it covers the cost of labor, of machinery, of the necessary buildings and conveyances, and of everything else that is required for the efficient operation on hand; it must also cover taxes and all other fixed costs, and still give the owners a fair return for the capital invested, which means a fair rent for the land, a fair salary for their work, and possibly a profit. This last is linked to the efficiency of the organization. Any revenue less than that will discourage some of the owners from utilizing their land, and by dropping out of the market the supply of Alphium will decrease, which, in turn, will tend to increase its price, and consequently the profit of those who remain in the market. As it is often the case, the raw material will be sold to those interested in the first phase of transformation and in so far as no particular commodity is meant, we are at liberty to assume that several changes in ownership will take place. Each successive owner will perform some special operation before selling the Alphium to the next. He will add to his cost that of the additional labor, machinery, and so forth, and will sell his products at a profit if he can, or at least at a price which will cover not only expenditures but a fair return for capital invested as well as a just salary for his effort. Again it stands to reason that those who are able to maintain a more efficient organization are apt to profit more than those who are laggard and inefficient.

Consider now this exchange from another angle. Whoever buys the raw material from the original owner of land must transport it to a locality where the succeeding transformation takes place. This locality may be only a few miles from Alpha, or hundreds or thousands of miles away. Again this transportation between Alpha and Beta, Gamma, Delta, and so forth, may be made by land, water, or air and may employ only one or thousands. Depending upon these factors, the cost of the raw material may differ from one locality when the methods of transportation are different. Of course, locality to another. The cost will also be different for the same for each locality the price will follow the law of supply and demand, so that the backward and incompetent organizations will drop from the market, and give others the opportunity to expand. But, independently of these discrepancies, the price of raw material will bear an approximate relation to the distance of the locality from Alpha. This assumption is justifiable if we consider that as the various enterprises cease to exist the method of transportation will be standardized for all, and tend to equalize the cost of transportation to the remaining enterprises. One can then visualize Alpha at the center of several concentric circles, each at a certain distance from the next. The total land covered by these circles will represent the sphere of influence of Alpha, and it will be assumed that, starting from the center, the cost of the raw material will tend to increase by the same amount from any one circle to the next. For simplicity say also that the price remains the same for all communities between two consecutive concentric circles, and that it increases some definite amount from one circle to the next. Let a be the cost per unit of weight, or volume, or whatever standard measure is chosen for Alphium for the area within the first circle. Assume also, given only one method of travel, that the cost of transportation from one circle to the next is equivalent to 10 per cent of a. The cost in Beta, located immediately after the fourth circle, will be $1.4a$.

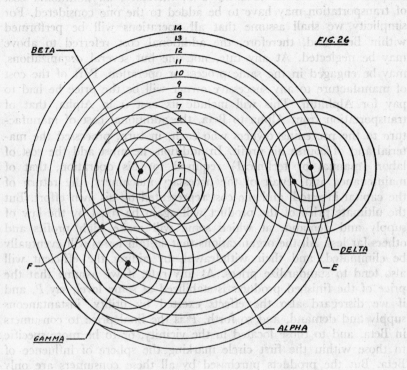

Likewise, between the eighth and ninth the cost will be $1.8a$. Beta represents an industrial center where Alphium is transformed into its finished stage. As several operations may be needed, some may be performed in other localities and, therefore, an additional cost of transportation may have to be added to the one considered. For simplicity we shall assume that all operations will be performed within Beta and, therefore, the additional cost referred to above may be neglected. At any rate, not one but several organizations, may be engaged in the same process or operation. Part of the cost of manufacture to any successive owner will be the price he had to pay for Alphium. This will include its cost a in Alpha, that of transportation from Alpha to Beta, the additional cost of manufacture to the preceding owners who each, in turn, processed the material and of course his profit. In addition, he must add the cost of labor (manual or technical) required for his operation, that of maintenance and repair of the necessary machinery, the return of the capital invested, and the cost represented by his own effort. But the ultimate price of the product will again be fixed by the law of supply and demand, at which some will make high profits and others far less. All the organizations that sustain losses will eventually be eliminated, and their withdrawal, by aiding the efficient will also tend to standardize prices. At any rate, if we assume that the price of the finished products is stabilized at some level, say P, and if we disregard also the effects exerted by utility, instantaneous supply and demand, and so forth, P is the final price to consumers in Beta, and to those located in the vicinity, or to be more specific to those within the first circle marking the sphere of influence of Beta. But the products purchased by all these consumers are only a small fraction of the supply; the remainder must find its way to localities at greater and greater distances from Beta. All the region where these products find a market represent the sphere of influence of Beta.

This again is represented by concentric circles around Beta, spaced at some distance, which for convenience may be assumed one hundred miles. The type of transportation, the labor, the capital invested, and the other factors required to move products from Beta to some other locality will affect the ultimate price to the distant consumers. For simplicity, it is assumed that only distance affects the price, in relation to that in Beta. One may say that the price tends to increase the same amount, no matter what the direction of its outward travel, and that it remains the same for all the communities included between two concentric circles. For convenience this increase in price from one circle to the next will be indicated as a percentage of the original price *a*. Let this increase by 8 per cent of *a*, or 0.08*a*, so that in a locality between 400 and 500 miles from Beta the price will be:

$$Pb + (0.08 \times 4) \, a.$$

On these assumptions one can state that the consumers placed at great distance from Beta will have to pay a higher price than those who are nearer. Thus far only the center of production in Beta has been considered. But, as is usually the case, many localities will have the equipment, knowledge, and manpower to turn out finished products equal or similar to those made in Beta. These manufacturers, being variously distant from Alpha, will pay more or less than those in Beta, depending on distance. Some of these places we shall name Gamma, Delta, and so forth. While the influence on prices exerted by distance generally holds, tariffs and other man-made obstructions to the natural flow of products may alter this order, and often one may find the price of raw material in places relatively close to Alpha to be considerably higher than in more distant localities. To convince our reader of the truth of this statement, he need only remind himself that raw material found in distant colonies is often far cheaper in the mother country than in nations considerably closer. Tariffs and other barriers prevent the normal flow between the colony and the nearer nations. This, however, is a topic due to be further discussed later on. For the present it will be assumed that the price of raw material in Gamma is bound to be higher than that in Beta, because of the greater distance from Alpha and will be found by the previously given formula. Like Beta, the industries and manufacturing centers in Gamma will make commodities similar or identical to those turned out in Beta, eventually to be sold to consumers in Gamma and her surrounding sphere of influence. This also holds for Delta and any other community with the requisite ability, equipment, and manpower, and provided also that such manufacture is sufficiently profitable to attract business people and capital.

Now besides the fact that the cost of raw material will be related to the distance from Alpha, the variation in living conditions in each locality, the price of labor, skill and efficiency of those engaged in the manufacture, the adoption of labor-saving devices, will all affect the final cost to the producers, even though the finished products are approximately the same. The final price reached in the several localities may thus be higher than, equal to or lower than in Beta, and will depend on the factors mentioned above. But, irrespective of prices, each of these localities will be the center of an independent and well-defined sphere of influence.

Referring to the diagram shown in page 527, Alpha is represented by the center of concentric circles spaced at a distance of one hundred miles apart. All this area is within the sphere of influence of Alpha. Therein we may assume localities Beta, Gamma, and Delta, at different distances from Alpha, as the manufacturing centers. Each has a sphere of its own that can also be represented by concentric circles around the locality in question. From the diagram it may be immediately noted that some (in this case those about Beta and Gamma) overlap each other. The effect of this overlapping will be better understood and appreciated by assigning a definite price reached by the products in the different manufacturing centers. This is explained in note 10-1.

For communities very close to any of these centers, for instance E in relation to Delta, it is easy to understand that their populations will find it to their advantage to purchase articles that originate from Delta, the center to which they belong. Similar products from other places will not be sought, because the large cost of transportation from other centers increases their price to such an extent that they become unable to compete with similar products originating from Delta. However, for communities like F, claimed by several manufacturing centers, the cost of transportation is no longer of paramount importance, and other factors may decide the choice. It is easy to see that people will prefer to buy from the center that charges less, even though further away than others.

NOTE 10-1

The distance of Beta, Gamma, Delta, from Alpha is assumed respectively 400, 800, and 1200 miles. If a is the cost of Alphium, the raw material in Alpha, and 10% is the percentage paid for transporting Alphium 100 miles, its cost in these manufacturing centers will be:

$$\text{Beta:} \quad a + 0.4a = 1.4a$$
$$\text{Gamma:} \quad a + 0.8a = 1.8a$$
$$\text{Delta:} \quad a + 1.2a = 2.2a$$

Difference in living conditions, in efficiency, and so forth, will vary the cost of finished products to the manufacturers of these centers. Assume that this additional item for the three communities is respectively: 1.2a, 1.5a, and 1.0a, then the final cost will be:

Beta: $P_B = 1.4a + 1.2a = 2.6a$
Gamma: $P_G = 1.8a + 1.5a = 3.3a$
Delta: $P_D = 2.2a + 1.0a = 3.2a$

Since price tends to become equal to cost, one may assume that 2.6a, 3.3a, and 3.2a represent also the price to the respective local consumers. But these products are also sold to more distant localities, and naturally the cost of transportation to those places must be added. At the opening of this discussion it was assumed that this cost is 0.08a for each 100 miles of travel.

Consider then locality E in the Deltan area of influence. As E is 200 miles from Delta the price of finished products will be:

$$P_E = 3.2a + (0.08a \times 2)a = 3.2a + 0.16a = 3.36a$$

3.2a is the price in Delta, and 0.16a the cost of transportation to E. Now to determine the price of the same products from the next closest center (Beta in this case). The distance between Beta and E is found from the diagram to be 1400 miles. Thus the price will be:

$$2.6a + (0.08 \times 14)a = 2.6a + 1.12a = 3.72a$$

2.6a is the price in Beta, and 1.12a the cost of transportation to E. Following the same reasoning, the cost from Gamma will be:

$$3.3a + (0.08 \times 16)a = 3.3a + 1.28a = 4.58a$$

It is evident from the above that, everything else being equal, the consumer in E will prefer to buy products from Delta, even though they may be cheaper in other centers. It can be safely said then that E definitely belongs in the sphere of influence of Delta to the exclusion of Beta and Gamma.

This cannot be said for other localities, for instance F which is 400 miles from Gamma and 600 from Beta. Repeating for F the calculation made for E, the price of products from Beta will be:

$$2.6a + (0.08 \times 6)a = 2.6a + 0.48a = 3.08a$$

The price from Gamma will be:

$$3.3a + (0.08 \times 4)a = 3.3a + 0.32a = 3.62a$$

From the above it is evident that everything else being equal, consumers in F will prefer to buy the products from Beta rather than from Gamma, even though the latter is much closer. This is because the Betan price is sufficiently lower than the Gamman to more than counterbalance the greater distance.

. . . .

In our analysis it was assumed for simplicity that the price of an article increases the same amount as it travels outward, and is the same for any community within the same two concentric circles around the center. However, this is not so in reality. A range of mountains, an unabridged river, the lack of good roads, the mode of transportation, may materially alter distances as well as cost of transportation from the basic figure derived from their geographical distance. Natural obstacles and shipping facilities distort the concentric circles drawn for the purpose of illustrating the rise in price from one region to another.

We are all familiar with topographic charts, in which points of equal altitude are connected by a continuous line that loops around and returns eventually to its origin. In such a map the peak of a mountain will be represented by a single point. Any one of these contour lines, looping about that point, but not actual circles, will represent points of equal height at a lower level than those on a curve closer to the peak. The summit can symbolize the manufacturing center and each loop will join the localities in which the price of the commodities from that center is the same. In representing the sphere of influence of a specific manufacturing place, imagine then a similar map with a succession of concentric loops which in places will be spaced considerably apart, while elsewhere will curve closer to each other. The nearing of these lines will reveal that a barrier of some kind (natural or man-made) increases the cost of transportation quite ·rapidly as the products go further outward, while their spacing apart shows that lack of natural barriers and good transportation facilities reduces such increase to a minimum. As before, the region between any two concentric loops will include all places where the prices of commodities from a certain center reach the same level. The spacing of the lines, more than aerial distance, will give an indication of the method and efficiency of transportation enjoyed by any community in relation to others. From the above it is easy to see that locality F, which was naturally attracted toward Beta, will turn toward Gamma if lack of roads, natural barriers or poor shipping facilities should increase the cost of commodities from Beta to a higher level than those from Gamma. Barring new changes in the various factors affecting that price, each center has a sphere of influence of its own, and the manufacturers of this zone will find it unprofitable to force their products upon localities that belong to another, because of their disadvantageous competitive position. They may do so only if willing to absorb heavy losses in an effort at eliminating the other center as a competing factor in the market. In studying the variation of prices reached by products in different localities the topographic chart has been used as an example. However, the map representing prices, unlike the chart, is bound to suffer many changes with the passing of time. Indeed many manufacturing centers and their respective spheres of influence, not only may change in shape, but also in size, and may even disappear altogether. The construction of a railroad, a tunnel that shortens the distance between two communities, a change in the method of transportation, are all factors that will alter the cost of commodities to such an extent that entire regions may be made to gravitate toward one center rather than another. The consumers of any disputed region may find it to their advantage to shift their purchases from one manufacturing center to another, and they will do so regardless of the damage that their choice may inflict upon the one that loses their support. Thus the zone they join will be greatly enlarged, and that of the rival correspondingly reduced.

ORIGINS OF LARGE CITIES AND IMPORTANT INDUSTRIAL CENTERS

In the discussion just finished Alpha was assumed close to the only source of raw material. If this is indissolubly bound up with the expanding needs of the area, additional labor will be necessary with the passing of time. The workers, of course, will live with their families, in or near the place and thus will require other people with diversified knowledge and ability to promote that comfort consonant with a civilized society. From this one can easily surmise that Alpha is bound to expand until it may become a large city. Besides Alpha, other places like Beta, Gamma and Delta can also grow, become communities, and gradually evolve into cities of considerable size and importance. What are the forces responsible for their development? Usually a river, the end of a valley, the vicinity of the sea, the possession of a good natural harbor, an important road junction, a good climate, and other factors that promote trade and exchange may well be the causes that change a small town into a large city. Of course, not all the cities have become such at the same time. Indeed, some in Europe and Asia have been important since time immemorial, while other communities, as some in the American continent, are expanding and becoming great centers of population under our very eyes. Of course, the forces that were at play in the formation of some of the oldest cities, like Florence in Italy, are different from those responsible for the great development of New York. On a map of any country it is relatively simple to recognize the forces responsible for the growth of each individual city. Such cities more often than not are also large industrial manufacturing centers. In analyzing these causes one can also recognize that different forces have acted for the development of different cities. This can be traced to the fact that with time, varied modes of life have been in vogue among people, and in turn have brought about corresponding needs and requirements. Again, certain cities reached maturity through centuries of slow and gradual growth, while others needed only a few decades to expand from an insignificant community into an important center. This discussion needs no proof or explanation as it belongs to common knowledge. The history of each city will give evidence of the forces that have made it what it is today. Be these as they may, such manufacturing centers are also the focus of affluence for a continuous stream of people. They come from near and far, and while many are attracted to the city because of the possibility of finding work directly in its industries, others, not directly concerned thereby, recognize that here is opportunity to utilize to better advantage their talents and the profession or trade in which they are proficient. The larger the population, the greater is the number of customers for the small business man, and likewise the salaries and wages available. Because of this continuous flow of workers and their families, directly or indirectly connected with the local industry, additional needs arise in the city, resulting in the attraction of still others, and further civic growth. Needless to say, the well-being of these people is directly linked to that of the industry flourishing there. Now in any of these centers the amount of commodities produced is generally based upon what can be sold, not only to local townspeople, but also to inhabitants of the vicinity.

ATTACHMENT OF PEOPLE TO THEIR CITY

In general, one may state that production governs the number earning a livelihood from that industry, as well as the size and sureness of their wages, the prosperity of the small business man, the profits of the owner of wealth, and the richness of the community. It is, therefore, natural that all living in any center, and this includes people in nearby towns, will feel a unity of interests, even though of different gradations, but still a unity of purpose, seeking that the area of their abode should flourish and reach higher levels, as their self-interest is naturally involved. That city becomes their own and the vast majority will share its fortune for better and for worse, because their families live and their homes are located there, together with most of their friends and acquaintances. Naturally, if conditions should change and vast sections of the population can no longer prosper or make a living, some will emigrate and establish their homes elsewhere, yet many will remain. This is why there are cities with a stationary or decreasing population, and in history there are also examples of cities being completely deserted, due to the fact that everything had changed to such an extent that life there was no longer possible. As a generality, however, it may be said that people have a tendency to be attached to their places of birth in the face of great hardships and uncertainties. How else could we explain the tenacity displayed by the thousands of families which for many centuries, generation after generation, continue living on the slopes of volcanoes when they know that at any moment their homes and possessions, not to mention their lives, may be overwhelmed and destroyed? How else explain the obstinacy of dwellers in poor lands at the fringe of deserts? This feeling of attachment has the effect of many sharing the fortunes of their land, and since all wish to improve their standard of living, they will go to almost any length to increase the well-being of their region, even if this should inflict losses upon other places. From this basic instinct, nationalism, that potent source of misunderstanding, and the cause of so much strife came into being.

ANALYSIS OF EFFECTS OF CONFLICTING SPHERES OF INFLUENCE

With some of the basic instincts of man clear in mind, and realizing his reactions to all that affects his immediate well-being, we may proceed with our exposition of the sphere of influence of a city. It has been shown how it starts and expands. As there may be several overlapping each other, any community located between two centers will naturally gravitate toward the one that sells at a lower price. It was also shown that the greater the distance the more expensive its commodities are apt to be, and by distance is implied also any physical impediment to the normal flow from the center to the community in question. These impediments are instanced by the absence of good roads, by ranges of mountains, etc. These conditions may change, through the construction of a bridge, tunnel, or a road which can divert the economic pull of a community from one center to another.

Reverting to the manufacturing center, it was shown how its well-being depends on the ability of its population to dispose of its products. Its wealth is in direct proportion to the amount of business which it can maintain, and it is to its advantage not only to continue the same output but to increase it, and this can only be done by expanding its zone of influence. Hence, it is obvious that it is to the advantage of any manufacturing center to improve its facilities so as to reach an ever-increasing number of consumers. As mentioned before, these facilities may be represented by better roads, better transportation, and by lowering the cost of production. But the policy adopted by Beta, in order to increase its sphere of influence may be, and usually is taken up by other manufacturing places, as their populations, with similar needs and requirements, are likewise intent upon the progress and advancement of their respective centers. In the present example there has been assumed for simplicity a single center from which raw material can be bought, and several manufacturing points producing the same products. Of course, this is not what happens in real life, as different centers actually turn out a variety of commodities. There are cases in which one kind of commodity is manufactured in one center and not in another, so that improvement of communications between them may be beneficial to both without endangering the interests of their manufacturers and their employers. Nevertheless, such occurrences are the exception rather than the rule, as very seldom are the economies of two different centers complementary to each other. As is usually the case, Beta may be manufacturing mainly one kind of commodity and less of another, and the reverse may hold in another place. It is possible, therefore, that an improved system of communication, unquestionably beneficial to both populations and to some manufacturers, may be detrimental to others. Of course, if this innovation happens to be detrimental to many local manufacturers or at least to the most influential among them, all kinds of obstacles will be raised against adoption, while, if it is beneficial, the project will go through. Thus, even when the people in general are benefited by such a change, there are individuals adversely affected because, as a result, they will have to stand a stronger competition from rivals in other centers. But with minor influence in the community, they will be powerless in the face of a determined majority. In order to better emphasize the interrelation of spheres of influence close to each other, it has been assumed that all centers turn out the same products, so that the advantage or disadvantage to any one will be better understood. With such an assumption, it is easy to see that any advantage any innovation may bring the population of any particular center, through the expansion of its field of influence, is bound to be harmful to the interests of an adjoining center, which has its field correspondingly reduced. If they are far apart, the chances are that the increase of one sphere does not damage in any way the interests of the other, and in such an instance humanity in general benefits by these improvements. But, for those centers that are closer together and their fields overlap each other, an increase in the sphere of influence of one center is bound to be accompanied by a decrease in that of another. It is easy to see that competition between them is bound to develop.

The decrease of the field of influence of any manufacturing center, needless to say, has unfavorable repercussions upon many of its population. Many products will be unsold and will have to be disposed of at less than cost, enterprises will go bankrupt, and the entire local industry may be thrown out of step and be affected in one way or another. Production will have to be curtailed, many will be thrown out of work, and this fact may far outweigh the advantage of reduced prices of the commodity from the other center. Even though less apparent, similar effects can be experienced by a nation. In cases where only the industry of a particular region is adversely affected by the expansion of the sphere of influence of a center located in another nation, it is probable that many who have lost a job as a consequence of competition from abroad, will find another job in an alternative industry in the community or elsewhere in the nation, and except for manufacturers forced into bankruptcy, the standard of living in general may even be improved. However, if the competition from abroad should affect not one but many industries, it might have disastrous consequences on the entire economic structure of the nation. There would be no new jobs for the unemployed, heavy losses would be suffered by many manufacturers, and as this means a depression, everyone must accept a lower standard of living.

Now that the subject of competition between industrial centers or between nations has been started, it must be stressed that no community and no nation will willingly submit to the inevitable without seeking to find remedies, and between nations may eventually involve war. One of the first steps will be that of striving to control the source of raw material. Reverting to the diagram of page 527, it is plain how advantageous it would be to such industrial centers as Beta, Gamma, or Delta to come into absolute possession of Alpha. Through this ownership it could then limit the amount of raw material going into any competing center, or this would be completely stopped if the competition should prove too excessive. It is this basic necessity that induces nations in general to acquire or arrogate vast amounts of lands and raw material, often far above their actual needs or physical capacity to exploit. Such wealth in their possession is not likely to be utilized by themselves immediately, and to some extent may even be rented to competing interests of other nations. Their ownership, however, gives them the privilege of stopping that flow if and when competition from abroad proves too severe. It likewise gives them the power to expand their sphere of influence whenever they desire, with no fear of economic reprisal.

The control of raw material is obviously the most direct and decisive method to defeat competition. A less effective alternative is through a decrease in cost of production. For simplicity it was assumed that all the raw material is located in Alpha, but since actually it is usually found in varying amounts in many localities, it would be extremely difficult for a single person or nation to own or control all of any specific raw material on earth. Any person or center may succeed, however, in controlling large portions, while the rest may be held by others. These latter, even though having some raw material on hand, may be unable to compete with the former, and the only way they can expand their sphere or prevent it from being reduced is to lower the price of their products. In a world of approximately equal technological knowledge such decrease in cost is often obtained by a lower wage scale, which means a lower standard of living.

We may now ask ourselves: Why does the poor community or nation feel this relentless urge to expand its field of influence, and thereby incur the retaliatory measures of the more fortunate centers? The answer is simple. The attainment of a better standard of living is one of man's basic instincts and goals and he will seek it even if confronted by great obstacles whenever and wherever possible. In a world with such a lack of intelligent planning and cooperation among nations, it is natural that each one should look after his own interests, and try to improve his lot whenever opportunity offers, often with no regard for other people's interests. Taking any average person, we know that within his limits he will do all he can to improve his financial standing and that of his family, in relation to the society or community of which he is a part. As the interest of each person is bound up with the welfare of his community and nation, it is natural that he should also use his skill and ingenuity to improve their standard of living. Indeed in a prosperous community or nation the opportunities for himself, his kindred, and their descendants will be greater. Such prosperity can only be attained by widening the sphere of influence, both of the community and of the nation. It is natural, therefore, that the most enterprising element in either should go to any limit to obtain that goal, and therein will receive the moral support and cooperation of all who have the same outlook and interests. To this end they will strive for any outcome beneficial to their community, and conversely hamper and halt, as far as they can, any change that seems detrimental.

It is understandable enough that such a desire should pervade nations and communities poor in raw materials and resources, but one finds the same urge among inhabitants of rich and flourishing regions. Because of that basic instinct referred to above, these more fortunate people also strive to improve their lot, no matter how good, and this can be accomplished by improving local economic conditions, while they will certainly oppose any change in any way unfavorable. If it were in their power, one can be sure that many of them would dispose once and for all of the competing centers no matter what the hardship inflicted on their people. If they do not do so, it is because somehow they feel that after all the complete economic bankruptcy of those centers would adversely affect their own fortunes. Such purpose, of course, is never expressed in open opinion as a feeling of restraint and veneer of civilization keeps people from expressing themselves openly on this subject. This, indeed, would be regarded as unethical, and would expose them to reprisal by those endangered. We can be sure, however, that this instinct is at the bottom of their subconscious minds, and is the prime mover of their actions, no matter how disguised. From an economic standpoint we do not mean that altruism and generosity are non-existent. In any nation and any community one finds many examples of true and whole-hearted goodness and abnegation, yet despite the many exceptions, all of such display is made to satisfy the inner ego. Frequently the wealthy philanthropist, who distributes millions of dollars to charitable organizations and the like, becomes cruel and ruthless if his dominant position in the community is in any way jeopardized. The old animosity between the haves and havenots, whether in a community or among nations, is nevertheless raging and relentless. Due to the lack of cooperation and coordination in modern society, whatever proves advantageous to one community or nation endangers the interests of other communities and nations, and this keeps people divided and suspicious of each other. The lower class fears and hates the upper; the poor nation hates and fears the rich one. In a world where arguments are settled by brute force rather than justice and tolerance, the average individual faced by danger and uncertainty, tends to ally himself with those who have similar fears and interests, and in that allegiance finds strength and support. For similar reasons alliances among nations are made. Here, however, the link is not between the poor and inconsequential nations against the rich and powerful. Any of the great powers could easily destroy any such combination, and, therefore, there would be no point to it. Instead, each weak nation tends to associate itself either with the one most feared, in a frantic effort at self-preservation, or, if not threatened, seeks the one from which the greatest economic advantages can be obtained. Such as it is, the similarity of interests among individuals which may be called collectivism is one of the basic forces that set apart classes among the citizens of any community or nation and generates nationalism within one nation against others.

SIMILARITY BETWEEN NATIONALISM
AND COLLECTIVISM

It is plain enough that nationalism and collectivism are one and the same thing. Their apparent difference stems from the fact that, while one applies to the activities of individuals and groups versus other groups of the same society and nation, the other applies to the activities of the individual of a nation versus other nations. Collectivism indicates the action of individuals within one community or one nation, when they join forces and talent with the purpose of defending and enhancing their common interests against other groups in the same community or nation. Similar feeling throughout the population becomes nationalism. Here, however, it is a matter of the entire population versus other nations. All in all, in both cases the feelings and the actions originate in similar needs and purposes, and the difference is merely in scale.

It may be asked if this characteristic is a product of modern society and its particular mode of life. One can safely reply in the affirmative. However, it must be added that not only our society but all those that preceded it had their share in the molding of this instinct, as the same forces have guided the actions of men since time immemorial. Similar circumstances and needs of the human race throughout its eventful history have developed a second nature in man which manifests itself, not only in the economic field, but in so many others as well that one can hardly conceive its absence. In its mildest form it may be called competition or rivalry. It is this second nature that generally makes us ally and identify ourselves with a particular group. The members may be living in one's town, or belong to one's race, religion, or nation, and this allegiance will manifest itself in important as well as inconsequential matters. We all are familiar with the feelings of partnership and animosity that arise among spectators at a football game who, as a generality, side up with the team that belongs to their city, or their section of the town, and in short with the one to which the spectator feels closer by instinct, no matter how flimsy the relationship may be. One personally may not know the players, but the fact that they represent one's section of the city, makes one take sides and root for the victory of his town, school, nation, race, and so forth. To carry the argument to absurdity, if people were living on Mars and a game could be arranged between Martians and Chinese, an American or a German would cheer the Chinese team for the simple reason that it represented his planet. Concluding, we may state that the instinct of ego and the instinct which draws people close to those who have identical interests are at the base of nationalism.

FORMS OF EXPRESSIONS IDENTIFIABLE WITH NATIONALISM AND COLLECTIVISM

While it would be erroneous to assume that all of us are like that, we must honestly admit that these instincts are real, and that they sway the thoughts, and actions of most people, no matter in what part of the world. Of course, while the feeling of friendly rivalry is harmless, to say the least, still such basic instincts are in great part responsible for many clashes between classes and nations, and needless to say the consequences are far more serious than those occurring on a football field.

Any one who identifies himself with the proletarian class, even though himself in possession of a steady and comfortable job, will unconsciously share the views and feelings of the other proletarians, and consequently of those who appoint themselves the leaders and spokesmen of the poor. Thus a man may love and respect his personal superior for his kindness and consideration to him, but this feeling will only be personal. The same gentle and kind master will be numbered among the tyrants as soon as important issues are at stake between the proletariat and the upper classes. The member of the proletariat sees in the other classes a gang intent upon depriving him and all other proletarians of their sacred and just rights to attain a higher standard of living, intent on keeping him and his fellow-workers forever subjugated and enchained. On the other hand, anyone who identifies himself with the upper class will by instinct share the views and the feelings of this group. In this struggle among classes he sees nothing but a criminal effort on the part of the proletariat to rob him and his fellow-capitalists, without reason or justification, of privileges which belong to them because of their birth, intellect, and ability.

Similar difference of opinion and outlook can be found in relations among nations where the poor country, through the words of its leading citizens, will accuse all who have plenty of monopolizing far more wealth than they need, and preventing the needy nation from raising its standard of living and making itself economically independent. Since everyone in an impoverished country stands to gain, although in different proportions, from any improvement that may come to their nation, all will unite in upholding this necessity, and will go to great lengths to justify the steps taken by their government if presented to them as motivated by justice and honor. The rich country, on the other hand, will not share this view. What is now in its possession may have been obtained either by peaceful acquisition or by wars fought in other periods for a righteous and worthy cause (the gaining of raw material being only incidental). At any rate, this wealth is theirs and has long been so; and if they enjoy a better standard of living than others, this fact should be ascribed exclusively to their sturdiness, initiative, and foresightedness, and certainly they see no reason why they should relinquish such advantageous position, acquired with so much effort, in favor of some country which does not and should not rank equally with their nation. Similar stands taken by the leaders of the various nations have, naturally, a large following among their respective populations, and since neither is willing to compromise unless on some inconsequential matter, the common ground for their understanding is non-existent. Despite the high-sounding phrases of the respective leaders, and the high ideals which seem to justify their actions and policies, the real aim pursued by each head of state is the one that benefits his country, irrespective of other nations' interests, and certainly they intend to retain and safeguard those advantages which justly or unjustly have been acquired over the heads of others.

GENERAL POLICIES FOLLOWED BY THE
GOVERNMENTS OF MODERN TIMES

This is the fundamental policy on which any modern government must stand or fall, and, indeed, it could not be different. No head of a state could retain his position for a single day if he should decide to uphold policies of true justice and equality. As mentioned before, the actual and cynical truth is never set forth to the people or to the world in general, for such a thing does not exist in government parlance; instead their policies, in regard to other nations, are always presented to the people as dictated by high principles and ideals. The people in turn, while instinctively conscious of the real truth, like to be lulled into believing that these beautiful ideals are actually the guiding elements, and either through plain ignorance of facts, or because they prefer to be deceived in such matters, will support and justify their government even when common sense places it in the wrong.

Parallel to this open and straight-forward policy there is, however, a secret and tortuous one. Screened by secrecy, a continuous jockeying for advantageous position and an incessant bargaining among nations is going on continually with the intent of depriving others of some specific raw material or economic advantage. This to the ignorance of the majority of the population which, being erroneously informed, often supports schemes which, if set forth clearly, would not be to the liking of many basically honest citizens, who incline little to monopolistic policies, whether followed by individuals, corporations, or by their own country as a whole. One method used by powerful neighbors to subjugate a weak and helpless nation is to promote uprising among its population, in order to justify before the world the necessity of intervention. As is often the case, in any country there are always individuals who for personal advantages are willing to betray their country and their people and, as they are unscrupulous and clever, they usually succeed in fomenting discord within their nation. Once they attain positions of importance they seek the aid of the powerful backer that was instrumental to their accession. As this well-organized and financially strong minority will pretend to speak for the complete population, their appeal will seem spontaneous to the outside world. With such a setting the powerful neighbor, on the lookout for this opportunity, acquires the supposed moral justification to enter the country and establish order and justice. This intervention may even be hailed and praised, as few within or without the country can refute the reasonableness and morality of this action. The victim, however, internally disorganized and helpless, loses its freedom, and is absorbed into the sphere of influence of the aggressor. As this cynical method has been successfully applied time and again, it is not necessary to cite the many examples coming to mind in proof of this account.

However, it does not deceive the leaders of other powerful nations, who are ever alert to safeguard the interests of their own class and incidentally of their country. The loss of the victim as a potential extension of their own sphere of influence is a real one, and further jockeying and bargaining will take place behind the screen of secrecy. This usually occurs amid the utter ignorance of the nation which is being partitioned or absorbed. Needless to say, its fundamental interests are not in any way considered or even taken into account. The nation standing aloof will ratify this aggression only if a positive economic advantage is granted in compensation. This is usually in the form of permitting the bystander to use the same method and tactics to subjugate some other helpless victim. Using such criminal methods, powerful aggressor nations come to dominate vast expanses of lands outside their immediate jurisdiction, and the fate of millions is thereby sealed beyond their own power to alter. The poor countries left defenseless against this procedure must resign themselves to the fact that "might makes right". Mind you, my reader, this method is used not only by your nation or mine, but by any one with the necessary power and opportunity, because the basic instincts of men are the same among all people.

However, should this policy be adopted by a nation not overly strong and brazen, its bargaining power is usually less, and since any expansion will somehow injure the interests of the powerful nations, this aggrandizement will be opposed and resisted. The real aims of this country will be made public to the world, and they will brand the audacious imitator as a disturber of the international peace. If it is still determined to carry through these plans, the others will then arouse sufficient enthusiasm at home to justify a declaration of war. Of course, the real issue, the fear that vested interests in the country may be endangered by the new competitor, is usually prevented from becoming a public issue. As long as the weaker nation is kept poor in resources and with a limited sphere of influence, there will be no fear that the field of influence of the strong will ever be reduced or endangered. With such intentions, how many wars have been waged in the past under the banner of justice and fair play? We have seen a great empire, holding under its power millions of heterogeneous peoples often seething and striving helplessly for liberty, wage war for the defense of other nations and peoples under the pretext of preserving the ideals of independence for all. England, the arch-champion of liberty and justice, the great defender of democracy, did not realize or wish to realize that she herself was keeping many peoples under political and economic subjugation. One can be sure that she is not contemplating either in the present or in the future ever relinquishing her overlordship without a fight. This must not be regarded as a deceitful and unwarranted misstatement on our part, inspired only by some particular prejudice or misconception of that great country, as this would not correspond to the truth. We need only cite a famous speech by Premier Churchill, delivered during the war, in which he very clearly defined the basic policy of the empire. That England may have to free some, even most of her colonies in the near future, possibly without any forcible action by other countries, will not disprove our contention. The rapidly changing conditions in our society, the loss of the balance of power to other nations and empires, the tacit but nevertheless powerful public opinion throughout the world, all combine to prepare the setting for this seemingly spontaneous granting of freedom. Let us not forget that these alone will be the real causes of such a capitulation. We, ourselves, in America had to fight for the liberty of which we are proud, and would still be an English colony if England had her say. While she happens to be the culprit in this instance, let us not relax in the belief that we would have been more generous in her position; and the same can be said of any other nation. The desire by any group to control as much raw material as possible, to the exclusion of others, is the expression of the basic selfishness of man, especially in a world in which cooperation is lacking.

SIMILARITIES BETWEEN NATIONS AND INDIVIDUALS

From what has been explained so far it can be concluded that relations among nations are similar to those that exist among individuals or groups and this could not be otherwise because after all the latter with their needs and desires form communities, and groups of these make up nations. To explain better this similarity one can point out the behavior of individuals or groups within one country, which can easily be detected in the behavior among nations, and eventually prove that what may tend to improve conditions among individuals would also tend to improve those among the nations. In previous parts of our study we have analyzed the methods and the forces that tend to create monopolies within one nation. Generally in a business circle numerous manufacturers are engaged in producing and selling the same kind of products. The fair competition with each other is highly beneficial to society, as it tends to bring the price to the same level as cost, weeds out the inefficient, and yields everyone a fair return for his labor. There is, however, a tendency on the part of many individuals or groups to extort excessive profits at the expense of the public through monopolies. The first stage of their operation is that of underselling a competitor in the open market, even at a financial loss to themselves. This operation has the purpose of driving the competing interests out of the market. As this is gradually accomplished, the underseller manages to buy or in some way control a greater portion of the means of production and sale, and his position becomes much stronger, both against his victim and would-be rivals. Since power breeds power, from an inconsequential start, he gradually becomes an absolute arbiter in his field, at liberty to set his price and profit, naturally at a decided loss to the public. Having eliminated competition there is no longer any urge on his part either to decrease the price or improve the quality of his products. The monopolist, in short, reaches the stage of being able to rake in money with little effort and no regard to the needs of people. That such tactics are unfair and dangerous to humanity goes without saying, and accordingly in most countries the government, under pressure, takes steps to curb and limit such action. These steps prove successful or otherwise, depending on the individuals who head the nation, naturally swayed by their basic interests and those of the class to which they belong. This condition is generally found within all nations.

Reverting our discussion to the family of nations, we can say that due to fortuitous circumstances, such as the winning of a battle either recently or many centuries ago, due to a treaty made by shrewd statements and politicians or because of the secret maneuvering, previously explained, various countries gained colonies rich in resources and raw materials, which they exploited and are now exploiting for their own benefit to the exclusion of others. Competition among nations, as among individuals in the endless struggle for betterment, was bound to develop in time and, as always the wealthier nations were able to expand their field of influence and restrict that of others, despite the efforts of the latter, because they could at any time raise economic barriers to block the flow of raw materials to all rivals. As the needs and instincts of our forefathers were similar to ours, wars of reprisal were waged in the past under all manner of pretenses, and the countries with resources, not only were usually victorious, but able to acquire additional wealth and colonies. This does not imply that these nations were able to retain indefinitely that position of pre-eminence. Like individuals, there is a continuous shift from one class to another, some of the poor becoming rich, and conversely some of the rich through various circumstances becoming poor.

As a proletarian enters the upper class he rapidly assimilates its traditional feelings, and absorbs the same interests of the class to which he now belongs. The same occurs among nations. This naturally refers to those who are at present in a pre-eminent position, but the same can be said for others which in the past occupied similar rank. Spain saw her days of grandeur centuries ago, and when at the peak of her power displayed the same characteristics and qualities that contemporary great powers now show. It is hard to foretell the fate of England. Notwithstanding her prominence in the past and her recent victory over Germany, the appalling losses she sustained during the war in devastated cities, slaughter of her people, and undernourishment among the survivors, has made possible the shifting of her leadership to other nations. Her empire seems to be seething more feverishly than ever with desires of secession and setting up of independent nations. Her leading class, because of her severe losses and imponderable factors that generate life cycles in the evolution of nations, seems unable to cope with and change the tide of events that tend to deprive them of their pre-eminence enjoyed for centuries. Of course, there is no way to foresee the future, and we may on the contrary witness a rebirth and regeneration of England. This is not the first time this great nation has appeared to totter and decline, either through internal disorgan-ization or because of staggering blows from without. Each time the indomitable spirit of its people has eventually found its equilibrium and revived its strength. Despite this genius for recovery, it remains on record that when in control of the main resources of the world, England was extremely stingy about sharing them, nor is there lacking reason to fear that similar policies would likewise be followed by the United States or by Russia should they succeed in turn to her world-dominating role.

At this stage of our study it is well to analyze the pros and cons of such a state of affairs. With England becoming even temporarily only a second-rate world power, with Germany losing her last vestige of empire, with France, Italy, Japan, and other nations economically crippled and helpless, the vast body of resources all over the world appears liable to come under the control of gigantic interests which in turn are led by small groups of determined men. In other words, with the passing of time, the monopoly of world resources seems to be passing into fewer and fewer hands.

Starting in the Middle Ages, when the civilized world was divided among relatively large numbers of individuals who composed the nobility, this system eventually was replaced by the nations, which in greater or less degree manifested power and competing influence against each other. At present the nations seem in the process of being replaced by mighty economic trusts, indeed empires, in which the will and the interests of the few will overrule the vast majority of the world's population. The similarity of the evolution that is now taking place among the nations and the monopoly that fre-quently occurs within one country is unescapable. Needless to say, both are detrimental to society in general, being both opposed to the fundamental law of division of labor.

One often finds expressed the opinion that it would be to Europe's advantage, and incidentally to that of all the world, if she could be conquered by one of the nations of that continent. All of them, by uniting their resources, would be able to prosper and raise their standard of living. With many reservations we academically agree with this opinion; however, in the past, as well as in the present, any nation that has displayed such a will has acted not with the purpose of aiding the entire population of Europe, but with that of improving its own standard of living to the exclusion of the others. It is for this reason that no nation has ever been able to conquer the indomitable spirit of those countries which, while poor, prefer their poverty to subjugation and slavery. It is this fear that keeps those nations so far apart from each other, but, of course, resistance is always proportional to the strength of the nation. What has been difficult for Germany seems to be easy for Russia, nowadays the dominant power of Europe. The majority of those nations which suffered such severe damage during the war, are now internally too disorganized and economically impoverished to resist successfully the incessant propaganda, the threats, and more subtle devices by the Russians. Europe at present seems to have become the main battlefield between the interests of Russia and those of the United States. Even though an American and, therefore, partial to this country, I must assert that no good will come to humanity as a result of this gigantic battle, no matter who is the winner. In greater or lesser degree any monopoly is bound to be detrimental to society.

To give an example of the consequences which monopoly will cause the average citizen of our country as well as of the world, we wish to point out the fact that many American commodities are nowadays sold abroad at a much lower price than in the United States. Cigarettes, automobiles, and many other articles, are examples of this statement. Numerous American manufacturers accept heavy losses abroad in order to promote their products in other countries. Thereby they succeed in running out of business hundreds of corporations elsewhere unable to sustain their competition. But do you think, my reader, that this loss is actually borne by those in the process of establishing world monopolies? Decidedly not. This loss is borne by you and me and by the millions of Americans who have to pay higher prices for that merchandise here to make up and more for that loss. And do you think that when all these monopolies are finally established that the prices will drop to a normal level? One cannot tell, but we are inclined to disbelieve such a turn of events. In the meantime, countries in which the native industry becomes further disorganized, due to this unfair competition, will be forced into another lowering of their standards of living, will experience greater unemployment, with more misery than ever, and eventually we will be forced to feed those populations out of our work and our salary to a far greater degree than at present. That such tactics tend to dislocate and distort economic conditions of the world is quite evident; that this and future generations will have to pay in lower standards of living is a matter of course; and under the illusive impression that by expanding our economic power to distant lands we generate better jobs for ourselves and our children, we tacitly approve our government's permitting some of our citizens to set up vast monopolies in various countries. These individuals, by using the overwhelming might of the dollar, come into possession of vast resources to which they have no right. Of course, one can say that if we don't, someone else will, and it is the great tragedy of our times that we do wrong in the effort to save ourselves from greater injury and grief at a later date. In other words, granted that monopolies are antisocial, we feel that, so far as we ourselves are concerned, it is better to have an American monopoly rather than a Russian, German, or other sort. Naturally similar reasoning is followed by the people of these other countries, and thereby the common ground in which the nations could get together becomes more distant than ever. This economic infiltration tends to destroy the productive power of other countries, until they cannot buy the vast output of our mass production. As they become insolvent they will also cease to be instruments of trade, their economy will lapse to a plain agricultural level sufficient only for their subsistence, and they will no longer be able to acquire our automobiles, refrigerators, and washing machines. As a consequence, our standard of living will sag, and all will suffer as a result of the selfish and short-sighted schemes of men, never satisfied, who devour the grain that should be sown for next year's crop.

As often stressed, we are neither against capitalism or labor, nor at the service of any interest, one nation or another; we realize the fallacy of many actions of men, and having at heart the progress of humanity as a whole, feel compelled to denounce wrong whenever it appears. For this reason we are not at all impressed by our rich and prosperous country's gifts and charitable contributions, made to alleviate the suffering of underfed populations elsewhere. Although the loaf of bread given today cannot be expected to feed them forever, we still feel deeply hurt and shocked when years later the same countries try to better their lot by using some of the methods we have resorted to ourselves. (The conquest of Abyssinia by Italy is a case in point.) As a result of this resentment we consider such countries not quite civilized, and as this feeling coincides with the interests of those who really control the world, the eventual reprisals become a simple matter of political manipulation.

Now supposing the average citizen of the world to be conscious of these incongruities, why does he willingly become a blind pawn in the leader's gamble for supremacy? It is because he is first of all a citizen of some particular country, and therefore morally bound by laws, religion, customs, and traditions, to uphold its interests first. Now there is invariably considerable latitude as to what the interests of a country really are. Distortion of facts, propaganda, and other devices are usually responsible for the crystallization of the public opinion along the desired lines. If a world-minded citizen comes to different conclusions and is courageous enough to say so, he may be considered a traitor, and with his family becomes liable to physical punishment, and death. Since no world organizations as yet exist for combining the opinions and efforts of such citizens, they are forced to go along with the others, and allowed to vent their feelings platonically among their friends when no danger threatens their country. The average citizen likewise must be condoned for not taking a more belligerent attitude toward the wrongs, perpetuated about him. As a rule he is poor, defenseless, and uninformed, and depends on the bounty of the cliques who keep him alive by giving him a job. His well-being, modest as it may be, depends on that of the rich. Anything that tends to damage the interests of the powerful few will also injure him and the rest of the population, inasmuch as factories may close, prices skyrocket, and all manner of misfortunes descend upon him. To climax all this he may even lose his only mode of making a living. The protection of the interests of the powerful becomes his own protection and preoccupation, and because of this, while an incessant attrition continues between rich and poor in any country, all join forces and fight shoulder to shoulder against any other nation or interest that threatens them and their standard of living. This is another form assumed by patriotism.

As the war, under whatever pretext, becomes a reality, people are slaughtered, property destroyed, vast damage caused, shameful cruelties perpetrated, and the inevitable famine, plague, and privation spread among millions until peace finally reappears. The vanquished nation lies bleeding in the dust under the heel of the victor, and is forced to accept his terms, no matter how severe or unjust.

If the rich country happens to be the victor, she will subjugate the poor country and will deprive the latter still further of its previous means of livelihood. Being guilty of losing the war, the defeated nation will be reduced to a level from which she never again can challenge or endanger the winner. Needless to say, the standard of living of the latter will be injured by the tremendous strain of the war, yet as its wealth has not been appreciably decreased, and possibly has been enlarged by annexation of new areas, close to her borders or colonial, this injury may be only a temporary setback. However, the drop in standard of living of the vanquished will be staggering, especially considering the destruction and devastation everywhere, the heavy indemnity in cash and commodities imposed, and the appalling loss in human life, only too probably including the strongest and ablest of the nation's youth. Time, however, is a great healer of wounds, and as the population slowly returns to a normal life, even though at a level far below pre-war times, the ancient animosity against the rich nation will inflame the passions of the people and precipitate a new conflict.

If the poor country, on the other hand, should happen to win the war, she will claim everything in sight and will not listen to any consideration as to what is just or unjust. The rich nation deprived of even the barest means to continue as a national entity, will be exposed defenseless to any demand, however extravagant, by the victor. Her industry, works of art, historical treasures, and Heaven knows what else will be bodily transported to the vindictive winner, and left deteriorating and unattended for lack of skill and appreciation. Needless to say, such vandalism, while merely a matter of prestige rather than of benefit to the victor, will more severely injure the defeated nation, and in general will be detrimental to humanity. But, of course, men cannot and will not look far ahead. The victorious nation drunk with new power and importance, will destroy or confiscate all the wealth within reach, even if she realizes her inability to utilize it to the best advantage for herself and mankind in general. Any such thought would be the least of her worries, and with her triumph will come the self-assurance that in time she can use her loot as efficiently as its former owner, but now to her benefit alone. The indiscriminate and methodical destruction that will take place in the subjugated nation will have telling effects on her shattered economic position, and naturally will injure the economy of her neighbors. But as "might makes right", the previously impoverished nonentity will now be busily engaged in establishing herself as an arrived power, engaged in bullying other small nations, cowing them into submission, and forcing them into her expanding sphere of influence. Any colony held by the loser automatically qualifies among the spoils of victory. Her own experience of lowliness and poverty will be forgotten, and quickly she will display the insolence and arrogance proper to a superior race and nation. In short, she is now a satisfied nation, and let no one dare to challenge that position.

Yet even if the victor is one which previously was poor and to some extent justified in waging that war, will people in general be benefited by this victory for which so much blood was shed and so much sacrifice endured? No. Naturally the prospective condition of the winning population will be brighter, but needless to say its betterment will also depend to some extent upon world economic conditions, and as is usually the case, wars do not leave it in a better shape than before. However, a small percentage of that population will have gained considerably because of the conflict. Bankers, industrialists, and the like, already relatively rich before the war, and in line to gain appreciably from their contribution to its waging, are also the ones likely to gain by victory because they have the ready cash to pay the government for appropriated wealth placed on sale at a fraction of its actual worth. All those who deal in such transactions are certain to better considerably their standing. However, the rank and file of the population will remain as poor as ever, and can only hope that in the near or distant future the industrial betterment of the country, as a result of all this acquired wealth, may eventually bring them prosperity. As to their immediate physical gain, one can be sure that this will be far smaller than the sacrifice and hardship they had to endure, not to mention the loss of friends and relatives. As wars are often followed by a general unsettled condition among all countries, depression usually sets in, so that all, rich and poor, winners and losers, must pay in proportion to the damage incurred in this expensive method of improving their conditions.

Unfortunately, conditions will not change or improve in the future, despite the high-sounding phrases of the leaders of each country. Real betterment cannot be achieved so long as selfishness and greed form the base of each nation's policy, nor until ways are found to harness and harmonize the vast energy of people, rich and poor, in all classes and nations. Nor can it be achieved until means are found to harmonize the efforts of all human races, allow each individual to contribute his best for himself and mankind, and prevent once and for all the destruction of human life and property. As previously noted, progress depends on an ever-expanding division of labor and what system could surpass that which apportions labor among the entire population of the earth?

THE FUTILITY OF TARIFFS AND OF WARS

In the section of this chapter just ended, we have stressed the fact that the welfare of a manufacturing center usually depends upon its ability to retain or to increase its sphere of influence. In cases where two such centers are far distant, the expansion of either will not affect the interests of the other, and, therefore, not result in friction, hostility, or reprisal. This cannot be said, however, when their zones overlap, for sooner or later a sense of rivalry is bound to arise over the possession of disputed areas. Likewise, it has been shown that the people of such areas will tend to buy from the center selling at a lower price.

Assuming for the present that competition between the two centers remains on a fair and just level, every effort will be made by the contending parties to adopt efficient methods of production and all kinds of labor-saving devices in order to lower costs. But any step taken by one center will usually lead to countermeasures by the other, likewise determined to hold or enlarge its sphere of influence. This general improvement of production and lowering of prices naturally is beneficial to society, even though constituting a constant strain upon the manufacturers, who are bound to live in an atmosphere of uncertainty and tension. In a world of "live and let live" one can visualize the contending parties reaching an understanding by which their fields of influence are clearly defined and settled. Once this agreement is reached, both groups are free to raise their prices to a level at which they make substantial profits at the expense of society. This is what actually happens when the centers are few in number, but fortunately for society there are actually hundreds of independent groups of individuals engaged in the manufacture of similar products, so that any agreement among them is very unlikely. As a result, individuals or centers able to lower costs of production below those of others can gain and expand, while many of their rivals, faced by heavy losses, must abandon the struggle and withdraw from the market. When such a condition appears within a country, the effect is more or less confined to manufacturers unable to keep up with progress. Their loss, however, will not affect the standard of living of the population in general. Indeed the laborers, while eager to see the source of their wages and livelihood prosper and expand, are nevertheless able to find other jobs should that industry fail. While not minimizing the far-reaching repercussions of such failures, we must admit that as a rule society stands to gain. Of course, frequently the failing industries are absorbed by other interests, and consequently the factories are saved from actual shut-downs. Of course, if this should tend toward the setting-up of monopolies, we know that other detrimental effects would soon appear, but this is immaterial in the present discussion. At any rate, when competition becomes unfair and degenerates into rivalry and cut-throat methods, we know that public opinion, backed by government regulations, will lessen the unfavorable effects of such tactics.

In our basic example upon page 524, it was assumed that the raw material, as well as the manufactured products, could move freely from one place to another, and that the cost to the final consumer would reflect the distance as well as the living conditions of the center where they were made. While not actually stated, the sphere of influence of the various manufacturing centers were considered as part of the same country where local laws and regulations were binding upon all. Actually certain centers may belong to different nations. From the standpoint of economics it is clear that any community or consumer will choose commodities which, other factors being equal, are the cheapest on the market. They may or may not originate from manufacturing centers located in the country in which the buyer lives. If a community gravitates toward a center belonging to its own nation, well and good, it is intrinsically bound to that center, and under fair and normal competition it is just that its citizens should prefer to buy from these places rather than elsewhere. There are, however, many instances in which communities of one nation gravitate toward centers that belong to other nations, either because they are closer, have good roads or other methods of transportation, or in consequence of factors immaterial to the present discussion. At any rate, whatever the reason, it will be to the consumer's advantage to buy from this foreign center, and he will do so if its products are allowed free and unhampered entry across the border.

The fact that community A buys from center C rather than B will injure the interests of manufacturers located in B. This in turn will react upon the employees of that industry, especially if it is compelled to retrench because of the choice made by the population of A. We wish to assume that one of the first steps taken by any industry in the effort to meet competition is that of introducing better methods of production, rather than to lower wages and consequently the standard of living of the workers. To the extent that the wages of employees in industries belonging to the same country or community are approximately the same, efficiency and better modes of productions are usually the deciding factors in meeting competition. This is not the case when competition comes from abroad. In this latter instance the wage scale may become the deciding factor favoring any center. In seeking survival the industry in *B* may be forced to lower the wage scale of its workers, but as this would be resented by the entire population, other methods will be chosen to counteract competition from *C*. One is the imposing of tariffs upon products coming from *C* as well as from the nation to which it belongs. For the purpose of simplifying this discussion we shall indicate this latter country as Beta, while Alpha will be that to which *A* and *B* belong. As explained elsewhere, the tariff is a device by which any importer from abroad must pay a specific sum either to the community or to the nation where the imports are to be sold. In cases where the tariff is moderate, this gives the manufacturers of center *B* the opportunity to hold their own against the competition of *C*. In addition to the fact that the former are still able to make a profit, their working and living conditions will not be affected, wages and salaries will be held high, and efforts to reduce the cost of the commodities will not be necessary. The population of *A*, with no special interest in the welfare of community B, will nevertheless be adversely affected by such a tariff, being now forced to gravitate toward *B*, where prices are higher.

The manufacturers, workers, and general population of *C* will also suffer from that tariff because the outward flow of commodities will be drastically reduced. The consequent reduction in price and curtailment of production will take the form of fewer available jobs as well as in lowering of standard of living. However, since center *C* is part of Beta, its plight is of no special concern to *B* or the government of Alpha. Neglecting, therefore for the present the influence on the population of *C*, we can still say that the tariff, while beneficial to the community and to the manufacturers of some specific center, is detrimental in greater or lesser degree to the rest of the nation, and especially to those who would normally buy products from abroad. Upon the strength of these opposing interests depends the adoption or rejection of this tariff. Frequently those who benefit most are the financially powerful manufacturers who have great importance in shaping the policies of the nation. The population of large and prosperous cities and the like, will also back up the industries within their community, as the source of salaries and wages. On this account they will minimize the advantage of saving slight sums when buying from abroad. To the extent that the people likely to oppose the tariff live in small communities near the border, and lack the similar influence at the polls as well as in swaying the affairs of the nations, it is easy to guess which group will decide that choice. Likewise, in order to avoid friction among the population, intensive propaganda and appeals to nationalism will be unleashed, urging adoption of the tariff and giving precedence to home products. This, in many instances, means that people are compelled to buy articles from hundreds of miles away when available and cheaper from just beyond the border. While in many instances such a policy is pursued in the honest conviction that it protects the standard of living of the population in general, it is equally true that such policies tend to perpetuate graft and inefficiency and are actually detrimental to the nation itself. As one of the immediate effects of the tariff is that of decreasing the supply for the same amount of demand the price will tend to rise, and while wages and salaries will remain unchanged, the profit of the manufacturers will be excessively increased. In other words, the enthusiastic support of the manufacturers for tariffs is not altogether prompted by humanitarian principles.

Now to apply tariffs to reduce competition from C is bad enough, but often they are raised to such a level that for all practical purposes the imports from that center will cease completely. Without discussing the loss to C, which remains no concern of Alpha, this fact gives the manufacturers of B a wide degree of monopolistic freedom, on the fallacious assumption of helping home industry.

The foregoing has been introduced into our discussion on the supposition that the same kind of commodities are manufactured in centers B and C. It is possible, however, that those produced in C cannot be duplicated by the manufacturers in B. Should such commodities be of luxury nature, the adoption of tariffs would affect only the rich. Some of the wealthy will continue buying the usual amount, irrespective of price, while others will buy less, but due to their nature and the fact that the poor are not affected, only the industry of C will suffer because of the inevitable reduction in sale, Occasionally such policies are adopted to encourage the production of vital commodities of inferior grade and of a substitute nature.

Here again the rich will still purchase the kind imported from abroad, while the poor must make shift with local trash. Monopolistic policies will be the consequence, within these limits, and the population in general is the obvious loser.

So much for the immediate effect on the people of Alpha as a result of tariffs imposed by their government, but it remains to consider the consequence of such a policy on the population of *C* as well as on Beta. As said, these measures are introduced by the government of Alpha when competition from *C* endangers the interests of influential individuals of that country. Tariffs have the effect of throttling a trade that had hitherto been expanding, and represent an abrupt reduction of the sphere of influence of *C*. This naturally means decreased production, shutdown of previously growing industries, unemployment, and other undesirable effects felt by the entire population of Beta. That this raising of barriers between the two nations should be unpopular in center *C* goes without saying. Now, there are several modes of reprisals to which *C* can resort to counteract such effects. First it will seek to lower the price of its products by introducing better methods of production, and if this is not sufficient, wages will be reduced. But as the tariffs can be raised at will, there is nothing to stop the government of Alpha from doing this when such reduction in price by the manufacturers of center *C* again overtakes center *B*. In this case, a limit will be reached at which no further reduction can be made without lowering standards of living in *C*, which cannot be done if discontent and disorders are to be avoided.

To the extent that any measure provokes countermeasures, it is understandable that Beta in turn, urged by similar interests and under the same misconceptions, will impose tariffs of her own upon commodities imported from Alpha, with the consequence that both populations will suffer in one way or another.

Now, were we to assume that all material is concentrated in either nation it could easily be seen that the wealthier has a great advantage over the other, because besides the tariff upon manufacturers she can limit the exportation of the necessary raw material. Obviously such a practice is bound to cause more hardship and economic chaos among the nations. Fortunately, no country has an absolute control over the raw materials of the world, or more ferocious wars would be the lot of mankind, but it is all a matter of degree and the present-day confusion among nations has its root in a condition severe enough to generate the unrest of our time.

It must be stressed that hundreds of different raw materials are needed to maintain the level of our civilization. Raw material is found in greater or lesser abundance almost everywhere in the world, constituting a great bargaining medium among the nations, and thus all lands can sustain various degrees of standard of living, even though in many cases the amount in their possession does not permit them either to compete successfully with others or to raise their living level above a certain minimum. Because of the urge impelling men to improve their state, the contest for the acquisition of natural resources, and quest of zones of influence goes on relentlessly not only among manufacturers and centers within a single nation but between entire countries, each seeking to take as much material as possible, at the expense of the others. Now, while competition among centers or individuals of any country results in weeding out inefficient enterprises, tending to advance progress and betterment among the people in general, this cannot be said for competition among nations, since here it is not always the most efficient nation that wins out, but the one which is more powerful and already in control of resources far above actual needs. In this latter case the elimination of competition is definitely harmful to humanity as a whole. As any nation loses out to another because of the impossibility of acquiring the desired products, its factories are certain to be closed and unemployment bound to increase. As a result, wages and salaries must be drastically reduced, and the general standard of living will be adversely affected. Moreover, all who lose their jobs cannot hope to find others in their community or elsewhere in the country, because general economic disruption has upset the life of the nation. As a consequence, sooner or later its choatic condition is bound to be felt by the others in one way or another.

Were we all aware of these facts, what method could we advance to eradicate conditions so detrimental to humanity? One must admit that with human nature as it is, with all the prejudices, feuds, and selfish interests imbedded in the instincts of the various peoples and more or less decisive in the affairs of the world, no betterment appears possible. Even with a League of Nations or United Nations, each country like each individual is concerned only with the immediate advantage that good fortune may secure, and makes the most of circumstances without considering one moment that conditions of the present may change and dominance pass to other nations in the future. As they in turn are sure to follow the same short-sighted policies, it can easily be foreseen that no good is in store for humanity in general.

We must bluntly state that we do not see any particular evidence either on the part of the League of Nations or United Nations to carry through their official profession of protecting and upholding sacred human rights. This is particularly true when interests of small and weak countries are unjustly endangered by the policies of the great powers. The United Nation is just another League of Nations with different name and location, but with similar ideals and organization. Despite the attitude that many will take toward our statement, and no matter the profuse and platonic expressions of great thinkers and leaders, we do not see in the activities of these organizations anything but a futile attempt on the part of the satisfied nations to preserve the status quo in the world today. Their effort is mostly intended to muzzle with methods short of war, the aspiration of unscrupulous great powers in their attempt of world domination. By gathering the approval and support of weak nations they try to create a world opinion in the hope that it may prove a restraining influence on the would-be aggressor countries. This was also the ideal and the attitude taken by the "Holy Alliance" of more than one century past where government of the then great powers tried to prevent the diffusion of liberal thinking and also to circumvent the imperialistic desires of Napoleon. While the merits or demerits of the aggressor nations are not the main topic of the present discussion, we must realize that any alliance based on false pretenses and on purely egotistic principles could not and will not endure the impact with reality. Sooner or later such alliance must give way to chaos and confusion. It was so with the Holy Alliance, it was so with the League of Nations and it will be so with the United Nations. In all these attempts of coalition among nations or better to say among the ruling minorities of the large and satisfied nations we see two definite purposes. One is that of satisfying their people and the world in general regarding their efforts to establish justice and fair play, the other is that of imposing a status quo among all nations, whatever the difference in their economic conditions. With these aims accomplished they think their idealistic goal is achieved. That this status quo might be utterly oppressive to others is no concern of theirs, and if it leads to jealousy, antagonism, and open strife let future generations take care of the problem as best they can. Once this order is established the status quo cannot be altered without infringing upon the spirit of the alliance and the culprit will appear to the world as a violator of peace.

As a generality the selfish rich, whether an individual or a nation, looks with scorn and contempt on those who today are weak and poor. Thereby he becomes the object of resentment and hate, but confident in his own strength, he is opposed to any change that may better conditions for others, even though he himself is not thereby injured in any way. He does not seem to take into account the fact that in the future he or his descendants might become poor and be in turn the object of despisal and detestation. This sums up the world today. If one looks below the veneer of respectability that obscures international manipulations and faces facts, reckons the consequences of policies, treaties, and the none too altruistic alliances among nations, he must conclude that conditions are neither improving nor likely to improve until some radical change is introduced that will do away with this jockeying and maneuvering for positions of power, and instead build cooperation and good-will among all men and nations. How this may be accomplished will be discussed in a subsequent chapter.

When economic relations between two countries become tense, and one begins to resent the effects of discriminating policies on the part of the other, while no peaceful method avails either to bring understanding or slacken strangulation, then actual conflict between the two nations is at hand. The explosive situation eventually needs but a spark to set either nation at the other's throat. Both countries will rely heavily on the patriotism and valor of their people. They will idolize their heroes and their deeds, including those acts which under normal circumstances are punished by law, but now are praised and made symbols of greatness. If such a war could rectify injustices and abolish animosity between the belligerents for good, we would be inclined to approve it even if an enormous destruction of property and a tremendous holocaust of human life should be its price, but unfortunately this is never the case, and while they fight under the illusion of upholding a just cause, more often than not the real motive is the rivalry between powerful interests in both countries bent upon the exclusive acquisition or retention of wealth.

As wars are bound to swing nations further apart, we must conclude that instead of leading ultimately to harmony and happiness, they merely breed more wars with no benefit whatever to humanity. This being the case, and history having taught the dangers and destructions involved, why do nations still resort to such methods to solve their differences? Again basic instincts are the sources of this senseless behavior. The selfishness and greed of man makes him ignore justice and covet what belongs to others. His primitive urges impel him to fight, not for the just share of worldly goods but for the outright mastery of all and the utter subjugation and degradation of the opponents.

Germany in her days of victory made it only too clear for what she was fighting when her vanquished victims came successively under her heel. Not only were their possessions destroyed or confiscated, but millions were murdered and martyrized merely to cripple those nations so that never again could they oppose the newly established master race. Can one feel that Germany is now faring much better than the people she had previously subjugated? While we may hope so, and refuse to believe that any civilized nation would permit sadistic and irresponsible individuals to commit human acts as many of the Germans did while in the saddle, we know that the Germans as a whole have a dark future ahead and will be compelled to a lower standard of living not apt to open their hearts and make them better citizens of the world. Indeed how could Germany become satisfied when she will be stripped of much of her wealth, when she will be forced to give up much of her land and property, and thus have a larger population to feed on less area, when she already is forced to yield slave labor to Russia and still is prevented from improving home conditions? Will Japan fare any better? Colonies she had gained at the end of the first world war have now been taken away. Undoubtedly she will be stripped of all land acquired even before that. How can one expect that such a nation will ever be satisfied when the reason for her continuously waging war was to enlarge her possessions and by that give better opportunity to her people? Will Italy fare any better than the others? Italy, poor and economically dependent upon others, may be forced to give up colonies settled long before the first war, which somehow represented a hope of self-sufficiency in the future. Will these methods induce good-will among men? No. We strongly doubt this outcome and even though on the surface there will be declarations of friendship and cooperation, hatred and vengefulness are the inevitable consequence of the policies pursued by the victors. Yet we citizens of conquering nations truly believe that the defeated peoples ought to be satisfied, and that what is required is merely either a new kind of government or a re-education in their mode of life and attitude toward neighbors. How a poor nation can live happily among rich and prosperous rivals no one has yet been able to answer. As we see it, even if the Axis states have fallen forever, others will take their place in the perennial quest for supremacy, and the world is bound to remain a perennial battleground as long as animal instincts are permitted to decide the fate of men. Should we then allow the vanquished to retain possession of the wealth for which they fought and lost? No, this is not in our mind, for there is no limit to such envious aspiration. We believe, however, that a system must be devised by which all will have a just share of world wealth in proportion to ability, ingenuity, and contribution to general welfare. If we could make the standard of living not entirely dependent upon basic wealth, if every nation could improve its condition without infringing on the rights of others, there is hope that a better understanding among nations will eventually be achieved.

Having reached the end of this analysis it is well to draw some obvious conclusions. It is evident that those economic forces in the world that spring from the endless variety of needs among all the people on earth give rise to conditions which no individual, group, or nation can guide and control. Because of this incessant quest for security and betterment, because of the relentless natural law of the survival of the fittest, because of the fact that retrogression or just plain stagnation means decay and disintegration, all people have drifted into a struggle that admits neither quarter nor appeasement. Lack of co-ordinating influences and unnecessary competition makes it imperative for each to expand in order to live. This in actual life usually is at the expense of others who in turn will react and use reprisals. As we see it this strife is bound to increase with improvements in technology and with the overlapping of the various spheres of influence which will come to represent the interests and the very life of larger bodies of populations in the world. We can easily see that a zone of influence may have as its center, not merely an industry or a city, but an entire nation. Essentially all such areas are based on the same needs, their only difference being in their magnitude and the number of people involved. If we should abrogate and completely cancel all laws controlling inter-relationship among the inhabitants of any single country, this being advocated by anarchists, it would soon lead to a situation in which entire regions and cities as well as individuals would resort to physical clashes. Lacking any superior authority invested in the government, each person would have to use all his strength to protect, not only his interests, but his very life. This was the case centuries past when many present-day civilized countries were divided into small states and principalities. Each separate state felt more often than not the necessity to arm itself and form alliances against neighboring rivals which seemed to threaten its interests. This, fortunately, is no longer the case, as most of these isolated units now form part of a nation and all have to abide by the guiding power of the federal or central government. The presence of such authority, not only serves as protection for those otherwise endangered, but is used as a restraining influence upon all who otherwise would infringe upon other people's interests. The condition among nations throughout the world nowadays corresponds to this chaotic era of the city-states or to a group of anarchistic individuals in which each feels constrained to be a law to himself to safeguard his life and rights, actual or imagined.

From the foregoing the necessity of a higher authority with the necessary power to enforce law, order, and justice becomes imperative if we are to lead the world from lawless chaos to stability in which all can live in peace and freedom.

CHAPTER XI

DESIRABILITY OF A FEDERATION OF NATIONS
UNDER THE SAME MODE OF LIFE

IN PREVIOUS CHAPTERS we have described the method proposed for improving conditions within a nation. Among the most important policies contemplated by this new mode of life we may mention the following:

(1) Positive forces are introduced to increase the standard of living of the population in general.

(2) A minimum wage, based upon the amount of supply, is calculated and enforced. Through this the standard of living of the poor assumes a major role in the advancement of all branches of society which will no longer be endangered by unscrupulous individuals who find it profitable to decrease rather than to increase available vital commodities.

(3) The present wage scale, based on ability and industriousness, is respected and maintained. This, because of the justice of remuneration in accordance with contribution toward society in general. The greater the contribution of each individual, the larger should be his compensation and, while his standard of living will be better than the minimum assured to the incapable, still it will not detract from that minimum.

(4) Any physically healthy person will always be able to obtain work, since the EW will find employment whenever industry is incapable of doing so. Projects undertaken by the EW will not be in competition with industry, but will be aimed toward increasing the role of private initiative and enterprise. With the serenity of mind proper to those who feel secure in their jobs and confident of their future, and with the self-respect inherent in those conscious of being a vital part of a society basically just and healthy, all will contribute their best to the improvement of society in general and of themselves and their families in particular.

(5) The basic freedom of the individual will be upheld and defended because all should be left free in their quest of happiness if their actions do not infringe upon the basic interests of others. His activities will not be forced or dictated, but aided and guided whenever help is sought, in the honest conviction that the welfare of the nation depends on the well-being of each individual.

(6) Standard of living will be measured by effort exerted as well as by amount of commodities and services enjoyed. We have seen how one of the strongest instincts of man, especially evident in the poorest part of society, is that of acquiring vital commodities for which they usually have to spend most of their earnings. As this is not sufficient for their need, they welcome additional work so as to increase the percentage of the theoretical amount. In their instinctive appraisal the increase in wages far surpasses the greater expenditure of effort, and is, therefore, profitable. It has been noted, however, that this excessive effort, often unregulated and blind, raises production to a level far above what the public is willing to absorb. The prices of these commodities, vital or otherwise will naturally drop and with them the profits of those responsible for the excessive production. It could be said that their gains are far surpassed by the additional effort, even though the latter is not generally considered by the individual quite often bent at the acquisition of food for his family. As such even though able to obtain a very modest return for his labor, he usually feels that his living conditions have improved, whatever the effort on his part. This, of course, is right so far as the individual is concerned, but not so for society that permits such a condition to exist, since the immediate result of the increased purchasing power, under a stable equilibrium, is that of raising the price of vital commodities. While this tends to increase the disparity between effort exerted and commodities obtained by those willing to work and strive, their gain will be at the expense of the others in the lower brackets of society, because the rich, whatever the price, will always be able to buy all they want at the expense of the poor. However, if a gradual increase of the stable equilibrium point is provided this necessity will gradually diminish and finally disappear. All those with many dependents, not only will become able to provide for them without undue increase in effort, but this effort will decrease with the passing of time as the equilibrium point reaches higher levels. Needless to say their standard of living will be favorably affected by both factors.

(7) All will be free in their honest quest of riches and while no

obstacle will be placed in their way, inheritance laws will withhold large fortunes from accumulating in the hands of the incapable and inept. Thereby much of the parasitic element in society which thrives on the effort of others will be greatly reduced. This does not mean that regulations be such that all their wealth will return to society. Generous bequests will be allowed, more than sufficient to maintain the highest standard of living in the nation, inferior only to that reserved for those who through toil, ability, and genius place themselves in the vanguard of society.

(8) The economic well-being of a community will be gradually transformed and made to blend with that of other communities. The wealth of the land will be utilized to the utmost in order to raise the relative living level to the maximum. This, in turn, will be greatly increased by preventing useless competition with neighbors and by concentrating on productions for which the community is best qualified. No pretense is made that all zones will attain the same standard of living. Those with more wealth and natural resources, if in possession of knowledge and technical ability are bound to surpass others not so generously endowed. It stands to reason that stones near the fire should be warmer than those more distantly placed. What men resent most is not the disadvantage resulting from their land being poor or far from natural resources, but the inferiority forced upon them by selfish manipulations of others who, by diverting the natural flow of products and materials, deprive them of what they consider their due.

In the new mode of life this injustice will no longer exist and, therefore, will cease to be a cause of attrition between communities and nations. Since a strict balance of trade will be maintained with the purpose of regulating the amount of products flowing from one place to another, the living level of each community will be related to the wealth of its land. In this none can feel robbed, discriminated against, or injured. However, as economic conditions of all areas will be closely interwoven, the well-being of each will materially add to the well-being of the others while its gains will not be at their expense. All will find it to their advantage to uphold any policy that enhances and improves the lot of those who are unfortunate. As a result the standard of living of each zone, while still linked to the basic wealth of the land, will be greatly enhanced by the amalgamation of interests among all zones.

(9) The new mode of life regards labor, or ability to perform work, a form of wealth which, like any other, must be utilized

wherever available for the benefit of mankind. In cases where a zone has too large a population for the land to support, its standard of living is bound to be low, especially when no help is received from the outside. This population, however, constitutes a potential wealth that should be used for the general good. Several methods are indicated to improve its conditions. New industries and enterprises with a fair chance of success can be sponsored and encouraged. The relatively low cost of labor within the zone will be a favorable factor in competing with industries outside the zones. This will also serve to counteract the greater cost of transportation of such material as must be imported. As the living condition of this population improves, the cost of production will also rise, and the competitive position versus industries outside the zone will tend to stabilize at a specific level which, if occasionally below that of others, will still surpass the original one. This level will result from a good balance between wealth of the land, labor wealth, and size of population. Secondly, the EW will subsidize projects intended to stimulate the productivity of the zone. As stated this, in one way or another, benefits them all. Thirdly, some labor will be encouraged to emigrate elsewhere as needed, and by decreasing the ratio between size of population and wealth of the land a better living will result for those remaining in the zone.

(10) Opening up of industries in the overpopulated zone, say A, will be done intelligently so as not to damage other zones or the federation itself. Each step must be part of a general program for the entire federation. Thus if an adjoining zone, say B, should also need such aid it is evident that the planned expansion in zone A would damage the interests of zone B. But if both are channelled toward the production of nationally needed commodities, those damaging effects will not appear. Where a zone is rich in resources, it could easily outdistance others in the sale of manufactured commodities. In such a case, while more emphasis will be placed on the sale of unfinished products and on greater purchase from the outside, working hours will be gradually shortened without decreasing wages. This will maintain a flow of commodities easily absorbed by the entire nation, and the standard of living of this zone will exceed others because each person will work less for the same purchasing power.

This will promote a perfect collaboration among zones with different natural resources. The rich area, by curtailing productivity, so as to increase that in others, contributed heavily to their well-being. In return the average citizen improves his standard of living through the reduction of working hours. On the other hand, the average citizen of the poor zone, while gaining a larger proportion of vital commodities must exert a greater amount of effort than the citizen of the rich one and in this respect will fare less well. This, however, is just and proper, since both receive the commodities necessary to their well-being. The large amount of work done by the citizen of the poorer zone only reflects the poorer condition of his land imposed by nature and not brought about by man. Needless to say, both types of zones gain by this union.

(11) No fear is felt that the industrialists of the rich zone will be unfavorably affected by the industries emerging in the poor zone. Indeed, many of them will be totally or partially owned and financed by these men, as they have the necessary capital for such enterprises. Irrespective of this they will gain greatly by the stable and progressive condition of business throughout the country. Of course, those who are incompetent may be actually endangered; however, if they should fail as a result of the new industries, we can be sure that sooner or later that would have been their fate even if those industries had not existed.

To the extent that a brighter prospect lies ahead of everyone in the nation, that the gain of an individual or class adds rather than clashes with that of another, and that all the zones in the country reach a higher standard of living through this closer amalgamation of interests we can visualize a happy and contented society. It is true that living standards within one zone or community will differ according to ability and aptitude, and among the zones will vary in proportion to the natural resources on hand. In either case the larger earnings of the individual and the high living level of the zone will be the result of a natural gift; intelligence and ability in the first, abundance of raw material in the second. This discrepancy will not be resented by the average citizen as no one will feel it is due to dishonest and egotistic activities. All will realize that whatever level of living they have attained, this is a direct result of cooperation and cumulative planning and that their well-being would be far lower if they were left alone with their limited resources.

POSSIBILITY OF UNDERSTANDING AMONG NATIONS

It now remains to analyze what can be done to establish justice and cooperation among nations so that the foundation can be laid on which humanity can securely rest and prosper. Nations, being agglomerations of peoples, are apt to be swayed by the same instincts and interests analyzed before and, therefore, bound to benefit by similar remedies suggested for one nation. Just as with persons of different classes who are living within one community or nation, we are confronted by wealthy and impoverished countries. By this is not meant that all of a rich country are wealthy and all of a poor one penniless. Even in the United States, easily the richest nation of the world, there is untold misery among millions, and in contrast, vast wealth can be found in the hands of a few in India who are surrounded by oceans of poverty and malnutrition. But, on the whole, some countries have a higher standard of living than others. Without denying merit where due, it must be admitted that it is in countries which have attained a higher degree of civilization that we find an ambitious and energetic population. As a general rule, education is widespread, and many of the advantages enjoyed result from hard work and co-ordinated planning. This high standard of living, however, achieved because of those qualities, can also be ascribed to an abundance of resources which permits and maintains a strong and healthy economic system. It promotes trade among citizens and nations, and brings into being remunerative work for many. In stating these facts we have no specific country in mind. We know that some have been able to attain a high degree of civilization seemingly without such resources, which would tend to disprove our statement. But one needs only to search more deeply into the causes of this apparent discrepancy to find the forces that yielded this advancement. These may have acted because of geographical location, climatic condition, or other phenomena which had a definite influence in the evolution of that population. But, as this does not pertain to the present discussion, the finding of these causes can be left to the reader who cares to search deeper into the subject. These nations, in any case, are the exception rather than the rule, and usually the richer the country, the higher the average standard of living is apt to be. It must be noted in passing that wealth is used here in its broadest interpretation, and besides its material form includes also the imponderable personal variety.

Undeniably, the prominent position of nations is the result, not only of definite efforts made by the present population, but of fortuitous circumstances and progressive steps taken by past generations. As the fortunate countries acquired this position, this also meant further progress and enlightenment for many of their people, making possible a rapid gain in knowledge and culture. From the time when only a few devoted their lives to science and research, greatly adding to the improvement of industry and technology, opportunity to enter the field was given to many others. Because of the many scientists engaged in the expansion of all branches of human activity, progress has been attained at a greater pace. This, in turn, has placed in the hands of these nations powerful instruments of war and destruction. This technical knowledge, however, has no connection with the moral evolution of man which in the last analysis is the only measure of growth and advancement. Unfortunately, in this respect, our society is little better than many civilizations of the past. Progress in this particular analysis refers only to that physical and technological advancement that gives the possessor a powerful instrument which, at his own discretion, can be used for good or evil. Since moral progress has not increased in the same ratio as technological progress, nations possessing technical power have not hesitated in the past as well as at present to subjugate independent societies under the most untenable and unjustifiable pretenses. By such methods vast reservoirs of riches have come into the hands of a few powerful countries while native populations have been left poor, and enslaved, reaping no benefit from their natural wealth. This apparent superiority of one nation or race over another, has in the process of time, given to those more advanced in technique the false impression that by nature they are superior to the others. The Romans felt superior to their slaves and so did the nobles in relation to their peasants. Those who belong to these supposedly superior nations do not realize, however, that the people of a backward country do not have the same opportunities as they have. Yet, sooner or later, these people will also arise. Fortunately, for mankind the craving for culture, the yearning toward the better things in life, cannot be confined or restricted to any one race or nation. In time these backward races and nations will rapidly ascend the ladder of progress. The means of transportation which greatly lessen distances, the commerce and trade among peoples, exert great influence in every part of the earth and carry with them the seeds of civilization and culture. This in turn kindles in the souls of men the desire for freedom, the desire to learn, prosper and improve standards of living. It may be conceded that in the most backward countries this only applies to a small fraction of the population, that which constitutes the upper class, probably because it is the only one in direct contact with foreign culture. This process, however, once started, cannot be stopped, and ultimately more of the people will clamor for a standard of living they consider their due, and nothing will divert this determination. Those nations and classes which, due to fortuitous circumstances, have started the march of progress earlier and thereby been able to acquire advantages which only ignorance on the part of the others have made possible, must realize that they are confronted by a gigantic awakening of the masses in almost every corner of the world. These masses more and more will assert themselves and claim their rightful place in the sun. This awakening may be compared to what takes place in the fields and forests when spring puts life into every tree, plant, and clod of earth. No matter what we may undertake to stop this process the forces of nature eventually assert themselves over the will of men. Mankind, in its relentless quest for betterment will soon reach a crossroads where a momentous decision must be made. The fate of present and future generations will rest on this, and we shall learn how far humanity will advance toward its final aspiration and goal.

One of these roads is the maintenance of the status quo in the world as found today. This opposes any change in relationship among individuals and among nations. If this is the path chosen, we will find nations, hitherto holding wealth to which they have no claim, but holding through intrigue and power, maintaining their position of leadership in the sense of being able to enjoy more supplies and comforts. This preeminence will likewise be due to the fact that they can compete successfully in the world market. The control of such a great amount of wealth allows them the alternative either to use only what is needed to their well-being, while withholding the rest, or apportion some of it, not in accordance with natural laws, but to their likes and dislikes, with the view of enhancing their immediate as well as their future exclusive interests. Their position, in other words, will be akin to a monopoly in which by eliminating actual or potential competitors, these nations can dominate the economic life of others, raise prices to a level far above actual costs, and thus inflict injury upon humanity in general. Of course, these nations, or rather their leaders, would prefer to have their colonies remain indefinitely in a dormant and subject condition. This would greatly simplify the control of their wealth. However, civilization, like the spring referred to above, is quietly spreading among these people, who in time will neither recognize nor respect the overlordship of outsiders. This process of awakening, accelerated by the inevitable contacts with other civilizations and countries, quite often seeking to undermine the preeminent position of the controlling nation, will make the natives, not only conscious of their rights, but also conscious of the fact that the wealth of their land is being depleted to raise the living conditions of outsiders while they, themselves, linger in a state of poverty, with no hope of peacefully winning that freedom for which all men aspire. Needless to say, their resentment will eventually flare up into open revolt. No doubt there are many exceptions. However, to be frank, most of the native populations of contemporary colonies are held in virtual slavery, and any concession given to them is not granted with the wholehearted initiative of the so-called mother country, but with reluctance because of the ever-louder demand both within and without.

Akin to the miserable situation of peoples in a state of servitude and slavery is the status of nations free and relatively rich but nevertheless too poor in comparison to the privileged ones. Lack of resources prevents them from using their available manpower to good advantage, and by that raise their standard of living. It is inevitable that such a state of affairs should cause friction and attrition because after all the basic instincts of men are similar among all nations and races, so that, if humanity maintains the status quo, we can be sure that our heritage will consist of strikes and revolts, wars and famines, sickness and suffering, which have ever proved effective brakes to progress and advancement.

The other road is that of promoting true justice among individuals and nations, in the honest realization that the welfare of each one is intrinsically bound up with that of the others.

We hope that the most civilized countries of the world will take the initiative in laying the foundations of the new society. This will raise rich and poor alike to an undreamed-of civilization and progress. We hope also that these nations, realizing that the new mode of life is advantageous to them, agree that for the good of all, no peoples should be subjugated to the interests of others, and accept the axiom that only by subdividing labor among a larger number of people and of nations, can real progress be achieved.

Trade barriers and other man-made regulations are often responsible for the contradictions whereby commodities are far cheaper in distant lands (usually the mother country) than places only a few miles from where they are found or fashioned. Besides the definite loss that may ensue to countries desiring more of these products such practices are antisocial and harmful to humanity.

Indeed the fact that any one country holds a greater amount of raw material, does not necessarily mean that their products will be sold for less to the ultimate consumer. We need to realize that pre-eminence in world trade should depend on two important conditions: (1) The country is far advanced in technology and ability to cut expenses, (2) the country is rich in raw material and, therefore, transportation costs are bound to be less than others. In both cases such advantages, being intrinsic to the nation, cannot arouse animosity among others.

We accept and support the higher rank in society acquired and maintained by individuals who possess high degrees of skill and intelligence, when this position has been attained through inborn ability and hard honest work, but not when obtained by force, intrigue or dishonest action. We also refuse to accept the pre-eminent position of those who are there because of their forefathers. This is all the more resented if they no longer possess the qualities of their ancestors.

The foregoing has been introduced at this point to emphasize the similarity of relations among individuals to those among nations. We feel confident, therefore, that just as the advocated mode of life is certain to improve relations among individuals, it will likewise improve those among nations.

We have already analyzed the advantages available to any nation that adopts the new principles of life, independently of the type of regime or culture of other countries. Consider now what would happen if several nations instead of one decide to make this change. Any such two nations, no matter where located, will form a close economic unit similar to the one that binds the inhabitants of any country. This stems from the fact that both nations embrace the same principles and ideals, and renounce forever egotistic international policies. By this they place their faith in the constitution of humanity, equal for all nations and all people, do not recognize narrow interests of individuals or minorities, no matter how powerful, but the rightful interests of all people within that system. One of the primary steps, of course, is that of gradually abolishing any economic barrier among them so that trade may freely circulate as within one country. Both nations, whether large or small, will be divided into zones of two or three millions population, due account made of the basic interest of the people. Cultural and ethnological technicalities, while important, must not jeopardize the first condition. Each zone, in other words, will be formed of one or more industrial centers and their immediate areas of influence. For each will be found an economic position with relation to the others and, as shown, this will be determined by the intrinsic wealth of the land, the average index, and the balance of trade. The same monetary system will be adopted by all, and will greatly encourage trade among them. Capital will also move freely, provided that it tends to better the economic position of a zone without impairing that of another. This means that citizens of any zone in any country may invest in industries in other zones of the same or different countries, with the specific understanding that this capital becomes an integral part of the economic life of the zone in which the industry is located, and follows regulations governing that zone. In other words, the outflow of money must conform to well-established rules which take into account the economic position of the zone itself. The division of any country into zones will follow directives earlier analyzed. As a zone is defined, the various branches of the EW will gradually introduce those forces that raise its standard of living. The officials of the EW may or may not be natives of that zone or country. The reason for this is that, since all zones and countries form an economic unit, shuffling of officials may prove beneficial because, having no particular ties with the population they serve, will be less swayed by graft or favoritism. On the other hand, the interests of the zone in relation to others will be protected because of the watchful supervision of the PW made of local members. At any rate, while this supervision will be unfailingly active, it will prove unnecessary because of the rigid rules within the EW which functions independently of nationality and predisposition of officials. As the activities of the EW will be known through the publication of periodic bulletins, anyone will be able to ascertain the economic position of his zone or community, and keep informed of the steps contemplated and taken.

For the calculation of the economic position of the zone indicated by P, the factors X, Y, and Z must first be determined. The method for the derivation of P is outlined in page 341 and does not need further elucidation. Depending on the size of this index, each zone will be entitled to a certain amount of assistance.

To make our point clear, suppose the United States, France, and Italy join in such a system, and that Sicily and the state of Georgia are two of the large number of zones making up these three nations. As previously explained, both zones will have a definite economic position given by the product of the three factors X, Y, Z. Now if the economic position of Georgia should be lower than that of Sicily, naturally Georgia is entitled to precedence in receiving assistance from the central government of the three nations. Yet, while the central branch will adopt policies which aim at raising the standard of living of Georgia, these policies will not detract from basic interests of other zones. Naturally they will vary, depending on circumstances, and may range from simple financial aid or introduction of new industries to finding work for the many unemployed either within or outside the zone, so as to relieve the effects of overpopulation. Such activities, however, will not prevent Sicily from receiving her due consideration because her economic position happens to be better than that of Georgia. As a matter of fact all zones in need of assistance will be entitled to it at the earliest possible time, but, of course, priority must be given those in more urgent need.

It is evident that the new mode of life, adopted at the beginning by one or more nations, will probably extend with time and enlightenment to an increasing number throughout the world. In joining the sister nations they will, naturally, become an integral part of the new economic system, and while they will retain their customs, religion, and culture, in an economic sense they will assume the same duties and privileges as the others. As the population of this federation will easily encompass hundreds of millions, it becomes evident that internal problems pertaining to some zone in the middle of the United States or of China cannot be efficiently settled (unless basic principles of the Constitution are involved) by the officials of the federation government. Such problems from all parts of the world would prove cumbersome and a stumbling block to the progress of the entire Federation. If the government of the Federation, because of its vastness, should become unduly burdened, the situation will be ripe for the division of the complete land into superzones. Each will be composed of nine zones and its officials, by assuming duties similar to those in the federation government, will devote their activity to matters involving their new economic unit. Only major issues will then go to the officials of the federation who, relieved of many details, will be in a better position to guide the destinies of humanity as a whole. The basic principles adopted for the formation of a zone will also apply to the superzone, the choice of the nine zones being dictated by economic considerations which take into account the basic interests of the zones involved. Ethnological and cultural considerations will only be secondary in that regard. Thus Europe, for instance (if all this continent should join the federation), could be easily divided into several superzones (the average population being 27 million). Now the fact that occasionally races must be either divided or joined with others will in no way imperil their interests or jeopardize their cultural heritage. This division is only made to expedite the solution of problems resulting from the policies intended to raise the general standard of living.

Returning to our instance, the assistance to be given either to Georgia or Sicily, much progress will be made by the zone itself through the normal operation of the local EW, while the aid of the Federation will be required only when the economic help of the respective superzones is not sufficient. The EW of each superzone will seek to increase the supply of vital commodities, decrease their cost of transportation, and introduce measures that enhance the economic situation of each community and zone belonging to that group. It is natural that commodities will be more expensive in one place than another. This will only result from cost of transportation and since no trade barrier will be raised against their natural flow, no resentment can be caused by such a condition. A strict balance of trade will be maintained among all zones and whenever industries can be located in one place rather than another for the general good, this will be done. Zones rich in material resources will naturally attain a higher standard of living. This will be apparent by the larger amount of commodities enjoyed, and by the fewer hours of work needed. It may seem that such zones would attract a large number of emigrants from less fortunate areas, but we do not fear such an outcome. Because of the fusion of interests among all zones, the standard of living of the poorest and richest areas will not be at such variance as can be found in modern society under our mode of life. As each zone is experiencing some degree of progress, the instinctive attraction toward one's homeland will be far stronger than any difference in standard of living. Of course, some change of population is inevitable, but this will not be sufficient to affect in one way or another the living levels of the zones concerned. In cases where it is advisable that many be moved elsewhere, the recipient zone will be in a region sparsely populated and rich in material resources. The native population, too small, poor, or backward to utilize their resources in full, will be greatly enhanced by such an influx, because new blood will be injected in the life of the zone which will raise it to a more important role in the economy and well-being of the federation.

POSITION OF A COLONY WITHIN THE FEDERATION

The procedure in the previous section will be followed when several nations of approximately the same stage of civilization and outlook decide to adopt the new mode of life. Some of these, however, may have colonies under their control. What should be the policy regarding these people? The granting of freedom is the only step consonant with basic human rights. Their dealings with the mother country or the others in the federation must be on the same level as those of any free state. This statement, however, must be made with some reservation. The unrestricted freedom mentioned above applies only to colonies which have reached a relatively high degree of civilization. The entrance into the federation, if they should so decide, will win them privileges as well as duties, equal to those of other members. We feel justified in stating that their willingness to join must be ascertained by a proper referendum, since the mother country by pledging herself to the new system of life, relinquishes the claim to speak for these people. Should the majority be opposed to such alliance, this will be permitted. In any case the fundamental principle of human rights must be upheld, irrespective of the interests of the federation.

This course, on the other hand, may not prove the best when dealing with a population markedly backwards and uncivilized. Such people, grossly ignorant and living on a plane much lower than that of any civilized society, will not be able to determine what is good or bad for themselves. In such a case the procedure naturally must differ, and will entail a waiting period in which this society, while not formally in the federation, will yet be within its economic system, as will be later explained.

Just as other member nations, each colony will be divided into zones determined either by size of land or population. Colonies well advanced in civilization will enter the community of nations with the same obligations and same rights as others. The voice of each of their zones will have the same weight regarding policies adopted. Their economic position will be the basis on which they may claim assistance from the federation. In zones whose population is still backward and uncivilized, the federation as a whole will become the trustee of both land and people. This trusteeship, however, should not last longer than necessary. As soon as any zone gives unmistakable evidence of being able to govern itself and has achieved a degree of national entity that will not permit it to become the prey of ruthless minorities, freedom will be granted by a general election held among the PW representatives of all the superzones and of the federation. It goes without saying that it will be given the opportunity to enter the federation on an equal basis with the others. Such elections will be taken at twenty-five year intervals, so that if any zone or colony, in the estimation of these representatives, has not reached the necessary level, its case must again be considered 25 years hence. We feel that in the life span of a nation this is an adequate period for gauging its advancement and progress. During this interval it will be assumed that it still needs assistance, advice, and protection. One of the most important steps will be that of educating the people and awakening them to the great advantage of civilization in_general. Religious and educational missionary organizations, free medical and hospital care, and other non-economic activities will be set up with financial aid from the federation government, and form the spear head of enlightenment and progress. These missionaries must mingle with the people, learn their language and customs, help them physically and morally, and prove able to win their confidence and friendship. Within a specified number of years they must exchange the citizenship of their mother zone for that of the new one if they want to retain that position. Because of their superior culture, it is likely that they will emerge as the upper class of this zone. As their interests will become intrinsically bounded with those of the adopted zone, thus raising level of culture and standard of living, the indigenous population will be favorably affected. In cases where the aboriginal population is small in comparison to the area, as they become more civilized, inducements will be offered to have them occupy only a part of the land. This will serve the double purpose of preparing for possible immigration from overpopulated zones and of preserving the homogeneity of the native stock. The federation, in accordance with a pre-established plan, will send representatives, officials, and the necessary personnel to govern and administer the land. At all times efforts will be made to include in the government many prominent citizens and local leaders as practicable. This will be done so that they may learn by experience and contact the new way of life, and in turn impart that knowledge to others. Their number will be gradually increased, and a corresponding reduction made of the outside representatives, according to the aforementioned plan. This reduction, based upon the progress made by the population, will be determined by periodic elections of five years among the PW representatives of the federation.

The judicial and executive power will always be invested in outstanding native citizens who will be under the jurisdiction of higher officials of the zone. Being in actual contact with the native population and, therefore, familiar with their way of thinking as distinct from that of the civilized world, this policy seems to be the best. The transition from the old to the new mode of life cannot be forced at too rapid a pace, or friction and resentment would be the natural consequence, retarding rather than accelerating the pace of progress. The needs of these nations at first will be considerably less than those of more advanced populations. To the extent that these zones are not actually an integral part of the federation, their people are exempted from such duties as taxes and other charges upon the citizens of other zones, for the maintenance of the federation government. For this reason they cannot expect financial aid in raising their standard of living. However, these zones will also maintain a strict balance of trade. The simple fact that raw material is being exported to all parts of the world means that gold or other commodities of equal value will enter the zone. No doubt most of this money will merely enrich emigrants who have found it convenient to become citizens of this zone. However, the laws of inheritance, which must also be strictly maintained for these regions, will tend to break up large estates and divide them among a larger number of people. This fact plus the positive help of the local EW which is bound to reach an ever larger portion of the indigenous population, will in time raise this society to a higher level of civilization.

The economic structure of these zones will naturally follow the usual pattern and will possess an index relating available supply to wages. At first this index (a) is bound to reflect the actual condition of the zone. This means that many commodities considered vital in distant places will probably be unknown here, or too expensive to be included in the list. Accordingly they will be omitted and will only be based on commodities known and appreciated by the population. There again the goal chosen will be some theoretical quantity (q). As the population advances, and commodities become abundant, the value of (q) will rise and gradually close the gap between this society and others in the federation. To be more specific, the requirements of the hypothetical family belonging to an advanced society are quite definite and well known. These requirements may include commodities which in other ages may have been unknown or only reserved for the rich, but, because of the high stage of civilization, they have come to be thought of as vital. They are needed to maintain good health and a given living standard. They naturally include most commodities of a local nature and their selection will depend both on the price they reach in the local market, and on the financial means of the hypothetical family. As to the backward society, many of these commodities will be unknown, and, therefore, will not affect their index one way or another. However, with the gradual evolution and with increased contact with other people, some of these articles will eventually be imported. At first they will be included with the luxury kind bought only by the rich, but with time and greater abundance they will become vital. The procedure is examplified by the electric light, ultimately introduced into a small community far from advanced industrial centers, and described in page 251. The natural resources of the zone will be utilized for the benefit of all. Prices of local raw materials will be the same for whoever enters the market, and will follow only the law of supply and demand. Of course, the management of industries in the zone must be in the hands of competent people, who may come from any part of the federation; this will also apply to the skilled workers. However, efforts must be made to use as much unskilled labor from the local population as possible. It is understood that all who come to live in this zone must become an integral part of the community and zone after a certain number of years, and share with the local population the economic ups and downs of the zone. By this we mean that as many newcomers will send money and other forms of wealth to their homelands without a compensating return, a condition of unbalance may develop within the zone. As noted, a tax, proportional to the unbalance, will be raised to counteract this tendency. Thus, while the individual remains free to use his wealth as he may choose, this additional tax will prove a brake upon an outflow that may bring poverty and hardship to the people of the zone. As its economic position improves in relation to others, this population, hitherto taxed for the specific purpose of sustaining the local government, will also be taxed in order to contribute toward the sustenance of the federation government. It is a matter of course that the latter assumes the duty of providing this zone any assistance it may need in the future, within the limits of this contribution. This will accelerate the process of civilization among the people, and hence be advantageous to them.

Under the increased standard of living of the formerly backward country, wages will rise and likewise costs to local and distant people, but as the population of the zone will be able to import more, this in itself will amply compensate for higher prices. The active part now taken by these inhabitants as producers as well as consumers will further the division of labor we cited as a prerequisite of progress and betterment.

If this colony is too large for the indigenous population, it has been noted how it may be induced to settle on suitable areas through financial help and other incentives. The rest of the country will then be opened to all overpopulated zones in the federation. The pioneering immigrants, ultimately becoming citizens of the new zones, will thus form another economic unit of the federation.

CASE OF A POOR AND OVERPOPULATED ZONE

Consider now a zone with a population far too large for its resources, and thereby reduced to a low level of living. It is an established fact that the lower such standards, the larger is the number of oversized families. While this appears a paradox, it is nevertheless true. Better living conditions with greater leisure and means of enjoyment are not usually linked with large families. Therefore, the improvement of economic conditions in a country seems to our mind a good method for checking the often unreasonable increase of population. Given a country poor in resources but densely populated, prevented by outside forces from expanding and thus attaining a higher standard of living, it will continually press against its neighbors, and sooner or later be driven to extreme measures for relief. But as the safety valve of emigration is introduced, some of the population will find a new and better life in other lands, and the internal pressure in the mother country will correspondingly decrease. As the disparity between the wealth of the land and the population tends to diminish, a higher standard of living will be attainable. This will check the excessive increase in population and the urge toward emigration will also lessen as no one is generally willing to leave family and home if he has opportunities to make just as good a living in his own country. With a more contented and less crowded population, the urge to aggression against other countries will abate, and the nation will harmonize with its neighbors in friendship and fair play. Among other positive improvements we wish also to mention the fact, even if of secondary importance, that as outflow to distant lands decreases, each country will retain the purity of race, language, and cherished customs even with free interchange between nations. As this thinning-out process relieves overpopulation, and a higher standard of living is gradually attained, the nation will become a positive factor in the regeneration of society and of humanity in general.

This, however, can only be achieved by adopting the new mode of life and joining the Federation of Nations. Upon entrance, the necomer will be expected to contribute her share to the universal well-being. This will be represented by the work her excess population can perform. As noted, many countries are in need of additional labor and if this exchange is wisely guided, the results are bound to be advantageous to all parties concerned.

Take, for instance, the United States of America in the early period of her expansion. It was the "Open Door" policy of the later 19th century that gave her the necessary manpower to carry through her phenomenal economic expansion, and by admitting new blood made her one of the leading nations of the world to which other civilizations look for assistance and guidance. If the Federation of Nations rises above petty interests and jealousies and the principle of emigration is incorporated in its code of life, this flow will naturally be channelled and regulated so that, without endangering any member, it will be of maximum benefit to the entire Federation. We also wish to remind the reader that, while at the onset this phenomenon may be of utmost importance, it will gradually decline as a better equilibrium is established between populations and wealth available, and as standards of living equalize throughout the federation. The improved living conditions in the originally over-populated nation under discussion mean a greater purchasing power, and more trade with other zones, which also stand to gain. The same nation, feeling the helping hand of others in stabilizing its economic equilibrium, will give unmistakable signs of contentment and peace. It will more heartily cooperate with others and uphold the new principles. By feeling closer to all peoples of the federation it will not hesitate to defend any member endangered by wanton aggression. Despite this new bond it will still retain its own individuality, customs, traditions, and religion.

Within the far-flung frontiers of this association of nations, as equilibrium among the various zones approaches, we shall see a scanty population in lands poor in natural resources, and a greater concentration in those more generously endowed by nature. The top limit of standard of living will far surpass the relative maximum and the discrepancy versus rich zones will be reduced to a minimum and mostly represented by a different amount of effort.

CASE OF A RICH AND ENLIGHTENED POPULATION

Any country which, at the present time, has the good fortune to own or control resources above its ability to use, and which has also a relatively high degree of civilization and standard of living, is the least likely to desire any change from the present condition. We stress this because the determined minorities governing such nations, being suspicious of the advocated mode of life or of any change that could even remotely jeopardize their privileged position, close their eyes to the simple truth and strive to swing the people to their way of thinking. These nations, having reached a high degree of self-sufficiency, are quite apt to have a favorable balance of trade. As their leaders will consider this situation extremely advantageous to their country in general and to themselves in particular, they will see no need of change. Assuming their sincerity and honesty, while these ideas may be true under present conditions of chaos and national selfishness, they must admit that this would not be the case if the new method ruled our way of life. Since the need for unified action is not only demonstrable but imperative, efforts should be made toward this end.

With the present set-up of society, even in the richest countries of the world, wealth is usually concentrated in the hands of the relatively few who are able thereby to provide many jobs offering good livelihood for large segments of the population. Yet even in these countries great poverty exists, and as times goes on, the destitution of the underprivileged makes itself felt with ever-greater intensity, making us conscious of the many improvements that could and should be made. Because the new mode of life improves all conditions, no matter what the level in the kaleidoscopic pattern of society, and cultivates good relations among inhabitants of the same country as well as between nations, we feel that with time and gradual enlightenment many in the population will recognize and accept its unquestionable advantages. By building up the necessary determination and persuasion, they will guide their country through this transition, not only for their benefit, but for that of humanity in general.

How will the life of these people, living in fortunate lands, be affected by the new mode? As the EW begins to function, and the country is divided into independent economic zones, large estates will gradually become available to a larger number of people. As stated, generous portions will be retained by the lawful heirs and their standard of living will not be appreciably lowered. However, the revenue of such estates, added to the taxes collected from the population in general, will enable the EW to carry out its program of economic advance. The new order will eliminate that parasitic part of society that thrives on the efforts of others, and while it will arouse in many the desire to work and produce, it will prevent the congenitally idle from obstructing the path of progress.

As the country shows a favorable balance of trade, we may surmise that a large portion of the payment for raw material and finished products is received in the form of gold rather than consumable goods and other forms of actual wealth. A good deal of this gold naturally is used to keep local industry going, and provides good wages and salaries for many, but the rest merely accumulates in banks and becomes the property of wealthy people who already have far more than they need or will ever utilize. The fact that gold instead of useful products is being exchanged indicates also that the people do not obtain the variety which such an outflow could sustain. Gold itself, not being a useful commodity in the sense of giving comfort and enjoyment, but only used as a medium of exchange, has no value in raising the local standard of living. We admit that a sizable portion of an individual's standard of living is based upon commodities of a luxury nature, such as elaborate houses, costly furniture, automobiles, and so forth, as well as by services which may include travel, theaters and other activities requiring much money. For this large sums are necessary. However, any amount beyond what the community can offer does not increase that standard, and is, therefore, wasted. It is not meant here to convey the idea that we are opposed to any kind of saving. Saving, as we see it, is the renunciation of a present enjoyment for a greater and better one in the future. This future enjoyment may be the ability to buy a home, provide for old age, send children to college, or in any way enhance the position of the saver. Under this concept saving is justifiable because it will finally fulfill its function. The waste to which we refer, and upon which we want to focus our attention, is found in the millions of dollars set aside every year as profit by the enormously rich who can never hope to use those dividends to increase their comfort. That money usually is sought only out of lust for power, although this is not always the case. Quite often wealthy men, owners of great fortunes and large industries, feel very strongly their responsibility toward their employees; and while their personal expenditures are far above the average citizen's, they are apt to re-invest the surplus in industry. Thereby, they feel that they are helping their community and nation because this increased capital provides more jobs and greater production. Under this misconception they are liable to use fair or unfair methods in increasing the zone of influence of their industry, often with marked injury to competing enterprises of their own or other nations. While their immediate goal of providing more jobs to citizens of their community may be achieved, the indirect damage done to humanity as a whole usually is never taken into account. Due to the haphazard nature of their production, and the lack of co-ordination among industries within and without the country, it is possible that the expansion of their industry may force others to retrench, either because of the unfair methods referred to above or through overproduction, so that their increased output means no real gain to society. Add to this the fact that their monopoly will be more strongly felt, and since this extra labor is probably withdrawn from more useful fields, it is plain that their extra money is not used for the best advantage of society. In other words, while the tycoons do not derive any particular benefit from the money they are re-investing, the problematic betterment they bring the few thousands to whom they provide livelihood is far outweighed by the economic dislocation that will ensue elsewhere. Now this profit, thus saved or poorly used, was acquired through the labor of thousands or even millions of people, working for hours to earn the wage or salary that maintains their particular standard of living. Assuming that the average person has reached the level consonant with his knowledge, aptitude and ability, the only way open to him to improve his position is to increase his working hours. We have seen at the beginning of this chapter, as well as elsewhere in our study, that many of those with a low standard of living welcome additional work in their effort to increase their purchasing power. This urge can be analyzed from still another angle. Granted the fundamental instinct to enhance their economic position, it is obvious that they would prefer to do so by increasing their ability and bargaining power rather than their effort. This, however, is not always possible, since while ability is usually bound up with aptitude and talent, and, therefore, constitutes a gift of nature, their bargaining power is affected by the number of others who have similar aims. Thus the only alternative available is that of increasing their effort. In their estimation the increased purchasing power and the definite objectives achieved will more than counterbalance the extra effort and accordingly prove profitable. While no appreciable effect will be felt when only a few workers are involved in such activities, this will not be so when their number increases. All this added purchasing power increases the pressure toward the acquisition of vital commodities. Since the rich will always be able to buy what they need, this added demand means that commodities previously bought by the very poor now go to those who succeeded in increasing their financial power, and thus what they gain is lost to the others. It is quite true that, with the increase in price, profits will appear and in time will add to the supply. As the prices, under a reduced pressure, revert to the original level, the very poor will again be able to buy their previous amount. Those who have increased their purchasing power have no doubt climbed one step on the social ladder, and by changing the pattern of society, made possible an increase in equilibrium point. This, however, does not cause any particular improvement on the part of the poor, who while previously forced to a still lower level, now merely return to their normal standard. In short, we can say that their condition, originally bad, oscillates to one that is worse and back to the bad. This, of course, when no technological advancement is involved. Regarding those who succeeded in strengthening their purchasing power, it remains to be proved that their standard of living has actually improved, since their gains were obtained through an increase in effort. In many cases it is plain that if their better financial position was won by a large increase in effort, the worker has actually decreased his standard of living. This is especially true when the fatigue is the main cause of sickness and poor health. Again, oftentimes, their efforts only go to increase the production of commodities that cannot find ready market and, therefore, their meager return, is far outweighed by their additional struggle. But in many cases this is a sacrifice made to provide for those they love and therefore we only feel respect and admiration for them. However, since this new equilibrium point is only maintained through this extra effort and the illusory gain for some means a definite loss for the others in their class, we must conclude that society is not improved by such a process. On the other hand, this increased production for an uncertain demand, while causing havoc among the population, has also unfavorable repercussions among other nations. All this because our modern society, being unable to promote a gradual increase in the economic equilibrium point, compels the average worker to exert himself unreasonably in the effort to improve his social condition.

If effort is injected in the consciousness of society, all will see that, for a definite amount of supply and consequent standard of living, the average worker will improve his well-being if the same commodities can be obtained through a decreased effort. This means that, while the purchasing power of the population must be maintained, the working hours, if feasible, should be gradually reduced to the distinct advantage of society in general. If we accept this as a basic concept of the future society, we can easily see that betterment can be attained through an increase in supply, a decrease in effort, or both. We know that in the future society there will be many with the urge toward longer hours of work. This, as aforesaid, is often an imperative necessity among the poor. But, as the supply will increase at a far greater rate than at present and through natural forces, many will gradually gain more of the vital commodities needed by normally required effort, and thus this social phenomenon, if not completely eradicated, will decrease to a point that will no longer influence the well-being of society. The decreased effort, coupled to its consequent decline in production, will open the door to commodities from elsewhere. In consequence the supply and the corresponding prices will not be materially affected. This will serve to diminish the profits of the local industries, which, as noted, were reinvested with no real enrichment of the owners nor of the community and nation in general. Thus a better standard of living for the population will result. Of course, while this method is justifiable if applied to the entire economic unit, such as a zone or superzone, it would cause unnecessary confusion if applied only to communities. It is obvious that in all cases where commodities, for which the zone is particularly proficient, are vital to other zones or nations, that supply not only must be maintained but if necessary increased through additional labor secured from non-vital industries of this or other zones. Such immigration naturally will be permitted as far as it will not unfavorably affect the local standard of living, and since the middle of the road seems to us the best, a moderate immigration, coupled with a reasonable reduction in working hours, will prove a definite economic progress for the zone and for humanity in general. Due to this controlled immigration the population will increase and with it the importation of commodities manufactured elsewhere, so that while the inhabitants will continue to obtain what they need, their balance of trade will decrease. We can conclude that this zone or nation, while improving, is also helping other zones and nations.

Regarding the capitalists and industrialists who will have to pay the same wages and salaries to a larger number of employees, it may seem that they would be adversely affected by such policies. On this we wish to make the following consideration. In cases where the local supply must be decreased, the EW will use its beneficial power in diverting these industries toward profitable channels, and consequently the owners stand to gain rather than to lose. As to those industrialists who feel that their profits are reduced because of higher wages to be paid, they must realize that profit is only the result of an unbalance between price and cost, and that as a generality these two factors tend to be equal. As the cost goes up the price will also increase, and those who have talent for reducing expenditure will still be able to make profits as before.

From this discussion we can see that a rich zone stands to gain by blending her economy with that of other zones. Besides increasing the index, she will also be able to decrease the amount of effort and, therefore, her people will enjoy more leisure than those of poorer zones. Of course, we cannot and should not expect a rapid improvement in the condition of any particular population as the new mode of life is adopted. Time will be required to set up the EW organization, while errors will result from the initiative of many who, imbued with humanitarian fervor, may see things in different ways, follow diverse paths, and slow down the process of betterment. But with greater experience and with a more enlightened population, that betterment will be no unreachable Utopia, but a certainty since honesty and good-will will be substituted for selfishness and shortsightedness, while hard work, cooperation and constructive planning will replace confusion and laissez-faire. The Constitution of Humanity will set up definite principles which, becoming the protector of human rights, incorporated in the laws of the land, will not permit too great a deviation from the chosen path. These variations, due to differences in interpreting these principles and laws, may depend on the human factor, but as all roads will be more or less converging, even if a longer route is taken, it nevertheless will finally lead to the chosen goal.

Under the guidance of great leaders, progress unquestionably has been made in the past, but in many cases only as a by-product of their effort to wrest power from others, this opening the way to new ruling minorities. As these new minorities have finally pushed up to the top, the tendency has always been to retain such power and control, even after their leadership has spent itself and lost its right of preeminence. To explain this social phenomenon, we must note that in the past as well as at present, the great majority of the population, while vitally dependent for its well-being on just laws and ethics, is usually incapable of exerting the proper pressure toward this goal. Much of this is due to the abysmal ignorance and ineptitude of the masses, their uncooperative attitude, and their apathy toward things to which they feel neither equal nor competent. Thus, they usually follow those who know how to coordinate their efforts. These leaders, endowed by nature with superior qualities, are able to discern their aspirations and needs, and serve as forces of progress and advancement. They eventually form a small and powerful minority placed at the top of society. Naturally no one will question their role while their contribution to society and humanity in general is so vital. That power is freely granted to them in recognition of their beneficial guidance. But this leadership, whether in terms of individuals or of classes, eventually spends itself. As its components lose those qualities which made possible the attainment and the retention of that prominent place in the body social, it is for the best of society that they should give way to others who, through their qualities and activities, acquire that right. This unfortunately rarely happens, and as usual the entrenched minority which has lost its ability for leadership, and often becomes obstructive to progress, must be dislodged by force before a new advance can be made. In passing, we wish to remind our reader that in the future society this condition will no longer exist. Anyone who possesses the necessary qualities of talent and leadership, will easily attain that position of responsibility for which he is qualified. For these people, their promotion will be facilitated as far as their contribution is essential to the general good, but merit and not birthright will be the sole guidance. Thus the new society will have at its summit a self-rejuvenating minority, elevated only for their achievement and greatness.

Reverting to the obstinate minorities who have lost the capacity to govern, this invariably has led to ruthless dictatorship and enslavement, the use of force and to the undoing of a great deal of what so laboriously had been built up or gained before.

Unfortunately humanity lacks and has usually lacked the kind of political leadership with the vision necessary to see things as they will affect distant generations. Policies have been developed with a specific and immediate objective. This has been done without ever considering their implications to other nations and societies or to future generations. Thus those policies, aside from the fact that they could not be applied to other nations and societies unless enforced and only for short periods of time, because basically detrimental to them, turned out also to be unbearable to the nation and society which they meant to protect. Of course, this could not have turned out differently if we consider that they had the specific goal of seizing or maintaining power within the narrow limits of a community, nation, or society, and being basically dictated by selfishness and greed, could not stand the impact of time and the test of general application. Often enough many such policies were also dictated by the force of events and circumstances, and, therefore, were ephemeral attempts of solving problems of the time. This was based on the theory that each nation should solve its own problem in its own way, and that the detrimental influence of these policies would have to be solved by the leaders of future generations.

Now this lack of coordination of purpose and efforts on the part of minorities of past generations, even assuming their honest intentions and good-will, could not help but produce strains and ruptures within our social body, which in turn has gone far to isolate nations and societies. Their efforts may be compared to those of frantic individuals who, independently of each other, attempt to repair some particular fissure of a dam upon which their immediate safety depends, without considering that the entire structure is giving unmistakable signs of falling to pieces. This kind of chaotic and un-coordinated waste of energy and effort, followed by our forefathers and ourselves, has left humanity wandering along dangerous and unknown paths, studded with rocks and unfathomable abysses and retarding its advance toward betterment and progress, which would undoubtedly be reached if a better road were chosen. The groups and factions forming society, with their endless and foolish rivalry, enforce reforms and policies which protect their interests to the exclusion of others. As long as the world is ruled by force rather than justice and wisdom, we cannot expect progress to occur smoothly and gently. In the future, no less than in the past, interests will be opposed to other interests, policies will be dictated to safe-guard strong and entrenched minorities, and as the nature of men cannot be expected to change rapidly, wars and strife may plague generations to come. What seems an advantage today may turn out otherwise tomorrow, and it seems to us that no gain will ever be valid either for a person or a nation if it involves a loss for other people or nations. Sooner or later, as fortune decides, the advantage may pass to others, leaving the person or nation in an intolerable position. In its turn a new cycle will start, and if we add up gains with losses it can be easily seen that no real advancement has been made. Referring again to the dam and the frantic efforts of those intent upon the repair of one particular fissure, and frequently pre-venting others from using their energy upon other flaws more vital to the survival of the entire structure, we must realize that real progress and betterment can only be attained if all efforts are joined and coordinated before being applied. This certainly should have a better chance of success.

We realize that the hardest battle will be that of convincing the minorities now entrenched and in control of the economic life of the nations. Wars are not instigated or desired by the poor. They result only from the clash of interests among the respective minorities, who, in their quest of supremacy, set the stage for useless slaughters. We can easily predict the arguments of these minorities all over the world against the adoption of the suggested mode of life.

In a rich country, where the standard of living is better than in others, the following points will probably be used.

(1) Since their nation is in so much better economic condition than others any fusion with these will unfavorably affect its standard of living.

(2) The admission of immigrants is bound to lower the wages of labor.

(3) The admission of cheap commodities from abroad will only mean the shut-down of factories and industries, with the consequent disastrous effects of unemployment and depression.

(4) The admission in the body social of such a large organization as the EW, more or less of a parasitic nature, since it does not actually contribute to the increased production and supply, means that it will have to be paid and fed by the public, already over-burdened by the cost of government.

(5) Fear will be injected into the heart of the small businessman, in order to make him believe that the competition of the EW impairs

and jeopardizes his free enterprise, and will eventually force him out of business.

(6) Fear will be aroused in the population in general to the effect that the policies of the EW could easily change into coercive methods and tyranny while intent upon molding the life of the nation along lines not consonant with the basic interests and aspirations of the people.

Anyone who has followed our study will easily find the requisite reply, and thereby expose the untruthful nature of all these statements. They will also realize that such an antagonism springs from definite causes and feelings. For some it will be because unfair methods of competition and monopolies will be no longer permitted or tolerated. For others it will spring from the fact that no great wealth will be allowed to accumulate in the hands of the inept and of those who are not willing to accept the responsibility that wealth imposes on them in relation to humanity in general. For others, still, it will be because their exalted position may be jeopardized if they do not happen to have the requisite ability and talent. As these will be the real causes of hostility we can be sure that they will be kept in the background in their condemnation of the new mode of life. To be sure, as individuals, they know the justice of this plan. They know also that, if cooperative and active, they stand to gain like all other members of society. Yet, as a group, the fact that they are already there will make them suspicious of any change or of philosophy that tends to break their strangle-hold on society and humanity in general. Their interests as a class will dictate their line of action. We do not mean that all in the upper classes will be hostile to the new mode of life. As a matter of fact we base our hopes of success upon their aid and cooperation, but it stands to reason that if antagonism exists it will be likely to derive its strength from this class more than others. Therefore, it is this shortsightedness and fear that must be met and overcome if an unobstructed road to progress is to be found for humanity.

In the poor country, where the small but powerful minority is extremely sensitive to anything that may affect its immediate advantage over the rest of the population, similar objections will be raised against the new mode of life. These minorities, now supreme in their respective countries, nevertheless unconsciously dream themselves some day the rulers of the world, when, through alliances, intrigue or the aid of their own misguided masses, they will succeed in the conquest of other nations, and by destroying other ruling minorities win that pre-eminence to which they feel called by destiny. As usual, the welfare of humanity has never a real place in their plan, and if humanity does prosper through strife and hardship, this is only incidental, and a by-product of forces that are at play in the world.

Since these minorities are part of humanity, and in so far that many among them are great leaders, efforts should be made to safeguard their interests and the standard of living that goes with their leadership. However, they must not endanger or jeopardize the betterment of others, and the mode of life now imposed on humanity must be superseded by a better one with or without their approval. As aforesaid, their cooperation in making this transfer possible is desired and sought because of its value, however, our words are addressed, not only to them, but to all open-minded individuals throughout the world, who like us want to see the dawn of a better era upon the face of the planet and the injustices of our present society come to an end.

If we could give life to a peaceful and enlightened association among these people all over the world, inspire them with enthusiasm and determination, and make them crusaders for this cause, no minority, however powerful, could stand for long the upsurge of humanity, now seething for justice and freedom.

It is true that with the proposed plan a period of adjustment among the various interests, whether within one or more nations, is imperative so that no tangible progress will be immediately felt. Nothing is achieved with a stroke of the pen, but even if the goal cannot be reached immediately, betterment will be felt in a relatively short time, and with the leadership and cooperation of all right-thinking men the future will be finally cleared of all kinds of obstacles and hindrances.

Let us take the United States of America as an example. This country enjoys at present a much higher standard of living than any other in the world. Wages are higher, and calculation of the index would also reveal America's fortunate economic position. Because of her vast resources the United States has a very favorable balance of trade, which indicates that more commodities are exported than imported. Since there must be equilibrium between the various kinds of wealth being exchanged, the difference is made up of gold, which flows in continuously from all parts of the world. Independently of the fact that money in the form of specie is near the vanishing point in other countries, warning us that such drainage cannot possibly go on forever, we know that sooner or later these countries will become incapable of buying from us. This will have telling effects on our future economic welfare and all the gold acquired through the labor of millions of Americans through hard work and mass production will not be sufficient to stop the inevitable depression. This gold, in other words, does not add to our well-being. It is true that some of this money finds its way to the pockets of the average citizen in the form of higher wages, and thus definitely adds to his standard of living, which, besides food and comfortable shelter, is based upon a greater amount of enjoyment and services. These include his ability to take long vacations and travel, and ability to pay for more expensive entertainment. However, much of this money merely accumulates in the hands of the rich, who, having already reached the maximum standard of living, either foolishly squander large sums without receiving enjoyment which such wealth could produce, or use it to expand an already too large industry. The contention is usually made that large sums are continually being used for the advancement of science and art, for charitable institutions and for finding better methods of production, which by decreasing costs enable more people of limited means to improve their standard of living. However, these wages are in payment for a definite effort exerted during the average 40 hour-week. Now the combined output of these workers more than suffices to supply commodities for the general public, and the excess must find its way elsewhere or industry would grind to a halt. Thus, we are foolishly building on a very unstable foundation because we pin our hopes of a continued prosperity on our ability to sell industrial surplus to foreign countries which, as we know, are either unable to ship us other commodities in exchange or lack the financial power to buy ours. Of course, this country has been making large loans to other countries so that these in turn may be able to make these purchases from us. How we can ever expect to be repaid is now beside the point. Most countries receiving such loans are poor in resources, and as a rule unable to repay us. Without appearing too pessimistic, we may just as well reconcile ourselves to the idea that this money is actually given rather than lent. There is, of course, no harm in this, as our country, holding vast reserves of gold, can easily afford that loss, especially if thereby we are able to keep our industry going and to reduce unemployment. But, assuming that such is our intention in making these loans, do we realize that in this we are actually doing work that others should do? If we give money in

order to sell commodities, it means that we are donating outright
to other countries supplies which we American workers must exert
much effort to produce. But this is not all. The fact that other
countries owe us money, which it is true they have no intention of
returning, gives us the right, actual or alleged, to interfere in their
internal affairs. This is bound to cause much misunderstanding,
ingratitude, and hatred, while our seemingly altruistic gestures will
go for naught. It seems to us, taking human nature as a base, that
the reactions of these people is justified and rational. They feel that
all loans granted them from time to time are not made to help the
economic condition of their country, but merely to maintain a
market for our surplus commodities. Thus the granting of a loan
becomes a purely private device on the part of this country to aid its
own economic and business well-being. Consequently they do not
feel any obligation. Again their indebtedness puts them at an economic
and moral disadvantage which they tend to resent, and when we
claim the right to direct their domestic affairs this resentment is
likely to assume more serious proportions. While on one hand they
wish they could pay and thereby regain their freedom of action and
self-respect, on the other hand they feel themselves unable to,
through lack of resources, and in consequence resentfully envy our
riches and wealth. Since it is the privilege of the rich to bestow
wealth (in this case loans), according to likes and dislikes, this fact
is not likely to arouse much friendship and cooperation. All this to
bolster a gigantic industry with the belief that it enhances our
standard of living, which requires us to slave away at the production
of great quantities of commodities, delivered overseas without any
compensating return or gratitude. But again, even assuming generosity
on our part, granting these loans do not make countries feel grateful
to us, because such aid in money or commodities is usually inadequate and falls short of their needs. It only tides them over a
while, after which new loans and commitments will be needed with
further sense of submission. This help, in other words, does not
provide the means of their economic freedom and self-sufficiency.
Yet, with all necessary means to do this, we are unwilling to take
such a step as we unconsciously fear future complications that might
jeopardize our pre-eminent economic position in the world, and
endanger a standard of living that takes into account only the
amount of wage (both in commodities and services), but not the
effort exerted. Misled by this false concept of standard of living we
feel that if we should enable others to manufacture commodities,

it would mean greater unemployment here without realizing that by decreasing the number of working hours for our entire population without decreasing wages, all would find work and retain their purchasing power. Our economic tradition is one that has no flexibility between effort and corresponding supply. The consequence of keeping people at work for a traditional number of hours per week is that a certain amount of commodities is produced. Since it is too large for our use, Americans cannot see how they can encourage other nations to increase world production, which would mean a still larger surplus in our own, with a corresponding rise in unemployment, fall of prices, and lowering of living standards. Consequently, we continue feeding millions in Europe and elsewhere in the world, and in return reap insincere friendship and ill-concealed antagonism. Now, if instead of charity we gave them the means of greater production thereby improving their standard of living through their own efforts, then and only then would we reach their hearts and win their friendship. Besides a great advance in world trade and commerce, beneficial to us as well as to them, the wealth of our land would make it possible for us to reduce our effort while earning the same amount of commodities and services. We can truly say that the wonderful standard of living reached by many of our citizens would be attained by many more if a more sensible attitude were adopted toward our fellowmen both at home and abroad.

Having established the fact that much of the gold reaching this country does not add to but actually detracts from our well-being, we can say that we are producing some commodities at a rate far exceeding the ideal amount for this country. It becomes evident that the hours of work should be reduced, and that our markets should be opened to foreign products which, being cheaper, would reach a larger percentage of the population. Of course, the purchasing power of the public should be kept constant and possibly increased, and this would mean a decided improvement in the average standard of living of the nation. It may seem from all this that the manufacturers and industrialists, because of outside competition, would no longer make the same profits. This is so only on the surface, as explained in other parts of this book. We must remember that almost any country is likely to have some special aptitude for producing better and cheaper commodities than others, either because of climatic conditions or through possession of materials more abundant than elsewhere. We are ourselves no exception, but wish to stress that our great wealth and technological training gives us a freedom of choice hardly equalled in any other part of the world. If willing we could easily divert our industry toward productions not in direct competition with those of other countries. As these do not possess the same freedom of choice, this attitude would give them the opportunity of expanding the production of those commodities for which they are best fitted if reasonably certain that their surplus would be bought by this country to fill the void caused by our shifting to other crops and manufactures. This would promote commerce among all nations, lower prices, and prove highly beneficial to the public in general. Now since the amount of effort on our part would not be changed but merely diverted in definite directions, this would not affect in any way our unemployment problem. If reduction in hours of work, at some later stage is considered as a solution for unemployment, it must be borne in mind that this economic phenomenon is chiefly the result of our reluctance to spread the essential effort among the entire population of our nation, naturally requiring a lessened individual effort. Since we have not altered the fundamental principle of supply and demand, profit would still remain the main spring of production, and those more efficient than others would inevitably realize higher profits. Now this can be attained only by adopting the new mode of life. In fact, without the friendly control of the EW, many manufacturers in their unregulated quest for profits would invade fields of production in which they actually have no right, and thereby bring about those economic dislocations which we are trying to erase.

In the tenth chapter we spoke of industrial zones of influence, and came to the conclusion that the prosperity of a community or of a nation is dependent on the size and vitality of its surrounding zone of influence. We said also that as zones of influence eventually overlap each other, sooner or later a clash will result for full possession of the disputed land. When one center succeeds in supplanting the other, the latter must retrench and relapse to a lower standard of living. For that analysis we considered one kind of raw material concentrated only in one locality, and if this was actually the case, what was said of those hypothetical places would apply in our own society. However, fortunately for humanity, this is not the case as raw material of one kind or another is found in almost any part of the world. At this time, however, we only had in mind to portray the economic forces that arise among communities and nations intent upon the raising of their standard of living. Since the inclusion of different kinds of raw materials as well as the places where they could be found would only complicate the analysis without affecting the basic forces involved, it was decided to consider only one place and kind of material. However, it must be understood that the forces resulting from such a condition are considerably stronger than those in a real society, and that their intensity is only proportional to the degree the actual condition approaches the hypothetical one. In the present study, however, more concern is given the remedies required to improve the relationships among communities and nations, and, therefore, a condition close to the actual must be considered.

Reviewing again the diagram on page 527, and assuming that different kinds and amounts of raw materials can be found, not only in locality A, but also in A$_1$, A$_2$, and so forth, let B, C, D . . . G still stand for manufacturing centers. Here again no particular restriction is placed upon the natural flow of material from one place to another, and the law of supply and demand, with the cost of transportation, are still the basic factors for calculating the price of raw material to the manufacturers in any of those centers. Thus, if we assume again locality A, we know that due to the forces of supply and demand developing in this community a price will be reached. As the material is being sent elsewhere its subsequent price will increase with distance. Let us deal first with one kind of raw material, which as aforesaid, will also be found in the other localities. Due to this new condition in the market, there will be communities in which the raw material from A costs more than from locality A$_1$. Consequently manufactureres of these communities will find it to their advantage to buy from A$_1$, instead of A. Now the actual separation of the zones is not a narrow line, allowing one to say that all on one side of it will buy from one center and those on the other side will buy from the other. Since supply and demand have a marked bearing on these prices, it can easily be seen that if the price rises in A, due to a sudden increase in demand, this will be felt throughout its zone, and at the border many previous customers will now find it profitable to buy from the other center. This is equivalent to a decrease in demand, and eventually will force prices in A to the original level. From the above, one must conclude that each zone of influence oscillates through periods of expansion and retrenchment, and that communities on the border, as well as in those places where the zones overlap each other, will accordingly shift purchases from one center to another. These pulsations, since they are related to instantaneous supply and demand, are bound to be small and will not materially affect the size of the zone if the price tends to stabilize at some particular level. By this it is meant to say that all communities close to one center will always be attracted by this center irrespective of the instantaneous changes in price. In any event it is assumed here that the manufacturer, no matter where located, will buy the raw material cheapest on the market and independently of its source.

Due to the new assumptions, we can easily see that the present condition is different from the one analyzed in chapter ten, since the industrial centers at a great distance from A will be able to obtain the same products from a nearer locality, and thereby be able to decrease their basic cost. This, of course, will not mean that purchases from A will no longer be made, as this will be decided by the price as well as the amount needed by the manufacturers. Indeed, it is reasonable to assume that if the rate of extraction in A1 is very small, and the need by the manufacturing center is very great, that the latter should depend on A as well as A1, for the amount needed. In any case a new equilibrium will be established among the various manufacturing centers, and their respective zones of influence will naturally be different from those in the previous analysis. As the new zones of influence take form, we will find again zones that are far away from all others. The surrounding population, because of the possibility of finding raw material much nearer, will be greatly benefited as the cost and consequent price to the public will be considerably lower. The same, of course, holds for the others, since the cost of transportation as well as a decreased demand in those localities where raw material is found is bound to decrease the original cost and the price to the public. But even so, there will still be areas of influence of different manufacturing centers overlapping each other, and, as the basic forces previously analyzed will still be present, competition sooner or later is bound to develop among them. Depending on circumstances, the time will come when one or more industrial centers will succeed in controlling ever more places where raw material is found. This gives them the power to limit the flow of products to those areas which endanger the free expansion of the centers under consideration. Assuming that certain centers, as B, C, and so forth, succeed in their plan, this means that other smaller regions are forced to retrench. This, of course, will weaken the economic structure of these populations, and sooner or later it is likely that the economic advance will be followed by a political one in which these small centers will be incorporated into the country where the expanding center is located. Among the effects brought about by this change we wish to mention the fact that the dominant minority of the defeated land will be forced to relinquish its power to that of the victor, and will gradually sink to the same level as the masses. The conquered population stands also to be adversely affected, especially if the two societies happen to be at different levels of civilization. They must relinquish many of their liberties, and besides receiving low wages, will see the resources of their land pass into the possession of other societies and civilizations not particularly interested in their economic welfare. This naturally will weaken the vitality of the expanding center, since internal discontent and sporadic uprisings will absorb an increasing amount of the activity of the victorious minorities. But for all practical purposes these lands which are gradually occupied and annexed become an integral part of the expanding area. This expansion does not necesarily stop here, as the greed of man knows no limits. As this new unit begins to overlap another, the same needs will generate new clashes and new enslavements. But independently of the vitality of a country, physical limitations, as to communications and sheer strength, will prevent this process from going on continually and take over all societies and all raw material. Therefore, any center that is at a safe distance from the expanding one, while crippled by its competition, will still have some access to raw material and, therefore, be able to maintain a modest standard of living, much lower, however, than if better opportunity to acquire supplies were available. From this one can conclude that the general condition of humanity will approach that considered in Chapter ten, depending on the amount of restriction on the natural flow of goods.

In all this discussion one kind of raw material has been considered, more or less concentrated in localities A, A_1, A_2—and so forth. But in reality we have not one but thousands of commodities, and while some have to be extracted from the ground, as for instance coal, iron, silver, and so forth, many more, such as food products, will depend on the quality of the soil, the climate, and the amount and intensity of cultivation being carried out by the population and accordingly always available. Thus the actual degree of economic strangulation exerted by a center which succeeds in cutting off the exportation of vital products needed for a high level of living will be considerably less effective than it would appear from a superficial analysis, especially when it includes the physical necessities of life such as food. Yet such strangulation will cause the inhabitants gradually to lose their ability to compete successfully in the open market and cause many manufacturers to withdraw after heavy losses. Consequently, the industry of this society may shrink and be able only to provide for the simplest local needs. This country or society, originally an industrial and progressive type, might then revert to farming and pastoral pursuits which, as we know permit only a much lower level of living. If these societies retain their aggressiveness and desire of betterment, it can be easily seen that they will resent this foreign imposition and exert all their power to extricate themselves from such an intolerable situation. This again will not bode well for the peace of the world.

Now the clash between zones here presented results from the fact that each center produces the same kind of articles which compete against each other in the open market of the world. This again does not represent the actual facts, as everyone knows that difference in raw material, soil, and climate found within each land will tend to make either center more efficient than the other in the manufacture of some specific article or commodity, and, therefore, in this particular field better prepared to withstand determined and frequently unfair competition from others. It is natural to assume that this center will produce in large quantity, or at least as much as compatible with the resources on hand, whatever wares find an easier market. For one thing, those engaged in such production will prosper because of their better competing position. However, even in this direction a limit will be reached, and because of the potential demand and high cost of imported manufactured products, many within the community will have to make articles for home consumption which depend on that kind of raw material that must be imported from other places. This activity, depending on the industriousness of the population, may constitute either a large or a small portion of its business operations. At any rate, it is in this field that strong competition with other centers will develop. Now the well-being of the community or manufacturing center, as explained, will depend on its ability to sell these products to an ever-increasing number of buyers. From this more wages and salaries will come, and money will be secured for the purchase of imported articles that increase the standard of living. As the competition from other centers becomes severe, and the necessary raw material more scarce due to restrictions imposed abroad, it is plain that these industries will have to retrench, and the damaging effect on the population will naturally be in proportion to the degree of retrenchment. Many will lose their jobs, and in one way or another become public charges and a burden upon the rest of the population. Social strain will appear, and the general standard of living will decline. In other words, even though this center utilized to the utmost its own resources, this is not sufficient to maintain the desired degree of standard of living, and the economic dislocation of this center again will be in proportion to the amount of restraint placed upon the flow of raw material.

The interferences referred to above, the consequent clashes of interests, and the competitions are mostly due to the lack of coordination in the activities of societies which, seeking to improve their standard of living and without originally intending any harm, chose methods and policies that eventually injure the basic interests of the people. Lack of understanding among them, and the inflexible economic structure of each nation which does not permit the shifting of production from one field to another without endangering the interests of the industries involved, are factors blocking that cooperation. When an industry and a nation embark on a chosen path, they usually do not find it easy to change their policy without causing internal disruption, and thus are apt to pursue their course, even if found detrimental to others, because at that time and contingency it seems the easiest and best to follow or at least too difficult to change. Those who are endangered, being also set upon their own betterment, are bound to react to all such policies with equally shortsighted countermeasures and, therefore, all will eventually spend most of their effort either in repairing the damage inflicted by others and devising ways and means for protecting themselves from additional blows or in inflicting blows to others for their problematic advancement. Due to this misplaced effort and to this waste of energy, the well-being of everyone, once near, is made more elusive than ever.

In our contemplated society this condition will no longer exist. One can easily see that if people and societies were guided by a just authority which, besides having at heart the good of the individual as well as humanity, was also able to channel and coordinate their efforts, their problematic betterment would become a certainty. As a result the world would soon witness the same societies and nations magically living in complete accord with each other. We have seen that an industrial center and a nation are enhanced by the expansion of their sphere of influence to more distant regions as it provides labor opportunity for many in the population. This effect, however, would be far surpassed if more emphasis were placed in raising the standard of living of the entire population. Even when one zone overlaps another, there is no reason why it should clash with it or damage the interests of the latter as a prerequisite of betterment. All know that from the same raw material hundreds of articles can be manufactured. Under the guidance of this higher authority it could be easily decided which article should be emphasized by one center and which by the other. It is plain that the interests of the two lands, rather than remaining opposed, would be made complementary to each other. As each center would derive its well-being from the manufacture of different kinds of products, it is evident that both could expand unhampered to a far greater degree than at present, and each could include the other industrial center without impairing in any way its interests and individuality. As each will concentrate upon the production of articles for which it is better qualified, their basic cost and ultimate price will also be cheaper, and as they will reach more people within and outside the community, this will mean a larger sphere of influence of that center. This, of course, will apply to articles of luxury which are beyond the control of the EW. Thus it may seem, in seeking to abolish competition among countries, that we are swinging to the other extreme by advocating the formation of huge trusts and monopolies, able at any time to raise their prices without fear of reprisal. That this is not so will be evident in the course of the following discussion.

The reader is probably aware by now of the necessity of the new mode of life and of the division of each country of the federation into zones of equal population. A statement was also made to the effect that each zone, in order to prevent unecessary competition, should concentrate on the production of articles for which it is best equipped, implying by this that the production of all other articles should be discouraged and forbidden. This statement, while true in spirit, must not be taken too literally. Elsewhere we have also strongly spoken of the necessity of competition as a prerequisite to progress. Competition, based on fair methods and carried out honestly, must be maintained, not only among inhabitants of the same, but of different localities. It should be organized and sponsored where absent and encouraged where languishing, but only to the point of maximum return. This means that it should be reduced if found to detract from the well-being of the population. Let us clarify the contradiction apparent between the two lines of thought developed in the last few paragraphs: that which takes as essential to progress a continuous expansion of the sphere of influence unhampered by restrictive regulations, and that which advocates more, rather than less, competition for the good of the people. First of all it must be made clear that the various zones of the federation, whether among one or several nations, will be more strongly linked economically than at present, for while commerce and trade will continue freely, the inhabitants will reach agreement readily, especially under the supervising guidance of the EW, as to which production should be increased or reduced. We know that the well-being of the people in each zone will be made ever less dependent on the fortune of any particular local industry. Due to the widespread range of both the local and the federation EW, work will be found for all, whatever the condition of the industry, and if one should fail, it will not mean hardship for everyone in that area. The greatest factor of betterment, to our mind, is the fact that the present stable economic equilibrium, due to the forces injected in the life of society, will continually advance to higher levels, allowing a steady increase in production and in purchasing power. In short, this new mode of life will accomplish the dual result of improving with time the condition of all, rich or poor, and extending the sphere of influence of the industries. This increase will be in the greater number of customers among the local population, and while the industrial sphere of influence may under certain circumstances spread to other countries and zones, success or failure in this respect will not affect the industrial well-being. It has been shown that for all vital commodities, as long as their scarcity factor is above unity, the larger the production the better, and even if other zones of the same or other nations are also engaged in this production, no real damage will be done the industry as long as the supply is easily absorbed. Competition in this field will be stimulating and helpful since it will eliminate inefficient industries without preventing better organizations taking their place, and thus preserve purchasing power. As a matter of fact, increase in production of vital commodities will actually be encouraged in every possible way, as this will improve the standard of living of the people without endangering the interests of any industry so engaged. Let us look at the problem from another angle. It has been noted that the products of any industry must find buyers, not only in the community and the immediate surrounding regions, but also in more distant places. As they reach these regions, obviously their basic cost will increase because to the original price must be added the cost of transportation. It is natural that prices there should reflect this condition, and, therefore, their scarcity factor is bound to increase with the distance from the original source. Now the rich of these distant communities are apt to buy what they need, irrespective of price, leaving the poor with that much less. Of course, one could say that a rise in production by the manufacturing center would increase the supply in this distant community and eventually lower its scarcity factor. This, however, while sponsored by the EW so as to improve the standard of living of the people in general, would not be the best or most economical method as far as this particular population is concerned. Indeed, a definite increase in production by the original center, whether through expansion of the facilities already available or addition of new organizations, is bound to spread according to some definite law among the people of its sphere of influence, so that the actual quantity received by the distant community, although having the same proportional increase, will be too small to bring sizeable betterment. It is plain that even a relatively small production within the community or nearby places will have a far greater effect on local conditions, and, therefore, we feel that the organizing of industry in the distant locality should be sponsored and encouraged. We feel also that the interest of the already established industry of this community is not in any way affected, because, due to the vital nature of the commodity, whatever amount reaches this population will be absorbed independently of the rate of production of the auxiliary unit. In other words, when it considers the production of vital commodities the EW should use every effort toward decentralizing this production as much as practicable, as this will tend, with the same increase on output, to better the condition of a far larger number of people. This solution becomes obvious when one considers the great need of vital commodities everywhere, although this is not the case for luxury products. As noted, the EW will have much less authority in this particular field, and cut-throat methods of competition are more apt to occur therein. But here again the influence of the EW, although not vital, will be of great assistance since it will be to anyone's advantage to accept the advice of an organization familiar with the actual condition of the market and with the trends apt to develop among different societies. As expressed before, by guiding the industries along those channels that tend to make the economic structures of the zones complementary to each other, each industry will be able to expand geographically to a much greater degree than at present. However, here also competition, as far as the point of maximum utility, must be sponsored and encouraged. Considering present conditions, we must remember that these industries, while engaged in the manufacture of commodities that do not affect the standard of living of the great majority of the population, still are an important factor as the means of livelihood for thousands or millions. It is because of this interdependence that such industries often engage in disastrous competitions with those belonging to other manufacturing centers, reaching thereby results with which we are all too familiar. But in the future this interdependence will be greatly reduced and the well-being of any particular industry will no longer be so vital to the life of the community. If some industry, through honest and legitimate competition, should decline and eventually disappear, others organized along more profitable lines will replace them, providing jobs for all affected by the shutdowns. With this concept in mind we can state that even in this field any article of a luxury nature is bound to be more expensive as it reaches distant places, and even though the rank and file may not be vitally affected, we see no reason why auxiliary industries should not be sponsored in these communities, especially if this will be beneficial to their well-to-do portion of the population. Of course, as mentioned before, such competition will be sponsored to the point of maximum utility which is represented by the stage where all manufacturers are able to derive a just profit, and therein all of them will do well to follow the advice of the EW, but in the last analysis the geographical expansion of the sphere of influence will be less important in the future than at present, for the following reason. Due to the continuous improvement of the stable equilibrium point more workers with the passing of time will be able to divert part of their earnings to the purchase of luxury commodities. Due to this new social force these industries are bound to increase sales to a far greater degree and the need of expanding their zones of influence to distant regions will not be so vital to them, and therefore, will no longer be greatly sought. Therefore, by a judicious apportioning of specialized products among different zones, without decreasing the competition so vital to progress, and by increasing the purchasing power of the people, these industries no less than those producing vital commodities will prosper without impairing the interests and the well-being of other manufacturers and zones.

Following this policy, the economies of the various zones, instead of competing against each other, would begin to blend and finally form a harmonious whole in which each would be encouraged to produce most of what it can turn out best and at the lowest price. The rich zones, as time goes on, will improve still further through an increase in range and amounts of products enjoyed. However, most of their gain will be in the decreased effort required of them. The poor zones, on the other hand, will make their gains mostly through a decided growth in commodities enjoyed, because the effort will remain the same or actually increase which means that many previously unemployed will now engage in production.

In conclusion the world must realize more and more that nations, no matter how far apart, are economically bound to each other, and whatever gain one of them may secure through selfish policies, this automatically becomes a loss to the others. Now if gains can be made by a country without injuring the economic standing of another, or if benefit be obtained by both, it is evident that jealousy and rivalry, so common with our mode of life, will soon change to friendship and cooperation.

RELATIONS WITH NATIONS OUTSIDE
THE FEDERATION

The preceding sections have considered the relations between nations within the federation, but since it cannot be expected that it should initially include all countries in the world, there remains the question of policies toward those that have not adopted the new mode of life. It has been shown how the nations that have entered the federation, whatever their wealth, civilization, and ability, by joining forces can give as well as receive great benefits not available under other forms of government. Such a fusion of interests, however, will not change in any way the individuality of the nations. This is both good and desirable. Indeed that division of labor, which is of paramount importance to progress, assumes as a fundamental truth that the individuals or groups (in this case nations) are basically different in aptitude as well as skill. By assigning to each those tasks which he or they can perform most efficiently, the best results for society in general will be secured. Any community to be prosperous and dynamic must have lawyers as well as engineers, capitalists as well as laborers, teachers as well as artists, doctors as well as sailors and so on. All these are engaged in specialized activities for which they are particularly adept and fitted, and it is only through their combined efforts that the community can advance and prosper. Similar reasoning, of course, applies to the community of nations. We mean by this that all those traits and qualities that assign a definite individuality to a nation should be protected like the individuality and freedom of the average man. Race, religion, customs, ways of doing things, are qualities that distinguish one country from another. Because of these factors the nation acquires a character and a mode of life that is dear to its people and in no way interferes with the progress of humanity. The population, by retaining these qualities, often the direct result of its nature, its climate, and its race, will be able to find its own equilibrium among the other nations. Changes due to the closer cooperation with each other are bound to occur, but these will be gradual, unnoticeable, and never imposed by any law or regulation. These changes will be the result of the closer amalgamation of interests and of the new attitude that individuals will assume toward other people and nations. At any rate all people will be free among free people, free to worship in their own way, free from fear and economic subjugations. They will form a compact and unified bloc that no outside force will ever be able to challenge, and will easily resist the propaganda and allurements of any other philosophy of life.

Returning to the basic discussion on hand, let us consider what attitude should be taken by a nation or a zone within the Federation toward another which is outside that economic system. With the purpose of making our thoughts clear on the subject we shall take into consideration a zone rather than a nation, and assume that it borders a country that does not belong to the Federation. In previous chapters we have seen that the individual in the new society will be left free to improve his standard of living, provided that he follows honest and honorable methods. The same, of course, can be said for a zone which will come to be regarded as an individual in the great agglomeration of nations. There may be occasions when certain commodities produced by neighboring countries outside the Federation reach in the market a lower price than similar products from other zones. Since the purchase of these foreign products no obstruction should be placed upon their importation, even though represents a benefit to the people living in the zone, it is plain that this may be detrimental to the interests of backward sister zones.

However, no matter where these purchases are made, the zone must keep the balance of trade, which is one of the musts in the new mode of life. At first one might be inclined to believe that such a policy, since it may be detrimental to other zones, will also be detrimental to the federation in general, and thus should not be advocated. This, however, is not so and the seeming paradox can be explained if we consider the great flexibility of the new order as well as its adaptability to new situations and conditions. It is plain that when such a situation arises, the EW of the backward zones as well as the EW of the federation will study the causes and apply the necessary remedies. If the methods of production of these commodities can be improved and their cost reduced, so as to partly regain their original sphere of influence, the cooperation of the EW will prove of great benefit to all the interested manufacturers, but if this is not the case, that production will be guided and directed toward more profitable channels, and in this the local as well as the federation EW will again prove of great assistance through their knowledge of the economic forces at work. If unemployment should develop because of this competition we know that many will find jobs in expanding industries with a favorable competing position, others will be absorbed by other zones, and the rest will be engaged in enterprises of a national character under the supervision of the various branches of the EW. In every case the population of the backward zones, irrespective of the fact that they will not feel the detrimental effects of foreign competition because of the action of the EW in providing jobs for all, is certain to gain since any improvement made by the local industry and any consequent reduction in prices is bound to be beneficial and helpful. If the zone is rich in material resources and the heavy cost of production is a result of the high wages and salaries, we know that with other corrective remedies a general reduction in working hours will be adopted within the zone which will go very far in preventing unemployment. This reduction in effort will tend to decrease the production of those commodities that are experiencing such a high degree of competition from abroad, and while the supplies available to the population will be the same as before, the decreased effort will prove a definite improvement in standard of living. The purchasing power of the population, however, will never suffer, and if we consider that the reduction in effort is the ultimate step brought by the foreign competition we see that the population of the affected zone actually stands to gain and improve. In other words, the Federation will have within itself the necessary instruments of adjustment to permit any zone or nation to take advantage of any benefit that may come from abroad and, in utter variance with the modern attitude, will have the ability to transform the present offsetting factors into actual benefits for all the zones. All that has been here said can be also expressed by a simple and obvious physical phenomenon that does not need elucidation or proof. We refer to the experiment of communicating vessels in which, no matter where the liquid is poured, the level will reach the same height in all. It is plain that this policy will exert a profound impression in the neighboring nations, especially among their middle and lower classes which constitute the vast majority of the population. Since this policy aids rather than antagonizes those countries, friendship and good will is bound to develop, and through example and actual proof of progress, the time will come when they also will ask to be admitted into the Federation of Nations.

We wish to add that when a nation decides to enter the Federation it becomes obvious that among other changes she should also be willing to accept its monetary system. It is easy to visualize the confusion within one country if several currencies should simultaneously be permitted to exist. The step is a necessary one because, while the nation will retain its individuality, it will still be a part of a large whole and the existence of two or more monetary systems in the federation would hamper the free flow of goods, with a consequent slowing down of progress and betterment. Of course, the transfer from one monetary system to another must be gradual and must not cause undue confusion and strain. This can be accomplished by the authorities by placing in circulation at suitable intervals increased amounts of the new currency while the old is being retired. If, nevertheless, some hardship should be caused to some, it will still be worthwhile in view of the great advantages which the country eventually will reap.

INFLUENCE OF INVENTIONS AND TECHNOLOGICAL ADVANCEMENT

As already explained, discoveries have been an important factor in the advancement of society. During the last 100 years they have been made at such an increased rate and have covered so many fields of human activity that one can truly say that there has been more physical progress in this period of time than in all recorded history. Of course, we are still at the beginning of a new era of achievement, and in the future we may expect additional progress that will raise society to undreamed of heights and further transform our mode of life. Some of these achievements will be in the form of better and cheaper commodities made available to a larger percentage of the population. However, if we take the past as a guide a great deal of hardship and maladjustment will have to be endured before this advance is actually obtained. All know that many scientific discoveries are made by persons of great intellect who constitute the driving force of mankind in its quest of higher achievements. These leaders, who often scorn personal wealth and ease form the nobility of the human race, and possess the necessary vision that keeps them constantly in search of new attainments in all branches of pure and applied science. The result of their efforts eventually emerges in new discoveries and inventions. Unfortunately their practical applications too often fall into the hands of those who, less idealistic, take advantage of patents to foster their own interests to the detriment of others. We have already expressed our views on the subject, and have justified this form of temporary monopoly since in the major proportion of cases only the desire of profit will encourage many capitalists to risk large sums of moneys that are necessary to transform inventions into actual commodities important to society. However, patents are only valid for a definite number of years, and even with the extensions granted for additional improvements and secondary changes, society as a whole eventually will reap their full benefit and, therefore, the present procedure does not endanger society as do others which we shall now analyze.

Inventions may be divided into three distinct classes. One kind consists of those inventions and discoveries that do not have an immediate useful application, and, therefore, must wait for still other developments before their influence is felt upon society in general. We have another kind which creates new fields of application such as the automobile, airplane, telegraphy, telephony, radio, and so forth. These inventions have created entirely new problems of study and entire new industries, and from a moderate start have eventually provided jobs and livelihood to millions of people. Yet a third kind is represented by those made with the purpose of improving already established industries. This gain or improvement is generally in the form of a lower cost of production. What previously required the labor of a large number of workers now is made by a machine or a new process which can produce the same amount of commodities with only a few employees in a matter of hours. This kind of improvement has been going on in thousands of different fields. While their introduction has helped in many instances to increase production to a level undreamed of at the time when only human labor was available, and has established entirely new jobs due to the often complicated nature of the new method of production, yet an increasingly great amount of labor has been displaced. Many workers with modest ability and experience have found it increasingly difficult to retain a job unless willing to take wages below the amount needed for the subsistence of themselves and their families. Frequently even this willingness is not sufficient, as appears from the fact that even in prosperous times we are faced by an ever-growing number of unemployed. We are concerned with the fate of the thousands who every day lose their jobs and livelihood through this relentless displacement. These people and their families find it extremely difficult to readjust themselves in the new structure of society, and by their enforced idleness and poverty cause new problems that cannot go unnoticed and unsolved. Society at present pays only scant attention to this all-important problem, and appears utterly unconcerned with the fate of these unfortunates who with their families and for no fault of their own are deprived of the means of subsistence. Since they are part of humanity, potential workers as well as consumers, the new mode of life sees that they secure jobs consonant with their ability, this not only for their good but for that of society in general. If society adopts the new mode of life, labor-saving inventions will no longer strike terror and dismay into the souls of millions. Any invention and technical improvement will then be welcomed by rich and by poor and will benefit humanity to a far greater extent than at present. In the future society the machine will revert to its natural function of helping rather than competing with man, who freed from long hours of monotony and drudgery, will be able to devote more time to higher attainments beyond the task of providing livelihood for himself and his family. This is a topic already analyzed in studying the new mode of life within one nation. It is natural that similar reasoning should also apply to the Federation of Nations, which will ultimately form a gigantic union of peoples with similar outlook and interests. These people, free from internal frictions, jealousies and wars, at peace with themselves and the world in general, will no longer feel the necessity of preventing the spread of new ideas and of knowledge, and of restricting for the sake of safety data regarding new discoveries and manufacturing methods. Since scientific talent is universal and not the monopoly of any race or nation, such exchange of knowledge will make it possible to advance at a far greater rate than at present and will eventually bestow boundless benefits to all people on earth.

CHAPTER XII

THE FUTURE GOVERNMENT

As a connclusion to this study it is well to present our visualization of the future government of the Federation. Before entering upon the subject, however, we must once more emphasize that if and when the new mode of life is adopted, many minds will contribute their talent, knowledge, and experience to our rather crude and imperfect framework, and many details, now merely suggested here, must be given shape and substance before our plan is put to actual test. Even after the new era has commenced, provision must be made for altering what may be found detrimental to society. With this essential understanding we can proceed with our description.

All that is good in our way of life must be retained where possible, and what is faulty naturally must be eliminated. New functions and activities must be added to make the future government subservient to and consonant with the ethics which will form the foundation of the future society. These additions must be simple and comprehensive, and must blend with what will be preserved.

The government, whether of a small community or of the Federation itself, will be divided into five main branches of a pyramidal nature, with definite and specialized duties of their own. They will exert a controlling influence over the activity of each other, and the limits of their respective spheres of influence will be set by definite rules, ideals, and ethics forming the Constitution of Humanity.

The "Economic Welfare Branch", or EW, whose activities we have already given in some detail, is one of these units. It will concern itself with the economic progress of society, bring into action those forces that promote advancement and introduce new moral standards in the relationship among individuals and societies.

Another unit of the future government, called the "General Welfare Branch", or GW, will concern itself with all activities intended to safeguard and protect the liberties of men, look after their comfort and well-being in other than an economic sense, and in short assume many functions of our present government.

The third will be the "People's Welfare Branch" or PW. It will defend and uphold the interests of the people versus the EW and GW if these should adopt or try to enforce policies which are at variance with the spirit and clauses of the Constitution.

The first two branches will consist of people fully qualified for their tasks. Their services, protected from political pressure, will be secured through competitive examinations or definite evidence of worth. Contracts of employment, especially for those in an executive capacity, will be valid for a definite number of years renewable if so desired by their superior. These contracts, however, will be liable to cancellation should they prove incapable of performing their duties.

In contrast, the members of the PW branch will be chosen by popular vote in such a way that while a consistent and homogeneous policy will prevail, new members will continuously enter this all-important branch of the government, keeping it consonant with the changing of times, trends and needs.

The fourth unit, called "Legislative Branch" or LB will study and discuss with other branches of the government new laws and regulations as they may be needed in the slow but gradual evolution of society and finally set them in legislative parlance. These new laws, naturally, must be within the spirit set by the Constitution.

The fifth unit, called "Judiciary Branch" or JB, besides the task of enforcing the laws of the land, will be the final interpreter of the Constitution as written at the time its verdict is given.

This suffices as a general outline of duties. It will now be in order to present a more detailed description of the functions and activities of the five branches within the community, the zone, superzone and Federation. There will be found at the end of this chapter a list of all the abbreviations used in this text to indicate divisions, departments and official position. This is for the purpose of eliminating the repetition of titles, bound to become monotonous and irritating to the reader. Obviously such abbreviations, becoming imbedded in the popular mind, would eventually be used for designating these units and officials.

COMMUNITY GOVERNMENT

A community of 100,000 is the smallest body we wish to consider as requiring a government. By this we mean that in a land dotted with small towns and villages, several such settlements must be grouped together until that population is approximately reached. In some lands the community will represent what in the United States we call the county. Of course, in sparsely populated regions such a requirement would mean a linking up of villages too far apart for easy communication, and in this respect the interests of the people would be jeopardized. On this account, and for such conditions only, the community may be made up of a smaller population, enjoying the same rights and prerogatives as the others. A large city, on the other hand, will be divided into several communities, in this case corresponding to boroughs or districts.

The reason for not being willing, as a general rule, to consider communities of fewer inhabitants than 100,000 is that the number of government employees will be more or less determined by the tasks they perform rather than by the size of the population, and subdivision into smaller entities would unreasonably increase the number of officials paid from the taxes levied on the people. The reason for not, as a general rule, considering units of larger population than 100,000 is that the efficiency and effectiveness of the community government decreases with the increase of the inhabitants whom it serves, and this naturally is paramount to the interests of the people.

The government of the community will be divided, as already mentioned, into its "Economic Welfare Branch" (CEW), "General Welfare Branch" (CGW), "People's Welfare Branch" (CPW), "Lesgislative Branch" (CLB), and "Judiciary Branch" (CJB). See Table 10, page 634.

COMMUNITY ECONOMIC WELFARE BRANCH (CEW)

A description of the activities of the local EW branch has already been given in the seventh chapter of this study, and needs little clarification. At its head there will be the Community Manager (CM) who, besides the immediate duties of the "Price Stabilization Division" CEW2-1 will assume within definite limits, the activities of the other divisions and groups of the EW, subject to referring to the higher zone authorities all problems not under his direct personal jurisdiction.

He will be above all the managers of the EW stores of the community, whether a city or agglomeration of villages, who in turn will hire from among the local population the personnel needed to discharge efficiently the duties of serving the public. The CM will also head an indefinite number of career men who will serve as aides in the various activities, besides preparing graphs and reports that, at definite intervals, must be forwarded to the zone authorities. The CM will likewise secure the services of additional assistants, locally chosen if feasible, to help him when special problems come up over and above the normal activity of the branch. Career men, being an integral part of the organization, may be promoted, transferred, or discharged only through recommendation to higher authorities, who are the final judges in this matter. The CM is himself a career man, and is appointed by the superior branch of the zone.

The CM, the managers of the various stores, and other key men in the organization will form the local "Executive Board" (CEWB). They will meet every few days to discuss matters of policy and distribution. The various groups of this branch, shown in a tabular from, have been given on page 328 to which we refer our reader.

COMMUNITY GENERAL WELFARE BRANCH (CGW)

The second branch of the community government will be referred to as the Community General Welfare Branch (CGW) and, as previously stated, will concern itself with problems of a general nature not under the direct jurisdiction and responsibility of the CEW, yet of paramount importance to a civilized community.

A Community Governor (CG) will head this branch of the local administration. His position will not be a political one and he will be hired, as we shall later see, by the third branch of the government after approval of the higher authorities of the zone. His contract of employment will be for four years, and he can be reappointed if his services prove satisfactory to the local third branch as well as to the higher authorities of the zone.

The CG will assume full responsibility for the activities of all members of this branch, and accordingly will have the authority to hire and discharge all employees under him.

As in any local government this branch will be divided into several departments. These and the title of officials are given in Table 11, page 634.

The Education Department (ED-CGW), composed of an indefinite number of officials, will devote its efforts to the smooth and efficient operation of the community grammar schools. It will see that they do not become overcrowded, suggest and supervise the construction of any new one when needed, provide for their facilities, furnishings, cleanliness, and upkeep, hire the necessary personnel, and settle their salary. This department will also maintain the public libraries, and in brief concern itself with the task of fostering public education and instruction.

The Police Department (PD-CGW) will ensure the safety of the citizens and their property within the community. Upon the apprehension of anyone who has committed or is in the course of committing a criminal act, it will turn him over to the Judicial Department, which we shall consider later in our text.

The Finance Department (FD-CGW) in accordance with information supplied by other branches of the government, will determine the necessary appropriations, and fix the tax rate accordingly. It will also be its duty to assess all property within the community.

The Health Department (HD-CGW) will supervise the improvement of sanitary conditions which may vary from the task of keeping the streets clean to that of providing mass injections for the population.

The Safety Department (SaD-CGW) will provide the necessary fire equipment for preventing conflagrations among a population of this size. Pulmotors and similar devices will also be under its jurisdiction. It will maintain suitable number of ambulances for rapid transportation of patients to community hospitals.

The Construction Department (CD-CGW) will care for and improve public property. Its duties will cover the construction of new streets as well as the repair of the old. It will attend the public parks, playgrounds, and the like; it will supervise the erection of new public buildings and the maintenance of government property.

Other departments will concern themselves with public transportation, water supply, elections, and, in cooperation with a division of the EW as well as with charitable organizations, care for the poor in the community.

Each of these departments will be under a department head who is a career man chosen by the CG and directly responsible to him. The personnel will be sufficient to assure the efficient discharge of duties, and whenever possible it will call on the voluntary help of the local inhabitants, as for instance in the safety, election, and health departments. All the members who are regularly employed will be chosen through a merit system and competitive examination. Employees thus appointed cannot be removed from office except for incompetency or dishonesty. The CG and all the departments' heads will constitute the Executive Board of the local GW or CGWB, and the frequency of their meetings will depend on the number and importance of the problems on hand.

COMMUNITY PEOPLE'S WELFARE BRANCH (CPW)

The third branch of the local government will be known as the Community People's Welfare Branch (CPW). The fundamental principle on which it is based has already been explained and analyzed in previous chapters. We shall deal now with the inter-relation between this and other branches of the government.

We have seen that the representatives composing this branch will be elected by the local population, chosen for their honesty, ability and integrity so as to ensure their being respected and esteemed by the great majority of the people. Their term of office will be twelve years, and the fact that they have been elevated to this important branch of the government will not link them to any petty interest in the community. These representatives cannot be discharged before their term is over, and as they cannot be re-elected, no matter how great their qualification, they will discharge their duties without thought of perpetuating themselves in their position by securing popular favor, or better to say that of determined minorities. Thus the people will choose them, not with any particular selfish objective, but for their integrity, common sense and judgment, and will give them the power to represent the community in all matters affecting the local population. Because of the trust invested in them these representatives assume the moral obligation to do their best in studying the merits and implications of the laws and regulations to be enforced within the community, and to use their power in accordance with their conscience and judgment. The fact that every four years one representative will be replaced by another will assure that this branch is constantly conscious of and in touch with new trends and needs, making it a true champion of the people. It is of vital importance, therefore, that great care be used in selecting these individuals. It may be stated also in passing that the method of replacing only one third of this branch at a time will permit a long range policy not apt to be swayed by the whims of the electors, who under animosity may choose exponents of unsound qualifications and aims. Thus any such representative, while exerting his proper weight, will be checked, if needed, by those who, having been previously elected and having gained experience, will be less apt to yield to idle impulses, and, therefore, serve as a moderating and restraining force.

We have already stated that each community will elect one representative every four years, and as the term of office is twelve, there will always be three representatives for each 100,000 population. These delegates will not be required to give up their own trade or profession, but will receive a small nominal salary. They will have under them a suitable number of permanent employees who will help them in attending to the necessary correspondence and other tasks connected with their duties. As a rule, a two to one majority vote will express the will of this body. Their titular head will be the senior representative (C-SR), who has already served eight years in this branch. He will officially be called the Community President (CP), and as his position will be similar to that of a city manager, he may be required to attend functions of a civic nature. However, his vote, in all matters discussed within the PW, will not carry greater weight than that of the other representatives. See Table 13.

It has been noted that a large city will be divided into a number of communities, depending on its size. Now we all know that there are problems and issues vital to the city as a whole, besides minor problems particularly important to various boroughs. In order to secure a uniform policy for such issues as affect the entire city, the representatives of the various communities will combine into a permanent single PW branch for the city, and elect a titular head or president (CP) among their senior members. City-wide measures can then be decided by balloting among the civic representatives, and a 2/3 vote among all of them will express the will of the people. For minor matters affecting individual communities this body will generally accept the decisions of the representatives of the community in question. If this should prove injurious to other communities of the city, the matter must be decided by the entire body and a 2/3 majority among all its members will prevail.

In passing, we wish to mention the fact that, like the PW, the other branches of the local government will also be united to represent the city as a whole. To be sure, the statement has been made that the government in a community with more than 100,000 population is not efficient. This applies, however, only to those communities that are made up of small villages and towns, which even though relatively near to each other may possess more diversified interests and involve greater logistic problems of communication than a corresponding population within a city. The necessary personnel of these branches will have to be sufficiently numerous to discharge their duties efficiently, but no more. Where this unification applies, the personnel should be smaller than if the city was divided into a group of independent communities each with its specified quota of employees.

In other parts of our study we have seen that one of the important duties of the PW representative is that of supervising the activities of the EW branch of the government as these affect the individual or the people in general. Whenever disagreement arises between any CPW representative and an official of the EW, these matters will be taken up by the CPW as a body, which will assume the responsibility of attending to their solution. If no agreement can be obtained, the matter must be referred to the higher branch of the zone. A similar procedure will be used for settling discrepancies between CPW representatives and officials of the GW branch. The difference, however, will rest in the fact that, while the CPW as a body has the authority to terminate the services of the CG, it does not have such authority over the CM. The reason rests in the fact that, while the CGW serves the population of the community and is more or less independent of other communities, the same cannot be said for the EW branch. It is of paramount importance that the EW should adopt a unified policy throughout the nation or federation. This policy must be dictated by the highest authority of this branch who has a clearer and wider perspective of the economic forces in the nation. This policy in turn must be followed more or less rigidly by the CM, who cannot be considered responsible for matters in which principles and policies are involved, and thus will not be coerced by entrenched interests of those communities. Should such a discrepancy arise, the matter must be referred respectively to the higher authorities of the PW and EW branch of the zone.

The CPW will select and hire the CG. At its discretion it may let the contract expire or draft a new one, depending on the merit of the official and on the interests of the community. Officials who at the end of their terms are out of a job may be requested, if desired by the CPW, to enter the fourth branch of the local government whose activities we shall analyze later. If such an invitation is not extended, a national bureau will place them, if possible, within other communities either in a position like the one relinquished or another with less responsibility. Since these individuals are career men in the government, every effort should be made to keep them employed, but, of course, their worth must be paramount, and if they lack qualities necessary to fill positions of responsibility, it is natural that they should accept lower ones in the vast structure of the government. The CPW moreover must have the authority to terminate the services of the CG if he proves unworthy of his rank, but in such a case a 2/3 majority is not sufficient, and if one of the three representatives should disagree, the question must be referred to the people through a special referendum. When an official has given a definite proof of incompetency or corruption and becomes the subject of such a disciplinary action, the intervention of the national bureau will no longer be valid. Times may arise when the local PW may try to enforce its will in matters strictly pertaining to the CG domain. If not resisted, this would result in the application of unsound policies. Because of the vast authority held by the PW over the CG, it is possible that the latter would be powerless in preventing such an outcome. For this reason, the CG must be given the right of taking the matter to the Zone Governor. If the ZG decides to side up with the CG, he must discuss the matter with the ZPW. It has been shown that the ZPW, if willing, may exert its authority over the PW representatives of the community.

COMMUNITY LEGISLATIVE BRANCH (CLB)

All the previous discussion assumes society as crystallized in some pattern in which the government employees carry out a specific set of laws and regulations. But we all know that changes of times and conditions will require new laws and regulations to cope with new needs and problems.

City Managers and Governors, as well as other important government employees, residents of the community, who have rendered faithful service and retired from active duty, will be invited to enter another branch of the community government and will become community Aldermen (CA). This body will form the Legislative Branch of the community government (CLB). In this capacity they will study and formulate new laws and regulations within the community. A Secretary (SE-CLB) will be the titular head. The CLB will convene at some special time of the year as set by the Secretary. The members composing this body will receive a small salary, with extra compensation when extensive work is required. If their number is limited, prominent citizens of the community may be included, after due approval of the CPW representatives.

The CLB will form committees to study the merits of any regulation brought to the attention of this body. Many of these measures will be suggested by the members themselves, as their knowledge and experience makes them particularly qualified for such initiative. Others may originate with officials of the community government and individuals or groups in the community. All these proposed ordinances must be sent to the Secretary, who will put them on record in the private files of the CLB. As aforesaid the CLB will convene when in the judgment of the SE-CLB a sufficient number of proposed measures have accumulated to warrant a new session.

Depending on the nature of the ordinance, it will be referred to the committee that specializes in that specific subject. The committee in turn, after due study and consideration, will prepare a report to be submitted to a general meeting of the CLB. If approved by the majority of the CA's (50% + 1), copies will be sent to the heads of the EW, GW and PW branches of the community government. The CM, basing his opinion on the report as well as upon discussions among the CEWB, may or may not approve the measure, and will forward his opinion to the CPW. Similar procedure will be followed by the CG who, in special cases, may secure also the opinion of his zone superior. We may be confronted by the following alternatives:

1) When all branches are in favor the signature of the three heads of the local government as well as that of the judge is required to ratify that regulation as a law.

2) Where the CG is opposed, one or more meetings between representatives of the three branches can be called under the chairmanship of the CP. At these, the pros and cons may be discussed, and depending on circumstances amendments may be suggested to assure the approval of all branches. In this case the proposed variations will be transmitted to the proper committee of the CLB for further study and the preparation of a new report. In cases of vital importance to the public blocked by an uncompromising attitude on the part of the CG, the CPW is given authority to place the problem before the people by asking for a referendum on the controversial issue. Likewise, the CG is given the right of referring the problem to the ZG who, as we have seen, has a definite way of exerting his authority versus the community PW. As the issue is placed in the hands of persons who are out of the heated field of discussion and excited personalities, they are apt to give an unbiased opinion. Of course, if the people, through the referendum, side up with the PW, the regulation must be accepted unless utterly opposed to the clauses and spirit of the Constitution because their will is paramount in all

other matters. It is natural that the CG will be absolved of any responsibility if the regulation should eventually turn out to be damaging to the people themselves. In cases where the CG is consistently obstructive to all kinds of reforms and in many cases overruled by his own superior at the zone, the PW is given authority by law to replace that official. Such a radical step, however, should be avoided if possible because, while the authority of the PW over the CG is necessary and vital to the well-being of the community, if too often applied the CGW would lose its effectiveness. After all, the CG in his attitude has the backing of other officials of his branch who are likewise expert and responsible individuals. Thus he should be given credit for possessing good reasons for taking such a stand. If no common ground can be found, and while waiting for the time when the CG's contract of employment will expire, the public should be consulted and be the final judge.

3) Where only the CM is opposed to the passing of the regulation, one or more meetings between representatives of the three branches can be called under the chairmanship of the CP. At these meetings the same procedure will prevail, to assure the approval of all branches. Should this be the case, the amendments will be sent to the proper committee of the CLB as in the previous instance. In vital deadlocks the matter, as explained before, must be referred to the higher branch of the PW of the zone.

4) Where both branches CEW and CGW are opposed while the CPW is in favor, a meeting similarly between the representatives of the three branches under the chairmanship of the CP can be called and a compromise sought. In cases of vital importance and uncompromising attitude of the other two branches, the matter again may be referred to the higher branch of the PW of the zone. In this case, however, the CPW branch loses its right of calling for a referendum or taking punitive action against the CG, or in any way attempting to enforce its will over that branch of the government.

Similar procedure will be followed in those cases in which the CPW is opposed to the adoption of the new regulation.

Assuming now that the ordinance is finally accepted by all branches of the local government, we have seen that the signature of the titular heads of the three main branches is not sufficient to make that ordinance law, and that the approval of the Judiciary branch is required. We shall now treat of this all-important branch of the government.

COMMUNITY JUDICIARY BRANCH (CJB)

Another important task that will fall on the CPW representatives is that of selecting the one or more judges within the community, depending on its needs and geographical size. These officials will assume the important responsibility of representing and enforcing the law. They will supervise civil as well as criminal cases. Trials may still be by jury. Several lower courts will be strategically located among the various towns and villages of the community. These courts may try petty offences against law and order, and disputes over properties or contracts which involve small amounts of money. In addition, there will be a higher court in the most important center, which will try criminal and civil cases too important to be heard by the lower. Others, naturally, will sit at the capitals of the zone, superzone, and federation, which will be discussed later.

Besides the paramount duty of law enforcement, the judges must shoulder the task of analyzing all new regulations issued in the community, to ensure that they are in accordance with the Constitution of the Federation. Being human, they may render different interpretations upon the law of the land from those of other judges on higher courts, and be at variance in their verdicts. To the extent that cases can be appealed to higher courts, this enables the CPW or any party that does not feel satisfied to reopen its case for review. However, the higher the court the more binding will be its decision, until the Supreme Court of the Federation is reached, which is the final authority in this field. The judges of the community are elected for life (until the retirement age) by the CPW representatives, and a new appointment will occur only when a vacancy appears. Their salary will be low and such a position may be sought by local lawyers mainly because of the prestige that it will entail. These judges, however, have the right to resign and return to private practice, or accept positions on higher courts. In either case, as already mentioned, the vacancy must be filled by the CPW. Failing health and incapacity to perform their duty for a prescribed interval of time will require the CPW to place them on the retirement list. In all cases the judge must be left free from political pressure and in no way subservient to private interests, since his decision, unless revised by a higher court, will be the law of the land.

A question may arise at this point as to who is going to enforce the law when no one appears in a position to take direct initiative in the matter. To be specific, the "Police Department" is under the direct control of the CG, who in certain circumstances must take orders from the CPW. Now the political pressure referred to above could equally be exerted by the representatives of the CPW who, as citizens of the community, are apt to be swayed by determined minorities into using it upon the judge. While the Constitution will allow varied interpretations of many clauses, provided that they converge upon accepted aims, there will be others strict, rigid, definite in their phrasing. Objectionable behavior or actions on the part of any one in the Federation, no matter how important his position may be, will call forth definite countermeasures established by law to block such conduct. In this particular case, if one or all of the CPW members, who are the highest officials in the community, should disregard the law by exerting coercion or the like, any citizen may report their action to the CG who, having verified the facts, will sign the warrant for their arrest, or himself become incriminated and punishable by law. The citizens who have first exposed this illegal act, if not satisfied with the action taken by the CG, may report him directly to his zone superior, who having also established the facts must order his arrest. The Chief of Police will attend to routine tasks of maintaining law and order. For the arrest of an official of the government he will need a signed warrant from the CG. Such a warrant signed by the Zone Governor will be necessary for the arrest of any official of his zone, but this will not be sufficient against an official of the superzone or Federation. Even the Federation Governor will be liable to be taken into custody if a warrant is signed by the heads of the FEW and FGW branches, namely the FM and FG, who, however, will not have similar authority over any other official within the Federation. Failure on the part of these two to take such an action will cause them to become liable to arrest through a warrant signed by the Chief Justice of the FJB after a majority of the Supreme Court has voted that action. Prisoners such as these important officials are not to be classed with the rank and file of other criminals, and will be held in a special detention place, with the time of their confinement prescribed by the courts. In other words, these cases will pass out of th jurisdiction of the EW2-5.

Any CPW official who has attempted coercion or other unlawful acts and been imprisoned, will not lose his status of representative, although his salary will not be paid during that period. When released from custody he can resume his position. Having lost face, he probably will shun further public activity in the community, which will remain without the full representation until the next election, when, as in other communities, only one candidate will be chosen. Such a state of affairs will follow from the fact that a PW representative is elevated to that position by the people, whose wishes must be respected and upheld. It will be up to them at the next election to make a better choice and demand higher standards from those they so honor.

Returning to the Community "Judicial Branch" we wish to remind our reader that in any criminal case either the judge or the jury may find the defendant guilty or not guilty. If the charge is proved against him, he must be transferred to the ZEW2-5 to pay his debt to society.

In describing the activities of the CLB it has been noted that no law can become valid unless signed by the judge of the community court. As soon as the three main branches of the local government have agreed upon a new law or regulation, it will be sent to the community judge for study from the standpoint of being consonant with the Constitution, and in this procedure he may obtain the advice of the other judges within the community. If he so desires, he may call a meeting of all the heads of the various branches, to consider changes and corrections. Once the judge is satisfied and has given his approval, his signature will be the first to be affixed to the law, followed by those of the CP, CM, and CG.

ELECTION OF THE CPW REPRESENTATIVES

We have seen that in special cases the CPW representatives of the community may be called to vote on matters not settled by a superior branch of the zone due to the votes being below required majority. A period of several months may be allowed them to study the subject. As such matters will become of general interest and public opinion will make itself felt through articles in the local and national press, popular gatherings, and letters to editors, this body may consider a special election or referendum, depending on the nature of the problem, and give the proper order to the CG who will transmit it to the "Community Election Department." When such a procedure is adopted it means that the CPW of this community disqualifies itself from giving its opinion in the matter, and the election returns must be forwarded to the special branch of the zone to be added to the votes of the other communities. After this is done the result of the election and the percentage of the voting population must be translated into percentages of the number of CPW representatives in the community.

In previous chapters of our study we have submitted what we feel to be a democratic method for determining the actual will of the people where, while a referendum will assume all equal at the polls, the normal election will take into account the age as well as the degree of culture and education of the voter. We all know that either in a referendum or an election only a percentage of those who are qualified to vote will actually go to the polls, while the others, either because they are detained or do not care, renounce this important privilege. We take it for granted that if an issue is clear and vitally important to the individual he, as a generality, will make every effort to vote, and otherwise the indication is that so far as he is concerned he does not care what the result of the election will be. Take for instance two groups of 100 people, and assume that the election result on some particular issue is the following:

First group: 90 in favor, 10 against.

Second group: 45 in favor, 5 against, and 50 have not voted and therefore are undecided.

The proportion of those in favor out of the number of persons that have gone to the polls in both cases is 90%, but, while in the first group all have voted and therefore have expressed their opinion, in the second group only 50% have done so. We do not feel that the election returns of both groups deserve the same weight and importance implied by stating that those in favor are 90% of the population. Naturally there will be cases, as in the election of representatives, in which the percentage that goes to the polls, while important, is not of great consequence, but there are others in which the knowledge of the true will of the people is vital, and hence the failure of an individual to vote must be given the proper weight. Obviously the election result of the second group must be interpreted that 45% (not 90%) are in favor of the issue, 5% are opposed and 50% undecided. We have seen that when the will of the people is not clearly expressed, as in this particular case, that the Manager of the EW branch of the government by law must be left free to follow the policy he may deem best. By using the second interpretation of the results, corrupt minorities will be prevented from taking advantage of popular apathy, and thus push through measures detrimental to the public in general. In stating that a majority of 65% is needed to repeal some decision of the

EW branch, we do not mean 65% of all who have voted but 65% of those who have the right to vote. Of course, in elections among PW representatives such a condition will not exist, because all of them are morally bound to vote and default will not be tolerated. If absent through duty or sickness, their vote must be sent through any of the normal channels prescribed by law, such as mail, telephone, and so forth.

As a matter of interest we wish to emphasize at this time that we do not feel that the election of candidates to federal positions in the United States is consonant with the true will of the people. Indeed, merely 50% plus one vote for the Democratic or Republican party, means that all the electoral votes for that state will go to the Democrats or Republicans. In other words, in states in which the population is equally divided the will and the interests of a vast proportion will not be directly represented in the affairs of the federal government. Nor is this all. Actually a small majority of votes in a state with a large number of electoral votes may, under certain circumstances, elect as President a candidate receiving a minority of the votes in the country. Let us explain this fantastic anachronism.

Assume an election among three states of the Union indicated as Alpha, Beta and Gamma, whose population is respectively 10, 4 and 4 million. Each state has an electoral vote for every 100,000 individuals, so that the respective totals will be 100, 40, and 40. As a result of the election suppose that in Alpha 4,990,000 vote the Democratic ticket and 5,010,000 Republican. Thereby all the 100 electoral votes of Alpha will be Republican. As pointed out, 4,990,000 individuals of this state lose their representation in the government, which cannot be called just. On the other hand the smaller two states are 100% Democratic, winning all electoral votes. The various results are given in Table 12, page 634.

Since the Republicans have 100 electoral votes against 80 for the Democrats, they win the election, even though their victory is based on the will of 5,010,000 against that of 12,990,000. Who can believe this system proper or just? It is quite true that in a country like ours, in which the two dominant parties control approximately the same number of votes, any election based on the true will of the people would send to the government an equal number of officials who represent different trends and interests. While this would be just and fair to the people, yet it would produce a feeble, uncertain and inconsistent policy, and no one could be called responsible, since each official would have to agree to many compromises not necessarily good for the country. Thus, while the present system may result in such a paradox as the one illustrated above, it still is far preferable to the chaotic condition that would be caused by the other. However, with the new mode of life, in which the economic needs of the people as well as their human rights are made the foundation of society, and accordingly incorporated in the laws of the land, division among Republicans, Democrats, or other parties will no longer exist because people will lack the economic incentive. The party system in other words will come to an end of its free will and accord. By this we do not mean that by adopting the new mode of life differences of opinion among the population will disappear, as this would be absurd and basically opposed to human nature. Given a goal, no matter how simple, there always will be different ways of approach. However, differences of opinion, being out of the economic field, will not be so sharply defined as at present and therefore will not jeopardize the common goal. Elections will merely express the choice of the people as to the path to be followed, and the presence of the representatives of the minority, no matter how large, will not hamper the course of government policies.

Returning to our description of the election of PW representatives, it must be noted that this will occur every four years. While only one representative will be chosen for a population of 100,000, four or more names will appear on the ballot, which will allow selecting among various candidates. Some months prior to election time, the names of all those who seek this position must be sent to the electoral board of the community. They may be submitted by the candidates themselves, or by groups and organizations in favor of a particular candidate. It will be one of the board's duties to eliminate from the list all who do not have the necessary requirements as to age and time of residence in the community. The list, when completed, will be made known to the public in general, and the would-be candidates and their supporters may start certain amount of campaigning. A primary election will then be held, and the four or more candidates (as prescribed by law), who have obtained most votes will become the official nominees for the regular election. The political campaign will then start in earnest, and at the general election the one who polls highest will become the representative of the Community for the next twelve years. As any of these representatives may advance later on to a higher branch of the PW the resulting vacancy will be filled by the candidate who received the next largest number of votes, serving only for one four-year term. In cases in which two or more candidates have received the same number of votes, the oldest among them will be chosen for that position. The choice for a higher branch of the PW applies only to the one who has just been elected to the CPW. The others who have already served more than four years in such capacity cannot, as a general rule, accept such promotion until their term of twelve years has expired. We feel that this is just and right because of the confusion that their leaving would cause the other two representatives of the community. Having served that length of time and acquired valuable experience, they could not easily be replaced by the junior representative. There may be cases, however, when the outstanding qualities of a senior representative qualify him for a far more important assignment, and this rule should be disregarded. We feel that the importance of the individual justifies the inconvenience of the community for the good of the nation. This promotion must be at least to a representative of the superzone or of the Federation itself. In such a case each of the remaining representatives will move up one grade, and the position left vacant will be taken by the candidate who received the next largest number of votes. The latter will be called Alternate Representative and insofar as he was not the overwhelming choice of the people, he must step aside at the next election in favor of the one who receives that majority. Each regularly chosen representative, however, will still serve his twelve-year term, and this means that those representatives who were advanced in the local PW branch will retain that position for eight rather than four years.

The representatives will be chosen through regular election instead of referendum because in such a case the considered and uncoerced will of the people must be sought rather than the sheer weight of numbers. As an overall picture of the PW branch in the community we may refer to Table 13, page 634.

The total number of representatives for each community is three. All community representatives of five adjoining communities will form one of the six CPW-C of the zone (15 Representatives).

All community representatives of one zone will form one CPW-Z (90 Representatives). See Table 8, page 334.

All community representatives of one superzone will form one CPW-S (810 Representatives).

All community representatives of the Federation will form the CPW-F (for s number of superzones the total number of Representatives will be given by s x 810).

1) A petition signed by 20% of the CPW-Z will force a decision of the corresponding ZPW to be brought to a general election of the CPW-Z.

2) A vote of 50% plus one of the CPW-Z will reverse a decision of the ZPW.

3) A petition signed by 20% of the CPW-S will force a decision of the SPW to be brought to a general election of the corresponding CPW-S.

4) A vote of 50% plus one of the CPW-S will reverse a decision of the SPW.

5) A petition signed by 20% of the CPW-F will force a decision of the FPW to be brought to a general election of the CPW-F.

6) A vote of 50% plus one of the CPW-F will reverse a decision of the FPW.

TABLE NO 10

COMMUNITY GOVERNMENT	ECON. WELFARE BRANCH	CEW
	GENERAL "	CGW
	PEOPLE "	CPW
	LEGISLATIVE BRANCH	CLB
	JUDICIARY "	CJB

TABLE NO. 13

TITLE OF THE COMMUNITY PW OFFICIALS	
COMMUNITY PRESIDENT	CP
" SENIOR REPRESENTATIVE	C-SR
" REPRESENTATIVE	C-R
" JUNIOR REPRESENTATIVE	C-JR
" ALTERNATE	C-AR

TABLE NO. 11

BRANCH	COMMUNITY GENERAL WELFARE DEPARTMENT			COMMUNITY GENERAL WELFARE OFFICIAL'S TITLE	
COMMUNITY GENERAL WELFARE BRANCH~CGW	EDUCATION	ED-CGW	COMMUNITY GOVERNOR CG	HEAD OF EDUCATION DEPARTM.	H-ED-C
	POLICE	PD-CGW		" " POLICE "	H-PD-C
	FINANCE	FD-CGW		" " FINANCE "	H-FO-C
	HEALTH	HD-CGW		" " HEALTH "	H-HO-C
	SAFETY	SₐD-CGW		" " SAFETY "	H-SₐD-C
	CONSTRUCTION	CD-CGW		" " CONSTRUCTION "	H-CD-C
	TRANSPORTATION	TD-CGW		" " TRANSPORTATION "	H-TD-C
	WATER SUPPLY	WₐD-CGW		" " WATER SUPPLY "	H-WₐD-C
	ELECTION	EₑD-CGW		" " ELECTION "	H-EₑD-C
	WELFARE	WₑD-CGW		" " WELFARE "	H-WₑD-C

TABLE NO. 12

STATE	TOTAL POPULATION	DEMOCRATIC VOTES	REPUBLICAN VOTES	ELECTORS	
				DEMOCRATIC	REPUBLICAN
ALPHA	10,000,000	4,990,000	5,010,000	—	100
BETA	4,000,000	4,000,000	—	40	—
GAMMA	4,000,000	4,000,000	—	40	—
TOTAL	18,000,000	12,990,000	5,010,000	80	100

TABLE NO. 14

ZONE GOVERNMENT	ECONOMIC WELFARE BRANCH	ZEW
	GENERAL	ZGW
	PEOPLE	ZPW
	LEGISLATIVE BRANCH	ZLB
	JUDICIARY	ZJB

TABLE NO. 16

TITLE OF THE ZONE PW OFFICIALS		
NUMBER	TITLE	
1	ZONE PRESIDENT	ZP
5	" SENIOR REPRESENT.	Z-SR
6	" REPRESENTATIVE	Z-R
6 {	" JUNIOR REPRESENT	Z-JR
	" ALTERNATE "	Z-AR

TABLE NO. 15

BRANCH	ZONE GENERAL WELFARE DEPARTMENT			ZONE GENERAL WELFARE OFFICIAL'S TITLE	
ZONE GENERAL WELFARE~ZGW	INTERIOR	ID-ZGW	ZONE GOVERNOR ZG	HEAD OF INTERIOR DEPARTMENT	H-ID-Z
	STATE	SD-ZGW		" " STATE "	H-SD-Z
	FINANCE	FD-ZGW		" " FINANCE "	H-FD-Z
	AGRICULTURE	AD-ZGW		" " AGRICULTURE "	H-AD-Z
	EDUCATION	ED-ZGW		" " EDUCATION "	H-ED-Z
	POLICE	PD-ZGW		" " POLICE "	H-PD-Z
	ELECTION	EₑD-ZGW		" " ELECTION "	H-EₑD-Z

ZONE GOVERNMENT

The zone, as explained earlier in our study, is composed of approximately thirty communities, and accordingly has a population of about three million. This figure is not absolute, and variation will be permitted from such requirement, depending on circumstances. An essential feature is that a zone should be an economic unit with a reasonable balance between city and rural population, in which the interests of any set of individuals are closely related to those of the others. On this account, given a city already having more than three million citizens, it is evident that a reasonable amount of surrounding area must be included, although the total population for the zone may surpass the theoretical number. For the same reason with a sparsely populated land, this requirement may entail the grouping of populations far apart from each other, often with no ethnological connection or community of interests, and here again the rule should be disregarded. However, there must be an absolute minimum for the population of a zone, below which it should not go. Since each zone will have a definite role in directing the affairs of the federation, we should not permit the forming of numerous undersized zones in sparsely populated lands as this would give them an unreasonable advantage at the expense of more populated areas. A case in point is the population of the Pacific Islands who, as we hope, will also join the Federation of Nations.

Furthermore, in regions with expanding populations there will be times when a new regrouping may become necessary for the benefit of the inhabitants who gain thereby a greater representation in the federation. This regrouping, however, must never be disassociated from the basic requirement of a zone which, as already stated, must represent an independent economic unit.

The zone, in the future mode of life, will be thought of in area of land and population as similar to many states in this country or provinces in various countries of Europe.

While a zone will be an integral economic unit, it will be a part of a superzone, made up of several such areas. Each zone will have definite rights and responsibilities, either to its communities or the superzone to which it belongs.

Like the community government, the zone government will be divided into five distinct branches. One will concern itself with problems of an economic nature, and will be called the EW branch of the zone, or ZEW. Another dealing with problems of a more general nature, will be called the GW branch of the zone, or ZGW. A third represents the total population of the zone, and like the corresponding unit in the community will be the guardian of the people's interests. Its name will be the People's Welfare Branch of the zone, or ZPW. The fourth unit, called the "Legislative Branch of the Zone", or ZLB, will perform similar duties as those described for the community government. The fifth or "Zone Judiciary Branch", or ZJB, will enforce the law within the zone and also be the interpreter of the Constitution. All this appears in Table 14, page 634.

ZONE ECONOMIC WELFARE BRANCH (ZEW)

The activities of this branch of the government have already been described, and need no further elucidation. It is important, however, to indicate the necessary connections that must exist between the ZEW and the other branches, so as to present a consistent and complete picture of the future government.

A General Manager (ZM) will be the head of this branch and will assume the responsibility of the entire organization under him. As to the four "Group Managers", one will head the group engaged in the collection of inheritances within the zone; the second will control the one that is devoted to the caring of the wealth that enters the trusteeship of the EW. The third will head the one that handles the distribution of wealth among the population. The fourth will head the policy group of the zone. Under these managers a number of career men and personnel sufficient to cope with the numerous economic problems will complete the staff of this important unit of the government.

The ZM is also the titular head of the EW branches of the various communities in the zone. He must follow definite policies adopted by superior authority and will be responsible for the steps necessary to put them into practice.

The ZM and the four Group Managers will form the "EW Executive Board of the Zone", or ZEWB. They will be aided by the division managers as well as the other officials who will attend such meetings in an informative capacity, but only upon request. Each individual in the organization assumes responsibility for all under him. Efficiency, integrity, honesty and ability are the fundamental requisites for holding the job. Promotion or demotion as a rule must be recommended by the immediate superior, but granted only by an official of higher position. We refer the reader to Chapter Seven, page 327, for a more detailed analysis of the activity of this branch of government.

Out of the revenue from inheritances and taxes collected within a community, a specific percentage must be sent the zone government, which will use it for its multiform activity. Another percentage will be sent the superzone, and the rest will reach the Federation Government. There will be cases when estates awaiting division cannot be assigned to any particular community, being located in different parts of the zone. Often the size and importance of the property may be such that it requires far more personnel and expert handling than the community is able to provide. In all such cases the zone will assume its charge until divided among the heirs and the public in general in accordance with our description in the fifth and seventh chapters. Such a case might be represented by an important industry concentrated within a community.

In the ZEW, all groups and divisions will be adequately represented, with the exception, perhaps, of the Price Stabilization Division which will have its chief representation in the community government. The reason for this is self-evident, for this division, due to the nature of its activity, will have the greatest contact with the public. As this contact will be greatly reduced in the government of the zone, its personnel will be correspondingly less.

The various groups and divisions of this branch, shown in a tabular form, are given in Table 6, page 328, to which we refer our reader.

ZONE GENERAL WELFARE BRANCH (ZGW)

This branch of the government, with the exception of problems of an economic nature coming under the EW jurisdiction, can be compared to the government of any state in this country. A Zone Governor (ZG) will be at its head. His position, like that of the ZM, is not political, he will not be elected, but hired by the third branch of the zone government with the approval of the superzone authorities. His term of office will be four years, and he can be retained in that position for additional terms if this is approved by the ZPW branch as well as by the superzone.

Within suitable limitations the ZG will assume complete responsibility for the activities of all this branch. He will have authority to hire or discharge any one in the ZGW.

The limitations referred to above deal with the relationship that must exist between this branch and the corresponding one in the superzone. While these connections will not be in any way comparable to those in the EW, and though allowance must be made for independent initiative on the part of each zone to govern itself according to its own way of life, there will be general policies that must comply with a master plan that includes, not only the superzone but the entire Federation. The same holds for the CG who in some respects must comply with the policy chosen by the ZG. In such fields as those of education, public health, delinquency, and the like, there are many instances in which a unified policy is not only desirable but essential to the well-being of society, and even though these activities are outside the economic field, they must be controlled by a centralized authority above community, zone, and superzone limits, lest chaos be the consequence. Should Community Governor be unwilling to comply with some special policy set by the Zone Governor and assuming that in his stand he has the approval of the local CPW, the ZG may still enforce his will by appealing to the ZPW. Since this branch fosters the interests of a far larger population than that of the recalcitrant community, it is quite likely that it will side with the ZG. We have seen in previous parts of our study how under certain circumstances the CPW-Z may annul the decisions made by the ZPW, and hence must conclude that the CPW-Z has greater authority. Clearly, as the CPW-Z is closer to the people, it is just that this should be so. This, however, applies for all the community representatives of the zone, taken as a body, but not for those of one community alone. Thus the ZPW must have full legal authority to enforce its policies on individual communities to the extent that they aid the interests of the entire population of the zone. It is understood that if the CPW-Z should side with the community, this body at some later date may annul the decision of the ZPW.

As in any state government the ZG heads various departments. These and the title of officials are given in Table 15, page 634.

The Interior Department (ID-ZGW) will cope with problems of a general nature within the zone that tend to unify the relationship between the communities under its jurisdiction. It will formulate laws on marriage and divorce, deal with religious problems, and represent the zone in disputes. Other activities may be typified by those connected in this country with the Bureaus of Geological Survey, of Fisheries, of Reclamation, of Mines, and so forth. Still another will be that of promulgating laws affecting intercommunities trade and commerce.

The Department of State (SD-ZGW) will handle problems affecting the zone in relation to others within the superzone, and in lesser degree with any other zone in the Federation. On given occasions, it will deal with problems affecting the zone versus surrounding countries outside the Federation. This will depend on the particular geographical location of the zone. We have seen also that the zone itself may initiate the necessary activity within the Federation for securing some particular beneficial treaty with a neighboring country. Delegations assigned by the Federation to this particular task will be extensively staffed by officials of the SD-ZGW particularly concerned. Such treaties, however, to become effective, must be approved by the highest PW branch of the Federation as well as by the highest EW branch, which in turn must supervise readjustments to avoid losses to the rest of the population.

The Finance Department (FD-ZGW) is in charge of the finances of the zone, but has no jurisdiction over the inheritances which, as we have seen, fall in the domain of the EW. This department superintends the collection of the revenue in the zone and is responsible for public debt operations. It will cooperate and, of course, comply with the Finance Department of the superzone.

The Department of Agriculture (AD-ZGW) gathers and publishes information on its specific subjects. Within the zone it establishes regulations regarding marketing, distributing, and so forth, and maintains the personnel necessary to conduct research directed toward improvement of the soil for food production. The Forest Service, which is part of this department, is responsible for the care and management of public woodlands, and in general assists the public in matters dealing with the cultivation of land.

The Education Department (ED-ZGW) establishes uniform rules for the elementary schools throughout the zone, and is also directly responsible for the high schools maintained in all important centers. Like the Education Department in each community it will hire the principals of schools, pass upon the selection of professors by the school board, determine their salary, administer the more important libraries in the largest centers, and in general provide for most aspects of public enlightenment.

The Police Department (PD-ZGW) will help corresponding units in the communities in all cases in which different communities are involved, and in general will handle problems of public safety within the zone. All who act against the law of the land will be apprehended and, depending on the nature of the offense, may be handed over to the Department of Justice of the zone or of the interested community for prosecution. Depending on the nature of the problem, this department will represent the zone in matters involving the government versus individuals or corporations. Another department (ELD-ZGW) will supervise elections within the zone and will promulgate laws effective throughout the communities.

Each of these departments will be under a career man chosen by the ZG and directly responsible to him. The personnel must be in sufficient number to assure the efficient discharge of its duty. All the employees will be selected through a merit system and competitive examination. All thus appointed can be removed from office only for incompetency or dishonesty, but not through political influence. The ZG and the various departments' heads will form the "Executive Board" of the zone (ZGWB). The frequency of their meetings will depend on the number and importance of the problems on hand.

As mentioned before, the ZG has the right to choose from among the qualified career men whomever he wants to head the various departments. Such appointments should not be considered promotions, reserved for the worthiest and for those who have been longest in the service, but as assignments. Indeed the ZG who shoulders the entire responsibility for this branch of the government, must be surrounded by men he has learned to respect and trust, and who are congenial with him, as this is the only way to ensure harmony and cooperation within the organization. As the term of ZG will last only four years, unless renewed by the PW branch, it is likely that many department heads will be replaced by a new ZG. If these ousted officials are chosen for similar positions in other zones, or because of outstanding qualities elevated to the superzone or the Federation government, well and good, but if not they could not revert to their previous jobs, already taken by others. Because of their talent, experience and knowledge, they will be invited to join the Legislative Branch (ZLB) of the zone, and continue to serve society. In this capacity they will be senators, holding this rank for life, or rather until retirement age. Their salary will be somewhat smaller than that of the department heads, and their duties will be defined later in this chapter.

PEOPLE'S WELFARE BRANCH OF THE ZONE (ZPW)

The third branch of the zone government will be called the People's Welfare branch of the zone (ZPW) and its activity has already been analyzed. Again we wish to emphasize the relation between this branch and the others in the government.

We have seen in the seventh chapter that its members will be chosen for a period of twelve years by a special election among the (CPW-Z) which is made up of all the PW representatives of the communities in the zone. These electors, subdivided into groups each forming five adjoining communities, will assemble at a specified time after the local election for the purpose of selecting nominees to the ZPW. Within limits these candidates may be chosen from among themselves, and the rest among the population in general on the basis of their merits and qualifications. The names of all who want to run must be submitted to the senior representative of the respective community, either by the would-be candidate or by groups and organizations backing some particular individual. At the assembly among the members of the five communities, all who lack the qualifications as to age and time of residence will be eliminated. In any case all candidates must be notified to the PW of the zone branch that their names have been received and considered, to prevent any representative from withholding that of anyone standing for office. As the weeding out is made, the names of the qualifying nominees will be made known to all the representatives and electioneering carried on among them. A few weeks later the representatives of the five communities will assemble again and the election will be held in earnest. On each ballot the name of four candidates will be written in order of preference, with each position equivalent to a given number of points. The one who receives the largest number will be elected representative of the zone. He will not be bound to any particular faction or interest. He cannot be discharged before his term of office is completed, and the fact that he cannot be re-elected, no matter what his contribution to the public welfare, will ensure that he will discharge his duties without the necessity of courting the favor of entrenched minorities. In other words, he will be elected for his integrity, judgment and honesty, and not to further some definite aim or interest. Conscious of this trust, he will feel the moral obligation to do his best for his people, yet whatever he does must be consonant with his conscience and with the spirit of the Constitution. Like the CPW, this body will be composed of junior representatives (Z-JR), representatives (Z-R), and senior representatives (Z-SR). This will assure a uniform policy not apt to yield to unsound whims of the population. However, unlike the representatives of the CPW, the members of the ZPW must give up their trade or profession and devote their undivided attention to the duties of their new position. A zone of average size (thirty communities), will have eighteen representatives, of which six will be elected every four years. The titular head of this branch, the zone President (ZP), will be chosen by the members themselves from among the six senior representatives, and in case of deadlock the oldest in age will qualify. This will occur when two consecutive votings fail to give anyone a majority. The zone representatives, like those in the CPW, cannot be replaced except in case of chronic illness, injury, or death, or if subsequently elected to a higher branch of the PW, and, therefore, generally must serve the full term. Housed in a special building of the zone capital, they will have under them a number of permanent employees to aid in carrying on the necessary correspondence and other activities involved in their duties. In minor matters and in those not involving new laws or changes in policies, a two-thirds majority suffices, and consequently indicates the will of the zone. As an overall picture of the PW branch in the zone, we refer to Table 16, page 634.

The total number of representatives for each zone is 18. All the zone representatives of one superzone will form one ZPW-S and their number will be $18 \times 9 = 162$. See Table 8, page 334.

All the zone representatives of the Federation will form the ZPW-F and their number will be 162s where s indicates the number of superzones in the Federation.

(1) The ZPW has jurisdiction as a body (50% + 1 vote) over 50% — 1 vote of all the community representatives of that zone (CPW-Z) and consequently over any CPW or CPW-C of the zone.

(2) A petition signed by 20% of the CPW-Z will force a decision of the ZPW to be brought to a general election of the CPW-Z.

(3) A vote of 50% plus one of the CPW-Z will reserve a decision of the ZPW.

(4) A petition signed by 20% of the ZPW-S will force a decision of the corresponding SPW to be brought to a general election of the ZPW-S.

(5) A vote of 50% plus one of the ZPW-S will reverse a decision of the SPW.

(6) A petition signed by 20% of the ZPW-F will force a decision of the FPW to be brought to a general election of the ZPW-F.

(7) A vote of 50% plus one of the ZPW-F will reverse a decision of the FPW.

The ZPW, being the people's representative, will naturally have a vital interest in what is being done by the other two important branches of the government. It has been emphasized that its influence over the ZEW, while important, will not be absolute and in major disagreements they must appeal to the respective superior authorities. This, because the policies of the EW apply to the complete population of the Federation, and, therefore, must comply with a general plan formulated by superior authorities for the general good. The influence of the ZPW over the ZGW will be, however, much more strict and exacting. Indeed, while many of the policies adopted by this branch must still comply with a master plan chosen by superior authorities of the superzone and Federation, still each zone will be left relatively free to govern itself as it wishes and, therefore, the will of its people, invested in the ZPW, must be more strongly felt. The ZPW, besides the task of selecting the ZG, with certain limitations, it may renew his term of office or cancel it altogether in the interest of the people. The limitations mentioned above refer to those cases where the ZG, certain of the soundness of his policies, gains the approval and support of the SG who may take the matter up with the SPW for the final settlement of his quarrel versus the ZPW.

One of the main duties of a zone representative is to protect the people in all matters injurious to their rights and interests. When any complaint is brought to his attention by a citizen, an organization, or a member of the CPW-Z, he must consider whether this complaint is justified in the light of existing regulations. If it is clear that an injustice is actually being done, he will approach the responsible official and discuss the matter. Chances are that a plausible explanation may be offered that may solve the difficulty, but if not he must persevere in his task. Depending on circumstances he may refer the matter to the ZPW at the regular meeting for further study and action. As in the CPW a delegation may be then sent to the official for further discussion. Depending on the turn of events the final settlement may be rapid or slow, but it will be just and it will comply with the spirit of the Constitution.

On occasion, issues being discussed by the members of the super-zone may fail to obtain a majority and qualify as the will of the people. In such instances the PW branch of the superzone dis-qualifies itself to deal with that problem and the issue is sent to the ZPW-S of the zone within that superzone. A period of months will be allowed in order that the ZPW-S members can familiarize themselves with the subject, during which time various representa-tives of the superzone advocating opposing lines of thought may be invited to explain and clarify their stand. Unless the solving of these problems is vital to the population, all such matters that come from the upper branch may be grouped, and at some specified time a general vote taken among ZPW-S members of the zone within the superzone, and the results made known to the public. Even here a specific percentage must be attained to indicate the will of the people, or the issue will be sent to the CPW-S for a new vote.

Another important task of the ZPW is inherent in the influence it exerts in the shaping of the new regulations that eventually become law within the zone. This brings us to the Legislative Branch of the zone.

LEGISLATIVE BRANCH OF THE ZONE (ZLB)

The ZLB will be composed of officials of the ZGW and ZEW who, having honorably completed their terms but failed to be reinstated to positions of the same rank or having decided to retire from active duty, are now out of office. Because of their vast experience and knowledge they must not be lost to society. Their continued cooperation is, therefore, sought in less taxing duties. The invitation to become a member of the ZLB will be extended by the ZPW, to which is left the option of selection. If the number of members is small the ZPW will also have the right to name pro-minent individuals of the zone whether or not they have been connected with the Government. These members will be called Zone Senators (S-ZLB) and while their work will be of great importance to society, it will not require their undivided attention. When the ZLB is not in session and the Senators are not due to attend to some special duty, they may return to their normal trade or profession. This body will convene at certain seasons to submit new laws. Some may originate with members of this branch, eminently qualified as they are for such initiative; others may be proposed by any official of the zone government or by groups of individuals if signed by at least six persons scattered throughout the zone. These submissions will be sent to the Secretary of this Legislative Body (SE-ZLB), who is likewise chosen for four years by the ZPW. The ZLB will divide itself into committees specializing in specific sets of problems. These will study the proposals and prepare a report for the titular heads of the other branches of the zone government. The procedure for making a new law will be similar to that in the community government. Here also full agreement among the branches is essential, and the signature of the titular heads as well as that of the judge is necessary to enact any law. There will likewise be eight alternatives as to agreement or disagreement among the three main branches, and in general what has been said of the community government applies also in this case.

JUDICIARY BRANCH OF THE ZONE (ZJB)

The ZPW representatives, besides their other tasks, have that of choosing the judges of the Zone Court who, as a body, will represent the highest authority in the zone and will convene in a special building or Court House at the capital. The Zone Court will be composed of five judges who hold office for life or until retirement. They have the right to resign or to accept appointment to a higher court. Only a two-thirds majority among the members of the ZPW is necessary for their nomination.

Cases of sufficient importance within the zone can initially be tried in this court, as well as those coming from a lower court. Here again cases can be appealed to a higher court if the contestants are not satisfied with the verdict. However, pending a new trial, its decision constitutes the law of the land, by which all concerned must abide.

The Zone Court, as already noted, has also the important role of deciding the constitutionality of measures passed by the other branches of the zone government, and the signature of the supreme judge is necessary to ratify any regulation as law in the zone.

The salary of the judges must be consonant with their elevated position and responsibility. Failing health and inability to perform their duties during a given prescribed length of time will authorize the ZPW to terminate their services and place them on the retirement list. The judges must be free from political pressure and in no way subservient to private interests. In general, what has been said for the Judiciary Branch within a community applies also in this case.

SUPERZONE GOVERNMENT

A superzone will as a generality be composed of nine zones, not necessarily adjacent. Since each zone has a government of its own, the convenience of contiguity is not an absolute necessity. The main role of the superzone government will be that of blending and co-ordinating the interests of the zones under its jurisdiction. In selecting the zones that will form a superzone this factor of contiguity will naturally be taken into account, and will be a desirable feature. Cultural level, race, religion, and basic interests, however, will be the major consideration, because they are important in fostering good will, cooperation, and unity of interests among the people of the superzone. At any rate such factors and considerations are not of supreme importance, because the interests of the various populations will be adequately protected by their own representatives, as well as by the Constitution of the Federation which is not influenced by difference in customs, race, or religion, and holds all equal under the same law.

The superzone may be thought of as equal in size and population to an average country of Europe. With each zone having about 3,000,000 inhabitants, the population of the superzone will be twenty-seven millions, approximately that of Spain or Poland. The population of the various countries in the Balkan Peninsula, for instance, may have to be joined into one or more superzones while nations like the United States, Russia, India, and China, would be divided into several superzones. The United States, for instance, could form five superzones with a name chosen for each one.

One of the main activities of the government of the superzone, besides furthering those measures that best serve the people under its jurisdiction, will be that of representing their interests in relation to other superzones within the Federation. Problems affecting the entire population of the superzone must be solved by this government rather than by those of the individual zones. The Constitution of the Federation must be such that it will assign specific fields of activity and responsibility to all the governments ranging from community to Federation, and none should be permitted to trespass upon the fields of others. Thus, specific matters pertaining to a community which do not conflict with the interests of those adjacent or with the spirit and laws of the Federation naturally must be left to the local government. However, if the interests of an adjoining community within the zone are endangered, it is evident that this will be for the zone to solve, and its authority must be recognized by all concerned. In the same way if the adjoining communities belong to different zones within a superzone, then it is for the latter to render judgment.

In a work of this kind we cannot go into extensive details as to the actual subdivision of duties among the various governments. If the new mode of life is finally considered, trained and specialized minds will devote themselves to the drafting of the "Constitution of Humanity" which will form the foundation of all laws, ethics, and fields of activity within the future society. Naturally, this will have to be done long before the new government reaches the stage of supplanting and superseding the present regime, no matter what its form and nature. For the present, however, we wish to give a general outline, subject to the revisions that must be made when the actual application is at hand.

The government of the superzone will be divided into five main branches which we shall indicate as the SEW, SGW, SPW, SLB, and SJB. All this appears in Table 17, page 661.

The nature of their duties as well as the general setup will be similar to the corresponding units of the zone, with the difference that their laws and regulations will be enforced throughout the superzone. This government will have the authority to supersede and annul regulations issued by individual zones if they infringe on basic rights of other zones or conflict with the laws made by the superzone. A more detailed analysis of the nature and relationships of its various branches follows.

ECONOMIC WELFARE BRANCH OF THE
SUPERZONE (SEW)

A General Manager (SM) will be the titular head of this branch of the government, taking the responsibility for the policies followed by his entire organization throughout the superzone. In other words, he heads the ZM of the various zones, and has authority to terminate their services for the good of the people. In contrast to the ZEW, the SEW will only be a policy making body and will be called "Central Branch". Its role will be that of coordination and leadership instead of directing details, which will be left to the individual zones. For instance, in cases where large estates spreading over various zones are to be divided, it is natural that the SEW be the final authority as to how this must be done, but it will not have the personnel either to take charge or to distribute this wealth among the population. Naturally numerous types of problems affecting different parts of the superzone will come to its attention, and accordingly the Central Branch will be divided into various groups specializing in different fields. Thus, one group will handle matters that concern inheritances, and supervise the activities of similar ones in the various zones, another will undertake the care of wealth entering the possession of the EW; while another attends to questions of distribution. Each group will be headed by a Group Manager who, while not outranking any ZM, will assist the SM in formulating policies and hence have great influence. As stated before, the SEW will be responsible for all the policies adopted, collect information as to trends within and without the superzone, and issue directives for the economic progress of the population under its jurisdiction.

Each zone will be called upon to contribute a percentage of its total revenue for the maintenance of the superzone government, and a good part of this will be used in fostering enterprises of a general nature throughout the superzone. Its personnel must be of the highest caliber, and sufficiently numerous, not only to give undivided attention to the shaping of policies, but also to expedite matters in the most efficient manner. Since the SM will hold a position of authority far superior to that of any ZM, it is clear that he must be acceptable to all the zones within the superzone as well as to the government of the Federation itself. This official will be under the direct supervision of the EW manager of the Federation (FM), who accordingly may transfer or terminate the services of any SM in the Federation. As any such positions become vacant, the FM will submit to the ZPW-S of the superzone a list of acceptable candidates. This branch in turn will weed out the names of those whom they do not wish to endorse. This information will be obtained by an election among all the representatives, and a list of the four or five candidates with the largest number of votes will be returned to the SPW. A similar election will take place here, and the list will be further condensed. From this the EW Manager (FM) will select the new SM, because the actual promotion or hiring must take place within the EW branch. This official, once chosen, will not be in any way subject to the directives of the SPW. In accordance with the all-embracing uniformity of policy, enforced throughout the Federation, the SM's will be directly responsible to the FM, who alone has authority to accept or terminate their services. The reason why the PW is given some voice in this choice is that at this level in the organization, it remains desirable that a citizen acceptable to the superzone be appointed to such an important position. Similar procedure could be used for the selection of the four Group Managers, final choice being made by the SM instead of by the FM. The various groups and divisions of this branch, as well as the title of the various officials are shown in a tabular form in Tables 24 and 25 at the end of this chapter.

GENERAL WELFARE BRANCH OF THE SUPERZONE (SGW)

This branch of the government will be similar to the corresponding one in the zone, differing only in the size of population it will serve. A Governor (SG) will be chosen as titular head by the SPW for a term of four years, and he can be retained in office for additional terms if so desired by the SPW and by the higher authorities of the Federation. Unless removed for incompetency, fraud, or criminal action, upon retirement he may be invited to become Senator of the superzone. Within due limitations (similar to those specified for the ZG), he will assume full responsibility for the activities of all members of the SGW, and naturally must have the right to select the heads of the various departments under him. In saying that the SG is responsible for the acts of all his employees we do not mean to imply that he must supervise their actions in detail. Such a task would overwhelm anyone. However, as instances of incompetence come to his attention he must prove to possess the necessary acumen to single out causes and the responsible individuals and, depending upon circumstances, show sufficient wisdom, courage, and leadership in taking the proper corrective measures. The most important departments of this branch, as well as the title of the various officials, are given in Table 18, page 661.

The State Department (SD-SGW), like the corresponding unit in the zone, will handle problems affecting the superzone in relation

to other superzones, and to some extent with countries that do not
belong to the Federation. The latter activity naturally will depend
on the geographical location of the superzone. The SD-SGW may
initiate the necessary procedure within the Federation for securing
a beneficial agreement with the neighboring country. When this
treaty will be of direct benefit to the entire population of the superzone, officials of this department will be adequately represented
at any meeting taking place between the Federation and the other
nation. Such treaties, however, to be effective, must be approved by
the FPW as well as by the FM, who must supervise any adjustments necessary within the Federation to avoid injury to the rest
of the population. While great freedom will be allowed each zone
or surperzone to negotiate any treaty they may wish for the benefit
of their population, due care must be taken that the other inhabitants
of the Federation are not in any way adversely affected. Thus any
zone or superzone can proceed with the drafting of such treaties,
but details will be modified or application delayed, to provide time
for other zones or superzones to readjust their internal economy to
the new situation. Tariffs, for instance, may be diminished gradually rather than abolished, and no unfair or discriminating treaty
will be tolerated by the Federation, as conflicting with the spirit of
the Constitution. It is a matter of course that the treaty must
also be approved by the SPW. The SD-SGW will also regulate and
supervise similar activities of the individual zones.

The Interior Department (ID-SGW) will be charged with problems
of a general nature within the superzone which facilitate relationships
between the zones under its jurisdiction. It will make laws and
regulations pertaining to trade and commerce. It will be responsible
for the care of its natural resources. Some of its activities will
correspond to those conducted in this country by the Bureaus of
Geological Survey, Fisheries, Reclamation, Mines, and so forth. To
the extent that similar work is done by the Interior Department of
each zone, this department will serve as their connecting link and
coordinator.

Now it is expedient that ID-SGW should have a definite authority
over the corresponding departments of the various zones, in order
to ensure a unified policy. In the vast majority of cases, of course,
this authority exerted by the higher branch will be approved and
endorsed, but obviously there may be cases in which disparity of
opinion arises between these branches. As the Interior Department,
or any other for that matter, in any zone is directly responsible

only to its ZG, it is natural that if such disagreement should occur that the matter be taken up with the latter who, as noted above, is responsible to the ZPW. In cases where the ZG readily agrees with the higher branch, and acts to comply with its policy, all will go well, but if agreement is lacking the dispute must be referred to the SPW who, as we shall see, has authority not only over the ZGW but also over the ZPW of each zone. Since the SPW represents the entire population of the superzone, it is quite likely that in the vast majority of cases it will side with the SG and act accordingly, but if not (and a 2/3 vote is required for confirmation of the SG's decision), the zone government must be left free from any dictate from the superzone.

The Finance Department (FD-SGW) will be in charge of the finance of the superzone. It will control the collection of revenue from the zones and will be responsible for public debt operations. In general, it will translate into law the policies handed down by superior authority.

The Department of Agriculture (AD-SGW) will have the same duties and responsibilities as the corresponding unit in the zone, and naturally its authority throughout the superzone and subjection to the higher branch of the Federation will parallel what we have outlined for other departments.

The Department of Education (ED-SGW) will establish uniform rules for the high schools of the superzone, and be directly responsible for the universities in the region. It will select the presidents of the various universities, pass upon and approve the nominations of professors by the university board, set their salary, maintain libraries, museums, and so forth, and in general cooperate with the zones regarding public education.

The Police Department (PD-SGW) will help its counterparts in cases where different zones are involved, and in general will concentrate upon public safety within the superzone. It will cooperate with the various PD-ZGW in financing schools and homes for children of delinquent parents, as well as for delinquents themselves. Likewise, it will cooperate with the same branch of the EW (SEW2-5) in establishing special schools for officers of the police force. This department will also act for the government of the superzone against criminals and fugitives from justice.

Another department will attend to elections within the superzone, and formulate laws and regulations calculated to establish a uniform pattern throughout the land.

Each of these departments will have as titular head a career man chosen by the SG, directly responsible to him and also acceptable to the SPW.

The Department personnel must be of such number and caliber as to ensure the efficient discharge of the manifold duties of this branch of the government. Promotions will be on a competitive basis, and no one can be discharged unless guilty of fraud or obvious incompetency, and will be protected from political pressure. The SG and the department heads will form the GW Executive Board (SGWB). The frequency of its meetings will depend on the number and importance of the problems on hand.

The SG, as already stated, must be left free, not only to choose the heads of the various departments, but also to change them if he consider it necessary. At the end of his four years of service his position may pass to another, who quite likely will dismiss many of the department heads. Some of these will probably be given positions in the Federation government because their outstanding records may have made them nationally known, while others will be made Senators and become part of the Legislative Branch of the super-zone. What has been said for a Senator of the zone applies also to a Senator of the superzone. He will be free to accept a more responsible position in the government if offered him, and naturally his salary will be suitable. No one should receive more than one salary at a time from the government. At the end of the new assignment, the rank and pay of Senator will revert to him. However, if his higher position happens to be one in the Federation government, at the end of his term he may become a Senator of the Federation.

PEOPLE'S WELFARE BRANCH OF THE
SUPERZONE (SPW)

The activity of this unit will be similar to the corresponding one in the zone. Its members will be chosen for a term of twelve years by a special election among the zone representatives. Each zone will send three representatives to the superzone, of which one will be elected every four years. Of the three individuals two may be chosen among the ZPW, and the other must be an outstanding citizen of the zone. Thus the total number will be 27, of which nine will be elected at a time. As an overall picture of the PW branch of the superzone we refer to Table 19, page 661.

The total number of representatives for each superzone is 27. All the superzone representatives of the Federation will form one SPW-F and, if s is the total number of superzones, the total number of representatives will be 27 x s. See Table 8, page 334.

(1) The SPW has jurisdiction as a body (50% plus 1 vote), over 50% minus one vote of all the zones or communities' representatives in the superzone and consequently over any ZPW or CPW of the superzone.

(2) A petition signed by 20% of the ZPW-S or CPW-S will force a decision of the SPW to be brought to a general election of any of those two bodies.

(3) A vote of 50% plus one of the ZPW-S or CPW-S will reverse a decision of the SPW.

(4) A petition signed by 20% of the SPW-F will force a decision of the FPW to be brought to a general election of the SPW-F.

(5) A vote of 50% plus one of the SPW-F will reverse a decision of the FPW.

The titular head of this branch, the President of the superzone (SP), will be chosen by the SPW among the senior members every four years. He will preside over all general meetings of the SPW, but the value of his vote will be the same as that of the others. His salary will be slightly higher, and he will also be compensated for expenditures suitable to his station. Being the first citizen of the superzone, he will have to attend public functions, represent the superzone, and in general maintain a station consonant with his eminent standing. For the election of the SP the same procedure will be adopted as for the zone government.

These representatives, like those already described, cannot be replaced except for permanent incapacity to discharge their duties, or if elected to a higher position in the Federation.

The death of any delegate or his promotion to an upper branch of the PW will leave his zone inadequately served. Accordingly, the candidate who received the next highest number of votes at the last election will succeed with the title of Alternate Representative (S-AR), and in that capacity will complete the four years' term, after which a regular one will be chosen. At this next election Alternate Representatives will have the right to seek the regular position. Instances will be considered of various cases. If a vacancy occurs in the position of (S-SR), the other two will advance in seniority, and with the (S-AR) the zone will still maintain the same representation. If it happens in the position of (S-R), only the (S-JR) need

FIG. 27

CASE 1: NORMAL ADVANCE OF PW REPRESENTATIVES

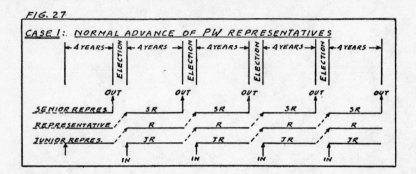

CASE 2: SENIOR REPRESENTATIVE OUT OR ELECTED TO SUPERIOR BRANCH OF GOVERNMENT

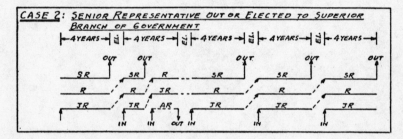

CASE 3: REPRESENTATIVE OUT OR ELECTED TO SUPERIOR BRANCH OF GOVERNMENT

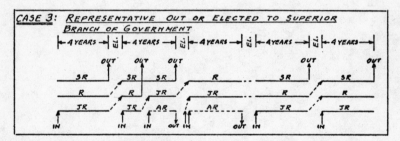

CASE 4: JUNIOR REPRESENTATIVE OUT OR ELECTED TO SUPERIOR BRANCH OF GOVERNMENT

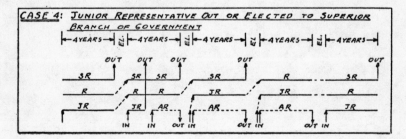

succeed in seniority, while the (S-AR) will take his place. At the next election two representatives must be chosen, of which the one polling the most votes will become (S-JR) while the runner-up becomes the new (S-AR). If the vacancy ensues in the position of (S-JR) an alternate or (S-AR) will take his place to the end of the four-year term. Then, as in the previous case, two representatives will be chosen of which one will become (S-JR) and the other (S-AR). Similar procedures follow at the next election. In order to make this seemingly complicated procedure more clear to the reader, we refer him to Fig. 27, page 654a, in which the various cases are preesnted in a diagrammatic form.

Each solid horizontal line stands for the term of office of the regular representative, and the dotted lines of the Alternate. The spacing between two adjoining lines represents the election which occurs every four years. What has been said for the superzone applies for the other governments of the Federation. No more than one representative can be elected from any one single group of three representatives. This is to say that there should never be more than one Alternate Representative at any one time unless death should make the filling of that vacancy imperative.

All the representatives are morally bound to keep abreast of all matters pertaining to the superzone in general, and to their zone in particular, and must vote whenever there is an election, as this is an important way for the zone to influence the affairs of the superzone. In those cases in which a representative is ill or unable to attend the election, his vote must be sent through any of the normal channels prescribed by law, such as mail or telephone, and the election results must be withheld until all the votes have been cast and counted.

While every representative must be guided by high principles of justice, honesty, and decency, which at times may force him to vote against the demands of his own electorate, it will be among his duties to defend the interests of individuals or groups in his zone who may feel injured by any particular policy of the other branches of the government. With this aim in mind it will be his obligation first to study the matter and see whether injustice is actually done. If he feels that anyone's rights are jeopardized, he must take up the matter with the proper official and seek the solution. In the case of uncompromising attitude on the part of the official, he must refer the matter to the SPW, so that pressure may be brought to bear either in awakening the official to the will of the people or in introducing revised regulations to correct the situation.

Besides this, the SPW as a body, has the important task of seeing that all new enactments do not infringe upon the people's liberties. In such matters they have a vast power, one which includes the right to remove the SG if required. When conflict of opinion occurs with the SM, it has not such power and must refer the complaint to the superior branch of the Federation. Hence if the SM, ZM, or CM of the government considered should persistently antagonize the corresponding PW branch of the government, even though within their rights, causing matters often to be referred to a higher branch, it would be wise for the immediate superior of the EW to replace the official by another who has more tact and can carry out the program of the EW without undue friction and misunderstanding.

It has been noted that in any election among representatives and upon questions of policy, the percentage for or against will have a definite weight in the effectiveness of that voting. If the majority of votes does not reach a specific percentage, the matter must be referred to a lower branch of the PW for additional study and a new election. This has the purpose of determining in important matters the true will of the people. The SPW, among other duties, will elect the (SG) and may extend his services at will. The election, however, as already stated, must be approved by the FGW.

The capital of the superzone, where these various branches will be located, need not coincide with that of any of the nine zones. It will be desirable to choose for it some central place in the superzone.

As mentioned already another important task of the SPW is to share in the shaping of new laws and regulations to be enacted within the superzone. This brings us to the Legislative Branch of the superzone (SLB).

LEGISLATIVE BRANCH OF THE SUPERZONE (SLB)

Like the zone and community government, the functions of the three main branches of the superzone assume society as crystallized in some particular pattern that does not admit change. It may seem at first that all should be interested in maintaining the laws written in the Constitution, but as explained before the Constitution, with the exception of those few basic and fundamental laws that must not be changed unless the mode of life is altered, will deal with ethics and aims to be attained, leaving its interpretation to the present as well as to future generations. Of course, it will have laws and regulations, so as to present a complete and rational set of rules to the present society. These, however, take into account only the needs of modern times and cannot possibly foresee or cover needs that may develop in future generations. Thus, the Constitution must be sufficiently elastic, having the necessary mechanism to adjust itself to new times and requirements. Needless to say that future changes must be introduced in a constitutional manner. Their instrument is found in the Legislative Branch (LB). This body, like the others previously considered, will be composed of the Senators (S-SLB) who may be officials of the SEW and SGW retired from active duty or temporarily without government assignment, and of prominent citizens of the superzone appointed by the SPW.

The introduction of any new regulation as well as the process of enacting a new law will be similar to that for the corresponding branch of the zone, and needs no elucidation. We wish to repeat that, while the new Constitution will be enforced throughout the Federation, it must allow some freedom to the governments of the various superzones. Indeed, we cannot expect that equal standards be imposed to all people in the Federation, who often enough will have different backgrounds and civilizations. To make our point clear on the subject, laws regarding bigamy, divorce, and so forth, which may appear just to people of western standards, may be utterly inconsistent and intolerable to a population in central Africa, and should this be part of the Federation, we cannot expect these Africans to accept forthwith ethics to which they are not accustomed. New regulations that may eventually evolve into laws within such a zone or superzone are bound to differ from those enacted in an area like New York, and the Constitution must respect such variations. In other words, with the exception of those fundamental laws referred to above, all people must be free to govern themselves as they choose, and the connecting link between such different inhabitants of the Federation must be economic ties, promulgated by the EW which, as seen, in many cases outranks the PW. Any radical change in the policy of the EW will affect basic clauses of the Constitution and as the effects will be felt by the entire population of the Federation, its application, as well as its changing into law will be harder to attain. This will give assurance that no one will be able to secure economic advantages at the expense of others.

While the core of the new laws and regulations will be formed within the Legislative body, we have seen that proposals for new legislation may be sent to the Secretary, in this case (SE-SLB), who will be the titular head of the branch, by an official of the government, and by the people themselves. Naturally some of the suggestions will have actual merit, and should be given the proper attention and consideration, ultimately after study and review eventually being incorporated among the laws of the land. Others may be fatuously foolish and inadequate. Since the originators are citizens of the Federation, they are entitled to proper courtesy and respect. After due acknowledgment the proposal must be sent to the proper committee and a copy forwarded to the PW branch. The committee, after a rapid consideration, may assign to any of its members the task of replying to the originator, showing the inconsistency and impracticability of the ideas, and if the sponsor withdraws the proposal the matter comes to a close. If the author is obstinate, his scheme may again be considered by the committee and referred to the assembled SLB. If the latter is unimpressed, a new reply will be sent, but if further persistency results, the case goes to the SPW which, being the mouthpiece of the people, has authority to reject it outright. No bid, however, no matter how absurd should be left to gather dust in the archives of the SLB, and all matters coming to its attention must be disposed of as rapidly as possible. Any such petition, to be within the law, must be signed by a certain number of citizens. Three signatures entitle it to be sent directly to the CLB for consideration. Ten signatures within one community will carry it to the zone government or ZLB, although if the signers are from all over the zone, only six are needed. The signature of 100 citizens in one community may send a petition directly to the government of the superzone, but if they are inhabitants of various zones only (6 x 9) equals 54 signers are required. One thousand signatures within a community serve to forward a petition direct to the FLB, but if they are scattered throughout the Federation, the required number becomes 600.

JUDICIARY BRANCH OF THE SUPERZONE (SJB)

The SPW, besides its other tasks above enumerated, has also that of choosing the judges of the Superzone Court who, as a body, form the highest authority in the superzone in this field, and will convene in a special court house at the superzone capital. This court will be composed of nine judges, one from each zone, who are elevated to this position for life, active until retirement or until incapable. At any time they may resign and accept a position in a higher court. Only a two-thirds majority among the members of the SPW is required for their nomination.

Cases of sufficient importance within the superzone can be tried for the first time in this court, and, of course, it will hear all that come up from lower branches. Here again cases can be carried to a higher court if sufficiently important, should the parties not be satisfied with the verdict. However, pending a new trial its decision is the law, and all concerned must abide with it.

This court, as already mentioned, has also the important task of deciding on the constitutionality of measures passed by the other branches of the superzone government, and the signature of the Chief Judge (CJ-SJB) is necessary to enact any law of the superzone. The salary of the judges of this court must be consonant with their position and responsibility, and lasts for life. Failing health and inability to perform their duty allows the SPW to place them on the retirement list. The judges, needless to say, must be free of political pressure, and not be in any way subservient to minority interests.

As already mentioned, this court represents the highest authority within the superzone, in the field of justice, law, and order; and depending on circumstances it may sustain or annul verdicts given by a lower court when they come before it. In general, the court will uphold the Constitution of the land as written at the initiation of the Federation, and likewise the amendments which from time to time are ratified by the people. In other words, no matter what may be the pressing necessity of a new law, these judges have the duty to see that the Constitution is respected in letter as well as in spirit. Only a referendum among the entire population of the Federation may change the statues of the Constitution, and thus reverse any decision of the court.

Due to their great influence in the life of society, their appointment, while actually made by the SPW, must have the approval of the various ZPW of the zone from which the judge may be elected. First the SPW will select a number of candidates from the zone that has lost the representation, and present it to that particular ZPW for study. As the names of candidates are weeded out, the superzone will have a reduced list from which the necessary appointment will be made. The SPW will have, however, the only say as to who shall be the Chief Justice among the nine judges elected.

As in other courts of the land, there will be matters in which the court will use its judgment as to the interpretation of the Constitution as it affects the superzone and its zones and communities. However, there will be matters of economic nature that will affect all the superzones, in which case they must abide by the decision taken by the Supreme Court of the Federation. We mean by this that if they should uphold or reject a law under the impression that it is within their domain, and then if it proves harmful to other parts of the Federation, the resulting dispute must be settled by the Supreme Court of the Federation, which may annul or uphold that verdict depending on its merits. The contending superzones, it goes without saying, must abide by the verdict of the Federation Court.

TABLE NO. 17

SUPERZONE GOVERNMENT	ECON. WELFARE BRANCH	SEW
	GENERAL " "	SGW
	PEOPLE " "	SPW
	LEGISLATIVE BRANCH	SLB
	JUDICIARY "	SJB

TABLE NO. 19

TITLE OF THE SUPERZONE PW OFFICIALS		
NUMBER	TITLE	
1	SUPERZONE PRESIDENT	SP
8	" SENIOR REPRES.	S-SR
9	" REPRESENTATIVE	S-R
9 {	" JUNIOR REPRES	S-JR
	" ALTERNATE "	S-AR

TABLE NO 18

BRANCH	SUPERZONE GENERAL WELFARE DEPARTMENT			SUPERZONE GENERAL WELFARE OFFICIAL'S TITLE		
SUPERZONE GENERAL WELFARE BRANCH~ SGW	STATE	SD-SGW	SUPERZONE GOVERNOR	HEAD OF STATE DEPARTMENT	H-SD-S
	INTERIOR	ID-SGW		" INTERIOR "	H-ID-S
	FINANCE	FD-SGW		" FINANCE "	H-FD-S
	AGRICULTURE	AD-SGW		" AGRICULTURE "	H-AD-S
	EDUCATION	ED-SGW		" EDUCATION "	H-ED-S
	POLICE	PD-SGW		" POLICE "	H-PD-S
	ELECTION	$E_\ell D$-SGW		" ELECTION "	H-E_ℓD-S

TABLE NO. 20

FEDERATION GOVERNMENT	ECON. WELFARE BRANCH	FEW
	GENERAL " "	FGW
	PEOPLE " "	FPW
	LEGISLATIVE BRANCH	FLB
	JUDICIARY "	FJB

TABLE NO 22

TITLE OF THE FEDERATION PW OFFICIALS		
NUMBER	TITLE	
1	FEDERATION PRESIDENT	FP
n-1	" SENIOR REPRES.	F-SR
n	" REPRESENTATIVE	F-R
n {	" JUNIOR REPRES.	F-JR
	" ALTERNATE "	F-AR

TABLE NO 21

BRANCH	FEDERATION GENERAL WELFARE DEPARTMENT			FEDERATION GENERAL WELFARE OFFICIAL'S TITLE		
FEDERATION GENERAL WELFARE - FGW	STATE	SD-FGW	FEDERATION GOVERNMENT FG	HEAD OF STATE DEPARTMENT	H-SD-F
	INTERIOR	ID-FGW		" INTERIOR "	H-ID-F
	WAR	WD-FGW		" WAR "	H-WD-F
	FINANCE	FD-FGW		" FINANCE "	H-FD-F
	AGRICULTURE	AD-FGW		" AGRICULTURE "	H-AD-F
	POLICE	PD-FGW		" POLICE "	H-PD-F
	ELECTION	$E_\ell D$-FGW		" ELECTION "	H-E_ℓD-F
	POST OFFICE	RD-FGW		" POST OFFICE "	H-RD-F

GOVERNMENT OF THE FEDERATION

In general the Federation government is similar in structure, as well as in duties to that of the zones and superzones, with some basic variations analyzed later in our text. We have seen that each zone and superzone has a certain amount of autonomy, and that within limits they may administer themselves as they see fit. This is just and proper, since the Federation will be an agglomeration of peoples of vast difference in culture, race, customs and religion. The unifying element will be a set of fundamental principles which, embodied in legislation, will be enforced by the government of the Federation, guarding the interests of the people as a whole.

In contrast to present-day methods in many nations, the Federation will derive its power, not from the members of one race, land, or class, but from all its inhabitants, and each one will have his part in steering the affairs of state.

Like those previously reviewed, the government of the Federation will be divided into five main units, which we shall indicate as the FEW, FGW, FPW, FLB, and FJB branches. All this appears in Table 20, page 661.

The nature of their activities will be similar to those of the corresponding units of the superzones, with the difference that they will range over the entire population of the Federation. A detailed analysis of their functions follows.

ECONOMIC WELFARE BRANCH OF THE FEDERATION (FEW)

The activities of this unit of the government have been analyzed before, and require little elucidation. It is essential, however, that we should point out the connections that must exist with the other branches.

A General Manager (FM) will be its titular head. He will shoulder responsibility for the entire organization throughout the land. In some respects his position will be the most important in the government, since the rate of progress will depend so greatly upon his leadership and vision. It is natural, of course, in such a vast organization as the EW, that he should not be expected to be thoroughly acquainted with every phase and detail necessary to further the welfare of the population. He will be accountable, however, for them to the extent that it will be he who selects the holders of positions of great power and responsibility. At any rate, as the Constitution will be clear, rigid and to the point, the human factor will no longer play such a prominent role in the solution of problems which involve fundamental and basic principles of human rights. By law it is decreed that everyone within the organization shall abide by definite rules when confronted by specific problems, and this is bound to ensure progress, independently of the type of leadership. These principles prevent any minority or entrenched interest from ever being able to secure privileges at the expense of the multitude. Accordingly, if they are rigidly applied, no one should feel discriminated against in any way as the Constitution gives unlimited freedom to honest and justified endeavor, but automatically resists corrupt and dishonest procedures that by spreading within the body social may bring about the downfall of society. But clear and rigid as these regulations may be, everyone knows that people are not perfect and it is possible that officials, even of the highest rank, sooner or later may succumb to corruption or misinterpret the spirit of the Constitution, allowing injustice to flourish openly or in secret. The EW is a closely knit organization which takes orders directly from the FM, while no other part of the government, even the PW, has the right to punish or dismiss any EW official even if guilty of corruption and fraud. Nevertheless in cases such as these the PW representatives have the right and the privilege to appeal to their immediate superiors, who can take up the matter with the superiors of the incriminated officials. Needless to say, these officials, once the accusations have been investigated and proved, have the authority to take whatever punitive action they consider in order. Failure to take such a course would render themselves liable to punishment by their own superiors, until culminating with the FM, who is directly responsible to the FPW branch of the government. Of course, actual criminal acts will be dealt with through the normal channels of the Judiciary Branch, so the maximum penalty any other official can inflict upon anyone under his jurisdiction is that of an outright discharge from the organization. Even so the actual dismissal cannot be made by the immediate superior of the culprit, but only requested by him and ultimately ordered by a higher official. Still there may be occasions on which the people's delegates, in their zeal for upholding the immediate interests of those whom they represent, forget that the EW is an organization beneficial to the entire population, and not subservient to any minority. Thus it is possible that friction and misunderstanding may ensue between the PW branch and an EW official, each honestly engaged in carrying out Federation directives. In such a case the EW official must be protected and upheld by his superiors. Of course, the PW representatives can always refer the dispute to their superior branch, but as this consists of delegates from vastly larger populations, it is apt to view the problem in wider perspective, and it is more likely than not that it would finally side with the EW. Needless to say, any such quarrel would be settled then and there. However, there may also be occasions when the controversy will reach still higher branches of the PW, at each successive level coming before individuals who represent the interests of yet larger societies, and, therefore, are more qualified to form a just and unbiased opinion. In extreme cases the case may reach the FM, who is directly responsible for the entire EW organization. Ultimately the Supreme Court of the Federation, as the highest authority in the land, may and probably will be called to give its verdict upon the matter, which will definitely settle the question. Our readers know that in cases where the PW and the population in general are very strongly in favor of or very strongly against an issue, a referendum can be held to amend the Constitution.

We have already stated and must now emphasize anew, that if an official of the EW during the normal discharge of his duties becomes the object of attack by the PW or the population in general, even though he is vindicated, if circumstances demand it he must be transferred to another community, zone or superzone. This should be done because it is expedient that the officials of the EW be able to carry out their duties and the policies by which they are guided without raising undue antagonism among the local population, whose interests are upheld by the PW. In other words, cooperation is paramount, and since all policies of the EW are fair and just to all concerned, it is evident that any friction that may develop results from the fact that the official has not made them clear and understandable to the people. It goes without saying that any employee or official of the EW who displays ignorance or incompetency becomes liable to be demoted or discharged.

The FM is the only official of the EW who will be hired from outside the organization. In the seventh chapter we described the method to be adopted for the selection of the first FM, to whom will fall the complicated task of giving form and substance to an organization which is merely visualized in this study. However, like his successors, he will be hired for a definite number of years (4), at the end of which he must give way to whomever the FPW chooses to elevate as his successor. It is understood that he may be reappointed for an additional four-year term, if desired by the FPW. It goes without saying that these individuals will be internationally known, of the highest caliber, and demonstrably great leaders. Since the FM assumes the responsibility for the entire organization under him, he must have the right and privilege to choose his assistants in his great task. Key positions, such as heads of sub-branches, managers of communities, zones, and superzones are out of the field of normal promotion. The reason is that these ranks require exceptional traits of character and leadership, innate with the individual and not apt to be acquired even by years of experience. Those blessed with these qualities sooner or later are bound to attract the attention of their superiors, who will confer upon them these positions of responsibility rather than to others honest, capable, and efficient, but lacking those prerequisites. Indeed such an individual should eventually be promoted from whatever position he may have within a community to a similar one in the zone and upward, but should never be chosen for a position in which leadership is paramount. This applies even to that of Manager of a community, for which leadership, tact, and understanding of human rights are far more important than culture and knowledge.

When the FM is replaced at the end of his term, naturally his successor will surround himself with his own choice of able assistants for whom he feels trust and respect. Thus every four years there is likely to be some reshuffling among the highest officials of the EW, which may spread downward throughout the organization. Some officials will remain in their positions, others will be advanced to higher rank, and the rest may become senators of the zone, superzone or Federation if invited by the corresponding PW branches, and thereby continue their service. Senators will always be free to accept positions in any branch of the government where vacancy occurs, for which they have qualifications acceptable to the new officials.

Proceeding with the activities of the EW branch of the Federation, we note that, like its counterpart in the superzone, it will consist only of the Central Branch, as its main duty will be that of coordination among the various zones and superzones. This branch, more than any other, will be responsible for the policies to be enacted throughout the land. The actual care of details, as already seen, will be left to the zones and communities throughout the Federation. This branch of the government will have available an adequate number of capable agents to be stationed anywhere to collect first-hand information for immediate transmission to headquarters. This will enable the FEW to issue the proper directives, especially when speed is essential, without waiting for such data to flow through normal channels, which would sometimes involve considerable delay. This will also add elasticity and effectiveness to the smooth functioning of the Federation.

Money from taxes and inheritances will support this branch of the government. Each community will be allowed to retain a substantial percentage of the total revenue, and the remainder will be sent to the zone government. This, in turn, will deduct another percentage and forward the rest to the government of the super-zone. A similar procedure will operate between the superzone and the Federation government. The funds reaching the Federation will not only pay the wages and salaries of all employees, but will be used also in fostering enterprises of major importance within its territories that cannot be sustained either by private initiative or by the governments of individual zones and superzones. Aid also will be given to zones or superzones in need, according to their economic index.

The various groups and divisions of this branch, as well as the titles of the various officials are shown in Table 24 and 25 at the end of this chapter.

As already stated, this branch will receive all kinds of information from every part of the Federation, and thus will be able to discern new economic trends upon which it will base farseeing directives. The personnel must be of the highest caliber and will reach their elevated position through successive promotions from lower branches and by demonstration of worth and capability. As to the selection of the four Group Managers of the Federation, the first requirement is that they be acceptable to the FM, but due to their great importance they must also win the approval of the FPW. Their selection will be made by the FM, who will submit to the FPW a list of prominent citizens (chiefly government employees) qualified for the position. The FPW will eliminate some and return the lessened list, from which the FM will make his choice. This will be his privilege because they must be first and last responsible only to him. The FM and the four assistants will form the Federation Executive Board (FEWB). In settling important questions regarding policies all the SM will be summoned to attend FEWB meetings with equal rank to the Assistant Managers.

GENERAL WELFARE BRANCH OF THE FEDERATION (FGW)

This branch of the government will be similar to the corresponding ones of the zone and superzones, with some important variations we shall point out later in our text. A Federation Governor (FG) will be its titular head, and his position will not be political. He will be elected by the FPW for a period of four years, with the usual understanding that his term can be renewed as often as the FPW and the Federation in general wishes. Unless discharged for incompetency or criminal conduct, at the end of his service he will be entitled to become Senator of the Federation, an appointment valid until retirement age, and enter the legislative Branch of the Federation, in which capacity his experience and knowledge of government affairs will not be lost to the nation. It is a matter of course that, as Senator, he may accept another responsible position in the government, and his salary will be the greater one of the two. The FG will assume entire responsibility for this branch, and has the right to select those who will assist in his work; the method being similar to that used for Group Managers of the FEW. His main duty will be one of leadership rather than attention to details, and what has been said for the SG will also apply. The most important departments of this branch, as well as the title of the various officials, are given in Table 21, page 661.

STATE DEPARTMENT (SD-FGW)

This unit, in many ways similar to the corresponding department of the superzone, will cope with cases affecting the Federation in relation to foreign countries. With the advice and cooperation of the EW it will sign treaties with other nations. Such agreements, to become effective, must be ratified by the FPW. We wish to say in passing that for treaties that may link the Federation to other countries, as for instance those regarding allegiance, if the necessary majority among the FPW should be lacking, ratification must be referred to successively lower branches of the PW until it may reach the people proper. This inevitable slow process will necessitate a longer study, permit a thorough analysis of the pros and cons, and prevent the association or alliance of the Federation with another nation without the knowledge and consent of the people. The Department of State will maintain ambassadors and consuls in other countries to represent the Federation. This Department, in short, will have the same role as that of any civilized country in the world today.

INTERIOR DEPARTMENT (ID-FGW) This will correspond to that of any zone and superzone, and serve as the coordinating link among them. In passing, it may be stated that the cultural progress of backward countries within the Federation will be one of the most important tasks of this department, which will closely collaborate with the governments of such zones or superzones.

WAR DEPARTMENT (WD-FGW) While the Federation will be a compact family of nations which have forever abandoned war as an instrument for settling disputes, and will go to great lengths to avoid quarrels with other countries, as it will have elasticity to cope with any economic influence from the outside, nevertheless strength and preparedness are essential to escape being dragged into wars elsewhere in the world. An aggressive conflict launched by the Federation is utterly unthinkable to us, and any war in which the Federation may become involved could only be one to repel invasion.

It should be one of its chief policies not to interfere with the internal affairs of another nation, provided that the latter's conduct does not disregard fundamental principles of justice and decency, nor radically depart from accepted codes of civilization. On this point it is well to state our opinion in full. Within a civilized community no one would think of condemning or in any way hampering the policemen in their effort to restrain or punish anyone guilty of a criminal act, even though the liberty of the individual stands as one of the basic principles of human rights. The freedom of one's fellowmen must be respected as long as it does not infringe upon that of others. Nor would anyone interfere with an individual, seeking to stop a parent from maltreating his children, even though the authority of father or mother should be respected and interference within a family avoided. Such intervention seems to us just and proper, within the rightful prerogatives of a civilized society. Because it is fundamentally similar we claim that humanity should have the moral right to prevent nations from committing acts of cruelty either against individuals or groups within or without their domains.

Upon the basis of fundamental principle we believe that our Federation of Nations, while opposed to any war caused by craving for power and economic domination, should stand forth as a champion of justice and defender of the rightful liberties. Accordingly, the Federation must not follow a policy of indecision and vacillation which, besides encouraging the evil, merely postpones greater tragedy. We visualize instead a dynamic Federation of Nations, fearless and unwavering, which will uphold basic human rights even if war ensues. In other words, we wish to see our Federation the great champion of subjugated peoples everywhere, with no selfish motive or desire of aggrandizement, for the rights of mankind should be defended wherever in danger, this being the only way to prevent unscrupulous minorities from taking power and bringing universal disaster. Once justice has been established, the Federation should abstain from asking or accepting economic advantages of any kind injurious to other nations, vanquished as well as victors. The Federation will not need to buy friendship. The gleaming example of friendship and cooperation among its heterogeneous populations, the unselfish and altruistic measures taken by its leaders, are bound to generate cordiality and good will among other nations, who gradually will realize the benefits of this new system of life, and of their own volition seek annexation.

Actual action, according to this fundamental attitude of the Federation toward other nations, will inevitably depend on conditions in general. First of all the defensive and counter-offensive power of the Federation must be sufficient to discourage any would-be aggressor. At the beginning we cannot expect that the Federation will include all the most powerful nations of the world, able, therefore, to prevent the waging of war without its consent. In its initial stage it will probably consist of only a few countries, and, therefore, will have limited strength. The first duty of its government will be, of course, that of organizing the defense of the Federation against possible aggressors. Besides the mustering of the greatest power within its ability, it should seek alliances with peace-loving nations cherishing similar ideals and also apprehensive of aggression. If their combined resources suffice to intimidate the would-be aggressor nation, well and good; if not, the Federation should never hesitate to take up arms no matter which allies suffer invasion. Only by strict adherence to principles can the Federation gain respect and friendship. It is true that some supposedly friendly nations may at times be swayed by different codes and principles from those avowedly proclaimed. Unfortunately, the world cannot be changed overnight, so unless the new policies are directly opposed to the aforesaid basic principles, such countries should still receive the support and cooperation of the Federation in their efforts to retain self-government and maintain the peace of the world. In short the Federation, due to its initially limited power, must perforce consider the necessity of compromise as every great nation does nowadays. However, as it becomes stronger, because of the entrance of new members, its reliance on foreign aid will gradually decline and she will be able to follow an independent course closer to her aims and ideals. From this it can be foreseen that a level will be reached when her military might can be finally reduced. This will follow when strong present-day potential aggressor nations join the Federation. As they solve their economic problems they will become peace-loving countries mindful of their neighbors' rights and liberties. The Federation will thus become a stabilizing factor in the world at large, and though no attempt will be made to force its mode of life upon others, its existence will prevent unscrupulous minorities of any country from subjugating and maltreating the weaker majority, it will prevent would-be aggressor nations from terrorizing and overrunning weaker nations.

No mention has been made of a department of war within a zone or superzone. Naturally, there will be none, and with the exception of a police force, existing to protect life and property within these geographical jurisdictions, no army or navy will be organized, as this is reserved for the Federation as a whole.

Most wars, past and present, started from economic maladjustments, which generated hostility and ill-will. As such unbalanced situations among sister zones or superzones will no longer exist, this will also suppress their necessity of maintaining armed forces against other members of the Federation, and hence no provision was made.

The WD-FGW will be headed by a Secretary of War (H-WD-F), who will take orders only from the FG, and will supervise necessary setup to make the Federation strong and secure. The military organizations will include career men in the upper branches and volunteers in the lower, being divided into as many specialized branches as are required by a modern organization of this kind. If necessary, the recruiting of additional troops and specialized talent may be made compulsory throughout the Federation. This Department will provide the soldiers, sailors, and airmen with leadership and technique of training, and be able to wage war with the highest degree of efficiency and effectiveness. No sacrifices in money or resources should be spared to place the Federation in a condition of a readiness to enter the international interplay of nations.

An act of aggression against any part of the Federation, major or minor, will be regarded as a declaration of war upon all its members. The enemy will be resisted, if possible, but in any case will ultimately be punished. The qualification of this statement needs exposition.

Due to the lack of compactness of the Federation in its early stages, there may be times when aggressors cannot be prevented from making their onslaught. As any nation may join the Federation, some of its members may be isolated outposts surrounded by hostile populations, but equally entitled to its protection. Suppose, for instance, that the United States and several South American republics form the first members, and in Europe only Switzerland has joined them. Thereupon all Swiss soil is guaranteed defense, no less than that of New York, California, or the South American member states. Then should a neighbor venture upon violent methods against Switzerland, within suitable limits the Federation will let the threatened country solve the controversy as she sees fit, offering its mediation, and without imposing economic sanctions. However, if actual invasion of Switzerland took place or other mode of outright attack, the entire Federation will move as one to open hostilities, even though actual contact at first may be difficult. This aid will be given as soon as the physical obstacles have been overcome. Due to the isolated location of Switzerland, she may suffer devastation before rescue arrives, but the determination of the Federation will ensure that justice finally triumph, proving beyond doubt that international banditry will no longer pay. Such a lesson would prevent other nations from embarking on a similar course.

The WD-FGW, similar in its set-up to any Department of War of any contemporary country, must be free (within restrictions analyzed in this discussion) to decide upon the strength of the army, navy, and air fleet; quality and kind of training; location of military outposts; and in all technical, strategic, and other types of defense problems. It will collaborate with the SD-FGW regarding the advisability of keeping a suitable number of troops, war material, and equipment in key locations within the Federation. To make this point clear, our previous example will serve: In a zone like Switzerland, surrounded by nations not in the Federation, it is natural that strong military forces and war equipment be kept there in readiness rather than in one located in the center of the United States, for the purpose of resisting the initial impact of any would-be aggressor. But, in general, we wish to stress that most military technicalities, as, for instance, amount and quality of training, type of equipment, and so forth, would be left to the war department, as best qualified for decision in the matter.

This freedom of action, however, is not to be interpreted as indicating that this department cannot be restricted and its activity channeled through directives in line with the ideals of the Federation. First of all, the Department of War must comply with and conform to directions issued by the FG, who in turn is responsible to the FPW. This department, despite its jurisdiction over military matters, especially the vital assignment of making the Federation as powerful as practicable within the limits of the financial allotment, will not concern itself with political matters and serves only as a responsive tool in the hands of those actually charged with guiding the destiny of the Federation. All draftees, needless to say, must swear allegiance to it as a whole. We have seen that acts of war against any part of the Federation or its allies, if such exist, are automatic declarations of war, and mean that this entire group of states will be brought to bear against the aggressor. Yet, there is also the possibility of using its power to protect from invasion other nations neither allied nor belonging to the Federation. Thus, if the Federation consisted merely of a few small South American republics, and a colossus like the United States (outside the Federation), should attack Canada, it is evident that despite its denunciation of such a criminal act, it will be powerless to deter the invader. In this case, intervention by the Federation, aside from the fact that it would not accomplish its purpose, would be extremely risky, to say the least. If its members, however, include one or more of the Great Powers, there would be no question which side it would take. Actually the possibility of the United States invading Canada, or Switzerland overrun by her neighbors, is very unlikely and remote, and the names of these countries are here used only as illustrations.

Considering anew a Federation of powerful nations, it is clear that its intervention in behalf of liberty and justice would prevent any invasion, hence taking an active part in international affairs is not only desirable, but necessary if it is to uphold its ideals. Although one wishes to believe that the second World War will prove the last fought among civilized nations, one cannot do more than hope that our discussion is only hypothetical. However, should this not prove to be the case and the Federation is forced to draw the sword in behalf of defense of human rights, we firmly believe that forever after this action by a great agglomeration of peoples will eradicate wars as a means of settling differences, so that in its results that conflict would be just and beneficial.

In saying earlier that the WD-FGW must be a responsive instrument wielded by those who steer the destiny of the Federation, it raises the question: Who are these people who can declare war against another nation even if it is not invading or directly threatening the Federation? This is what we shall now explain. If the world situation becomes critical and public opinion veers toward intervention, the FPW, as the body acting with the highest authority in government affairs, will order an election among the PW representatives. This means that all delegates whether from community, zone, superzone, or Federation, cast their votes for or against war, either in person or by mail. All votes will have the same weight, and their verdict will be decisive. Depending on circumstances, such an election may take weeks or only a few hours. Public sentiment will already be known, and taken into account because all community representatives, who constitute the great majority in the PW, will feel morally bound to vote according to the definite desire of their constituents. In case of doubt they have means of ferreting out that sentiment through a referendum within their community. We feel sure that as the people in the course of time come to appreciate the wonderful achievements made possible through the new mode of life, they will also acquire the courage and determination to stand by their ideals despite all dangers, and yet act also with wisdom rather than impulsiveness in opposing the foe, so that their risk and sacrifices will not be undertaken in vain. On this point we wish to stress that the opinion of the FPW has paramount value. Officials who have reached the supreme position in the government will have far-reaching confidential information regarding the power of the Federation versus that of other nations, so that should it be hopelessly weak, the election will not be ordered at all, in order to avert the consequences of the generous enthusiasm of the people.

In itself the PW branch of the Federation is the only qualified body that can take the initiative necessary to declare war upon another nation. This does not include the case of actual attack or invasion, when there would be no need to consult the wishes of the people. If the poll of the representatives yields a score as low as fifty per cent plus one, this suffices to bind the entire Federation. Once war is declared, the WD-FGW will be granted the authority essential to carry it through to victory.

TREASURY OR FINANCIAL DEPARTMENT (FD-FGW) This will be far more important than the corresponding units within a zone or superzone. Besides the nominal task of administering the financial structure of the Federation as a whole, it will have that of issuing detailed directives to the various departments of zones and superzones to facilitate their interrelations. It will also be the only body authorized to print or coin money and establish a unified monetary system. Another important duty will be that of supervising taxation, with the assistance and collaboration of the financial departments of the zones and superzones. Only when all the essential expenditures of the government units, from those of the community to those of the Federation, are accurately ascertained, will it be possible to calculate rates for each zone, community, and citizen. We have already expressed our views regarding the type of taxes that should be levied, especially those in indirect form, but the opinion of qualified experts should be the deciding factor.

A further responsibility of the department will be that of the financial readjustment of any country entering the Federation. This will be necessary because only one monetary system must exist for its diverse populations.

The question may arise as to the kind of currency chosen for our future society. While this problem is one for the experts to solve, whose wisdom we need not question, this occasion is taken to set down our views for the record.

It goes without saying that any complicated currency, such as is now used in the British Empire, based on a subdivision from the pound down to the penny, should be disqualified as desirable for the Federation. We would prefer instead a simple monetary unit such as the dollar, franc, or lira, which have a decimal basis and, therefore, are easy to understand. It should be based on gold, and if all held in the vaults of the government and the banks is not sufficient to maintain the proper volume of trade, both domestic and foreign, other metals such as silver, copper, and the like should also be recognized as legal tender. We do not pretend to be experts of the subject, yet always think of gold and coinage in general as continuously representing the same amount of fundamental wealth, while ordinary commodities follow in value the law of supply and demand. This, of course, is not true since heavy exports of gold or great expansion of the amount on hand, as when new mines are put into operation, affect its value like that of any other commodity. The reason for this change is that when people in a community or nation obtain large quantities of gold, they are apt to buy commodities ordinarily bought by others and thereby cause scarcity, so that the price of commodities rises even though the supply remains the same. This means that the value of gold compared to that of these commodities has lessened. This may benefit the new owners of gold, but not at least immediately, the rest of the population which naturally resent the influence of the new rich. However, we can say that while this phenomenon may cause economic dislocation and hardship in some sections of the present society, which is based on a stable equilibrium point, it will not do so in the future society where that point will be further advanced by this increased demand, and, therefore, any dislocation will only be brief and limited.

This, however, is not the only simplification we wish to urge, as there are other reforms beyond the field of finance that would eventually add to the well-being of the average individual.

First of all the centimeter-gram-second system (CGS), with some modifications to which we shall refer later, should be introduced throughout the Federation. Since it is based on a decimal subdivision of the quantities involved in the measurement of physical phenomena, so vital to humanity in general, this adoption would greatly help the average person better to visualize these scientific details, and, therefore, prove beneficial to society because less confusion and more efficiency would ensue. In note 12-1 we have given an example of the merits of the CGS versus the English system now currently used in the United States. Specifically we have taken the case of measuring distances. Other physical phenomena such as speed, force, power, and so forth could have been taken to prove our point. The chief advantage of the metric system rests in the fact that units are divided into tenths and hundreds of parts. This enables fractional distances to be expressed in decimals, which are far easier to manipulate in the addition, subtraction, multiplication, and division of two or more quantities.

NOTE 12-1

Take a distance of five miles, using the unit of length in vogue in the United States. Now any person familiar with it will have no difficulty in visualizing this distance. However, one mile is equivalent to 1,760 yards, to 5,280 feet, to 63,360 inches. Distances, of course, are not always given in miles or fractions thereof, and often are expressed in yards, feet, or inches. Any of them is used for distances within reasonable limits. Thus, we speak of a book being two inches thick, a room twenty feet long, a street thirty yards wide, and so forth, and no one would think of giving a distance between two cities in inches, because the accepted unit for this purpose is the mile. However, in the process of calculation, distances often add up to values beyond the limits being used, and they become almost meaningless unless converted to the proper unit. Such procedure, when time is valuable, is usually long, tedious, and essentially unnecessary. In these units five miles become 8,800 yards, 26,400 feet, or 316,800 inches.

In the CGS system this distance of five miles is equivalent to 8.045 kilometers. As one kilometer is equivalent to 1,000 meters, one meter to 100 centimeters, and one centimeter to 10 millimeters, this means that five miles can be expressed as 8,045 meters, 804,500 centimeters, or 8,045,000 millimeters. It is true that 8,045,000 millimeters is as meaningless as the 316,800 inches of the English system, but the change of millimeters to kilometers for the final visualization of that distance is done easily and swiftly by moving the decimal point the proper number of places. Needless to say, another advantage appears in the fact that no matter which unit is chosen, the digits representing that distance are always the same.

. . . .

The usual argument against the adoption of this system in this country is that the transfer involves many changes (machines, tools, gauges, and so forth) besides the fact that the majority of our mechanics and engineers have been accustomed for many years to the old standard of measurements and naturally would resent the change. This, however, should not prove an unsurmountable obstacle, especially when the life of the country is being reorganized, and in view also of the fact that many countries of Europe and elsewhere, which we hope will enter the Federation, have already taken this technical step and could not possibly be expected to relapse to our cumbersome system.

At the beginning of this discussion we commented that the CGS standards of measurement should have some modification. This refers to the third unit of the system—that used for the measure of time. This has been passed on to us from our forefathers, and like others based on obsolete needs, making it no longer consonant with our modern society and retained only by tradition and that ingrained inertia which opposes all change.

The day will still remain the basic unit of time, being that of a complete rotation of the earth about its axis, but it can be divided into decimal parts instead of such an arbitrary number as 24. The day should be divided into ten equal parts, each containing one hundred minutes, and in turn these divided into one hundred seconds. Then the new second would be a hundred thousandth part of the day instead of the eighty-six thousandth, and while it will be approximately equal to our present second, the new system will have the marked advantage of permitting a rapid conversion from one unit to another without ponderous mental calculations often open to error. In note 12-2 we give an example of its merits compared to the one used at present.

NOTE 12-2

With the present standard of measurement, in order to change any number of seconds into days, they must first be put into minutes, then into hours, and finally into days by wearisome calculations. With the new standard the change can be made while reading the number in a fraction of a second, by shifting the decimal point in the figure recording the entire time left or right, depending on the chosen unit. For instance, 7,644,252 seconds measured in the proposed system, and final result of calculations, can be thought of as written in the following manner: 76-4-42-52. This can be done if we divide the number starting from the right into two, two and one digits. Once this mental division has been made, we can say that this interval, originally given in seconds, consists of 76 days, 4 hours, 42 minutes, and 52 seconds. The number of each unit will appear in the original figure, which counts in seconds. If the number is to be given in hours and fractions thereof, the numbers of days and new hours may be grouped together (764) and show the total number of new hours, while the number of minutes and seconds will form the fraction, and the new complete time will be 764.4252 hours.

If one wishes to make a similar transformation in the present system, he must first change the seconds into minutes, thus: 7,644,252/60 equals 127,412 minutes plus 32 seconds. These in turn must be expressed in hours: 127,412/60 equals 2123 hours plus 32 minutes. The hours in turn must be changed into days, thus; 2123/24 equals 88 days plus 11 hours, so that the original 7,644,252 seconds can be expressed by 88 days, 11 hours, 32 minutes and 32 seconds, a result reached by long and tedious calculation. Moreover the digits representing the various units as 88, 11, 32, and 32 do not appear in the original number of seconds, a distinct disadvantage compared to our new method.

. . . .

The division of the day into 10 new hours instead of 24 at first may cause considerable confusion while people readjust to the new standard. Those who work from eight o'clock in the morning to five in the afternoon will be occupied from 3.3 to 7.1 and in time associate such figures with an actual period of the day. At preesnt 12 Noon gives the sensation of being the middle of the day, in the new system this number will be superseded by 5. Its reasonableness and simplicity with the clocks and watches designed accordingly, would accelerate the process of adjustment. Naturally the hours of work would be revised to be reckoned by simple numbers, as from 3 to seven, instead of 3.3 to 7.1, with wages and salaries to match.

If the new hour should prove unduly long compared to the one of the present system, and arouse extensive objection, the day could contain 100 instead of 10, each unit equivalent to 24 of our minutes. We do not think, however, that this would be a disadvantage because quite often engineers and scientists must deal with times considerably smaller than one second. In the consciousness of the general public the new minutes would probably supersede our second as it would be 8.6 times as large.

The basic advantage of the proposed system is that time, together with distance and mass, would be given in a decimal form and as they represent the units on which all others are based, the change from one expression to another would be greatly simplified, and this would in itself accelerate progress.

Another change of similar nature is the division of a circle into 100 degrees rather than 360. This also for the purpose of simplifying calculations in the construction of tools, machinery, and so forth. The degree would contain 100 minutes, each of 100 seconds, giving 1,000,000 of the latter units instead of 1,296,000 to a circle. These changes, of course, are not part of the text and are merely given here as suggestions. They should doubtless be adopted during the interregnum. This dissertation, however, detoured us from the analysis of the Federation government.

OTHER DEPARTMENTS IN THE FEDERATION GOVERNMENT

The Departments of Agriculture, Police, and so forth, will parallel those already described for the zones and superzones, and also will be similar to equivalent branches of contemporary governments.

Each will be headed by career men chosen by the FG and directly responsible to him. Naturally these officials will have risen within the GW organization, reaching preeminence through talent and competitive examinations, and becoming internationally known. As earlier stated, the rank of a department head cannot rest on qualifications alone, as the candidate for appointment must be acceptable to the FG as to personality and mutual respect, to ensure team work among those shouldering burdens of state. Thus, he may come from among those on the lower rungs of the ladder. Except for the departments heads, who can be replaced at will by the FG, employees can be discharged for incompetency or similar charges made by their immediate superiors, but such removal takes place only by higher officials. This arrangement avoids allowing personal animosities to wreck the career of an otherwise honest and efficient employee who does not view things in the same light as his immediate superior. Direct interviews will precede discharge or transfer to another department. This will ensure justice and simultaneously salvage the services of an otherwise satisfactory employee. Needless to say, should the incriminated individual be definitely proved corrupt or inefficient, his discharge must be final.

The FG and department heads will form the "Board of the GW Branch" (FGWB), holding meetings as frequently as required by conditions and problems. The term of office of the FG is four years, renewable if his qualifications are outstanding. Otherwise another official of the organization will be elected by the FPW, and in turn he will have the right to select as department heads capable individuals whose qualities he knows and appreciates. The outgoing FG and any replaced heads of departments may take positions of less prominence, or become Senators of the Federation (S-FLB), and thereby join the (Legislative Branch).

In contrast to what often happens in present-day society, anyone who through merit has been able to reach high rank becomes a permanent asset to humanity in general. Such a man's services will always be of great value, and should be retained as long as the individual is physically and mentally fit. With his great experience in government affairs, his membership in the FLB should prove of great value in framing new legislation for the Federation. The rank of Senator should, of course, last for life even though in time the holder of this honor may no longer feel able to take active part in this body. We feel that anyone who has done so much for society should be relieved for the rest of his life from the necessity of providing for his livelihood. Any Senator will be at liberty simultaneously to fill another position in the government, his salary being the more remunerative of the two, but will not be allowed to draw more than one pay.

PEOPLE'S WELFARE BRANCH OF THE FEDERATION (FPW)

The third unit of the Federation government is the People's Welfare Branch, and its operations will be similar to those in zones and superzones. Its members will be elected for twelve-year terms by the PW of the zones (ZPW-F) after due approval by the PW of the superzones (SPW-F). This is a somewhat different procedure from that used in the lower governments, and the reason will appear later on. The candidates will be chosen from either the representatives of the zones and superzones or among outstanding citizens. The same freedom of action will apply and each representative first of all must be responsible for the good of the Federation, that of the zone he represents, being only second in importance. High moral principles and the courage that must be displayed in the upholding of justice against selfish minorities, internal or external, are vital qualities to be sought.

There will be three representatives for each zone, giving the FPW as many members as in all the superzones. The reason for this large number is that the Federation will consider questions from all corners of the world requiring immediate attention and solution. On this account the FPW must be sufficient to allow division into committees with specialized fields. Again the zone rather than the superzone has been chosen as the unit from which to send these officials because it is closer to the people. As an overall picture of the PW branch of the Federation (FPW), we refer to Table 22, page 661.

The total number of representatives is given by $3n$ where n stands for the number of zones in the Federation.

(1) The FPW has jurisdiction as a body (50 per cent plus one vote) over 50 per cent minus one vote of all the superzones, zones, or communities, representatives in the Federation and consequently over any SPW, ZPW or CPW of the Federation. See Table 8, page 334.

(2) A petition signed by 20 per cent of the SPW-F, ZPW-F or CPW-F will force a decision of the FPW to be brought to a general election of any of those three bodies.

(3) A vote of 50 per cent plus one of the SPW-F, ZPW-F, CPW-F will reverse a decision of the FPW.

Obviously matters affecting any zone should be aired before the entire Federation through zonal delegates since they are familiar with the local situation and interested in solving its problems. The interest of the people should be paramount, and this cannot be left to delegates only indirectly linked to the local population. The reason for requiring the approval of the representatives of the superzone is to ensure that only citizens of outstanding qualities and ability are chosen, and it is natural that they should not only be known and respected within the zone, but also throughout the superzone, for both of which they will take their seats. As in previous instances only one-third of this branch will be elected every four years, unreplaceable, unless incapacitated through sickness, permanent injury, or the like. Appeals for retirement must originate among the representatives of the same zone, granted at the meeting of the FPW through an inner election, and signed by the Federation President (FP). But as long as the delegate is willing to vote, even though unable to discharge other duties, he should be retained. The importance in his vote rests on the fact that different interpretations will be placed upon percentages of votes for or against issues, and it is vital that each expresses the will and views of his people. Of course, in many issues affecting far away zones it is understandable that a delegate may wish to abstain. If he should do so, he would still exert his weight in the solving of problems. As this solution may be opposed to his conscience as well as to the basic interests of his zone, we feel that, no matter what the source and the kind of issue, he has the moral obligation to study its implications and merits and then vote according to his conscience and the basic interests of the population in general which he, in that capacity, represents.

A great deal of time and energy will be spent by each delegate in following up matters affecting his zone and its inhabitants in relation to the Federation Government. Because of this he may frequently have to confer with officials of other branches in order to settle complaints and rectify any damage or injustice suffered by any of his constituents. Usually any wrongs will be readily recognized by his colleagues and a remedy found, thereby closing the issue. Where this fails it will be because of different interpretation of the law and, therefore, specific instructions given to local officials. In such a case the representative will take the matter up with the other two from the zone, and eventually with the FPW as a whole, if they feel that injury is being suffered either by citizens or organizations. The FPW in turn will assign the complaint to the qualified committee, which will go to the bottom of the problem, ascertain and verify the facts, and then prepare a report to be submitted to all the delegates in the Federation. These will thereby become familiar with the dispute, and at the next meeting of the FPW, when the report will be officially introduced and voted upon, be able to cast an intelligent and unbiased vote. We know that this may be all-powerful in forcing the other two main branches to change their practices or policies. When the issues are such that they involve basic principles and the vote among the FPW is so heavy that the lower branch of the PW is precluded from taking an active part, the matter must be submitted to the Federation Court, which is the highest authority in the land upon the interpretation of the Constitution. The verdict of this body will be the law of the land, binding upon all parties concerned.

Besides the duties enumerated above, the FPW has also the important task of seeing that new laws do not infringe upon the rights of the population in general, and in such matters it has a vast power, since no regulation can become law without its consent, and in the last analysis has also the authority to terminate the services of the FG and FM if it should so decide. The proportion of votes required for this step will differ, and for the FM requires at least a 90 per cent majority. If it is greater than a certain minimum, but less than 90 per cent, the matter must be referred to the lower branches of the superzones. The reason for the high percentage is that unless the FM is definitely proved inefficient or incapable, he must be given ample power and initiative in order to coordinate the economic forces of the Federation without kowtowing to powerful minorities, or to representatives not fully familiar with the problem on hand. Humanly it is possible that selfish groups, aided by the press, may succeed in confusing issues to such an extent that some lawmakers may be won to their side and resenting the obstinate attitude of the FM, seek his removal. But not all will fall to such schemes, and at the final showdown will vote in behalf of the FM. However, when the vote is overwhelmingly against the FM, this will be a clear indication that this dissatisfaction is not engineered, but truly signifies the will of the people in which case the FM must comply with the law by relinquishing his place.

As to the FG, his position, while of great importance, is not so vital to the population of the Federation, and, therefore, he can be more easily removed. Even in this case, however, a definite majority is necessary, and if the vote is not below a certain minimum the question must be referred to the representatives of the superzones.

Every four years the FPW will elect the President of the Federation (FP), who will be one of the senior members of this branch. Similar procedure to that in the zone and superzone should be used. The FP is theoretically the highest citizen of the Federation, who will receive ambassadors from other countries, and in general duplicate the duties of a King or a President. While he will preside at all meetings of the FPW, his vote will not have greater weight than that of any other representative of this branch. His signature, with those of the FM, FG, as well as the CJ-FJB, is necessary to make a law valid throughout the Federation.

LEGISLATIVE BRANCH OF THE FEDERATION (FLB)

The FLB, like those previously considered, will be composed of the Senators (S-FLB), who may be officials of the FEW and FGW retired from active duty and temporarily without government assignment, besides prominent citizens of the Federation invited and appointed by the FPW. This branch will promulgate new laws and regulations as new needs become evident for the welfare of the Federation. For the purpose of subdividing the task of studying and analyzing new legislation, the FLB will divide itself into several committees, each to specialize along certain lines, including individuals expert in each field. A secretary (SE-FLB), elected from among the members, will become their titular head. He will hold office for a period of four years, and will coordinate the work of all the committees. He will keep the archives, and files of regulations placed on the agenda. It will also be his duty to assign each type of new legislation to the qualified committee for review and the preparation of reports. New regulations may be sent in writing to the SE-FLB by any member of the FLB. The procedure for the drafting of a new law will be similar to that described for the zone and superzone. As already mentioned, all laws drafted by the FLB must apply throughout the Federation, and, therefore, be limited to fields that do not violate the rights of the zones and superzones to govern themselves according to their mode of life, customs, race and so forth. In other words, since the Federation may eventually include the majority of the nations on earth, the zones will come to be considered as individuals of a community in which each must be protected and aided, and his liberties upheld and respected as long as they do not conflict with those of any other.

While the FLB is the only branch of the Federation government in which new laws are given form, ideas may be presented by any important official of the other branches of the government by following the prescribed rule of submitting the regulation in writing to the SE-FLB. Other proposals, as we have seen, may come from the people themselves if sufficient signatures are available. The FLB will convene only in certain seasons of the year, and at other times when a special session is in order. This will be ordered by the SE-FLB. All proposals must receive as rapid consideration as possible, their merits analyzed and acted upon and not left in abeyance as often as is the case at preesnt.

JUDICIARY BRANCH OF THE FEDERATION (FJB)

The FPW will also have the important task of electing the judges of the Federation Court (FJB) whenever a vacancy develops in this important branch of the government.

The FJB will represent the highest judicial authority within the land, without whose approval no law in the Federation can be enforced. We have seen, however, that new laws within a community, zone, or superzone can be made and enforced, without ever coming to the direct attention of this Court. However, there may be cases in which fundamental clashes on the interpretation of the Constitution may arise in which some of the parties, dissatisfied with the verdict of a lower court, appeal the issue higher and higher until it may reach the FJB. This Court, being the supreme authority in this field, renders verdicts which are final unless the Constitution is changed. In other words, the FJB, while lacking authority to promulgate new laws or any way to enter the turmoil of society, will remain aloof and uphold the spirit of the Constitution as it stands when the verdict is given, and thus will be its most powerful guardian and interpreter. The FJB will be composed of as many judges (J-FJB) as there are superzones, but not less than nine and always an odd number, to prevent deadlock. While the choice of a J-FJB from each superzone of the Federation is desirable, this should not be a strict rule since the character, experience, and ability of the man elevated to this lofty office are much more important than geographical background. This, however, will be a matter for the representatives of the FPW to decide. The reason for increasing the number of judges of the FJB becomes evident when we consider that with the expansion of the Federation their duties will multiply. On any issue fifty per cent plus one will constitute the opinion of the Court. The judges of the Court, including the Chief Justice (CJ-FJB), are elected for life, and remain active only until retirement age. They must be lawyers of exceptional knowledge and qualities, internationally recognized in their field, and of such character and integrity that they can dissociate themselves from the love of their land, prove completely impartial, and deliver an unbiased interpretation of the Constitution irrespective of consequences.

CAPITAL OF THE FEDERATION

It is self-evident that the activities of the government of the Federation must be carried on with close collaboration among its various branches. It is, therefore, important that all be located in some central place that will become the capital of the Federation. The vast building of the now defunct League of Nations in Geneva, the skyscrapers constructed for the United Nations in New York, or any other edifice on earth that has ideal geographical and climatic location could easily become its home. It is desirable, however, that such a capital should be chosen at or near the center of the entire population of the Federation, which at present is only a hypothetical entity. Thus any choice we here suggest may prove erroneous, especially if the country in which it is located is one that does not wish to enter the Federation. But as we are dealing with hypothesis, no objection can be taken if we express our opinion on the subject.

Were the entire population of the world to join this Federation of Nations, we feel that this capital should be somewhere in Europe, the logical continent available. Being close to Asia and Africa, and still nearer than these to America, Europe more obviously qualifies as the aforementioned center of population than that of any other continent. Assuming now that Europe is actually selected, we would immediately exclude any northern city because of their inclement weather in winter. For the same reason we would exclude any city too far South as too warm in summer. This capital again should be of easy access both from land and sea, and for this and climatic reasons we would suggest any city either on the Italian or the French Riviera. The list of the possible locations would then be reduced either to Genoa, or Marseilles, each with an ideal climate and yet of easy access from any part of the continent. Again either of these major cities has the advantage of possessing a harbor with modern facilities, able to take care of the large passenger ships necessary to carry government officials to and from distant parts of the Federation. It is true that nationalistic feeling might prevent the selection of any of these cities, but assuming that the Riviera is chosen as the ideal location, both Italy and France could be persuaded to grant sufficient land near their mutual borders to form a zone within which the new capital could be built. This procedure would be similar to the historic one in the United States of America where land was taken from Virginia and Maryland for the construction of the Federal City, as called by the first President. Modern technology and expert engineering would easily solve any difficulty which nature could interpose to such a plan. Obviously, however, it will not be the entire population of the world at first, but likely only a few nations which will launch the Federation, so the capital must be at or near their center. After this choice, its location should not be changed unless this should be desired by the great majority of the population, and the Constitution revised accordingly.

A local government with a police force which may symbolically include all races in the population of the Federation will maintain law and order within the capital. It will receive its financial support from the Federation, cooperate with its government when important functions and parades must be held, look after the physical necessities of a well-kept city, such as cleanliness, lighting, parks, recreation, buildings, and so forth, and safeguard lives and property of the citizens of the community.

GENERALIZATIONS ON THE GOVERNMENT OF THE FEDERATION

We have also another important subject to discuss while describing the government of the Federation; that of the language to be used by the officials who fill its positions and come from distant places, often different in culture and civilization. The national languages of the Federation will be all those of the peoples who have joined it. This means that all the laws and regulations will be translated into as many languages as there are nationalities in the realm. It follows as a matter of course that one of the prerequisites of obtaining high rank in the Federation government will be the mastery of many languages, so that anyone who attains an important office will be able to make himself understood by as many people as possible. This, of course, cannot be very well insisted upon for the PW representatives who, while part of the government, are quite in a class by themselves. They are elected by the people for their character, honesty, and knowledge of their land, not for prowess in languages. Because of this we realize that often the free exchange of thoughts and ideas among members of different nationalities will not be fluent and easy. In committee meetings and in large assemblies there will be on hand translators and interpreters who will give the necessary assistance. Each candidate for any position in the government will enumerate the languages he understands and those in which he is sufficiently proficient to address an audience. From these data the chairman of a committee will decide on the language to be used, choosing the one which requires the least number of interpreters. But whatever language is used during the meeting, the report must be translated and published in all the languages of the Federation.

There will be occasions on which several men of different nationalities must discuss matters of common interest. If they know the same language, they probably will waive the assistance of interpreters, but if one member of the group is not familiar with the language used by the others, an interpreter will be required on his account. No doubt this will mean much wasted time, but most problems before the government of the Federation, while of far-reaching importance to the entire population, will not be of such nature that immediate solution is required, and the time spent in making issues clear to everyone will be more than repaid in the good will and cooperation that is bound to ensue. We realize also that heads of departments and sub-branches may come from different countries, and in turn will have under them employees of various nationalities, but the aid of the numerous interpreters and translators, and the requirement of the knowledge of several languages, a qualification for holding high positions in the government, will simplify and speed up their work a great deal and the outcome will be less impracticable than it may seem at first. It also follows that the schools throughout the Federation must emphasize the study of languages to a far greater extent than at present, and naturally it must be compulsory for those pupils and students who seek careers in the government.

Returning to our description of the FPW, we wish to point out that anyone elected to such a position for as long as twelve years will eventually get out of touch with his public at home, who may be thousands of miles distant. As this would not be right, we propose the following procedure. Each zone sends three delegates to the FPW to take part in governing, but also to represent the zone itself. In rotation each would be given the privilege, indeed the duty, to spend three months each year in his zone. Thus, he will be in touch for at least that length of time with his people, discuss policies with them, and if necessary deliver speeches in the different communities of his zone. In addition, while at home, he will review complaints and the like with citizens and organizations within the zone, obtain their points of view in various matters, and with his knowledge of government affairs be able to give the proper advice or information. In matters that line up the individual against the Federation government itself, he will officially receive the complaint, but must refrain from offering a hasty opinion until he has become thoroughly familiar with all the details, which he will not be able to do until he has gone over the matter with the proper official at the capital. At any rate, he cannot be coerced or imposed upon if, after reviewing the case, his views do not coincide with those of the people who made that complaint. When confronted by such cases he must use tact and judgment to decide how to handle the situation. It is reasonable to assume that as he was raised among his people, and likely to possess similar background, he may unconsciously incline toward their views, which is natural enough, but when back at the capital besides conferring upon the matter with the official in charge, he should also sound out the opinion of other zone delegates, and by approaching the problem with an open-minded attitude, his common sense will show when his cause is wrong. If the complaint is justified, he probably will win the support of others, who are there to redress injustices wherever they may come from, and thus will have a good chance to straighten things out. Otherwise he will do well to avoid forcing the issue, because it will probably be killed within the FPW.

CONCLUSIONS

We have been witness in the past three decades to two wars in comparison with which all others in history seem insignificant. On the surface it may seem that they were fought because of some specific incident: the invasion of Serbia by the Austrian Empire in the first world war, and the destruction of Poland in the second. While these aggressions on the part of powerful nations against peace-loving countries were bad enough, other forces and interests figured in the outbreak as well as in the spreading of these conflagrations, adding to the tremendous holocaust in human life. The mode of life in one nation versus that in another has played a prominent role in calling millions to the battlefield. The re-establishment of freedom in the conquered countries has been also another principle publicized for that purpose. We do not question the noble intentions and good faith of the leaders who had the responsibility of winning the first world war, but while the fields were still red with human blood most of the high principles gave way to selfishness, vengeance and plunder. While freedom was restored to some, subjugation and privation were imposed upon others. The annexation of lands and seizing of privileges was carried on openly with heartless disregard for human rights. People were made to suffer for the crimes and errors of their leaders. How could we expect that the world should have become resigned to the many disparities brought about by the will of the victorious nations? The second world war was almost inevitable when the Versailles Conference was in session, and its arrival only awaited the necessary interval of preparation, and the regrouping of interests for the attempt at revenge.

This appalling holocaust, at the present writing, has ended, but since human nature has not changed, since injustices are still being continued and imposed upon, and so many have been and will remain poor and unjustly punished, the seeds of a third and even more devastating war are being planted in the heart of millions who, for no fault of their own, see their future impaired with no hope of an eventual ascent. It is also distressing to witness how the line-ups are taking form for a third ordeal sometime in the future. While the basic interests of the vanquished are ignored and utterly disregarded, while these countries are made subservient to the over-lordship of the few powerful nations, to their whims and impracticable theories, the interests of the small countries are partially considered and defended, and only when they do not clash with those of the great powers who have emerged victorious. The spheres of influence of the conquerors have been further extended to the far corners of the earth as a result of their victory, and because in so many areas they overlap each other, ominous clouds are already looming on the horizon.

Let us not rest in the complacent belief that those instruments of war that seem so frightful and inhuman will not be used because of our advanced civilization. The submarine was an instrument of war internationally condemned by another generation because of its savage and indiscriminate destruction. That the submarine was used in the second world war on a far greater scale than before is a matter of general knowledge, and one can be sure that its effectiveness will increase as time goes on, no matter how people may feel about its inhumanity. However, we have now entered an entirely new era in which submarines, artillery, airplanes, and the other contrivances of war fade in importance compared to the new weapon of death, the atomic bomb. The tragedy of this discovery does not rest in the fact that it has been invented at all, as the ability to split the atom and the release thereby of undreamed-of energy may mean in the immediate or distant future an unfathomable advancement in our mode of life. The tragedy, we repeat, rests in the fact that such power should become available to man while morally and spiritually unprepared to use it for his own good, and through his barbaric instinct, apt to use it instead for destructive ends. The possibilities of such a weapon in the hands of unscrupulous people blinded by hatred and greed, can hardly be overestimated. That this weapon, now that it has been discovered, is here to stay is self-evident; that it will be used in any future major war must also be taken for granted; and it is almost a certainty that it will be further improved and finally become able to exterminate vast populated areas in a fraction of a second. On this account it is not only desirable but imperative that the future of humanity find solid and lasting foundations, it is imperative that new respect for ethics and a new mode of life be introduced to harmonize and regulate relations among individuals and nations if we wish to avoid the annihilation of our culture and civilization.

It is useless to say that no one in the future will have the ruthlessness and barbarism to use the atomic bomb, especially when wars nowadays, having become a matter of life and death for entire nations, are apt to encourage frenzied and frantic efforts for preservation. Let us also remember that, unfortunately for mankind, the atomic bomb has already received its baptism of blood, and this was done by one of the most enlightened and civilized countries in the world. Needless to say, this historical precedent will be taken as justification for future destructions and devastations.

We do not claim perfection in the advocated new mode of life, but if adopted, we would no longer fear those forces that cause chaos and disruption, nor the depressions which at short intervals of time upset the economic balance of society because such evils would no longer exist.

As we see it, humanity has gone through a succession of sharp and spasmodic convulsions in her eventful life. Civilizations in the past have blossomed and flowered, only to be replaced and supplanted by those which, after their cycle, in turn gave way to others. Wars have been waged under all kinds of pretences, entire races and populations have been annihilated or annexed, people in their quest of domination have conquered and subsequently been conquered, and the law of the strong has reigned supreme while the poor and the weak have suffered and succumbed. Yet in all this turmoil, humanity has definitely advanced and progressed as the centuries passed. This makes us conscious of the fact that peoples and leaders, no matter their power and determination, have never been able, unless for a limited time, to change the course of humanity, which derives its momentum from forces that reside in the innermost recess of man.

Wars, revolutions, extortions, and enslavement somehow, no matter their causes and aims, can always be identified with the will of the few being imposed on the many. True enough, it may have seemed that some of these phenomena were originated by the spontaneous initiative of the many trying to escape the servitude and the oppression of the few, yet even in such an eruptive and world-wide convulsion as the French revolution, it was still the will and the leadership of the few that gave the soul and the mind to a cataclysm that was to obliterate a ruling class that had enjoyed undeserved privileges since time immemorial. Many of these leaders, generous and brave, gave the masses the honest conviction that they were breaking forever the chains of servitude, yet with them there were also others who, taking the fundamental needs of the people as a springboard to power, were actually aiming at the acquisition of that brutal and powerful force, vested in an obedient and ignorant populace, that could be used, not to break those chains, so immaterial to them, but to enthrone themselves in those conditions from which the old ruling class had been dislodged. No doubt during these eventful years humanity made sizable strides toward better conditions of life, but these improvements were small compared with the massacres and destructions that went on during that period. The world after the French revolution was left almost as bad as before, and more wars, more suffering had to be endured before the industrial era eventually raised society to the level it holds today. Now whether the revolution was the cause of this progress, or this would have come about even if the revolution had not taken place are questions we are not able to answer. We know that events do change the course of history, that some have beneficial effects while others have not, so that, while clashes of interests and ambitions give rise to causes and effects, their influence is only temporary and meanwhile that instinct in mankind which we call hope gives humanity that force and perseverance to forge ahead no matter where those violent events may have led. We believe that the instinct of betterment is in the innermost nature of man. He has had it since time immemorial, and will retain it as long as he roams on earth. As a result, even though mankind may suffer delays and setbacks through wars, famine, plagues and oppressions of tyrants, as soon as the offsetting forces abate, the pre-determinate path is resumed toward her glorious and distant goal.

Once the vague outline of the ultimate goal is identified and cleared, once the ideals and principles of the future society are established and imbedded in the consciousness of men, no human force, no atomic bomb, no instrument of destruction and war can deflect and restrain the longing for that ultimate attainment. Yes, individuals may be eliminated and killed, entire populations massacred and destroyed, but that light in the human heart will never flicker or perish. The teachings of Christ, even though poorly applied and understood, nevertheless are powerful beacons on which we may direct our course and our life and even though quite often incapable to steer toward them because of our great immaturity, yet they represent our hope, our guidance, our standards to which we compare and measure our actions and efforts.

Now that this should be so is our great fortune, and salvation, and this realization alone makes us confident of the future. No matter how seriously the progress of humanity is retarded or deviated, it cannot be radically changed, and since we are all part of humanity, all vitally concerned in her progress and betterment, if not for ourselves at least for our children and distant descendants, it becomes our duty to do all we can to bring order and sanity out of the present chaos and confusion.

At the end of our study we feel that this book would not be completely finished if nothing were said about religion and its influence upon mankind. The fact that no reference has been made on religion must not be construed as a gross neglect on our part. If we consider that the new philosophy and advocated mode of life is intended for the entire human race, so extensively divided by innumerable creeds, it becomes obvious that religion has no place in a study of this kind. Yet, the fact that religion, in the past as well as at present, has had and has a powerful influence in the evolution of society, in many cases adding powerful forces in the shaping of its progress while in others being the main cause of much terror and suffering, imposes upon us the duty of not completely neglecting a force which has such a vast influence on the future of mankind.

Of course, religion, no matter in which form, is the manifestation of the subconscious aspiration of the humble as well as of the great toward the higher Being that guides and controls all that exists. This aspiration is found in the very nature of man and because of its universality it cannot be discarded as the mere hallucination of the weak or the imposition of the strong but should be taken as one of the manifestations of God. True enough, this aspiration, this inner force that raises man toward the supreme Being is apt to take different forms and be expressed by different behavior and conduct. Yet, while these do not disprove the existence of God, they only show the limitations of men. Different experiences, nature, background, and stages of civilization have all contributed to direct people to various paths presumably leading to God. And why not? Can we honestly say that only one road can lead one person from one place to another? Can we honestly say that God with his supreme wisdom and love will condemn all those who, in their effort toward Him do not happen to take that path especially prescribed by social institutions? We do not think this to be so. As in many other activities and fields, man has had the tendency to give unnecessary and undeserved importance to details, forms and inconsequential minutiae, rather than try to comprehend the scope and the aim of the complete whole and as such apt to condemn others who do not happen to subscribe to his actions and way of thinking. This goes to prove the yet limited ascent made by man on the long ladder of evolution, shows how easily he can still be swayed from looking and persevering toward the main goal ahead. This effort made by humanity, this sublime aspiration toward the supreme Being, therefore, is often distorted by unnecessary practices and dogmatism that blur the beauty of that effort and in the name of religion many deeds are being done of which humanity cannot honestly be proud. Taking the point of view of a Christian, can we honestly think that men like the Mahatma Gandhi of India should be forever condemned or in any way unfavorably compare in the presence of God with many Christians who go through life only giving lip service to their religion and complying with the form rather than the spirit of the teaching of Christ? Again we do not think this to be so. To be sure, the day when humanity will follow the same creed and religion will be the dawn of a new and better era on earth, this, however, not because it will be closer to God but because a powerful and destructive force will come to an end, a force that since time immemorial has placed men against men and in its wake has promoted hatred, intolerance and misery.

We like to compare humanity to a group placed in an enclosure, this being surrounded by thick and misshapen panes of glass which tend to distort all on the outside. It is plain that while all these people are conscious of the light filtering through, all will disagree as to the actual form and shape of the object emitting the light. This will depend on their position in the enclosure, intuitiveness and imagination. The light and the object, we can be sure, is the same yet all will disagree and still be positive of their own interpretation. In short all religions have a common denominator represented by the instinctive desire of man to aspire to higher levels of morals and goodness. This is the light that makes us conscious of God and needless to say this is the basic concept that should be adopted in gauging people and their actions irrespective of their creed and religion. As man further advances, time will come when he will learn to smooth and polish that glass in which he is now enclosed and the actual image of God will be finally revealed to him in its true grandeur and splendor.

The tendency on our part is to believe that the religion we have learned to follow is the only one that leads to God. On this account, either we use all efforts in forcing our belief to others or actually take the stand that all those who happen to be affiliated to other religions will be forever condemned. Under this misconception if we do not consider them as being actually out of the human race, they still represent people who, depending on circumstances, we feel free to desecrate and rob or do not represent people with which we like to have anything in common. Given the proper mass hysteria this feeling of repulsion has led many people to the stake and in various periods of history has made possible the inquisition in Spain, the ghetto and massacres in Poland, the untouchable in India, the KKK in America, the crucifixion of Christ. This is a clear indication that mankind is still in a stage of childhood and that much progress is still needed for its growth and its coming to age. For all this, of course, religion is not entirely to blame and that economic feeling of unsecurity that tends to form classes and nationalities in the world must also share that responsibility.

What can and should be done to improve this condition would transcend the purpose of our book. We cannot hope that the day when all people on earth will gladly accept the same creed and religion is close at hand as for this much ground work, much give and take has to be done by those who lead humanity. This union, naturally, must first be promoted among these leaders so that they in turn may guide their followers toward that reunion. We wish to visualize the day when all churches, temples, and places of prayer permit exponents of other religions to come in rotation to their places not to emphasize the good of their creed but that of still other religions. This would greatly help to dispel intolerance and prejudice and bring much needed enlightenment. We wish to visualize also the day when the leaders of the various religions rather than enforce and emphasize set and inconsequential rules such as to what one should or should not eat at some prescribed day of the year, help instead the people of their parish in their normal problems of the day, help them to grow and mature. Such deeds and attitudes on the part of the leaders would unquestionably help humanity out of its moral and spiritual confusion and by this build the foundation for future growths and achievements.

In conclusion we can say that this book is dedicated to all who do not wish to see their dear ones sacrificed on the altar of war, to those who want real justice and righteousness among men, to those leaders who, with the clear and shining goal ahead, summon the self-sacrifice and determination to enlighten all people and all races here and everywhere, and by winning the simple as well as the great eventually reach all people on earth.

With a new consciousness of human rights, with a stronger faith in ultimate human attainment and destiny, the path to higher and more brilliant horizons will be wider and clearer, and the gradual improvement of society will no longer be left to chance and uncertainty. Man will again become master of his environment, and above all with those new moral forces that will teach him justice, magnanimity, and love, he will rise in nobility and in stature, and assume his proper place in the wonderful framework of nature.

TABLE NO. 24

	GROUP	SUBGROUP	COMMUNITY	ZONE	SUPERZONE	FEDERATION
GOVERNMENT — **ECONOMIC WELFARE EW**	POLICY EW1	DIVISION				
		UPPER	Few Career	ZEW1-1	SEW1-1	FEW1-1
		INNER	MEN	ZEW1-2	SEW1-2	FEW1-2
		LOWER	CEW1	ZEW1-3	SEW1-3	FEW1-3
	DISTRIBUTION EW2	PRICE STABILIZ.	CEW2-1	ZEW2-1	SEW2-1	FEW2-1
		INDUSTRY REG.		ZEW2-2	SEW2-2	FEW2-2
		LABOR CONTROL		ZEW2-3	SEW2-3	FEW2-3
		HOSPITALIZ.		ZEW2-4	SEW2-4	FEW2-4
		DELINQUENCY		ZEW2-5	SEW2-5	FEW2-5
		RECREATION		ZEW2-6	SEW2-6	FEW2-6
	MAINTENANCE EW3	HOUSE		ZEW3-1	SEW3-1	FEW3-1
		LAND		ZEW3-2	SEW3-2	FEW3-2
		INDUSTRY		ZEW3-3	SEW3-3	FEW3-3
		SALE		ZEW3-4	SEW3-4	FEW3-4
		FINANCIAL		ZEW3-5	SEW3-5	FEW3-5
	INHERITANCE EW4	HOUSE		ZEW4-1	SEW4-1	FEW4-1
		LAND		ZEW4-2	SEW4-2	FEW4-2
		INDUSTRY		ZEW4-3	SEW4-3	FEW4-3
		ART		ZEW4-4	SEW4-4	FEW4-4
		LAW		ZEW4-5	SEW4-5	FEW4-5
GENERAL WELFARE GW		DEPARTMENT				
		STATE		SD-ZGW	SD-SGW	SD-FGW
		INTERIOR		ID-ZGW	ID-SGW	ID-FGW
		WAR				WD-FGW
		FINANCE	FD-CGW	FD-ZGW	FD-SGW	FD-FGW
		AGRICULTURE		AD-ZGW	AD-SGW	AD-FGW
		EDUCATION	ED-CGW	ED-ZGW	ED-SGW	
		HEALTH	HD-CGW			
		SAFETY	SaD-CGW			
		CONSTRUCTION	CD-CGW			
		TRANSPORTATION	TD-CGW			
		POLICE	PD-GGW	PD-ZGW	PD-SGW	PD-FGW
		ELECTION	E$_l$D-CGW	E$_l$D-ZGW	E$_l$D-SGW	E$_l$D-FGW
		POST OFFICE				P$_o$D-FGW
		WATER SUPPLY	WaD-CGW			
		WELFARE	WeD-CGW			
PEOPLE'S WELFARE PW			3 REPRESENT. FOR EACH COMMUNITY — CPW	18 REPRES. (3 FROM EACH 5 COMMUNITIES) — ZPW	27 REPRES. (3 FROM EACH ZONE) — SPW	71 REPRES (3 FROM EACH ZONE) — FPW
LEGISLATIVE BRANCH LB			SECRETARY & SUFFICIENT ALDERMEN — CLB	SECRETARY & SUFFICIENT SENATORS — ZLB	SECRETARY & SUFFICIENT SENATORS — SLB	SECRETARY & SUFFICIENT SENATORS — FLB
JUDICIARY BRANCH JB			ONE JUDGE & PERSONNEL CJB SEVERAL LOW COURTS LC-JB	ONE COURT 5 JUDGES (1 FOR EACH 5 COMMUNITIES) ZJB	ONE COURT 9 JUDGES (1 FROM EACH ZONE) SJB	1 COURT-MINIMUM 9 JUDGES 1 PER SUPERZONE UNEVEN NUMBER FJB

TABLE NO. 25

TITLE OF OFFICIALS				INITIAL OF OFFICIALS			
				COMMUNITY	ZONE	SUPERZONE	FEDERATION
ECONOMIC WELFARE EW — MANAGER ~ M	1st GROUP MANAGER 1GM	1st Div. Manager 1st Group	COMMUNITY MANAGER ~ CM (Few career men in EW1 and EW2-1)		ZONE MANAGER ~ ZM · Z1GM	Z1DM1G	SUPERZONE MANAGER ~ SM · S1GM	S1DM1G	FEDERATION MANAGER ~ FM · F1GM	F1DM1G
		2nd " " " "		Z2DM1G	S2DM1G	F2DM1G
		3rd " " " "		Z3DM1G	S3DM1G	F3DM1G
	2nd GROUP MANAGER 2GM	1st " " 2nd		Z1DM2G (Z2GM)	S1DM2G (S2GM)	F1DM2G (F2GM)
		2nd " " " "		Z2DM2G	S2DM2G	F2DM2G
		3rd " " " "		Z3DM2G	S3DM2G	F3DM2G
		4th " " " "		Z4DM2G	S4DM2G	F4DM2G
		5th " " " "		Z5DM2G	S5DM2G	F5DM2G
		6th " " " "		Z6DM2G	S6DM2G	F6DM2G
	3rd GROUP MANAGER 3GM	1st " " 3rd		Z1DM3G (Z3GM)	S1DM3G (S3GM)	F1DM3G (F3GM)
		2nd " " " "		Z2DM3G	S2DM3G	F2DM3G
		3rd " " " "		Z3DM3G	S3DM3G	F3DM3G
		4th " " " "		Z4DM3G	S4DM3G	F4DM3G
		5th " " " "		Z5DM3G	S5DM3G	F5DM3G
	4th GROUP MANAGER 4GM	1st " " 4th		Z1DM4G (Z4GM)	S1DM4G (S4GM)	F1DM4G (F4GM)
		2nd " " " "		Z2DM4G	S2DM4G	F2DM4G
		3rd " " " "		Z3DM4G	S3DM4G	F3DM4G
		4th " " " "		Z4DM4G	S4DM4G	F4DM4G
		5th " " " "		Z5DM4G	S5DM4G	F5DM4G
		EXECUTIVE BOARD	CEWB	ZEWB	SEWB	FEWB
GENERAL WELFARE GW — GOVERNOR ~ G		HEAD OF STATE DEPART.	COMMUNITY GOVERNOR ~ CG	ZONE GOVERNOR ~ ZG	SUPERZONE GOVERNOR ~ SG	FEDERATION GOVERNOR ~ FG
				$H\text{-}SD\text{-}Z$	$H\text{-}SD\text{-}S$	$H\text{-}SD\text{-}F$
		" " INTERIOR "		$H\text{-}ID\text{-}Z$	$H\text{-}ID\text{-}S$	$H\text{-}ID\text{-}F$
		" " WAR "				$H\text{-}WD\text{-}F$
		" " FINANCE "	$H\text{-}FD\text{-}C$	$H\text{-}FD\text{-}Z$	$H\text{-}FD\text{-}S$	$H\text{-}FD\text{-}F$
		" " AGRICULTURE "		$H\text{-}AD\text{-}Z$	$H\text{-}AD\text{-}S$	$H\text{-}AD\text{-}F$
		" " EDUCATION "	$H\text{-}ED\text{-}C$	$H\text{-}ED\text{-}Z$	$H\text{-}ED\text{-}S$	
		" " HEALTH "	$H\text{-}HD\text{-}C$			
		" " SAFETY "	$H\text{-}S_aD\text{-}C$			
		" " CONSTRUCT. "	$H\text{-}CD\text{-}C$			
		" " TRANSPORT. "	$H\text{-}TD\text{-}C$			
		" " POLICE "	$H\text{-}PD\text{-}C$	$H\text{-}PD\text{-}Z$	$H\text{-}PD\text{-}S$	$H\text{-}PD\text{-}F$
		" " ELECTION "	$H\text{-}E_eD\text{-}C$	$H\text{-}E_eD\text{-}Z$	$H\text{-}E_eD\text{-}S$	$H\text{-}E_eD\text{-}F$
		" " POST OFFICE "				$H\text{-}P_oD\text{-}F$
		" " WATER SUPPLY "	$H\text{-}W_aD\text{-}C$			
		" " WELFARE "	$H\text{-}W_eD\text{-}C$			
		EXECUTIVE BOARD	CGWB	ZGWB	SGWB	FGWB
PEOPLE'S WELFARE PW		PRESIDENT	CP	ZP	SP	FP
		SENIOR REPRESENTATIVE	C-SR	Z-SR	S-SR	F-SR
		REPRESENTATIVE	C-R	Z-R	S-R	F-R
		JUNIOR REPRESENTATIVE	C-JR	Z-JR	S-JR	F-JR
		ALTERNATE "	C-AR	Z-AR	S-AR	F-AR
LEGISLATIVE BRANCH LB		SECRETARY	SE-CLB	SE-ZLB	SE-SLB	SE-FLB
		ALDERMAN	A-CLB			
		SENATOR		S-ZLB	S-SLB	S-FLB
JUDICIARY BRANCH JB		CHIEF JUSTICE	CJ-CJB	CJ-ZJB	CJ-SJB	CJ-FJB
		JUDGE	J-CJB	J-ZJB	J-SJB	J-FJB
		JUDGE OF LOWER COURT	J-LC			

(Left margin vertical label: TITLE OF GOVERNMENT OFFICIALS)

INDEX